FREDERICK DOUGLASS

THE NEGRO
IN OUR HISTORY

BY

CARTER G. WOODSON

AND

CHARLES H. WESLEY

TENTH EDITION
(Further Revised and Enlarged)

ILLUSTRATED

THE ASSOCIATED PUBLISHERS, INC.
WASHINGTON, D. C.

Printed in the United States of America

PREFACE

This book was written five years ago and would have been published at that time, had not the high cost of printing during the World War rendered its manufacture too expensive. A few pages have been added to bring the work nearer to the present date, but the leading facts as set forth herein appear as they were originally written.

The purpose in writing this book was to present to the average reader in succinct form the history of the United States as it has been influenced by the presence of the Negro in this country. The aim here is to supply also the need of schools long since desiring such a work in handy form with adequate references for those stimulated to more advanced study.

In this condensed form certain situations and questions could not be adequately discussed, and in endeavoring thus to tell the story the author may have left unsaid what others consider more important. Practically all phases of Negro life and history have been treated in their various ramifications, however, to demonstrate how the Negro has been influenced by contact with the Caucasian and to emphasize what the former has contributed to civilization.

The author is indebted to Mr. David A. Lane, Jr., who kindly assisted him in reading the entire proof.

CARTER G. WOODSON.

WASHINGTON, D. C.
April, 1922.

Second   Printing—1923

Third   Edition—1924

Fourth   Edition—1927

Fifth   Edition—1931

Sixth   Printing—1937

Seventh Edition—1941

Eighth   Edition—1945

Ninth   Edition—1941

Tenth   Edition—1962

PREFACE

The demand for additional copies of this volume has been so great that this Tenth Edition has been authorized by the Association for the Study of Negro Life and History and issued by the Associated Publishers. Fourteen years have passed since the last edition. These years have witnessed the most rapid changes of history in the life and status of the darker peoples in the United States and in the areas abroad. With the momentum of change increasing so rapidly, and with the development of our nation into a dominant world power, the need was present for a text which would describe the amazing advance of the Tenth American. The status of colored Americans has become far different from what many Americans and people abroad believe it to be, and these facts should become a part of the educational process, if we are to have a world of peace. Good texts in the general history of the United States are available for use, but the neglects, innuendoes and omissions concerning the people of color are disturbing to students of human relations. This edition has been planned to give correction to these partial views of the history and culture of the darker people, so that the resulting picture can be truthful and well rounded.

The authors, with related backgrounds in historical training and association in research, writings and publications, have shared similar views, but these do not preclude interpretations different from their own by teachers and students who will use the volume for study and reading. A bibliography of selected references is included in this edition.

CHARLES H. WESLEY

Washington, D. C.
November, 1961

CONTENTS

ix

x   Contents

INTRODUCTORY
CARTER G. WOODSON
SCHOLAR — TEACHER

We are almost too close in time to present an accurate view of Carter G. Woodson among scholars and teachers. The measure of the achievement of one whom we consider as a great scholar can be made with completeness not only by his work but also through the critical and creative achievements along similar lines of a subsequent generation of scholars. These scholars draw upon his discoveries and conclusions and build paths leading to new truths. Smoller, the German historian, has stated that "History is in league with genius." In other words, as the nation and the people pass along the years, the individual and his work grow the greater. Then it becomes difficult to separate fact from fiction. The lives of the great men of American History have been of this pattern in developing halo and glory. Men and women who are often discounted or regarded as average persons develop with the passing years into those who are greater. Truly, in this respect, history is in league with genius.

The fundamental principle of our history makes itself manifest in the life and career of Carter G. Woodson. However, in his case we do not have to wait for the years to place him among the scholars, although we do not know how the future will rank all of his historical writings. The discovery of new historical materials, the re-interpretations and the re-writing of history have led to re-appraisals of many a man's work. Nevertheless, we can now make our

appraisal, with certainty, concerning Woodson. We do not
have to ask for the fictionist, the poet and the builders of
dreams to create his greatness. He has been a builder of his
own monument.

There are several characteristics of the scholar-teacher
which were typical of Woodson and these give him a place
among scholars, which is exactly what Woodson was in the
truest sense. His life and career were denials of the assumption that the scholar-teacher cannot be a capable
administrator and organizer. For he was a discoverer of
truth, an organizer of truth, a contributor to truth, a disseminator of truth and a defender of truth. Those of us
who have worked with him know that he had in a special
way these attributes of scholarship. He had marked intellectual ability in literary production, keen judgment of
men and the rare ability of clearing the path of minor
issues in order that major ones might have the right of
way. He was persistent in argument and almost dogmatic.
One could dissent from his views but he must be prepared
to battle with him. He had a serenity which sustained him
in adversity and in loneliness. He came to his end with
courage, as he closed and locked his door and gave acquies-
cence to death. We shall think of him as a distinguished
scholar-teacher of this generation.

Woodson came into the field of historical scholarship
from the field of education at a time when his work and
point of view were needed in the interest of truth. From
the coal mines of West Virginia, he went to the Douglass
High School in Huntington, Berea College in Kentucky,
the University of Chicago, the Sorbonne in Paris, and Harvard University's Graduate School, from which he received
the doctorate in 1912. In this work of preparation and in
his subsequent career, he displayed characteristics of the
scholar.

The main purpose of the graduate schools of a quarter

of a century ago was the education and development of scholars. In fact, it was known as "a school for scholars." At that time the attainment of the college degree was the terminal point for the average citizen and the prospective teacher. The potential scholars then carried on their work beyond the bachelor's degree in the graduate school. Woodson was one of these.

This situation by itself is no longer in general existence. Large numbers now are enrolled in the graduate schools. Many are there to secure the graduate degrees which will give their possessors advances in salary, rank and position, which are obviously desirable objectives. The scholarly purpose of the past is not forgotten but it is not always the superior objective. Others have not secured jobs after the award of the bachelor's degree and, having the funds, enter the graduate school for a year or more of study. This school has become a kind of preparatory school for better teachers, better administrators and more cultured citizens. All of these ambitions are worthy purposes, but the single ambition of the past, creative scholarly endeavor, has difficulty in surviving. When it does survive, in perhaps one-half of the cases the candidate for the doctorate so exhausts himself in the development of his dissertation that it is his last contribution to knowledge. Carter G. Woodson was not of this type of scholarship.

There were five characteristics which placed him among the scholar-teachers of his day. These are also the characteristics which typify the finest scholarship of our day. Those who look forward to the scholarly life, entrance into graduate school and continuous contributions to knowledge would do well to emulate him.

First, He Was a Discoverer of Truth. He came on the scene at a period in the development of historiography when, as Oswald Spengler says, "Race and environment were the two main rival keys that were offered by would-be

scientific nineteenth century western historians for solving
the problem of the cultural inequality of various extant human societies, and neither key proved, on trial, to unlock
the fast-closed door.'' While there was no evidence to show
that race was a basis for the historical advancement of peoples, the assumption was made that this was true, because
of the facts at hand concerning some racial groups and the
lack of facts concerning others.

Woodson did not set out deliberately to become a scholar. He seems to have been almost pressed into scholarship
by these strivings for explanation in society. He had tested
historical knowledge as it related to various peoples. His
studies, travels and experiences in Europe, Asia, the United
States and the Philippines had expanded his personal
knowledge of languages, literatures and cultures. He had
seen that scholars had selected the facts which they desired
to include in their published works and had neglected others. In fact, it is well known that this was an acknowledged
method of historians even in the twentieth century. He
knew also, as Henri Pirenne, Belgian historian, has stated,
''The account of perceivable historical facts is still infinite-
ly far from being complete. Enormous gaps appear in it
at first glance.''[1]

As a result of the omissions and neglect of others, he
then became a rebel against the learning of the scholars in
the universities, after having tested this knowledge against
fundamentally valid truths discovered through his own life
experience. With an exceptional intelligence, a keen insight and an originality beyond the average, he undertook
the discovery of truth about the peoples of color in Africa,
their descendants across the seas and in the United States.
He did not want the Negro people to meet the ''awful fate

[1] Stuart A. Rice, *Methods in the Social Sciences* (Chicago, 1931),
p. 440.

of becoming a negligible factor in the thought of the world.''[2]

There had been others who were similarly convinced of the errors, weaknesses and neglect of historians and students of society but either they had not had the opportunity of probing deeply in the assembled knowledge of the schools as had Woodson, or they had been led off into the bypaths of racial defense and racial crusading. They had not remained steadfast in the pursuit and discovery of historical truth with the same singleness of purpose. One of those who had was George W. Williams, author of *History of the Negro Race in America from 1619 to 1880, Negroes as Slaves, as Soldiers and as Citizens,* published at New York, 1882, in two volumes. This work of Williams was the outstanding contribution having the earmarks of scholarship to the general subject of the Negro's total contribution to American history until the rise of Woodson. There were contributions to the slave trade, slavery emancipation, group organization, and selected phases and periods of history which helped to piece together a more effective story. But Woodson's *The Negro in Our History* first published in 1922 provided basic materials for college and secondary school uses drawn from many individual studies of the Negro people in Africa and the Americas.

Woodson insisted upon the discovery of the complete truth, and when he came upon partial truth, he did not hesitate to abandon the false. Two instances will illustrate this position. I recall that a brochure put out by the Association carried the statement that a pilot of one of the three ships of the fleet of Christopher Columbus was a Negro. From the sentimental point of view, such an incident had significance for the Negro. Woodson began to dig for the truth. Each of us worked on the problem from his own angle. He came up with the view that this was not true and

---

[2] *Journal of Negro History,* X (October, 1925), p. 600.

of the Negro as Reflected in Letters Written during the Crisis, 1800-1860, published in 1926; and the *Works of Francis J. Grimké,* published in 1942.

His scholarship as a contributor was demonstrated further through his revelation of the mistakes and imperfections of other writers by his more adequate interpretation and presentation of the facts, his corrections of generalizations and methods of developing conclusions.

He Was an Organizer of Truth. He was not only a scholar pursuing the truth but he was also an organizer of truth. His organization, in Chicago, Illinois, on September 9, 1915, of the Association for the Study of Negro Life and History was the first organized effort of Negroes, as Woodson stated, "to treat the records of the race scientifically and to publish the findings to the world." The brief record of these proceedings is as follows:

9/9/15

A meeting called by Dr. Woodson for the purpose of considering definite plans for the organization of a society, which should publish a magazine devoted to the study of the Negro, was held in the office of the Executive Secretary of the Wabash Avenue Department of the Chicago Y.M.C.A. Those present were C. G. Woodson, G. C. Hall, A. L. Jackson, W. B. Hartgrove, and J. E. Stamps. Dr. Hall was elected temporary chairman, J. E. Stamps, temporary secretary. The proposed constitution was read, and after alterations adopted. A permanent organization was formed, and the following officers were elected: Dr. G. C. Hall, President; J. E. Moorland, Secretary-Treasurer; C. G. Woodson, Director of Research and Editor. In addition to the above named officers the Executive Council will be J. A. Bigham, A. L. Jackson, Miss S. P. Breckinridge, and G. N. Grisham.

The editorial staff will consist of six or eight persons to be selected by the Editor and approved by the Executive Council.

A motion prevailed that in a reply to a request from Dr.

Moorland we offer to cooperate with Howard University along lines satisfactory to the Executive Council.

J. E. STAMPS[3]

I was then an instructor at Howard University and a cooperation was undertaken then, which has lasted through the years. Dr. Rayford W. Logan, Chairman of the Department of History at Howard University, has served as Director of Research and Editor, of the Association.

While Woodson was an organizer of real ability, he was a person of single mind and action, and one might say that he was of the successful, lone-wolf type. He acted on his own and was willing and capable of accepting responsibility. This type of action was typical from the beginning of his career. He brought out the first issue of the JOURNAL OF NEGRO HISTORY on January 1, 1916, about three months after the organization of the Association, without even a consultation with his Executive Council. As a result, one member of the Council resigned. In spite of the prediction that the JOURNAL would not live, it has continued through the years and not a single issue has been missed. The first issue was published at a cost of four hundred dollars, most of which were personal funds taken from his salary as a teacher at the Armstrong High School of Washington, D. C. During the first three years, annual deficits continued to be made up from Dr. Woodson's small salary. The JOURNAL is now in its forty-fifth year and is practically self-supporting.

Shortly thereafter, Dr. Woodson organized the Associated Publishers, a private publishing corporation with 90-odd per cent of the stock held by himself. This organization was planned as a publishing agency for both the publication and the sale of books. Another ultimate source of income for the Association was also assured in this way.

He was interested in the difficulties which Negro scholars

[3] *Ibid.*, XXV (October, 1940), p. 422-423.

faced in the publication of their works of scholarship. After stating that the Negro scholar faced a lack of provision by foundations for the publication of the results of his researches, he said: "The Negro faces another stone wall when he presents such scientific productions to the publishing houses. They may not be prejudiced, but they are not interested in the Negro. We understand that the more serious the work is the less chance it has for reaching a large reading public. Yet scholarship must be advanced by these strictly scientific works. This represents a very dark prospect for the rapidly increasing number of young men and women who are prepared for creative work but receive no encouragement whatever. In this way the cause of Negro scholarship has dreadfully suffered in spite of the one-sided method of the foundations in trying to broaden the minds of Negroes teaching in their own schools. What is the use of knowing things if they cannot be published to the world? If the Negro is to settle down to publishing merely what others permit him to bring out, the world will never know what the race has thought and felt and attempted and accomplished and the story of the Negro will perish with him."[4]

His successful organization of membership campaigns, and the financial appeals, mark him as more than the scholar of the ivory tower. His collections of materials, notably the vast store of materials which he has assembled for his Encyclopedia Africana, is another significant aspect of his ability as a scholar-organizer. He collected disciples, young men and women who were invited to his meetings and who loved the cause even more than the master, but at the same time they admired him and his abilities. Many became of themselves pioneers in selected areas of Negro scholarship in the social scenes. He gave his movement a philosophy and built an organization for it.

4 Woodson to Wesley, June 19, 1937, Washington, D. C.

He was a Disseminator of Truth. Through the channels of the Association and his personal contribution he spread the truth about the Negro people. He saw that the effective transmission of the truth had to be accompanied by a dissemination among the scholarly and the non-scholarly groups. Some books were for one group and some for the other: *The Journal of Negro History* for the scholarly inclined and the *Negro History Bulletin* for another group. The latter was not a popular endeavor but it was for teachers and students, particularly in the secondary and elementary schools. He answered letters calling for information and gave answers to historical questions in a wide correspondence. He knew that there had to be a wide dissemination in order to secure the understanding, the appreciation and the support of his work. Often, when he endeavored to popularize the knowledge of the Negro, he found it difficult for he appealed to many whose convictions were settled about the position, past, present and future, for the Negro. He became a popularizer but he did not vary from the standards of genuine scholarship nor was his intellectual discipline impaired by these efforts on the public platform. Nevertheless, he declined to exploit Negro History even for the support which came from such exploitation. He would be a disseminator of truth but not for the returns which would come from it. He believed in the "saving and popularizing of the records of the race that it may not become a negligible factor in the thought of the world."

His Negro History Week posters, dating from 1926, his latest Negro History Week Kit, his annual circulars and news releases were other channels used for the spread of truth. His concept of his work was that "truth must be dug up from the past and presented to the circle of scholars in scientific form and then through stories and dramatizations that will permeate our educational system."

He was a Defender of Truth. It was inevitable that this

trait should develop in his life, for truth and truth-seekers seem to have to engage in struggles with the false and its supporters. Defenders of truth use intellectual weapons which are planned to have power to overcome error. The presentation of facts is not sufficient to secure their acceptance. Facts must be supported, fought for and generalizations made from them based upon that which appears to be evident truth.

While he was a Defender, there was also in him a modest sensitivity, for he wrote in 1944:

I always feel relieved when satisfied that I am not to be held up to ridicule by persons who do not understand the sacrifices which I have made to help the Negro by leading him to think rather than to follow the dictates of the poor whites, who are exploiting the race as friends of the lowly, and Negro politicians who likewise misuse and mislead the Negro.[5]

Woodson also went further into this point of view when he stated that there had appeared in the JOURNAL OF NEGRO HISTORY and in publications of the Association materials which some persons did not "desire to see come to light." He said:

Here and there, therefore, were heard complaints expressing dissatisfaction with the policy of telling the whole truth and nothing but the truth regardless of whom it affected. One interracial agency, assuming authority to dictate the leadership of the Negro race in all matters in America and in Africa, became most vicious in its attacks. This agency prepared a memorandum setting forth the reasons why the Association for the Study of Negro Life and History should not be further supported and clandestinely circulated it to lop off the supporters of the Association. Finally, it had the effect of depriving the Association of the assistance of all foundations and the rich people, who had formerly assisted the undertaking.

5 Woodson to Wesley, September 15, 1944, Washington, D. C.

Observing as early as 1930 that such was the situation with respect to financial support, the Director began to organize the Negroes of the country to obtain from them what the interracialists had succeeded in diverting from this effort.[6]

He opposed the efforts of any of these groups to use the Association and its channels for their own causes. He fought against the so-called "traducers" of the Negro and against those who would make of the Association a channel of propaganda, for his cause was the scholarly presentation of the truth. He declared:

The Association always makes a sharp distinction between the study of the Negro and the agitation of the race problem. There is no effort to minimize the importance of the agitation for the rise of the Negro to the level of citizenship, but the Director and his coworkers have always been willing to leave that as a field in which the propaganda organizations may operate. In this way, the extension efforts of the Association have been directed successfully through those channels which assure a sane presentation of the past of the Negro as it bears upon the present.[7]

He declined to permit those whom he thought to be associated with some of the foundations to direct or modify the work of the Association. He had received assistance from several foundations and interested individuals, but he resented any attempt to dominate the pursuit of truth by him and his coworkers. He declared in 1940:

This is a most unfortunate situation in the modern world where wealth is boundless, but those who have been favored with fortunes are not usually interested in the promotion of the truth. Often when financial support is given, such strings are attached as to prevent the research into matters which may prove prejudicial to economic interests. In the case of the Negro there appears also the added handicap

[6] *Journal of Negro History*, XXV (October, 1940), p. 425-426.
[7] "Annual Report of the Director," *ibid.*, XXXI (October, 1946), p. 388.

from those opposing the teaching of doctrines which may interfere with white supremacy. What is desired in such quarters is to suppress the whole truth and to publish such a portion of it as will not change the present way of thinking.[8]

He often fought against the tradition of inferiority in the education of Negro youth and against those who would rob the Negro population in the United States of faith in themselves, and others of the faith which they could have in them. His *The Mis-Education of the Negro,* published in 1933, was directed against the agencies of education which failed to recognize and make use of the truth about the Negro. He knew that there was underemphasis in this connection, but he was also aware of overemphasis.

Here was a man who was a scholar but he was more than this. He was a discoverer, a contributor, an organizer, a disseminator, and a defender, all in the cause of truth. With his life and work he expressed a fundamental belief in the touchstone for scholars in history as well as for all people—''Ye shall know the truth and the truth shall make you free.'' Carter G. Woodson embodied these truth concepts, and the truths of his soul go marching on. May those who read these pages also join the procession of truth seekers!

[8] *Ibid.,* XXV (October, 1940), p. 423-424.

CHARLES H. WESLEY

THE NEGRO IN OUR HISTORY

CHAPTER I

THE UNKNOWN AFRICAN ORIGIN

MOST historians know practically nothing about the Negroes in Africa prior to their enslavement, and there has been little systematic effort to study them.[1] The world has long looked at Africa "through the eyes of human sentiment or dividends." Men have invented all sorts of arguments based upon estimates **Africa unknown.** of "physical phenomena as conceived by phrenology and physiognomy, using signs and symbols to describe every part of the man—from the heel to the skull—to prove the mental and moral inferiority of the Negro." There have been few to enlarge upon the physical inferiority of the Negro, however, inasmuch as the Negro is regarded as belonging to the most vigorous portion of the human family.

The fact is that we know less about Africa than about any other part of the world. With the exception of Egypt and the Red Sea shore, Africa is difficult of access because of its plateau formation and unnavigable rivers. The

[1] For more extensive treatment see W. Z. Ripley's *Races of Europe*, J. Deniker's *Races of Men*, J. Finot's *Race Prejudice*, F. Ratzel's *The History of Mankind*, Franz Boas's *The Mind of Primitive Man*, Spiller's *Inter-Racial Problems*, C. Bucher's *Industrial Revolution*, Casely Hayford's *Ethiopia Unbound* and his *Native Institutions*, James Bryce's *Impressions of South Africa*, Leo Frobenius's *The Voice of Africa*, and G. Sergi's *The Mediterranean Race;* David Randall-Maciver, *Medieval Rhodesia;* E. W. Blyden, *African Life and Customs;* J. P. Johnson, *The Stone Implements of South Africa* and *The Prehistoric Period in South Africa.*

1

ancients knew more about Africans who came into the
Mediterranean world than they knew of the Africans in
**Access
difficult.**
their home.   Homer mentions the Ethiopians
as "the farthest removed of men."   Herodo-
tus said that the Phœnicians visited parts of the continent

SLAVERY AMONG THE ANCIENTS

as far as the equator six centuries before Christ.   About
450 or 500 B. C. the Carthaginians established trading
posts on the Atlantic Coast of Morocco and probably
reached Sierra Leone and the Gold Coast.   Frequent in-

ternational commercial intercourse took place on the Nile
and the Red Sea. The East Coast as far as Zambesi was
known to the ancient Europeans. Ptolemy's geography
indicates that the ancients had almost accurate knowledge
of the Nile from its very source. Then there appeared
evidences of closer contact in the permanent settlements like
the Greek colonies, Cyrene and nearby cities, and those of
the Phœnicians at Utica and Carthage. These figured
conspicuously in the history of the ancient world, but did
not penetrate the continent. The slave trade made Africa
uninviting; and, on the other hand, the fight on the slave
trade attracted attention thereto. Mohammedanism, dis-
puting the progress of Christianity, also kept out the modern explorer.

A CONGO NATIVE

Until about 1850, Africa in the
mind of the modern world was a
series of coast lines. **A series of coast lines.**
Americans and Eu-
ropeans are still practically on
the outside looking at the continent through a glass darkly.
The coast contact, such as it was,
figured in the history of the
world. The East Coast of Africa
was early visited by Arabs.
Then came the slave traders of
the Mohammedans as a result of
the rise of Moslems. They took
Northern Africa by the eighth
century and threatened Europe,
only to lose their foothold there
and some of their conquest in the southern Mediterranean.
They crossed the Sahara into the Soudan, and pushed their
way as far as the Zambesi, roughly speaking, to ten degrees
north latitude. Christian slave traders succeeded the Mo-

hammedans but their traffic restricted them to the coast. Neither Europe nor America had any definite knowledge of the interior of Africa until after 1870 when Stanley had explored the back country.

It is only recently that there has been a tendency to study the African and his continent scientifically, and scholars in large numbers have not as yet turned in this direction. For this reason **Superiority Myth.** a majority of the people of Europe and America still regard the African as a heathen below the lowest of the human family. The supposedly low depths of the native Africans emphasize the so-called heights which the whites have attained. As a matter of fact, however, the African civilization does not suffer in comparison with the civilization of other members of the human family. All

An African Youth

have intermingled and borrowed, the one from the other. In science, then, there is no such thing as race. In anthropology and psychology there are no such myths as inferiority and superiority of races. Because of lack of opportunity in an unhealthy environment, some may not have accomplished as much as others more favorably circumstanced; but, wherever the climatic conditions and the opportunity for development have been similar, the cultures of various members of the human families have tended to be very much alike. Even in the case of different climatic conditions the record of man tends to support this parallelism. The early civilization of the African, for example, did not differ much from that of the primitive Greeks or that of the early Romans. Looking at the native African through a glass darkly, however, the American or European is apt to conclude that because the African is physically unlike the white man he is not worth while and his achievements are not significant. This wrong impression has come from innumerable books of travelers, officeholders, and missionaries presenting more misinformation than truth.

Travelers in Africa have been largely casual observers who go through the country rapidly. Because of its infelicitous climate and strange civilization differing so widely from that of their home countries they have not wanted to tarry there long. Very few of them have seen much of the interior of the **Misrepresentations.** continent. What they have to say about Africa, then, is very much like that of the Pullman car observations of tourists spending a few hours among the Negroes in our own South only to return home to pose as authorities on the race question.

A CHAIR

Public functionaries, as a rule, have been less dependable than the travelers. While having the opportunity for more careful observation, they have been biased by their position. If the political institutions of the natives differ **Misconception of Africa.** very much from those of the mother country, the natives have not shown capacity for political organization. If their industrial system does not harmonize with the projected exploitation by the conquerors, the natives are lazy and shiftless. If the victims of their greed do not readily wear the foreign yoke, they are cruel savages who should be destroyed that the interlopers may have full sway without the mischievous interference of the aborigines.

From the missionaries, whom we must concede as being disposed to be an honest and upright class, we cannot expect any more truth about Africa than we obtain from travelers and public functionaries. In a few of these missionaries' accounts, however, one does see some tendency toward fair-mindedness and an effort to rise unto the appreciation of the African's contribution to civilization. But some of these authors use exaggerating language, contradicting themselves in praising the natives in one place and denouncing them in another. They often blame the natives for the faults of a system decaying in the transition to another under European occupation. Furthermore, it would be unwise to expect that partisans of a certain religious **Unscientific** system seeking to uproot another can be **accounts.** depended upon to report definitely on the virtues of the people whom they would proselyte. The missionary is the very sort of man who would be more than apt to go to the extreme of denying the existence of anything significant in the civilization of the so-called heathen. If he had a favorable impression of the natives' religion and morals he would thereby be disqualified for missionary effort. The missionary naturally thinks that what the heathen is to-day is the very thing which he should not be, and that the mission of the apostle is to make him what he ought to be. The books written by most of these missionaries, therefore, are largely worthless in arriving at an appreciation of African culture. Peeved because of the meager results in converting the heathen, missionaries too often condemn the stubborn-hearted as hopeless pagans.

The missionaries do not realize that they are often trying to supplant a system superior to their own.

The trouble in this case results from the belief that differences in culture imply superiority or inferiority. The Africans do not build their houses, tend their flocks, herd their cattle, train the youth, or appease the **Differentness** gods in the same way as the Europeans or **misunderstood.** the Americans. Then, they must be inferior beings fit only for the exploitation of their so-called superiors or swept from the face of the earth if they resist the interlopers. It seldom has occurred to these foreigners that some achievements of modern civilization now referred to as steps forward in the development of the human race may be rued to-morrow as a backward stride toward barbarism. A hundred years from to-day many of the present customs of Europeans and Americans will be ridiculed and lamented by their descendants. Even to-day the modern world is rising like a seething mass to overthrow the present economic system to go back to the communistic basis of society so well worked out among the Africans.

In view of what has been said above, one might naturally inquire as to what is the African civilization. "Nothing," the majority of Europeans and Americans would reply, "except a backward system leavened here **An important** and there with ideas from abroad." No state- **inquiry.** ment, however, can be farther than this from the truth. It is an evidence of ignorance to think that all parallelism in culture shows borrowed ideas. Groups of persons in the same climate and similarly circumstanced will develop very much alike, although the one may be ten thousand miles removed from the other. The pottery, tools, weapons, and musical instruments of the one resemble those of the other. As one writer has well said, one bereaved in Berlin would tend to express his grief very much in the manner in which a native of Oceania would give vent to this feeling except that the former might evince a command of more beautiful language. Equalize the circumstances of the two and the method of expression will show more parallelism. Unable to understand this, pseudo-scientists have tried to trace migrations of culture from the "higher" to the "lower" races when they have no facts whatever to support their fallacies.

CONGO POTTERY

Most assuredly one group has borrowed from another; but the fact must be established by satisfactory evidence. **Foreign influences.** For example, scholars say that the Negro taught the Mediterranean world the use of iron. It has been established that Africans near the heart of the continent were the first to learn the use of the valuable metal. It has also been proved that these Africans had commercial intercourse with the seats of civilization around the Mediterranean. It is reasonable to conclude then, that the Africans gave this unusual impetus to early progress. The missionary was wrong, however, when he claimed that the Muganda natives in Central Africa had learned bathing from the English. Promptly asked by one of them what is the English custom, he replied: "A bath every day." The native rejoined: "Well, a Muganda has one every evening as well." As a matter of fact some Europeans and Americans do not bathe more than once in six months. Yet this missionary thought that the Muganda habit of cleanliness was borrowed from the English.

The foreigner here, too, often makes the mistake of confusing advance in culture with brain improvement. On this false ground most of the argument for superiority or inferiority of races is made. Environment and opportunity have been the large factors in making prog- **Mistakes so** ress. Scientists have proved that one stock **easy in ob-** has no more mental capacity than any other. **servations.** "The mind," says one authority, "is nothing but a means of manipulating the outside world.

Number, time, and space conceptions and systems become more complex and accurate, not as the human mind grows in capacity, but as activities become more varied and call for more extended and accurate systems of notation and measurement." Unable to see virtue in the civilization of these natives, however, Europeans proceed to remake them or kill them off. While they may not be

A NATIVE

killed in warfare, they are just as easily killed off by the disruption of their socialistic, communistic manner of life, without which the native cannot exist. Many African tribes, therefore, have thus been exterminated very much in the same manner in which the Red Men in America have met their fate.

To understand Africa, moreover, the continent itself must be studied. In considering the forces effective in making the civilization of Africa it is well to note that **Features of Africa.** although it is the second continent in size, it has such few inlets that it has the shortest coastline of all. Some historians will therefore inform us that owing to this lack of good harbors, Africa, through commerce, has not had sufficient contact with the outer world to keep its civilization abreast with that of other continents. Although Africa has valuable land, it suffers from the handicap of being in the main a high elevated tableland with rapids and falls, rendering difficult the approach from the outer world; and the four great rivers, the Zambesi, the Niger, the Congo, and the Nile, are not sufficient to furnish facilities for transportation even in the interior. Africa lies in the part of the tropical world where, because of its peculiar location with reference to the directions of the winds, the climate is unusually warm and dry except in the region drained by the Congo. There the abundant rainfall produces conditions very much like those in other parts of the torrid zone.

Because of these peculiar geographic conditions there exist various civilizations determined largely by the areas in which they have developed. For general purposes Africa **African civilizations.** may be divided into three zones. Stretching from a little above the equator to the south of that circle is the region of the heaviest rainfall and consequently the most abundant vegetation. There may be found swelling streams flowing through forests teeming with animals, natural crops, and an abundance of fruits serving as food for man. On that account there is no struggle for life. Above and below this zone are two others of less rainfall and consequently less vegetation. There it is necessary for man to cultivate the fields in order to make a living. Still farther beyond the limits of the

The Unknown African Origin

A SCENE ON THE NIGER

last-named zones are areas of much less vegetation. In the North, there is practically none at all on account of the lack of rain. In the sections of little rainfall man must earn a living by pasturing cattle and the like.

A CONGO CHIEF

What, then, are these various civilizations which have sprung up in these respective zones as a result of environment? Those Africans who have lived under the equator where there is no struggle for life have not made much advancement. In that section it has not been possible for necessity to become the mother of invention. Those living in the areas requiring cultivation of the soil have made the most progress of all. It has been necessary for them to bring under their control certain

Environment as a factor. forces of nature to increase the food supply which nature in that zone niggardly yields. The dwellers in the arid regions are handicapped by being restricted to merely one industry from which returns are obtained with increasing difficulty. While under such circumstances the achievements of the people in one or two respects may reach a high stage, they must remain a backward stock for lack of proper environment and opportunity.

This situation throws much light on slavery and its concomitants in Africa. As there is not very much of an effort to earn a living in the region under the equator, slavery in that section seldom extends beyond that of women who are usually attached to men as wives. A rich man in need of labor secures **Slavery in Africa.** additional wives to supply that need, and a wife is easily obtained in a land where every woman is supposed to be attached to some man. In the case of wars, too, when male

CAPTIVES TO BE ENSLAVED

captives are taken they can be easily disposed of as slaves for the reason that they are not needed in the economy of the country. Some few of such captives are sacrificed because they are not accustomed to work and cannot be trusted to fight for a new nation. Foreign slave trade found an opportunity here.

In the zone farther north there is much demand for the labor of slaves. A living is obtained there with more difficulty than in the equatorial zone. The effort on the part of one to shift arduous labor to the shoulders of another results in the enslavement of the weak to do the work of the strong. In the arid zone a slave class is not considered indispensable, since it cannot easily maintain itself there and at the same time support superiors. As all of the population must work, free rather than slave labor is the rule.

The people of Africa inhabiting these various zones are commonly known as the black race. Yet, because of climatic differences, men in these parts became widely different from each other. Later they have tended to blend in various migrations. We are told that there was a movement of peoples and of civilizations from Asia into Egypt and from Egypt up the Nile into the interior of Africa, and **The move-** again from Egypt westward to the Atlantic **ment of** near the Gulf of Guinea. There was, too, a **peoples.** backward movement from the West to the East, causing a conflict, a fusion, and a destruction of cultures. Out of this chaos developed the Bantu, self-styled "the people," a warlike nation which came from the Northeast and imposed its sway and language on all of Southern Africa.

In the north the controlling forces centered for some centuries in Egypt. Although commonly regarded as a **Egypt and** country of Asiatic civilization, Egypt, like **the North.** other parts of Africa, was molded in this crucible of cultures. It was the land of mixed breeds or persons comparable to Negroes passing in this country as people of color. One-third of the Egyptians, however, were distinctly black. History seems to indicate that that country was first settled by a Negro tribe that mingled later with the Mediterranean people coming from the north. There came into contact with them the Greeks, the Italians, and Carthaginians. The Greeks were thereby influenced to the extent that investigators contend that the civilization of Greece had African rather than Asiatic origin.

Some scientists are even of the opinion that original man evolved in Africa rather than in Asia. The African, more over, has left traces of a very early culture. Recent studies based upon actual excavation in Africa have led to startling conclusions. There have been discovered from place to place relics indicative of an interesting culture in this continent during prehistoric times.

Primitive man in Africa.

Leo Frobenius believes that on the west coast of Africa there developed in the prehistoric era the Atlantes, an advanced nation of superior culture. This nation had reached a stage very much like that of ancient Greece and Rome.

An Axe of Authority

All of Africa, however, just as most of other parts of the world, was not settled by people of exactly the same type. The records of archæologists indicate that the primitive African was not necessarily black, but of an Asiatic type of Negroid features. There are certain records which lead to the conclusion that at one time the peoples of Africa were largely of the mulatto type. To-day the natives of Africa are not generally black but exhibit in their racial characteristics many of the divergencies found among the people of color in the United States. There are in the main such types as the small primitive stock, the larger forest Negro in the center and on the west coast, and the tall blacks in the Soudan.

African peoples.

In the course of time people tend to become a hybrid group just as it has happened in Europe and America. The **Races in Africa.** efforts to promote racial integrity have begun too late. All Africans except those in the extreme North, however, were Negroes. This means that they were persons who, although not purely black, nevertheless had a larger percentage of Negro blood than that of any other stock. Biased investigators referring to these, however, identify them as whites if they happen to discover evidences of advanced culture even if such persons have a small percentage of Caucasian blood. The inconsistency of the position is that these Negroid persons brought into contact with Europeans and Americans elsewhere are all designated as Negroes and treated as an inferior group when they aspire to economic and social equality among whites. It can be proved that neither the majority of the Egyptians nor of the natives in Northern Africa were actually black people. In the same sense it can be established that the so-called Negroes of America are not actually black people, or that because of their interbreeding with Indians and Negroes Americans are not thoroughly white. If the Egyptians and the majority of the tribes of Northern Africa were not Negroes, then, there are no Negroes in the United States. If the biased writers must claim connection with the early tribes in Northern Africa they should be equally as willing to do the same with respect to the so-called Negroes of America.

In Central and Southern Africa, however, there can be no question as to the existence of the typical black man. The Pygmies, a primitive stock, lived in Central Africa. These primitive people are said to have covered the country from the Sahara to the Zambesi-Congo and from the coast to the Atlantic. They were a dwarf-like **The Pygmies.** people of from 4 feet 2 inches to 4 feet 6 inches in height. They lived largely by hunting with bows and arrows. It is thought that they represented a culture anterior to that of the Stone Age; but this requires further proof.

Other primitive peoples of prehistoric age were the Bushmen and Hottentots in South Africa. They have left striking evidences of their culture showing that they were among the first of men to advance in civilization. The Bushmen lived on the flesh of animals. They did not cultivate the soil. They hunted game with poisoned arrows. Relying largely upon these

Bushmen.

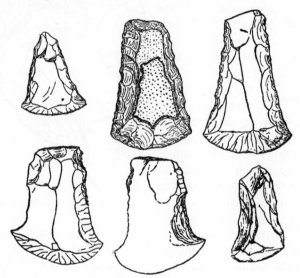

IMPLEMENTS OF THE STONE AGE

means to find a subsistence, they became masters of the knowledge of poisons and antidotes. They were not cannibals. They dwelt in caves. Because of their artistic turn of mind they painted the walls of the caves in which they lived. Some of this rock painting is still preserved. Their music showed progress in rhythm. They had a folklore exhibiting thought and poetical fancy. As a people they were said to have wonderful power of endurance, remarkable alertness, keenness of vision, and a highly developed sense of hearing. In government the political organization did not extend beyond that of a clan ruled by a chief. Their religion was a fetishism. They practiced monogamy rather than polygamy.

The Hottentots appeared in Southern Africa later than the Bushmen. They were of a larger stature than the Bushmen. They were noted for their buoyancy of spirit and fitfulness of feeling. For this reason it is not surprising that they were

Hottentots.

given to merry-making, singing, and dancing. At the appearance of the new moon, it is said that members of this tribe danced and sang without intermission the whole night and poured

A PRODUCT OF THE STONE AGE

forth libations in honor of Phœbus. They possessed unusual power of imagination. They had also a lore of heavenly bodies to which they assigned names. Like the Bushmen, they were remarkable for their hardihood and power of endurance. They also used the poison arrow in hunting and in war. But they did not develop this to the degree observed among the Bushmen. Unlike the Bushmen, they were pastoral in their habits. They lived largely upon the horned cattle, sheep, and goats rather than altogether upon hunting. Yet they were not disinclined to the chase. They kept dogs for this particular purpose, both for the sport of it and for providing themselves with a variety of food.

In the pastoral stage the Hottentots, of course, enjoyed food of a higher class than that of the Bushmen. The Hottentots feasted on the milk and the flesh of domestic animals. They also ate roots, wild fruits, and certain vegetables. In dress the Hottentot was restricted to skins and fur karosses of animals. These extended from the waist to about the level of the knees. Like the Bushmen, too, they had no use for permanent dwellings, inasmuch as they went from place to place to find pasturage for their cattle. Their houses, therefore, consisted of huts made of sticks, set in the ground and then bent and bound together and cov-

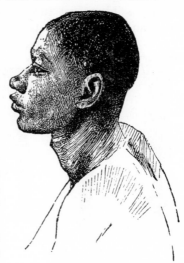

One of the Types

ered with mats and rushes. Settled in a place for considerable time, they had a form of government consisting of tribes and clans under separate chiefs. The Hottentots and the Bushmen suffered from the rise of the powerful Bantu. The Bushmen were practically destroyed by the Dutch when they established their colonies in South Africa.

The Bantu, the most important stock that developed in South Africa, consists of three ethnical groups of tribes. The details do not interest us here. They were **The Bantu.** the result of an extensive admixture of the various tribes of Africa and possibly had some infusion from invaders from Asia. They are, therefore, referred to by some scientists as a hybrid group. In most cases they have preserved valuable traditions of families, tribes, and clans except where certain wars have destroyed their records and dismembered the nations. They trace their history without much difficulty. This, of course, is not possible to get through books but by means of tradition and the monuments of the country.

KNIVES

The chief occupation of the Bantu is agriculture. They raise principally millet, Kaffir corn, or Indian corn. Africans, it is said, introduced it into America as they did tobacco centuries before the whites ever **Occupations** reached the Western Hemisphere. They also **of the Bantu.** raise pumpkins, melons, the sweet reed, sugar cane, and beans. Business developed among them to the extent that exchange was necessary. In their transactions they used cattle, sheep or goats as a medium of exchange. Their agriculture was largely primitive, however, and was carried on mainly by women inasmuch as the men devoted themselves to warfare. The weapons which they generally used were the spear and the shield.

The government of these people was strictly patriarchal,

very much like that in tribes governed by a sort of king. He was the chief magistrate, the military commander, the supreme justice, and the most high priest. Under him served petty chiefs of the clans making up the tribe. Under these were the heads of the **Institutions.** families which in their local jurisdiction exercised practically the same powers as the chief of the tribe. This social order was very much like that of the early Greeks and Romans. The Bantu tribes, however, never had a strong centralized government like those of modern times. The Bantu lived in village communities ranging from 50 to 500 and sometimes to 1,000 persons. Each village was independent of the others socially, economically and politically. The head of the community was a headman, a viceroy representing the supreme ruler of the tribe. The village in which the chief lived, of course, was the metropolis of the

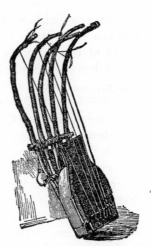

AN AFRICAN LYRE

nation. This system appeared at its best under Chaka, the hardy Zulu chieftain and the most efficient military leader known to so-called primitive people; under his successors, Dingaan, Cetewayo and Dinizulu; under Moselekatze, followed by Lobenguela in Matabeleland; under Moshesh, the builder of the Basuto nation; and under Khama II, the ruler of the Bamangwato. All these leaders proved to be a thorn in the side of the Boers and British who finally took the land of the Bantu. Other Africans, however, had shown more capacity for political organization and welded the tribes into nations of village communities.

CHAPTER II

AFRICAN INSTITUTIONS A BACKGROUND

THE ease with which the Negro thrives in centers of modern civilization, in contradistinction to the destructive effect of this influence on the belated peoples like the Indians, has evoked admiration and comment. In the begin-

The African background. ning of the treatment of the rôle played by the Negro in our history, then, it may be well to examine briefly the situation in Africa with a view to determining exactly what accounts for the facility with which the culture of the Negroes brought to Europe and America has so easily fused with the culture generally known as that of the white man. Has the culture of the Negro anything in common with that of the modern nations, or is the Negro merely imitative, as is often asserted by many writers?[1] History says that the African is the father of civilization.

A thorough knowledge of African institutions, therefore, is essential to understanding the African's contribution. Let us direct attention, then, to this neglected aspect of the story. In some parts of Africa the state has reached an advanced stage. Among the military tribes of the East the

African government. government tends to be despotic inasmuch as a dictator is necessary in time of war. Such is not the situation where the people lead a peaceful life.

---

[1] The best authorities on African institutions are the following: E. W. Blyden's *African Life and Customs;* Casely Hayford's *Gold Coast Native Institutions;* S. M. Molema's *The Bantu, Past and Present;* and Leo Frobenius's *The Voice of Africa* in two volumes. Hundreds of other persons have written on African institutions, but most of them could not understand what they saw or heard.

The king, therefore, does not rule with absolute sway in all parts of the continent, as so many writers on African institutions have tried to make the world believe. The king is often a limited monarch. His position is sometimes hereditary, but in many cases he is chosen by a council of state. For proper cause, in some of these parts, the people through their chosen representatives may depose the king and choose another. The king's power, however, is real. The head of each community or province belonging to the state must respect the authority of the king. He is the commander-in-chief of the forces of the state and he is the arbiter of all

A Powder Flask

disputes arising among the provinces of his jurisdiction But the local governments of his province seldom suffer from interference on the part of the king.

The king, surrounded by courtiers, maintains himself with usual pomp in his home. His household is controlled by a number of chieftains performing various functions like those of stool-bearers, sword-bearers, criers, butlers, huntsmen, farmers, and physicians. Then there are the body-guard of the king and other

The King.

military bodies functioning through a sort of a department of war. It must not be thought, however, that the African king is merely a war chieftain. His problem is rather that of maintaining the peace. The peace is often disturbed by interference with national institutions. Most of the wars in Africa are fought to prevent such tampering with the customs of the country. Travelers and others in misrepresenting Africa, however, have said that these wars have been waged merely to supply the demand for slaves. Captives in war have been sold as slaves, but the wars were not waged for such a purpose. The selling of captives as slaves is a sequel rather than a cause of war.

The same may be said about the sacrifices of human be-

AN ANTELOPE HORN TRUMPET

ings in ancient Africa. Among some Africans there are certain religious ceremonies involving the sacrifice of human beings. Victims thus offered up, however, consist of **The** criminals convicted of certain infractions of **sacrifice.** the law and kept for execution in connection with religious rites. These are supposed to have a deter-

INTERESTING ROCK PAINTING

rent effect upon those permitted to witness the ordeal. While innocent persons have been thus dispatched to appease the gods, there is no general custom of sacrificing unoffending people. Here the Africans do no more than the Hebrews when "Samuel hewed Agag in pieces before the Lord or when David delivered to the Gibeonites the seven sons of Saul to be hanged before the Lord."

The institutions of the Africans are worked out on the socialistic basis. In keeping with the customs of the village community of the ancient world, strict communism or socialism is carried out on the family basis. The clan is merely a family expanded. All males of the same blood dwell to-

A BANTU DANCE—ROCK PAINTING

gether. They bring their wives to live with their kindred rather than separate on marrying. This **Interesting** means that the village is made up of several **customs.** joint families each occupying a distinct ward, at the head of which is the oldest male member of the family group. Just as the village is a coöperative union of families, so is the tribe a coöperative union of villages. The underlying principle of the whole scheme is that of brotherhood established on social and economic equality. All institutions exist for the good of the many rather than for the benefit of the few.

In this system, therefore, no labor is requited. Everybody is supposed to work and everybody has the right of enjoying the fruits of the common labor. There can be

Equality.

no extremely rich, and there can be no extremely poor. Such a thing as capitalism or pauperism cannot exist in this society. Individualism has no place here. Collectivism is the underlying law of the

A DAGGER

communistic and socialistic system. Private property, however, does exist in these parts. While land is free to all, some things like cattle are subject to private ownership. Yet, inasmuch as all of these things come under the protection of the tribe, they are regarded as belonging in a sense to the chief. The owner considers himself merely a sort of steward enjoying the use of a possession of the king. What he gains in excess of the average share may be distributed among his relatives; but on his death the clan often decides the question of inheritance.

Africans have a system of education with much merit. Leo Frobenius had never been in a country where he heard so much of education, and he never saw a place where it was more systematically carried out. There is no formal school training in native Africa except the discipline of two societies found in most communities. The one for the boys is under the direction of a fatherly old man, and that for the girls under a trustworthy matron. They are

Methods of instruction.

carefully instructed in physiology and hygiene with special reference to fatherhood and motherhood. It is the ambition of every male to produce offspring. It is the desire of every woman to become a mother. As the clan or tribe needs strong men for its protection, this tendency is encouraged.

Early in life, about the regular school age in modern countries, the African boy begins his education. He is required to look after the kids, the young goats, and to make observation in agricultural methods. The boy is required later to tend larger animals and finally to herd cattle. He also undergoes circumcision very much like that of the Hebrews. The girls of the same age begin the study of household and domestic duties such as supplying the family with water, cleaning the house, pounding the corn, and preparing food. They continue at this sort of training until they reach the age of becoming housewives. After having been under strict supervision of matrons who have instructed them in the rudimentary instructions of motherhood and have taught them the duty of wives to their husbands, the course terminates with ceremony. This consists mainly of dancing. In preparation for this dance, a thing which is a part of the training, they paint their faces with bewildering colors.

A Knife

In marrying the African youth has an eye single to the good of the communistic state. In keeping with the custom among most people of such a stage of civilization, the ceremony is arranged after the contract is made by the parents of the young people. They themselves have very little to do with it. The groom is accustomed to give a number of cows, goats,

Marriage.

sheep, or the like, to the parents of the girl he has chosen. These, however, are not intended as an actual purchase of the wife, as maligners of Africans often say. They are rather intended as a means of securing the wife against ill treatment. If ill used, she can leave her husband and return to her father, but these gifts are not returned. Of course, there are cases of an actual purchase of women as happens

in any slaveholding country like the Southern United
States before the Civil War. There is no more of an actual
purchase in such marriage arrangements in Africa, however, than in some of the dowry contracts common in
Europe and America to-day.

The marriage ceremony, like others, is usually celebrated
with dancing. The most of this festive performance is

ANOTHER SORT OF DANCE

not according to any particular rhythm, but resembles
rather a confused and independent jumping in which all
participate. Members of the families concerned, however,
are accustomed to stage also a more graceful exercise in
keeping with the art, the description of which has found its
way into modern literature. The musical instruments are
drums, horns, reed and stringed instruments.

Connected with marriage sometimes, too, is polygamy.

As women do most of the work to release the men **for** hunting and the protection of the state, a man's wealth may be determined by the number of wives he has. The husband, however, usually concentrates his attention on one of the group. She is his household manager. The others are treated mainly as servants. This also has been misunderstood and referred to as backwardness when compared with the monogamy sup- **Polygamy.** posed to be practiced among the Christians. As a matter of fact, however, polygamy is not found among all Africans. Where it is found, all men are not economically prepared to indulge in it. A man cannot easily support more than one wife. Polygamy, then, is restricted largely to the official class and the well-to-do, as it illegally exists to-day among such elements in modern countries. Some tribes, moreover, practice monogamy in preference to polygamy.

Polygamy, moreover, grows out of their peculiar socialistic system. Because of frequent wars so many soldiers are killed off that there are more women than men. Polygamy is practiced, then, because of the benefit resulting to the state in the production of sufficient able-bodied men to protect it. As a rule a woman must attach herself to some man. Polygamy in Africa, moreover, renders impossible spinsterhood and prostitution, which exist among the so-called civilized people. The Africans practice openly what Europeans and Americans practice clandestinely. There are no loose women among the people of Africa. Every woman has her own marital connection and recognizes the tie as binding. There are cases of moral lapses, but no evidence of a general profligacy of sexes. Delinquents are deterred therefrom by the strict laws punishing adultery with maiming, mutilation, or death.

In another way, too, the Africans have often been misunderstood. Travelers have occasionally referred to them as thieves and liars. Examples of their mendacity consist

mainly of efforts to mislead the foreigner whom they sus-
pect as desirous of doing some injury to them or to their
Morals of tribe. If, for example, the foreigner inquires
Africans. as to the right road to the house of the chief,
the native invariably sends him in the contrary direction.
If he wants to know the distance to a certain town, the
native informs him that it is about twice or three times as

far as it actually is; and
when he has gone as far
as directed another na-
tive may inform him
that he is on the wrong
road. To weaken their
enemies, moreover, peo-
ple in this stage are ac-
customed to take cattle,
goats, sheep, or other
property; for while they
weaken the tribe from
which they are taken
they strengthen their
own particular group.

AN AFRICAN STOVE

Any person able to contribute thereby to the welfare of
the tribe is considered a leader of worth, and may rise to
the chieftaincy of the tribe. These things were customary
among the American Indians, and the Americans find
them so to-day among the Filipinos. The custom differs
very little from that of Europeans and Americans; for
they have one code of law and ethics which they follow
when dealing with other races and a different code in dealing with their own kind.

In their own group, living among themselves, the Africans consider an untruth a sin. Any one disturbing the
property of another, moreover, becomes a criminal, subject
to the severe penalty of a fine, imprisonment or even death.

In fact, locks and safes which are necessary in America and Europe are not required among the uncontaminated natives of Africa. The patterns of morality of the Hebrews and certain Africans, the Kaffirs, for example, are strikingly coincident. The Kaffirs have laws to meet every crime committed. "Theft is punished by restitution and fine; injured cattle, by death or fine; false witness, by a heavy fine; adultery, by fine or death; rape, by fine or death; poisoning or witchcraft, by death and confiscation of property; murder, by death or fine; treason or desertion from the tribe, by death and confiscation."

POTTERY

Running throughout the system underlying the life of the African native is his religion. He adheres to this, even to the very letter of the law as handed down by his forefathers. Roughly speaking, we may say this religion is a belief in a world of spirits and an effort to be guided by them. The African believes in God. He **African** believes that man is immortal. His spirit **religion.** can never die. Since the beginning of time, then, the world has become filled with spirits. Man can therefore commune face to face with the spirits of the departed. Referring to the custom on the Gold Coast, Casely Hayford says: "You should watch him as he takes offerings of food and drink to the graveside. There he carefully sets a chair for the dear one gone before, then places the meal in order, and pours out a libation, addressing the spirit of the departed the while. He earnestly believes that the spirit of the departed relative hovers around him by day as well as by night, and he has both the physical and the spiritual sense to perceive its presence. He sees in the mammiferous bat, winging its flight from room to room at night in the home once dear to the loved one, who is supposed to dominate it, a kindly providence which does not leave him all forlorn in his grief, but sends the spirit of the departed back occasionally to watch and to protect. He even speaks to it in endearing terms at times, and would fain believe that it understands and is in full sympathy with him. You may sneer at the seeming simplicity of the native mind, but the Aborigines believe that there are mysteries in this world yet unrevealed to man. He, the Native, implicitly believes in ghosts, and has many an authentic story to tell of some strange visitation which he has experienced. Nay, more, his sense of smell detects the presence of a ghost in a house."

Speaking further on this wise, the same author says: "Mark you, he does not look to communion with the gross, material matter that lies mouldering in the grave; but he looks to that indefinable something beyond which has defied the reason of mankind for all time. He **Communion with the spirit.** looks beyond his present squalid surroundings to a world hereafter where he will meet every member of his family, and particularly those whom he has dearly loved, and where he will meet with them in joyous intercourse as he has done in this world. It matters not what happens to-day, since to-morrow may find him in the grave and at rest with his forefathers. In this happy frame of mind he goes through life contentedly, free from

carking care, and wonders sometimes at all the excitement
and ado of men of another race. And as for a material hell,
the scarecrow of the missionaries, he merely smiles at such
a suggestion. Is there not trouble enough in this world?
God knows there is. Why should God add trouble to
trouble?''[1]

In Africa one finds a varying conception of God. Among
some strictly African natives, in Yorubaland, however,
Leo Frobenius found these ideas of divinity: ''The idea
of the generative and fertilizing godlike force is so persistent that it is not confined to human beings; but, on
the contrary, the first-fruits of every spring-   **God in**
sowing, the firstlings of stock-raising without   **Africa.**
any exception, again become the share of the deity in the
form of sacrificial offerings in return for having been by
him begotten. And not only so, many other things go to
prove the significance and inevitability of the idea that
the Deity must necessarily be the originator of all succes-
sive generations. And, therefore, almost all the prayers of
Yorubans, all their rituals, always culminate in the petition
for fruitfulness of their fields, the blessings of children in
their families, and aid in every kind of propagation.

''Now, an Orisha (a god) can just as well have his home
on a grand altar, rich in symbolic ornamentation, as in a
naked, little hut. He is manifest in it and to no lesser degree than in the control of the natural agencies in which he
mythologically dwells. The River God is not the river;
he only animates it, he is effective in it, proceeds from it.
And the Sun God is not the actual sun; the   **Nature**
divinity lives in the sun. Every Orisha has   **as God.**
taken up his abode in his natural attributes, and may, if
he so will, leave them, move about amongst his family, and
there plant the seeds of blessing and abundance of increase.
Precisely in the same way he can inspire, i.e., enter into,

[1] Casely Hayford, *Gold Coast Native Institutions*, 101-103.

those specially destined to receive him, so that they behave as though possessed.''[2]

[2] The African story of the creation, although found in various versions, differs little from that of the Hebrews. In it appears also the idea of the fall and redemption of man. Leo Frobenius found in Africa one running like this: "At first there was no earth. There was Okun (or Olokun), the ocean, a water stretched over all things. Above it was Olorun. Olorun, the Orisha of the sky, and Olokun, the Orisha of the sea, were coeval. They contained (or possessed) all that there was. Olorun had two sons. The first one's name was Orishalla (the same as Ostaballa, who here is also simply called Orisha); the younger's, Odudua. Olorun summoned Orisha. He gave him some earth. He gave him a hen with fingers (? claws) (Adje-alesse-manu). He said to him, 'Climb down' (or, go down to earth), 'and make the earth upon Okun.' Orisha went. On the way he found some palm-wine. He began to drink and got drunken. Then he slumbered. Olorun saw this. Then Olorun summoned Odudua and said to him: 'Thy (elder) brother has got drunken on his way down below. Go thou, take the sand and the hen with five fingers and make the earth upon Okun.' Odudua went. He took the sand. He went down and laid it on the sea. He put the hen with five fingers on it. The hen began to scratch and spread the sand about and forced the water aside. Ilife was the spot where this took place, round, which, at first, the sea still flowed. Odudua ruled the land of Ilife as its first king. The sea of Ilokun grew less and less and ran away through a small hole from there a hole from which to this day one can fetch the holy water—much water and it never fails. It is called Osha. Now, Orisha was very wrath that he had not created the earth; he began to wage war against Odudua. They contended for a long time, but then made peace. They both went underground and were never seen again."
  A second version runs thus:
  "In the beginning the earth was not. There was only water. Olorun sent down Oshalla. He gave him a ball of sand on his way. He said: 'Spread this out upon the face of the waters.' Oshalla went. On the road Oshalla picked up a flask of palm-wine. He tasted it and said: 'This is good.' He drank while going. Whenever he was athirst he drank a mouthful. He drank the first mouthful very early. Then he grew weary, went to sleep and forgot what Olorun had bidden him. Then the other Orishas took a mirror (Awo-aje), looked into it and saw that Oshalla had been drinking down below, gone to sleep and forgotten Olorun's behest. Thereupon Olorun sent Odudua, saying: 'Do thou what I told Oshalla to do.' Odudua was a strong man. He took a ball of earth with him. He descended. He made the earth and pushed the water aside. Olorun then gave Odudua a hen, called Adje-alesse-mahun; it was a hen with five fingers; it pushed the water back so that it became the sea. When Odudua and Oshalla had finished their work, they went into the earth

This religion is administered by a priestcraft of which the king himself is head. However, the actual administration of the system is not generally interfered with by the king. With this religious effort the priests unite the function of the medicine men. Working in this way the priests treat both mind and body. **African priestcraft.** The training of the priest begins in early childhood by sending him to another community to undergo training for a number of years. This consists of the study of things spiritual and also the use of herbal remedies. The completion of this training is celebrated with an exciting dance in which the fetish is said to come upon him. Some of these medico-priests have been known to cure diseases which have baffled the skill of European physicians. They are experts in herbal treatment. These medico-priests, however, like most of those operating among primitive people, clothe their operations with sufficient secrecy to make the people believe in their power to do many things which are impossible. Although the laity may detect the imposition, the office of the priest is so sacred among the Africans that they do not expose them when caught.

Studying this religious system, in which there is so much good in spite of the irrational ideas involved, one can see the reasons for the ease with which the Negro has accepted Christianity. The religion of Jesus is an Oriental production. It easily appeals to the mind of the Negro, which is also Oriental. The mind of the white man is Occidental. He has, therefore, failed to understand and appreciate Christianity. The study of the African religion, too, leads one to understand how it is the greatest impediment to the missionary work in that continent. It is extremely

at Ilife where they had begun their labors, and were turned to stone. Since then men worshiped these stones. Oba-diu is the high priest of Oshalla. Odudua is greatly feared. So powerful is this Godhead that before the people in Ilife can speak the name of Odudua, they must slay a sheep and drink its blood."

difficult for the native to abandon his own religion when it
so permeates the life of the people that to do so means a
declaration of hostility to the king, the most high priest,
Difficulties of and a repudiation of all of the traditions of
missionaries. the native's forefathers. It is almost impossible to change the religion of a man without changing the
other elements in his civilization. For this reason it has
been said that one railroad is worth a thousand missionaries.
But such an innovation as a railroad or steamboat brings
many evils in its train. In thus changing the civilization
of these people by foreign aggression they fall victims to
social diseases, intemperance, prostitution, and race hate.

CHAPTER III

AFRICANS IN HISTORY WITH OTHERS

CONSIDERED from the continental point of view, however, the life of the African is complicated. Being the second largest continent with various sorts of climate, Africa presents all of the aspects of life in other regions. Above we have tried to indi- **Occupations of Africans.** cate the chief interests of the people by the designation of certain zones. While this is helpful, there are so many exceptions to be made that we should not consider these terms as absolutely conclusive. Africans have been and are now doing things very much in the same manner as we find them done by other peoples similarly circumstanced. In a short sketch like this, moreover, it is impossible to figure out accurately the occupations or industries of all the people of a continent. Considered as a whole, however, there are certain pursuits which may be thought of as typical of large areas of that continent. Cattle raising is one of the chief industries of Africa. This is marked by the kraal, or cattle pen, found in almost every village of the cattle zone. This is a sort of center of the commercial life of the people. The majority of Africans look upon their cattle, sheep, or goats as the most valuable property. They often use them in exchange as we do money. Some sort of farming, too, is general among most Africans, although not that of modern times. They cultivate maize, rice, millet and vegetables. Nature enables them to produce easily

also yams, ground nuts, pumpkins, melons and beans.
Such fruits as the plantain, banana, orange, and the mango
flourish there as in other tropical countries. Coffee, too,
may be produced in large quantities. Africans have not
been generally interested in their mineral wealth except
in making use of iron.[1] Some have exploited gold.

In the construction of their homes the natives of the
rainy region seem to have followed the model of the "ant
hill." There the native, like the ant, has had to look out
for himself in building his hut high enough to be beyond
Home the reach of the rising water. The homes of
construction. the natives are thatched huts built sometimes
upon beams of hard wood like ebony or mahogany found
in abundance in certain parts of Africa. Softer woods

AN ANT HILL

would be quickly de-
stroyed by the termites
which feast thereupon in
that climate. In their
villages the homes of the
tribal chiefs and wealthy
may be more imposing
structures. The arrange-
ment of these homes in
clusters or sometimes ac-
cording to design presents
an interesting picture.

In facing the forces of nature to wrest therefrom a
livelihood, Africans have given a lesson to the so-called

[1] For more extensive treatment see J. Deniker's *Races of Men,*
J. Finot's *Race Prejudice,* F. Ratzel's *The History of Mankind,*
Franz Boas's *The Mind of Primitive Man,* Spiller's *Inter-Racial
Problems,* C. Bücher's *Industrial Revolution,* Casely Hayford's
Ethiopia Unbound and his *Native Institutions,* James Bryce's *Im-
pressions of South Africa,* Leo Frobenius's *The Voice of Africa,*
G. Sergi's *The Mediterranean Race,* Felix DuBois's *Timbuctoo,
the Mysterious;* Lady Lugard's *A Tropical Dependency,* and David
Randall Maciver's *Medieval Rhodesia.*

civilized world. In the industrial arts they have shown conclusively that they were once the greatest metal workers of the world. Developing as such, the Africans were the first to smelt iron and use the forge. To this **Industrial** race, therefore, belongs the credit for the gift **arts.** of the most useful thing to man. Upon its use has been established the civilization of modern times. We cannot imagine ourselves without the use of iron unless we think of the most barbarous state of the prehistoric period when men dwelt in caves and lived by pillage and plunder. In the all-wise plan by which our destiny is determined every race has the capacity for certain definite contributions. The discovery of iron is the outstanding contribution of the Negro.

AN AFRICAN HOME

It is a grave error to think of Africans altogether as people working in the rough. In the use of metals the Africans have not restricted themselves to crude methods. By practically all persons who have made a study of the industrial arts of the African, we have a high estimate of what they have produced. Their pottery, **Metal** basketry, implements, and weapons show the **workers.** highest of skill and the keenest appreciation of the beautiful. Although deprived of foreign contact, they have shown here a capacity in industrial arts beyond that of anything contemporaneous in Europe. Their cutlery not only compares favorably with that of Sheffield, but even shows workmanship and inventive genius unexcelled in the modern world.

Advancing still further, the African, even with limited evidence available, has sufficient to show that he has equaled, if not excelled, all others in fine arts. According **Fine arts.** to the evidence brought to light by such investigators as Schliemann, Sir Arthur Evans, Giuseppe Sergi and our recent scientists, the stimulus to Greek art came from Africa. In evidence the archæologists offer the figures of Sherbro and the megaliths of Gambia. These indicate a superior culture which we have seldom considered as possible among Africans. Further evidence has been supplied in the discoveries of stone implements belonging to the prehistoric period in South Africa. Other discoveries in Rhodesia are decidedly convincing as to the unusually artistic mind of the African. Probably the most striking of all these discoveries is that of the antique works of art of Benin described by Pitt Rivers and Felix von Luschan. These works were brought to light as a result of the punitive expedition sent upon this town

A HANGING LAMP IN BRONZE FROM BENIN

at the mouth of the Niger River in 1897. They represent a fine art of such an early stage that there is no actual record as to the date of its production. In the usual fashion Europeans thought of this art as resulting from European influence. Further investigation, however, has

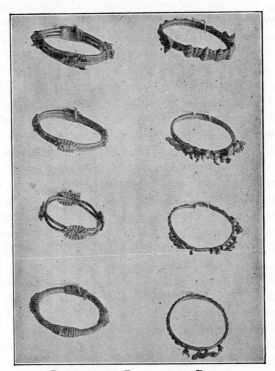

BRACELETS IN BRONZE FROM BENIN

shown that these productions are characteristically African. They could not have resulted from European influence because they belonged to an early period when Europeans were savages.

Although the Africans have made unusual contributions to the dance, music, and sculpture, however, some of the

most advanced nations have not succeeded in political organization. Yet Africa itself is not a fair test of the political possibilities of the Negro. In the first place, as stated above, the continent is cut off from the rest of the world by an unbroken coast line of a plateau area permit-
Political ting few navigable rivers. Having had such
organization. little opportunity to profit by contact with other parts, Africa deserves unusual credit for the political institutions which it has independently developed. While immensely rich in vegetable oils, fibers, gums and hard-woods, foreigners found those things too accessible else-where to warrant the hardships necessary for invading the all but impenetrable interior of Africa. At that time, moreover, little difference in the situation resulted from the gold and diamonds which to-day crown Africa as one of the richest of the continents. These are treasures which have come into their own in modern times.

In the interior of Africa itself nature provided other handicaps to political organization. Both the climate and the physiographic features of the continent indicate the difficulty of developing political institutions. On the West
Handicaps to Coast, for example, most of the land is so
progress. low and marshy, so full of small streams and prodigious growth that travel is decidedly difficult. Road building is almost impossible in this section, and in the case of clearing a path, nature is so prolific here that in a few days the rapid growth will close up the thoroughfare. Unsuitable, too, for horses and mules, which easily fall victims of the tsetse fly, the problem of transportation is still more complicated. The highest form of political organization attainable under such circumstances, there-fore, is that of a tribe ruled by the chief. Occasionally, too, there may arise a chieftain with sufficient following to bring under his sway a number of these tribes to form a kingdom. Yet empires have risen in the West.

On the East Coast, however, nature renders possible a more extensive development of political institutions. While the climate is the same, the country is somewhat open and the means of communication are far better **African** than on the West Coast. Nature somewhat **kingdoms.** favored the Sudan and Dahomey. Northeast of Dahomey, the Fulahs, similarly circumstanced, established a number of kingdoms which manifested evidences of ability to endure.

A CUSTOM—ROCK PAINTING

Between Bamako on the Upper Niger and Siguiri Mandingoes, under their great king Gonga Musa, built the Manding, or Melle, the most extensive African empire of its day. To the east of Melle appeared also the Hausa kingdom resembling a federation very much like that of Switzerland. West of Lake Tchad developed the kingdom of Bornu, which has enjoyed its growth largely since the invasion of the Mohammedans, about the year 1000.

It will no doubt be interesting, therefore, to trace briefly the rise and fall of some of these empires. The highest of these civilizations centered in the Nile region, with Ethiopia around the head waters of that river and **The Negro in** Egypt along the lower. "Ancient Egypt **the Empires.** knew the Negro, both bond and free," says Chamberlain, "and his blood flowed in the veins of not a few of the mighty Pharaohs. Nefertari, the famous Queen of Aahmes, the King of Egypt, who drove the Hyksos from the land and founded the 18th Dynasty (*ca.* 1700 B.C.), was a Negress of great beauty, strong personality, and re-

markable administrative ability. She was for years associated in the government with her son, Amen-hotep I, who
succeeded his father. Queen Nefertari was highly venerated and many monuments were erected in her honor; she
was venerated as 'ancestress and founder of the 18th
Dynasty' and styled 'the wife of the God Ammon,' etc.
Another strain of Negro blood came into the line of the
Pharaohs with Mut-em-ua, wife of Thothmes IV, whose

A MYTH—ROCK PAINTING

son, Amen-hotep III, had a Negroid physiognomy. Amen-
hotep III was famous as a builder and his reign (*ca.* 1400
B.C.) is distinguished by a marked improvement of Egyptian art and architecture. He it was who built the great
temple of Ammon at Luxor and the colossi of Memnon.
Besides these marked individual instances, there is the fact
that the Egyptian race itself in general had a considerable
element of Negro blood, and one of the prime reasons why
no civilization of the type of that of the Nile arose in
other parts of the continent, if such a thing were at all
possible, was that Egypt acted as a sort of channel by
which the genius of Negro-land was drafted off into the
service of Mediterranean and Asiatic culture. In this
sense Egyptian civilization may be said, in some respects,
to be of Negro origin. Among the Semitic peoples whose
civilizations were so numerous and so ancient on the shores
of the Mediterranean and throughout Western Asia, the

Negro, as in Egypt, made his influence felt, from the lowest
to the highest walks of life, sometimes as a slave, sometimes
as the freest of citizens. As cup-bearer, or confidential
adviser, he stood next to kings and princes and as faithful
eunuch he enhanced and extended the power of the
other sex in lands where custom confined them to the four
walls of their dwellings, or restricted to the utmost their
appearance and their actions in public. And women from
Ethiopia, 'black but comely,' wives or favorite slaves of
satraps and of kings, often were the real   **Influence**
rulers of Oriental provinces and empires.   **abroad.**
Nor have the Negroes in these Asiatic countries been absent from the ranks of the musician and the poet, from
the time of Solomon to that of Haroun al Raschid and
beyond in the days of emirs and sultans. One must not
forget the Queen of Sheba, with her dash of Negro blood,
said, together with that of the great Solomon, to have been
inherited by the sovereign of Abyssinia. When under the
brilliant dynasty of the Ommiades (661-750 A. D.), the
city of Damascus was one of the glories of the world, its
galaxy of five renowned poets included Nosseyeb, the
Negro. And we can cross the whole of Asia and find the
Negro again, for, when, in far-off Japan, the ancestors of
the modern Japanese were making their way northward
against the Ainu, the aborigines of that country, the leader
of their armies was Sakanouye Tamuramaro, a famous
general and a Negro.'' [2]

The story of the Negro restricted to Africa is still more
interesting. Ethiopia and Egypt were at first united, but
in the course of time separated as two distinct empires.
There were various wars between the Egyp-   **Ethiopia and**
tians and the Ethiopians when the former   **Egypt.**
were trying to wrest the country from the invaders of the

[2] *Atlanta University Studies, Select Discussions of Race Problems,* pp. 86-87.

north. The affairs of the Ethiopian and Egyptian empires did not apparently become separate until during the Middle Empire of Egypt, when Nepata and Meroe became centers of a largely native civilization. The new empire, however, continued its wars against the Ethiopians and gradually incorporated the country, until Ethiopia finally became subject to that land. In the course of time, however, Ethiopia asserted itself, easily overran Egypt, and appointed a son of the king of Ethiopia to rule the land of the Pharaohs. Ethiopia once ruled Yemen.

The Negro was then at his best as a constituent factor in the affairs of the Egypto-Ethiopian empire. When, however, the country was conquered by the Assyrians and then by the Persians, Egypt became subject to the invaders from Asia, whereas Ethiopia continued its way. Ethiopia was again invaded by a Greek influence from the East and the influence of the tribes from the Soudan on the West, but the Ethiopian language and government tended to endure. Ethiopians persistently gave trouble **The Egypto-Ethiopian empire.** to the Romans, who undertook to subdue them and failed thoroughly to do so because of their interior position. This country lay asleep during the Middle Ages. In later years it took the name of Nubia. After having experienced various conquests and subjugations resulting in changes which have not yet succeeded in blotting out altogether its ancient civilization, it finally became known as Abyssinia.

With the exception of what the historian Herodotus has left in fragmentary form, not much is known about the early nations established on the Niger or the Soudan. They are connected in history with Ethiopia and **Soudan and the Niger.** Egypt as centers of culture distinctly African. The first extensive accounts date from the approach of the Mohammedans about the year 1000. The Mohamme-

dans came largely as traders and gave much stimulus to
the rise of commerce among these people. The invaders
did not utterly change the civilization, but they influenced
the life and history of the people. Drawing no color line,
these Arabs accepted the blacks as equals and carried
some of them to Arabia. This gave rise to the Arabised
blacks represented by Antar. In Arabia he became the
military hero and one of the great poets of Islam. Carrying their civilization later into Spain, the Africans attained distinction there also. A Negro poet resided at
Seville, and a Negro founded a town in lower Morocco.

In the eleventh century the Moslems found in the west
the far advanced kingdom of Ghana, which they conquered
after much resistance. The natives had an army of two
hundred thousand men and sufficient wealth **The Kingdom**
to support it. When this kingdom declined **of Ghana.**
in the thirteenth century, Melle superseded it and added
greatly to its wealth by the expansion of its commerce
through welcoming the Mohammedan traders. The Mohammedans found evidence of advanced civilizations even
in the Congo, and learned that the Zulu chiefs, whose
armies swept southeastern Africa, exhibited unusual power
of military organization.

Among the city states where this exceptional culture
was discovered was that of Jenne. From this the modern
name Guinea has been obtained. This city experienced
as usual, migrations and movements frequent **The State**
in other parts of Africa, resulting in the de- **of Jenne.**
struction of many of the evidences of civilization. But,
according to several travelers, there was found an advanced
culture in their terra-cotta industry, in their achievements
in clay, stone and iron, in their glass beads, earthen and
glassware, and in the dexterity of their weaving. This
civilization shows the city group like that around Timbuktu

and Hausa. These cities had a government largely like that

Timbuktu. of an autonomy of modern times—what we would call the social and industrial state, but of an essentially democratic order. Of considerable importance was the Mossi Empire made up of five states which in some form endured for many centuries as a distinctly Negro organization.

There developed also the progressive state known as Ashanti. In the orgies of war and sacrifice of human beings, Dahomey, it is said, exhibited

Ashanti and Dahomey. a striking contrast to the city democracy of "elevated religious ideas, organized industry and noble art." Backward conditions rendered the country so weak that it finally developed into a region of internecine strife which paved the way for the lucrative slave trade carried on by the Christian nations. Yet Dahomey was in many respects a country of progress. The people

ARMS AND ORNAMENTS

as a rule were good farmers and skilled in mechanic arts. Some Dahoman kings were rulers of great ability.

In the regions of the Great Lakes flourished other centers of civilization. There were found evidences of advanced culture in the mining of silver and gold and in trade in precious stones. These Africans were the first to smelt iron and to use it as the great leverage of civilization.

The Lake Region. They had useful iron implements, erected well-constructed buildings and fortifications, made beautiful pottery, and worked extensively in the

various metals. As indicated by their utensils and implements, they had made much more advancement in religion
than some of the other tribes. They had temples of significance comparing favorably with those of the Greeks and
Romans. The government established was based on
slavery. The people devoted themselves to
agriculture and to industries.

There emerged, too, the large kingdom of
Songhay, covering the period from the year
700 to 1335 A. D. This nation, according to
Es-Sadi, the author of the *Tarikh Es-Soudan*,
had three well-connected dynasties known for
their great warriors who extended the
territory of the empire, and statesmen who
distinguished themselves in ad- **The Kingdom**
ministering its affairs. After **of Songhay.**
resisting the Mohammedans for some time,
the sixteenth king was converted to their faith
about the year 1000. Among the greatest of
these rulers was Soni Ali, noted for his military exploits and his success as a statesman.
The country again saw something like a
return to a golden age under another distinguished ruler called Askia Mohammed. He brought the
country into contact with Egypt and the outer world, and
finally marched against neighboring empires, which he
conquered and ruled with a provincial system very much
like that of Rome. He established schools of learning and
promoted the study of law, literature, the natural sciences,
and medicine.

A CYLINDRICAL
VESSEL

In the end, however, this empire fell into the hands of
undesirable rulers. According to the pious annalist, "All
was changed in a moment. Danger took the place of serenity, destitution of abundance; trouble, calamities and

violence succeeded to tranquillity. Everywhere the populations began to destroy each other. In all places and in
every direction rapine became the law, war spared neither
life nor property, nor the position of the people. Disorder was general, and it spread everywhere till it reached
at last the highest degree of intensity.'' ''Things continued thus,'' adds the historian, ''until towards the moment
in which the Songhay dynasty approached its end, and

A CHOPPER

its empire ceased to exist. At
this moment faith was ex-
changed for infidelity; there
was nothing forbidden by
God which was not openly
done. Men drank wine, they
gave themselves up to vice.
... Because of these abomina-
tions, the Almighty in His
vengeance drew down upon
the Songhay the victorious
army of the Moors, whom he
brought through terrible suf-
ferings from a distant country. Then the roots of this
people were separated from
the trunk, and the chastise-
ment they underwent was
exemplary.''

All of these facts set forth, however, show that African
culture prior to the exploitation of the New World was in
many respects like the culture of Europe. The natives
African far removed from the equator had reached
culture. the stage of easily earning a subsistence by
using iron implements. European nations were late in
learning this. In art and architecture they had advanced

far beyond the primitive stage, in literature their achievements attained the rank of the world's best classics in the *Tarikh Es-Soudan,* and in religion and morals most of them kept abreast with the times. In government the Africans united the best in democracy and monarchy. Theirs was a slave society, but there was a healthy sentiment against the exploitation of men. With the thinking class, birth did not differ from birth; "as the freeman was born so was the slave." "In the beginning," said a pious African, "our Lord created all; with Him there is neither slave nor freeman, but every one is free." "To love a king," the African thought, "is not bad, but a king who loves you is better." And it sounds a little socialistic to hear the proverbs, "If thou art poor do not make the rich man thy friend," "If thou goest to a foreign country, do not alight at a rich man's house," or "It is better to be poor and live long than rich and die young."

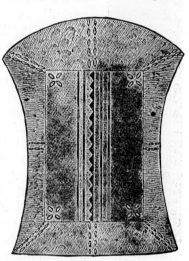

A SHIELD

The African mind, too, exhibited evidences of philosophy not to be despised. The native philosopher found three friends in "courage, sense and insight." The African realized that "the lack of knowledge is darker than night," that "an ignorant man *African proverbs.* is a slave," and that "whoever works without knowledge works uselessly." "Not to know," he believed, "is bad;

not to wish to know is worse." Adhering to a high standard of morals, the African taught the youth that "there

is no medicine for hate" and that "he
who bears malice is a heathen; he who in-
jures another brings injury to himself."
To emphasize opportunity the moralist reminded his fellows that "the dawn does
not come twice to wake a man." To teach
politeness he asserted that "bowing to a
dwarf will not prevent your standing erect
again." In emphasizing the truth, he asserted that "lies, however numerous, will
be caught by truth when it rises," and
"the voice of truth is easily known." The
African warned the selfish man that "if
you love yourself, others will hate you; if
you humble yourself, others will love you."
Among the Africans there was a belief that
"a man with wisdom is better off than a
stupid man with any amount of charm and
superstition." Such sentient expressions as
"A butterfly that brushes against thorns
will tear his wings," and "He who cannot
move an ant and yet tries to move an ele-
phant shall find his folly," have the ring of

AN ORNA-
MENTAL VESSEL
IN BRONZE
FROM BENIN

the plantation philosophy developed in the
United States. The proverbs "When the fox
dies, fowls do not mourn," and "He who
goes with a wolf will learn to howl," exhibit more than
ordinary mental development.

CHAPTER IV

FOREIGN AGGRESSION

It happened that centuries ago, when the civilization of the blacks was not unlike that of the emerging modern Europe, Africa was disturbed within by migrations and from without by foreign aggression. Such a movement overthrew the Roman Empire and destroyed **Disorder in** its civilization. Being too weak to resist **Africa.** invaders while dealing with enemies at home, Africa yielded to the attacks of the restless nations. When the Bantu hordes had destroyed the peace of the African empires, there appeared the Mohammedans on the East Coast in quest of slaves to supply their harems and armies.[1]

During the seventh and eighth centuries the Mohammedan religion well established itself in Western Asia and began to take over Northern Africa. At first Africans already enslaved were bought from their masters and used in war, as was the custom throughout Europe and Asia. When, however, there came a demand for a larger number of slaves than could thereby be supplied, they were seized by well-planned methods involving the enslavement and depopulation of large districts of Africa. This led to the overthrow of African nations long since established as centers of culture and the rise of other states committed to the policy of profiting by the lucrative slave trade.

[1] For this aspect of the subject the following are helpful: Sir Charles Lucas's *The Partition of Africa;* T. K. Ingram's *History of slavery and Serfdom;* John R. Spear's *The American Slave Trade;* F. H. Buxton's *The African Slave Trade;* and T. Clarkson's *African Slave Trade.*

This trade finally reached the very interior of the continent and became the most cruel traffic in human flesh theretofore known to the world. It is only of late that it can be said that this Mohammedan slave trade has been actually

Mohammedan slavery. checked. It remained as a disgrace to certain Eastern nations during the latter part of the nineteenth century and even into the twentieth. Slavery among the Mohammedans, however, was not altogether a

An African Forge

hopeless condition. If the slave professed faith in Islam he might become a communicant in that connection, enjoying equality with the richest and the best, accepted on the principle of the brotherhood of man.

Finally came Europeans, too, working their way to the Far East and Australia by way of the Cape of Good Hope. Marco Polo's account of Cipango, or Japan, was a stimulus. This undertaking was a conspicuous development of the Renaissance which resulted in the discovery of America.

Foreign Aggression

TIMBUKTU

The moving spirit in the early enterprise was Prince Henry of Portugal, who sent out men to trade in gold dust and Negro slaves. They proceeded sometimes under **Coming of the** the pretext of converting the heathen. Prince **Portuguese.** Henry died in 1460; but others pushed the exploration as far as the Equator by 1471 and reached the Congo by 1484. Two years later Diogo Cam went a thousand miles south of the Equator and "set up a stone cross on the border of Hottentot land. Then came Bartholomew Diaz, who was driven by storm beyond the Cape of Good Hope in 1486. Vasco da Gama doubled the Cape in 1497 and explored the coast as far as Mombasa and Melinde. He proceeded thence to Calicut in India in 1498. The Portuguese established strongholds on the bay of Arguin and at Elmina on the Gold Coast. They extended their influence into Angola and Mozambique and even learned something about parts of the interior of Africa.

The French, following close upon the Portuguese, if not preceding them, made a settlement in the Canaries in 1402. They later entered the region of the Senegal. The English made an unsuccessful attempt to trade with the Guinea coast in 1481. William Hawkins, the father of Sir **Other** John Hawkins, ventured to trade in slaves **troubles.** on the coast from 1530 to 1532 and in 1553. Then came his bold, plundering son, who in 1562 took more than a hundred slaves from Guinea to Santo Domingo. Uniting religion with the slave trade, he ordered his crews to "serve God daily" and "to love one another." He went first to Hispaniola with three hundred Negroes whom he traded for pearls, hides, and other products. The second voyage was more hazardous, and he failed in the third. In spite of his murderous plundering, however, his chronicler entreats that "his name be praised forevermore, Amen."

Foreign Aggression

AN AFRICAN VILLAGE

Yet men of the type of Hawkins are not to be unsympathetically condemned. In that day there was no sharp distinction between a pirate and an honorable seaman. Some of the sea rovers held commissions of their "God-fearing sovereigns" who promoted these popular enter-

Piracy and commerce.

prises. Most races, moreover, have not yet emerged from the stage of primitive civilization when right was restricted to one's blood kin. If strangers within the gates could not be murdered, there was no moral law restraining one from abusing the subjects of non-Christian nations. Menendez believed that his slaughter of captives was for the glory of God. Francis Drake, the notorious plunderer of his time, commended his lieutenant "to the tuition of Him that with His blood redeemed us."

This importation of the Negroes, however, was not their first contact with the Western Hemisphere. Long before the Teutonic elements established a claim to North America the Africans had visited its shores and penetrated

The Negro and the discovery of America.

the interior. According to Leo Wiener, of Harvard University, the Africans were the first to discover America. He has found in the American language the early African influence in words like "canoe," "buckra," and "tobacco." They could not have been brought from any other part of the world. African fetishism, too, resembling a custom among the American Indians, has been considered another reason for believing that Africans saw the shores of America centuries before the Teutons had developed sufficiently to venture so far on the high seas. Inasmuch as scientists now claim that there once existed on the western coast of Africa a very advanced people who influenced even the civilization of the Mediterranean World, they have little doubt of their having extended their culture across the Middle Passage. Africa, it will be remembered, is nearer to America than Europe.[2]

Negroes, moreover, have a place among the exploits of the European pioneers who many years later explored North and South America. Pedro Alonso Niño, a pilot of the fleet of Columbus, has been referred to as a Negro, but this has not been proved. Voyages with Cristobal de la Guerra and Lúis de la Guerra are also accredited to Niño. In the discovery of the Pacific Ocean, Balboa carried with him thirty Negroes, including Nuflo de Olano. In the conquest of Mexico, Cortez was accompanied by a Negro, who, finding in his rations of rice **The Negro** some grains of wheat, planted them as an **with the Span-** experiment and thus made himself the pioneer **ish explorers.** in wheat raising in the Western Hemisphere. Negroes assisted in the exploration of Guatemala and the conquest of Chile, Peru, and Venezuela. Negroes accompanied De Ayllon in 1526 in his expedition from the Florida Peninsula northward and figured in the establishment of the settlement of San Miguel near what is now Jamestown, Virginia. They accompanied Narvaez on his ill-fated expedition in 1527 and continued with Cabeza de Vaca, his successor, through what is now the southwestern part of the United States. They went with Alarcon and Coronado in the conquest of New Mexico.[3] They were ordered to be imported by De Soto, the explorer of the lower Mississippi.

One of these Negroes wrote his name still higher in the hall of fame. This was Estevanico, or Little Stephen, the explorer of New Mexico and Arizona. Estevanico was a

[2] *Journal of Negro History*, IX, 1-17; Channing's *A History of the United States*, I, 116-117.

[3] By 1540 a Negro in Quivira, Mexico, had attained the priesthood. At Guamanga in 1542 Negroes constituted a brotherhood of the True Cross of Spaniards.

member of the unfortunate expedition of Narvaez who undertook to reduce the country between Florida and the Rio
Little   de las Palmas, in Mexico. Overcome by mis-
Stephen.   fortune, only four of the expedition survived. One of these survivors was Estevanico. Referring
to Cabeza de Vaca's instructions to this Negro, Channing
says, "He ordered him to proceed in advance for fifty
or sixty leagues and to report the probability of success
by sending back wooden crosses. If the news which the
Negro gathered was of moderate importance only, he was
to send back a cross the size of the palm of his hand; if
the news were better, the cross might be larger. Four days
later an Indian came into camp with a cross as tall as a
man. With him was another Indian, who told the friar of
seven large cities with houses of stone and lime, some of
them four stories in height. The portals of the principal
houses, he said, were ornamented with designs in turquoise.
Other crosses greeted Fray Marcos, another member of the
expedition, as he journeyed onward. Instead of awaiting
the coming of his chief at the appointed distance, Estevanico pushed on to the wonderful city, where he was at
once murdered. Indian traditions still tell of his coming
and his going; of how he related to those in the city that
he was the messenger of two white men, one of whom was
skilled in things of the heavens. The Indians at once
made up their minds that he was a liar, for it was incredi-
ble that a black man should be the agent of two white men.
They set him down for a deceiver and also found that he
was greedy, without morals, and a coward. Seeking to
escape, they fell upon him and killed him; if they had got
hold of the white men and the attendant Indians, they
would doubtless have massacred them also—"a curious
slaughter of red, white, and black."

The Negroes followed with the French close upon the
trail of Cartier and Champlain. They appeared with the

Jesuits in Canada and the Mississippi Valley during the seventeenth century. They later consti- **Negroes and** tuted a considerable element of the pioneers **the French.** in Louisiana. In these regions as elsewhere the Negro assisted in the exploration of the country and contributed much to the establishment of legal claims by actual settlement.

The chief interest of the whites here, it must be remembered, was the enslavement of the blacks. The "Christians," like the Mohammedans, justified their enslavement of foreigners taken as captives in war. But **Christian** in the eighteenth and nineteenth centuries, **slavery.** when the Europeans were engaged in the exploitation of the New World, slaves were no longer merely taken over as a sequel of war but became also an object of commerce to supply the colonies with cheap labor. This change of attitude was justified by the Christian world on the ground that, although it was contrary to an unwritten law to enslave a Christian, this principle was not applicable to the unconverted Negroes. Driven later from this position when numerous Negroes accepted Christianity, they salved their consciences by a peculiar philosophy of the officials of the church. These ecclesiastics held that conversion did not work manumission in the case of the Negro who differed so widely from the white man. The substance of this was soon incorporated into the laws of the colonies and the decrees of the Bishop of London, the spiritual head of the colonial church.

An important stimulus to these developments was the slave trade. Europe was in the midst of a commercial revolution. They wanted new routes, new methods, and new commodities. Slaves were considered an important commodity. Prior to the operation of the slave trade for the purpose of exploitation, however, there had been sufficient infiltration of the Negroes into southern European countries to make their presence no exception to the rule.

African slaves in Europe. African slaves were brought to Spain, and this trade was further extended by the Portuguese when they conquered the Mohammedans of North Africa. After the extensive explorations of Prince Henry, the Portuguese ships were bringing to that country more than seven or eight hundred slaves every year to serve as domestic servants and to work the estates evacuated by the Moors. Slaves were so common in the city of Seville in 1474 that Ferdinand and Isabella nominated a celebrated Negro, Juan de Valladolid, as the "mayoral of the Negroes" in that city.[4]

This slavery in the Iberian peninsula, of course, was of a mild form. Despite the suggestions of men commercially inclined, the Christian Queen Isabella had refused to permit the traders to embark upon the enterprise as a commercial one. Furthermore, to prevent the spread of heathenism and to promote religion, she allowed only **Slavery in Spain.** Christian Negroes to be carried to the colonies.[5] At the death of Isabella, however, King Ferdinand, who was less interested in the Negroes than was his companion, gradually yielded to the requests of the merchant class, and allowed the importation of unconverted Negroes into the Spanish colonies. But Ferdinand did not give extensive privileges to all persons desiring to bring in Negroes. At times he undertook to check the trade. In the reign of Charles V, Bishop de las Casas urged a plan for importing Negroes to take the place of the enfeebled Indian slaves. This plan, once adopted, became the policy of the Spaniards in dealing with the Negroes in their colonies. When the Spaniards became committed

[4] W. E. B. DuBois, *The Negro*, p. 146.
[5] C. G. Woodson, *The Education of the Negro Prior to 1861*, p. 19.

to the policy of slaveholding, however, they found themselves handicapped by having no foothold in Africa. They had to depend on the slave traders of other nations, especially the English. This explains the "Asiento," one of the important provisions of the Treaty of Utrecht in 1713. In closing the War of the Spanish Succession, this agreement secured to the English for a number of years the monopoly of the slave trade with the colonies of Spain.

The English, however, never got a foothold on the African coast until they established their authority on the Gambia about 1618. The Dutch made a voyage to Guinea in 1595. In 1617 they took possession of the island of Goree and in 1624 obtained their great desideratum in establishing a fort on the Gold Coast. The Danes reached the Gold Coast probably about 1650 and built Christiansbourg Castle. Near the close of the seventeenth century a Brandenburg company built one or more forts on the Gold Coast. After holding them for two generations they disposed of them to the Dutch.

The Portuguese influence in Africa, however, was predominant during these years. The Spaniards, on the other hand, ruled in Central and Southern America by virtue of the Papal Bull and the Treaty of Tordesillas, which divided the newly discovered lands between these nations. Other nations were in Africa on sufferance only. Thus the power of the Portuguese **The Portuguese predominant.** continued until it was broken by the Dutch in the wars culminating in 1637. They then took Elminia on the Gold Coast and drove the Portuguese from West Africa north of the Equator except from Gambia and certain islands. At the same time the Portuguese were being driven south by the Arabs on the east coast. By 1700 they lost all of their territory there except Mozambique. They were able to keep only Angola on the west coast. The Dutch trading companies then had their day during the first half of the

seventeenth century. The Dutch East India Company was
the most successful corporation of its kind in existence.
One of the ships of the Dutch brought upon this country
an evil when in 1619 it sold the colonists at Jamestown,
Virginia, twenty Negroes. The Dutch West India Company followed in 1621 for further exploitation in America.

The Dutch, however, were not permitted to come into
permanent possession of all they had taken over from the
Portuguese. The English made inroads here as a result
of the naval war successfully closed with the Peace of
The Dutch on Breda in 1667; and a war between the French
the coast.   and the Dutch in 1672 ended with the transfer of Gorée to France. The English slave trade then became an organized business operated by special companies
beginning with such a grant as early as 1618. Another
was made to a company of this sort in 1631. In 1662 there
vas chartered the Royal Adventurers trading into Africa.
This corporation was reorganized in 1672 as the Royal
African Company with the monopoly of the slave trade
between the Gold Coast and the American colonies. So
profitable did the trade become, however, that as a result
of a general demand the trade was thrown open to all English vessels. This brought in vessels from New England,
especially from Boston and Newport. The slave-trading
corporations maintained a line of vessels plying between
America and certain forts established on the Guinea coast.
The French operated in the region of the Senegal, the
Slave-trade   English on the Gambia, and the Dutch and
corporations. English on the Gold Coast. At first the task
of obtaining the slave cargo was largely that of the captain. On landing, he traded his trinkets or rum for slaves.
He sometimes kidnaped Africans, even the princes, who
drove their captives in war to the coast to be sold. This led
to hazardous encounters with armed Africans. They found
it necessary thereafter, then, to systematize the buying by

KANO

establishing factories along the coast to have the slaves on hand before arrival. In the course of time the slave trade in the interior of Africa was highly developed. Wars being waged at that time supplied captives offered as slaves for the market. When captured they were brought to the coast and sold to the representatives of the companies with vessels in port for their exportation. They

INSPECTING A CAPTIVE

were not usually natives of the countries along the coast. In fact, Africans of these ports were seldom sold for this purpose except when a rival nation captured the slaves of the masters living in a hostile section. Some of the slaves supplying this demand were brought from the distant countries in the interior of Africa.

The commodities given in exchange for these slaves were generally sent out from manufacturing centers like Newport and Boston in New England, and from Bristol and

Liverpool in England. In 1726 Bristol, Liverpool and London had 171 ships engaged in the slave traffic. These vessels carried iron bars, rum, cloth, shells, crystal beads, brass pans, and foreign coins, to be exchanged for slaves. The slaves thus purchased had been driven to the coast in coffles, sometimes for distances of more than one thousand miles. They had to cross a country which had practically no facilities for transportation except those with which nature had endowed it. As it was necessary to go most of the way walking, and as the means of subsistence were not always to be secured, many of the captives dropped dead from thirst and famine. Those who succeeded in surviving the ordeal of this drive to the coast were presented for sale on arrival only to face other horrors of the "Middle Passage." Sometimes forced into a crouching position, sometimes compelled to lie down, captives accepted as valuable were shackled and herded together like cattle in ships. The space generally allowed for the standing room of a slave was just a few square inches. Ventilation was usually inadequate, clothing was limited, the water was insufficient, and the food was spoiled. Crowded thus together in the lower parts of an unsanitary vessel, many of these unfortunates died of various complaints before reaching America. Occasionally the trusted Negroes on board would start a riot

BRANDING A NEGRO WOMAN SLAVE

Horrors of the Slave Trade.

to liberate themselves by killing their captors, but the system was finally reduced to such a safe procedure that little fear therefrom was experienced. After the slave trade was declared criminal the traffic became most in-human. Prior to this time a slaver had to exercise some care with these captives, for a loss of too many would have made the voyage unprofitable. But the restriction on the trade so increased the price of slaves thereafter that a loss of some of them could be more easily borne.

These slaves, however, were not brought in large numbers directly to the continental ports. Slave labor did not at first seem very profitable along the Atlantic. In the West Indies, devoted to the production of cane sugar so much in demand at that time, African slaves were welcomed. In these islands they were exchanged mainly for such raw materials as molasses. They could secure a slave in Africa for about 100 or 120 gallons of rum valued at about $50 or $60. They would sell him in the West Indies for from $100 to $200, or for molasses worth this amount. Brought by the slavers to our ports, the molasses was manufactured into rum. To supply this demand for rum **Slaves carried to the West Indies.** manufacture Newport had twenty-two distilleries. With this rum the ships set out to Africa again on their triangular route connecting with the commercial centers in three widely separated parts of the world.

In the West Indies the Negroes were successfully exploited so as to make those islands the wealthiest colonies of the world. In the course of time, however, after having been well broken in, and in some cases after having taken over a considerable portion of the western civilization, a number of these slaves were brought from the West Indies to the United States. Some of them had then learned to read and write two or three modern languages. When, however, such mentally developed Negroes proved to be the source of discontent and insurrections, the **American** colonists deemed it wiser to import slaves in their crude form directly from Africa.

As to exactly how many Negroes were thus brought away from Africa, authorities widely differ. When the slave trade was in full swing 50,000 or 100,000 were brought over every year. Some authorities believe that not more than 5,000,000, while others contend that 10,000,000 Africans were expatriated. But to figure out the ex- **The enormity** tent to which this process of depopulation **of the trade.** affected Africa, one must bear in mind that for every slave imported into America at least four or five others had to meet death in the numerous wars, in the inhuman drive to the coast, and in the cruel shipment in unsanitary ships hardly suitable for importing hogs. Africa probably lost more than 50,000,000 natives. When we think of how the First World War conscription of 4,000,000 men upset the economic and social life in our own country, we can easily estimate the effect of the loss to Africa of 50,000,000 of its inhabitants. This, to some extent, accounts for its decline.

The source of these Negroes will be of much interest. They came in the main from Guinea and the Gold Coast. Very few came from the East Coast of Africa. The slave trading nations did not control that part of the continent. Among these slaves were a few of the most intelligent of the Africans, the Senegalese, with an infusion of Arabic blood. They were especially valuable for their work as mechanics and artisans. Then there were the **Sources of** Mandingoes, who were considered gentle in **the slaves.** demeanor but "prone to theft." The Coromantees brought from the Gold Coast were hearty and stalwart in mind and body. For this reason they were frequently the source of slave insurrections. It was said, however, that the Coromantees were not revengeful when well treated. Slavers brought over some Whydahs, Nagoes and Paw

Paws. They were much desired by the planters because they were lusty, industrious, cheerful and submissive. There came also the Gaboons. They were physically weak and consequently unsuited for purposes of exploitation. The colonists imported, too, some Gambia Negroes, prized for their meekness. The Eboes brought from Calabar were not desired, because they were inclined to commit suicide rather than bear the yoke of slavery. The Congoes, Angolas and the Eboes gave their masters much trouble by running away. Among the Negroes thus imported, too, there were a few Moors and some brown people from Madagascar.

Sometimes an African of high social standing was thus kidnaped and brought over. In the possession of Michael Denton of Maryland there was found a slave who observed the custom of praying five times a day according to the requirements of the Mohammedan religion. An ignorant white boy, seeing him kneel and bowing in the direction of Mecca, threw sand in his eyes and so impaired his sight as to invite an investigation of his habits. It was discovered that he was an orthodox Mohammedan and an Arabic scholar. Hearing this, James Oglethorpe interceded in his behalf, had him liberated and taken to England. There he was accorded all of the honors due a man of learning. He was associated with a professor of Cambridge in the translation of oriental manuscripts and through him he was introduced to some of the most desirable people of England. This was probably the record of Job, a slave in Maryland in 1731-1733, a Fula, brought from Futa in what is now French Senegal. He could write Arabic and repeat the whole Koran.[6]

6 Thomas Bluett, *Some Memoirs of the Life of Job the Son of Solomon the High Priest of Boonda in Africa;* London 1816. Francis Moore, *Travels into the Inland Parts of Africa*, London 1738.

CHAPTER V

THE SITUATION IN TROPICAL AMERICA

THE lot of the slave in tropical America was most unfortunate. Owing to the absentee ownership, the inefficient management of the plantations, and the paucity of white women to serve as restraining influences on masters, the system of slavery developed in the West Indies proved to be of a cruel sort. The slaves were treated **The slave** more as brutes subjected to a process known **in the** as "breaking in." Some were assigned to **West Indies.** work among well-seasoned slaves, and a few were given individual tasks. When they became well "broken in" they were grouped by families in separate quarters. These were surrounded by small tracts of land on which they were required to raise their own food. Such things as clothing, dried fish, molasses, rum and salt, which they could not easily produce, were issued from the plantation commissary. They went to work in gangs, some cultivating sugar cane, some toiling in the mills and stills, some laboring at handicrafts. Others were placed in domestic service.[1] On the continent their lot was a little easier.

As few implements had been introduced and the planters

---

[1] The conditions in the tropics facilitating the increase in the slave trade are treated in T. K. Ingram's *History of Slavery and Serfdom,* John R. Spear's *The American Slave Trade,* W. E. B. DuBois's *Suppression of the African Slave Trade,* B. Mayer's *Captain Canot or Twenty Years of an African Slaver,* R. Drake's *The Revelations of a Slave Smuggler,* Bryan Edwards' *West Indies,* T. Clarkson's *History of the Abolition of the Slave Trade,* 2 Volumes, and the *Journal of Negro History,* XI, 584-668.

of that day did not easily take to labor-saving devices, most
of the cultivation of the crops was done with the hoe. This
Drudgery fatal. required the hardest of labor. Under these
conditions the slaves could not develop into
a robust class. Worst of all, many of them died as a result of this drudgery. While the death-rate was unusually
high, the birth-rate was exceptionally small. There was
no provision for taking care of the African newborn.
Speaking of Jamaica, a surgeon said that one third of the
babies died in the first month, and few of the imported
women bore children. A contemporary said that more
than a quarter of the babies died within the first nine days
of "jaw fall," and another fourth before they passed their
second year. The Negro women had to work hard and the
planters themselves encouraged them in sexual promiscuity.
Such a habit is not conducive to reproduction. This
meant that the colonies had to depend on the importation
of new African slaves. The slave trade to supply the demand for such labor was thereby stimulated. The planters
ceased therefore to purchase male and female slaves in
equal numbers, as had been the custom, inasmuch as the
breeding of slaves there apparently failed.

Negroes, moreover, proved to be susceptible to the diseases of white men. Lacking time to establish an immunity
against such maladies, the unseasoned slaves died in large
numbers. They suffered especially from colds and measles
Ravages of diseases. which, considered ordinary complaints in the
case of the white men, proved fatal to these
Africans. Travelers and planters mention in their accounts such other troublesome diseases as lockjaw, yaws,
cocoa-bag, guiney worms, smallpox, leprosy, hereditary
venereal diseases, menstrual obstructions, promiscuous
venery and ulcers. The excessive use of new rum aggravated these complaints and contributed to the sterility of
the early slave population. To supply this need, an author-

ity estimated that a planter with 100 slaves would have to import six a year. Others estimated it at a figure as high as from a third to two-thirds. This, of course, varied according to the treatment of the slave with respect to food, housing conditions, and alloted labor. Toward the end of the eighteenth century, however, the average life of the slave was estimated at from fifty to sixty years.

A CHAIN GANG

The treatment of the slaves in Tropical America is reflected by the code developed there. Among the English the slave was early declared by law as the personal property of his master. The child followed the condition of the mother. Slaves had no right of locomotion except subject to the will of their owner. The patrol system authorized all persons to punish slaves absent from their **Law of** plantation without required passes. In the **slavery.** course of time this penalty for running away was so increased that in some cases the fugitives would suffer death.

In the case of mutiny or rebellion, they were subject to the rigors of martial law. Slaves were not allowed to have weapons, nor to assemble in public meetings. For striking a Christian, the slave could be subjected to severe corporal punishment. For unusual crimes they suffered death. There were cases of punishment by being mutilated, broken on the wheel, or burnt alive. The sale of alcoholics to slaves was prohibited.

Certain precautions as to the comfort of slaves were taken, moreover, for otherwise they might prove unprofitable to their masters. By law they were allowed so much clothing and at least as much as a specified quantity of food. There had to be drawers and caps for the men and petticoats and caps for the women. Such regulations as these were especially featured in the slave code of Barbados, which decidedly influenced the slave codes of the Southern States. Barbados was the first prosperous slaveholding colony of the English.

The lot of the slave in Tropical America, too, was aggravated by absentee ownership. The overseers in charge of the plantations were required to produce the largest crop possible. This in turn, of course, necessitated their **Evils of absentee ownership.** driving the slaves to the utmost in order to secure the largest return from their labor. The owners of these plantations residing in Europe might sometimes be won to the idea of reform, but the good words which they might periodically utter out of compassion for the slave had little effect in improving the economic situation far away in the New World. In the course of time, however, the lot of the slave under the English in Tropical America seemed to improve. The tendency was from slavery unto serfdom. Some of the cruel measures fell into desuetude. Planters, becoming more kindly disposed toward their slaves, permitted them to acquire property. They sometimes owned not only hogs, cattle and sheep, but also land. The custom of the country permitted masters to bequeath to their slaves some of the property which had been accumulated as a result of their faithfulness to their owners. This change was effected as a result of the humanitarian movement in England which took the form of agitation for the abolition of the slave trade and the improvement of the condition of the slave. West Indian slaves, then, sometimes tended to become servants.

Among the Portuguese, Spanish and French colonists the condition of the blacks became still more favorable. The very letter of the slave law among the Latins resembled that of the English; but the home countries in these three cases insisted on humane treatment of the slaves and were more generous than the English in offering bondmen opportunities to toil upward. The slaves as such fared much better than they did on the English planta- **The enlight-** tions. Whereas, the English never treated **enment of** the slaves with familiarity, nor smiled upon **the slaves.** them, nor spoke to them except when compelled, the Latins addressed them with mildness, handled them kindly, and treated them as members of the human family. The tendency of the Latins to interbreed with the blacks and their custom of recognizing and elevating their mulatto offspring, moreover, offered a way of escape to a large number of Negroes. But some of the English actually sold their offspring by Negro women. A large number of bondmen in Latin-America, too, secured their manumission by meritorious service and thereafter had the status of freemen.

Among these fortunate Negroes there was in Guatemala, in the seventeenth century, a freedman who had accumulated much wealth. He had secured his liberty by paying his kind master a handsome sum for his freedom. Thereafter he bought a large farm and considerably increased his holdings by making other purchases. He lived in Agua Caliente, a little Indian village on the road to the city of Guatemala. This was that part of the country then said to abound with gold, a treasure which the Spaniards had for many years sought in vain. Although the sources of this Negro's wealth were cattle, sheep, goats, and his trade in butter and cheese with the City of Guatemala, the Spaniards persisted in believing that his wealth came from the hidden treasure.[2]

A thrifty freedman in Guatemala.

In his travels through this tropical region, Sir Thomas Gage found a still more interesting Negro of this class. While sailing along the Atlantic coast of Costa Rica, Gage's ship was captured by two corsairs under the flag of the Dutch, who were then struggling against Spain for their freedom. The commander of this ship was a mulatto named Diaguillo, a native of Havana. His mother lived there. Because of maltreatment by the Governor of Campeche, to whom he was attached as a servant, this mulatto desperately ventured to swim to one of the Dutch ships near by. Offering himself to serve the Dutch against those who had abused him, he easily ingratiated himself into their favor. Soon thereafter he married a Dutch girl and arose to the position of captain of a vessel under the command of the famous and dreadful commander named Pie de Palo. Coming aboard the ship on which Gage was sailing, the corsair took four thousand pesos' worth of jewelry and pearls and deprived the individuals of their personal belongings. But because of Gage's ministerial profession Diaguillo permitted him to retain some books, pictures and clothes. He said to Gage: "If fortune to-day is on my side, to-morrow it will be on

The Black Corsair.

---

[2] *The Journal of Negro History*, Vol. I, p. 395; and Sir Thomas Gage's *Voyages*, Part 3, Ch. II.

yours, and what I have won to-day, that I may lose to-morrow.'' Diaguillo then prepared a luxurious dinner, to which he invited Gage. Thanking the crew for the good luck they had procured him, the corsair took leave of the captives.[3]

The most interesting example of the enlightened Negro of this class in the West Indies was Francis Williams. He was the son of one John Williams, liberated in 1708, and ranked among those persons in the island against whom slave testimony was forbidden. These same privileges were later extended to other members of his family. Consequently they were respected by the whites among whom they socially moved. We have much more information about the son, Francis. The family was of such good report, and the youth Francis had exhibited so many evidences of mental capacity, that early in the eighteenth century the Duke of Montague, desiring to put to test some of his opinions about the capabilities of the Negro, had Francis instructed in an elementary school in Jamaica. He then sent him to an English grammar school to prepare for Cambridge University. After some years Francis Williams completed his education at that institution and returned to Jamaica between 1738 and 1748.

Francis Williams, the scholar.

Impressed more than ever with the truth that a Negro trained in the same way as a white man will exhibit the same intellectual attainments, the Duke of Montague sought further to advance his protégé by securing for him a seat in the Jamaica Council. This proposition, however, was opposed by Governor Trelawny. He contended that admitting a black man to the Council would excite restlessness among the slaves. Whether or not

The Duke of Montague.

³ *The Journal of Negro History*, Vol. I, p. 395; and Sir Thomas Gage's *Voyages*, Part 3, Ch. II.

the governor was diplomatic or prejudiced is not known. He did add a Negro detachment to the army employed in Jamaica, but he never permitted the ambitious youth to sit in the Council. Williams settled in Spanish Town, the capital of the island, and during the rest of his life conducted a classical school. In this position he made a reputation for himself as a schoolmaster and figured somewhat prominently as a poet. The only evidence of his attainments in this field, however, consists of a Latin poem which conforms in most respects to the standard of that age. It seemed that the ambitious poet was not very popular among his own people, as he was regarded as haughty and opinionated. He treated his fellow blacks with contempt and entertained a rather high opinion of his own knowledge. He was frequently charged with being a sycophant and racial toady who said and did much to the detriment of his race.[4]

This better situation of a few Negroes was due also to the fact that a large number of slaves in remote parts of the West Indies and Latin-America asserted themselves and escaped to uninhabited districts to declare and maintain their independence. In **The Maroons.** parts where the Negroes were as numerous as the whites, these fugitives often jeopardized the very life of the colony. As such, they were known as Maroons. They had few arms that the primitive man did not possess, but because of their resourcefulness and power in military organization they became a source of much terror throughout Latin-America.[5] In the small colony of Guatemala in the seventeenth century there were as many as three hundred such Negroes.

---

[4] The career of Francis Williams is treated in *The Journal of Negro History*, Vol. II, pp. 146-159. A better account may be found in William James Gardner's *History of Jamaica*, p. 31; and in Edward Long's *History of Jamaica*, p. 234.

[5] Dallas, *History of Maroons*, p. 26.

They had resorted to the woods and could not be subdued by the forces sent against them.

The greatest enterprise of the Maroons, however, was exhibited by the little Negro Republic in Brazil, Palmares. Professor Charles E. Chapman calls it the Negro Numantia, because its career resembles so much that of Numantia against which the Romans fought for a number of years before they could invade the beleaguered city. Because of the self-asserting spirit of certain Portuguese slaves, many of those imported from Guinea escaped to the forests. They established their villages called *quilombos*, the type to which Palmares, in the Province of Pernambuco, belonged. It was not long, however, before this town extended its sway over a number of others settled by persons of the same antecedents. At one time it was reported to have a population of twenty thousand, with ten thousand fighting men. Palmares, the name also of the capital of the republic, was surrounded by wooden walls made of the trunks of trees and entered by huge gates. It was provided with facilities for wide surveillance and sentry service.

In the course of time the population of this village gradually increased because of the eagerness of slaves and freemen to try their fortunes in the forests. In the beginning they maintained themselves by a sort of banditry, taking food, slaves and women, whether mulatto, black, or white. They later settled down to agriculture, and established seemingly peaceful trade relations with the Portuguese settlements in the less hostile parts of Brazil. Palmares then developed into a sort of nation, uniting the desirable features of the republican and monarchical form of government. It was presided over by a chief executive called the *Zombe,* who ruled with absolute authority during life. "The right to candidacy."

says Professor Chapman, "was restricted to a group recognized as composing the bravest men of the community. Any man in the state might aspire to this dignity providing he had Negro blood in his veins. There were other officers, both of a military and a civil character. In the interest of good order the *Zombes* made laws imposing the death penalty for murder, adultery and robbery. Influenced by their antecedents, they did not discontinue slavery, but they put a premium on freedom. Every Negro who won his freedom by a successful flight to Palmares remained free, whereas those who were captured as slaves continued as such in Palmares."

This Negro Republic, however, was an unnatural growth in the eyes of the Portuguese. It was considered a resort for undesirable aliens who constituted an ever-increasing danger to the prosperity of Brazil. In 1698, therefore,

The destruction of Palmares. Governor Caetano de Mello of Pernambuco ordered an expedition to proceed against the city. These brave blacks met the invading forces and indisputably defeated them. Returning later, however, with a formidable army of seven thousand men under the command of a more competent soldier and provided, too, with adequate artillery, the Portuguese reached the city after some difficulty and placed it in a state of siege. The defense of this city was heroic. "After the Portuguese had breached the walls in three places," says the annalist, "their infantry attacked in force. They entered the city, but had to take it foot by foot. At last the defenders came to the center of Palmares where a high cliff impeded further retreat. Death or surrender were the only alternatives. Seeing that his cause was lost beyond repair, the *Zombe* hurled himself over the cliff, and his example was followed by the most distinguished of his fighting men. Some persons were taken, but it is perhaps a tribute to Palmares, though a grewsome one, that they were all put to death; despite the value of their labor it was not safe to enslave these men. Thus passed Palmares, the Negro Numantia, most famous and greatest of the Brazilian *quilombos.*" [6]

After the destruction of Palmares and the suppression of other attempts of the Negroes to strike for freedom, they became resigned to their fate as slaves in Brazil as elsewhere in the Western Hemisphere. Among these Latin people, however, soon developed a movement for the amelioration of the condition of these bondmen and for their ultimate emancipation. This did not work out as early in Brazil as it did later in distant parts of North America; but the elevation of the Negro to the status of freedom and citizenship was effected in Brazil with less bitterness, and members of this race met little obstruction across their path of progress. Brazilians of African blood later rose to usefulness and renown in music, architecture, literature, science, and government. Brazil produced brilliant Negro soldiers, following the example of Henrique Diaz who distinguished himself as a hero in winning that country from the Dutch in the 17th century. Years thereafter Negroes received the greatest honors of the nation, even that of being president of the Republic.

[6] *The Journal of Negro History*, Vol. III, pp. 31-32.

CHAPTER VI

SLAVERY IN A STRUGGLE WITH SERVITUDE

THE cruel system of exploiting Africans in Tropical America did not reach the slave States until the cotton gin and other mechanical appliances instrumental in effecting the industrial revolution made slavery seemingly profitable.[1] The first Negroes brought to the continental colo-

Slavery patriarchal. nies were few, and they served largely as indentured servants so closely attached to the homes of their masters that they were treated like members of the families. They had the same status as that of the white felons and convicts imported into this country to serve a definite period. After serving their master a few years the indentured servant could become free. This happened in the case of some of the first twenty Negroes brought to Jamestown in 1619. It has been said, moreover, that Anthony Johnson, probably one of these Negroes, not only gained his freedom but became a slaveholder himself. Between slavery and servitude there was no clear distinction in the English language at that time. A man described as a servant might be a slave, and vice versa. The status of a slave was unknown to English law. Slavery gradually evolved in America by custom. It has been shown conclusively that the Negroes were gradually debased from

[1] Slavery in its first form is briefly treated in Channing's *History of the United States*, II, 336-400. The slaves' opportunities for enlightenment are presented in C. G. Woodson's *The Education of the Negro Prior to 1861*, 18-150. See also Bryan Edwards' *History of the West Indies;* Sir Harry Johnston's *The Negro in the New World;* and the *Journal of Negro History*, I, 132-150, 163-216, 243-264, 399-435; II, 78-82, 105-125, 186-191, 229-251, 411-422, 429-430; III, 1-21, 22-28, 33-44, 45-54, 55-89, 211-328, 335-353, 381-434.

putin

indentured servitude to slavery.[2] Slavery as such was not legally recognized in Virginia until 1661. At that time the Negro was considered as held to the permanent service of his master, "incapable of making satisfaction for the time lost in running away by addition of time." *+ increased*

The importation of Negroes gradually increased, however. Negroes were brought from the West Indies to *son the majority of the colonies from.*

THE DASH FOR LIBERTY

Massachusetts probably as early as 1636. The records show the actual importation of Negroes in 1638, and Massachusetts passed her first regulation in regard to slavery in 1641. It was **Coming of** restricted to **Negroes.** the forced servitude of lawful captives taken in just wars. In 1646, however, Massachusetts rather set its face against slavery when she ordered returned to Africa at public expense two slaves brought in by one cruel John Smith from the Guinea Coast. Connecticut had no special interest in slavery during the earliest period. The colony merely used it as punishment for Indians in providing that those incurring the public displeasure should be shipped out and exchanged for Negroes. In developing its attitude toward slavery, Rhode Island provided in 1652 that all slaves brought into the colony should be liberated after serving ten years. In 1703 and 1708, however, Rhode Island legally recognized slavery in penalizing vagrancy and taxing the trade. This colony became the chief slave-

[2] *Journal of Negro History*, VIII, 247-231.

trading center in the country. New Hampshire was largely passive in this respect. In 1714 it enacted a measure respecting the conduct of slaves and masters.

The Dutch West India Company introduced slavery into the New Netherlands about 1650. By indentured service arrangement, however, some of them became free. In the hands of the English in 1664 there came some restrictions in New York in the new code of laws providing **Slaves in** that no Christians could be held as slaves ex- **the colonies.** cept when adjudged thereunto by authority or when selling themselves. Such regulations were abrogated later, however, when slaves rather rapidly became Christians. The Bishop of London, the head of the colonial church, and the lawmaking bodies of the colonies came to the rescue with decrees and ordinances to the effect that although the Negro might accept Chrisianity, his conversion would not work manumission.

New Jersey seems to have followed the fortunes of New York in accepting slaves from the Dutch. The colony took legal action in sanctioning the institution in 1664. Delaware had slaves during these years, too; but the colony did not formally recognize the institution until 1721. Maryland definitely legalized permanent slavery at the session of its legislature of 1663-1664.

We hear of Negroes in Pennsylvania as early as 1639; but by a provision in its Charter to the Free Society of Traders in 1682 they had an outlet to freedom through the expiration of terms of indentured service. In 1688, **The German-** moreover, their lot was doubtless improved **town protest.** by the protest of the Germantown Quakers against slavery.[3] Although nothing definite was then done,

---

[3] This document was signed by Gerhard Hendricks, Franz Daniel Pastoruis, Dirck Op den Græff, and Abraham Op den Græff. Nothing definite, however, was done.

the Quakers renewed their opposition in 1696. By 1700, however, the Negro seemed definitely on the decline from servitude to slavery and his status as such was recognized by law that year. While the lawmaking body prohibited the selling of Negroes out of the colony it determined their status as slaves. Importation was checked by a duty on slaves brought in after 1700 and the tax was doubled five years later. Unsuccessful attempts were made in 1712 and 1715 to prevent importation altogether by excessive duties, but these were disallowed in England.

Farther south the development was not so very different. North Carolina, like some of the other colonies, had slavery before it knew it as such. The colony took cognizance of the institution in 1715 when it established a system of slave control. Slaves came into **Slaves in the** South Carolina so rapidly after its sanction **Lower South.** in 1682, however, that there was fear that, outnumbering the whites, the slaves might rise against their masters. This happened in 1720 and several times thereafter. Importation, therefore, was checked by prohibitive duties as in the case of 1740. At the same time white immigration had to be encouraged. The treaty of Utrecht, granting the English a monopoly of the slave trade, opened the way for such large importations that some of the colonies were in danger of being "Africanized." Georgia, therefore, was to be a free frontier colony because in this important position it needed free labor and could not spare time to guard both the frontier and Negroes. But apparently outstripped in economic development by slaveholding colonies, Georgia began importing slaves in 1749. In 1755 and 1765 Georgia worked out a regular slave code.

This sketch above brings out the fact that slavery as a system of exploitation was not seriously thought of in the colonies until near the end of the seventeenth century. England had not then a strong foothold on the West Coast of Africa and had not the monopoly of the slave

Slow expansion of slavery. trade conceded in the Treaty of Utrecht. Furthermore, the development of the colonies during the early years was not so rapid as to require much more cheap labor than what could be supplied by the white indentured servants. The economic urge, moreover, required time to overcome the scruples of the early settlers with respect to man-stealing. Some colonies tried to forbid the traffic. Americans trading in slaves during the early years, too, left most of them in the West Indies. English slave traders still farther removed from the effects of an excessive slave population, however, had no such sentiments as those of some Americans with respect to the trade. The British administration regarded slaves as essential to a colony. Measures enacted by the original thirteen to prohibit the traffic were abrogated by the home Government on the ground that the colonies had no authority to interfere with a trade so profitable to Englishmen.

At the same time, too, the other European nations championed the traffic and supplied their colonies accordingly. Negroes, as we have observed above, were with the Spanish and Portuguese settlers throughout Latin America. They were brought in as constituents of the very first

Slave trading popular. settlement of Florida at St. Augustine. Certain Negro fugitives taken over from the English plantation of St. George, in South Carolina, were settled just outside of St. Augustine as a community known as the settlement of Gracia Real de Santa Teresa de Mosé. They had their own public officers, their priest, and their own militia to defend the community. This settlement was destroyed by soldiers sent from Georgia about 1741.

In Louisiana under the French, moreover, the Negroes also increased. Here, as in Spanish America, there was not so much of that fear of the Teuton that he might be overcome by the slave. Because of the more favorable attitude of the Latins many Negroes could become free, and race prejudice did not always prevent them from rising to equality in the community. In 1721 there were 600 Negroes in Louisiana and 2,020 in 1745. In 1729 Governor Perier wrote of prodigies of valor performed by fifteen Negroes armed to fight the Indians. The very next year, however, we hear of Negroes there, who, realizing their prowess in arms, turned the tide the other way. They were plotting with the Indians to annihilate the whites and take over the country. The plan failed. Samba, the leader, and several of his companions were broken on the wheel; and a woman, charged with being their accomplice, expiated her offense on the gallows.

Negroes in Louisiana.

The slave, as it will appear elsewhere, was rebelling against being reduced lower and lower in the social order until he constituted the lowest element in society with no social or political rights which the others needed to respect. Slaves tended to be regarded as property, taxed and disposed of by will as other chattels. Indentured servants were subject to poll tax, and the contracts under which they served rather than themselves were considered as property. In 1748 and 1753 Virginia defined slaves as imported non-Christians but provided that the definition should not apply to Turks and Moors on good terms with England and with proof that they were free in that country. According to this code, moreover, conversion to Christianity could not result in the freedom of the slave. Intermarriage of the races was forbidden. Manumission was restricted to liberation for meritorious service. A Negro could not enslave any other person than one of his own color. Dealings with slaves could be had only through their masters. Both fugitive servants and slaves could be apprehended, imprisoned, and

The slave code.

advertised for as any other property lost or stolen, and they could be whipped for escaping from their masters. Slaves rebelling, conspiring with free Negroes or indentured servants, or administering medicine, should be put to death. The right of assembly was restricted. Slaves who would not abandon "evil habits" might be dismembered. Any Negro who lifted his hand against a white man received thirty lashes on his bare back. Testimony of Negroes was admissible only in the case of a capital offense charged to a slave. Even in that case the judge warned the witness beforehand that if he falsified he would be pilloried, his ears would be cut off, and he would get thirty-nine lashes. Negro criminals were tried by special courts without the assistance of a jury.

This code of Virginia tended to become the law of all of the slaveholding colonies, modified to suit local conditions. In 1693 the government of Philadelphia ordered the constable to arrest all Negroes "gadding about" on the first day of the week. Such offenders were to be imprisoned until the following morning and given thirty-nine lashes. South Carolina and Pennsylvania followed Virginia in providing special courts for Negroes charged with burglary, murder, and the like. They might be whipped, branded, deported, or put to death.

Politically the Negro in the colonies was almost a nonentity. In colonial days few colonists could exercise the right of suffrage or hold office unless they had a certain acreage or some other property, belonged to a particular church, or met a special requirement. Only one white man out of every fifteen in this country could vote, even as late **Political** as 1800. Some few free Negroes comply- **rights.** ing with these conditions exercised this right. These distinctions were then based on economic conditions and not on color. When race discrimination required that the Negroes be deprived of the right to hold office and to vote it had to be done by special enactments. Such a code had to be worked out step by step. During the increase of race prejudice and the debasement of the majority of Negroes to a lower status, the colonies gradually restricted the civic and social rights to the whites. In this the colonies generally followed the English laws for vagrants and servants and the Barbadian slave code. In most colonies Negroes were excluded from the militia. The laws generally provided, however, that the child should follow the condition of its mother. This meant that a child born of a slave would be a slave although the father might be free, and that a child born of a free mother would be free although the father might be a slave. Some of the colonies, however, were late in taking the extreme position of antagonism to the Negro, and several never had this attitude altogether. For example, Negroes voted in North Carolina and Tennessee until 1834.

In the course of this debasement, too, an effort was made to degrade the Negro below the Indian. A law of Virginia in 1670 made distinction between the slavery of Negroes and that of Indians. The measure provided that when Indians were sold the terms should be such as applied in the case of selling Englishmen into service, **The Negro and** and it secured to the Indians the protection **the Indian.** of the laws of England. Although the Indian himself gradually lost favor, the laws of this same colony tended nevertheless to give him a higher social and civic position than that of the Negro. This tendency continued in all colonies until the Indians caused the whites so much trouble by such uprisings as that giving rise to Bacon's Rebellion in 1676 that they were no longer considered more desirable than Negroes. This was especially true after they began to join with the Negroes in conspiracies against the whites. The Indian as a slave, however, was not tractable and the colonies tended to refrain from enslaving them. The laws of Massachusetts and Pennsylvania in 1712, of New Hampshire in 1714, and of Rhode Island in 1715, will show this point of view.

Out of the association of these reds and blacks subjected to the whites came a new class of Negroes commonly known as the mustees, or mestizos, and it became necessary for laws and legal documents citing persons of color to give **Mustees and** in detail all of these various designations. **mestizos.** Later no distinction was made between them and other persons of color, however, and they passed as a part of the free Negro population. Evidences of their presence in Virginia appeared at an early date. In 1734 John Dungie, an Indian of King William County, married Anne Littlepage, a mulatto daughter of the wealthy Edmund Littlepage. He himself was occupied as a sailor, and his wife, a free woman, was the heir of considerable wealth. It was difficult to hold the Indian in the status of slavery. The Indian tended to find equal privileges or to be regarded a troublesome foe.

Because of the numerous uprisings of Negroes, too, the colonies began to think of the Negroes as being as untractable as the Indians. The former not only joined with **Early** the latter in conspiracies against the whites **uprisings.** but started insurrections themselves. This danger became pronounced after the wholesale importation of slaves brought enough of the unyielding Africans to start easily an uprising in the interest of freedom. This was one of the reasons why the colonies prohibited or restrained the importation of slaves. The disturbances of the unconquerable African recruits caused them to live in eternal dread of servile insurrection.

Some of these early uprisings deserve mention here. In 1730 a Negro in Malden, Massachusetts, plundered and burned his master's home because he was sold to a man in Salem, whom he disliked. In 1731, slaves being imported from Guinea by George Scott of Rhode Island, asserted themselves and murdered three of the crew. Captain John Major of Portsmouth, New Hampshire, in charge of a cargo of slaves, was thus murdered with all of his crew the following year. Captain Beers of Rhode Island, and all his unfortunate co-workers except two, suffered the same fate when on a similar voyage a few years later. Before leaving the West Coast of Africa in 1735 captives on the *Dolphin* subdued the crew and by explosion destroyed both their enslavers and themselves in the effort to escape.

Blows at sea.

In the colonies themselves this rebellious spirit in the Negro continued. In the Northern Neck of Virginia in 1687 and in Surry County in that State in 1710 Negroes worked out plots for the overthrow of slavery. In 1722 two hundred Negroes assembled in a church near the mouth of the Rappahannock River, Virginia, to kill the white people. When the plot was discovered they fled. Hearing that Governor Spotswood would free all Christianized Negroes on his arrival there, certain of them started an insurrection in Williamsburg, Virginia, in 1730.

Troubles in Virginia.

Escaping from their masters in South Carolina in 1711, a number of armed Negroes maintained themselves by marauding expeditions from their base on the frontier. The Governor of the colony, terrified by their raids, advocated amending the Negro act to cope with the aggravated situation and offered a reward of £50 for Sebastian, their Spanish Negro leader. His final capture brought relief to the whites. There was a small uprising in that State in 1720, resulting in the execution of three Negroes. In 1730 there was to be organized warfare between the races. Each slave was to kill his master and then the Negroes would proceed to dispose of all other white persons whom they met. For

Uprisings in South Carolina.

this effort the leaders met the usual fate. In 1739, how-ever, three other such plots developed in that State in St Paul's Parish, in St. John's, and in Charleston. With this, however, the Spaniards seemed to have had some connec-tion. They were at that time embarrassing in every way possible the British plantations to the north of them. In the conflicts which took place twenty-five Negroes were killed. The Negro leaders and others to the number of 34 were shot, hanged, or gibbeted alive. Not deterred by this drastic punishment, the Negroes in the same section staged a repetition of this in 1740. The leader was a shrewd man named Cato. They proceeded from place to place, taking possession of firearms and burning houses. After they had successfully performed their mission in terrorizing the whites in a radius of ten miles they were overpowered by the militia where they halted to indulge in drinking, sing-ing, and dancing. More than 20 white persons were killed and, as a result, the leaders were all put to death. A special act of the State in 1740 checked the importation of Negroes by imposing a duty of £100 on Africans and £150 on the Negroes from the colonies. Even this did not put an end to such uprisings, for in 1754, C. Croft, of Charleston, had two of his female Negroes burned alive because they set fire to his buildings. In 1755, Mark and Phillis, slaves of John Codman of Charleston, having learned that their master had made them free by his will, poisoned him to expedite matters. Mark was hanged and Phillis was burned alive.

Believing that the necessity for maintaining surveillance over Negroes at the time of combating the Indian on the frontier was sufficient reason for preventing the importa-**The Georgia** tion of slaves, Georgia soon had reasons for **situation.** regretting that it had receded from this posi-tion. In 1728 a plan to kill the whites of Savannah brought into the field a body of militant Negroes. Because of dissension in the ranks they met defeat. Soon thereafter, however, the colony contrived to meet the exigencies of this situation.

Farther north, where we do not now think of the Negroes as being numerous, there were sufficient of them for such an effort. In 1712 New York was shocked from its very foundation by the discovery of the Negro plot to destroy the whites with fire and sword. The school of Elias Neau, maintained for the education of the Negroes, **Plots in** had to be temporarily closed. The excitement **New York.** did not subside until it was known that eighteen of the leaders had been hanged and others deported or broken on the wheel. In 1741 the Negroes repeated the effort in New York City. They proceeded to the slaughter by burning the city to kill the white people to get possession of their property and free the Negroes. Four white persons implicated were executed. Of the one hundred and twenty-five Negroes arrested, thirteen were burned, eighteen hanged, and seventy-one deported. In 1723 some desperate Negroes planned to burn the City of Boston. So much fear was experienced that the city had to take precaution against "Indians, Negro or Mulatto Servants, or Slaves." The Negro tended, then, to be regarded as a slave to be exploited or an outcast to be dreaded.

This apparently fixed attitude toward the Negro continued in the leading colonies. By the end of the seventeenth century the Negroes were abandoned to develop the best they could in their isolation in the New World. As agricultural interests of the colo- **The Negro** nies attracted the larger number of slaves **on his own** they were gradually removed from close con- **initiative.** tact with the masters and therefore had but little opportunity for improvement as did those who continued as house servants. In this neglected condition the master class ceased to think of the Negroes as capable of spiritual or mental development. Some never thought of the Negro as possessing a mind or soul. In 1756 Andrew Burnaby reported that the people of Virginia hardly regarded the Indians and Negroes as human beings, and that it was almost impossible to convict a white man for killing a Negro or an Indian.[4]

Against this system, which held the blacks in perpetual servitude and prevented the elevation of free persons of color to the dignity of citizenship, persons of sympathetic tendencies persistently protested.[5] There was some anti-slavery sentiment from the very beginning of the introduction of slavery into the original thirteen. Here and there in the colonies there were persons who seriously objected to the rigor to which the slaves were subjected in the development of the industries of the New World. These first protests, however, were largely on religious grounds. The objection was that the exploiting methods gave the Negroes no time for mental development or religious instruction. Men who had at first accepted slavery as a means of bringing these heathen into a Christian land where they might undergo conversion to the faith, bore it grievously that selfish masters ignored the right of the Negroes to be enlightened.

Antislavery sentiment.

This antislavery sentiment, however, was not due primarily to cruel treatment of the slaves. In fact, the first Negro slaves were largely house servants, enjoying the treatment usually received among the ancient patriarchs. Some of them were indentured for a certain period, and

[4] Andrew Burnaby, *Travels Through North America*, p. 31.
[5] The early antislavery movement has been well treated in M. S. Locke's *Antislavery in America from the Introduction of the African Slaves to the Prohibition of the Slave Trade*, in Alice D. Adams' *Neglected Period of Antislavery in America*, and in the annual reports of *The American Convention of Abolition Societies.*

even the slaves during the eighteenth century had many opportunities for obtaining freedom. The free Negroes had a social status of equality with that of **Mild attack** the poor whites, but the latter had little **on slavery.** chance for full citizenship. A bold attack on slavery, therefore, did not follow, for most of the objections raised during the eighteenth century were economic or political rather than sentimental. Certain antislavery advocates considered slavery prejudicial not only to the interests of the slaves themselves but to those of a country desirous of economic and political development. Efforts were first made to keep the institution out of Georgia because slaves were not vigorous enough to furnish defense for a frontier colony and would starve the poor white laborers. William Usselinx proposed to prohibit its introduction in the Swedish settlements because African slave labor would be less profitable than that of the European.

More striking than these arguments were those of the Puritans and Quakers, based on religious principles.[6] The religious element believed in slavery as connected in some way with religion. Although not advocates of social equality for the blacks, the New England colonists believed in equality before God and, there- **Puritans.** fore, in the freedom of the body. The Puritans thought that slavery was the particular offense that called down the avenging wrath of God; but not wishing to make money of it, they sought at first to restrict it to lawful captives taken in just wars. They felt that it was an impediment to salvation in that the souls of the captives were often neglected. "Remember," said Richard Baxter, whose

---

[6] For a lengthy discussion see M. S. Locke's *Antislavery in America from the Introduction of the African Slaves to the Prohibition of the Slave Trade*, pp. 1-157, and C. G. Woodson's *The Education of the Negro Prior to 1861*, Ch. III. Valuable information may be obtained from *The Journal of Negro History*, Vol. I, pp. 49-68; Vol. II, pp. 37-50, 83-95, 126-138.

thought influenced the Puritan, "that they are of as good a kind as you; that is, they are reasonable creatures as well as you, and born to as much natural liberty. If their sins have enslaved them to you, yet Nature made them your equals. To go as pirates and catch up poor Negroes or people of another land, that never forfeited life or liberty, and to take them slaves, and sell them, is one of the worst kinds of thievery in the world." Having the same idea, Roger Williams protested against the enslavement of Pequot Indians in 1637. John Eliot and Cotton Mather attacked the institution because of its abuses. In 1701 Justice Sewall presented his convincing argument against it in his essay entitled *The Selling of Joseph.*

Among the Quakers, who, unlike the Puritans, believed in social equality as well as equality before God, the antislavery movement met with more success. The Quakers **Quakers in earnest.** noticed especially the cruel treatment of slaves and the vices resulting from the system. They also endeavored to prove that the system was prejudicial to the interests of all in that it prevented the poor whites from finding employment, promoted idleness among the rich, cut off the immigration of industrious Europeans, and precluded the prosperity of whites already in the land.

These religious antislavery attacks, of course, were met by various other arguments. Some said that Negroes were slaves because of the curse of Canaan; others because they **Proslavery and antislavery arguments.** were ignorant and wicked. They might, therefore, rejoice over their opportunity to be led to Christ through enslavement by the Christian white race. Ralph Sandiford inquired: "If these Negroes are slaves of slaves, whose slaves must their masters be?" [7] Elihu Coleman, replying to the argument that Negroes should be enslaved because of their wicked-

[7] Ralph Sandiford, *Brief Examination,* Ch. IV, p. 5.

ness, said: "If that plea would do, I believe that they need not go far for slaves as now they do." [8] Seeing that the difference of race was the main thing, the Quakers of Germantown, Pennsylvania, said in 1688: "Now, though they are black, we cannot conceive there is more liberty to have them slaves, than it is to have other white ones. There is a saying that we shall do to all men like as we will be done to ourselves, making no difference of what generation, descent or color they are. Here is liberty of conscience which is right and reasonable. Here ought also to be liberty of the body." [9] This argument was further elaborated by George Keith, John Hepburn, William Burling and Benjamin Lay. All of these were men of influence in shaping the thought of the Quakers with respect to slavery.

This protest against slavery tended to become more and more religious. Sandiford said: "Shall we go to Africa for bread and lay the burden which appertains to our bodily support on their shoulders? Is this washing one another's feet, or living by the Gospel, or maintaining liberty and property? And to live on an- **Ralph Sandi-** other's labor by force and oppression, is **ford's attack.** this loving mercy? And to keep them slaves to us and our posterity to all eternity, is this walking humbly with God?" [10] Denouncing all slaveholders as sinners, Benjamin Lay said: "Slaves are bound to them; so are they to the Devil, and stronger, for as death loosens one, it fastens the other in eternal Torment if not repented and forsaken." He styled as a sort of devils **Benjamin Lay.** that preached to hell rather than to Heaven those ministers who, in leaving their homes on Sunday to preach the "Gospel of glad tidings to all men and liberty to the captives,

[8] Elihu Coleman, *Testimony*, p. 17.
[9] Germantown Friends' Protest Against Slavery in A. B. Hart's *American History Told by Contemporaries*, Vol. II, Section 102, pp. 291-293.
[10] Ralph Sandiford, *Brief Examination*.

directed the slaves to work to maintain them in pride, idle-ness, laziness and fullness of bread, and sins of Sodom.''[11]

These arguments were not merely empty protests but ideas translated into action by the Quakers. They promoted manumission by individual owners, and by 1713 worked out a definite scheme for the liberation of the Afri-**Manumission** cans and their restoration to their native land, **promoted.** after having been prepared beforehand by instruction in religion and the fundamentals of education. Their protests against the purchase of Africans seriously impaired the market for slaves in Philadelphia by 1715, and decidedly checked the importation of slaves into Pennsylvania in 1743.

In this effort there figured two important characters among the Quakers, Anthony Benezet of Philadelphia and John Woolman of New Jersey. Born of Huguenot parents persecuted as heretics in France, Benezet readily sympa-**Benezet and** thized with the oppressed Negroes in **Woolman.** America. He considered the world his country and all mankind his brethren. In several treatises he warned the world of the calamitous state of the enslaved Negroes, endeavoring to show that such a practice is inconsistent with the plainest precepts of the Gospel, the dictates of reason, and every common sentiment of humanity. In the struggle for the rights of man he boldly advocated the emancipation of the slaves and their elevation through practical education and religious instruction. John Woolman, his contemporary, and Quaker to the manner born, was no less courageous in his attack on the institution. Having traveled through the colonies where slavery was pronounced, he became embittered against the institution. Wherever he went he bore eloquent testimony against ''slavekeeping, preaching deliverance of the captive.'' He refused to eat food or wear clothes produced by slave

[11] Benjamin Lay, *All Slave-Keepers Apostates,* pp. 92-93.

labor. Living up to his high ideals of freedom, he refrained from accepting the hospitality of slaveholders. He actually retired to seclusion in Pennsylvania and led a most eccentric life.

In later years the work of the Quakers became more effective. Most of the slaves of Quakers in New England and the Middle States were manumitted by moral suasion and religious coercion by the time of the American Revolution. The same followed among the Quakers in the Southern States not long after the close of the century. No such effective work was accomplished by any other body of Christians. Among the Congregationalists there were heard such protests as that of Samuel Hopkins of Newport and that of Ezra Stiles, later the president of Yale College. Samuel Webster of Salisbury, and Nathaniel Niles and William Gordon, of Roxbury, also attacked the evil, but at that time their group did not make an organized effort for the extermination of the system.

Results among the Quakers.

CHAPTER VII

SLAVERY IN ASCENDANCY

IN spite of these conditions, however, the slave population continued to increase. There were about 6,000 Negroes in Virginia in 1700, and they so rapidly multiplied as factors in the widely extending tobacco culture that in 1760 one-half of the inhabitants of that colony were blacks. To supply the need for cheap labor in the production of rice and indigo, the blacks increased so fast in South Carolina after 1730 that Negroes soon exceeded the whites and outnumbered them two to one in 1760. This increase tended to degrade the position of the white servant, to "cause pride and ruin the industry of our white people, who, seeing the race of poor creatures below them, looked down upon them as if they were slaves."[1]

There were not many Negroes in the northern part of the United States. Pennsylvania had a considerable number, however, for William Penn himself owned slaves. A **Few slaves in the North.** few toiled on the farms along the Hudson, and the number in the city of New York reached 6,000 when the whole population was 40,000. Boston was one of the centers in New England to which some Negroes were brought, but a still larger number doubtless landed at the ports connecting more closely with the West Indies. Many of these went to Newport and thence they gradually scattered to other points. In 1748 South Kingston had 1,405 whites, 381 Negroes and 193 Indians. New

[1] Almost any of the monographs on slavery of the various States contain useful information on early slavery in America. *The Journal of Negro History*, I, pp. 163 to 216; VIII, pp. 247-283, however, is especially helpful there.

England, however, because of its economic condition, never became the home of many slaves. In 1770, when there were 697,624 slaves in the thirteen States, only 3,763 of these were in New England. At that time 36,323 of the slave population lived in the Middle States and 656,538 in the South.

This result was not strange; for the colonies were merely commercial enterprises, and the slave trade was profitable to the European promoters. In 1770 there were in England itself not less than 15,000 slaves brought in by traders as attendants and servants. There was no decided check to this influx until the famous Somerset decision. Somerset had run away from **Slavery in** his master **England.** in Virginia. When captured he was to be shipped to Jamaica, where he was to be sold.

GRANVILLE SHARP

A writ was procured by Granville Sharp, however; and there followed a hearing which finally brought the question before Lord Mansfield. He gave the opinion that the state of a slave is so odious that it can be supported only by positive law **The Somerset** to that effect. Such law did not exist in **decision.** England.[2] He therefore ordered the slave to be discharged. Liberal as this decision was, however, it did not seem to have any effect on the colonies, although the subsequent struggle for the rights of man in this country

[2] Hurd, *Freedom and Bondage,* I, 189-191.

tended to do much to direct attention to the condition of the Negro.

There were then in the American colonies many slaves whose condition constituted an exception to the rule. The slaves as a whole were much better treated at that time than they were during the nineteenth century. Most of them were then given some opportunity for enlightenment **Exceptional** and religious instruction. Embracing these **slaves.** opportunities, many of them early established themselves as freemen, constituting an essential factor in the economic life of their communities. Some became artisans of peculiar skill; others obtained the position of contractors; and not a few became planters themselves who owned extensive estates and numbers of slaves. Sir Thomas Gage found a number of such planters of color in Guatemala in the seventeenth century; the mixed breeds of Louisiana produced a number of this type. Even the English colonies along the coast were not always an exception to this rule, as is shown by the case of Anthony Johnson in Virginia, already mentioned as a Negro servant who attained the status of a slaveholder himself. Andrew Bryan, a Negro Baptist preacher, was widely known as a slaveholder in Savannah, Georgia, before 1790.

These exceptions resulted largely from the few white men who became interested in the welfare of the Negroes during the seventeenth and eighteenth centuries. Among these **The clergy** were Paul le June, a Jesuit missionary in Can**and** ada, Le Petit and François Phillibert Watrum **the blacks.** of the same sect in Louisiana, Alphonso Sandoval in Havana, Morgan Goodwyn in Virginia, Thomas Bacon in Maryland, and George Keith in Pennsylvania. Some of these liberal workers coöperated with the Society for the Propagation of the Gospel in Foreign Parts, to which the Negroes were indebted for most of their early enlightenment. These reformers contended that the gospel was sent also to the slaves and that they should be prepared by mental development to receive it. With the increasing interest in education it became more restricted to the clergy and such other well-chosen persons recommended by them and attached to the churches.

It was soon evident, however, that little could be effected in the enlightenment of these blacks without first teaching them the English language. In almost every case, therefore, during the eighteenth century, when the clergy undertook the teaching of the gospel among the blacks, it involved also instruction in the fundamentals of education, that their message might have the desired effect.[3] In fact, in some of the colonies, the Negroes were about as well provided with schools as the whites.[4] The first school for the education of the whites in the Carolinas was established in 1716, and a school for the education of the Negroes was established in 1744. There were in a few colonies, schools not only for free Negroes but for slaves. They were sometimes taught in the classes with the children of their masters. In some cases, when the Negroes experienced sufficient mental development to qualify as teachers themselves, they were called upon to serve their masters' children in this capacity. In the eighteenth century there were schools for Negroes in almost all of the cities and towns where they were found.[5]

It was fortunate for the Negroes that many schools of the middle colonies were conducted by the indentured servant class of low estate. It looks rather strange that our fathers should commit such an important task **Convicts as** to the care of the convicts taken from the **teachers.** prisons in England and indentured in America. Yet this

---

[3] *The Journal of Negro History*, I, 87, 233, 361, and 492, and II, 51.
[4] Woodson, *Education of the Negro Prior to 1861*, Chapter II.
[5] *Ibid.*, 10-150.

was the case. Jonathan Boucher said, in 1773, that two-thirds of the teachers in the colony of Maryland were such felons.[6] As these were despised by the whites of the higher classes, they were forced to associate with the Negroes. The latter often learned from them how to read and write, and were thereby prepared to enlighten their own fellow men. Negro apprentices, moreover, as in the case of David James, a free Negro bound out in Virginia in 1727, had the right to instruction in the rudiments of learning and the handicrafts.

The location of some of these schools established for Negroes will be of much interest. Samuel Thomas undertook the instruction of certain Negroes in the Goose Creek Parish in Charleston, South Carolina, in 1695. A school **Early schools for Negroes.** for the more extensive instruction of the Negroes was established there in 1744, with Harry and Andrew. These young men were the first of the Negro race to be employed as teachers in America. Further interest was shown in the enlightenment of the slaves in that section by gentlemen and ladies of consequence. This was especially true of Eliza Lucas, later the wife of the renowned Justice Pinckney. Encouraged by the appeal of Benjamin Fawcett in behalf of the instruction of the slaves, the Rev. Mr. Davies devoted much of his time to this work among the Negroes in Virginia. So did Hugh Neill and William Sturgeon, ministers in Pennsylvania. Elias Neau had a school for Negroes in New York as early as 1706. Anthony Benezet began to hold evening classes for them in Philadelphia in 1750. The settlers of New England then tolerated the instruction of the slaves along with their own children.

The evidences of the mental development of the Negroes

---

[6] Jonathan Boucher, *A View of Causes and Consequences of the American Revolution*, 39.

of that day are found in the words of the masters themselves. In offering slaves for sale and advertising for
fugitives, masters spoke of their virtues as Intellectual
well as their shortcomings. Judging from development.
what they said about them in these advertisements, one
must conclude that many of the eighteenth-century slaves
had taken over modern civilization and had made themselves useful and skilled laborers. Some of them had a
knowledge of the modern languages, the fundamentals of

AN ADVERTISEMENT OF A RUNAWAY SLAVE

mathematics and science, and acquaintance with some of
the professions. It was a common thing to refer to a slave
as being smart and exhibiting evidences of having experienced most of that mental development which usually results from what we now call a common school education.
Some spoke "good English," in contradistinction to others
who spoke "very much broken English." In other cases
the fugitive would be credited with speaking "proper English" or speaking "very properly."

Brought in from the West Indies, where they had been
in contact with all nationalities of Europe and had not

been restricted in their development, many of these slaves had picked up more than the mere fragments of education.

Slaves with some knowledge. It was not unusual to find a slave speaking Spanish, French and English—and exceedingly good English. William Moore had a slave who spoke Swedish and English well. Philip French of Philadelphia had another who spoke Dutch and good English; and John Williams, of the same state, owned a Negro who spoke very good English and was very fluent in his talk. Another type of this sort was a slave who escaped from Charleston in 1799. He spoke both French and English fluently, was very artful, and succeeded in passing as a freeman. A better example was a slave of Thomas May of Maryland, whom his master considered plausible and complacent. He could speak good English, a little French and a few words of High Dutch. He had been in the West Indies and in Canada, serving as a waiting-man to a gentleman, and had thereby had the opportunity of getting acquainted with the different parts of America.

In addition to the mere knowledge of how to express themselves fluently in the modern tongues, a considerable number of the fugitives advertised in some parts had **Slaves able to read and write.** learned to read and write. Advertising for a Negro, named Cato, Joseph Hale said that "he speaks good English and can read and write." Another said: "He is an artful fellow and can read and write, and it is probable that he may endeavor to make his escape out of the Province." And still another was described in the terms: "He can read and write and it is likely that he may have a counterfeit pass." An examination of hundreds of advertisements for fugitive slaves during the eighteenth century shows that almost a third of them could read and write.[7]

---

[7] For a treatment of the eighteenth-century slave see *The Journal of Negro History*, I, 175-189.

Another evidence as to the favorable condition of the Negroes during the eighteenth century is their economic condition. The kind of garments they wore and the manner in which they lived throw much light on this situation. In some cases they lived in houses, enjoying the same comforts as their masters. In other cases their quarters were much better than those then provided for the poor whites in Europe and for the indentured servants in the colonies. Some masters did not take much care of the latter, since, when their term of service expired, they would no longer be of use to them.

According to the testimony of most masters in the advertisements for fugitives, they were well attired. For example, a master of Philadelphia in 1721 said that his slave escaped, wearing "a dark brown colored coat and jacket, a pair of white fustian breeches, a gray milled **Slaves** cap with a red border, a pair of new yarn **well dressed.** stockings with a pair of brown worsted under them or in his pockets." A slave owner in Maryland spoke of another fugitive as having "a black cloth coat, a high hat, white flannel waistcoat, a checked shirt, a pair of everlasting breeches, a pair of yarn stockings, a pair of old pumps, a worsted cap, an old castor hat, and sundry other clothes." A Boston master in 1761 lost a slave, who had, "when he went away, a beaver hat, a green worsted coat, a close-bodied coat with a green narrow frieze cape, a gray coat, a black and white homespun jacket, a flannel checked shirt, gray yarn stockings, a flannel shirt, a bundle of other clothes, and a violin." White persons at that time were not generally better clad.[8]

In not a few other cases these fugitives are mentioned as persons who had not only an ample supply of clothing, but considerable money. John Dulin, of Baltimore, advertised

[8] *The Journal of Negro History*, I, 203.

in 1793 for a slave supplied with ample funds. The context of the advertisement indicates that the money was

Slaves in good circumstances.

earned by the slave while hiring his time. Referring to another fugitive, a master said: "As I expect he has a sum of money with him, probably he may get some one to forge a pass for him and pass as a free man." Some Negroes were widely

THE FAITHFUL SLAVE

known, as they were serving as mechanics and artisans. A few of them became contractors on their own account, overseers for their masters, and finally freemen established in business for themselves.[9]

In the absence of restrictions which characterized the oppressive slavery of the following century, they had entered many of the higher pursuits. Some of these Negroes were serving as teachers and preachers, and a few were en-

[9] *Ibid.,* 203.

gaged in such practice of medicine as was then common in this country. Referring to one of his slaves, in 1740, James Leonard of Philadelphia said he could "bleed and draw teeth, pretending to be a great doctor and very religious, and he says he is a churchman." In 1797 James George of Charleston, South Carolina, had a slave who passed for a doctor among

Slaves in higher pursuits.

THE PUNISHMENT OF A RUNAWAY SLAVE

his people and, it was supposed, practiced in that capacity about town. Negroes were serving as privateers and soldiers in the army during the colonial wars and had learned so much about the military contests for possession in the New World that the English feared the close relations between the French in the West and the slaves of the colonies along the coast. This might eventually lead to an understanding between the French and the slaves to the effect that the latter might cross the mountains into French territory.

Probably the most striking evidences of the favorable situation of the slaves during the eighteenth century is their close relation with the poor whites. The most of these, at that time, were indentured servants. Reduced to **Slaves and** the same social status by common lot in servi- **poor whites.** tude, these two classes were equally treated in many parts. This was especially true of the colonies around the Chesapeake Bay. The slaves and the inden- tured servants followed the same occupations, had the same privileges and facilities, and experienced together the same pleasures. Living on this common plane, these two classes soon proceeded to intermarry. In 1720 Richard Tilghman of Philadelphia complained that his mulatto slave, Richard Molson, had run away in company with a white woman named Mary, who, it was supposed, passed as his wife, and with a white man named Garrett Choise, and Jane, his wife. A mulatto servant man in Philadel- phia named Isaac Cromwell absconded with an English servant woman named Anne Greene in 1745. Two years later, Ann Wainrite, a servant woman of New Castle County, escaped, taking with her a Negro woman.[10]

These close relations between the blacks and the inden- tured servants later caused unusual dissatisfaction. Laws were therefore enacted to prevent this interbreeding of the races. In 1661 the preamble of such a law in Maryland **Dissatis-** said, "And forasmuch as divers free-born **faction.** *English* women, forgetful of their free condi- tion, and to the disgrace of our nation, do intermarry with negro slaves, by which also divers suits may arise, touching the issue of such women, and a great damage doth befall the master of such Negroes, for the prevention whereof, for deterring such free-born women from such shameful

[10] *The Journal of Negro History*, I, 206.

matches, *be it enacted:* That whatsoever free-born women shall intermarry with any slave, from and after the last day of the present assembly shall serve the master of such slave during the life of her husband; and that all the issues of such free-born women so married, shall be slaves as their fathers were. *And be it further enacted:* That all the issues of *English,* or other free-born women, that have already married Negroes shall serve the master of their parents, till they be thirty years of age and no longer.''[11]

This, however, did not seem to prevent the miscegenation of the two races. Planters sometimes married white women servants to Negroes in order to transform such servants and their offspring into slaves. This happened in the case of Irish Nell, a servant woman brought to Maryland by the proprietor and sold later to a planter when he returned to England. The proceedings instituted to obtain freedom for her offspring by her Negro husband occupied the attention of the courts of Maryland for a number of years. The petition was finally granted. This procedure was especially legislated against in 1681, by a measure which penalized this custom then obtaining among the planters. Yet the interbreeding of the two races was not apparently abated by this procedure. The public was burdened with so many illegitimate mulatto children that it became necessary to frame laws to compel the persons responsible to maintain these unfortunate waifs, and to make the Negroes or the white persons concerned servants or slaves for a certain number of years.

Miscegenation.

In Virginia it was necessary to take the same action. Hugh Davis was whipped there in 1630 because he was guilty of defiling his body by lying with a Negro. In 1622

---

[11] This social status is more extensively treated in *The Journal of Negro History,* I, 206-216, and II, 335-353.

the colony imposed fines for fornication with a Negro, but did not restrict intermarriage until 1691. According to **Efforts to separate the races.** this law, if any free English woman should have a bastard child by a Negro or mulatto, she should pay the sum of fifteen pounds sterling. In default of such payment she should be taken into the possession of the church wardens and disposed of

ENTERTAINMENT

for five years. Such illegitimate children should be bound out as servants until they reached the age of thirty. If the woman in question happened to be already in servitude, five years were added to the term for which she was then bound. This same law was further elaborated and extended by the Virginia law of 1753. Here, however, it developed, just as in the case of Maryland, that these laws failed to remedy the prevailing "evil." That State also found itself with an unusually large number of illegitimate mulatto children on its hands. The officials hit upon the plan of binding them out. This was done in the cases of David James in 1727, one Malachi on a plantation, and another free Negro in Norfolk county in 1770.

North Carolina also undertook to put an end to this miscegenation. That colony provided in 1715 for the usual laws restricting the intercourse of the two races. Clergymen officiating at mixed marriages were penalized. These precautions, however, failed to meet the requirements. The custom continued in North Carolina just as it had elsewhere, in spite of the fact that the law of 1741 legislated against "that abominable mixture and spurious issue, which hereafter may increase in this government by white men and women intermarrying with Indians, Negroes, Mulattoes or Mustees." It was enacted that if any man or woman, being free, should intermarry with such persons, he should be fined fifty pounds for the use of the parish, and any white servant woman found guilty of such conduct should have two years of service in addition to the time for which she was already bound out.

This custom obtained in other parts where the Negroes were found in smaller numbers. Because of the scarcity of such population it was checked with greater difficulty. Massachusetts enacted a law against it in 1705. Pennsylvania took action in 1725. These laws were **Difficulties in separating the races.** extended and made more rigid in the course of time, as the custom gave more and more dissatisfaction. It was a long time, however, before it had very much effect in New York, and still longer in Pennsylvania. This intermixture endured. The anti-miscegenation law was repealed in Pennsylvania in 1780, and mixed marriages became common. But when the ardor of the revolutionary leaders had become much diminished towards the close of the eighteenth century, there set in a decided reaction against miscegenation. It was therefore extensively agitated throughout communities where Negroes were found in large numbers, and various petitions came from those sections praying that intermarriage of the whites and blacks be prohibited.

Persons who professed seriously to consider the future of slavery, therefore, saw that miscegenation, and especially the concubinage of white men with their female slaves, introduced a mulatto race whose numbers would

The danger of miscegenation to slavery. become dangerous if the affections of their white parents were permitted to render them free. The Americans of the future would thereby become a race of mixed breeds rather than a white and a black population. As the lust of white persons for those of color was too strong to prevent race admixture, the liberty of emancipating their mulatto offspring was restricted in the slave States, but the custom of selling them became common.

These laws, therefore, eventually had their desired effect. They were never intended to prevent the miscegenation of the races, but to debase black offspring to a still lower status. In spite of public opinion Negro males, under other circumstances, might intermarry with the poor

Laws finally effective. white women. The more important objective, too, was to leave the women of color without protection against white men. They might use them for convenience, while white women and black men would gradually grow separate and distinct in their social relations. Although thereafter the offspring of blacks and whites did not diminish, instead of being gradually assimilated to the type of the Caucasian, they tended to constitute a peculiar class, commonly called people of color. This class had a higher social status than that of the blacks but became finally classified, with all other persons of African blood as Negroes.

These various elements of the so-called Negro population were at first designated according to the custom in the West Indies. "The Kingston parish register of baptisms," says Prof. Pitman, "mentions black or Negro, mulatto, sambo, quadroon, mustee or mestee, brown, 'of color,' and Indian. The mulatto was the offspring of a white man and a black woman; the mulatto and a black produced a sambo; from the mulatto and a white came the quadroon; from the quadroon and white the mustee; the child of a mustee by a white man was called a musteefino. The children of a musteefino in Jamaica were free by law and ranked as white persons to all intents and purposes." Others there, as on the American continent, suffered from the pagan requirements of caste in a frontier country advertised as Christian.

There were made efforts also to restrict contact of slaves with the free Negroes. One means employed was the embittering of one against the other. The free Negro was encouraged to think himself better than the slave. On the other hand, the slave was taught to hate the free Negro because of his haughtiness in his superior position. The poor whites, another undesirable class in the slave society, were handled very much in the same way. The Negroes, therefore, continued to become a hopeless class doomed to exploitation by the whites.

In the lowest status possible in the social order the slaveholder could content himself with the thought that the Negro thus debased could not rise from the position assigned him. The gap was to be widened by improving the whites while leaving the Negro to his fate. He must be left out of the political and social order. Little account was taken of the Negro then except in a few liberal centers. Slaves were not even required to marry according to law. Morals were vitiated by the breaking of home ties in the operation of the slave trade and by remating in the interest of the masters. When married according to form it was usually an extra legal ceremony of words of caution as to how to conduct themselves in the interest of their owners. This was sometimes followed by a feast in the kitchen of the plantation house, or a collation no more expensive than a morsel and cup of tea or coffee.

These unions, such as they were under the circumstances, were often considered just as binding and sacred as the marital ties effected by legal ceremony; and there were masters who insisted upon the marriage of slaves according to law as required of the whites. Court records in Massachusetts, New York, and Virginia supply such evidence. At the same time there were sympathetic persons and religious workers brave enough to attack the system which permitted the development of loose morals, and they thereby accomplished some good. Their efforts did not avail as much as they might have for the reason that the detribalized Negroes in being brought from Africa presented a more difficult problem since they were not permitted to be Europeanized in America. It is a gross violation of the truth in which ignorant, loose writers on the Negro some time indulge, however, when they try to make it appear that the Negro family was non-existent except so far as being held together by the mother who became attached to first one man and then another. The moral sense of the imported Negro African rebelled against any such promiscuity. While there were cases of Negroes debased to such a low level, these undesirable conditions did not obtain everywhere.

CHAPTER VIII

THE case of the neglected Negro, was not hopeless. Efforts in behalf of the race became more successful in later years. This was due not altogether to the forceful preachments of the sects, but also to the new impetus given the movement by forces set to work during the period following the French and Indian War and culminating in the spread of the nascent social doctrine which effected the American Revolution.[1] The British, as a result of the military triumph of Wolfe at Quebec and Clive in India, had come into possession of vast territory. Parliament, under the leadership of Grenville, Townshend and North, hoped to incorporate these conquests into the empire. These ministers hoped to defray the expenses incident to the execution of the plan by enforcing the Navigation Acts, which had all but fallen into desuetude. Long since accustomed to freedom from such restraint, the colonists began to seek in law and history facts with which they disputed the right of Parliament to tax America, and on the basis of which they set forth theories justifying the religious, economic and political freedom of man.

During this period the colonists of the more democratic

After the French and Indian War.

---

[1] For a lengthy discussion see M. S. Locke's *Antislavery in America from the Introduction of the African Slaves to the Prohibition of the Slave Trade*, pp. 1-157; and C. G. Woodson's *The Education of the Negro Prior to 1861*, Ch. III. Valuable information may be obtained from *The Journal of Negro History*, Vol. I, pp. 49-68; Vol. II, pp. 37-50, 83-95, 126-138.

order obtained first toleration and finally religious freedom for their more popular sects. These were the Quakers,

**Toleration
and the
Negro.**
Methodists, Baptists and Presbyterians. Most
of these at that time accepted the Negroes as
human beings and undertook to accord them
the privileges of men. For the Negroes this meant larger
opportunities for religious development and intellectual
progress, and finally, citizenship in the more liberal colonies. Political leaders, imbued with the idea of the unalienable rights of man, joined these religious bodies in the
struggle for the freedom of the Negroes. These efforts of
religious groups, formerly operating independently along
parallel lines, finally culminated as one united movement.
The freedom justified by the Bible reached common ground
with the liberty which the patriots discovered in John
Locke's *Second Essay on Government*.

In this struggle certain spokesmen grew bolder with assertions tantamount to what the conservative element branded
as radical utterances the consequences from which few at

**The rights
of Man.**
that time could estimate. In 1767 Nathaniel
Appleton insisted that the slaves should not
only ''be treated with a respect agreeable'' but that the institution should be abolished. If the West Indies, as some
then contended, could not be cultivated without slave labor,
''let them sink then,'' said he, ''for it is more honorable to
seek a support by begging than by theft.'' [2]

Playing their part in the anti-slavery drama, the Presbyterians took the position that slavery was wrong because
it subjected the will of the slave to that of the master. The

**Presby-
terians.**
Baptists often attacked the institution with
such zeal that some of them became known as
the Emancipating Baptists. The Methodist Episcopal
Church, influenced by John Wesley, declared at its conference in 1786: ''We view it as contrary to the golden law of

[2] Nathaniel Appleton, *Considerations on Slavery*, p. 19.

God and the prophets, and the unalienable rights of mankind, as well as every principle of the Revolution, to hold in deepest abasement, in a more abject slavery than is perhaps to be found in any part of the world, except America, so many souls that are capable of the image of God.'' [3] Strenuous efforts were then made to excommunicate slaveholders and especially those known as ministers. [4]

This success, however, was not necessarily due to the work of the clergy of the liberal sects. It was their effort supported by those political leaders who applied the principles of the Declaration of Independence to **Political** the Negro. The same theological doctrines **leaders and** and political theories which impelled the colo- **the Negro.** nists to rise against the home country to establish the free government and religious liberty caused them also to contend that it was wrong for the whites to exploit the blacks. In many cases the foremost advocates of the rights of the colonists were also advocates of the freedom of the Negroes. However, there were some who contended that the principles of the Declaration of Independence did not apply to the Negroes, as slaves were not constituent members of our society.

Finding it difficult to harmonize their holding men in bondage with the assertion of the right of all men to be free, however, the revolutionary leaders boldly met the question. When James Otis was arguing the **Meeting** case of the Writs of Assistance, showing the **the issue.** immunity of the colonists from such violation of the laws of nature, he did not forget the Negroes. He said they should also be freed. It is little wonder, then, that John

---

[3] Lucius Matlack, *History of American Slavery and Methodism,* p. 29.

[4] While the Quakers, however, discouraged the growth of the institution among their people, and actually exterminated it, the other sects kept the question in its agitated state until it finally divided several of them before the Civil War.

Adams, who heard the argument, shuddered at the doctrine taught and the consequences that might be derived from such premises. Patrick Henry soon discovered that his own denunciation of the clergy and other agents of royalty in America was broad enough to establish the right of the Negro to freedom, and later expressed himself accordingly.

Thomas Jefferson, the philosopher of the Revolution, found among other grounds for the justification of the re-

The position of Jefferson. volt against Great Britain that the King had promoted the slave trade. Jefferson incorporated into his original draft of the Declaration of Independence an indictment of George III to the effect that he had violated the "most sacred rights of life and liberty of a distant people, who never offended him, captivating them into slavery in another hemisphere or to incur miserable death in their transportation thither." Though not so outspoken, there stood with Jefferson almost all of the fathers of the American Revolution, even those in the South, like Henry Laurens, George Wythe, George Mason, and George Washington. These men supported Jefferson in 1776 in the immortal declaration "that all men are created equal, that they are endowed by their Creator with certain unalienable Rights, that among these are Life, Liberty and the pursuit of Happiness."

This new interest in the Negro during the American Revolution secured to the race an appreciable share in defending the liberty of the country.[5] One cause of the

The new freedom and the Negro. Boston Massacre was that a slave, out of love of country, insulted a British officer. Negroes were in front rank of those openly protesting against the quartering and billeting of British

---

[5] This military history is well treated in W. B. Hartgrove's *The Negro Soldier in the American Revolution,* in *The Journal of Negro History,* Vol. I, pp. 110-131.

soldiers in Boston to enforce the laws authorizing taxation in the colonies. In the clash itself Crispus Attucks, another Negro, was one of the first four to shed blood in behalf of American liberty. During the war numbers of Negroes, like Lemuel Haynes, served as minute men and later as regulars in the ranks, side by side with white men. Peter Salem distinguished himself at Bunker Hill by killing Major Pitcairn, a number of other Negroes heroically rescued Major Samuel Lawrence, and Salem Poore of Colonel Frye's regiment acquitted himself with such honor at this battle of Charlestown on June 17, 1775, that fourteen American officers commended him to the Continental Congress.

The organization of Negro soldiers on a larger scale as separate units soon followed after some opposition. The reasons for timidity in this respect were various. Having the idea that the Negroes were savages who **Negro units** should not be permitted to take part in a **proposed.** struggle between white men, Massachusetts protested against the enlistment of Negroes. The Committee of Safety, of which John Hancock and Joseph Ward were members, had this opinion. They contended that inasmuch as the contest then between Great Britain and her colonies respected the liberties and privileges of the latter, the admission of any persons but freemen as soldiers would be inconsistent with the principles supported and would reflect dishonor on the colony. Although this action did not apparently affect the enlistment of free persons of color, Washington, in taking command of the army at Cambridge, prohibited the enlistment of all Negroes. The matter was discussed in the Continental Congress and as a result Washington was instructed by that body to discharge all Negroes, whether slave or free. When the enlistment of Negroes came up again in the council of the army, it was unanimously agreed to reject slaves and by a large majority to refuse Negroes altogether. By these instructions Washington, as commander of the army, was governed late in 1775.

Many of the colonists who desired to avail themselves of the support of the Negroes were afraid to set such an example. They were thinking that the Brit-**Fear of arming Negroes.** ish might outstrip them in playing the same game and might arm both the Indians and Negroes faster than the colonies could. A few were of the

THE DEATH OF CRISPUS ATTUCKS, MARCH 5, 1770

opinion that the Negroes, seizing the opportunity, might go over to Great Britain. On this account the delegates from Georgia to the Continental Congress had grave fears for the safety of the South. They believed that if one thousand regular troops should land in Georgia under a commander and with adequate supplies, and he should proclaim freedom to all Negroes, twenty thousand of them would join the British in a fortnight.

As a matter of fact, they had good reason for so think-ing.   When Lord Dunmore, governor of Virginia, was driven from the colony by the patriots, he summoned to his support several hundred Negroes to assist   **Negroes** him in regaining his power. He promised   **armed by** such loyalists freedom from their masters.   **British.** The British contemplated organizing a Negro regiment in Long Island. Sir Henry Clinton proclaimed in 1779 that all Negroes in arms should be purchased from their cap-tors for the public service and that every Negro who might desert the ''Rebel Standard'' should have security to follow within the British lines any occupation which he might think proper.

These plans, moreover, were actually carried out in some parts.   The British made an effort to embody two Negro regiments in North Carolina. Between 1775 and 1783 the State of South Carolina lost 25,000 Negroes, **Negroes with** who went over to the British. Probably three- **the British.** fourths of all the Negroes then in Georgia were lost to the Americans. One-third of the men by whom Fort Corn-wallis was garrisoned at the siege of Augusta were Negroes loyal to the English. A corps of fugitive slaves calling themselves the King of England's Soldiers harassed for sev-eral years the people living on the Savannah River, and there was much fear that the rebuffed free Negroes of New England would do the same for the colonists in their sec-tion.

It was necessary, therefore, for the leaders of the country to recede from this position of refusing to enlist Negroes. Washington within a few weeks revoked his order prohibit-ing their enlistment.   The committee in the **Negroes** Continental Congress considering the matter **enlisted.** recommended the reënlistment of those Negroes who had served faithfully, and Congress, not wishing to infringe upon what they called States' rights, was disposed to leave the matter to the commonwealths. Most men of foresight, however, approved the recognition of the Negro as a soldier. James Madison suggested that the slaves be liberated and armed. Hamilton, like General Greene, urged that slaves be given their freedom with the sword, to secure their fidelity, animate their courage, and influence those remaining in bondage by an open door to their emancipa-

PETER SALEM AT BUNKER HILL

tion. Henry Laurens of South Carolina, then in eternal dread of the disaffection of the slaves, said he would ad-

Proposal of Henry Laurens.
vance those who are unjustly deprived of the rights of mankind to a state which would be a proper gradation between abject slavery and perfect liberty, and would have a corps of such men uniformly clad and equipped to operate against the British. John Laurens, the son of Henry Laurens, was permitted by the Continental Congress to undertake such enlistment in South Carolina, but when he brought his plan before the legislature he was defeated by a "triple-headed

monster that sheds the baneful influence of avarice, prejudice and pusillanimity in all our assemblies." [6]

In other parts of the country, however, the interest in the Negro was such that they regained their former standing in the army. Free Negroes enlisted in Virginia, and so many slaves deserted their masters for the **Negro soldiers** army that the State enacted in 1777 a law **in Virginia.** providing that no Negro should be enlisted unless he had a certificate of freedom. But later many Virginia slaves, with the promise of freedom, were sent to the army as substitutes for freemen. To prevent masters of such Negroes from reënslaving them, the State passed an act of emancipation, proclaiming freedom to all who had enlisted and served their term faithfully, and empowered them to sue in *forma pauperis,* should they thereafter be unlawfully held.

In his strait at Valley Forge, Washington was induced by General Varnum to enlist a battalion of Negroes in Rhode Island to fill his depleted ranks. The **Solving the** Rhode Island assembly acceded to this re- **problem in** quest. The State gave every effective slave **the States.** the liberty to don the uniform on the condition that upon his passing muster he would become absolutely free and entitled to all the wages, bounties, and encouragements given to any other soldier. Connecticut undertook to raise a Negro regiment, and New York in 1780. The latter promised masters the usual bounty land to purchase their slaves and proclaimed freedom to all bondsmen thus enlisting for three years. This sort of action governed the enlistment of Negroes in New Hampshire. There it tended to exterminate slavery. In 1781 Maryland resolved to raise 750 Negroes to be incorporated with the other troops. At the suggestion from Thomas Kench, Massachusetts considered the question of organizing in separate battalions the Ne-

[6] Sparks, *Writings of George Washington,* VIII, 322, 323.

groes serving in the ranks among white men. It was believed that in units by themselves they would exhibit a better *esprit de corps* and that a larger number would enlist; but, as the suggestion led to a heated debate in the legislature and to blows in the coffee houses of Boston, nothing definite was done.

The services rendered by these black troops showed both patriotism and valor. On July 9, 1777, a Negro soldier under the command of Colonel Barton at Newport captured at great peril Major General Prescott

Opinions as to Negro bravery.

of the British army. Of the battle of Monmouth, of June 28, 1778, Bancroft said, "Nor may history omit to record that of the Revolutionary patriots who on that day offered their lives for their country more than 700 black men fought side by side with the white." Referring to the behavior of Negroes who fought under General Greene, Lafayette said that in trying to carry the commander's position the enemy repeated the attempt three times and was often repulsed with great bravery. "At the passage of the ferry," said the Marquis de Chastellux, "I met a detachment of the Rhode Island regiment, the same corps we had with us last summer, but they since have been recruited and clothed. The greater part of them are Negroes or mulattoes; but they are strong, robust men and those I have seen had a very good appearance." "Had they been unfaithful or even given way before the enemy, all would have been lost," said Dr. Harris, a veteran, in praise of the Negroes in the battle of Rhode Island on August 29, 1778. "Three times in succession they were attacked with more desperate valor and fury by well-trained disciplined troops and three times did they successfully repel the assault, and thus preserved our army from capture." According to Lecky, "the Negroes proved excellent soldiers in a hard-fought battle that secured the retreat of Sullivan when they three times

The Negro and the Rights of Man

By His Excellency

GEORGE WASHINGTON, Esq;

General and Commander in Chief of the Forces of the United
States of America.

THESE are to CERTIFY that the Bearer hereof
Bristo Baker Soldier
in the *Second Connecticut* Regiment, having faithfully
served the United States *from April 8th, 1777 to
June 8th, 1783* and being inlisted for the War only, is
hereby DISCHARGED from the American Army.

GIVEN at HEAD-QUARTERS the *8 June 1783*

G Washington

By His Excellency's
Command,

REGISTERED in the Books
of the Regiment,

Adjutant,

THE above *Baker*
has been honored with the BADGE of MERIT for *Six*
Years faithful Service.

HEAD-QUARTERS, June *12* 1783,

THE within CERTIFICATE shall not avail the
Bearer as a Discharge, until the Ratification of the definitive
Treaty of Peace; previous to which Time, and until Proclama-
tion thereof shall be made, He is to be considered as being on
Furlough.

GEORGE WASHINGTON

FACSIMILE OF AN HONORABLE DISCHARGE OF A NEGRO SOLDIER
FROM WASHINGTON'S ARMY

drove back a large body of Hessians.'' Negro troops sacrificed themselves to the last man in defending Colonel Greene when he was killed at Points Bridge, New York, on May 14, 1781. Other Negro soldiers both on land and sea, recruited from the colonies along the Atlantic and from the West Indies, helped to force Cornwallis to surrender at Yorktown on the 19th of the following October.

Some of these Negro soldiers emerged from the Revolution as heroes. A Negro slave of South Carolina rendered Governor Rutledge such valuable services in this war that by special act of the legislature in 1783 his wife and children were liberated. Because of his unusual fortitude and valor in many skirmishes in the South, in one of which he was severely wounded, the State and the people of Georgia honored Austin Dabney. He received a pension from the United States Government and by an act of the legislature a tract of land from Georgia. He subsequently accumulated considerable property, attained a position of usefulness among his white neighbors, had the respect and confidence of high officials, and died mourned by all.

The result of the increasing interest in the Negro was soon apparent. The Continental Congress prohibited the importation of slaves. With the exception of South Carolina and Georgia, a general effort in the extermination of
The progress of emancipation. slavery was made during the revolutionary epoch. The black codes were considerably moderated, and laws facilitating manumission were passed in most of the colonies. In 1772 Virginia repealed a measure forbidding emancipation except for military service. About the same time Maryland prohibited the importation of slaves and in like manner facilitated emancipation. New York, New Jersey and Pennsylvania prohibited the slave traffic. Vermont, New Hampshire and Massachusetts exterminated slavery by constitutional pro-

vision; Rhode Island, Connecticut, New Jersey, New York and Pennsylvania washed their hands of the stain by gradual emancipation acts; and the Continental Congress excluded the evil from the Northwest Territory by the Ordinance of 1787.[7] So sanguine did the friends of universal freedom become that they thought that later slavery of itself would gradually pass away in Maryland, Virginia and North Carolina.

To prepare the freedmen for this new opportunity, schools were established in almost all large groups in towns and cities. Efforts were made to apprentice such blacks to trades, to place them in the higher pursuits **Preparation for** of labor, and to develop among them a class **emancipation.** of small farmers who might be settled on unoccupied lands west of the Alleghenies. The friends of the Negro looked to education and religion as the leverage by which they might be elevated to the status of white men. Here and there there had been some effort in the education of the Negroes during the colonial period; but, after the revolutionary movement was well on its way, this undertaking became more systematized. It was, therefore, productive of more satisfactory results. There was an actual education for the social betterment of practically all of the Negroes who thus became free.

[7] This prohibitory clause was:
There shall be neither slavery nor involuntary servitude in the said territory, otherwise than in the punishment of crime, whereof the party shall have been duly convicted: *Provided always,* That any person escaping into the same, from whom labor may be lawfully claimed in any one of the original States, such fugitive may be lawfully reclaimed and conveyed to the person claiming his or her labor or service as aforesaid.

Be it ordained by the authority aforesaid: That the resolutions of the 23d of April, 1784, relative to the subject of this ordinance, be, and the same are hereby, repealed, and declared null and void.

Done by the United States, in Congress assembled, the 13th day of July in the year of our Lord 1787, and of their sovereignty and independence the twelfth.

Education was regarded as a right of man. Dr. McLeod seriously objected to the holding of slaves because it de-

Education a right of man. stroyed their intellectual powers. David Rice in attacking the institution complained that the master thereby deprived them of the opportunity to have instructing conversation and for learning to read. Thomas Jefferson, having in mind the gradual emancipation of slaves, hoped that the masters would permit them to be prepared by instruction and habit for self-government, the honest pursuit of industrial and social duty. Negroes were voting and holding office. In fact, this was the halcyon day of the Negro race prior to the Civil War. Never had so much been done before in behalf of the blacks, never had there been such opportunities for developing their power to function as citizens. So much impetus was then given to the cause of the Negroes that, despite the reaction following this epoch, they retained their citizenship intact in most parts of the North and even late in parts of the South. Negroes voted in North Carolina and Tennessee until 1834.

The strongest impulse to general improvement of the Negroes, however, came through the new religious bodies. In this social upheaval they attained not only toleration

Religious freedom. but freedom. As there was less ground for antagonism to the development of the Negroes in this direction, many of them became socially equal with the white communicants; and some Negro churchmen, trained by pious persons, preached to audiences of the Caucasian race. Among these was Jacob Bishop. He so impressed his co-workers that near the close of the eighteenth century he was made pastor of the first Baptist church (white) of Portsmouth, Virginia. William Lemon was preaching at this time to a white congregation at Pettsworth, or Gloucester, Virginia. Some recognition by whites was given during these years to Henry Evans and Ralph Freeman of North Carolina, to Harry Hosier of Philadelphia, Black Harry of St. Eustatius, and Lemuel Haynes, an intelligent Negro preacher to white people in New England. Andrew Bryan, contemporary with Jacob Bishop, preached occasionally to the whites, but devoted his life to religious work among his own people. He was the successor to George Liele, who, under the **George Liele** rule of the British in Savannah, had founded **and Andrew** the first Baptist church of that city. Liele **Bryan.** went with them to Jamaica, where he established the first Baptist church in that colony. Bryan's task, however, was not so easy as that of Liele. The Americans who succeeded the British in authority at Savannah persecuted Bryan. They whipped him whenever he attempted to preach. In the course of time, however, he obtained the support of a few kind-hearted whites, who interceded in his behalf and secured for him the permission to preach without interruption. His work thereafter made progress, and extended to Augusta through the coöperation of Henry Francis and others.

During these years, too, thanks to this religious influence, the liberation of the slaves and their elevation to a more important position in society assumed a form different from that of emancipation through military service. The struggle for the rights of man resulted in the organization of the first abolition society in Pennsylvania in 1775. The membership of this organization consisted largely of Quakers. The movement did not gain much force during the Revolutionary War for the reason that abolition was being worked out to some extent along other lines. The very **Abolition** next year after the signing of the treaty of peace **Societies.** closing the war, abolition interest among the Quakers and their co-workers was renewed. With John Jay as president the New York Manumission Society was established in 1785 to promote the liberation of slaves and to protect those already freed. They had in mind then the liberation of those kidnaped and unlawfully held in bondage. The Pennsylvania Abolition Society started in 1775 was reorganized in 1787 with Benjamin Franklin as president. As many as twelve such organizations were reported in 1791. New Jersey organized another in 1792. Seeking to concentrate their efforts upon the sources of authority in this country, nine of these abolition societies delivered to Congress on December 8, 1791, a memorial inveighing against the slave trade. Undaunted by the refusal of Congress to take action in this case and encouraged by the faith of those within their ranks, these nine local bodies organized in 1794 the American Convention of Abolition Societies. Their two important objectives were to increase the zeal and efficiency of the individual societies, and to assume the responsibility in regard to national matters.

Operating locally, these societies became a fighting force in behalf of the Negro. In cases of oppression they appealed to the courts for the relief of this despised class. Negroes unjustly imprisoned and kidnaped, and illegally held in bondage, were freed here and there wherever these abolition societies operated. Not restricting their efforts to **The method of** the freedom of the slave, they undertook also **abolitionists.** to prepare them for the duties of citizenship. Negroes were taken into the meetings of the Quakers and other abolitionists to undergo religious instruction. Some were placed in school or apprenticed to trades. When properly equipped they were turned over to a committee charged with placing them in positions of usefulness and in settling them in comfortable homes in the community. They were freely advised from time to time as to how to conduct themselves in such manner as to win the favor of the public. They were told to attend church, to acquire the rudiments of education, to learn trades, to deal justly with their fellow men, to be simple and frugal in all their habits, to refrain from the use of alcoholics, to avoid frolicking and idle arguments, to marry according to legal requirements, to save their earnings, and to demean themselves in proper manner toward their respective communities.

In this effort for the uplift of the Negroes these friends had the moral support of reformers abroad. Fighting for the abolition of the slave trade and for the improvement of the Negroes in the British colonies had for some years been an important concern of Thomas Clarkson, William Wilberforce, Granville Sharp, and Zachary Macaulay in England. They organized there a society for the abolition of the slave traffic in 1787. Influenced by the example of these men there started in France the following year the Society of the Friends of the Blacks. Among the persons coöperating then were Le Comte de Mirabeau, Le Marquis de Lafayette, Condorcet, Jean Pierre Brissot, Clavière, and later Sieyés, Pétion, Grégoire, Robespierre, and the Duke de la Rochefoucauld.

The idea of improving the Negro as a preparation for emancipation had some weight even in the distinctly slaveholding areas when connected with the idea of colonization. Some larger slaveholders agreed with Thornton, Fothergill and Granville Sharp in the plan for educating Negroes for colonization in Africa. Others believed with Anthony Benezet, T. Brannagan, and Thomas Jefferson, that after adequate instruction they might be settled upon the lands of the public domain west of the Allegheny Mountains. Both Lafayette and Kosciusko undertook to settle manumitted slaves as freemen on plantations to educate them for service to their race and nation. Lafayette after failing to induce George Washington to join with him in the experiment undertook it at Caen, which failed because of the confiscation of his property during his changing fortunes of the French Revolution. Kosciusko left all his property in America as a fund for the same purpose, but on account of subsequent wills which others claimed that he made, such property was otherwise disposed of by the federal courts.

Men like Daniel Davis, and Benjamin Bush, however, insisted upon the right of the Negro to be educated whether he should remain here or be deported for colonization. **The right to** Their position was immediately attacked by **be elevated.** those who insisted that the Negro was mentally inferior to the white man, and, therefore, could not be equipped to function as a citizen. To this John Wesley replied that if they were dull, their stupidity was due to the inhuman masters who gave them no opportunity for improving their understanding, "for the Africans were in no way remarkable for their stupidity while they remained in their own country." William Pinkney insisted that Negroes are no worse than white people under similar circumstances, and that all the Negroes need to disprove their so-called inferiority is an equal chance with the more favored race. Buchanan informed these "merciless aristocrats" "that the Africans whom you despise, whom you inhumanly treat as brutes and whom you unlawfully subject to slavery with tyrannizing hands of despots are equally capable of improvement with yourselves."

Franklin considered the idea of the natural inferiority of the Negro as a silly excuse. He conceded that most of the blacks were improvident and poor. He believed, however, that their condition was not due to deficient under- **Mental** standing but to their lack of education. He **capacity.** was very much impressed with their achievements in music. So disgusting was this notion of inferiority to Abbé Grégoire of Paris that he wrote an interesting essay on "Negro Literature" to prove that people of color have unusual intellectual power. In this sketch he made honorable mention of Phyllis Wheatley, Benjamin Banneker, "Othello," Angelo Solimann, Thomas Fuller, James

Derham and others. Grégoire knew not Jupiter Hammon, a religious versifier in New York. Another writer discussing Jefferson's equivocal position on this question said that one would have thought that "modern philosophy himself" would not have the face to expect that the wretch, who is driven out to labor at the dawn of day, and who toils until evening with a whip over his head, ought to be a poet. Benezet, who had actually taught Negroes, declared "with truth and sincerity" that he had found among them as great variety of talents as among a like number of white persons.

Had these defenders of the Negro been better informed, they could have recorded that the distinguished Chevalier de Saint-Georges was knighted by Louis XVI, because of his unusual achievements as the director of the orchestra at the Grand Opera in Paris. They might have mentioned, too, Lislet Geoffroy, who attained such distinction as a man of thought that he was admitted to the French Academy. "Among the favorites of Peter the Great and his famous consort Catharine, was an Abyssinian Negro educated in France, to whom

GUSTAVUS VASA, a talented African

was attached the name of Hannivalov. He became a general and received other honors from the Russian government. He married the daughter of a Greek merchant, and his son became a general of artillery, who built the harbor and fortress of Cherson. The great grandson of Hannivalov was A. S. Pushkin (1799-1837), perhaps the greatest of all Russian poets.[8] In Spain, where considerable

[8] For further information on Pushkin see *The Journal of Negro History* VIII, 359-366.

diluted Negro blood came in with the Moors, we find a remarkable record of the black man. Juan Latino became its great Latin Scholar, and Juan de Pareja, a painter. In one of the churches of Seville are to be seen four beautiful pictures (Christ bound to a column, with St. Peter kneeling at his side; St. Joseph; St. Anne; Madonna and Child), the work of a mulatto, Sebastian Gomez, the slave, then the pupil, companion and the equal of his master, the great painter

PHILLIS WHEATLEY

Murillo, who had him made a free citizen of Spain, and at his death (1682), left him part of his estate." [9]

In the circle of Intellectual Negroes there stood out two characters more prominent than most blacks in America. These were Phillis Wheatley [10] and Benjamin Banneker. [11] Phillis Wheatley was a slave in a Boston family that gave her every opportunity for improvement. After receiving instruction for a few years she mastered the fundamentals of education and made unusual advancement in the study of Latin and History. In the very beginning of her career she exhibited the tendency to write poetry. She attracted the attention of the most prominent people of that day who had to concede that she had de-

Phillis Wheatley.

[9] *Atlanta University Publications*, No. 20; *Select Discussions of the Race Problem*, 87-88.

[10] R. R. Wright, *Phillis Wheatley*.

[11] Henry E. Baker, *Benjamin Banneker* in *The Journal of Negro History*, Vol. III, pp. 99-118.

cidedly demonstrated that Negroes had possibilities beyond that of being the hewers of wood and drawers of water for another race.

Benjamin Banneker was a character of more genius than that with which many of his white contemporaries were endowed. Born in Maryland, of a free mother and slave father, he was free. At that time, a Negro of this class exercised most of the privileges accorded white men. Banneker attended an elementary school. Upon the moving of the well-known Ellicotts to his neighborhood about the time he was reaching his majority, Banneker had made such advancement in science and mathematics that Mr. George Ellicott supplied him with books. Studying these works, Banneker developed into one of the most noted astronomers and mathematicians of his time. He was the first of all Americans to make a clock, and he published one of the first series of almanacs brought out in the United States. These meritorious achievements made him so prominent that he was sought and received by some of the most prominent men of the United States. Among these were James McHenry, once Vice-President of the United States, and Thomas Jefferson. The latter was so impressed with his worth that he secured for him a place on the commission

BENJAMIN BANNEKER'S ALMANAC

Benjamin Banneker.

that surveyed and laid out Washington in the District of Columbia.

The striking evidence of the mental endowment of certain Negroes caused Thomas Jefferson, the well known popular authority on philosophical matters in that day, to change from certainty to doubt with respect to the mental inferiority of the Negro. He was not impressed with the poetry of Phillis Wheatley and considered it beneath the dignity of criticism. Writing to General Chastellux in 1785, however, Jefferson, said that although the Negro in the position in which he was at that time was not equal to the white man in mind and body that "it would be hazardous to affirm, that, equally cultivated for a few generations, he would not become so."

In 1791 Jefferson addressed to Banneker these words: "Nobody wishes more than I do to see such proofs as you exhibit, that nature has given to our black brethren talents equal to those of the other colors of men, and that the appearance of a want of them is owing merely to the degraded condition of their existence, both in Africa and America. . . . I have taken the liberty of sending your Almanac to Monsieur de Condorcet, Secretary of the Academy of Sciences at Paris, and member of the Philanthropic Society, because I considered it as a document to which your color had a right for their justification against the doubts which have been entertained of them."

With respect to Banneker Jefferson said in addressing thus the Marquis de Condorcet: "We have now in the United States a Negro, the son of a black man born in Africa and a black woman born in the United States, who is a very respectable mathematician. I procured him to be employed under one of our chief directors in laying out the new Federal City on the Potomac and in the intervals of his leisure, while on that work, he made an almanac for the next year, which he sent me in his own handwriting, and which I enclose to you. I have seen very elegant solutions of geometrical problems by him. Add to this that he is a very worthy and respectable member of society. He is a free man. I shall be delighted to see these instances of moral eminence so multiplied as to prove that the want of talents observed in them, is merely the effect of their degraded condition, and not proceeding from any difference in the structure of the parts on which intellect depends.''

To Banneker himself Jefferson said in referring to the slaves: ''Nobody wishes more ardently than I do to see a good system commenced for raising the condition both of their body and mind to what it ought to be, as fast as the imbecility of their present existence, and other circumstances which cannot be neglected, will admit.''

To Henri Grégoire, who had sent Jefferson a copy of his *Littérature des Nègres* the latter wrote: ''Be assured that no person living wishes more sincerely than I do to see a complete refutation of the doubts I have myself entertained and expressed on the grade of understanding allotted to the Negroes by nature, and to find that in this respect they are on a par with ourselves. My doubts were the result of personal observation on the limited sphere of my own State, where the opportunities for the development of their genius were not favorable, and those of exercising it still less so. I expressed them, therefore, with great hesitation; but whatever be their degree of talent it is no measure of their rights. Because Sir Isaac Newton was superior to others in understanding, he was not therefore lord of the person or property of others. On this subject they are gaining daily in the opinions of nations, and hopeful advances are making towards their reestablishment on an equal footing with the other colors of the human family. I pray you, therefore, to accept my thanks for the many instances you have enabled me to observe of respectable intelligence in that race of men, which cannot fail to have effect in hastening the day of their relief.''

Yet Jefferson showed his insincerity in saying later to Joel Barlow: ''Bishop Grégoire wrote to me on the doubts I had expressed five or six and twenty years ago, in the *Notes on Virginia,* as to the grade of understanding of the Negroes. His credulity has made him gather up every story he could find of men of color (without distinguishing whether black, or of what degree of mixture), however slight the mention, or light the authority on which they are quoted. The whole do not amount, in point of evidence, to what we know ourselves of Banneker. We know he had spherical trigonometry enough to make almanacs, but not without the suspicion of aid from Ellicot, who was his neighbor and friend, and never missed an opportunity of puffing him. I have a long letter from Banneker, which shows him to have had a mind of very common stature indeed. As to Bishop Grégoire, I wrote him a very soft answer. It was impossible for doubt to have been more tenderly or hesitatingly expressed than that was in the *Notes on Virginia,* and nothing was or is further from my intentions, than to enlist myself as the champion of a fixed opinion, where I have only expressed a doubt. St. Domingo will, in time, throw light on the question.''

CHAPTER IX

INDEPENDENT EFFORTS

PRIOR to the American Revolution the Negroes were not
sufficiently well developed to be mutually helpful. The
institutions of the country were in the hands of the whites.
There was therefore little opportunity for concerted action
among the Negroes. The American Revolu- Negroes weak
tion, however, marked an epoch in the de- at first.
velopment of the Negro in the United States. The struggle
for the rights of man set working certain forces which
all but indicated the dawn of a new era. In spite of the
reaction which followed the Negro held this ground for
years to come. In the considerable number of schools established for the education of the Negroes and the churches
founded by them the race had its opportunity for independent thought and action. Granted larger economic opportunities in preparation for gradual emancipation, they
could more easily carry out plans to supply their peculiar
needs. Negroes readily manifested interest also in the
efforts to manumit members of their race and to secure
justice for those illegally held in bondage.[1]

In education they ceased to be altogether recipients of
the favors of the whites. Now and then there appeared
ambitious Negroes who had qualified themselves as teachers. As such they not only served their own particular
group but also the whites. At that time   Showing
prejudice was one of caste rather than of   initiative.
race. Men were not generally restricted on account of
color; and whatever the attitude of the government

[1] These facts are covered in detail in Woodson, *Education of the
Negro Prior to 1861*, pp. 93-178, and *The History of the Negro
Church*, pp. 40-121. See also *A Century of Negro Migration*, pp. 1-60.

141

might be in the matter that had little bearing on the question, inasmuch as education at that time was a private undertaking at the expense of the persons concerned. The Negro as a private school-teacher, moreover, had a social standing about as high as that of a teacher of any other group. Few persons otherwise engaged aspired to teach except from the missionary point of view. The profession was largely restricted to those suffering from physical handicaps or otherwise undesirable. In 1773, according to Jonathan Boucher, two-thirds of the school-teachers in Maryland were the imported felons and convicts brought from Europe to serve here as indentured servants.

The independence of the Negro manifested itself even in the exceptional ambition to rise to usefulness in professions. As early as 1740 there was a Negro in Pennsylvania

Negroes in professions. advertised as qualified to bleed and draw teeth, "pretending to be a great doctor." In 1797 there was another in South Carolina posing as a doctor among his people and practicing in that capacity about town. Near the end of the century there appeared in Philadelphia a regularly recognized Negro physician known as James Derham. He was born in Philadelphia in 1762 where he was taught to read and write. Employed occasionally by his master to compound medicines, and to assist him with his patients, he learned the profession. Sold as a slave to Dr. George West, a surgeon in the 16th British regiment during the Revolutionary War, he further developed in the medical profession. At the close of the War he was sold to Dr. Robert Dove, of New Orleans, where he had still more opportunity in this line and obtained his freedom on liberal terms. He became so well grounded in the art of healing that he soon built up a business in New Orleans paying him $3,000 a year. Of him Dr. Benjamin Rush said: "I have conversed with him upon most of the acute and epidemic diseases of the country where he lives and was pleased to find him perfectly acquainted with the modern simple mode of practice on those diseases. I expected to have suggested some new medicines to him; but he suggested many more to me. He is very modest and engaging in his manners. He speaks French fluently and has some knowledge of the Spanish language.''

Endeavoring to provide for their own social life, too, the Negroes easily became interested in fraternal organizations. The pioneer in developing the Negro in this direction was Prince Hall, the father of Free Masonry among the Negroes in North America. Hall was born September 12, 1748, at Bridge Town, Barbados, British West Indies. His father, Thomas Prince Hall, was an Englishman and his mother was a free woman of French descent. **Prince Hall and the Masons.** He was apprenticed as a leather worker in which he made unusual progress. Desirous of visiting this country, he came to the United States in 1765 at the age of seventeen. Although in a foreign country where he had neither friends nor education to help him on his way he applied himself industriously at common labor during the day and studied privately at night. Upon reaching the age of twenty-seven he had acquired the fundamentals of education. Saving his earnings, he had

PRINCE HALL

accumulated sufficient to buy a piece of property. He joined the Methodist Church, in which he passed as an eloquent preacher. His first church was located in Cambridge, Massachusetts. There he built up a prosperous congregation.

Desiring to learn the secrets of Free Masonry even during revolutionary times, he found his way to the quarters of General Gage on Cox Hill in Boston. He was admitted to the military lodge and advanced to the degree of Master Mason prior to the actual Revolution. Along with him there were associated others who later obtained a charter under which they finally operated with limited power. Their membership was increased from time to time by accessions from New York, Pennsylvania, and foreign countries. Hoping to enter into the full rights and powers in this country, Hall presented such a petition, which was refused on account of color. He then turned to foreigners for what he had been refused in his own country. The separation from England intervened. He nevertheless entered actively in the war and acquitted himself with credit. At the close of the struggle he renewed his effort to secure a charter for the Negro Masonic lodge. Addressing the Grand Lodge of England with such a prayer on March 2, 1784, he received a prompt reply granting the dispensation. The warrant was delayed. It was not actually delivered until 1787. The lodge was then organized and the officers duly installed. From this organization there sprang up others which soon necessitated the establishment of the Grand Lodge in Massachusetts. In the multiplication of lodges, too, a similar need developed elsewhere. The movement was well established in Philadelphia and Rhode Island in 1797. It was on its feet in New York in 1812 and the District of Columbia and Maryland in 1825. This same movement led to the organization of the Grand United Order of Odd

Fellows among Negroes in 1843. The society was established under a dispensation obtained by Peter Ogden from the order in England. Because of racial proscription in America these Negroes had **Peter Ogden.** been barred from the Independent Order of Odd Fellows, a purely American craft.

In the religious world the independent movement among

PETER OGDEN

Negroes had a better chance. The church was a more popular institution than the school or lodge. The majority of men in those days aspired to salvation. After the triumph of toleration and religious freedom, there were few to interfere with the institutions designed to prepare the multitude to this end. Prior to this change in the religious sentiment of the country, however, there was little thought as to the Negro in the administration of the church. The clergy of the sects dominant during the colonial **The church an** period were either inaccessible or unsym- **inviting field.** pathetic toward the Negro. The Anglicans, succeeded by the Protestant Episcopalians, would not countenance such a thought as that of a Negro rector; Catholics, more kindly disposed to the race, did not work in that direction; and neither did the Presbyterians nor the Quakers make sufficient inroads among them to justify the elevation of Negroes to commanding positions in these respective circles.

In the case of the Methodist and Baptist churches, however, the Negro had a better chance. These denominations socialized the Gospel. They presented it in such a simple form and with such a forceful appeal as to reach both the **Methodists and Baptists.** illiterate poor whites and the Negroes. Extensively proselyting these elements, the Methodists and Baptists rapidly developed as national forces in the United States after the American Revolution. Later, however, a considerable number of these poor whites became rich and in some cases slaveholders. They thereupon easily lost their sympathy for the Negroes. In these once antislavery churches, then, the race problem soon had its first battle. There were those who desired to restrict the Negro merely to passive worship. He was merely to heed the word and live. Finally, they tended to restrict members of the race to certain pews, to a separate section of the church, or to a different building.

Having enjoyed for some time the boon of freedom in the church, moreover, the Negroes were loath to give up this liberty. The escape of a young Negro, a slave of Thomas Jones, in Baltimore County in 1793, is a case in evidence. Accounting for his flight, his master said: "He **Reaction in the church.** was raised in a family of religious persons commonly called Methodists and has lived with some of them for years past on terms of perfect equality; the refusal to continue him on these terms gave him offense and he, therefore, absconded. He had been accustomed to instruct and exhort his fellow creatures of all colors in matters of religious duty." Another such Negro, named Jacob, ran away from Thomas Gibbs of that State in 1800, hoping to enlarge his liberty as a Methodist minister. His master said in advertising him as a runaway: "He professed to be a Methodist and has been in the practice of preaching of nights." Another Negro preacher of this type, named Richard, ran away from Hugh Drummond in

Anne Arundel County, that same year. Still another, called Simboe, escaped a little later from Henry Lockey of Newbern, North Carolina.

This was the beginning of something more significant. The free Negroes in the North began to assert themselves.

RICHARD ALLEN

They contended that they were not necessarily obligated to follow the fortunes of the white churches. Such self-assertion early culminated in the protest of Richard Allen, the founder of the African Methodist Episcopal Church. Richard Allen was the very sort of man to perform this great task. He was born a slave of Benjamin Chew of Phila- **Richard Allen.** delphia, but very soon thereafter he was sold with his whole family to a planter living near Dover, Delaware. There he grew to manhood. Coming under Christian influence, he was converted in 1777 and began his career as a minister three years later. Struck with the genuineness of his piety, his master permitted him to conduct prayers and to preach in his house. The master himself was one of the first converts of this zealous man. Feeling after his conversion that slavery was wrong, Allen's master permitted his bondmen to obtain their freedom. Allen and his brother purchased themselves for $2.000 in the depreciated currency of the Revolutionary War. Richard Allen then engaged himself at such menial labor as a Negro could then find. He cut and hauled wood while preaching at his leisure. Recognizing his unusual talent, Richard Watcoat on the Baltimore circuit permitted Allen to travel with him. Bishop Asbury frequently gave him assignments to preach. Coming to Philadelphia in 1786, Allen was invited to preach at the St. George Methodist Episcopal Church and at various other places in the city. His difficulties, however, had just begun. Yet he could not but succeed, because he was a man of independent character, strict integrity, business tact, and thrifty habits. When he spoke a word, it was taken at its face value. His rule was never to break a promise or violate a contract.[2]

The special needs of his own people aroused him to action in their behalf. He said, "I soon saw a large field open in seeking and instructing my African brethren who have been a long-forgotten people, and few of them attended public worship." Starting a prayer meeting in Philadelphia, he soon had forty-two members. Encouraged thus, he proposed to establish a separate place of worship for the people of color, but was dissuaded therefrom by the protest of the whites and certain Negroes unto whom he ministered. Only three of them approved his plan. Preaching at this church with such power as to move his own people in a way that they had never been affected before, however, he attracted so many that the management proposed to segregate the Negroes. The church undertook to carry out this plan drastically even to the extent of disturbing Richard Allen, Absalom Jones, and William White by pulling them off their knees while they were in the attitude of prayer. The Negroes, therefore, withdrew from the church in a body.

2 When he purchased the property for the Bethel Church on Lombard Street near Sixth the majority of the committee refused to accept it. Allen, having given his word so to do, kept it at a great personal loss.

This was the beginning of the independent Free African Society, organized by Richard Allen and Absalom Jones. At first, however, this organization was not so much a church as it was a social uplift organization. It appeared that Jones and Allen soon had differing plans, for the former finally organized the African Protestant Episcopal Church of St. Thomas, while the majority of the persons seceding from the St. George Methodist Episcopal Church followed the standard of Allen in effecting the independent body known as the Bethel Church. Allen purchased an old building for the Bethel Church and had it duly dedicated in 1794. He organized also a Sunday School and a day and night school, to which were sent regular ministers by the Methodist Conference. Allen was ordained deacon by Bishop Asbury in 1799. He later attained the status of elder. Negroes of other cities followed Allen's example. They organized what were known as African Methodist Episcopal Churches in Baltimore, Wilmington, Attleboro, Pennsylvania, and Salem, New Jersey. Having maintained themselves independently for some time, these African societies soon developed sufficient leaders to effect the organization of a national church. A conference for this purpose was called in Philadelphia in 1816. The most important transaction of the Philadelphia meeting was the election of a bishop. Upon taking the vote the body declared Daniel Coker bishop-elect. But for several reasons he resigned the next day in favor of Richard Allen, who was elected and consecrated by regularly ordained ministers.

The first independent Negro Methodist church.

The movement made rapid progress. With the establishment of the New York conference the limits of the connection extended eastward as far as New Bedford, westward to Pittsburgh, and southward to Charleston, South Carolina. There-

Progress of separate churches.

after, however, there was little hope of success in the South. The African Methodists there met with some difficulty under the leadership of the Rev. Morris Brown, who established in Charleston a church reporting 1,000 members in 1817 and 3,000 in 1822. Because of the spirit of insurrection among Negroes following the fortunes of Denmark Vesey, who devised well-laid plans for killing off the masters of the slaves in 1822, these communicants were required to suspend operation. Their pastor, Morris Brown, was threatened a n d would have been dealt with foully, had it not been for the interference of General James Hamilton. He secreted Brown in his home until he could give him safe passage to the North. There Morris Brown very soon reached a position of prominence, even that of bishop in the African Methodist Episcopal Church.

JAMES VARICK

Another secession of the Methodists from the white connection was in progress in other parts. A number of Negroes, most of whom were members of the John Street Methodist Episcopal Church, in New York City, took the first step toward separation from that connection in 1796. They had not been disturbed in their worship to the extent **Zionites separate.** experienced by Richard Allen and his co-workers in Philadelphia, but they had a "desire for the privilege of holding meetings of their own, where they might have an opportunity to exercise their spiritual gifts among themselves, and thereby be more useful to one another.'' Such permission was obtained from Bishop Francis Asbury by a group of intelligent Negro Methodists. Their white friends appointed as their adviser Rev. John McClaskey, who instructed them how to proceed in drawing up the articles of government. A charter was secured in 1801 and bears the signatures of Peter Williams and Francis Jacobs. This was the beginning of the African Methodist Episcopal Zion Church. A number of such congregations were established.

This church had not proceeded very far before there arose some dissension in the ranks. The supporters of Bishop Allen, moreover, appeared at the opportune moment, when the Zionites in New York City were without a building and were also without the direc-   **Causes for** tion which they had formerly had from the   **doubt.** white Methodists. The latter were disturbed by a schism resulting from differences as to church government and property. There soon came a time when it was necessary for the Zionites to decide exactly what they would do. This being the case, an official meeting was held on August 11, 1820, for the purpose of considering the serious state of the church. Being desirous, however, to proceed regularly rather than radically, these African Methodists sought ordination and consecration through some branch of the Christian Church. They sent a committee to make such a request of Bishop Hobart of the Episcopal Church, but he was unable to serve them. They then appealed to the bishop of the Methodist Church, but they were put off in one way or another. They thereafter appealed to Methodist conferences in Philadelphia and New York and were finally refused. The Zionites were then reduced to radical measures in that they finally had to ordain their own deacons and elders. Becoming thus aggressive, the

Zionites, like the Allenites, had taken the offensive. They extended their operations through missionaries. Under the leadership of such men as James Varick, George Collins, Charles Anderson, and Christopher Rush, they drew up

CHRISTOPHER RUSH

the doctrines and discipline of the African Methodist Episcopal Zion Church in America. They elected a number of elders, and finally organized in 1821 a national body, of which James Varick became the first bishop in 1822.

Before the Negro Methodists perfected their organization by which the influence of their churches might be permanently extended throughout the country, the Baptists had been locally trying to do the same thing. The Harrison Street Baptist Church was organized at Petersburg, Virginia, in **Early Baptist** 1776; and another Baptist Church at Wil- **churches.** liamsburg, Virginia, in 1785. The first African Baptist Church was established in Savannah in 1785, with the second Baptist Church in that City following fourteen years later. The African Baptist Church of Lexington, Kentucky, appeared in 1790. There was founded a mixed Baptist Church in the Mound Bayou, Mississippi district, in 1805, by Joseph Willis, a free Negro, born in South Carolina in 1762.[3] In the City of Phila-

---

[3] A man of fair education, Willis was a power in that State as early as 1798. We hear of him in Louisiana in 1804. Mississippi

delphia on May 14, 1809, thirteen Negro members who had for some time felt that it would be more congenial for them to worship separately, were dismissed to form the first African Baptist Church. On June 19, 1809, the use of the First Baptist Church (white) was given them for the meeting at which they were constituted an organized body. The main trouble with the First Baptist Church (white) seemed to be that it had suffered from having its antislavery ardor dampened during the reaction following the Revolutionary War.

When the African Baptist Church of Philadelphia was being organized, the same movement was culminating likewise in Boston. Prior to 1809 the Baptists of color had worshiped along with their white brethren. The church record of November 1, 1772, says: "After **Early workers** divine service, Hannah Dunmore and **Among Baptists.** Chloe, a Negro woman belonging to Mr. George Green, were received into the church." Speaking about this relation, this document says: "Our records have many notices of baptisms and marriages among the Negro people and until early in the present century there was a large group of them in the church." But the desire for independence and a more congenial atmosphere so obsessed them that they sought to form an organization of their own. This was finally effected in 1809 under the leadership of the Rev. Thomas Paul, a native of Exeter, New Hampshire. His labors, however, were not restricted to that city. He frequently made preaching excursions into different parts of the country where his "color excited considerable curiosity." Being a person of very pleasing and fervid address, he attracted crowds. It was while he was pastor of the Church in Boston, that in 1808 he organized in New York City the congregation now known

sent two ministers to ordain him in Louisiana in 1812. He organized the Louisiana Baptist Association and was chosen as its moderator in 1837.

as the Abyssinian Baptist Church and served it from June
to September of that year. After this Josiah Bishop and
others had charge of this very promising work in the
metropolis of the nation.[4]

That the independent church movement among Negroes
should be directed toward Methodism and Baptism requires some consideration. In those parts of the country in
which most Negroes were found, the dominant communicants among the whites were at first Episcopalians, the
successors to the rites and ceremonies of the
Anglican Church. Among some of the best
friends of the Negroes, moreover, were the
Presbyterians, who often extended the blacks the same
hand of welcome as did the Quakers. Whether the failure
of the Negro to be attracted to them was due altogether
to the emotional nature of the Negroes to which the
Baptists and Methodists appealed, to chance, or to the
wisdom of the leaders of the independent church movement among the Negroes, is a much-mooted question.

Causes of the independent movement.

The Episcopal Church, moreover, could hardly attract
large numbers of Negroes. Its discipline was ill-suited to
the undeveloped Negro. Its ministers had been among the
first to offer the Negroes religious instruction, but it had
lost favor by refusing to give Negroes the consideration

---

[4] Paul's interest in the Negro was not limited to those in this
country. In 1823 he presented to the Baptist Missionary Society of
Massachusetts a plan for improving the moral and religious condition of the Haitians. His plan was received with considerable
enthusiasm and he was appointed as a missionary and sent to that
country for six months. President Boyer of the Republic of Haiti
and other public functionaries kindly received this missionary. There
he soon met with some success in edifying a few pious people who
seemed gratified beyond measure by his ministrations. Writing
home, he frequently mentioned "the powerful precious soul-reviving
seasons" which he and the few disciples on the island enjoyed. Because of his lack of knowledge of the French language, however, he
could not reach a large number of the inhabitants of that island.
He was, therefore, compelled to leave Haiti with the regret that he
could not do more for its general welfare.

which they enjoyed among the Methodists and Baptists. Furthermore, the Episcopal churchmen refused to make slavery a matter of discipline. Consequently their work among the Negroes was restricted to such establishments as St. Thomas in Philadelphia, St. Philips, organized in New York in 1818, and the St. James, established later in Baltimore.

The independent movement among other Negro communicants was not so pronounced. In the first place there were not many of them, although various sects welcomed the Negroes and contributed much to their uplift. In the case of a more ritualistic church like the Catholics, to which Negroes were attracted only in small numbers, there was no opportunity offered for the development of the Negro along independent lines. Among the Congregationalists were found most of the ardent friends of the Negro during the first half of the nineteenth century. Consequently, there was little reason for an establishment separate from their fellow white communicants. A separate church of this faith among the Negroes did not appear until 1829 when there was organized the Dixwell Avenue Congregational Church in New Haven.

Negroes in ritualistic churches.

There were many other Negroes who without very much independent organization to support them nevertheless accomplished much in demonstrating the initiative of the race. For more than a generation, Andrew Marshall continued the efficient work among the Baptists of Savannah begun by George Liele and successfully developed by Andrew Bryan. For more than forty years, a pioneer Negro preacher, one ''Uncle Jack,'' went from plantation to plantation in Virginia to preach to whites and blacks. Henry Evans, a free Negro preacher of Virginia, happened to stop at Fayetteville, North Carolina, while on his way to Charleston. Ex-

Henry Evans.

pounding the Gospel on Sunday while working at the trade of shoemaking during the week, he so stirred up the town that the officials prohibited him from preaching. He won so many friends, however, that this order was recalled. He developed the work there to the extent of having a sufficient following for a church by 1790. He labored successfully among both races in that field until 1810. At this time Black Harry, another Negro preacher, had so impressed the public that Dr. Benjamin Rush pronounced him the greatest orator in America. Bishop Asbury often took him as his companion because his forceful preaching attracted a larger audience than the bishop himself could draw, for, says John Ledman, "Harry was a more popular speaker than Mr. Asbury or almost any one else in his day."

Out of Tennessee had come another Negro preacher of this type. This was John Gloucester, who had been the body servant of Gideon Blackburn of that State. Moved by his unusual gifts as a scholar and a preacher, his master **John Gloucester.** liberated him that he might engage in the ministry. He came to Philadelphia where he began his life's work as a missionary exhorting from house to house. He then preached in a schoolhouse and finally had sufficient converts with whom to establish the First African Presbyterian Church in Philadelphia in 1807. This work he promoted with unusual success until 1822 when he passed away.

In this class of preachers there were those who accomplished certain definite things worthy of attention. Among these a prominent place should be given to John Stewart. **John Stewart, the apostle to the Indians.** He was born of free parents in Powhatan County, Virginia. There he received some religious instruction. On coming to Marietta, Ohio, he came under the influence of the Methodist Episcopal Church. Believing that it was his mission to serve the world as a preacher, he proceeded to the arduous task of converting the Indians of Lake Erie. After overcoming the opposition of William Walker, the Federal Agent, he returned to the Wyandot Indians, at Upper Sandusky. Because of his enthusiasm and preaching with unusual power in proselyting Indians, the Methodist Episcopal Church granted him the support which his work required. They established there a mission station, and actual education with instruction in mechanic arts and agriculture soon followed. With other workers coming to his assistance Stewart saw his efforts crowned with remarkable success as he, on account of unusual labor, began to decline in 1822. He had nevertheless made himself the pioneer of the Methodist Episcopal Church in its mission work among the Indians.

Still more ambitious was the work of Lemuel Haynes. He was the son of a Negro by a white woman. He was born in 1753. His mother, because of the stigma attached to her child of color, deserted Lemuel in infancy. He later became an apprentice in the family of Lemuel Haynes, a white man who transferred him to one a preacher David Rose, of Granville, Massachusetts. to whites. Lemuel was placed at school. Conspicuous in the curriculum which he had to follow was religious instruction. Before his education could be completed, however, he had to answer the call to the colors and served with distinction in the Revolutionary War. Upon returning to his home among his good people he was often called upon on Satday evenings to read from collections of sermons to prepare the minds of the family for the more serious worship on the Sabbath Day. Availing himself of the opportunity to study religious books, he soon developed much knowledge of things spiritual. One Saturday evening, therefore, when asked to read a sermon from one of the divines, he read one of his own. As this sermon had a new ring and a thought that David Rose had never heard before he inquired as to whose sermon it was. Lemuel had to confess that it was his own sermon. The community, then, realized that it had in Lemuel the possibility of an unusual preacher. He was soon given the opportunity to exercise this gift. However, there were those who were disinclined to accept the ministry of a Negro. One white man who came to a church to hear him preach out of curiosity

LEMUEL HAYNES

endeavored to show his disrespect by keeping his hat on. He confessed thereafter, however, that before Lemuel Haynes had spoken five minutes it seemed to him that the greatest man he had ever seen was preaching to him from that pulpit. And thus he was finally received throughout that section in New England. He preached to the whites at Torrington, West Rutland, Manchester, and at Granville, in New York.

He served also as a missionary in the destitute sections of New England. While thus engaged he showed his unusual ability in engaging in the theological discussions of the times. This was about 1815. He was especially interested in that of the Stoddardian principle of admitting moral persons with credible evidence of grace to the Lord's Supper. Everywhere he acquitted himself with honor. He is remembered to-day by the white people of that section, who recently honored him with a monument.[5]

[5] *The Journal of Negro History*, IV, 22-32.

Farther South during these years there was before the public a preacher of unusual distinction—John Chavis, a full-blooded Negro of dark-brown color. He was born in Oxford, Granville County, North Carolina, in 1763. Making upon his hearers the impression of being unusually gifted, they sent him to Princeton. Under Dr. Witherspoon he was educated there as a Latin and Greek scholar. He devoted some time also to the study of Theology, and on his **John Chavis, a preacher and teacher.** return from Princeton engaged in the ministry. In 1801 the Presbyterians referred to him as a "black man of prudence and piety, in the service of the Hanover Presbytery as a riding missionary under the direction of the General Assembly." We find him stationed in Lexington, Virginia, in 1805. Afterward he returned to North Carolina. Referring to him as a man of that early day, Paul Cameron, a white man of note, said: "In my boyhood life at my father's home I often saw John Chavis, a venerable old Negro man, recognized as a freeman and as a preacher or clergyman of the Presbyterian Church. As such he was received by my father and treated with kindness and consideration, and respected as a character." Mr. George Wortham, a lawyer of Granville County, said: "I have heard him read repeatedly. His English was remarkably pure, containing no 'Negroisms'; his manner was impressive, his explanations clear and concise, and his views, as I then thought and still think, entirely orthodox. He was said to have been an acceptable preacher, his sermons abounding in strong common sense views and happy illustrations, without any effort at oratory or sensational appeals to the passions of his hearers." Thus he continued as a minister in having the respect and coöperation of both races until as a result of Nat Turner's insurrection, the preaching of Negroes was prohibited. He thereafter engaged in teaching until the time of his death. In this capacity he served the most aristocratic white people of that State in teaching their sons and daughters. In the end he counted among his former students W. P. Mangum, afterward United States Senator; P. H. Mangum, his brother; Archibald and John Henderson, sons of Chief Justice Henderson; Charles Manly, later Governor of that commonwealth, and Dr. James L. Wortham of Oxford, North Carolina.

CHAPTER X

THE REACTION

THE impetus given the uplift of the Negroes during the struggle for the independence of the country was gradually checked after 1783, when the States faced the problem of readjustment. In the organization of governments the States came to the conclusion that it was nec- **Emancipation** essary to restrain men to maintain order and **checked.** that they had to depart from some of the theories on which the Revolution was fought. In the elimination of the impracticable from the scheme of reconstruction after making peace with Great Britain, the proposal for the emancipation of the slaves was no longer generally heeded. In those colonies where the Negroes were not found in large numbers they were emancipated without much opposition and some of them were made citizens of the new States. But in those where the Negroes constituted a considerable part of the population there followed such a reaction against the elevation of the race to citizenship that much of the work proposed to promote their welfare and to provide for manumission was undone.[1]

Certain States of the Upper South did support the movement to abolish the slave trade. The prohibition of the slave trade in Delaware, Maryland, Virginia, **Slave trade** and North Carolina, however, did not neces- **in the South.**

[1] M. S. Locke, *Antislavery in America*, pp. 157-166; K. H. Porter, *A History of Suffrage in the United States*, Chs. II and III, C. G. Woodson, *The Education of the Negro Prior to 1861*, Chs. VI and VII; F. Bancroft, *Slave-Trading in the Old South;* and A. D. Adams, *The Neglected Period of Antislavery in America, passim.*

sarily show a humanitarian trend. The reasons for such action were largely economic. Industry there had reached a settled state, and the influx of more slaves, they believed, would lead to a decrease in the value of slaves, cause the supply of Southern products to exceed the demand, drain the States of money, and constitute a sinister influence on Negroes already broken in. If imported without restriction the trade might force upon the communities a larger number than could be supported and, instead of promoting slavery, might make instant abolition necessary.

The country, moreover, was far from being antislavery. The Congress of the Confederation had very little to do with slavery, as it did not care to interfere with the rights of the States. Slavery as a national question, however, appeared in the adoption of the Ordinance of 1787, providing for the organization of the Northwest Terri-

Slavery and the Ordinance of 1787.

tory. The sixth clause of that document provided that neither slavery nor involuntary servitude, except for punishment of crime, should be permitted in the said territory. This was enacted, of course, prior to the adoption of the Constitution of the United States and may seem to have no bearing thereon; but, as its legality was questioned on the ground that no such power had been granted to the Continental Congress by the States or by any provision in the Articles of Confederation, it requires special attention. It is of importance to note that it was defended on the untenable ground that it was a treaty made by the States forming the Confederation rather than an agreement of the States to be organized in this territory thereafter. The best which can be said for it, however, is that it was merely a legislative act of Congress.[2]

[2] All of these aspects of the Ordinance of 1787 are thoroughly discussed in J. P. Dunn's *Indiana; A Redemption from Slavery*, ch. vi; and in Chas. Thomas Hickok's *The Negro in Ohio*, chapter on the Ordinance of 1787.

The Convention of 1787, called to frame the first constitution of the United States, desired to take very little interest in the antislavery movement in the organization of
the new government. Oliver Ellsworth of Connecticut and
Elbridge Gerry of Massachusetts thought the   **The Conven-**
question of slavery should be settled by the   **tion of 1787.**
States themselves. When this question came more prominently before this body, however, it had to be considered
more seriously. It was necessary to consider a regulation
for returning fugitive slaves, the prohibition of the slave
trade, and the apportionment of representation. When the
South wanted the Negroes
to be counted to secure
larger representation on
the population basis, al-
though it did not want
thus to count the blacks
in apportioning federal
taxes, some sharp debate
ensued. But the Northern
antislavery delegates
were not so much at-
tached to the cause of
universal freedom as to
force their opinions on
the proslavery group and
thus lose their support in

BENJAMIN FRANKLIN, an advocate
of freedom

organizing a more stable form of government.[3] They
finally compromised by providing for representation of the
States by two Senators from each, and for the representation of the people in the House by counting all whites and
five Negroes as three whites. Another compromise was
made in providing for the continuation of the slave trade
until 1808, when it should be prohibited, and for a fugitive

[3] *The Journal of Negro History,* Vol. III, pp. 381-434.

slave law to secure slaveholders in the possession of their peculiar property.

Immediately after the Federal Government was organized there seemed to be a tendency to ignore the claims of the Negro. In 1789 the Quakers, at their annual meeting in Philadelphia and New York, adopted certain memorials praying the action of Congress in adopting measures for the abolition of the slave trade and, in particular, in restraining vessels from being entered and cleared out for the purpose of that traffic. There came also a memorial to the same effect from the Pennsylvania Society for the Abolition of Slavery, bearing the signature of its president, Benjamin Franklin. This led to much discussion of the slavery question; but by a vote of 43 to 11 the memorials were referred to a special committee which reported March 5, 1790. On the 8th the report was referred to the committee of the whole where it was debated a week. Several amendments were proposed and given consideration in the House. Finally, by a vote of 29 to 25, the reports of the special committee and of the committee of the whole house were ordered to be printed in the Journal and to lie on the table. The principle of non-interference with slavery set forth in this report determined for a number of years the reactionary attitude of Congress with respect to slavery.[4]

The Negro a negligible factor.

4 The report of the Special Committee was: The committee to whom were referred sundry memorials from the People called Quakers; and also a memorial from the Pennsylvania Society for promoting the Abolition of Slavery, submit the following report:

That, from the nature of the matters contained in those memorials, they were induced to examine the powers vested in Congress, under the present Constitution, relating to the abolition of slavery, and are clearly of the opinion,

First, That the General Government is expressly restrained from prohibiting the importation of such persons "as any of the States now existing shall think proper to admit, until the year one thousand eight hundred and eight."

Secondly, That Congress, by a fair construction of the Constitution are equally restrained from interfering in the emancipation of

Congress refused also to intervene in behalf of certain manumitted Negroes of North Carolina, who after having been given their liberty by the Quakers were again reduced to slavery. The only action of this sort taken by Congress during its early operation was to pass the **Non-intervention by Congress.** Fugitive Slave Law of 1793. This measure provided that a master might seize his absconding slave taking refuge in another State, carry him

slaves, who already are, or who may, within the period mentioned be imported into, or born within any of the said States.

Thirdly, That Congress have no authority to interfere in the internal regulations of particular States, relative to the instruction of slaves in the principles of morality and religion; to their comfortable clothing; accommodations, and subsistence; to the regulation of their marriages, and the prevention of the violation of the rights thereof, or to the separation of children from their parents; to a comfortable provision in cases of sickness, age, or infirmity; or to the seizure, transportation, or sale of free negroes; but have the fullest confidence in the wisdom and humanity of the Legislatures of the several States, that they will revise their laws from time to time, when necessary, and promote the objects mentioned in the memorials, and every other measure that may tend to the happiness of slaves.

Fourthly, That, nevertheless, Congress have authority, if they shall think it necessary, to lay at any time a tax or duty, not exceeding ten dollars for each person of any description, the importation of whom shall be by any of the States admitted as aforesaid.

Fifthly, That Congress have authority to interdict, or (so far as it is or may be carried on by citizens of the United States, for supplying foreigners) to regulate the African trade, and to make provision for the humane treatment of Slaves, in all cases while on their passage to the United States, or to foreign ports, as far as it respects the citizens of the United States.

Sixthly, That Congress have also authority to prohibit foreigners from fitting out vessels, in any port of the United Sates, for transportation of persons from Africa to any foreign port.

Seventhly, That the memorialists be informed, that in all cases to which the authority of Congress extends, they will exercise it for the humane objects of the memorialists, so far as they can be promoted on the principles of justice, humanity, and good policy.

REPORT OF THE COMMITTEE OF THE WHOLE HOUSE

The Committee of the Whole House, to whom was committed the report of the committee on the memorials of the People called Quakers, and of the Pennsylvania Society for Promoting the Abolition of Slavery, report the following amendments:

Strike out the first clause, together with the recital thereto, and

before any magistrate, and secure from that functionary authority to return the slave. Congress refused on this occasion to provide any safeguards to prevent the enslavement of free Negroes. No sympathy could then be expected from the North, for while that section considered the institution an evil, it had not in the least increased its love for the Negro; and evidences of unrest among Negroes did not make conditions more favorable. The North did not want the Negroes, and those southerners who had advocated their emancipation were confronted with the question as to what should be done with them when freed.

This problem was aggravated by the uprising in Haiti, or Saint Domingue. The successful rebellion of the Negroes there brought such a dread of servile insurrection among the slaveholders that many of them opposed the continuation of the slave trade. And even in the radi-

---

in lieu thereof insert, "That the migration or importation of such persons as any of the States now existing shall think proper to admit, cannot be prohibited by Congress, prior to the year one thousand eight hundred and eight."

Strike out the second and third clauses, and in lieu thereof insert, "That Congress have no authority to interfere in the emancipation of slaves, or in the treatment of them within any of the States; it remaining with the several States alone to provide any regulations therein, which humanity and true policy may require."

Strike out the fourth and fifth clauses, and in lieu thereof insert, "That Congress have authority to restrain the citizens of the United States from carrying on the African trade, for the purpose of supplying foreigners with slaves, and of providing by proper regulations for the humane treatment, during their passage, of slaves imported by the said citizens into the States admitting such importation."

Strike out the seventh clause.

Ordered, that the said report of the Commitee of the Whole House do lie on the table.

See Text of both reports in the *House Journal,* 1st Cong., 2d Sess.; the report of the special committee is also in the *Annals of Congress,* 1st Cong., II, 1414, 1415, and in *Amer. State Papers, Miscellaneous,* I, 12. Full reports of discussions are in the *Annals;* condensed in Benton's *Abridgment,* I. See also von Holst's *United States,* I, 89-94; Parton's *Franklin,* II, 606-614; Wilson's *Rise and Fall of the Slave Power,* I, 61-67.

cally proslavery South, as in the case of South Carolina, it was specifically provided that no slaves should be imported from this disturbed area in the West Indies. As a matter of fact, however, many refugees from Haiti did come to the ports of Baltimore, Norfolk, **Refugees** Charleston, and New Orleans. They sowed **from Haiti.** seeds of discord from which came most of the uprisings of Negroes during the first three decades of the nineteenth century.[5]

The story of the Haitian insurrection made a deep impression on the minds of a few Negro leaders. The situation in Saint Domingue was a complication. The **Haitian** eastern end of the Island was Spanish and **revolution.** the western, French. Further difficulty resulted from having in this French portion 50,000 Creoles, an equal number of mulattoes and about a half-million Negroes of pure African blood. All elements desired to avail themselves of the equality guaranteed French citizens by the General Assembly of the French Revolution. The mulattoes first asked for the extension of these rights to them. After being baffled by the grant ambiguously phrased, they finally heard the decree extending to the people of color of free ancestry the rights and privileges of citizens. The whites, incensed by this liberality on the part of the French Republic, precipitated revolution in the island by espousing the cause of the French King.

Thereupon, the slaves struck for freedom on August 23, 1791, and killed off their masters in large numbers. Hoping to undo this work, the Conventional Assembly of France abrogated the order extending the rights of **The uprising.** citizens and sent troops to put down the in-

[5] These uprisings are set forth in Joshua Coffin's *An Account of the Principal Slave Insurrections.* See also Edwin V. Morgan's *Slavery in New York* (American Historical Association Report, 1895), pp. 629-673; and E. B. Greene's *Provincial America* (The American Nation), Vol. VI, p. 240.

surrection. In the struggle which followed during the next two years, the Negroes tended to join the mulattoes to fight the master class. Thousands of persons were killed in the meantime and much property was destroyed. Santhonax, sent from France with Polverel to restore order, thereupon issued a proclamation of freedom to all slaves who would uphold the cause of the French Republic. This

TOUSSAINT LOUVERTURE

proclamation through the coöperation of Polverel, in charge at Port - au - Prince, gradually spread throughout the Island.

At this juncture there forged ahead an unusual character. This was Toussaint Louverture, an experienced soldier, forty-eight years old. He had been at first in command of royalist troops. He abandoned the royalist standard in 1794 to serve the Republican cause after the favorable

decree of the Assembly. He was promoted to the rank of general of the brigade in 1796. The following year he was put in full command in Saint Domingue.

Toussaint Louverture. Proceeding to handle matters efficiently, he immediately forced the surrender of the English invading the island. In somewhat similar fashion through the commercial aid of the United States, he expelled his rival Rigaud from the country. He then cleared the way for full civil military authority by imprisoning Roume, the agent of the Directory. He next subdued the Spanish part of the Island and proclaimed a constitution grant-

ing him power for life and the right of naming his successor.

This triumph of Toussaint Louverture upset one of the
dreams of Napoleon Bonaparte. As First Consul, he was
trying to make himself the head of a French empire. In
1800 he induced Spain to retrocede the Louisiana territory
to France. Saint Domingue was to be a stepping stone in
this direction. He sent his brother-in-law, General Le
Clerc, with twenty-five thousand soldiers to enforce the
claims of France in Haiti. Saint Domingue, thus upset by
Toussaint Louverture, seemed to Napoleon an **Napoleon's**
impediment of Republicanism tainted with **dream upset.**
American ideas. As a matter of fact, however, the Government established by Toussaint Louverture was less democratic than that of Napoleon. Le Clerc appeared upon the
scene in 1802. He betrayed Toussaint Louverture into
a conference on a French vessel on which he was transported to France only to die of neglect in the prison of
Joux. The French immediately proclaimed the annulment
of the decree of liberty to the slaves. This, however, did
not end the resistance to the French army. Toussaint Louverture's task of arousing his people had been too well
done. The French army was decimated not only by guer-
rilla warfare but the yellow fever. Before the end of the
year 1802, six-sevenths of Le Clerc's army had perished,
including the General himself. In the meantime, the
much delayed retrocession of Louisiana by Spain was effected. The United States Government, moreover, was
anxious to obtain this territory as an outlet to trade in the
West. This had been interfered with often by the closing
of the Mississippi to the trade of the Americans in the
Middle West. Jefferson, through the negotiation of James
Monroe, made a final effort to purchase this territory. In
the unfortunate outcome in Haiti, the disaster in Egypt,
and the inability to reach India, Napoleon could see his

dream for a world empire a failure. He, therefore, disposed of the territory to the United States in 1803.

The slavery question was immediately brought prominently before the country in the effort of antislavery groups to exclude the institution from the new lands thus acquired. It was provided that in acquiring the territory of Louisiana from France the privileges and immunities enjoyed by those citizens under the government of the French would be guaranteed by the United States. This led to some future constitutional questions. Inasmuch as Louisiana was slaveholding prior to the purchase, the institution was thereby perpetuated in that territory. On the other hand, many of the Negroes of that territory belonged to the body of citizens exercising the same rights as the whites. When, a few years thereafter, Louisiana followed in the wake of the other reactionary States of the South and undertook to restrict the privileges of the free Negroes, it was contended that the action of the State conflicted with this treaty. Free persons of color who were citizens at the time of the purchase were guaranteed the full enjoyment of the privileges which they had under the French régime. On the occasion of the enforcement of a law of the State depriving certain free Negroes of the right to attend school, this question was brought up in Mobile in 1833. At the time of the purchase this city belonged to the Louisiana territory. By special ordinance of the city council, therefore, these citizens were exempted from the operations of this law.

The Louisiana Purchase.

The chief cause of this reaction, however, was not fear of influences from without. The cause was primarily economic. During the second half of the eighteenth century, inventors, beginning with Watt, who built the first steam engine, brought out such mechanical appliances as the wool-combing machine, the spinning jenny, the power-loom, and finally Whitney's famous cotton gin. These revolutionized industries in the modern world. In facilitating the making of cloth these appliances so increased the demand for cotton as to expand the plantation system requiring a large increase in the importation of slaves. The cotton gin was a machine of revolving cylinders, one for tearing the lint from the seeds and another arranged to remove the lint from the first cylinder. It simplified the process of seeding cotton, and in releasing labor for production multiplied its output in a few years. Cotton cloth was thereby cheapened and the demand for it so rapidly increased that the South became a most inviting field in which was rooted one of the greatest industries of the world. Before the end of the second decade of the nineteenth century the States of the lower South became inalterably attached to slavery as an economic advantage in supplying the cheap labor it required. They began to denounce those who persisted in dubbing it an evil.

AN EARLY COTTON GIN

With this increase in the demand for slaves there came numerous petitions for the reopening of the African slave trade in the lower South. The Northern and Middle States early prohibited the slave traffic, holding it **Increase in** as a grievance against George III that they **the demand** were not permitted to do so earlier. Mary- **for slaves.** land prohibited it in 1783. North Carolina checked it by a rather high import duty in 1789, and South Carolina proscribed it by law for sixteen years. Georgia alone took no action except to provide for its own security in prohibiting the importation of insurrectionary slaves from the West Indies, the Bahamas and Florida, and to require free

Negroes to furnish certificates of their industry and honesty.

An early effort was made to repeal the prohibitory provision against the traffic in South Carolina, but it was defeated. Those interested in the trade proceeded to smuggle slaves along the coast, and the efforts to enforce the prohibitory law were without success. Finally, in 1805, after much persistence, the slave-traders in that State carried their point. They put through the bill to remove all African restrictions but continued the exclusion of Negroes from the West Indies and slaves from other States failing to have certificates of good character.

The action of South Carolina was interpreted as opening the door for all of the atrocities formerly practiced by the slave traders. North Carolina, New Hampshire, Vermont, Maryland and Tennessee, therefore, requested **The slave trade objectionable.** their Congressmen to make an effort to have the Constitution of the United States so amended as to prohibit the importation of Negroes from Africa and the West Indies. Congress refused to act in this case, not only because it had become reactionary, but because the time provided by the Constitution for the abolition of the slave trade would arrive in 1808. At the next session of Congress bills to prohibit the trade were introduced, but no action was taken.

In 1806 Jefferson took up the question in his annual message, urging Congress to interpose its authority to withdraw citizens of the United States from all further partici- **Jefferson on abolition.** pation in those violations of human rights which had been "so long continued on the unoffending inhabitants of Africa."[6] Senator Bradley of Vermont promptly introduced a bill with the provisions that interstate slave trade along the coast should be prohibited after the close of the year 1807 and that importa-

6 *Annals of Congress,* 1806-1807, p. 14.

tion of slaves should be a felony punishable by death.[7]
In the House, where proslavery Congressmen managed
the framing of the bill, it prohibited importation, provided
fines and forfeitures of the slaves from abroad on board
such vessels, and authorized the sale at public auction of
slaves thus smuggled in. As it was evident that this bill
would not prevent the enslavement of the blacks concerned,
Sloane, of New Jersey, proposed to amend the measure
so as to free the slaves thus forfeited. This proposition
to turn loose in the South Negroes just from Africa evoked
from Early, of Georgia, the prophecy of the prompt extermination of such Negroes in the Southern States. But
speaking for his people, Smilie, of Pennsylvania, felt that
he could not tolerate the idea of making the Federal Government a dealer in slaves. Such an act, thought he, would
be unconstitutional. After some excitement, this provision
was stricken out.

An effort was then made to substitute imprisonment for
the death penalty, only to cause much more confusion.
After more exciting discussion the House laid aside its bill
for the one from the Senate, from which it
promptly eliminated the death penalty and **Efforts in behalf of slave trade.**
provided a penalty of imprisonment of not
less than five nor more than ten years. The prohibition
as to participation in coastal slave trade was also eliminated. The bill was then passed and sent back to the Senate.
The Senate accepted this with the modification that the
coastal trade provision be applied only to vessels of less
than forty tons. There was still some opposition from
Early, of Georgia, because he thought the bill in that form
futile for the prevention of smuggling from Florida. John
Randolph believed it interfered with a man's right of private property. The bill as passed penalized with imprison-

[7] The debate on the prohibition of the slave trade is treated in
W. E. B. DuBois's *Suppression of the African Slave Trade.*

ment the importation of slaves from abroad, prohibited the
slave trade along the coast in vessels of less than forty tons,
required of larger vessels conformity to certain stipulated
regulations, and placed smuggled slaves, when seized, at the
disposal of the State where they might be landed.

This law, of course, was a victory for the lower South
then demanding an increase in the slave labor supply.
With these evasive provisions favoring State control, the
measure was never effective and the illicit
trade flourished throughout the South without much interference. It was not long be-
fore the prohibition of the slave trade was very much like
that of the prohibition of the sale of alcoholics in our day.
It was an easy matter to smuggle slaves into the country at
the Southern ports. This was especially true of Fernan-
dina and Galveston. Through a well connected number of
points reaching into the interior and crossing the Indian
reservations, the Negroes were carried wherever they were
desired. By connection with certain Spanish Islands in
the West Indies, especially with Cuba, ships engaged in
this traffic sailed under the Spanish flag. For convenience
they might assume the colors of almost any nation, since
these slave traders represented different nationalities.
Madison complained of this trade in 1810 and Congress
enacted in 1818 another measure prohibiting the traffic.
The proslavery interests at that time, however, were so
influential that the measure was so worded as to be weak
and ineffective. This was the culmination of the reaction
against the Negro. For economic reasons the South had
pitted itself against the Constitution. That Negroes might
be further exploited by the whites that section had finally
secured a majority sufficiently lacking in moral courage to
crush the spirit of the fundamental law. In the hands of
persons out of sympathy with the Negro, it was impossible

*Victory for
the proslavery
group.*

to secure a conviction under these laws until the Civil War.

From this stimulated traffic there followed not only the enslavement of a large number of helpless Africans, but also of some of the learned and most aristocratic of the tribes. One of these distinguished Africans brought thus into this country was Lahmen Kebby from Futa. He was liberated in 1835 after having been held as a slave for 40 years in South Carolina, Alabama, and other Southern States. In Africa he had served as a schoolmaster after having pursued a long course of preparatory studies. He said that his aunt was much more learned than he and ''eminent for her superior acquirements and for her skill in teaching.'' ''Schools,'' he said, ''were generally established through the country, provision being made by law for educating children of all classes, the poor being taught gratuitously.''[8] Finally there was another Fula, Omar ibn Said, sold into slavery in the Carolinas about 1807. At first he had a kind master, but at the death of his owner his lot was hard. He, therefore, became a fugitive. Arrested as a vagrant, he was imprisoned in Fayetteville. Writing in Arabic on some coals while confined in the Cumberland County jail, probably making thus an appeal for succor, he attracted attention as a remarkable man. General James Owen, brother of Governor John Owen, bought Omar and carried him to his home in Bladen County. There he was treated more as a distinguished freeman of color than as a slave. He was at first a devout Mohammedan and faithfully read the Koran that he might religiously live up to the principles of the Prophet; but Omar gradually became interested in Christianity. He later made a profession of faith in this religion and attended the country church near Owen's estate. He lived until after the Civil War. A slave of this type (it might

[8] *African Repository*, XIII, 204; *Methodist Review*, XLVI, 77-90.

have been Omar Ibn Said himself) was taken to the University of North Carolina, sometime before the Civil War, to instruct one of its professors in the Arabic language and literature.[9]

[9] *The American Historical Review*, XXX, 787-795.

CHAPTER XI

As a sequel and a cause of the reaction came the bold attempts of the Negroes at insurrection.[1] Unwilling to undergo the persecutions entailed by this change of slavery from a patriarchal to an exploitation system, a number of Negroes endeavored to secure relief by refreshing the tree of liberty with the blood of their oppressors. The chief source of these uprisings came from refugees brought to this country from Saint Domingue in 1793 **Slave** and from certain free Negroes encouraged **insurrections.** to extend a helping hand to their enslaved brethren. With the news of the first uprising of the blacks in that island in 1791 Negroes of Louisiana were emboldened to do likewise. On account of disagreement as to time and dissension in the ranks the plan failed. Twenty-three suspected slaves were hanged and exposed to public gaze to produce a deterrent effect on the minds of others.

The first effort of consequence was the bold plot in Virginia in 1800. The full name of the author of this plot was Gabriel Prosser. He was faithfully assisted by his brother named Martin and by Jack Bowler. They finally worked out a far-reaching plan with the first day of September as the date to assemble. The Negroes in and near Richmond were to march upon the city, seize the arsenal, strike down the whites, and liberate the slaves. This plan was frustrated by a fearful storm on the appointed day and by a slave who disclosed the secret to save the life of

---

[1] For additional information as to the rising of slaves see Joshua Coffin's *Slave Insurrections*, and Higginson's *Travelers and Outlaws*.

his kind master. However, there were echoes from it in a projected riot in Suffolk county and in some exciting scenes in Petersburg, Virginia; in Edenton, North Carolina; and in Charleston, South Carolina. Bowler surrendered without much resistance and Gabriel fell into the hands of his pursuers in a few weeks. Six of the accomplices were sentenced to execution on the twelfth of the month and five others on the eighteenth. Prosser himself was executed on the third of October. Twenty-four others, some of whom were innocent, suffered the same fate.

The uprising had been so deliberately planned that it was thought that white men were concerned with it; but, according to James Monroe, an investigation showed that there was no ground for such a conclusion. It was discovered, however, that the plotters had given orders not to destroy any of the French in the city. It was brought out, then, that these Negroes, through channels of information, had taken over the revolutionary ideas of France and were beginning to use force to secure to themselves those privileges so highly prized by the people of that country.[2]

The insurrectionary movement was impeded but could not be easily stopped. At Camden in 1816 a considerable number of Negroes planned another uprising. Betrayed also by a "faithful" slave, the Negroes saw themselves terror-stricken at the execution of six of their leaders. Some years later at Tarboro, Newberne and Hillsboro, North Carolina, there developed other such plots of less consequence. A plot to destroy the city of Augusta, Georgia, in 1819, resulted in the execution of the leader named **Other plots.** Coot. For some years these outbreaks were frequent around Baltimore, Norfolk, Petersburg, and New Orleans.

In 1822, however, Charleston, South Carolina, was the scene of a better planned effort. The leading spirit was

[2] *The New York Daily Advertiser*, Sept. 22 and Oct. 7, 1800.

Denmark Vesey, an educated Negro of Saint Domingue. His name was Telemaque, reduced later among illiterates to *Telmak* and finally to *Denmark*. He knew both English and French. With some money which he won in a lottery in 1800 he purchased himself from his owner, Captain Vesey, who had brought him to Charleston. He successfully established himself thereafter as a carpenter, and accumulated property to the amount of $8,000. From Saint Domingue he had brought new ideas as to freedom. He easily won the confidence of the slaves and for the next generation endeavored to inculcate in their minds discontent with their lot. Operating here in Charleston where free Negroes were to some extent a privileged class, many of them able to read and write, Vesey and his co-workers stirred up a considerable number. They often met in a church in Hampstead, one of the suburbs of Charleston. Instruction was given in things bearing on the struggle for liberty, literature styled incendiary was circulated, and the leaders of the Saint Domingue revolt were probably approached for aid. These Charleston Negroes read with interest the debate on the Missouri Compromise. The official report was that ''materials were abundantly furnished in the seditious pamphlets brought into the State by equally capable incendiaries, while the speeches of the oppositionists in Congress to the admission of Missouri gave a serious and imposing effect to his machinations.''[3]

The recruiting of the Negroes for seventy or eighty miles around was to begin about the Christmas of 1821. On the second Monday in July, 1822, when most of the master class would be absent for the summer vacation, the attack was to be made. Lists of thousands of recruits were drawn up, money was raised to purchase arms, and a blacksmith

[3] See *The City Gazette and Commercial Daily Advertiser*, August 21, 1862; *The Norfolk and Portsmouth Herald*, August 30, 1822; *The Education of the Negro Prior to 1861*, pp. 156-158.

was engaged to make pikes and bayonets for the incipient attack. The conspirators hoped, however, to obtain a larger supply by raiding the arsenal in the city.

Here again, however, the history of Negro insurrections repeated itself. A slave hearing about it, told his master. Officials, at first, could hardly believe all that which was divulged. Some of those implicated were exonerated when first examined. By the day set for the rising, however, the plans had all been disclosed. The city then ran wild with excitement. And well might this be so, for by this time the authorities had learned that some of the most respectable free Negroes and slaves enjoying the highest confidence of the public were deliberately planning to kill all of the whites of the city. Denmark Vesey, Peter Poyas, Ned Bennett, Rolla Bennett, Balleau Bennett, Jesse Blackwood, Gullah Jack, and others, thirty-five in all, were hanged; forty-three were banished.

An extensive scheme for an insurrection, however, came in 1828 from David Walker of Massachusetts. In an address he appealed to slaves to rise against their masters. To bring out the causes of the intolerable condition of the Negroes Walker mentioned ''our wretchedness in consequence of slavery, our wretchedness in consequence of ignorance, our wretchedness in consequence of the preachers of the religion of Jesus Christ, and our wretchedness in consequence of the colonization plan.'' Walker said: ''For although the destruction of the oppressors God may not effect by the oppressed, yet the Lord our God will bring other destruction upon them, for not unfrequently will he cause them to rise up one against the other, to be split, divided, and to oppress each other, and sometimes to open hostilities with sword in hand.'' [4]

David Walker's appeal.

The most exciting of all of these disturbances, however,

[4] David Walker's *Appeal.*

did not come until 1831. In August of that year Nat Turner, a Negro insurgent of Southampton County, Virginia, feeling that he was ordained of God to liberate his people, organized a number of daring blacks and proceeded from plantation to plantation to murder **Nat Turner's** their masters. His chief co-workers were **insurrection.** Henry Porter, Hark Travis, Nelson Williams, Samuel

NAT TURNER

Francis, and Jack Reese, Nat Turner was born the slave of Benjamin Turner, October 2, 1800, the very year in which perished Gabriel Prosser of like fame. Precocious as a youth, Nat Turner early learned to read and made progress in the study of the Bible and religious literature. He learned also to make paper, gunpowder, and pottery. He developed into a man of steady habits. He spent much time fasting and praying and communing with the spirit. Voices, he believed, spoke to him. He said he saw drops of blood on the leaves, and had visions of black and white spirits arrayed in a serious combat. In this mystified atmosphere he heard a voice saying: "The Serpent is loosed. Christ has laid down the yoke. You must take it up again. The time is at hand when the first shall be the last and the last shall be the first." [5]

An eclipse of the sun following close thereupon was

[5] Drewry, *Insurrections in Virginia;* and *The Journal of Negro History,* V, 208-234.

interpreted as the sign for the insurrectionists to begin. The slaying was ordered as soon thereafter as was convenient. They dispatched first the owners in that vicinity. Although they succeeded in carrying out their designs for the first night, most of the company frustrated their own plans by making noise resulting from intoxication. Nat Turner, himself, however, never indulged in strong drink; and he gave explicit instructions against committing outrages. They were decidedly weak the next day. After delaying they were dispersed by a company before they could reach Jerusalem, the county seat, to get the much needed arms and supplies. The following day the insurgents met another attack, and still another the next, when the group was finally dispersed. Nat Turner made another effort to assemble his men again, but did not succeed. With some provisions he then hid himself nearby under a fence from which he emerged only at night. Here for six weeks he evaded his pursuers, although State and Federal troops were scouring the country to find him. Detected by two Negroes attracted to the spot by a barking dog, Nat Turner had to change his hiding place for the less secure fields. Seen again by another on October 30, he surrendered. He was convicted on the fifth of November and executed on the eleventh. It is said: "He exhibited the utmost composure through the whole ceremony; and, although assured that he might, if he thought proper, address the immense crowd assembled on the occasion, declined availing himself of the privilege; and, being asked if he had any further confessions to make, replied that he had nothing more than he had communicated; and told the sheriff in a firm voice that he was ready. Not a limb or muscle was observed to move. His body, after death, was given over to the surgeons for dissection."

This uprising caused a reign of terror in Virginia. "Labor was paralyzed," says an author, "plantations abandoned, women and children were driven from their homes and crowded into nooks and corners. Negroes were tortured to death, burned, maimed, and subjected to nameless atrocities. Slaves who were distrusted were pointed out; and if they endeavored to escape they were ruthlessly shot down. In less than two days 120 Negroes were killed, most of them by ordinary man hunters who shot them as persons in pursuit of game. One individual rejoiced that he had been instrumental in killing between ten and fifteen.

"A party of horsemen started from Richmond with the intention of killing every colored person they saw in Southampton county. They stopped opposite the cabin of a free man of color engaged in cultivating his field. They called out: 'Is this Southampton County?' He replied: 'Yes, sir, you have just crossed the line by yonder tree.' They shot him dead and rode on.[6] A slaveholder went to the woods accompanied by a faithful slave who had been the means of saving his master's life during the insurrection. When they reached a retired place in the woods the man handed his gun to his master, informing him that he could not live a slave any longer and requested him either to free him or shoot him on the spot. The master took the gun in some trepidation, leveled it at the faithful Negro and shot him through the heart."[7] The Federal and State troops under Lieutenant Colonel Worth, Brigadier General Eppes and General William H. Brodnax, called out to restore order, aided and abetted the slaughter of the Negroes instead of securing protection to all.

Only sixty-one white persons were killed by the conspirators. After the general slaughter fifty-three Negroes were arraigned, seventeen of them were convicted and executed, twelve convicted and transported, and ten ac-

---

[6] *Journal of Negro History*, V, 212; Higginson, *Outlaws*, 300.
[7] These quotations are all from the *Journal of Negro History*, V, 208-234.

quitted. Three of the four free Negroes subsequently tried were executed and one discharged. An effort was made to connect David Walker and William Lloyd Garrison with this rising, but no such evidence could be found. Garrison disclaimed any connection with the insurrection. Probably there would have been more consolation for the masters if they could have thought that slaves by themselves were incapable of concerted action.

The excitement beyond the borders of Virginia was almost as wild as in the State itself. There were conflicting rumors as to the deeds of Nat Turner and the supposed raids and attacks of various members of his band in places far removed from Southampton county. North Carolina was shaken to the very center by the rumor that Wilmington was to be burned. The excitement did not subside until four Negroes were shot down in cold blood and their heads were exposed to public gaze to terrify the Negro population. In Georgia there arose similar confusion from the report that Macon was to be attacked by a force of Negroes. In South Carolina, Governor Robert Y. Hayne, who had begun his fame in that State by suppressing the Denmark Vesey uprising of 1822, had to issue a proclamation to quiet the people. Alabama was disturbed by the rumor that the Indians and the Negroes were about to start an attack on the whites. New Orleans was likewise moved by the report that there were 1,200 stands of arms in a black man's home in that city.

The results from this uprising were far-reaching. There were those Virginians who looked upon slavery as an impossibility as long as Negroes would so willingly risk their lives for freedom. Such persons, therefore, advocated emancipation. Petitions to this effect were sent to the State legislature, and the resolution to inquire into the expediency of gradual emancipation not only precipitated an interesting debate but the vote thereon showed that there was some antislavery sentiment in the State. Thinking people insisted that something had to be done when things had come to such a pass that "men with pistols in their hands had to lock their doors and open them in the morning to receive their servants to light their fires."

In other parts, where it was still believed that slavery was a safe and profitable institution, the result was the other way. This uprising had been sufficient to convince most of the South that if slavery was to be successful, the one thing needful was to close up the avenues of information to the Negroes. The first effort in this direction was to extend the slave code so as to penalize a number of deeds which theretofore had not been punishable by law. The majority of the slave states already had adequate regulations to keep down insurrections. But the fear resulting from this uprising **Stringent measures in the South.** had a direct bearing on other laws which followed. The Southern

BLACK WOLF, AN INDIAN CHIEF, 1827

States enacted more stringent measures to regulate the travel of slaves, to make them ineffective in assembling for insurrectionary purposes or for information obtained through contact with other persons or from schools. These stringent measures applying to travel and assembly were not restricted to slaves but made applicable also to the free Negroes and mulattoes. The wording of these laws varied. They usually provided, however, that it would be unlawful for Negroes above a certain number, usually five, to assemble without the permission of their masters, not even for worship, unless the services were conducted by a recognized white minister or observed by "certain discreet and reputable persons."

Most of the State legislatures took some action in this respect at their next session. Governor McArthur of Ohio recommended that the legislature prohibit by law the influx of free people into that State. Maryland provided a board of managers to use a fund for the removal of the free people of color to Liberia. Delaware prevented the use of fire-arms by Negroes, revived the law against the coming of free Negroes and mulattoes into the State, prohibited the meetings of blacks after ten o'clock, and forbade non-resident Negroes to preach. Tennessee also forbade the immigration of free Negroes. Georgia restricted the grant of credit to free Negroes, and prohibited all Negroes from preaching or carrying firearms. North Carolina, like Virginia, prohibited free Negroes from preaching. By constitutional provision in 1834 North Carolina and Tennessee prohibited Negroes from voting or holding office. Louisiana strengthened her slave code with respect to the instruction of mischievous slaves. Alabama prohibited free Negroes from settling in the State and provided a penalty for those who might teach Negroes to read and write. In 1834 South Carolina reënforced its law prohibiting the teaching of slaves to read and write and forbidding the employment of a person of color as a salesman in any house, store, or shop, used for trading. In 1838 Virginia provided that any Negro leaving the State for the purpose of education should not return to the State as a resident.

In many of the Southern States, however, the effort was made not only to regulate the traveling and assem-

bling of the free Negroes but to get rid of them entirely.
Some States merely gave them so many days to leave.[8]
The Missouri General Assembly enacted in **Free Negroes**
1819 a law providing that there should be no **driven out.**
more assemblages of slaves or free Negroes or mulattoes,
mixing or associating with such slaves for teaching them
to read. When that State framed its constitution on being
admitted to the Union it incorporated a provision to prevent the immigration of free Negroes into that State.
Louisiana had prohibited the immigration of free persons
of color in 1814, and in 1830 excluded such persons from
the State. In 1830 Mississippi followed in the footsteps of
her sister State. In cases where free Negroes were not
driven out, certain stringent measures to safeguard the interests of the slaveholders materially interfered with the
personal liberty and economic welfare of these persons of
color. Not quite so much of this legislation disgraced the
statue books of Kentucky, Maryland and Tennessee, but
public opinion there sometimes had the same effect.

The resistance of the Negroes to established authority
during these years assumed also another form. Inasmuch as
the Indians were hostile to the whites who gradually forced
them to the West, a considerable number of Negroes of the
pioneer spirit continued to escape to that **Negroes among**
frontier. The large majority of Negroes, **Indians.**
uninformed as to the geography of the country and un-
acquainted with the Indian, of course, could not avail themselves of this opportunity. The infelicitous climate of the
mountains and swamps to which the Indians were driven
proved also to be another deterrent force in the mind of the
Negro. Yet from the very beginning in the commonwealths
near the Atlantic coast there was much fear that the Negroes might join with the Indians. But the expected did

[8] See C. G. Woodson's *A Century of Negro Migration*, p. 40; and
The Education of the Negro Prior to 1861, pp. 151-178.

INDIAN MAN AND WOMAN IN DANCING DRESS

The customs of the Indians resembled somewhat those of the Negroes in Africa. This supports the contention of those who believe that Africans visited the shores of America more than a thousand years ago and influenced the civilization of the aborigines of this continent.

not always happen. The number joining the Indians, however, became sufficiently considerable to justify mention here.[9]

In 1786 the Continental Congress adopted an ordinance systematizing Indian affairs through the organization of two large districts. One lay north of the Ohio and west of the Hudson and the other south of the Ohio and east of the Mississippi. The very next year an Indian reservation in Virginia was accused of harboring an "idle set of free Negroes." It was pointed out that the proportion of Africans with Indian blood seemed to be about equal, for Indian women were married to black men and Indian men were married to black women. About the same time Negro slaves were escaping from the Carolinas and Georgia across the frontier into Florida where they came under the protection of the Indians.

In the lower Indian district, south of the Ohio and east of the Mississippi, lying also west of certain seaboard slave States, there was considerable danger of the loss of slaves. Furthermore, the effort to return such slaves proved to be unusually difficult after the interbreeding had **Fugitives** gone to the extent of making these Negroes **demanded.** and their children important factors in the Indian communities. Sometimes when compelled to give up the Negro women who were thus reclaimed by the white slaveholders the Indians refused to give up their children by such women inasmuch as they were a part of their own blood. One of the charges brought against the British at the close of the Revolutionary War, and even at the end of the War of 1812, was that in connection with Indians they had thus encouraged the escape of the Negroes to their lines. This matter was not settled until 1828. Georgia

[9] The general facts of the Indian-Negro question are given in the following: John T. Sprague's *The Florida War*; Joshua R. Gidding's *Exiles of Florida*; Samuel G. Drake's *Aboriginal Races*.

filed such a complaint against the Creeks in 1789. This practice was continued from year to year very much to the discomfort of the colonists in the South. The matter finally came to a head in the case of the Creeks in 1813, when, advised by the British, they attacked Fort Mins on the Appalachicola River and massacred a large number of citizens. They were, therefore, attacked by Andrew Jackson, who decisively routed them in Alabama in 1814 and forced them to sue for peace. Further trouble came in 1815, when about 1,000 Negroes from Georgia took charge of the fort which the British commander abandoned upon his return to England. Strengthened by the accession of some Creeks, this Negro fort became a menace to the peace of the slaveholding settlements. The Spanish, in whose territory this fort was, were called upon to destroy it. As no satisfaction came from this source it was necessary for Jackson to order General Gaines to destroy it in 1816. This order he carried out in most disastrous fashion.

The conflicts with the Creeks became easily connected with a more serious trouble with the Seminoles in 1817. The next year Jackson invaded the Florida territory, destroying things as he passed, and almost brought this nation into a war with Great Britain by hanging unceremoniously two British subjects trading there with the Indians. Some relief was offered the whites in this quar-

Conflicting troubles.   ter by the treaty of Indian Spring of 1821. In this the Creeks ceded to the Federal Government in the interest of Georgia about 5,000,000 acres of land. One of the important provisions of this treaty with the Creeks, who received a stipulated sum, was that the Federal Government should hold therefrom a fund to pay for such slaves as had escaped from Georgia to the Creeks since the year of 1802. This fund was administered in dishonest fashion by deception and fraud, which left a dark blot on American Indian diplomacy. After the

Florida territory was finally turned over to this country in 1821, moreover, the same dishonor characterized our methods employed in moving the Indians from the most valuable lands. To carry out such a design the Federal authorities forced upon the Indians another treaty at Fort Moultrie in 1823. One stipulation was: "The chiefs and warriors aforesaid, for themselves and tribes, stipulate to be active and vigilant in the preventing the retreating to, or passing through, the district of country assigned them, of any absconding slaves, or fugitives from justice; and further agree to use all necessary exertions to apprehend and deliver the same to the agent, who shall receive orders to compensate them agreeably to the trouble and expense incurred."

FOUR LEGS, AN INDIAN CHIEF, 1827

Instead of settling matters this treaty aggravated them. Certain Indian chiefs never consented to this treaty and suffered themselves rather to be driven into exile. Forced into this precarious position, moreover, the Indians were further harassed by white raiders seeking to reclaim fugitives and to enslave free Negroes living **Forced** among the Indians. Many of the Negroes born **treaties.** among the Indians and others whom they had purchase. were snatched from them. Being unaccustomed to matters of business requiring receipts and contracts, they could not make a case when such a matter sometimes came before

AN INDIAN FAMILY

While Americanized Negroes did not enjoy so much the life of the Indians, they found this lot much better than the drudgery of slavery. The flight to the Indians was the only way of escape available for the crude newcomers who had no opportunity to learn anything about the interior.

the courts. Even before such tribunals neither the Indians nor the Negroes had any chance for justice. The inhuman raiders concerned, moreover, thought to get rid of the Indians in this district altogether by memorializing Congress for their complete removal beyond the Mississippi. Inasmuch as Humphreys, the Indian agent, had not been successful in turning over to the whites Negroes to whom they had no legal claim, his removal was effected by 1830. Andrew Jackson, too, although a staunch unionist with respect to nullification, supported state rights in protecting the supposed rights of these Georgians on the frontier. He was, therefore, a warm advocate of removal beyond the reach of the whites. The situation was further aggravated by the refusal of the Federal Government to sympathize in any way with the claims of the Indians. The only consideration they received was an explanation that the Federal Government desired to protect them only in the case that they were removed from the jurisdiction of these slave States. The agitation for the return of the Negro slaves, moreover, was kept up through this period, as a reason for removal, inasmuch as the Indians were disinclined to return fugitive Negroes who had become connected with them by ties of blood. In 1829 the Cherokees were induced by the Federal Government to go west. Three years later the Creeks found themselves compelled to do likewise.

There remained the Seminoles, however, still to be reckoned with. The complaint was that they had not returned fugitive slaves. The Seminoles were finally forced to sign the treaty for removal west of the Mississippi on the terms set forth in the Agreement of Payne's Landing in 1832. In that treaty Article VI says: "The Seminoles, **The Seminole** being anxious to be relieved from the repeated **War.** vexatious demands for slaves, and other property, alleged to have been stolen and destroyed by them, so that they may remove unembarrassed to their new homes, the United States stipulate to have the same property (properly) investigated, and to liquidate such as may be satisfactorily established, provided the amount does not exceed seven thousand ($7,000) dollars.'' An additional treaty was forced upon them at Fort Gibson, Arkansas, in 1833, when seven chiefs, according to agreement, examined the country. It is significant that along with the chiefs was the Negro interpreter known as Abraham. However, although the Senate of the United States ratified both treaties and urged the actual removal, the Seminoles repudiating the officiat-

Negro Abraham.

NEGRO ABRAHAM

ing chiefs as deceivers, did not easily bestir themselves in that direction. This, together with the further reports of the slaveholders that the Seminoles were not returning fugitive slaves, irritated the Federal Government. It, therefore, prepared to force the removal of these Indians. This precipitated what is known as the Second Seminole War.

In this struggle there happened upon the scene one of the most distinguished characters in Indian-Negro history. This was Osceola. He was the child of parents whose identification is difficult. He was born a leader of men. He easily ingratiated himself into favor with all.

Osceola, a man of power. Although not legally a chief himself, he won upon all Indians with whom he came into contact and made himself the most important person in the tribe. Arrayed against him, however, he had the Federal Government, among the functionaries of which there was little sympathy for the oppressed. One of them, however, Congressman Giddings, from the Western Reserve, anticipating his later stand for freedom, said with respect to this Florida trouble: "I hold that if the slaves of Georgia or any other State leave their masters the Federal Government has no consti-

tutional authority to employ our army or navy for their recapture, or to apply the national treasure to repurchase them." There could be no question of the fact that the war was very largely one over fugitive slaves. To Giddings it seemed a cruel procedure to return to inhuman masters slaves who had become attached to the Indians among

AN INDIAN WARRIOR

whom they had lived. Yet, it was earnestly insisted by the slave power that the thing paramount in the removal of the Seminoles was to prevent the increasing danger of servile insurrection among the Negroes.

Cases of the actual stealing of innocent Negroes, moreover, are not wanting. The kidnapers openly did this in the case of twenty slaves owned by Chief **Kidnaping** Econchattimico. In 1835, John Walker, an **Negroes** Indian chief, spoke of other such raids upon his property by whites from Columbus, Georgia. He began by inquiring, "Are the free Negroes and the Negroes belonging to this town to be stolen away publicly, and in the face of law and justice, carried off and sold to fill the pockets of these worse than land pirates?"

Appearing upon the scene when the agent of the Federal Government insisted upon the removal of the Indians in keeping with the forced treaties, Osceola urged them to take a definite stand against the encroachment of the **Second Semi-** whites. In fact, when threatened with the **nole War.** consequences resulting from such a refusal Osceola actually defied the Federal Government. To overcome the influence of Osceola, the agent made further efforts for inveigling the chiefs into signing other agreements which they themselves did not understand. As they could not be publicly induced to come to such an agreement the agent of the Federal Government accomplished the same by secret conferences. He imposed certain restrictions upon the Indians to make their stay uncomfortable and urged preparation for their removal.

The crisis was reached, however, when a certain kidnaper carried back to captivity Osceola's wife, the daughter of a fugitive mulatto slave woman who had married an Indian chief. Reprimanding Thompson, the agent, for such an injustice, Osceola was arrested and imprisoned. By shrewdness, however, he effected his own release by deceiving Thompson to the extent of making him believe that Osceola had changed his point of view with respect to the removal and would induce the Indians to act accordingly. Osceola then hurried his preparations for war. The Indians themselves, however, became gradually divided into those in favor of the migration and protected by the Federal Government and those who, on the other hand, were ready to fight to death for their land. While some were preparing for removal, others were preparing for war.

Troops were soon upon the scene, and Osceola himself had his own soldiers lying in wait for Thompson. They finally killed him one day while he was taking a walk. The die was cast. At that very time other Indians, attacking American troops led by Major Dade himself, annihilated his command.

Our interest here in this story lies in the report that Negroes were fearlessly fighting in the ranks of the Indians. Then came the account that one lieutenant was tomahawked

OSCEOLA

by a Negro. Another said that a Negro named Harry had a band of 100 warriors. In all of these engagements **The Negro always a fighter.** the Negroes and Indians fought bravely. Their case, however, was hopeless. After the coming of Major General Thomas Jessup, who believed in uncivilized warfare, the Seminoles and their allies had no chance. This commander resorted to bloodhounds and hang-ing. He authorized plunder on the grounds that all the Indian property captured belonged to the corps or detach· ment making it. He even imprisoned an embassy from the Indian lines seeking conference with the authorities to devise means by which the removal might be worked out satisfactorily. This shows the utter breakdown of the so-called treatment of the Indians as independent nations and furnishes striking evidence of the selfishness of the American whites. After this war the resistance of the Indian was futile. The Seminoles were soon compelled to take up their abode on the other side of the Mississippi. In this position there could be little fear of servile insurrection of the Negroes. Most of their Indian allies were too far removed from the slave plantations. The institution of slavery was further secured and the South could more fearlessly face the country with its program to make cotton king.

CHAPTER XII

A DECLINING ANTISLAVERY MOVEMENT

THE early antislavery workers were not so aggressive as those of the second quarter of the nineteenth century, and they later lost some of their ardor. They did not contemplate instant abolition. The machinery for promoting the uplift of the Negroes, as further stated by them, had to do with methods of gradual emancipation.[1] According to their scheme, they raised funds to pur- Gradual chase slaves, encouraged their emancipation, emancipation. and provided for prospective freedmen opportunities for mental development and religious instruction that they might properly function in society on becoming citizens. These bodies maintained, moreover, a sort of vocational guidance committee in each locality to look out for apprenticing Negroes to trades and to find employment for them in the various fields when they had developed into efficient mechanics. The friends of the Negro, however, tended to diminish until few could be found.

The gallantry shown by the Negro soldiers in the War of 1812 added little to their desirability. Their record was soon forgotten by the exploiting and bloodthirsty class. This second war with England started from trade restrictions, the impressment of American seamen in the British service, and the failure to give up western forts

[1] The early antislavery movement has been well treated in M. S. Locke's *Antislavery in America from the Introduction of the African Slaves to the Prohibition of the Slave Trade*, in Alice D. Adams's *Neglected Period of Antislavery in America*, and in the annual reports of *The American Convention of Abolition Societies*.

as promised in the treaty of Paris and Jay's treaty. Additional hostility to England, however, was engendered by the outbreak of the Indian troubles in territory which white settlers going west desired. The Americans had difficulty in holding the Indians at Tippecanoe in 1811 because they were supplied with munitions of war from Canada. The Negroes were then asked to play their part.

The Negro in the War of 1812.

Negroes made a record for valor displayed in this struggle on land and sea. They fought bravely under Perry and Macdonough. An officer of this war writing of a naval engagement said: "The name of one of my poor fellows who was killed ought to be registered in the book of fame, and remembered with reverence as long as bravery is considered a virtue. He was a black man by the name of Johnson. . . . When America has such tars she has little to fear from the tyrants of the ocean."

Reduced to necessity of husbanding all resources, Andrew Jackson appealed to the Negroes in preparing for the battle of New Orleans. He said "Through a mistaken policy, you have heretofore been deprived of a participation in the glorious struggle for national rights in which our country is engaged. This no longer shall exist.

Negro soldiers with Jackson.

"As sons of freedom, you are now called upon to defend our most inestimable blessing. As Americans, your country looks with confidence to her adopted children for a valorous support, as a faithful return for the advantages enjoyed under her mild and equitable government. As fathers, husbands and brothers, you are summoned to rally around the standard of the Eagle, to defend all which is dear in existence." [2]

---

[2] He said also: "Your country, although calling for your exertions, does not wish you to engage in her cause without amply remunerating you for the services rendered. Your intelligent minds are not to be led away by false representations. Your love of

Three months after this proclamation when the battle of New Orleans had been successfully fought, Jackson could say: "To the Men of Color.—Soldiers! From the shores of Mobile I collected you to arms,—I invited you to share in the perils and to divide the glory of your white countrymen. I expected much from you; for I was not uninformed of those qualities which must render you so formidable to an invading foe. I knew that you could endure hunger and thirst, and all the hardships of war. I knew that you loved the land of your nativity, and that, like ourselves, you had to defend all that is most dear to man. But you surpass my hopes. I have found in you, united to these qualities, that noble enthusiasm which impels to great deeds.

"Soldiers! The President of the United States shall be informed of your conduct on the present occasion; and the voice of the Representatives of the American nation shall applaud your valor, as your General now praises your ardor. The enemy is near. His sails cover the lakes. But the brave are united; and, if he finds us contending among ourselves, it will be for the prize of valor, and fame its noblest reward."

The Negroes, too, had otherwise figured in the war. Inasmuch as the British Government followed the same policy of carrying away Negroes as in the case of the Revolutionary War, this question proved to be a trouble-

honor would cause you to despise the man who should attempt to deceive you. In the sincerity of a soldier and the language of truth I address you.

"To every noble-hearted, generous freeman of color volunteering to serve during the present contest with Great Britain, and no longer, there will be paid the same bounty, in money and lands, now received by the white soldiers of the United States, viz., one hundred and twenty-four dollars in money, and one hundred and sixty acres of land. The non-commissioned officers and privates will also be entitled to the same monthly pay, and daily rations, and clothes, furnished to any American soldier."

some one in the negotiations closing the second war with England. It was pointed out that many were induced to **Negroes with** run away and others were captured in battle. **the British.** From the Dauphin Islands, said to be without the limits of the newly acquired Louisiana territory, the British took many Negroes. A large number went over to the British ranks, also as a result of the proclamation of the British Admiral, Cochrane, proclaiming free all such fugitives. The first article of this treaty, therefore, provided that all possessions whatsoever taken by either party during the war or which might have been taken after the signing of this treaty shall be restored without delay and that these possessions should be destroyed. It specified, moreover, that artillery, public and private property originally captured in the forts of the United States should not be carried away. Negroes were carried away by the British even after the treaty had been signed. All of them were not declared free. The British sold some into the West Indies. The question was a difficult one because of difficult constructions of the clauses of the treaty by the representatives of the two different nations. It was not finally adjusted until 1828, when the claimants were awarded $1,197,422.18 largely for slaves whose indemnity a reactionary Federal Government had long sought.

The inevitable effect of the reaction was sectionalism. In proportion as there developed free labor in the North as a result of the industrial revolution, which at the same time, led to the extension of the plantation system, requir-**The results** ing more slaves, the South and the North **of the** became gradually estranged. The open viola-**reaction.** tions of the act prohibiting the African slave trade and the impetus given the domestic traffic to supply these plantations with Negroes, led to the bold attack on the institution during the first quarter of the nineteenth century. The cotton gin, although invented as early as

1793, had just then begun to do its work. During the first antislavery period there were no violent protests, as the workers concerned contented themselves with making an occasional speech or with writing for a newspaper an article inveighing against the institution and setting forth plans for exterminating the evil. A considerable portion of the abolition literature which influenced public opinion appeared in the *Genius of Universal Emancipation,* published by Benjamin Lundy. Through this organ the sentiments of a large number of antislavery people living in the Appalachian highland found expression. There were descendants of the Germans and Scotch-Irish immigrants who came to this country to realize their ideals of religion and government. They differed widely from those of the aristocratic planters who maintained a slavocracy near the coast. A few of these settlers of the uplands were gradually indoctrinated in the tenets of slavery in the proportion that the institution extended towards the mountains, but a large number of them continued even until the Civil War to work for the destruction of the institution. Out of this group developed a number of active manumission societies in North Carolina, Tennessee and Kentucky.

Later we see the tendency not only to regard the institution of slavery as an economic evil but to consider it as a sin of which the Christian people should be ashamed. In 1810 Louis Duprey informed professing **Slavery an** Christians that the great transgressions of **economic evil.** slave commonwealths would lead to overwhelming judgments of God. David Barrow, of Kentucky, denounced in a pamphlet the inconsistency in the use of religious formulas in connection with the bequests of slaves, and advocated immediate emancipation. About the same time, John D. Paxton, a preacher in Kentucky and Virginia, believed in the "moral evil of slavery and the duty of

Christians to aid slaves and free them.'' Daniel Raymond of Maryland branded slavery as a ''foul stain on our national escutcheon, a canker which is corroding the moral and political vitals of our country.'' Declaring slave traffic a curse to the master, John Randolph, of Virginia, said in Congress in 1816, ''Do as you would be done by.

ANOTHER SORT OF SLAVERY

Every man who leaves that great high road will have the chalice which he himself has poisoned—the chalice of justice, even-handed justice—put to his own lips by the God of nature, who does not require abolition societies to carry his purpose into execution.''

The strongest influence against slavery which had hitherto developed, as already observed, however, came from the Quakers. After ridding themselves of slavery they were strenuously working to abolish the institution in other parts during the first decade of the nineteenth century. They had used passive means, however, in **Antislavery** reaching their ends, and for that reason had **Quakers.** not gained very much ground. Yet they had done effective work in Virginia and North Carolina, and when they could not operate there as they desired they sent their slaves and others to the Northwest Territory where they had a new opportunity. It is doubtless due to their influence in North Carolina that a distinguished man like Judge William Gaston could call on the State to extirpate slavery. They, no doubt, had much to do with the fact that a proposal to abolish slavery in the North Carolina General Assembly failed only by the casting vote of the speaker, and that the institution was strongly attacked in the Virginia Convention in 1829-30, and in the legislature the following year.[2]

THOMAS JEFFERSON, an antislavery reformer

The spirit of antislavery, however, was declining in the South throughout the first half century of the republic, although a free discussion of the system was extended by the debate of the question of slavery in the territories.

[2] C. G. Woodson, *Education of the Negro Prior to 1861;* S. B. Weeks, *Southern Quakers and Slavery,* and R. R. Wright, *Negro Rural Communities* in *The Southern Workman,* Vol. XXXVII, pp. 158-166.

In this contest the proslavery and antislavery forces clashed.

Antislavery cause in the South.   The question throughout these years was whether or not the public lands in the West should be thrown open to slave labor. By that time it had become evident that the South was preparing to defend its peculiar system, whereas the North, in the interest of free labor, had unconsciously become radically opposed to the extension of slavery. In so expressing itself in its defense of the institution, the South alarmed the whole country. Thomas Jefferson, seeing slavery as an evil, said: "I tremble for my country when I reflect that God is just." While there was manifested less interest in the Negro at that time than formerly, the thinking public was more deeply impressed than ever with the idea that slavery was a problem which required serious consideration.

These protests, however, were scattered and they had little effect, for the abolition movement gradually became a sectional one. The antislavery societies which held wide **The decline of the antislavery movement.** sway until about the beginning of the nineteenth century lost ground from year to year. The lower South early exterminated such sentiments; and, in the Border States, where they had had extensive influence, they soon claimed only a few adherents. In 1827 there was one such society in Connecticut, none in Delaware, two in the District of Columbia, twelve in Illinois, eight in Kentucky, eleven in Maryland, two in Massachusetts, one in New York, fifty in North Carolina, four in Ohio, sixteen in Pennsylvania, one in Rhode Island, twenty-five in Tennessee, eight in Virginia. Less than a decade later almost all southern States in which most of these societies had developed ceased to support them, and the American Convention of Abolition Societies became largely a northern organization.

Against this system of oppression, however, a few prominent men of the South continued to protest. Judge J. B.

WORKING WITH THE HOE

O'Neall of South Carolina felt that it was shameful to
prevent the blacks from obtaining sufficient knowledge to

read the Bible. Daniel R. Goodloe, of North Carolina, was
of the same opinion. Southerners of the most radical type,
moreover, did not like to live under the stigma

Protests of sympathetic Southerners. with which they were branded by William
Jay, who charged them with having closed up
the Bible in denying the Negroes the revelation of God.
Some opposition was shown therefore; and in certain parts
it was found impossible to execute restrictive measures because of the healthy public opinion against them.

The untoward condition of the Negro in the country resulted from the unusually rapid spread of cotton culture
and the extension of slavery into the uplands of the South

Spread of cotton culture. where it had been considered impracticable. The people of the frontier section,
who had early constituted the opposition to the aristocratic pretensions of the slaveholders near the coast,
gradually became indoctrinated in the tenets of the slaveholding aristocracy and began to develop the same thought
as to politics and religion as obtained near the coast. In
the seaboard States, the interior of which lay among
rugged hills or beyond seemingly insurmountable mountains, the hopes of democracy lingered longer because of
the difficulty experienced in extending slavery beyond these
barriers; but even these parts had to yield ground to the
growing evil, despite the warning given by statesmen in
the prolonged debate resulting in the admission of Missouri.

In the same way the introduction of the culture of sugar
in Louisiana accelerated the trade in that territory. By
an additional act of Congress dealing with the prohibition

The sugar industry. of the slave trade in that State a loophole was
left in the law so that it was construed to
permit the importation of slaves from the other parts of
the United States. Slave traders in some of the Border
States where the worn-out soil made the system unprofitable, moreover, supplied the Louisiana Territory in spite

of restrictions to the contrary. They evaded the laws by purchasing slaves ostensibly for employment at home, but only to be sold later in Louisiana after a brief stay to comply with the letter of the legal requirements. The result was an influx of speculators buying sugar land and bringing in slaves. Before the nineteenth century was far advanced the increasing number of estates developed and their large production placed the culture of sugar in the front rank of the industries of the South.

In this situation, then, the South soon reached the position that slavery is not an evil and by no means a sin, and that the only use to be made of a Negro is to impress him into the service of the white man. No care was taken of the blacks as of persons to be elevated, for they were to be beasts of burden. Negro women were often worked too hard to bear children, and it mattered not if they did not, since it was deemed less expensive to drive an imported slave to

THE NEGRO CALLS A HALT

The situation in the South. death during a few years and buy another in his place, than to undertake to increase his efficiency by methods of improvement. Slaves were herded in pens like cattle; they were sold to do hard labor from the rising to the setting of the sun; they were given quarters no better than the stables for animals; and they were fed upon the coarsest food known to be given to human beings. To prevent their escape, police control was effected by a patrol system. This governed their going and coming so as to prevent them from assembling for help or from securing assistance or advice from sympathetic white friends and free Negroes.

A COTTON SCENE ON A PROSPEROUS PLANTATION

The extension of the cotton culture by the expansion of slavery was essentially connected with national development. Old political parties tended to pass away and national issues furnished the line of cleavage.
Cotton and slaves. Men were doing big things on a large scale. The main question was how to do them. While Northern pioneers were moving into the Middle West, Southerners and their slaves went into the Southwest. Some of the

latter moved also into Southern Ohio, Indiana and Illinois. The opening up of these new lands relieved the seaboard slave States in two ways. It offered opportunity to the poor whites who could not easily compete with the large slaveholders living near the coast. It also solved the problem of relieving these States of the excess of slave population which could no longer be supported on the worn-out lands near the Atlantic. Unaccustomed to the scientific agriculture which requires fertilization and rotation of crops, these seaboard slave States found themselves trailing behind the progressively industrial North. Devising schemes, then, for the solution of this particular economic problem, Southerners like James G. Birney, John G. Fee, Cassius M. Clay, and Daniel R. Goodloe, brought forward proposals for the abolition of slavery and the colonization of the Negroes. Such ideas tended to widen the gap between the uplanders and the rich planters near the coast.

In practically all of the seaboard slave States the planters along the Atlantic, controlling the governments by virtue of their property, had persistently fought the liberal extension of suffrage and the reapportionment of representation. They were afraid that the mountaineers would tax slavery out of existence. When, however, the opening of the West brought this relief, the antislavery movement decidedly declined in that section. Many of the slaveholders, formerly thinking of slaves as a burden, replenished their purses, not only by selling off slaves in excess of those whom they actually needed, but also by breeding slaves for the market. In certain parts they paid special attention to the production of fine-looking mulatto Negro girls. These were very much in demand by young white slaveholders who moved into the Southwest without their families. It is said that in Tazewell County, Virginia, a slaveholder kept as many as four Negro women for each one of his three sons to supply this demand.

Exactly how important this movement was may be observed by noticing the rapid increase of the population in the Southwest. According to the census of 1790 there were in all the West, exclusive of Georgia, 109,368 inhabitants. In 1815 the same territory had a population of 1,600,000. Few immigrants could be included in this report, inasmuch **Rapid development.** as Europe was then at war. In 1791 only 38 bales of cotton were produced. In 1809 the production reached 218,723 bales. In 1816 the country exported $24,106,000 worth of cotton sold at the price of $0.28 a pound. With this rapid development it was soon possible for States carved from this territory to meet the requirements for admission to the Union. Indiana and Illinois came into the Union respectively in 1816 and 1818. They were practically accompanied by Alabama, and Mississippi to the south of them.

This plan, however, could not be worked out until an adjustment of certain claims was made with respect to the territory east of the Mississippi known as the lands of the Yazoo companies. In keeping with the claims to land lying directly west of the original thirteen, Georgia insisted that this was her territory. As the land had never been definitely surveyed, conflicting claims ensued. Much more **Yazoo land claims.** trouble arose, however, from bribery and the corrupt deals entered into by the Government with these land companies. In the midst of these conflicting claims, of charges and countercharges, Georgia ceded all of these lands to the United States in 1802. The State received in return a narrow strip of land just south of Tennessee, $1,250,000, from the proceeds of such sales of lands, and the assurance that the national government would extinguish the Indian titles in Georgia as early as the same could be peaceably accomplished on reasonable terms. The whole area was then organized as the Mississippi territory with the understanding that it would be admitted as a

State as soon as it had 60,000 inhabitants. Having to grapple with the problem of removing from the territory, the Creek, Chickasaw, and Choctaw Indians, the population did not at first increase rapidly. Persons migrating went preferably to Georgia itself and to Louisiana. When this question of eliminating the Indians was finally adjusted by Jackson's victory over the Creeks in 1814 and the other victories over them in the first and second Seminole Wars, the territory became un-usually inviting. As a result, therefore, there could be carved out of this territory the State of Mississippi in 1817 and Alabama in 1819.

THE MOTHER AND CHILD

This expansion of popu-lation stimulated national development along pro-slavery lines. The im-petus given such nation-alism by the outcome of the War of 1812 could not be counteracted by antislavery agitation. The average American's heart swelled with pride to know that his country was increasing its area by foreign aggression. The reminder that this eventually meant merely an ex-tension of the evils of slavery was not suf- **The purchase** ficient to check that movement. Such rapid **of Florida.** territorial growth, moreover, tended to strengthen the bonds of union in which the majority of the people of this coun-try were beginning to believe. The first important step, thereafter, was to secure another natural boundary by the purchase of Florida from Spain in 1819 for $5,000,000.[3]

The most strenuous effort in this direction was the acquisition of Texas in spite of the danger of troublesome complications with aggressive foreign powers. The American Government made an unsuccessful effort to buy the

COTTON PICKERS AT THE CLOSE OF THE DAY

country. Growing more rapidly than Mexico desired, Texas was able to establish its independence in 1836. The citizens

Texas question. of Texas then seemed to the slave States patriots fighting for liberty; and numerous citizens of such commonwealths moved into the territory, taking their precious species of property with them. Texas was easily recognized as an independent nation. The country as a whole, however, paid little attention to the immigration

[3] For this acquisition there could be given many reasons. For a number of years Florida had been an asylum for fugitive slaves who found life much more satisfactory there among the Spanish and Indians than in the seaboard slave States. In trying to reduce the Seminoles there to order, moreover, Andrew Jackson had almost plunged the nation into a war with Great Britain by hanging two of its citizens supposedly implicated in troubles in that territory. Furthermore, the territory was needed for the expansion to a natural boundary in the Southeast. It was actually turned over in 1821.

of proslavery Americans into Texas and did not take so seriously the danger involved in the revolution so near to our border, which might lead to the expansion of slavery. When this proslavery country applied for admission to the Union, however, the matter became a formidable question. Andrew Jackson, who hoped to perpetuate his policy against the United States Bank by the election of Martin Van Buren to the Presidency, would not inject this question into the campaign of 1836. Thereafter, however, it was a burning issue which would not down. It helped the proslavery party somewhat to say that England and France were meddling in Texan affairs, and had induced Mexico to recognize its independence. However, it did not help the proslavery group very much to circulate the report that England was to advance money to free slaves in Texas in return for a guarantee of interest on a loan. Americans were not anxious, of course, to have any European country so near to our border, either as the owners of territory or promoters of trade. Several treaties for the annexation of the republic of Texas were presented, then, but all failed until 1845. As a result of the triumph of the Democratic party on an annexation platform in the election the previous year the republic was admitted as a State of the Union. To make good the annexation of this territory which Mexico had never given up, James Knox Polk actually picked a quarrel with Mexico not only to strengthen the claim to Texas, but to acquire other territory. This Mexican War **The Oregon** of two years, moreover, closed with the ces- **territory.** sion of territory in the Southwest, now included in as many as eight States. With the addition of the Oregon territory in 1846, the country had finally expanded to natural boundaries on the Rio Grande and the Pacific. Then came the contest of slave and free states for the extension of slave and free labor, respectively.

CHAPTER XIII

SLAVERY AT ITS WORST

THE plantation system resulting from the industrial revolution, the cause of the radical reaction, made slaveholding a business of apparently tremendous possibilities.

The rise of the plantation. Large sums were invested in the enterprise, and the South entered upon its career as a borrowing section. There was a rush of southern white men from the older States along the coast to the fertile cotton lands of the Gulf district as soon as they were opened for settlement. Many came almost empty-handed, but the majority of those taking up large tracts of land brought their slaves with them. The number of slaves increased forty or fifty per cent between 1810 and 1820, and they came thereafter in droves.[1]

On their way to the Southwest the slaves experienced the usual hardships of a long drive. The interstate traders placed the children in wagons and forced the men and women to walk from twenty-five to fifty miles a day. Often traders encountered on the way bought some of the slaves in transit, after subjecting them to such an examination of their teeth and other parts as to determine their age and health. Featherstonaugh mentions his meeting in southwestern Virginia a camp of Negro slave drivers just packing up to start. He said:

The internal slave trade.

[1] A. B. Hart, *Slavery and Abolition*, Chs. IV, V, VI, and VII; U. B. Phillips, *American Negro Slavery*, pp. 151-401; W. E. B. DuBois, *The Negro*, Ch. IX; M. B. Hammond, *The Cotton Industry; Debow's Review;* Williams Wells Brown, *The Rising Son*, 265-318; G. W. Williams, *History of the Negro Race in America*, Vol. I, pp. 115-324; and J. B. McMaster's *History of the United States*, VII, pp. 238-370.

"They had with them about three hundred slaves who had bivouacked the preceding night in chains in the woods. These they were conducting to Natchez, on the Mississippi River, to work upon the sugar plantations in Louisiana. It resembled one of the coffles spoken of by Mungo Park, except that they had a caravan of nine wagons and single-horse carriages for the purpose of conducting the white people and any of the blacks that should fall lame. The female slaves, some of them sitting on logs of wood while others were standing, and a great many little black children, were warming themselves at the fire of the bivouac. In front of them all, and prepared for the march, stood in double files about two hundred men slaves, manacled and chained to each other."[2]

Referring to one of these parties, Basil Hall said: "In the rear of all came a light-covered vehicle with the master and mistress of the party. Along the roadside scattered at intervals we observed the male slaves trudg- **A drove** ing in front. At the top of all, against the **of slaves.** sky line, two men walked together apparently hand in hand, pacing along very sociably. There was something, however, in their attitude which seemed unusual and constrained. When we came nearer accordingly, we discovered that this couple were bolted together by a short chain riveted to broad iron clasps secured in like manner around the wrists."[3]

Josiah Henson, a Negro brought into this traffic said: "Men trudged on foot, the children were put into the wagon, and now and then my wife rode for a while. We went through Alexandria, Culpepper, Fauquier, **Josiah** Harpers Ferry, Cumberland, and over the moun- **Henson.** tains to the National Turnpike to Wheeling. In all the

[2] G. W. Featherstonaugh, *Excursion through the Slave States*, Ch. I, p. 120; F. Bancroft, *Slave-Trading in the Old South*.
[3] Basil Hall, *Travels in North America*, Ch. III, pp. 128-129; and *Journal of Negro History*, VIII, 367-383.

taverns along the road were regular places for the droves of Negroes continually passing along under the system of internal slave trade. At the places where we stopped for the night, we often met Negro drivers with their droves, who were almost uniformly kept chained to prevent them from running away. I was often invited to pass the evening with them in the bar-room—their Negroes in the meantime, lying chained in the pen, while mine were scattered around at liberty."[4]

JOSIAH HENSON, prototype of
Uncle Tom's Cabin

Edwin L. Godkin said: "The hardships these Negroes go through who are attached to one of these migrant parties baffles description. They trudge on foot all day through mud and thicket without rest or respite. Thousands of miles are traversed by these weary wayfarers without their knowing or caring why, urged on by whip and in full assurance that no change of place can bring any change to them. Hard work, coarse food, merciless flogging, are all that await them, and all that they can look to. I have never passed them staggering along in the rear of the wagons at the close of a long day's march, the weakest furthest in the rear, the strongest already utterly spent, without wondering how Christendom, which eight centuries ago rose in arms for a sentiment, can look so calmly on

Hardships.

4 Josiah Henson, *Uncle Tom's Story of His Life*, p. 53.

at so foul and monstrous a wrong as this American slavery.''[5]

This migration, of course, had a disastrous effect on the seaboard States from which so many masters and their slaves were drawn. Industry was paralyzed on the lower Atlantic coast. There were the worn-out lands with deserted homes once characterized by abun- **The decline of** dance and luxury, ruined and distressed **the seaboard** debtors wondering how to find relief, hu- **States.** miliated planters with no way of escape but migration. Efforts at fertilization to rebuild the waste places were tried, and with this the slave States near the Atlantic experienced a sort of revival about the middle of the nineteenth century. This was due also, some think, to the demand for slaves as laborers on the railroads which at that time were being constructed to unite the South and to connect it with the West.

To supply the Southwest with slaves, however, the domestic slave trade became an important business, and the older States which suffered from the migration devoted themselves to slave breeding for this market. **Slave** This flourished the more because of the restric- **breeding.** tions on the African slave trade. In the work entitled *Slavery and the Internal Slave Trade in the South,* it is estimated that seven of the older States annually exported 80,000 to the South. These were Virginia, Maryland, North Carolina, Kentucky, Tennessee, Missouri and Delaware. Professor Asa Martin thinks that Kentucky furnished 5,000 a year. One writer estimates the number of slaves exported from Virginia at 120,000. It is difficult to figure out numbers, however, for the documents bearing on the sale of slaves did not always determine exactly what their destination would be. Men sometimes bought them appar-

---

[5] *The North American Review,* Vol. CLXXXV, pp. 46, 47.

ently for private use, concealing their ultimate aim to sell them South. Except when forced by economic necessity, or some case of insubordination, certain masters refused to sell their slaves if they knew that they would have to undergo the tortures of servitude in the cotton and sugar districts. It is also difficult to determine who were the interstate slave traders. Almost all commission merchants

A SLAVE AUCTION

dealt in slaves as in any other property, and they were not anxious to be known as being primarily interested in a work which was in no sense popular among the more nearly civilized slaveholders.

Some of these masters, in advertising slaves for sale, specifically stated that they were not to be sold out of the State. Persons who were bold enough to proclaim them-

Slaves sold south.

selves as such traders were mentioned with opprobrium in the older slave States.[6] The

---

[6] I. E. McDougle, *Slavery in Kentucky* in *The Journal of Negro History*, Vol. II, pp. 226-230; and F. Bancroft, *op. cit.*

presence of such traders in Winchester, Virginia, in 1818, evoked the comment: ''Several wretches, whose hearts must be as black as the skins of the unfortunate beings who constitute their inhuman traffic, have for several days been impudently prowling about the streets of this place with labels on their hats exhibiting in conspicuous characters the words, 'Cash for Negroes.' '' Some time in the thirties of the last century a master of Danville, Kentucky, sold a Negro woman to a regular slave trader. Upon learning this, threats of a mob to do him violence compelled this master to go in quest of the trader, from whom he repurchased the woman at a decidedly increased price.[7] Yet, intense as this feeling was, Delaware was the only slave State to legislate against the interstate slave trade. Maryland, Kentucky and Louisiana undertook somewhat to regulate it.

This enlightened minority could not stop this traffic, and for a number of centers in the Border States it became a source of much revenue. Dealers bought up slaves in the local markets and confined them in jails, **A source of** taverns, warehouses or slave pens, while **revenue.** awaiting buyers from the Southwest. The average slave pen had an administration building for the slaves, a court for the women and one for the men, with gates, barracks, and eating sheds. Some of the slave pens, however, were no more than stables for cattle or horses. On the convenient day they were placed on the sales block and auctioned off to the highest bidder. The slaves themselves, sometimes for personal advantage in determining their buyers, aided or impeded the sale by singing their own praises or proclaiming their shortcomings. Thus they spent weeks and months until the owner drove a bargain with a trader, who removed them in coffles to their home in the rising cotton kingdom.

[7] *The Journal of Negro History,* Vol. III, p. 229.

In this way the Negroes were made the means of exploiting the new Southwest by accelerating the westward movement from the South. The slaves were thereby taken from a declining section, where they had become such a burden that these States would have necessarily become antislavery, had they remained. These blacks were carried to the cotton district, where they were apparently profitable servants in developing a new industry. The 85,000,-000 pounds of cotton produced in 1810 doubled by 1820, doubled again during the next decade, and doubled still once more by 1840. This was then about two-thirds of the cotton production in the world. After that period there was no question as to our leadership in the production of this raw material.

What, then, was the plantation system, serving as the basis of this large cotton industry? This was the method of cultivating an estate of hundreds and sometimes thou-**The** sands of acres. The administration centered **plantation.** in the residence of the planter or, in case of absentee ownership, in the home of the manager of the estate. Nearby stood the stable, smoke-house, corn-house; and a little farther away appeared the garden, potato field, watermelon patch, and the like. Somewhat distant from this central building were the homes of the slaves, commonly known as quarters. In most cases these were rude huts, often with dirt floors and so poorly constructed as to furnish little protection from bad weather. Furniture was generally lacking unless the few stools and the beds of straw be worthy of such designation. In some cases the slaves were allowed to till a patch of ground on which they produced their own vegetables. Some few of them were permitted to raise chickens or hogs. They had to look after these personal affairs at night, on Sundays, or holidays, as their whole time was otherwise required in the service of their masters.

In the case of just a few slaves the master often worked with them. On larger plantations, however, slaves worked in gangs under masters or their overseers, if the owners had sufficient holdings to afford such supervision. **Slaves at** In the culture of rice the work could be so **work.** divided as to assign it as tasks by holding each slave responsible for a definite accomplishment. Some few planters, like McDonogh of Louisiana and Z. Kingsley of Florida, ran their plantations on something like the self-government basis. Slaves were thrown largely on their own initiative to earn what they could. The control was vested in courts, the personnel of which were slaves. The administrative officers were also bondmen carrying out the mandates of these tribunals. Isaiah T. Montgomery of Mound Bayou, Mississippi, was taught with white children and trained as an accountant to serve in this capacity on the Mississippi plantation of Joseph Davis, the brother of Jefferson Davis.

As a plantation was a community in itself, it had to be governed as such. On large plantations managed by men of foresight, definite rules were drawn up to determine the procedure of overseers and slaves. These were intended to maintain the government of the slaves, to pro- **Plantation** duce the largest crop possible, and at the same **management.** time to exercise such care over the bondmen as not to lose any of them by unnecessarily harsh treatment and neglect of their health. On some plantations, however, masters either worked to their own detriment by driving their slaves to an untimely death, or accomplished the same through overseers in the case of absentee ownership. This was often true in cases in which overseers were paid by giving them a share of the crop. The abuses practiced by these managers caused many planters to brand them as being a negligent, selfish, and dishonest class. The situation was not any better when the slaves were placed under a Negro driver. Some say it was worse.

Slaves were not generally cared for when sick. Women in pregnancy were more neglected than ever, and some worked too hard to bear healthy children. Many slaves **The care** were not given sufficient of the simple corn-**of slaves.** bread, bacon and salt herrings they were allowed; and a still larger number were not adequately

A PLANTATION

clothed. Negroes supplemented their rations by hunting and trapping at night. Some of them, by working at night, accumulated means by which they added to the meager provisions generally supplied from their plantation commissary. A few hoarded considerable sums with which they purchased their freedom and made their way to free States, if not permitted to remain after manumission. Others had to steal to obtain a subsistence, and parsimonious masters even encouraged them to do so.

Above all, punishments were crude and abusive. Because it would be prejudicial to their own economic interests, masters no longer mutilated Negroes or destroyed them on the wheel, as in the eighteenth century, unless it was absolutely necessary; but flogging, unmerciful beating, and even burning at the stake sometimes followed. In cases of unruly Negroes they were sold **Punishments.** South, where they faced the alternative of either yielding or being punished to death. The runaway slaves were hunted with dogs. When brought back they were put in heavy iron shackles or collars and sometimes subjected to such tortures as drawing out the toe-nails. Those persisting in resisting their masters were occasionally murdered. These conditions, however, differed from plantation to plantation, according to the custom of the masters.

Little relief from such a condition could then be expected when the church itself all but approved this régime. This was brought out in the case of Charleston, South Carolina, to which the African Methodists, after their **Restrictions** withdrawal from the whites, summoned Ne- **on religious** groes to be ordained to serve in that city. **affairs.** This freedom of action was too much for the South. The independent church movement there was stopped. Meetings were prohibited and the bishop, his exhorters, and immediate followers were ordered to be imprisoned if they did not depart from the State, while others were fined or given a number of lashes. As Negroes were forced thereafter to accept what accommodations were given them in the white churches, they gradually yielded room to the increasing membership of the whites until the blacks were ordered to the galleries or compelled to hold special services following those of the whites. A refusal of Negroes to give up to the whites prominent seats long occupied by them in a church in Charleston, South Carolina, led to their ejection by a group of white youths. When criticized for this these young members behaved so unbecomingly that nine of them had to be expelled; but to show their attachment to caste one hundred and fifty others left with them.

Unsuccessful efforts were then made to establish separate churches for the slaves, like the Calvary Church in Charleston, and the African Baptist Church in Richmond. For **Negro churches.** feigned reasons the legal endorsement for the latter was not given until 1855, and then on the condition that a white minister be employed. In the churches in the cities in the Border States, however, there was more religious freedom among the slaves. There was a Baptist Church in Lexington, Kentucky, in 1830. George Bentley, a Negro minister of polemic distinction, was preaching to the most enlightened whites as well as blacks in Giles County, Tennessee, in 1859. Out of a debate on baptism lasting more than four days he emerged victor over a white minister in that county challenging him to a discussion of the principles of baptism. He numbered among his communicants the best white people of the community and received from them a salary of about $600 a year. In the large cities there was still more religious freedom. Washington Negroes had several churches early in the nineteenth century, and Baltimore had ten churches for slave and free Negroes in 1834. In the neglected districts, however, the Negro was left in his heathen state.

The awful lot of the Negro became more pronounced as the churches which formerly championed the cause of the Negro tended to become, according to James G. Birney, **Proslavery church.** "The Bulwarks of American Slavery." By 1836 the Methodist Church, which at first attacked slavery, took the position of disclaiming "any right, wish, or intention to interfere in the civil and political relation between master and slave, as it existed in the slaveholding states of the union." Northern churches here and there were closing up their Negro pews or gradually eliminating the Negro membership altogether.

There were, moreover, southern churchmen who were busy writing treatises on the inferiority of the Negro and the wisdom of Providence in subjecting them to servitude in keeping with the Noachian "Cursed be Canaan." Preaching to Negroes, they explained the ancient proclamation: "Japheth shall dwell in the land of Shem and Ham shall be his servant." "Servants, therefore, obey your masters." They were faithfully supported in this theory by an array of pseudo-scientists. Such misinformed authors were producing numerous books explaining in detail the various ways in which the "woolly-headed, flat-nosed prognathous race" differed from the better selected Caucasian. Such nonsense, however, should not detain the student of history except so far as it is necessary to note how near the public mind sometimes approaches insanity. No scholar now accepts any such theory as the inferiority or superiority of races.

As all of the members of the national churches could not easily come around to this point arrived at through fictitious ethnology and anthropology, there followed in these ranks a schism which was really the beginning of the disunion. If people can not coöperate along religious lines it is very difficult to find a point of agreement to supply the necessary cohesion **The schism.** of a united nation. The knell of the Union was sounded, then, not first in the bombardment of Fort Sumter, but in the separation of the churches into northern and southern jurisdictions. In 1844 and 1845 the Baptists divided on the question of sending out slaveholding missionaries. There followed about the same time a similar separation of the Methodists because of a difference of opinion as to whether James O. Andrew, who-held the of-

fice of bishop, could at the same time remain in the possession of slaves whom he had acquired by marriage. Uniting
slaveholding with the deeds of the just men to be made
perfect, the cotton section said "yes" and established
churches to translate to eternal bliss the souls of men
who wrung their bread from the sweat of others' brows.

After this reaction the slaves were not generally allowed
any chance for mental development; and, of course, they
could not learn to appreciate Christianity. Planters in
Enlightenment some parts, thinking that the teaching of
prohibited. religion might lead to the teaching of
letters, prohibited it entirely. The best slaves could then
do for mental development was to learn by contact and
by stealth. Many a sympathetic person taught slaves to
read. In some cases private teachers were bold enough
to maintain Negro schools This was actually done in
Savannah, Charleston, and Norfolk.

How some of these slaves learned in spite of opposition
makes a beautiful story. Knowing the value of learning
as a means of escape and having a longing for it, too, be-
Stealing cause it was forbidden, many slaves continued
learning. their education under adverse circumstances.
Some of them, like Frederick Douglass, had the assistance
of benevolent whites who were a law unto themselves;
others studied privately and even attended school. Children of the clergy, accustomed to teach slaves to read the
Bible, were generally regarded as enjoying an immunity.
Some private teachers among the whites encouraged
Negroes to steal away to secret places where their operations were shielded from the zealous execution of the law.

The majority of these enlightened slaves, however,
learned by contact, observation and dint of energy.[8] Many
of them were employed at such occupations as to develop

[8] C. G. Woodson, *Education of the Negro Prior to 1861*, Ch. IX.

N. Rillieux

Evaporating Pan.

Nº 4.879

Patented Dec. 10. 1846

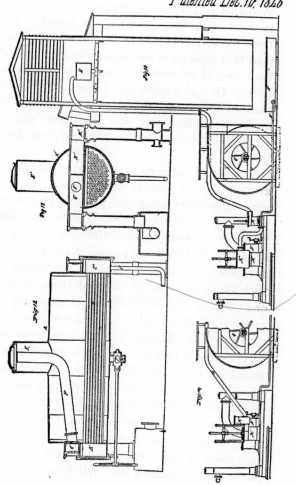

sufficient mental power to "read, write, and cipher."
"Blazon it to the shame of the South," said Redpath, "the
Learning by knowledge thus acquired has been snatched
contact.   from the spare records of leisure in spite of
their honest wishes and watchfulness." Many, like Robert
Williams and Albert T. Jones, stole enough to enable them
to read with ease. Lott Cary heard a minister preach
from the third chapter of St. John, and on returning home
read that passage of scripture, although he had never before
been taught to read and had not hitherto made such an
effort. Dr. Alexander T. Augusta of Virginia learned to
read while serving white men as a barber. W. S. Scarborough, of Wilberforce, was taught by one J. C. Thomas,
a cruel slaveholder of the bitterest type living in Macon,
Georgia.

In spite of their circumstances a few slaves experienced
another sort of mental development. Being in a rapidly
growing country where the pioneers had to make use of the
Inventions   forces of nature, here and there a slave be-
of slaves.   came an inventor. According to the opinion
of Henry E. Baker, an examiner in the United States Patent Office, slaves made certain appliances, experimenting
with the separation of the seed from cotton, which, when
observed by Eli Whitney, were assembled by him as the
cotton gin. Freedmen, during these years, were more successful. While James Forten, a free Negro of Philadelphia,
was making a fortune out of his new device which he perfected for handling sails, Henry Blair, of Maryland, interested in labor saving, patented two corn harvesters in
1834 and in 1836. Norbert Rillieux, a man of color in
Louisiana, patented an evaporating pan by which the re-
fining of sugar was revolutionized. There is much evidence
that some of the inventions brought out by white persons
in the South prior to the Civil War were devices invented

by Negroes. The slave as such, according to an opinion of Jeremiah S. Black, attorney-general of the United States in 1858, could not be granted a patent. The reason was that the slave could neither contract with the government nor assign his invention to his master. Confronting this problem, when Benjamin T. Montgomery, a slave of Jefferson Davis, was on this ground denied a patent on an invention, the President of the Confederate States secured the enactment of the law providing for patenting inventions of slaves.[9]

In spite of these notable exceptions under this exploitation system, however, the Negro race became an element with which the whites would not deal as man with man. The whites were restrained by law and public opinion from accepting Negroes as their social equals. The miscegenation of Negro **Negroes socially proscribed.** men and white women was penalized as a high crime, although there were always a few instances of such association. Abdy, who toured the country from 1833 to 1834, doubted that such laws were enforced. "A Negro man," said he, "was hanged not long ago for this crime at New Orleans. The partner of his guilt—his master's daughter—endeavored to save his life, by avowing that she alone was to blame. She died shortly after his execution."

With the white man and the Negro woman, however, the situation was different. A sister of President Madison once said to the Reverend George Bourne, then a Presbyterian minister in Virginia: "We Southern ladies are complimented with the name of wives; but we are only the mis-

[9] This law was:

And be it further enacted, That in case the original inventor or discoverer of the art, machine or improvement for which a patent is solicited is a slave, the master of such slave may take oath that the said slave was the original; and on complying with the requisites of the law shall receive a patent for said discovery or invention, and have all the rights to which a patentee is entitled by law.

tresses of seraglios."[10]   But the masters of the female
slaves were not the only persons of such loose morals.

A weakness of the white man. Many women of color were prostituted also
to the purposes of young white men and over-
seers.   Goodell reports a well-authenticated
account of a respectable "Christian" lady of the South,
who kept a handsome mulatto female for the use of her genteel scn, as a method of deterring him, as she said, "from in-
discriminate and vulgar indulgences."   Harriet Martineau
discovered a young white man who on visiting a southern
lady became insanely enamored of her intelligent quadroon
maid.   He sought to purchase her, but because of her unusual worth the owner refused to sell the slave.   The young
man persisted in trying to effect this purchase and finally
informed her owner that he could not live without this
attractive slave.   Thereupon the white lady sold the woman
of color to satisfy the lust of her friend.

The Northern States were also showing an antagonistic
attitude toward miscegenation.   This was especially true
of Pennsylvania.   In 1820 a petition against the custom was presented to the legislature of Pennsylvania.
A mixed marriage was the cause of a riot at Columbia
in that State in 1834; and another had the same result in
the riot in Philadelphia in 1849.   In 1838 members of the
Pennsylvania Constitutional Convention engaged in a
heated discussion of the custom.   The agitation there,
however, was generally ineffective.   Race admixture continued as is evidenced by the fact that one-fifth of the
Negroes in the State in 1800 were mulattoes and that in
1860 this proportion had increased to one-third.   This had
been brought about in spite of the fact that public sentiment against Negroes in the North had so developed as to
afflict them with many of the evils from which they suffered in the South.

[10] *The Journal of Negro History,* Vol. III, p. 350.

Against the hardships of the system numerous slaves rebelled. So thoroughly had they become intimidated after Nat Turner's fate that most of them did nothing to injure their masters; but they endeavored to make their escape into the woods, too often only to be brought **The runaway** back after a few weeks' adventure. Offering **slave.** in its advertisements some attractive reward, the news-

THE PURSUIT

papers quickly proclaimed the news of a runaway. White men, assisted with firearms and bloodhounds trained to run down fugitives, hunted them like game even in the North. That section, struck by the inhuman methods to recapture slaves, passed personal liberty laws to prevent the return of the Negroes apprehended, as many of these were kidnapped free persons taken under pretext of being runaways.[11]

[11] These Laws are collected in Hurd's *Law of Freedom and Bondage.*

These laws, however, were nullified by the decisions of the federal courts and the Fugitive Slave Law of 1850. This undertook to impress into the service of slave-hunting men who were conscientiously opposed to the institution. The North was then the scene of the most disgraceful deeds. These aroused the consciences of the people and swelled the ranks of the abolition minority which at one time seemed to decline to meet premature death.

The efforts of the slaves to escape from bondage, however, were unusually successful in the Appalachian mountains, where there had been retained a healthy sentiment against slavery. The mountaineers of North Carolina, Kentucky and Tennessee organized antislavery societies during the first quarter of the nineteenth century. When that movement became unpopular they generally supported the cause of colonization. This seemed a good solution of the immediate problem of the Negro; for the frontiersmen were not particularly attached to the unfortunate race. They believed that the institution of slavery was an economic evil of which the country should rid itself by a system of gradual emancipation as soon as possible. When, however, the conditions of the Negroes in the South became so intolerable that it was necessary to flee for larger liberty in the Northern States, they found it easy to make their way through this region where the farmers were not interested in the institution. It was of some help, too, that slaves could easily hide in the mountains and in the limestone regions which furnished comfortable caves. The promoters of the Underground Railroad, therefore, offered them a way of escape by extending their system southward through the mountains of these States so as to connect with the fugitives escaping thither. These lines led through Kentucky into Ohio, Indiana and Illinois, and connected with the Great Lakes. Along this route fugitives passed

Fugitives.

The Underground Railroad.

into Canada, under the guidance of persons like the daring Josiah Henson, Harriet Tubman, and John Brown.[12]

A few slaves in the South, however, did not suffer sufficiently to want to escape. Slaves in urban communities were occasionally better situated than other bondmen. Employed in the trades and domestic service affording close contact with their masters, they were economically better off than the free Negroes whom they often doomed to poverty by crowding them out of the various pursuits of labor. There was scarcely any industry in which slaves did not engage, and in most cases to the exclusion or at the expense of the poor whites as well as of the free blacks. Some

Town slaves.

HARRIET TUBMAN

contractors owned their workmen just as masters owned the Negroes on their plantations. Master mechanics less favorably circumstanced hired slaves. In a few cases slaves were employed under the direction of an enterprising master mechanic who took contracts, managed the business, and reported to the master at certain periods. It was soon learned, however, that a slave as such easily competed with free Negroes and whites. It was, therefore, necessary for the masters to grant such bondmen the larger freedom of

[12] W. H. Siebert, *Underground Railroad*, p. 166. See also *The Journal of Negro History*, VII, 235-241 and 377-379.

profit-sharing or of hiring themselves to stimulate them **to** greater endeavor. This custom proved unsatisfactory **to** white mechanics. In several States, then, laws were passed to prevent the hiring of slaves to themselves. But this custom continued in spite of strenuous efforts to the contrary, as the enforcement of it would have materially restricted the use of slaves. Many slaves thus employed were cheated in the end by dishonest contractors, but others more fortunately situated contrived thereby to purchase their own freedom and that of their families. To do this many Negroes worked at night after finishing their tasks by day. But this privilege served as another reason for legislation against this custom. It would lead to an increase in the number of free Negroes who might promote servile insurrection.

In the city, too, it was possible for the Negroes to maintain among themselves certain social distinctions based upon their advantages of contact with the whites and the amount of culture they had taken over. Those employed **Social** in the higher pursuits of labor and as domes-**distinctions.** tic servants to the rich whites were enabled by the working-over of cast-off clothes and imitating their masters' language and airs, to lord it over the crude slaves of the fields. In culture the less fortunate Negroes were further separated from these urban free blacks than the latter were from the whites. In their social affairs house servants sometimes had much liberty and apparently experienced much joy. They so impressed travelers with their contentment in this situation that some concluded that the Negroes had no serious objection to their enslavement.

The South had finally succeeded in hedging in the Negro so that he might forever afterward do the will of **Slavery, the** his master. But this seemingly sane method **undoing of** of developing the South was what resulted in **the South.** its undoing. Since migration of slaveholders promoted a segregation of planters of the same class, moving under similar conditions and to the same section, it made reform almost an impossibility; and in preventing the immigration of white laborers into the slave States the system became so strongly intrenched that it had to be attacked from without. In the first place, in the effort to exploit black men it transformed white men into reckless beings. The system, moreover, promoted the formation of wasteful habits. It prevented the growth of towns and cities, it shut out industrialism, and it made the South dependent on the North or European nations for its manufactures. While the North was receiving an influx of free laborers the South was increasing unnecessarily its slave labor supply, indulging in unwise investments, and overstocking the markets with southern staple crops. In making labor undignified, moreover, it reduced the poor whites to poverty, caused a scarcity of money, cheapened land, and confined the South to one-crop farming at the expense of its undeveloped resources.

The economic interests of the two sections, therefore, began to differ widely during the thirties. When Missouri asked for admission to the Union, the struggle which ensued emphasized these differences. Prior to this pe- **Differing** riod slavery had well established itself in that **interests.** territory. When everything had been arranged and Congress was about to pass the bill providing for its admission, James Talmadge, a representative from New York, upset things by offering an amendment providing that slavery should not be allowed in that territory. This led to a fiery debate participated in by the stalwart defenders of the proslavery section of the country and by the Congressmen of the North, who, although at that time unprepared to advocate a general abolition of slavery, were convinced that it was an evil and desired to prohibit its expansion. It was pointed out by the antislavery element that a part of the State of Missouri lies farther north than the mouth of the

Ohio River, above which slavery was prohibited by the Ordinance of 1787 organizing the Northwest Territory.[13]

The main question was whether or not Congress had any right to limit a State coming into the Union. Decidedly it had, but it was necessary to argue the question. It was brought out that in the admission of the State of Louisiana Congress imposed certain conditions requiring that the State should use the English language as its official tongue, should guarantee the writ of habeas corpus and trial by jury, and should incorporate into its organic laws the fundamental principles of civil and religious liberty. They could have pointed out, too, that Ohio was required to comply with a number of requirements, among which was the use of certain of its lands in the Western Reserve and in the southeast.[14]

The antislavery group, moreover, contended that inasmuch as Congress is required by the Constitution to guarantee to each State a republican form of government it **Binding a State.** was necessary to prohibit slavery because of its incompatibility with that form of government. The proslavery party supported their cause on the ground that to impose a restriction on a State would place it on a basis of inequality rather than that of equality with other States. The privileges enjoyed by one State should be enjoyed by all. If one had the right to hold slaves, all should enjoy the same privilege as they had when all were admitted to the Union. It was further contended that powers not delegated to the United States Government

[13] There are discussions of the constitutional question growing out of slavery in Herman von Holst's *The Constitutional and Political History of the United States of America*, in John W. Burgess's *Middle Period* and his *Civil War and Reconstruction*, and in James Ford Rhodes' *History of the United States*, Chs. VI and VII. Burgess and Rhodes, however, are generally biased.

[14] Restrictions were also imposed later on California when it was provided that the duties on goods imported there should have to be fixed according to terms set forth in the amendment to the regular navy act.

nor prohibited to the States were reserved to the States. The question as to whether a State should hold slaves, therefore, was reserved to that commonwealth and Congress had no right to interfere therewith.

It was asserted also, as was admitted thereafter, that the restriction against slavery in the Ordinance of 1787 was not binding on those States of the territory that had been admitted to the Union, and that they could **The Ordinance** introduce slavery when they desired.[15] The **of 1787.** pro-slavery leaders believed that the expansion of slavery would be a benefit to the country rather than an evil. It would provide for an extension of the system; it would reduce the number held by each person and, therefore, would bring the slave into more direct and helpful contact with the master. The agitation was quieted for the time being by a compromise. This permitted Missouri to come into the Union as a slave State but prohibited the institution north of the parallel thirty-six thirty constituting the southern limit of Missouri.

Another important question came forward in the Missouri debate when the question had been all but settled, that is, when the State had framed a constitution in keeping with the instructions given in the enabling **The** act, but had incorporated into this document **citizenship** a clause providing for the exclusion of free **of Negroes.** Negroes from that commonwealth. This provision was seriously attacked by the friends of freedom. They argued that inasmuch as these Negroes were citizens of the United States, no State had a right to restrict their privileges, as such action would conflict with the Constitution of the United States, which guarantees to the citizens of each commonwealth all the privileges and immunities of citizens

[15] J. P. Dunn. *Indiana; A Redemption from Slavery*, pp. 218-260; N. D. Harris, *The History of Negro Servitude in Illinois*, Chs. **III, IV** and V; and B. A. Hinsdale, *Old Northwest*, pp. 351-358.

in every other commonwealth. This drove home the **real** truth which the country had not before realized, that there was such a thing as citizenship of the United States in contradistinction to citizenship in a State, and that the citizenship of the United States is more than citizenship of a State. When a citizen, therefore, immigrated into and settled in another State, according to the Constitution he should not lose the right to be treated as a citizen of that commonwealth. When this involved the rights of the Negro it was certainly startling to the representatives of the South; and Missouri, for that reason, if for no other, was less inclined than ever to change that provision of its Constitution. The matter was settled by a second compromise to counteract the effect this clause might have. This provided that nothing therein contained should be so construed as to give the assent of Congress to any provision in the Constitution of Missouri which contravened that clause in the Constitution of the United States which declares that the citizens of each State shall be entitled to all of the privileges and immunities of citizens in the several States.

Slavery again showed its far-reaching effects. During the first three decades of the nineteenth century, the South, in the natural order of things, became a section de-**Slavery and** pendent solely on its peculiar institution, a **the tariff.** district devoted entirely to agriculture and almost solidly organized in defending such interests. For this reason the South developed into a mere plantation. The North, on the other hand, in view of the shipping industry, its commerce, and the manufacturing, which of necessity grew during the War of 1812 and decidedly expanded thereafter, developed a number of business and industrial centers desirous of protecting their industries by imposing certain duties on goods imported from Europe. This caused a shift in the positions of the leaders of these two sections. Whereas, in 1816, John C. Calhoun was an advocate of a protective tariff and Daniel Webster was a free trader, in 1832 Webster was in favor of import duties and Calhoun had constructed a policy of free trade. With the support of the West, desiring a protective duty on its hemp and the like, the manufacturing districts were able to secure the enactment of tariff-for-protection measures in 1824, 1828 and 1832.[16]

Against the protective tariff the commonwealths of the South began to argue that it was discriminatory and therefore unconstitutional, and that it imposed a tax upon one section for the benefit of the other. Con- **Opposition to** gress, as the South saw it, had no right to **the tariff.** legislate in behalf of one section at the expense of the other. So bitter did the South become because of this seeming imposition that in 1832 South Carolina undertook to nullify the tariff law. South Carolina took the position of Kentucky and Virginia in 1798, that a State had a right to obey or to nullify a law passed by Congress, if, in its judgment, it found out that that law was prejudicial to the interests of the State concerned.

It was made clear, moreover, that South Carolina was of the opinion that this country was not a union but still a confederation loosely held together very much as the States were under the Articles of Confedera- **A union or a** tion. A State, therefore, as long as it chose **confederacy?** to be bound by the terms of the Constitution could continue to do so; but if at any time it felt that the union with the other States was undesirable, it could of itself, or in connection with a number of States constituting a majority, call a convention representing the same power by which the Constitution was ratified and declare the severance of the ties that bound them to the Union.

It was necessary, therefore, for the Union to take high

[16] See Calhoun's speech in the Appendix.

ground for its own self-preservation. Although Andrew Jackson, then President of the United States, did not hold any brief for the tariff himself, he could not countenance the act of nullification. He, therefore, threatened to use force should South Carolina refuse to obey the laws of Congress. This matter, like others threatening the foundation of the Union, was settled by a compromise brought forward by Henry Clay. It was enacted that the duties would remain as they were under the law of 1832, but by a gradual process would be diminished until they reached the rates acceptable to South Carolina.

Slavery brought out also another economic question in connection with internal improvements. It was difficult for a slaveholding section to expand as rapidly as the manufacturing and commercial parts of the country. In **Internal improvements.** the all but phenomenal growth of the North and West there was an urgent need for canals and roads to tap the resources of the interior. As the South in its slow development did not feel this need and thought that it would not generally profit by these improvements, it usually opposed them. The proslavery leaders held that the United States Government had no authority to make such improvements and the States had not the required funds. This opposition resulted from the observation that these improvements were unifying influences. They strengthened the Union at the expense of the South, which hoped to hold the axe of secession over the heads of the Unionists. The disunionists had a precedent for this in the Hartford Convention of 1815, when New Englanders threatened the country with secession because of their dissatisfaction with the trade restrictions imposed during the War of 1812.

CHAPTER XIV

THE FREE NEGRO

WHILE the fate of the slaves in the South was being determined, there was also a considerable number of free persons of color whose status was ever changing. Few people now realize the extent to which the free Negro figured in the population of this country prior to the Civil War.[1] Before slavery was reduced from a patriarchal establishment to the mere business of exploiting men, a considerable number of Negroes had secured their freedom, and the fruits of the American Revolution, effective long thereafter in ameliorating their condition, gave an impetus to manumission. In some colonies Negroes were indentured servants before they were slaves, and became free upon the expiration of their term of service. The result was that there were in this country in 1790 as many as 59,557 free people of color, 35,000 of whom were living in the South. During the two decades from 1790 to 1810, the rate of increase of free Negroes exceeded that of the slaves, and the proportion of free Negroes in the black population increased accordingly from 7.9 per cent in 1790 to 13.5 per cent in 1810. After this date the tendency was in the other direction because of the reaction against the Negro, which brought about a restriction on manumissions.

The status of the free Negro.

[1] John H. Russell, *The Free Negro in Virginia, passim;* E. R. Turner, *The Negro in Pennsylvania;* F. U. Quillin, *The Color Line in Ohio, passim;* C. T. Hickok, *The Negro in Ohio, passim;* C. G. Woodson, *A Century of Negro Migration,* pp. 1-100; the *Journal of Negro History,* I, 1-68, 99-100, 203-242, 302-317, 361-376; II, 51-78, 164-185; III, 90-91, 196-197, 360-367, 435-441, and *Negro Population in the United States, 1790 to 1915.*

Between 1810 and 1840 the Negro population almost doubled, but the proportion of the free Negroes remained about the same. Because of further restriction on manumission and the more secure foundation of plantation slavery with rigid regulations to prevent the fugitives from escaping, this proportion of free Negroes in the black population decreased to 11.9 per cent by 1850 and to 11 per cent by 1860. While the Negro population as a whole doubled its percentage of increase, then, that of the free blacks declined. It became smaller in parts of the North and declined to one-fourth of the rate of increase between 1800 and 1810. In 1860 the rate of increase was about one per cent a year. It is worthy of note, however that there were 434,455 free Negroes in the United States in 1850 and 488,070 in 1860. At this latter date 83,942 of these were in Maryland, 58,042 in Virginia, 30,463 in North Carolina, 18,467 in Louisiana, 11,131 in the District of Columbia, 10,638 in Kentucky; in short, 250,787 in the whole South. About 50,000 of these had attained the independence of being heads of families by 1830, while a few thousand other free Negro families were reported among the white families as servants.[2]

Slow increase.

This increase of free Negroes was largely a natural growth. There had been, of course, some additions by purchases of freedom and the acquisition of new territory. Only a few immigrated into this country, for merely 7,011 free Negroes enumerated in 1860 were born abroad. Some idea as to the extent that other factors figured in this may be obtained from the fact that 1,467 Negroes were manumitted in 1849 and 1,011 became fugitives. In 1859 there were 3,000 manumissions and 803 fugitives. The census of 1860 shows

Increase a natural growth.

2 See Woodson's *Free Negro Heads of Families in the United States in 1830.*

that probably 20,000 manumissions were made during the decade between 1850 and 1860.

Negro Population, 1790 to 1860

Census Year	Total	Free		Slave	Decennial Increase			
		Number	Per cent		Number		Per cent	
					Free	Slave	Free	Slave
1860	4,441,830	488,070	11.0	3,953,760	53,575	749,447	12.3	23.4
1850	3,638,808	434,495	11.9	3,204,313	48,202	716,958	12.5	28.8
1840	2,873,648	386,293	13.4	2,487,355	66,694	478,312	20.9	23.8
1830	2,328,642	319,599	13.7	2,009,043	85,965	471,021	36.8	30.6
1820	1,771,656	233,634	13.2	1,538,022	47,188	346,660	25.3	29.1
1810	1,377,808	186,466	13.5	1,191,362	78,011	297,760	71.9	33.3
1800	1,002,037	108,435	10.8	893,602	48,908	195,921	82.2	28.1
1790	757,181	59,557	7.9	697,624	......	....	....	....

The statistics of the Negro population between 1790 and 1915 suggest as an explanation for this decrease that the free people of color were much older and therefore subject to a higher mortality rate; that they were **Sex** less normally distributed by sex and, there- **distribution.** fore, probably characterized by a marital condition less favorable to rapid natural increase. Among the Free Negroes at each of the five censuses, from 1820 to 1860, there were fewer males than females, whereas the distribution as to sex among the slaves remained about equally divided between the two. While this does not altogether account for the disparity, it doubtless had something to do with the situation; for the Negroes manumitted were, as a majority, men, and those who contrived to escape were largely of the same sex. Furthermore, masters controlled the slave supply so as to add what number they needed from whichever sex seemed deficient.

The customs and regulations restraining the slaves did not generally apply to the free people of color even when so provided by law. Some of them were closely connected with former masters, who gave them more consideration than that shown by many others who sold their **The status of** own flesh and blood. In spite of the law to the **free Negroes.** contrary, a few such benevolent masters maintained schools for the education of their mulatto children. When that became unpopular they were privately instructed or sent to the North for education. Charleston, South Carolina, affords a good example of the interest manifested in the free people of color by the sympathetic citizens. They winked at the efforts of the free blacks to educate their children in well-organized schools in defiance of the law. In the State of Louisiana, where many of these mixed breeds were found, their fathers sometimes sent them to Paris to avail themselves of the advantages of the best education of that time.

These free Negroes were not all on the same plane. In the course of time they experienced a development of social distinction which largely resembled that of the whites. There were freedmen in possession of a considerable amount of property, others who formed a lower class of mechanics and artisans, and finally those living with difficulty above pecuniary embarrassment. Among those in the large cities social lines were as strongly drawn as between the whites and the blacks, and the antipathy resulting therefrom was hardly less.

The well-to-do free Negroes were not merely persons with sufficient property to form an attachment to the community. Many of them owned slaves, who cultivated their **Progressive** large estates. Of 360 persons of color in **freedmen.** Charleston, 130 of them were assessed with taxes on 390 slaves in 1860. In some of these cases, as in that of Marie Louise Bitaud, a free woman of color in New Orleans, in 1832, these slaves were purchased for personal reasons or benevolent purposes, often to make their lot much easier. They were sometimes sold by sympathetic white persons to Negroes for a nominal sum on the condition that they be kindly treated. In 1830 there were reported to the United States Bureau of the Census 3777 Negro heads of families who owned slaves. Most of these

Negroes lived in Louisiana, Maryland, North Carolina, South Carolina and Virginia.[3]

Some of these instances are enlightening. A colored man in 1818 bought a sailmaker in Charleston. Richard Richardson sold a slave woman and child for $800 to Alexander Hunter, guardian of the Negro freeman, Louis Mirault of Savannah. Anthony Ordingsell, a free man of color, sold a slave woman in the same city in 1833. A Charleston Negro who purchased his wife for $700 sold her at a profit of $50 because she would not behave herself. To check manumission, as in Virginia in 1806, laws restricting it were enacted. Difficult conditions were imposed on such sympathetic and benevolent owners. Thereafter these freedmen were to be sent out of the State unless their former masters agreed to support them and guaranteed their good behavior.

Some other Negroes of less distinction accomplished much to convince the world of the native ability of the Negroes to extricate themselves from peculiar situations and to make progress in spite of opposition. Samuel Martin, a benevolent slaveholder of color residing at Port Gibson, Mississippi, purchased *Undistinguished free Negroes.* his own freedom in 1829, and thereafter purchased two mulatto women with their four children, brought them to Cincinnati in 1844, and emancipated them. Another Negro named Creighton, living in Charleston, South Carolina, accumulated considerable wealth which he finally decided to devote to the colonization of the Negroes in Liberia. Offering his slaves the alternative of being liberated on the condition of accompanying him to Africa or of being sold as property, he disposed of his holdings. Only one of his slaves accepted the offer, but Creighton closed up his business in Charleston, purchased for the enterprise a schooner of his own, and set sail for Liberia in 1821.

[3] See Woodson's *Free Negro Owners of Slaves in the United States in 1830.*

Among the prosperous free Negroes in the South may be mentioned Jehu Jones, the proprietor of one of the most popular hotels in Charleston and owner of forty thousand **Wealthy** dollars' worth of property. There lived **persons of** Thomy Lafon in New Orleans, where he ac- **color.** cumulated real estate to the amount of al- most half a million dollars. In the same city was a woman of color owning a tavern and several slaves. A Negro in St. Paul's Parish, South Carolina, was said to have two hundred slaves, and a white wife and son-in-law, in 1857. In 1833 Solomon Humphries, a free Negro well known by men of all classes in Macon, Georgia, kept a grocery store there and had more credit than any other merchant in the town. He had accumulated about twenty thousand dollars' worth of property, including a number of slaves. Cyprian Ricard bought an estate in Iberville Parish, with ninety-one slaves, for about $225,000. Marie Metoyer, of Natchi-toches Parish, possessed fifty slaves and an estate of more than 2,000 acres. Charles Roques of the same community left in 1848 forty-seven slaves. Martin Donato, of St. Landry, died in 1848, leaving a Negro wife and children possessed of 4,500 arpents of land, eighty-nine slaves and personal property worth $46,000.

These Negroes, however, were exceptions to the rule. Most well-to-do free Negroes in urban communities be-longed to the artisan class, and there were more of them **Prosperous** than one would think. In southern cities most **mechanics.** of the work in the mechanic arts was done by Negroes. There was less discrimination in this field in the South than in the North. Contrasting the favorable conditions of southern Negroes with that of those in the North, a proslavery man referred to Charleston, South Carolina, as furnishing a good example of a center of un-usual activity and rapid strides of thrifty free Negroes. Enjoying these unusual advantages, the Negroes of Charleston early in the nineteenth century were ranked by some as economically and intellectually superior to any other group of such persons in the United States. A large portion of the leading mechanics, fashionable tailors, shoe manufacturers, and mantua-makers were free Negroes, who had "a consideration in the community far more than that enjoyed by any of the colored population in the northern cities."

What then was the situation in the North? The fugitive slave found it difficult. Most Negroes who became free as a result of manumission had been dependents so long that they had lost their initiative. When thrown upon their own resources in the North where they had to make opportunities, they failed. In increasing the number of those seeking economic opportunities in the North, more- **Hardships in** over, they so cheapened the labor as to make **the North.** it difficult for the free Negroes already there to earn a livelihood. They were, therefore, branded by the writers of the time as the pariahs of society. There was, in fact, as much prejudice against the free Negroes in parts of the North as in the South. This feeling, however, resulted largely from the antipathy engendered by the competition of the Negroes with the large number of Germans and Scotch-Irish immigrating into this country a generation before the Civil War.

Some few Negroes facing these conditions returned South and reënslaved themselves rather than starve in the North. A larger number in the South, however, were enslaved against their wills for such petty of- **The return to** fenses as theft and the like, which almost any **the South.** poverty-stricken man would be liable to commit. They were ordinarily arrested as suspected fugitives, or for vagrancy and illegal residence, and finally sold for jail fees. As Negroes in these cases were not allowed to testify in their own behalf, the official arresting a free Negro generally preferred against him whatever charge best suited his convenience and disposed of the Negro accordingly. Eighty-nine were sold in Maryland under the act of 1858 justifying such reënslavement. Much of this repression was instituted for intimidation to keep the free Negroes down that they might never join with slaves in an insurrection.

How did the situation of the free Negro compare with that of the white man? In the first place, the freedman was not a citizen in any Southern State after **Restrictions.** 1834 and was degraded from that status in certain States in the North. In most States free persons of color had the right to own and alienate property with some limitations. They could even own and sell Negro slaves. Statutes and customs, however, prohibited them from owning whites as servants, and during the intense slavery agitation of the thirties this right of holding Negroes as slaves was gradually restricted to whites. This was due to the benevolent use made of it by certain Negroes, who purchased more than their wives and children. For fear of improper uses, too, free Negroes in the South were not allowed to own such property as firearms, dogs, fire locks, poisonous drugs and intoxicants. As they were prohibited from serving in the State militia, they would have no need for firearms. The Negro, moreover, had a weak title to property in himself. If the Negro's right to be free were questioned, the burden of proof lay on him.

In some cases, however, the free Negroes had a little chance in the courts. The freedmen had the remedy of *habeas corpus.* They could bring suit against persons **Some** doing them injury, and in the case of seeming **privileges.** injustice in a lower court they could appeal to a higher. When charged with crime the free Negro had the right to trial by jury and, after indictment, could give bond for his liberty. After Nat Turner's insurrection in 1831 the right of jury trial was restricted in several southern States to cases punishable by death. It must be remembered, however, that the Negro could not expect a fair trial; for, consistent with the unwritten primitive law of the white man in dealing with the blacks, judgment preceded proof. In the case of ordinary misdemeanors the lot of the free Negroes was no better than that of the slave. Corporal punishment in these cases was administered to the Negroes without stint, whereas a white man guilty of the same offense would be required to pay a fine. In most cases of felony the punishment for a white man and a free Negro was the same in the beginning, but the reaction brought on certain distinctions.

At times the free Negroes could go and come to suit themselves. During the ardent slavery agitation, however, it was necessary for them to exhibit their free papers when questioned. They were later restrained from moving from one State to another or even from one county **Egress and** to another without securing a permit. **regress.** Nearer the middle of the nineteenth century it was unlawful in some Southern States for a free Negro to return to the State after leaving. He might be spoiled by contact or education.

Although forcing the free Negroes to a low social status, the local government did not exempt them from its burdens. In Virginia, free Negroes were required to pay a poll tax of $1.50 in 1813 and $2.50 in 1815. In 1814, 5,547 free Negroes in that State paid $8,322 in taxes, and in 1863 they paid $13,065.22 in poll taxes. The Negroes in Baltimore paid $500 in school taxes in 1860, although their chil. dren could not attend the city schools. Most States incon sistently taxed the free Negroes in the same way.

Socially the Negro, whether slave or free under the eco.

nomic régime, was an outcast. Prejudice based on color rather than on condition made him an object of oppro-

The Negro an outcast.

brium in the nineteenth century, in contra-distinction to his condition a hundred years earlier. In the seventeenth century there followed miscegenation of the races. In the eighteenth century free Negroes still experienced some interbreeding and moved socially with the whites in certain parts. In the nineteenth century all social relations between the whites and the free Negroes became about the same as those of the former with the slaves.

No laws prevented the intermarriage of the free Negroes and Indians. Squaws accepted Negroes for husbands, and Indian men commonly had black wives. Extensive mis-

Interbreeding with the Indians.

cegenation of these stocks was experienced in most states in the South. As these two races in common were undesirables among the whites, the one early manifested sympathy for the other. This was evidenced by the fact that in the massacre of 1622 in Virginia not an African was killed. In the raids of the Indians on the settlers of Louisiana, Negroes often acted in concert with them. Efforts had to be made to separate the Negroes from the Indians, when the former eagerly resorted to their reservations as places of refuge. In some cases the Negroes on these estates survived the Indians, who became extinct.

Free Negroes mingled more with the slaves, however, than with any other class. This was not the condition in the beginning. Some slaves disliked free Negroes because conditions had made the former apparently the inferiors of the latter. But in the course of time, when the free

Relations of free Negroes and slaves.

Negroes dwindled in number and their chances for education and the accumulation of wealth grew less, the social distinctions between them and the slaves diminished and they associated with and married among them. This became common in the nineteenth century. In fact, when the question of employment became serious, it was often advantageous for a free Negro to marry a slave wife. This attachment too often prevented a free Negro from being expelled from the State by the hostile laws when he had this all but permanent connection with the community. A master would not force him to leave for fear that he might induce his family to escape.

The accomplishment of this task of reducing the free people of color almost to the status of the slaves, however, was not easy. In the first place, so many persons of color had risen to positions of usefulness among   **Exceptions** progressive people and had formed connec- **to the rule.** tions with them that an abrupt separation was both inexpedient and undesirable. Exceptions to the hard and fast rules of caste were often made to relieve the people of color. The miscegenation of the races in the South, and especially in large cities like Charleston and New Orleans, moreover, had gone to the extent that from these centers eventually went, as they do now, a large number of quadroons and octoroons, who elsewhere crossed over to the white race. As the status of the Negroes remained fixed, however, while that of the poor whites changed, the close relations formerly existing between these classes gradually ceased.

The free Negro was in many respects a disturbing factor in the economic system. White laborers did not care to compete with them. The free Negro usually won in the contest, for the reason that his standard of **A disturbing** living was lower and he could work for less. **factor.** Moreover, being almost defenseless before a hostile public, he could be more easily cheated and was, therefore, to be preferred. According to testimony, however, they were of economic worth. Yet others called them idlers, criminals, vicious vagabonds, a vile excrescence and the like. These opinions may not be taken seriously when there are so many others to the contrary.

In the North the Negroes were likewise socially and, in **Successful** addition to this, economically proscribed. Yet **Negroes.** they usually succeeded in permanently establishing themselves wherever they had an opportunity.[4]

NEW YORK AFRICAN FREE SCHOOL, No. 2, built a century ago

Joseph C. Cassey and William Platt became enterprising lumber merchants in Western New York; Henry Topp came forward as a leading merchant tailor in Albany; and

[4] For other instances of free Negroes making economic progress, see William Wells Brown's *The Black Man*, M. R. Delaney's *The Condition of the Colored People of the United States*, Alexander Mott's *Biographical Sketches*, W. J. Simmons's *Men of Mark*, C. G. Woodson's *A Century of Negro Migration*, and *The Journal of Negro History*, under the caption *Undistinguished Negroes*.

Henry Scott of New York City founded and promoted for a number of years one of the most successful pickling establishments in that metropolis. Along with him arose Thomas Downing, a caterer, and Edward V. Clark, a prosperous jeweler. Other Negroes were building churches, establishing schools, and editing newspapers promoting the interests of the people of color.

In Pennsylvania, where Negroes were found in large numbers, more evidences of progress were noted. The Negroes of Philadelphia had taxable property to the amount of $350,000 in 1832, $359,626 worth **Evidences of** in 1837, and $400,000 worth in 1847. They **progress.** had established before emancipation more than a score of churches with which were connected more than a hundred benevolent societies and a number of schools. Five hundred of these Negroes were mechanics, and a considerable number ranked as business men. Among the latter developed James Forten, a sail manufacturer; Joseph Casey, a broker; and Stephen Smith, a lumber merchant. William Goodrich of New York was investing in railroad stock. Benjamin Richards of Pittsburgh was accumulating wealth in the butchering business, and Henry M. Collins of the same city was developing a real estate enterprise of considerable proportions.

Little progress in the education of the Negroes, however, was noted during these years. With the exception of some clandestine operations there were few schools for slaves and free Negroes in the South, after the fears resulting from the insurrectionary movement. Most of such schools were in towns and cities. Julian Troumontaine taught openly in Savannah until 1829 and clandestinely thereafter until 1844. The Union army in **Negro** 1864 discovered that a Mrs. Deveaux had been **schools.** secretly teaching Negroes there for thirty years. Such a school taught by a white woman was discovered in Norfolk in 1854. There was a private Negro school in New-berne about this time, and still another in Fayetteville, North Carolina. John Chavis was teaching whites and blacks in that State. There was not much interference with secret Negro schools in Charleston, Wilmington, Norfolk, and Petersburg prior to the Civil War. Years before emancipation Simeon Beard conducted a Negro school in Charleston. In Baltimore, Louisville, and New Orleans there was no serious objection to private Negro education. In 1847 W. H. Gibson was teaching in a day and night school in Louisville. In New Orleans the education of the free people of color was regarded as necessary. In the North, too, especially in the cities, most Negro communities had some of the facilities of education. Abolitionists, Quakers, and other sympathetic groups maintained here and there a few Negro schools. When the idea of education at public expense became incorporated into the laws of Northern States some of them allotted a portion to the education of the Negroes in separate schools. In 1829, however, Ohio excluded Negroes from the benefits of public education and did not recede from this position until 1849. Indiana did the same in 1837 and reënforced the prohibition in 1853 by a provision that the names of Negro children should not be taken in the school enumeration and that the property of Negroes should not be taxed for school purposes.[5]

Outside of the large cities of the North, too, there were few Negro schools sufficiently developed to offer thorough instruction. The urban Negro schools began early in the century. There was a school for Negroes in **Schools in cities.** the house of Primus Hall in Boston in 1798, and the city opened a primary school for Negroes in 1820. There were three such in Boston in 1828, one in Salem, one

---

[5] In Woodson's *Education of the Negro Prior to 1861*, this subject is treated in detail.

in New Haven, and one in Portland, Maine. Rhode Island legally provided for Negro schools in 1828 and Connecticut in 1830. The African Free Schools of the New York Manumission Society organized in 1787 developed considerably by 1810 and still more by 1814. The State Superintendent of Schools began to open special schools for Negroes in 1823. The State provided for them by law in 1841. The African Free Schools were taken over by the New York Public School Society in 1834 and organized as a system. With further public support, these schools became the best of their kind in the country.

In Pennsylvania there were several private Negro schools supported by Quakers and sympathetic friends, but in 1818 some public aid was given to Negro schools in Columbia and Philadelphia. By the act of the legislature in 1834 a system of public schools thereby established offered the Negroes further help, but they were deprived of it until 1854. It was fortunate then that in 1839 Richard Humphreys left $10,000 to endow a school for the vocational education of Negroes. This became the Institute for Colored Youth. Removed to the present site, it is known as the Cheney School for Training Teachers. Lewis Woodson had a successful school in Pittsburgh in 1830, and it was not surpassed by any other there until Charles Avery gave for Negro education a fund of $300,000, from a part of which was established Avery College in that city in 1849. In Cincinnati, the Negroes had a school in 1820. They had a better one in 1834. In 1844 came the Rev. Hiram Gilmore, who established there a high school. In 1856 the Methodists established Wilberforce near Xenia. Negroes in the District of Columbia first studied privately with white friends, but in 1807 George Bell, Nicholas Franklin, and Moses Liverpool built the first Negro schoolhouse in the capital of the nation. No public support for such an institution could be obtained in a proslavery atmosphere.

Elsewhere, however, there was always some question about the public support of Negro education, even in the North where it had been provided. Men did not care to be taxed to educate the children of poor whites and Negroes. The first public schools for whites were not well provided for; and those of the Negroes were further neglected. The public was hardly able at that time to provide one efficient system for all. Negroes and their friends fighting for their freedom, then, attacked also caste in the public schools. They did not make much progress in this direction in the Middle States or the West. In Massachusetts, however, thanks to the agitation led by Wendell Phillips and Charles Sumner, caste in the schools was abolished in 1855.

Caste in schools opposed.

CHAPTER XV

THE free Negroes, moreover, exhibited not only the power to take care of themselves in old communities, but blazed the way for progress of the race in new commonwealths and in all but forbidden fields. In the Northwest Territory, where many free Negroes from the South were colonized, their achievements were no less significant. Luke Mulber came to Steubenville, Ohio, in 1802, hired himself out to a carpenter for ten dollars a month during the summer, and went to school in the winter. At the expira- Instances of tion of three years he could do rough carpen- success. try work and had about mastered the fundamentals of education. With this as a foundation he rose to a position of usefulness among the people of his town. Becoming a contractor, he hired four journeymen and did such credit- able work that he was often called upon to do more than he could. David Jenkins, of Columbus, Ohio, was then a wealthy planter, glazier, and paperhanger. One Hill of Chillicothe was its leading tanner and currier.

In Cincinnati, where, as a group, the Negroes had their best opportunity, many made rapid strides forward. By 1840 the Negroes of this city had acquired $228,000 of real estate. One Negro was worth $6,000; another, who had purchased himself and family for $5,000 a Achievements few years prior to 1840, was worth $1,000. in Cincinnati. Another Negro paid $5,000 for himself and family and bought a home worth from $800 to $1,000. A freedman who was a slave until he was twenty-four years of age, then

259

had two lots worth $10,000, paid a tax of $40, and had 320 acres of land in Mercer County, Ohio. His estate altogether was worth about $12,000 or $15,000. A woman who was a slave until she was thirty then had property worth $2,000. She had also come into potential possession of two houses, on which a white lawyer had given her a mortgage to secure the payment of $2,000 borrowed from this

A SECONDARY SCHOOL IN MERCER COUNTY, OHIO, admitting
Negroes in 1842

thrifty woman. Another Negro, who was on the auction block in 1832, had spent $2,600 purchasing himself and family. He had bought two brick houses, valued at $6,000, and 560 acres of land in Mercer County, Ohio, said to be worth $2,500.

Out of this group in Cincinnati came some very useful Negroes. Among them may be mentioned Robert Harlan, the horseman; A. V. Thompson, the tailor; **Statistics.** J. Presley and Thomas Ball, contractors; and Samuel T. Wilcox, the merchant, who was worth $60,000 in 1859. There were among them two other successful Negroes, Henry Boyd and Robert Gordon. Boyd was a Kentucky freedman who helped to overcome the prejudice in Cincinnati against Negro mechanics by inventing and exploiting a corded bed. The demand for this bed was extensive throughout the Ohio and Mississippi valleys. He had a creditable manufacturing business in which he employed twenty-five men.

Robert Gordon, the other Negro there, was doubtless a more interesting character. He was born the slave of a rich yachtsman in Richmond, Virginia. His master placed him in charge of a coal yard. He managed it **A shrewd** so faithfully that his owner gave him all of **business man.** the slack resulting from the handling of the coal. Selling this to local manufacturers, he thereby accumulated thousands of dollars in the course of time. He purchased himself in 1846; and, after inspecting several Negro settlements in the North, went into the coal business in Cincinnati. Having then about $15,000, Gordon made much more progress in this coveted enterprise than his competitors desired. They thereupon reduced the price of coal so as to make it unprofitable for Gordon to continue in the business. He was shrewd enough to fill all of his orders at the white coal yards by making his purchases through mulattoes who could pass for white. Soon there followed a general freezing on the Ohio River, which made it impossible to bring coal to Cincinnati. Gordon then sold out his supply at advanced prices. This so increased his wealth that he was later in a position to invest extensively in United States bonds during the Civil War and afterward in real estate on Walnut Hills in Cincinnati.

This economic progress would have been greater had it not been for race riots in communities in which free Negroes lived. On January 1, 1830, a mob drove eighty Negroes from Portsmouth, Ohio; 1,200 Negroes left Cincinnati for Canada as a result of the riot of 1829, and others lost life and property in the riots of 1836 and 1841.

Riots. The disastrous effects of this unsettled state were further aggravated by the Fugitive Slave Law of 1850. Many fugitives and their relatives residing in the free States moved immediately into Canada after the proclamation of this measure as the law of the land. Within thirty-six hours thereafter forty Negroes left Massachusetts for Canada. The Negro population of Columbia, Pennsylvania, decreased from 943 to 437. A **The fugitive slave law.** Negro settlement at Sandy Lake in the northwestern part of that State was broken up altogether. Every member of a Negro Methodist Church, eighty-two in number, including the pastor, fled from a town in New York to Canada. The Negro churches of Buffalo lost many communicants. One in Rochester lost one hundred and twelve members and its pastor; and another in Detroit, eighty-four. Some Negroes stood their ground and gave battle. Such was the case of the Christiana tragedy in Lancaster County, Pennsylvania, where Edward Gorsuch was killed and his son wounded by free Negroes whom they tried to enslave.

Those Negroes who dared to remain in the free States to defy the slave catchers were not thereafter in a frame of mind to promote their economic welfare, so great was the **Personal freedom a concern.** demand on their time for maintaining their freedom. In fact, the main concern of many leaders among the free Negroes and their sympathizers was aiding fugitives to reach free soil. William Craft, escaping from Macon, Georgia, with his handsome quadroon wife who effected their escape by posing as his owner, caused unusual excitement in the North until this heroic dash for freedom ended with their flight to England. Then followed the arrest of Daniel as a fugitive in Buffalo, where the Federal commissioner remanded him to his claimant. Hamlet was captured by his pursuers in New York City while the arrest of Jerry in Syracuse was stirring the whites and blacks throughout the North. Shadrach, claimed as a slave in Boston, was imprisoned but almost miraculously Seeking fugitives. spirited away to Canada. Thomas Simms, arrested later, however, was returned to slavery. This was done to please those who feared the southern threats of secession if the Fugitive Slave Law was not enforced, and to satisfy Boston business men who did not care to lose their trade with the South. Then for a similar reason came the return of Anthony Burns, a Baptist clergyman, arrested at the instance of Charles F. Suttle of Virginia; but two hundred special policemen had to be sworn in to restrain

ELLEN CRAFT, a fugitive disguised as her master

citizens who considered the law an infringement upon personal liberty. The Dred Scott decision, denying that the Negroes were citizens and making slavery national and freedom sectional, was the climax of these invasions of human rights.

Thousands of fugitives, however, were never apprehended. They were generally well directed through the free States by the agents of the Underground Railroad conducted by Quakers and militant abolitionists. This was not any well-known route controlled by a well organized body. It was rather a number of Christian people scat-

The Underground Railroad. tered throughout the free States but united with their common purpose to promote the escape of fugitives by clandestine methods in defiance of the proslavery laws of the United States. There were near the border important stations which were al-

WILLIAM STILL, an agent of the Underground Railroad

ways furnishing much excitement in the pursuit and capture. These stories have been related by William Still, in charge at Philadelphia, Levi Coffin, the station master at Cincinnati, and William Whipper, the moving spirit at Columbia, Pennsylvania.

Effective work was done in the Northwest Territory. Through this section extended numerous routes from Kentucky and Tennessee to Canada. Josiah Henson and Harriet Tub-

man used these routes in conducting fugitives to freedom. The career of the latter in this hazardous enterprise was

Harriett Tubman. unusually romantic. Born a slave in Maryland but endowed with too much love of freedom not to break the chains which held her, she became in the North the most venturesome worker in the employ of the Underground Railroad. When her co-workers had much fear as to her safety, she dared to go even into the very heart of the South. Once she returned to her old home in Maryland, where she met her master along the road, but easily contrived to prevent him from recognizing her. She did so much to aid the escape of fugitives and to rescue freedmen from slave hunters that the aggrieved owners offered for her a reward of $40,000. For these unusual exploits and her service as a spy during the Civil War she became known as the "Moses" of her people.

After the first excitement caused by the execution of the Fugitive Slave Law, conditions became a little more favorable for the Negroes in the North. Forcing upon the country try a radical proslavery policy which men formerly indifferent as to the issue could not accept, the southern leaders made friends for the Negroes in the North. The effort to impress the North into the service of recapturing fugitive blacks tended to raise up champions of individual liberty. The North had enacted personal liberty laws to counteract this slave-hunting, but these had failed. Sympathetic whites could not then go into the heart of the South to aid the

MYRTILLA MINER

blacks, but in the border States, and especially in cities like Baltimore and Washington, much was done for the improvement of Negroes through the many churches and schools established for their special benefit. Among many other workers promoting this cause was Myrtilla Miner, for years a teacher of girls of color in the District of Columbia and the founder of the first girls' school of methods in Washington.

In spite of all of their difficulties some of the northern

free Negroes attained national prominence.[1]   Among those first to appear after the reaction was Dr. James McCune Smith. He was a distinguished graduate in medicine of the University of Glasgow and for years a practitioner in the **Prominent** city of New York. Dr. Smith was of mixed **Negroes.** breed, of about equal proportions of Caucasian and African blood. In stature he was somewhat thick and

DR. JAMES McCUNE SMITH.

DR. JAMES McCUNE SMITH

corpulent. He had a fine head with a broad and lofty brow, round, full face, firm mouth, and dazzling eyes. As an educated man given to writing, he was easily drawn into the discussion on the race question. His knowledge of history, science, and literature enabled him to treat the question in a scholarly way. He was also an eloquent speaker who always made himself clear and talked to the point.

In the field of writers there stood two other men as the first actual historians produced by the race. These were William C. Nell and William Wells Brown. There was **William C.** then so much talk about the Negroes that **Nell.** men wanted to know more about the achievements of the race. These writers supplied this need. Nell was a native of Boston, a man of medium height, slim, gen-

---

[1] These persons of color are given more honorable mention in Simmons's *Men of Mark,* in William Wells Brown's *The Black Man,* and in his *Rising Son.*

Blazing the Way

FREE NEGROES IN THE CRISIS

CHARLES L. REASON   WILLIAM WHIPPER

PHILLIP A. BELL   CHARLES B. RAY

teel figure, quick step, elastic movements, a thoughtful yet pleasant brow, and thin face. Chaste in his conversation and devoted to literature, he passed as a man of learning with the reputation of being a person of unimpeachable character. Nell wrote a book, entitled *Colored Patriots of the American Revolution,* a volume containing numerous facts of the history of the race. He wrote other books of less importance and collected data which made him the best informed man in this field during his time.

WILLIAM WELLS BROWN

William Wells Brown, the other writer, was born in Lexington, Kentucky, in 1816. His mother was a slave and his father a slaveholder. Serving in St. Louis in an office of Elijah P. Lovejoy before the editor was forced to go to Alton, Brown received his inspiration and start in education. He moved North, where he took an active part in the work of the Underground Railroad. From 1843 to 1849 he served as **William Wells Brown.** a lecturer of the American Antislavery Society. He then visited England and France. There he came into contact with such lovers of freedom as James Houghton, Richard Cobden, Victor Hugo, and M. De Tocqueville, as set forth in his *Three Years in Europe.* Brown then published *Clotelle: or the President's Daughter,* a narrative of slave life in the Southern States. He studied medicine during these years, but never practiced much. He was busily engaged in advancing the cause of freedom. He was a regular contributor to the *London Daily News, The Liberator, Frederick Douglass's Paper,* and *The National Antislavery Standard.* In 1854 Brown published *Sketches of Places and People Abroad.* His claims as an historian, however, are based on *The Black Man,* which appeared in 1863; *The Negro in the Rebellion,* published in 1866; and *The Rising Son,* brought out in 1882. Up to the time of George W. Williams, Brown had done more than any other writer to popularize Negro history.

The Negro also showed a tendency toward independent political action. He was not working through any of the leading political parties at that time, but nevertheless tried to change the attitude toward the Negro by influencing the thought of the nation. The first effort in this direction was by way of the printed page. By the end of the second generation of the nineteenth century there were a considerable number of Negroes quali- **Early Negro press.** fied to read as well as speak intelligently as had been the case of Negro preachers mentioned above. This literature was of a controversial sort, however, criticizing in the main the proslavery group and the American Colonization Society. In this case the Negro writers were trying to embody the sentiment expressed in the various resolutions of meetings of free Negroes held throughout the North to denounce the deportation program of the American Colonization Society. Among the persons thus expressing themselves honorable mention should be given to John B. Russwurm, Charles B. Ray, and Samuel Cornish. These were the pioneers in the development of the Negro press.

After completing his education at Bowdoin College, John B. Russwurm, the first Negro to receive a degree

from a college in the United States, began in 1827 the
publication of *Freedom's Journal.* This was the first

Freedom's   Negro newspaper published in this country.
Journal.   At the same time Russwurm edited another
paper, entitled *The Rights of All.* The publication was a
neatly printed and creditable organ presenting the program
of the Negro in America. Russwurm later joined the colonizationists and went to Liberia where he creditably served
as an educator and a governor of one of the provinces.

In 1837 there appeared another Negro newspaper entitled *The Weekly Advocate,* edited by Samuel E. Cornish
and owned by Phillip A. Bell. The name of this paper
was changed that same year to *The Colored American.*
Like *Freedom's Journal,* its columns were filled with ex-

The Colored   cellently selected and original matter. It
American.   boldly advocated emancipation and the elevation of the Negroes to the status of citizens. In these
efforts the editors had the coöperation of the distinguished physician and scholar, Dr. James McCune Smith.
The papers continued equally as effective under a later
editor, Charles Bennett Ray, then serving as a Presbyterian minister engaged in the Underground Railroad enterprise and the antislavery cause. Years later

Growth of   there came *The Elevator,* ably edited at
the press.   Albany by Stephen Myers; *The National
Watchman,* conducted in similar fashion at Troy, New
York, by William G. Allen and Henry Highland Garnet;
The People's Press, edited by Thomas Hamilton and John
Dias in New York; *The Mystery,* by Martin R. Delany;
The Genius of Freedom, by David Ruggles; *The Ram's
Horn,* by Willis A. Hodges; *The Anglo-African,* by various
editors; and *The North Star,* by Frederick Douglass. The
name of the last mentioned was later changed to *Frederick
Douglass's Paper.* Various other papers of shorter dura-
tion came and went in the battle of words incident to the

Blazing the Way

A Negro Newspaper Edited a Century Ago

antislavery and colonization agitation. Finally came *The Christian Recorder,* established in 1856 by Bishop Jabez Campbell. This is still in existence and boasts of being the oldest Negro newspaper in the United States.

The Negroes, however, began about 1830 to work through a national organization. This developed into an annual national convention. It was the most formidable effort made by the Negroes during that crisis. In reply to the suggestion that the Negroes emigrate under the protection of the American Colonization Society, a few bold thinkers **Negro annual** like Peter Williams, Peter Vogelsang, **conventions.** Thomas L. Jennings and Richard Allen, proposed a convention of the leaders of the Negroes in the United States. A preliminary meeting was held in Philadelphia on the 15th of September, 1830. Delegates from seven States were present. Richard Allen was made president; Dr. Belfast Burton of Philadelphia and Austin Steward of Rochester, vice-presidents; Junius C. Morrell of Philadelphia, secretary, and Robert Cowley of Maryland, assistant secretary. This led to the first actual convention of the people of color. It was held at the Wesleyan Church in Philadelphia from the 6th to the 11th of June, 1831. At this time delegates from only five States were present. As Richard Allen, one of the prime movers, had passed away by this time, the control of the movement seemed to come into the hands of enterprising young men. There were present such rising characters as John Bowers of Philadelphia, Abraham D. Shadd of Delaware, William Duncan of Virginia, William Whipper of Philadelphia, and Thomas L. Jennings of New York. The convention made a favorable impression. It attracted some of the most distinguished men of the time. Among these were Benjamin Lundy, S. S. Jocelyn, Arthur Tappan and William Lloyd Garrison. By resolution the convention took the position that there should be a national meeting of the representatives of the free people of color, that the settlement of the Negroes in Canada be continued, that efforts be made to improve the "dissolute and intemperate condition" of the Negroes "and that the program of the American Colonization Society, in the wanton waste of slaves and property in carrying out its unconstitutional and un-Christianized policy be resisted."

The Negroes tended thereafter to meet in annual convention, often in Philadelphia, but sometimes in other cities of the North. With the exception of a few years, for various reasons which cannot delay us here, these meetings were regularly held from 1830 until the Civil War. They were usually addressed by some of the Concerted most distinguished men of the race and by action. white men in sympathy with the cause. The convention annually sent out an address to the Negroes encouraging them to struggle upward and at the same time so to demean themselves toward their fellow men as to win the public favor. Memorials praying for the abolition of slavery and the improvement of the free people of color were annually sent to the State legislatures and to Congress. Eight States were represented at the meeting in 1832 with as many as thirty representatives. There were fifty-eight delegates present in 1833. About this time the people of New Haven prevented this convention from establishing there a manual labor school for Negroes. In 1834 Henry Sipkins, a leader of prominence, was president. About forty delegates attended. By 1836 the movement had been substantially established by the increase of vital issues of the day like the Prudence Crandall affair in Canterbury, Connecticut; the agitation of the Lane Seminary in Cincinnati; and the expansion of slave territory. The convention, however, seemed to conflict with or to coincide with another for American Moral Reform, led by William Whipper. Associated with him were James Forten, Robert Purvis, Walter Proctor, John P. Burr, Jacob C. White, Joseph Cassey, Reuben Ruby, Samuel E. Cornish, and later John F. Cook. State conventions like those held in Ohio, Massachusetts, Connecticut, New York and Canada claimed also the attention of these advocates of freedom.

ALEXANDER CRUMMELL

There were at this time before the American public a number of other prominent Negroes ministering to other needs wherever necessary. There appeared Ira Aldridge, the successful Shakespearean actor; Edmonia Lewis, the sculptor; Edwin M. Bannister and William H. Simpson, painters of promise; James M. Whitfield, George M. Horton, and Frances E. W. Harper, writers cf popular verse; [2] Charles L. Reason, the educator called in 1849 to the chair of Mathematics and Belles Lettres of New York Central College; and George B. Vashon, a graduate of Oberlin, admitted to the bar in 1847. Vashon, however, devoted himself to education at New York Central College, where he distinguished himself in teaching the classics.

Some of the useful preachers were William P. Quinn, Alexander W. Wayman, Jabez Campbell, Daniel A. Payne, Peter Williams, William Douglas, Sampson White, M. **Prominent** C. Clayton, Alexander Crummell, and Henry **ministers.** Highland Garnet. The two last mentioned were the Negro students because of whom the academy at Canaan, New Hampshire, was unceremoniously closed in 1834 and the building dragged to a swamp. Alexander Crummell, a man of unadulterated blood, attracted unusual

[2] White and Jackson, *Poetry by American Negroes*, 1-26

attention. He happily combined with his commanding appearance and fluent speech a liberal education in the classics and theology obtained at Cambridge University, England. He made an impression by delivering in England in 1848 an address on the life and character of Thomas Clarkson. Crummell emigrated to Africa in 1852, but returned to this country in 1873 to engage in work in Washington.

Henry Highland Garnet was a dynamic force during this critical period. He was educated at the Oneida Institute under Beriah Green. He became a popular Presbyterian preacher and lecturer, but did not come into his own as a leader until he delivered to the Convention of Colored Americans at Buffalo, in 1843, his famous address on the Negro.

HENRY HIGHLAND GARNET

Recognized widely thereafter as a man of influence on the platform, he went to England in 1850 to carry his message. From that point he proceeded to Jamaica to toil as a missionary. He served as a Presbyterian minister in Washington and New York City, and for a few years was the president of Avery College. He died in 1882 while minister to Liberia.

In these ranks unselfishly toiled David Ruggles, J. W. C. Pennington, Samuel R. Ward, and Josiah Henson. Ruggles was a man of African blood, medium size, gentle address and polite language. He resided in the city of New York. There he became an eternal enemy of slaveholders bringing to that city servants, whose escape to freedom Ruggles often effected by means of the Underground Rail-

David Ruggles. road. Deeply interested in moral, social and political progress of the free Negro in the North, Ruggles published for several years *The Mirror of*

J. W. C. PENNINGTON

Liberty, a quarterly magazine advocating the rights of the Negroes. In this work he exhibited unusual wit and logic in hurling blows at his opponents, as is well evidenced by his pamphlet, entitled *David M. Rees, M.D., Used Up.* In this Ruggles exposed the fallacy of the ardent colonizationists who had advocated the expatriation of the Negroes.

J. W. C. Pennington was born a slave in Maryland. He was a man of common size, of unadulterated blood and of strongly marked African features. Slightly inclined to corpulency, he had an athletic frame and a good constitu-

J. W. C. Pennington. tion. He had no opportunities for early education, but after his release from bondage he so applied himself to the study of the languages, history, literature and theology that he became a proficient preacher in the Presbyterian denomination. He served as pastor of a church in Hartford, Connecticut, where he won distinction as a preacher and a lecturer. He then made several trips to Europe to attend Congresses at Paris, Brussels and London. On these occasions he was invited to preach and speak before some of the most refined and aristocratic audiences of Europe. In recognition of his scholarship, the University of Heidelberg conferred upon him the degree of Doctor of Divinity.

Samuel R. Ward, thanks to aid received from Gerrit Smith, obtained a liberal education in the classics and in theology. For several years he acceptably served a white congregation of the Presbyterian denomination at South Butler, New York. He was a black man, standing about six feet in height, distinguished by a strong voice, and energetic gestures. He shared with Frederick Douglass the unusual honor of being one of Samuel R. the most popu- Ward. lar orators of his day. He directed his appeals to the understanding rather than to the imagination; but, says a contemporary, "So forcibly did they take possession of it that the heart yielded." Ideas formed the basis of his method. His greater strength lay in knowing that words and ideas are

SAMUEL R. WARD

not inseparable. He never endeavored to be ornamental, although he was not inelegant. He was concise without being abrupt, clear and forcible without using extraordinary stress. Thus equipped for the deliverance of his great message, he preached or lectured in all the churches, halls and schoolhouses in Western and Central New York. His work extended to other parts of the North and to Jamaica and England.

Josiah Henson had neither the intellect nor the natural gifts of some of these men, but served as an example of **Josiah** the capability of the Negro. His experiences in **Henson.** slavery were so strange and peculiarly romantic that on hearing his story Mrs. Harriet Beecher Stowe recon-

HARRIET BEECHER STOWE

structed and embellished it so as to produce the famous narrative known as *Uncle Tom's Cabin.* That he was the original Uncle Tom, however, has been disputed. Josiah Henson settled in Canada and then rendered service in promoting the escape of 118 Kentucky slaves by means of the Underground Railroad through Ohio and Indiana. He thereafter devoted himself to preaching and education among his people. Serving with him was Hiram Wilson, one of the founders of the British-American Manual Labor Institute. Henson engaged also in business in Canada, lectured throughout the North in behalf of the emancipation of the slaves, and finally visited England, where he was received by some of the leading men of that country and by Queen Victoria.

CHAPTER XVI

COLONIZATION

IN the proportion that slavery became an exploitation effort merely for the enrichment of the whites, the free Negroes who lived in the South became more and more undesirable in the eyes of the planters.[1] Debased to a lower status, the free Negroes naturally thought of making an effort to extricate **The cause.** themselves from these circumstances. They could not forget their former state when slavery was of a patriarchal order. During the first two or three decades of the nineteenth century, therefore, many Negroes gradually found their way to the North. They were first aided in the migration by masters philanthropically inclined, and especially by the Quakers. Seeing that their manumitted slaves had little chance for elevation in the midst of a slave society, some Quakers sold out their holdings in the South and moved to the Northwest Territory to establish them as freemen. On this free soil the Negroes soon faced other all but insurmountable obstacles. Then came with more force the thought of settlement in Africa.

From the earliest times there had been some interest in

[1] The story of colonization is given in documentary form in *The African Repository*, the official organ of the American Colonization Society. The attack on colonization is presented in William Jay's *An Inquiry Into the Character and Tendency of the American Colonization Society*. See also J. H. B. Latrobe's *Liberia: Its Origin, Rise, Progress and Results;* John H. T. McPherson's *History of Liberia;* Frederick Starr's *Liberia; Description, History, Problems;* C. G. Woodson's *Century of Negro Migration,* Chapter IV; and *The Journal of Negro History,* Vol. I, 276-301, 318-338; II, 209-228; V, 437-447; VIII, 153-229.

Africa. It had been thought that the slave trade having its roots among the Africans themselves could be thoroughly exterminated only by thoroughly Christianizing the Africans. With this in view, the Rev. Samuel Hopkins **Early interest** of Newport, Rhode Island, proposed to Ezra **in Africa.** Stiles, later president of Yale, the sending of well-educated Negroes to Africa. Stiles seemed to think that an actual colony should be founded. Later we hear of two Negroes sailing as missionaries to Africa in 1774. The idea seems to be that of establishing a mission. Nothing definite followed because of the revolutionary upheaval which severed the economic and political connections between this country and Europe. But the idea remained in the mind of Hopkins. The idea sprang up, too, in the various antislavery societies which followed after the American Revolution. There was not at that time any clear-cut distinction between the colonizationists and the emancipationists.

From the very beginning of the antislavery movement there was an effort to provide for restoring the Africans to their native land. Such a scheme was developed by Quakers under the inspiration of George Keith as early as 1713 and was forever thereafter kept before the people throughout America. In the beginning this idea was that of those persons sympathizing with the Negroes and desiring to ameliorate their condition by emancipation. Such persons, however, were unable to think of incorporating them into their own society to live with the whites on a plane of equality.

The scheme was further advanced by Fothergill and Granville Sharp, and was given a new meaning by Anthony Benezet. Having much confidence in the intellectual **Promoters of** power of the Negroes, he felt that they might **colonization.** be colonized nearer to the white people. His proposal was that they should be settled on the western lands, which were ceded to the Congress of the Confederation. In this he was supported by a number of noted men of his time, chief among whom were Thomas Brannagan and Thomas Jefferson. During the Revolution, however, the manumissions of Negroes had led to the emancipation of a sufficiently large group of intelligent ones to justify the expectation that their liberation was not an experiment, should they be prepared by education and religious instruction. The number of Negroes receiving their freedom during this time did not render necessary an urgent agitation for colonization abroad.

At this time, moreover, opponents of the slave trade, like William Wilberforce, Thomas Clarkson, and Granville Sharp in England were actually promoting the settlement of Negroes in Sierra Leone on the west coast of Africa. The population of this colony was being increased by certain Negroes carried from the West Indies and from Canada. David George, a pioneer Baptist preacher in Georgia, went by way of one of the West India Islands and Nova Scotia to Sierra Leone.

In the proportion as the Negroes showed evidence of plotting insurrections in protest against the ever-increasing encroachment of slavery the idea of colonization became more pronounced in the minds of the slaveholding class. It grew in the minds of free Negroes, more- **The coloniza-** over, in the proportion as they were forced **tion idea.** by law to leave the South for centers in the North. There was extensive correspondence on deportation between the Governor of Virginia and the President of the United States immediately after Gabriel Prosser's insurrection there in 1800. The governor was authorized by the legislature to take up the question of colonizing "persons obnoxious to the laws, or dangerous to the peace of society." Although the President of the United States could find no solution of the problem he addressed to Rufus King, then United States Ambassador to the Court of St. James, a communication suggesting asylum for such Negroes in Sierra Leone. Inasmuch as the infelicitous condition of Sierra Leone did not justify the importation of American Negroes, some of whom had already proved troublesome to that colony, the problem had to be otherwise solved. In 1805 the General Assembly of Virginia embodied another proposal in a resolution to the United States government praying that free persons of color and others emancipated thereafter be settled upon some portion of the Louisiana territory. But, when in the westward movement of population thousands of whites rushed into the Southwest, the idea of settling freedmen in such territory soon vanished from the American mind.

The acuteness of the Negro problem, however, revived speculation in other experiments for its speedy solution. Deportation seemed then more feasible than ever. Another stage in the transplantation of the free Negroes therefore was soon reached. Because of their being apparently a menace to slavery free Negroes were driven out of the South by legislation and public opinion either immediately or within a specified time. This forced into the North such a large number of free Negroes that there arose a strong protest from various communities. Some of them agitated prohibiting the immigration of Negroes into their commonwealths. Negroes were then coming into the North in larger numbers than could be easily absorbed; and coming, too, at the time when thousands of foreigners were immigrating into this country, they caused an intense race prejudice to develop against their group. From these two forces—that is, the effort to drive the Negroes from the South and the attempt to turn them away from the North —came a great impulse to the movement to colonize Negroes abroad. The condition of the free Negroes was such that it would seem that they should have been willing to go. They were proscribed by employers who preferred whites.

They were denied consideration in the courts when they appealed to them because of imposition by ill-designing persons. They were subject to the attacks of mobs spurred on to action by almost any petty offense committed by one of the free population of color.

The desire for the colonization of the Negroes abroad, therefore, became even more widespread. Foreigners then crowding the free blacks out of the industries in the North hoped to remove them from the field of competition. Many slaveholders believed that the **Projects abroad.** then ever-increasing important institution of slavery could be maintained only by removing from this country the most striking argument for its abolition, the free Negro. Colonization, therefore, received a new impetus. The movement was no longer a means of uplift for the Negro but rather a method of getting rid of an undesirable class that slavery might be thoroughly engrafted upon the country.

Up to this time, however, there had not been any unifying influence to give the movement the support adequate to its success. The various advocates of the deportation of the Negroes had done little more than to **No concerted action.** express their views. A few had set forth some very elaborate plans as to how the machinery for the transportation of the Negroes abroad could be easily worked out. Replying, in 1811, to Ann Mifflin, desiring an opinion on the matter of African colonization, Thomas Jefferson said that he considered it the most desirable measure which could be adopted for the gradual drawing off of the black population. "Nothing," thought he, "is more to be wished than that the United States should thus undertake to make such an establishment on the coast of Africa." Unwilling, however, to content himself with this mere discussion, Paul Cuffe, a New England Negro known to the high seas, transported and established thirty-eight Negroes on the west coast of Africa in 1815. This was the first actual effort at colonization by Americans, and it served as an unusual stimulus to the movement. Cuffe recommended, however, that the region around the Cape of Good Hope he selected for colonization.[2]

Paul Cuffe.

PAUL CUFFE, the first actual colonizer

The colonization sentiment thereafter continued to grow. In the mountains of Tennessee and Kentucky, where the infiltration of slaves had made it impracticable for those emancipators in the mountains to continue to attack the institution, there developed a number of flourishing colonization societies which stimulated the movement. The Union Humane Society, an organization founded by Benjamin Lundy of Tennessee, had for one of its purposes the removal of Negroes beyond the pale of the white man. The same sentiment was expressed in Kentucky in its colonization society in 1812 and 1815. This body requested of Congress that some territory be "laid off as an asylum for all those Negroes and mulattoes who have been and who may thereafter be emancipated within the United States, and that such donations, allowances, encouragements, and assistance be afforded them as may be necessary for carrying them thither and settling them therein, and that they be under such regulations and government in all respects as your wisdom shall direct." The Virginia Assembly had taken up with the President of the United States, in 1800,

In the West.

the question of colonizing emancipated slaves and free Negroes. Encouraged by Charles Fenton Mercer, a slave-holder of colonization tendencies, the body passed a resolution in 1816 asking the American Government to find a place of asylum on the Northern Pacific coast on which to settle free Negroes and those afterwards emancipated in Virginia.

That very day a number of persons who for years had been thinking along this line met in Washington to effect a permanent organization. Among those present who had fostered the cause of colonization was Samuel J. Mills. While a student at Williams College he had become interested in this movement and, associating with others, had formed a missionary society to this end. Coming from Andover to Princeton to continue his preparation for the ministry, he became so interested in the work that he established at Parsippany a school to prepare Negroes for African colonization. Mills had likewise stirred up Robert Finley, a Presbyterian pastor, who **Organization.** had served as president of the University of Georgia and had been in touch with Paul Cuffe. Finley had called at Princeton the first colonization meeting. At the larger meeting held in Washington were Hezekiah Niles, the editor of the famous *Niles Register;* Elijah J. Mills, a congressman of Massachusetts; and Elisha B. Caldwell, clerk of the United States Supreme Court. Among others who attended this meeting in Washington were Henry Clay, the compromiser; Francis Scott Key, the author of the "Star Spangled Banner"; John Randolph, a member of the United States Senate from Virginia; Judge Bushrod Washington, a brother of George Washington; and Charles March, a congressman from Vermont. The first general conference of the colonizationists held in the home of Elisha B. Caldwell was devoted largely to prayer for the success of the enterprise. An address was delivered by

Henry Clay, who discussed the delicacy of the question and explained the purpose of the meeting and the condition on which he had attended. The principal address, however, was delivered by Elisha B. Caldwell. Various views were expressed indicating that although the members from the North had in mind the interests of the free Negroes, those from the South were primarily concerned with getting rid of this element to fortify slavery.

LOTT CARY

Bushrod Washington was chosen president, and the machinery was constructed for the extension of the work of the Society into all States. In the course of time, therefore, we hear of several States having colonization societies, and in some of them they were organized in ordinary towns. The purposes of these organizations varied according to the personnel of the management and the section of the country in which the society was founded. The national organization established *The African Repository,* the organ of the Society and in that way made its declaration of its purpose to the whole world. Masters were not necessarily urged to free their slaves, but each community was called upon to take steps to provide for the transplantation to Africa of all slaves who might be liberated at the will of the masters concerned or purchased for this purpose.

Plans to extend colonization.

The Negroes were not to be consulted in the matter. Their destiny in this case was to be in the hands of their rulers who did not consider the opinions of Negroes themselves as worthy of any special attention in launching the movement to deport them to the land of their ancestors. Doubtless for this reason Paul Cuffe, who was the first successful African colonizationist, apparently grew cold toward the proposal near the end of his career.

It was finally decided to expedite colonization in Africa. The United States Government was approached, and the matter received the attention of President Monroe, who submitted it to Congress. Upon his recommendation it was agreed to purchase in Africa certain territory lying near the Senegal River on the western coast. In making this purchase accordingly the country was designated as Liberia because it was to be the land of freedom. Its capital was called Monrovia in honor of James Monroe, the president of the United States under whom it was founded. The territory finally brought under control was an area of about 43,000 square miles between Sierra Leone and the French Ivory coast. The territory is cut into four unequal sections by the Cavalla, the St. John, St. Paul and Mano rivers. The natives there were of the Mandingo, the Vai, the Kpwessi, the Kru, the Grebo, the Bassa, the Buzi, and the Mano tribes.

The problem then was to produce in the United States a number of intelligent Negroes who might constitute a nucleus around which a government could be established in Liberia. As the colonizationists had learned from experience that it was necessary to begin with the youth, better institutions of learning for Negroes were established for this purpose. Occasionally one would hear of a southern

Preparation of colonizationists.

planter who freed his Negroes and sent them to eastern schools to undergo such education as would prepare them for higher life in their new home in Africa. Here we see that the blacks were encouraged to develop the power to work out their own salvation. It gave an impetus to the movement for more thorough education of the Negroes at the very time when the South was trying to restrict them in such opportunities. Those Negroes to be sent out were to be trained in the manual arts, science, and literature, and in the higher professions. The Society, however, soon found itself in a dilemma of telling the people of this country that, because the free Negroes were a depraved class they could not be elevated in this country, while at the same time encouraging these Negroes and their friends to promote the education of the few to be deported that they might have that same

JOHN B. RUSSWURM.

JOHN B. RUSSWURM, first Negro to receive a degree from an American college

mental development which the whites in this country considered necessary for citizenship.

The colonizationists soon found themselves facing other difficulties. The very people for whom Liberia was established arrayed themselves against it.[3] It was in vain that some contended that it was a philanthropic enterprise,

[3] L. R. Mehlinger, *The Attitude of the Free Negro Toward African Colonization* in *The Journal of Negro History*, Vol. 1, pp. 276-301.

since the meaning of colonization varied, on the one hand, according to the use the slaveholding class hoped to make of it and, on the other hand, according to the **Difficulties of** intensity of the attacks directed against it. **colonization.** The abolitionists and the free people of color opposed the Society because of the acquiescent attitude of colonizationists toward the persecution of the free blacks both in the North and the South.

The inconsistency of the position of colonization was logically exposed by William Lloyd Garrison in his *Thoughts on African Colonization.* He showed how utterly impossible it was to deport such a large number of persons. In this way Garrison anticipated Frederick Douglass, who summarized the situation, saying that "individuals emigrate but nations never." Garrison pointed out that there was no more reason for thinking of the Negroes as being natives of Africa and therefore deserving deportation to that continent than of thinking of the whites as being natives of Great Britain. He could see no reason, moreover, for persecuting the free Negroes to the extent of making it so intolerable for them that they would have to emigrate. He branded as a falsehood a statement that the Negro population constituted a dangerous element. He further charged with infidelity those who argued that the racial situation could never be improved in this country because of the inefficacy of Christianity in converting white men to the principles of brotherhood. He said that the Colonization Society was founded upon selfishness and that it was antagonistic to instant emancipation. It apologized to slaveholders, it recognized slaves as property, it ultimately aimed to drive out the blacks from this country, it slandered the character of free Negroes, it declared the elevation of the black people impossible in America while claiming it was possible in Africa, and it tended finally to misinform and dupe the whole nation into a scheme worked out in the interest of slaveholding.[4]

Almost before the colonization societies could be organized, therefore, the free people of color of Richmond, Virginia, thought it advisable to denounce the movement. They said that if they had to be colonized they preferred to be settled "in the remotest corner of the land of their nativity." They passed a resolution requesting Congress to grant them a portion of territory on the Missouri River. About the same time nearly three thousand free Negroes of Philadelphia took even higher ground. They claimed this country as their native land because their ancestors were the first successful **The protests** cultivators of its soil. They felt themselves **of Negroes.** entitled to participation in the blessing of the soil which their blood and sweat had moistened. Moreover, they were determined never to separate themselves from the slave population of this country as they were brothers by "ties of consanguinity, of suffering and of wrongs." In 1831 a Baltimore meeting of free Negroes denounced the American Colonization Society as being founded more upon selfish policy than in the true principles of beneficence and, therefore, as far as it regards the life-giving principles of its operations, it was not entitled to their confidence and should be viewed by them "with that caution and distrust which happiness demanded."

The free people of color in Boston inquired of those desiring to send them to Africa because they were natives of that land: "How can a man be born in two countries at **The feeling** the same time?" Referring also to the pro-**in Boston.** posal to stop the slave trade by the establishment of a colony on the western coast of that continent, they said: "We might as well believe that a watchman in the city of Boston would prevent thievery in New York;

[4] Garrison, *Thoughts on African Colonization.*

or that the customhouse there would prevent goods from being smuggled into any port in the United States." The Negroes of New York declared about the same time that the colonizationists were men of mistaken views, that their offer to colonize the oppressed free people was unjust, and illiberal, and tended to excite prejudice in the community. The free Negroes of Hartford, Connecticut, referred to the absurd idea of sending a nation of ignorant men to teach a nation of ignorant men. They asked, moreover, "Why should we leave this land so dearly bought by the blood, groans and tears of our fathers? This is our home; here let us live and here let us die."

ROBERT PURVIS

Some of the most distinguished men were effectively using the rostrum and press to impede the progress of the American Colonization Society. The best example of concerted action against the colonization movement, however, came from the annual convention of the free colored people, held first in Philadelphia in 1830 and afterward in that and other cities annually until the Civil War. The moving spirit of this enterprise was James Forten, **Support of distinguished men.** ably assisted by Robert Ray, James Cassey, Robert Purvis and James McCrummell. They early took the ground that they were unable to arrive at any other conclusion than that the doctrines which the Society inculcated were "suitable to those who hold religion in direct violation of the golden rule, and that the inevitable tendency of this doctrine was to strengthen the cruel prejudice of their enemies and retard their advancement in morals, literature and science—in short, to extinguish the last glimmer of hope and throw an impenetrable gloom over their former and more reasonable prospects.''

This feeling of antagonism of the free people of color manifested itself also in New York in 1848. W. S. Ball, **An incident** who had been sent to Liberia by the free **in New York.** people of Illinois, undertook to report there to a colonization meeting as to the lay of the land. In expressing himself as to the attractions and opportunities of that country he was interrupted by one Morrell. He approached the platform and addressed the meeting, saying that the question as to colonization and the Liberia humbug had been settled long ago. The audience was then disturbed with hisses and jeers, and finally with yells for a fight, until the room was thrown into pandemonium and the meeting broken up in disorder.

In 1852 there was held in Baltimore a pro-colonization meeting. After some sharp discussion, it was decided to examine the different localities for emigration, but preferably that of Liberia. Liberia became the bone of contention. Very few Negroes were willing to go **Colonization in** tion. Very few Negroes were willing to go **Baltimore.** to that country, and a majority of the Negroes in Baltimore were opposed to colonization of any sort. As these delegates had come from various parts of Maryland and did not voice the sentiment of the people of Baltimore, they were hissed and jeered from an outside meeting. This developed almost into a mob, intimidating the delegates to the extent that they were not permitted to exercise that freedom of thought which the exigencies of the hour required. Another meeting of the Baltimore citizens denounced this assembly as unrepresentative and proceeded to proclaim the determination of the Baltimore people to oppose the policy of permanently attaching the free people of color to this country.

Colonization seemed destined, then, to have rough sailing.

Although the movement had the coöperation of an unusually large number of influential men both in the South and in the North, it failed to carry out the desired object of taking the free Negroes over to Africa. From 1820 to 1833 only 2,885 Negroes were sent out by the Society. More than 2,700 of this number were taken from the slave States and about two-thirds of these slaves manumitted on the condition of their emigrating. Of the 7,836 sent out of the United States by 1852, 2,720 were born free, 204 purchased their freedom, 3,868 were emancipated in view of removing them to Liberia, and 1,044 were liberated Africans sent out by the United States Government.

The failure of African colonization.

CHAPTER XVII

SCHEMES FOR DEPORTATION

In the midst of the oppression of the free Negroes and the necessity for finding an immediate remedy, however, other schemes for colonization now came forward. There was proposed a colony of the Negroes in Texas, in 1833, prior to the time when the State became overrun with **Other schemes.** slaveholders. The opportunities of this country seemed to indicate that there was some reason for considering this plan feasible. But others thought that it would never suit Negroes on account of the fugitives there from Mexico and the presence of a superior race of people there already speaking a different language and having a different religion. There was some talk, too, of the transplanting of a number of Negroes to British Guiana. It was thought that because Santo Domingo had become an independent republic, it would prove to be an asylum for the free people of color in this country, as Jefferson a number of years before had predicted.[1]

This tendency towards the West Indies was stimulated by the dearth of labor there resulting from the emancipation of the slaves. Thanks to the untiring efforts of Wilberforce and his co-workers, this was effected by 1833. The West Indies offered inducements to Negroes immigrating into these islands. Among these was Trinidad, which received a number of Negroes from Baltimore, Annapolis, and Philadelphia. Jamaica, with its many opportunities, placed her claims for these refugees and sent her agents

[1] C. G. Woodson, *A Century of Negro Migration*, pp. 67-80.

into this country to proclaim the beauties of her civilization and the opportunities of the land. So favorable did this scheme become that the colonizationists had to redouble their efforts to prevent an unusually **The danger of** large number of Negroes from going to Eng- **the exodus.** lish-speaking colonies. Living on a plane of equality with

the whites and enjoying the rights of citizens, they as freemen, would become too powerful factors in the hands of the British, should they again undertake to wage war against the United States.

The most successful colonization, however, was a sort of transplantation proposed earlier by Anthony Benezet, Thomas Brannagan and Thomas Jefferson. This was the migration to **Migration** distant lands **to Canada.** in America, especially to

WILLIAM WILBERFORCE, the anti-slavery leader in England

British America.[2] Canada had served as an asylum for slaves who had made their escape into that country, but during the period of the cruel oppression of their class free Negroes began to migrate there in large numbers. They secured land for farms, built homes, constructed churches, established schools and, in fact, covered a considerable portion of southern Ontario. In spite of the cold climate, the abolitionists and the free Negroes themselves usually considered it more practicable for Negroes to

[2] W. H. Siebert, *The Underground Railroad from Slavery to Freedom.*

settle there than to avail themselves of the opportunities offered by the American Colonization Society in Africa.

Nearer to the Civil War there were established in Canada a number of Negro communities and towns. They exhibited the evidences of civilization found in other parts. **Progress in** The Negroes themselves gave proof of what **Canada.** might be done, should their race as a whole be given the opportunity to make of itself what it would. They had learned to cultivate the soil, market their products, and engage in local manufactures. They were not only coming into contact with the commercial centers of the Northern United States but had begun to export and import from abroad. Out of these colonies in Canada emerged a number of intelligent Negroes who thereafter became factors in the progress of their race.

In the course of time, however, when the conditions of the free Negroes in Canada did not seem so inviting, a larger number of them began to think that colonization **Recrudes-** elsewhere was a necessity, although few of **cence of** them believed that they should go to Africa. **colonization.** To deal with this question there was organized in 1853 a national council of the leading Negroes, which attracted representatives from as many as twelve State conventions. So divided on this question had the Negroes become, however, that only those persons who believed in colonization somewhere were asked to attend. Among the persons thus interested were William Webb and Martin R. Delany, of Pittsburgh; Doctor J. Gould Bias and Franklin Turner, of Philadelphia; Augustus R. Green, of Allegheny, Pennsylvania; James M. Whitfield, of New York; William Lambert, of Michigan; Henry Bibb and James Theodore Holly, of Canada; and Henry M. Collins, of California.[3] Frederick Douglass, an uncompromising enemy to colonization, criticized this step as uncalled for, unwise, unfortu-

[3] *The Journal of Negro History*, V, 437-447.

nate, and premature. "A convention to consider the subject of emigration," said he, "when every delegate must declare himself in favor of it beforehand as a condition of taking his seat, is like the handle of the jug, all on one side." James M. Whitfield, the writer of verse, came to the defense of his co-workers, and kept up a literary duel with Douglass for a number of weeks.

MARTIN R. DELANEY, an author, physician, and leader before the Civil War

The convention was held accordingly. In it there appeared three parties, one led by Martin R. Delany, who desired to go to the Niger Valley in Africa, another by James M. Whitfield, whose interests seemed to be in Central America, **Expeditions sent out.** and a third by Theodore Holly, who showed a preference for Haiti. The leaders of the respective parties were commissioned to go to these various countries to do what they could in carrying out their schemes. Holly went to Haiti and took up with the Minister of the Interior the question of admitting Negroes from the United States.

Before any results from these deliberations could be obtained there appeared evidence of considerable interest in emigration. This was especially true of Illinois and Indiana, from which commissioners **Interest in the West.** had been sent out to spy the land. This is evidenced, too, by the sentiment expressed by delegates attending the

Cleveland Convention in 1854. The next colonization convention was held at Chatham, Canada West, in 1856. One of the important features of this meeting was the hearing of the report of Holly, who had gone to Haiti the previous year. From this same meeting Martin R. Delany proceeded on his mission to the Niger Valley in Africa. There he concluded a treaty with eight African kings, offering inducements to Negroes to emigrate. In the meantime, James Redpath had gone to Haiti and accomplished some things that Holly failed to achieve. He was appointed Haitian Commissioner of Emigration in the United States, with Holly as his co-worker. They succeeded in sending to Haiti as many as two thousand emigrants in the first expedition in 1861; but, owing to their unpreparedness and the unfavorable climate, not more than one-third of them remained.

Looking backward at the movement, the laymen will doubtless consider the colonization effort a failure. The schemes for the settlement of Negroes in Central and South America went awry. The settlements in Canada were apparently successful, but several of them were all but broken up immediately after the Civil War when so many of the Negroes returned to the United States to enjoy the benefits of Reconstruction. The bearing of the undertaking on the other efforts for the uplift of the Negro, however, makes it one of historical importance. Furthermore, there **Liberia.** was one apparently successful effort at colonization. This was Liberia. It has endured as a republic down to the present time. As such its history becomes a unit in itself and should not long detain us here in our story.

Some few facts in the development of this country, however, require brief mention. The republic, as pointed out above, was the outgrowth of the American Colonization Society established in Washington, D. C., in 1816. In

Schemes for Deportation

THE MESURADO LAGOON

November of the following year that body sent out Samuel J. Mills and Ebenezer Burgess to select a place for settlement. On their way they enjoyed in England the hospitality of the African Institution which was already promoting the colony of Sierra Leone. They were thereby introduced to certain persons in that colony that with their coöperation the task of the American commissioners might be facilitated. They selected Sherbro Island. On this voyage Mills died and Burgess returned with a favorable report. Nothing definite was done thereafter until 1819, when the United States government in the effort to prevent the smuggling and the sale of recaptured Africans by slave traders appropriated $100,000. Samuel Bacon, of the American Colonization Society, and John Bankson were then sent to take eighty-eight emigrants to Sherbro Island. Among them were Daniel Coker, who first elected bishop of the A. M. E. Church, later resigned in favor of Richard Allen. Disease and disaster followed in this case, resulting in the death of most of the colonists and in that of the agents themselves. The few persons who remained repaired to Sierra Leone. In 1821 there went out twenty-one other immigrants under the direction of J. B. Winn and Ephraim Bacon. After tarrying some time at Fourah Bay they decided upon a more hospitable site at Cape Montserado. On account of the bad weather and the fever which they could not easily withstand so many of these colonists died that this expedition also proved a failure. They had succeeded, however, in reaching the present site of the capital of the republic.

That same year in November there came Eli Ayers as agent of the Society and Captain Robert F. Stockton, of the United States Navy. They were sent out to explore the land. They examined the coast as far as Mesurado Bay and approached some of the native chiefs for a grant of land. They succeeded in purchasing the mouth of the

Mesurado River and Cape Montserado and some portion of the back country. Most of the colonists were then removed from Fourah Bay, while some refused to go. **Early** They were eventually taken over by the Eng- **struggles.** lish. The pioneers then had some trouble with certain English seamen and with the natives who desired to abrogate their treaty granting the land for settlement. Fortunately there appeared at the opportune moment Boatswain, a chief from the interior, who denounced the treachery of these natives and promised the colonists that they would be protected, and they were. The colony then made a permanent settlement at Cape Montserado. This was the actual beginning of the Liberian republic.

The troubles of the colony had just begun. The natives were hoping still to get back the territory which they had ceded, and the agent in charge became discouraged and left. Fortunately, again another Negro appeared upon the scene. This was Elijah Johnson, one of the colonists. He had come to Africa to stay and intended to fight it out on that soil. In this position he was warmly **Trouble** supported by Lott Cary, a Negro Baptist **multiplied.** preacher from Virginia, who arrived there about this time. Unfortunately Cary was killed in an explosion while preparing for the defense against the natives in 1828. He rendered the colony valuable service.

On August 18, 1822, however, there appeared another great leader who contributed much to the establishment of that colony. This man was Jehudi Ashmun from Vermont. He arrived with fifty-five immigrants. Although he had no intention of remaining, he decided to do so because of the exigencies of the hour. The rainy season and fever again did its fatal work and a large number of the colonists succumbed. Among these was the wife of Ashmun. He prepared, however, for the defense of the colony and met an attack of the natives with diminished forces.

Bringing a field piece into action, however, he succeeded in driving the enemies back. With help from a British vessel passing by, the colonists succeeded in withstanding a second attack, but it was only by diplomacy that they prevented the English from taking the colony in the name of the king of Great Britain. Further relief came from an American vessel arriving in 1822. Additional supplies arrived from the United States the following year. In 1823 Dr. Eli Ayers returned and took up the apportionment of land and the reorganization of the colony. Ashmun had fallen into discredit because of his efficient way of doing things, and wished to withdraw from the colony. But the colonists rallied to his support the following year, and things moved on more prosperously.

The coming of R. R. Gurley in 1824 to look into the conditions marked another epoch in the history of the colony. To restore order there was established a constitution for the government of these settlements. There was to be an agent of the American Colonization Society in charge. Under him would serve all officers annually elected. There would be also a vice-agent, two councilors and two justices. The peace would be maintained by two constables and a defense unit of twelve privates, two corporals and one sergeant. Thereafter things became more encouraging, because the American Colonization Society sent out new immigrants and supplies twice a year after 1824. Fortunately there came a more industrious and intelligent class of colonists.

Organization.

The colony still had troubles. The slave traders disregarded the rights of the colonists. Ashmun had fearlessly attacked the slave traffic and for this reason had become unacceptable to some supporters of the Colonization Society. This trade flourished all around the Liberian settlements. After being worn out with the trials of this unusual undertaking, Ashmun himself retired to America in bad health and died in New Haven soon after arrival. This was a misfortune, for the colony needed Ashmun when much disturbed by the Dey-Gola War of 1832. But in spite of these difficulties the settlements still expanded. The colonization societies of the various States became active and sent out numerous settlers under their special protection. It was deemed necessary therefore to provide for a permanent government. By official request, Prof. Greenleaf, of Harvard, drew up a constitution for the "commonwealth." Under the government set **Organization** forth in this constitution all except one of the **a necessity.** important settlements were gradually brought. These were Montserado, Grand Bassa, and Sinoe. The exception was the colony of Maryland. This was ruled by an independent government first by James Hall, a white man, and later by John B. Russwurm, until 1857. Because of trouble there at that time it was deemed expedient to come under the protection of the general government. The first governor of the combined settlement was a white man, Thomas H. Buchanan. He began his term of office in 1838. Buchanan, however, was the last white man to exercise such authority there.

In 1847 Liberia was forced by encroachments from the French and English to assume the position of independence. The United States Government failed to protect the colony from such encroachments, although it had repeatedly used the land as a dumping ground for "restored African captives" in the crudest **Independence** form, and thereby hampered the early prog- **declared.** ress of the country. A Constitutional Convention therefore was called in 1847. A declaration of independence was promulgated and the proper instrument of government was framed. This was modeled after the Constitution of the United States.

The first person elected president was a Negro who had

emigrated from Virginia to Liberia. This was Joseph Jenkins Roberts. He proved to be a sympathetic, energetic and efficient administrator. He served the country from 1848 to 1855. Under him independent Liberia had an encouraging beginning. The details of the administration of his successors, Stephen Allen Benson, David B. Warner and James S. Payne need not delay us here. England

MONROVIA

recognized the independence of Liberia in 1848, and France in 1852. Other European States did likewise soon thereafter; but, because of the proslavery interests in control of the United States Government, this country did not grant Liberia such recognition until 1862.

As to the actual success of Liberia there can be no doubt. Instead of being evidence of the Negroes' failure in political organization the record of Liberia is evidence to the contrary. No colony which has endured has ever been beset with more difficulties than those which have afflicted Liberia. In the first place, the colony was established by ill-prepared emigrants. It was not a philanthropic experiment to show what the Negro could do. Some few members of the American Colonization Society had this idea, but they tended gradually to become a non-entity in the enterprise. The United States Government instead of endeavoring to make Liberia a member of the family of nations, used it as a dumping ground for recaptured Africans and for the settlement of poverty-stricken free Negroes removed from the Southern States to perpetuate slavery. In spite of all of these untoward circumstances, however, the first century of Liberia compares favorably with the first century of the Virginia colony. This first of the English colonies on the American continent did not penetrate the interior until 1716 when Governor Spottswood conducted his expedition to the West. The Virginia colony lagged behind in social and economic development; it did not believe in general education; and fifty years after its settlement Governor William Berkeley could "thank God that there were no free schools in the province." Liberia stood for education and social uplift and fought the slave trade which Americans diligently fostered. When we make due allowance for the fact that the Virginia colony antedated that of Liberia two centuries, we must think also of the infelicitous African climate, the foreign aggression, and the lack of help from without. Liberia, the land of the African, then, compares favorably with Virginia, the land of the Anglo-Saxon.

CHAPTER XVIII

ABOLITION

BECAUSE of the hard lot of the Negro, the opposition to slavery was fanned into such a flame during the thirties that the movement could no longer be properly designated as antislavery. It was abolition, an effort to effect the immediate emancipation of the slaves, since to hold them in bondage was contrary to the law of God.[1] Colonization was too slow in solving the problem. The most formidable leader of this radical reform was William Lloyd Garrison. He came forward with the argument that slavery was contrary to the natural rights of humanity, had bad effects upon the southern whites, and handicapped the whole Union, not only as an evil but as a sin.[2] Coming at a time when the world was again stirred by the agitation for the rights of man in Europe, this radical movement secured much more attention than it would have otherwise received. Men were then concerned with the better treatment of paupers, convicts, and lunatics. Reformers were directing their attention to special education for dependents and delinquents. Intemperance was becoming a serious problem. The rights of the laboring man were then claiming all but national attention, and women suffragists were taking front rank

Marginal note: William Lloyd Garrison.

[1] William McDonald, *Select Statutes*, 385-437; A. B. Hart, *Slavery and Abolition*, 152-295; his *History Told by Contemporaries*, IV, 24, 42, 72-143; William Jay, *Miscellaneous Writings;* W. P. and F. J. Garrison, *William Lloyd Garrison, passim;* F. L. Olmsted, *Back Country;* F. A. Kemble, *Georgian Plantation, passim;* D. R. Goodloe, *Southern Platform;* H. von Holst, *History of the United States,* III; J. B. McMaster, *History of the United States,* VI, 567-571.

[2] See Appendix for extract from the *Liberator.*

among the reformers. It was helpful to the Garrisonian movement, too, that new fields of opportunities were then opening in the North and West. With the growth of foreign trade, there arose a need for that sort of labor which the unskilled slave could not furnish. Appearing then at this time, Garrison could more easily arouse the people of the whole country as to the inevitable doom of a slaveholding nation.

WM. LLOYD GARRISON

Basing his fight on moral grounds, however, and contending that slavery could not be defended, he evoked the censure of the proslavery people. **Slavery a moral evil.** They became just as radical and fiery in the defense of the institution as he was in attacking it. After having been forced out of Baltimore because of his antislavery utterances he went to Boston and founded the *Liberator*.[3] The result was such a clash of words and a multitude of threats that it seemed likely that the South might secede. This feeling was further intensified by a number of uprisings among Negroes during the first three decades of the nineteenth century, culminating in Nat Turner's insurrection in Virginia in 1831. But intense as this excitement became, Garrison could not be hushed. His very words will give a better idea as to the earnestness of his purpose. He said, "I shall strenuously contend for the immediate enfranchisement of our slave population. I will be as uncompromising as justice on the subject—I am

[3] Almost any work on abolition deals largely with the career of William Lloyd Garrison, but the standard biography of the reformer is Wendell Phillips Garrison and Francis Jackson Garrison's *William Lloyd Garrison,* the story of his life told by his children.

not wrong, I will not equivocate, I will not retreat a single inch and *I will be heard.*"

The *Liberator* at that time, of course, could not have a very wide circulation, but it did find sufficient friends interested in the cause to maintain the publication. Garrison showed that he was by nature a journalist whose opportunity was unexcelled. He always suc-

Garrison as a journalist. ceeded in making his newspaper lively by conducting editorial combats and infuriating his antagonists. His work was made more effective by his impassioned

LEWIS TAPPAN

oratory. "No banderillero," says a writer, "ever more skillfully planted his darts in the flanks of an enraged bull!" Garrison had no mercy on slaveholders, accepted no excuses for their institution, and did not distinguish between those of the patriarchal order and those exploiting the slaves. Intensely interested in his cause, he breathed the very earnestness of his truths in everything that he said. Returning from one of his meetings he remarked: "The whole town has known of freedom. Every tongue is in motion. If an earthquake had occurred it could not have excited more consternation."

To promote the cause effectively national organizations soon seemed a necessity. On October 29, 1833, therefore, there was issued by Arthur Tappan, Joshua Leavitt, and Elizur Wright, officers of the New York Antislavery Society, a call for antislavery representatives to meet in Philadelphia on the fourth of the following December. Sixty delegates appeared and adopted a constitution,[4] together with a declaration of sentiments, the original draft

---

[4] See Appendix for a copy of this constitution.

of which was drawn by William Lloyd Garrison. This organization for some years thereafter served as a clearing house for the expression of abolition sentiment; but because of serious differences arising in the ranks, it had to share the field with an American and Foreign Antislavery Society meeting the requirements of those who could not conform with the methods and procedure of the American Antislavery Society.

WENDELL PHILLIPS

Along with Garrison worked a number of radicals. There stood Wendell Phillips, a well-made, re- **Wendell** markably **Phillips.** graceful person of expressive countenance with a sort of fascination in the soft gaze of his eyes. He attracted attention wherever his beautiful musical voice was raised in behalf of the slave. Had he been interested in some other element than the Negro, he would to-day be known to history as the superior of Pitt, Sheridan, or Burke. Although having bright prospects for a future as a popular public man, he early chose the part of abolition. He could not respect the church which compromised on slavery; he gave up the practice of law because he could not swear to support a constitution legalizing slavery; and he refrained from voting because he could not participate in a proslavery government.

A number of others aligned themselves with these cham-

pions of liberty. There was the brilliant scholar, Edmund
Quincy, not so eloquent as Wendell Phillips, but none

**Other co-
workers.**
the less staunch in his advocacy of freedom.
There appeared also Francis Jackson, one of
the first to stand by Garrison when the mob broke up his
antislavery meeting in 1835. Maria Weston Chapman,
another of this group, contributed much to the support of
abolition by raising funds through the Antislavery Bazaar.
Charles F. Hovey, the abolition merchant, gave large sums
to support the cause. Eliza Lee Follen, a poet, sang of
liberty and freedom. Sydney Howard Gay, the polished
writer, boldly advocated instant emancipation. William
J. Bowditch, a scholarly lawyer, used his talent to promote
freedom. With sketches of intelligent Negroes, Lydia
Maria Child gave the race a hearing in circles formerly
closed. Thomas Garrett kept the same fires burning in
proslavery Delaware.

Prominent in this group was Samuel Joseph May, a
graduate of Harvard College and Divinity School. He
abandoned a promising career in the church to promote
the antislavery cause, although he did find time to fill Unitarian pulpits in Brooklyn, Connecticut; in South Scituate,
Massachusetts; and in Syracuse. He participated in the
meeting in Philadelphia where the American Anti-Slavery
Society was organized. May sympathized with Garrison
and was one of the signers of his "Declaration of Sentiments." This document presented the principles upon
which the right of man to freedom is based and issued a
call to all men to promote emancipation. May served the
Society as an agent in 1834 and 1835. Next he functioned
as the general agent of the Massachusetts Anti-Slavery
Society for eighteen years. He assisted in the formation
of the New England Anti-Slavery Society. In these efforts
he was mobbed five times. He became also the conductor
of the Underground Railroad at Syracuse, New York. May

Abolition

ANTISLAVERY APOSTLES

ABBY KELLY FOSTER
LUCY STONE

STEPHEN S. FOSTER
GEORGE THOMPSON

was one of the few who stood by Prudence Crandall in Canterbury, Connecticut, when by special enactment she was imprisoned because she dared to admit girls of color to her academy. He made his home a place of refuge for fugitive slaves and opened his church to any intelligent lecturer who carried the message of freedom.

To promote this cause a corps of workers were **Antislavery lecturers.** required to serve as lecturers in the field. These had to do the most difficult work of winning the public to the movement. Hissed and jeered by proslavery sympathizers, hurling upon them rotten eggs, sticks and stones, these agents unselfishly performed their task. Some neither asked nor received any compensation; others gave their time and paid their own expenses. Among these

PRUDENCE CRANDALL

lecturers who thus toiled was Abby Kelly Foster, the Joan of Arc of the antislavery movement. She was a slim but **Abby Kelly Foster.** well-proportioned and fine-looking woman of bright eyes, clear voice. She drew such life-like pictures of the black woman in chains that one could not hear her without shedding tears. A logical, forceful speaker, successful with irony or argument and quick at repartee, Mrs. Foster usually convinced her audience or discomfited her opponents. Along with Mrs. Foster went her faithful husband, Stephen S. Foster. He was one of those who did not despise the cause in its day of small things. He labored incessantly to promote the work. But, because of his unusual zeal and honest method of "hewing to the line and the plummet" he became the most unpopular of the antislavery agents. Yet he always told the truth, did not overstate a question, and usually proved his point.

LUNSFORD LANE, a native of North Carolina, who lectured in the North against slavery

There were others scarcely less active. The eloquent Charles C. Burleigh, one of the most successful debaters championing the cause of the slave, would **Less active** have been **lecturers.** almost as effective as Wendell Phillips had he not spoken rather fast. Burleigh rendered the cause much aid as a lecturer and the editor of *The Pennsylvania Freeman.* Lucy Stone, an unprepossessing but pleasant woman of medium stature, round face, sparkling eyes, and with her hair cut short, became with her abundance of enthusiasm one of the most active abolitionists. She moved the people by forceful arguments and pathetic appeals. Susan B. Anthony, later known to greater fame as an advocate of woman suffrage, stood out as an eloquent abolition speaker with few equals. Andrew T. Foss left his pulpit to devote all of his time to abolition. Sallie Hollie put so much Scripture and prayer into her appeals that few refused her a hearing. Oliver Johnson, the ready debater, accomplished writer and eloquent speaker, not only served on the platform but at times edited *The Herald of Freedom, The Antislavery Standard*, and *The Antislavery Bugle*. Henry C. Wright devoted the best years of his life to the cause. The Grimké sisters, daughters of a prominent citizen in Charleston, South Carolina, left the South that, without interruption, they might bear witness against slavery. Charles B. Stebbins, the acute thinker and able speaker, also decidedly aided the movement. Nathaniel P. Rogers, with his penetrating mind, dealt hard blows at slavery through *The Herald of Freedom*. William Goodell and Theodore F. Weld exposed the institution by publishing works on slavery. James Miller McKim, a promoter of the Underground Railroad, was once the moving spirit of the Antislavery Society in Pennsylvania. There he was ably assisted by the untiring and eloquent Mary Grew.

LUCRETIA MOTT

Abolition was put on its feet in Pennsylvania, however, by Lucretia Mott.[5] She was a woman of faultless head, thoughtful countenance, beaming eyes, and full voice. Hesitant in speech at the beginning, she then easily grew

James and Lucretia Mott. eloquent. Assisted by a husband giving his means and time to the work, Lucretia Mott stirred up the people. Abolitionist to the manner born, she endeavored to effect a proscription of the prod-

5 A. D. Hallowell, *James and Lucretia Mott; Life and Letters.*

ucts of slave labor by discouraging the use of clothing and foods produced in the South. She carried with her, to sweeten her tea, sugar produced by free labor rather than run the risk of having to use that produced by slaves. A woman of culture and conversant with the conditions obtaining among the slaves, she attracted the attention of the indifferent observer and impressed upon his mind a new thought of the man far down. In her attack on slavery no abolitionist was more fearless, none more successful in presenting the cause.

Yet eloquent as was the appeal of white men in behalf of the slave, **Charles L. Remond.** the abolitionists soon realized that the Negro pleading his own cause could wield effective blows against slavery. The first Negro to be called to this service was Charles L. Remond. Until the rise of Frederick Douglass he was probably the ablest

CHARLES LENOX REMOND

representative of the Negro race. He was small of stature and of spare build. He was neat and genteel in appearance. He possessed a pleasing voice and early attained rank as an acceptable speaker. A free-born Negro himself, he felt more keenly the prejudice against his class than he did the persecution of the slaves. He confined his speeches largely to the desired change in the attitude of the whites toward the people of color. So proud was he of being a free man of color that he often boasted that he had not a drop of slave blood in his veins. He contributed to newspapers and magazines frequent letters and articles exhibiting clearness, force, and depth. It was said that no other man could put more real meaning in fewer words. Remond, thus equipped for his task, was employed by the Antislavery Society as a lecturer for about thirty years. In 1840 he attended the Convention of the World Antislavery Society in England, and remained abroad two years to lecture in Great Britain and Ireland. He made a very favorable impression.

SOJOURNER TRUTH

Other Negroes also were successful. William Wells Brown thus served the Society from 1843 to 1849, and some years thereafter Lunsford Lane of North Carolina. Sojourner Truth, as a coworker of the abolitionists, seemed to acquire miraculous power. Given to certain "mysterious communings" she could stir audiences with her heavy voice, quaint language and homely illustrations. But another Negro thus employed was more successful. He was not merely a Negro asking for the rights of freemen, but the intelligent, Frederick emancipated slave going through the country Douglass. as the embodiment of what the slave was and what he might become. He was then not only the thing discussed by the abolitionsts, but the union of the lecturer and his subject. Endowed, too, with philosophical insight and broader intellect than most men, he soon developed an effective oratory with which nature had enriched his gifts. This man was Frederick Douglass.[6]

Unlike Remond, Douglass had much originality and unadorned eloquence rather than a fine flow of language. When the country, therefore, had heard Frederick Douglass, Remond became a second-rate man. This soured the spirit of the latter; and he fell a victim to speaking disparagingly of his co-worker. But Remond was not the only anti-slavery orator to pale into insignificance on the approach of the "eloquent fugitive" from slavery in Maryland, for the people preferred to hear Douglass. And well might they desire to see and hear this man. He was tall and well made, with a fully-developed forehead. He was dignified in appearance, polished in his language, and

The success of Douglass.

FREDERICK DOUGLASS

gentlemanly in his manner. A contemporary said: "He is a man of lofty reason, natural and without pretension; always master of himself; brilliant in the art of exposing and abstracting." Another said: "In his very look, his gesture, his whole manner, there is so much of genuine,

[6] See Frederick Douglass' *Narrative of the Life of Frederick Douglass, as an American Slave,* and his *Life and Times of Frederick Douglass from 1817 to 1882.*

earnest eloquence, that you have no time for reflection. Now you are reminded of one rushing down some fearful steep, bidding you follow; now on some delightful stream, still beckoning you onward. In either case, no matter what your prepossessions or oppositions, you for the moment, at least, forget the justness or unjustness of the cause, and obey the summons and loath, *if at all,* you return to your former post.''

CHAPTER XIX

FURTHER PROTEST

For economic reasons instant abolition was gradually gaining ground in the western part of the country. There had always been much antislavery sentiment in the mountains of North Carolina, Tennessee, Kentucky, and Western Virginia. When the intolerable condition of **Abolition in** the Negroes in the South made it impossible **the West.** for the persons in that part of the country to do for the Negroes what they desired, they moved into the Northwest Territory where they could carry out their plans for the uplift of the blacks. Accordingly, there arose a number of antislavery societies in these mountains. Among the persons operating as the nucleus around which this sentiment developed were such men as Benjamin Lundy in Tennessee, James G. Birney in Kentucky, and Daniel R. Goodloe in North Carolina. Such ideas tended to influence the youth, too, as it happened in the case of the students in Maryville College in Tennessee. More than half of them had become antislavery by the year 1841. The same was true of Berea College in Kentucky, which developed from a group of students influenced largely by Cassius M. Clay, the antislavery editor, and John G. **In Kentucky.** Fee,[1] the abolition orator and founder of that institution. This school was established in 1855 to promote the principles of freedom. Its charter began with these words: "God hath made of one blood all nations that dwell upon the face of the earth."

[1] John G. Fee's *Antislavery Manual.*

As this sentiment tended to spread in the proportion that the antislavery leaders of the western slave States were forced to go North, there was made possible a better chance for abolition in centers where it had been considered dangerous. In Lane Theological Seminary in Cincinnati, the ardent discussion of slavery led to a sort of upheaval **Lane** resulting in a division of the students. Theo- **Seminary.** dore F. Weld, one of this group, actually espoused the cause of Garrison and undertook to translate into action his theories of Negro uplift by actually teaching colored children. As Lane Theological Seminary was then attended by a number of southern students, a separation of those who had thus become divided was necessary. When the trustees tried to prevent further discussion of slavery four-fifths of the students withdrew. Fifty-four asserted their right to a freedom of discussion of this important topic, and under leaders like Asa Mahan and John Morgan retired to the Western Reserve where they established Oberlin College.[2]

In that same section of Ohio, however, antislavery societies had already flourished under the leadership of Samuel Crothers, John Rankin, and Elizur Wright, later **The Western** a professor in the Western Reserve College. **Reserve.** These antislavery centers, too, were further strengthened by the coming of James G. Birney[3] from Kentucky, from which he had been driven because of his antislavery utterances. He first established in Cincinnati, Ohio, the *Philanthropist,* a newspaper which wielded great influence in preparing the minds of the people of this country for a fair discussion of slavery. Here his life was

[2] This is narrated in the *First Annual Report of the American Antislavery Society.*

[3] James G. Birney, *The American Churches, the Bulwarks of American Slavery;* and William Birney, *James G. Birney and His Times.*

SOUTHERN ABOLITIONISTS

BENJAMIN LUNDY   DANIEL R. GOODLOE

JAMES G. BIRNEY

JOHN G. FEE   CASSIUS M. CLAY

several times endangered and his press was twice broken up and destroyed.

Another group of abolitionists deserve honorable mention. These were reformers of a milder sort, who could neither tolerate radicalism nor approve the methods of some of the less ardent antislavery group. Among those taking this position was Dr. William Ellery Channing, a Unitarian minister of much fame in Boston and Newport. His appeal was **William E. Channing.** to the intellect rather than to the emotion. In presenting his case he wrote essays on slavery. He made a forceful argument as to the evil of the institution, but suggested some remedy other than instant abolition. Along with Channing may be mentioned scores of writers like **Frederika Bremer, Frances Kemble,** Henry Wadsworth Longfellow, and James Russell Lowell. John G. Whittier wrote "radical" poems.

GERRIT SMITH

There were abolitionists who, in addition to appearing on the platform, otherwise rendered the cause valuable service. Among these were Arthur and Lewis Tappan, successful merchants of New York. For years they had supported the cause of colonization but, seeing that it did not reach the root of the evil, abandoned that movement to promote abolition. More prominent than these was

Gerrit Smith of Peterboro, New York, a son of an ex-slaveholder. At first Gerrit Smith had restricted his efforts at uplifting the Negroes to what could be effected through the colonization society. Becoming more interested in the behalf of the Negroes and also developing in his mind anti-land monopolist tendencies, he devised the scheme of improving their condition by transplanting them from the city to small farms in the country. He, therefore, addressed a letter to Charles B. Ray, Dr. J. McCune Smith and Theodore S. Wright, prominent Negroes of New York City, to secure from them the names of Negroes whom he might thus colonize on **Gerrit Smith.** his lands in certain counties in southeastern New York. This list was accordingly given and the enterprise undertaken; but, because of the infelicity of the soil and the lack of initiative on the part of the Negroes, it failed.

The more intense the abolition agitation grew, however, the more sectional the movement became. Backward as the institution of slavery seemed, the South became more and more attached to it and would not countenance any attack on it. Not only was the old-time abolitionist **The South** in danger there after 1840, but the ordinary **proslavery.** observer who suggested moral suasion held his social position by precarious tenure. Cassius M. Clay was driven out of Lexington, Kentucky, by proslavery citizens who could not tolerate the antislavery sentiments expressed in his *The True American.* Upon receiving some copies of the *Emancipator,* which he loaned to white friends while in Washington, Dr. Reuben Crandall of New York was arrested and imprisoned on the charge of inciting a riot among the slaves. After waiting trial eight months in jail, he was declared not guilty. An English traveling bookseller was whipped and driven out of Petersburg, Virginia, in 1832, because, not knowing the temper of the South, he dared to say at the time of the Nat Turner insurrection excitement that the blacks as men were entitled to their freedom and should be emancipated. Amos Dresser, a student of Lane Seminary and of Oberlin College, was whipped and expelled from the State of Tennessee because, while selling books in that State, he had a copy of the *Emancipator* wrapped around a Bible left in a Nashville hotel.

Abolition in the South, therefore, ceased to be openly agitated. The radicalism of Garrison tended to solidify the South against the struggle for free institutions. His advice to Negroes to educate their children, to build up

Abolition quelled in the South.

their own trades, aid the fugitives, and to qualify as voters, stirred up the South. There it was believed that, if both races were free, one would have to be driven out by the other or exterminated. Southerners caused alarm by the false rumor that the abolitionists advocated the amalgamation of the races. But Jay did not think that white men would have to select black wives, John Rankin disclaimed any such desire for miscegenation, and Channing thought we have no right to resist it and it is not unnatural. Other abolitionists frankly reminded slaveholders that they were largely responsible for the miscegenation which had already taken place.

Southerners were successful, too, in promoting their cause by raising the complaint of the circulation of incendiary publications. These portrayed by pictures, cuts and drawings, the cruelties of slavery to acquaint the bondmen with the awful state to which they were reduced. Because of the crass ignorance in which most Negroes were kept, however, these publications, as a rule, never reached them. With the exception of a few like Samuel Green, a free Negro, in Maryland, who was sent to the Maryland penitentiary for having in his home a copy of *Uncle Tom's Cabin,* there were not many instances of Negroes making use of these publications.

Moderate abolitionists in the South thereafter either abandoned their plan or coöperated with the colonizationists in seeking an opportunity for the national development of the Negro abroad. Radical aboli- **Martyrdom of** tionists either left for the North or re- **abolitionists.** mained in the South to entice Negroes to escape from their masters by way of the Underground Railroad. As this was a rather dangerous risk in the South where such action was heavily penalized, many of these persons almost suffered martyrdom in behalf of the fugitives. Jonathan Walker was branded with a hot iron for aiding the escape of a slave. In 1841 Thompson, Burr and Work, abolitionists from Illinois, were sentenced to serve a term in the Missouri penitentiary for persuading slaves to escape from the town of Palmyra. In 1844 L. W. Paine, a Rhode Island machinist working in Georgia, was thus imprisoned six years for the same offense. In 1846 John L. Brown was condemned to be hanged for aiding fugitives, but the sentence was commuted to a whipping. Daniel Drayton, captain of a vessel upon which he permitted seventy-seven slaves to try to escape from their masters in the District of Columbia, lost his health while he was being almost starved there in confinement in an unsanitary prison cell. Another of these sympathizers, Delia Webster, a young lady from Vermont, teaching in Kentucky to find an opportunity for thus aiding fugitives, was sent to the penitentiary for two years. Calvin N. Fairbank, her accomplice, was sentenced to serve a term of fifteen years in the State prison. When pardoned by Governor John J. Crittenden, he immediately resumed his work in defiance of law and public opinion. In 1852 he was imprisoned the second time for fifteen years. He was not released until 1864, when the sympathetic Acting Governor Richard T. Jacobs, taking advantage of the absence of Governor Bramlette, pardoned Fairbank. Charles T. Torrey, a graduate of Yale and Andover Theological Seminary, went to Annapolis to report a slaveholders' convention. For this he was arrested and required to give bond for his good behavior. Some years later, upon being charged with having assisted a slave in escaping from his master, Torrey was convicted and imprisoned in a Maryland penitentiary, in which he died.

Exactly what the abolitionists accomplished is difficult to estimate. Some are of the opinion that the radicals did the cause of emancipation more harm than good. Few white men of that day felt that the slaves could be instantly emancipated. Most advocates of freedom had thought of gradual methods. The radical reformers who stirred up the whole country with the idea of immediate **Achievements of the abolitionists.** abolition set the conservatives against emancipation. The agitation itself, however, was hopeful. It showed that the country had developed a feeling of nationalism. A man living in Boston had begun to think that to some extent he was responsible for an evil obtaining in South Carolina. It resulted, therefore, in inciting a large number of antislavery people to greater activity and enabled the abolition societies to unify their efforts throughout the North by organizing and stimulating local bodies. All of these helped to make possible the destruction of slavery.

In the beginning the abolitionists had a hard struggle. They were opposed by the German and Irish immigrants who were hostile to friends of Negroes because of their competition with these foreigners in menial service in cities. By this same anti-abolition element Negroes manumitted by John Randolph of Roanoke were driven away from their homes in Mercer County, Ohio. The North, moreover, did

Further Protest

WHITE MARTYRS IN THE CAUSE OF ABOLITION

DANIEL DRAYTON
CALVIN FAIRBANK

L. W. PAINE
CHARLES T. TORREY

not take seriously the agitation for the abolition of slavery in a section closely connected with its financial and manu-

Radical abolition. facturing centers. Others, who had no such interests, moreover, regarded the abolition agitation as a direct blow to the Union. The reformers attacked the provision in the Constitution for the continuance of slavery. Citizens in Southern States, considering these onslaughts as intended to disturb the peace in their commonwealths, declared that it furnished sufficient ground for withdrawal from the Union. In several of the Northern States, therefore, legislation was proposed to penalize as an offense against the peace of the State discussions "calculated to excite insurrection among the slaves." Some undertook to brand the efforts of the abolitionists as acts of sedition. As the abolitionists made good their right of free speech, however, they were not hampered much in the North by such laws.

As it was therefore necessary for the opponents of the abolitionists to express themselves in some other way, they resorted to mob violence. During the years from 1834 to 1836 about twenty-five or thirty efforts were made to break

Anti-abolition riots. up abolition meetings. There was an anti-abolition riot at Clinton Hall in New York in 1833. Then followed a number of riots, culminating in the destruction of the property of the abolitionists in 1834, when the same sort of violence broke out in Utica and Palmyra. When George Thompson, the experienced spokesman of the abolitionists in England, came to this country to further the cause, and had himself advertised to speak in Boston, the so-called friends of the Union organized a mob; but Thompson, having had notice as to what they hoped to do, failed to appear. William Lloyd Garrison, who had the courage to attend, found himself in the midst of a riotous crowd whom the mayor, despite his efforts, could not control. When the mayor made known his inability to control the mob, the crowd ran Garrison down, put a rope around his body and pulled him through the streets of Boston. "The man," said an observer, "walked with head erect, flashing eyes, like a martyr going to the stake, full of faith and manly hope." To save his life, the mayor sent Garrison to the Charles Street jail, where with some difficulty he was rescued from the mob.

In Pennsylvania the cause of abolition had much opposition, despite the healthy antislavery sentiment among the Quakers. The city of Philadelphia was **Disorder in** being rapidly filled up during these years **Pennsylvania.** with German and Irish workers, who were hostile to Negroes. A mob burned Negro homes there in 1820; another tried to drive the Negroes out of the city in 1830; and still another destroyed both lives and property in 1834. It was somewhat difficult thereafter to find a place there for abolition meetings. Negro churches closed their doors to these agitators, not because they could not appreciate the impetus the abolitionists gave the cause of freedom; but, knowing that any building in which an abolition meeting was held might be burned, the Negroes had to exercise precaution. To solve this problem, the abolitionists constructed a building of their own, known as Pennsylvania Hall, but when it was noised abroad that Garrison and other abolitionists had addressed a meeting there, on May 16, 1838, there was formed a mob which broke open the doors, set fire to the building, and prevented the authorities from extinguishing the flames. Pittsburgh had such an outbreak the following year.

In the western part of the United States, where the abolitionists were equally bold, the same sort of riotous condition obtained. In 1836 a mob tried to drive the Negroes out of Cincinnati. Four years later another disorderly group endeavored to do the same thing in Portsmouth, Ohio. In 1836 a mob, long since enraged because of the advocacy of abolition in the *Philanthropist,* edited by James G. Birney, destroyed his office in Cincinnati and tried to take **Riots in** his life. In 1841 there developed a race war which **the West.** resulted in the expulsion of a number of Negroes after their property had been destroyed. In Alton, Illinois, the place in which Elijah P. Lovejoy had sought refuge for his abolition efforts, when he had been forced to leave St.

SENATOR JOHN P. HALE

Louis for criticizing the burning of a Negro at the stake, the same violence broke out. After his press had been twice destroyed, his building was attacked by a mob on November 7, 1837. He returned their fire but, on waiting patiently on the outside for the exit of Lovejoy some time thereafter, the mob shot him dead. The jury appointed to inquire into the guilt of the offenders required only ten minutes to bring in a verdict of not guilty.

Instead of preventing the rise of abolition, as was expected, these efforts rather tended to increase the sentiment in the North against slavery. In some of the State legislatures there began to appear a number of antislavery members, and very soon **Results of** even in Congress. John P. Hale first took a **riots.** stand against slavery in the Senate. In 1838 there came to Congress the downright abolitionist, Joshua R. Giddings of the Western Reserve. William Slade of

Vermont, an antislavery man, was sent to that body in 1840. There appeared, too, Thomas Morris, a United States Senator from Ohio, who rendered the cause much assistance. The abolitionists then had the opportunity to gain national recognition as a body primarily interested in elevating the moral life and atmosphere of the country. But they were far apart in their procedure. Their radical utterances denouncing the Constitution as a proslavery document, while others argued that it was antislavery, did their cause unusual harm.

Salmon P. Chase insisted that the Constitution is an antislavery document, and made the institution a black forgery. Replying to the arguments of the proslavery element that slavery was maintained by the Federal Constitution, some others, although **Radical leaders increased.** not advocates of instant abolition, insisted that a higher law than the Constitution protested against the action of Congress in the premises. According to the law of human nature "no greater crime against human beings can be committed than to make them slaves." While Garrison, in 1835, called God to witness that the abolitionists were not hostile to the Constitution [4] of the United States, in 1843 he declared "that the compact which exists between the North and the South is a covenant with death and an agreement with Hell, involving both parties in atrocious criminality, and should be immediately annulled." There still remained milder abolitionists like William Jay and Channing, who disavowed the extreme theory. The cause of abolition, however, continued to suffer; for it had not only failed to interest a majority of the people in the North but had furnished sufficient radicalism upon which the proslavery spokesmen could stir up the country with threats of disunion and terrorize the gradual emancipationists in the South.

[4] See the appeal of a Southern matron in the Appendix.

CHAPTER XX

SLAVERY AND THE CONSTITUTION

DURING these years important constitutional questions grew out of the encroachment of slavery and its haughty pretension to national precedence. By 1830 the abolitionists had become unusually aggressive and were organizing **The right of** throughout the country to make a bold attack **petition.** on the institution. They were then presenting to the State legislatures and Congress various petitions asking, among other things, for the abolition of slavery in the District of Columbia. These petitions at first were received and then refused favorable consideration. In the course of time they had been more easily disposed of by merely being referred to a committee which permitted them to die a natural death. However, upon the occasion of a petition of John Quincy Adams, long known as the only spokesman in behalf of free speech in Congress, the House voted to refuse such petitioners a hearing. This implied that a reasonable portion of the citizens of the United **John Quincy** States were denied the right of petition guar**Adams.** anteed by the Constitution of the United States.[1] Adams contended that these petitions must be received, heard, and referred to a committee; but when he insisted that there should be a report from the committee

---

[1] John W. Burgess, *Middle Period*, Chs. IV, X, XI, XIII, XVIII, XX; J. B. McMaster, *History of the United States*, VIII, pp. 473-521, 438-512; James Schouler, *History of the United States*, V, 389-433; T. C. Smith, *Parties and Slavery, passim;* James F. Rhodes, *History of the United States*, III, IV, V, VI; William McDonald, *Select Statutes*, I, 343, 365-372, 385-390, 397-454; II, 35-38, 42-43, 113; A. B. Hart, *American History Told by Contemporaries*, III, 574-655; IV, 122-192.

and a vote upon that report it looked too much like an insult from the antislavery party. He was, therefore, threatened with censure in the House in 1837.[2]

It is well to keep in mind, however, that Adams was not an antislavery man. His career had shown proslavery

tendencies.[3] In the Senate in 1807, when the prohibition of the slave trade was **The record** brought be- **of Adams.** fore that body, he voted against the measure. As a member of the mission negotiating the treaty with Great Britain, by which the War of 1812 was closed, he demanded compensation for slaves who had been carried away from their masters by the British Army.

JOHN QUINCY ADAMS, the champion of free speech

During his incumbency as Secretary of State he was unfriendly to the proposal of Great Britain for a slave trade treaty in the interest of the Africans, and as President he manifested no particular interest in the bondmen. Throughout his struggle for the right of petition in Congress, therefore, he was interested, not in the work of abolitionists but in defending the right of the people of his section to free speech.

When the House, in 1835, tabled an antislavery petition presented by John Quincy Adams, Henry A. Wise, of Virginia. took occasion to remark: "Sir, slavery interwoven.

[2] John W. Burgess, *The Middle Period;* A. B. Hart, *Slavery and Abolition;* and Herman von Holst, *Constitutional and Political History of the United States.*

[3] See the speech of John Quincy Adams quoted in the Appendix.

with our very political institution is guaranteed by our
Henry A. Constitution, and its consequences must be
Wise. borne by our northern brethren as resulting
from our system of government, and they cannot attack
the institution of slavery without attacking the institutions
of the country, our safety and welfare.'' In December of
that same year Slade of Vermont took occasion to remark
that as a constitutional right an abolition petition should
be printed, and that Congress had power to prohibit slavery
in the District of Columbia. He believed, moreover, that
the progress of abolition must be necessary to preserve the
balance of the situation or, rather, to restore it. When a
few days later two other such petitions were presented by
Morris, of Ohio, and Buchanan, of Pennsylvania, John C.
Calhoun declared such a memorial ''a foul slander on
nearly one-half of the States of the Union,'' and urged
''that a stop be put to that agitation which had prevailed
in so large a section of the country and which, unless
checked, would endanger the existence of the Union.'' Congress did not grant the desire of John C. Calhoun, but did
vote to reject the prayer of the petition.

Southern members immediately thereafter secured a special ''gag rule'' that, without being either printed or referred, all petitions, memorials, resolutions, propositions
or papers relating in any way or to any extent whatever
''Gag Rule.'' to the subject of slavery or the abolition of
slavery should be laid upon the table and
that no further action whatever should be had thereon.
The proslavery advocates had taken the advanced position
that Congress could not legislate on slavery in the District
of Columbia and that the wishes of the slave States border-
ing on the District of Columbia took precedence over the
power of Congress to legislate for the District. Yet the
Constitution provides that Congress shall make no law
abridging the freedom of speech or the rights of the people

peaceably to assemble or to petition the government for the redress of grievances. Adams, therefore, held the resolution to be a direct violation of the Constitution of the United States and the rules of the House and of the rights of his constituents.

A new stage in the discussion of the right of petition in Congress was reached when, in 1837, there were presented resolutions from Vermont legislature praying that slavery be abolished in the District of Columbia. In **A petition** accordance with the Southern idea of State **from a State.** rights, no State could be questioned in presenting any petition to Congress, although citizens might be restrained therefrom. Driven to such an extremity then, Rhett of South Carolina summoned his Southern co-workers to a meeting to devise a plan for peaceably dissolving the Union. They finally agreed, however, to undertake the enactment of a law providing for a more successful "gag rule." This declared it "the solenm duty of the government to resist all attempts by one portion to use it as an instrument to attack the democratic institutions of another."

At this time Henry Clay and Daniel Webster, two of the weakest men in this country, were dodging the slavery question. Largely for political reasons, neither one of these compromisers had the moral courage to take a stand on the issue. Henry Clay, who declared that he **Webster and** was not a friend of slavery, preferring rather **Clay.** freedom for all men, nevertheless considered the petitions for the abolition of slavery "a great practical inconvenience and annoyance" from which he hoped the people in the North would desist. In 1830 Daniel Webster considered domestic slavery one of the greatest evils, both moral and political. In 1836 he felt that it was the duty of Congress to take care that the authority of this government be not brought to bear upon slavery by any indirect interference. He later announced that as to slavery he would do nothing to favor or encourage its further extension.   Yet with regard to abolition he felt that it had taken such strong hold on the consciences of men that, if it were coerced into silence, he knew nothing, even in the Constitution or in the Union itself, which would not be endangered by the explosion which might follow.   Hoping to become president,

he later tended to become neutral, and bartered his birthright by an unsuccessful attempt to swallow the Fugitive Slave Law of 1850.

Growing bolder from year to year, the South during this period finally

Calhoun, the proslavery leader.

became solidly organized under the leadership of John C. Calhoun.   He had departed from his early position of nationalism to defend the institution of slavery.   In 1836 he boldly declared that

JOHN C. CALHOUN

"Congress has no legitimate jurisdiction over the subject of slavery either in the District of Columbia or elsewhere."[4] He believed that the abolitionists had no right to discuss slavery at all, that Congress should pass affirmative laws for the protection of slaveholders against abolition by mail, and that the Northern States should be prohibited from engaging in the agitation.   He insisted that "the conflicting elements would burst the Union asunder, powerful as are the links that hold it together.   Abolition and the Union

4 See Appendix for J. R. Giddings's attack on this policy.

cannot co-exist; come what will, should it cost every drop
of blood and every cent of property, we must defend
ourselves.''

Calhoun found for the South a safety valve in championing the desirable policy of expansion. The State of
Texas, developed under direction of proslavery men led
by Samuel Austin and Samuel Houston, be- The Texas
came an independent slaveholding section de- question.
siring annexation to the Union. This extension of our
territory could not be eas-
ily defeated, although the
purpose was to secure
slave territory. Joshua
R. Giddings, the first
militant abolition mem-
ber of Congress, however,
showed in a speech at-
tacking slavery, in 1841,
exactly how the admis-
sion of Texas would in-
crease the power of the
South and affect the eco-
nomic history of the
whole country.[5]

Many constitutional
difficulties were encoun-
tered, too, after some of

JOSHUA R. GIDDINGS

the States had abolished slavery. The South continued to
have trouble with fugitives escaping from its ports. It
was always easy, moreover, for a few slaves The return
to arrange with the Negro cooks and stewards of fugitives.
on vessels to conceal them as cargo and deliver them to
some agent of the Underground Railroad on arriving in the
North. In 1837 the schooner *Susan,* sailing from Georgia,

[5] See Giddings's speech in the Appendix.

permitted a Negro stowaway to escape on reaching a port in Maine. The State of Georgia preferred charges against the officers of the ship and undertook to take them into custody, but the Governor of Maine refused to honor the requisition on the grounds that they had left Georgia before they were charged with the crime. Three sailors coming

WILLIAM H. SEWARD

into New York with the slave they helped to escape from Norfolk in 1839 were similarly protected by Governor William H. Seward. He despised the institution of slavery. This caused a prolonged controversy between the chief executives of the two States and the expression of much bitter feeling on both sides. Virginia finally passed a law restricting commerce with the State of New York; and Mississippi and South Carolina, doing likewise, proposed "to unite with other States in any measure of resistance or redress."

Because of the disturbances resulting from the Negro insurrection in 1822, South Carolina passed certain "Negro Seamen Acts" requiring all Negroes on vessels to go to jail on arriving in port and to remain there until their vessels set sail again. These acts were earnestly protested against by Northern States and by England, because they interfered with the constant commercial intercourse between States. The measures were re-

Seamen Acts.

FRIENDS OF THE FUGITIVES

JOHN NEEDLES · · · · · · ABIGAIL GOODWIN
GRACE ANNE LEWIS · · · · DANIEL GIBBONS

laxed with reference to England, but with respect to the Northern States they continued as law. Thinking that it would be advisable to make a test case of this legislation, antislavery members of the Massachusetts legislature sent Samuel Hoar to intercede in behalf of a Negro thus deprived of his rights in that State. Upon arrival Hoar was notified that his life was in danger for the reason that he was ''an agent coming in not as a citizen of the United States but as an emissary of a foreign government hostile to the domestic institutions and with the sole purpose of subverting its internal policy.''

The South undertook also to indict as criminals violating the laws of the States persons who, although they did not come within the limits of the States, had by way of mail **Defense of** or message incited insurrection or aided slaves **slavery.** to escape from their masters. William Lago, a free Negro, was thus indicted in Kentucky. The Supreme Court decided that the governor of the State had a moral right to surrender Lago, but that the Federal Government had no power to compel him to do so. Joseph P. Mahan, a Methodist minister of Brown County, Ohio, was indicted by a grand jury of Kentucky for having aided the escape of certain slaves. Upon receiving a requisition from the Governor of Kentucky, the Governor of Ohio issued a warrant for the arrest of the minister. Not long after, however, the Governor of Ohio became convinced that the warrant had been issued without authority because Mahan had never been in Kentucky. The grand jury of Tuscaloosa County thus indicted R. G. Williams of New York in 1835, and the chief executive called upon Governor Marcy of New York to surrender him. The requisition was refused for the reason that Marcy could not see how a man could be guilty of a crime in Alabama when he had never been there. Rewards were offered for abolitionists like Arthur Tappan, and the State of Georgia appropriated

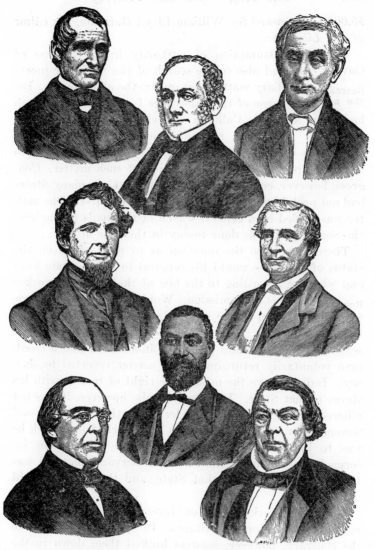

PROMOTERS OF THE UNDERGROUND RAILROAD

WILLIAM WRIGHT	E. F. PENNYPACKER
SAMUEL RHOADS	
J. M. McKIM	JOHN HEMAN
JOHN HENRY HILL	
WM. H. FURNISS	BARTHOLOMEW FUSSELL

$5,000 as a reward for William Lloyd Garrison, the editor of the *Liberator*.

This same assumption of authority in the defense of slavery extended also to the search of the mails for incen-
Searching   diary matter sent out by the abolitionists. Be-
the mails.   cause of the annoyance from which the South had long suffered, Calhoun introduced, in 1836, a bill providing that mail matter other than letters touching the subject of slavery should not be delivered in any State prohibiting the circulation of such matter. Congress, however, could not pass such a law, since many States had not prohibited the circulation of such matter. The matter was settled by a general search of the mails throughout the South, just as is done to-day in the time of war.

There arose also the question as to what effect on the status of the slave would his removal to a free State have and whether, according to the law of that State, it worked
Removal to   his manumission. Would he be free on his re-
a free State. turn to the slave State from which he went? In Massachusetts slavery was forbidden for any cause, whereas in Missouri and Louisiana it was held that a freedman voluntarily returning to his master reverted to slavery. Indiana gave the master the right of transit with his slaves in that State. In Pennsylvania, however, it was not allowed. When John H. Wheeler of North Carolina passed through that State on his way to New York, from which he was to proceed to Nicaragua, Passmore Williamson informed Jane Johnson, the attendant servant, that she was free under the laws of that State, and the courts upheld that opinion.

During the darkest days of slavery many more fugitives escaped to the Northern States. In spite of sentiment to the contrary, however, masters hunted them down in the North and demanded of the local courts their return to slavery. State officers often refused to carry out these mandates, and certain Northern commonwealths passed personal liberty laws to impede these efforts by granting alleged fugitives a trial by jury. In Ver- **Personal** mont and New York local officials were de- **Liberty Laws.** prived of jurisdiction in such cases, and State attorneys were required to act as legal advisers for Negroes thus accused. Ohio, however, egged on by the mob cruelly treating free Negroes migrating from the South to that State, enacted in 1839 a Fugitive Slave Law more drastic than the Federal measure of 1793. Some excitement was caused in 1837, however, when a Kentucky slave, Matilda, who, without being asked any questions, entered the service of James G. Birney at Cincinnati, was claimed and surrendered as a fugitive. Despite the appeal to the Supreme Court by such valuable counsellors as Salmon P. Chase and William H. Seward, John Van Zandt was fined $1,200 in 1840 because he rescued one of nine slaves who had escaped to the other side of the Ohio River.

An epoch was reached in the execution of the Fugitive Slave Law, however, when Edward Prigg of Maryland undertook to return from Pennsylvania the fugitive Margaret Morgan. Because Prigg seized her **The Prigg** without first instituting proceedings in the **Case.** courts of the State, he was arrested for violating the Pennsylvania statute against kidnaping. Upon appealing to the United States Supreme Court, however, the opinion was given that the owner had a right to recover the slave, but that the act of 1793 could not be construed as making its execution an obligation of the State officials. Following this decision John Shaw of Boston refused not long thereafter to grant a writ of habeas corpus in ac- **The Latimer** cordance with the State personal liberty law **Case.** to remove Latimer, a fugitive, from custody of the Federal authorities. There followed such a storm of protest, however, such an array of abolitionists against the authorities thus administering the law, that an observer of the trend of the times could easily see that feeling was running too high to calm the people of the North. They were then openly resisting the execution of Federal law. The southern people bore it as a grievance, therefore, that by the application of personal liberty laws the enemies of their basic institution could deprive them of their property. They urged, therefore, the enactment of a more stringent measure which eventually culminated in the passage of the Fugitive Slave Law of 1850.

CHAPTER XXI

THE IRREPRESSIBLE CONFLICT

SLAVERY became more troublesome for the United States at home when it involved the country in entanglements abroad. As the British Government gradually emancipated its slaves in the colonies after 1833, there was a tendency on the part of slaves and their sympathizers to seek refuge in those parts when carried on the high seas. For years very little effort had been made to stop the numerous violations of the slave trade, despite the fact that European governments had repeatedly called upon the United States to unite with them to abolish this traffic in men. When the ship *Comet,* in 1831, carrying slaves, and bound for the United States, was wrecked at the Bahamas, they were brought ashore and set free on the ground that the British Government did not recognize slavery on the high seas. Similar instances occurred in the case of the *Encomium* in 1835, and the *Enterprise* and the *Hermosa* in 1840. The United States Government promptly demanded an indemnity, contending that the accidental presence of the vessels in British waters did not interfere with the relation of master and slave; but, doubtless for the reason that emancipation was not at that time completed in the West Indies, Great Britain granted the United States, in 1840, an indemnity of $115,000 for the slaves of the *Comet* and *Encomium.* Nothing was granted for the others. The only consolation our government received was to declare it a violation of international law for which no redress could be obtained.

> International entanglements.

> Slavery on the high seas.

There took place on the high seas, moreover, a number of mutinies of slaves which, the proslavery element believed, required intervention on the part of the United States. One of the most significant of these cases was that of the *Amistad*. There were on board the schooner fifty-four Negroes who were being carried coastwise from Havana to Neuvitas on the island of Cuba in 1839. Under the leadership of the African,

L'Amistad.

JOSEPH CINQUE

Joseph Cinque, the Negroes murdered the passengers and the crew with the exception of two Spaniards spared to steer the vessel toward freedom. After roaming on the high seas a few days, the vessel came ashore for water and provisions at Culloden Point on the east end of Long Island, and was espied and taken possession of a short while thereafter by Captain Gedney of the United States Navy. Joseph Cinque, the leader, undertook to escape, but finally yielded. The captives were then brought before the United States Circuit Court in Connecticut, presided over by Andrew T. Judson. As the proceedings lasted for some months, Cinque with some companions was turned over to certain abolition teachers, who so thoroughly grounded him in the fundamentals of education that he developed into a man of considerable intelligence and showed natural ability as an orator. The outcome of the case was that, although Van Buren was ready to remand them, the Supreme Court on appeal decided that the Negroes, being free when they left Havana, were violating no law in killing those trying to enslave them. They were therefore set free.

The mutiny of the slaves on the *Creole*, en route from Richmond to New Orleans, in 1841, gave rise to another Congressional inquiry in which the right of the United States to exercise authority over slaves on the high seas was questioned. The leader was Madison Washington. He had made his escape from slavery in Virginia to Can- **The Creole** ada, but on re- **Case.** turning to rescue his wife had been captured and started South for sale. The one hundred and thirty-four slaves overpowered the officers of the vessel, killed one, and directed the ship to the British port, Nassau. There they were held to await instruc- tions from the British Govern- ment. When proslavery men in

CHARLES SUMNER, a fear- less advocate of democracy

Congress sought to have these Negroes returned to their masters on the ground that they were legally held at the time of their departure, Charles Sumner [1] insisted that the slaves became free when taken, by the voluntary action of their owners, beyond the jurisdiction of the slave States. On the other hand, Daniel Webster, then Secretary of State, contended that inasmuch as slaves were recognized as property by the Constitution of the United States, where slavery existed, their presence on the high seas did not

[1] See Appendix for Sumner's ideas.

effect a change in their status. The matter against Great Britain was drawn out into ten years of negotiations and was finally settled in 1853 by arbitration. It was provided that the British Government should pay an indemnity of $110,000 for having permitted these Negroes to go free.

To combat this view Joshua R. Giddings, an antislavery member of Congress, offered in connection with this case in 1842 resolutions to the effect that "slavery, being an abridgment of the natural rights of man, can exist only by force

Giddings' or positive municipal law." [2] Botts of Vir-
Resolutions. ginia thereupon secured the adoption of a resolution to the effect that "this House holds the conduct of said member altogether unwarranted and unwarrantable, and deserving the severe condemnation of the people

[2] Giddings' resolutions were:

1. *Resolved*, That, prior to the adoption of our Federal Constitution each of the several States composing this Union exercised full and exclusive jurisdiction over the subject of slavery within its own territory, and possessed full power to continue or abolish it at pleasure.

2. *Resolved*, That, by adopting the Constitution, no part of the aforesaid powers were delegated to the Federal Government, but were reserved by and still pertain to each of the several States.

3. *Resolved*, That, by the 8th section of the 1st article of the Constitution, each of the several States surrendered to the Federal Government all jurisdiction over the subjects of commerce and navigation upon the high seas.

4. *Resolved*, That Slavery, being an abridgment of the natural right of man, can exist only by force of positive *municipal law*, and is necessarily confined to the territorial jurisdiction of the power creating it.

5. *Resolved*, That when a ship belonging to the citizens of any State enters upon the high seas, the persons on board cease to be subject to the slave laws of such State, and therefore, are governed in their relations to each other by, and are amenable to, the laws of the United States.

6. *Resolved*, That when the brig *Creole*, on her late passage for New Orleans, left the territorial jurisdiction of Virginia, the slave laws of that State ceased to have jurisdiction over the persons on board said brig, and such persons became amenable only to the laws of the United States.

7. *Resolved*, That the persons on board the said ship, in resuming their natural rights of personal liberty, violated no law of the United States, incurred no legal penalty and are justly liable to no punishment.

of his country and of this body in particular." Giddings was, therefore, twice censured by the proslavery Congress. To show the attachment of his district to free institutions, however, he resigned and appealed to his constituents in the Western Reserve. They immediately returned him with a large majority.

The interpretation of the constitution brought other problems. In the development of the proslavery policy which dominated this country up to the Civil War, the South actually forced the nation into a struggle with Mexico to acquire territory for the extension of slavery. **The Wilmot Proviso.** A rather serious question arose when an act appropriating money for the purchase of territory from Mexico was blocked by David Wilmot's amendment providing that in the territory to be thus acquired slavery should be forever prohibited. This amendment caused much trouble years thereafter. Introduced from session to session, it became the nemesis of the proslavery party in quest of new territory. The proviso evoked from the proslavery advocates the claim that Congress had no

8. *Resolved,* That all attempts to regain possession of or to re-enslave said persons are unauthorized by the Constitution or laws of the United States, and are incompatible with our national honor.

9. *Resolved,* That all attempts to exert our national influence in favor of the coastwise slave trade, or to place this nation in the attitude of maintaining a "commerce in human beings," are subversive of the rights and injurious to the feelings of the free States, are unauthorized by the Constitution, and prejudicial to our national character.

See *Text* of the resolutions in *House Journal,* 27th Cong., 2d Sess.; for the resolution of censure, *ib.,* p. 580. For the discussions see the *Cong. Globe,* or Benton's *Abridgement,* XIV. The diplomatic correspondence regarding the *Creole* is in the *House Exec. Doc.* 2, 27th Cong., 3d Sess., pp. 114-123, and *Senate Doc.,* 1, pp. 116-125. See also von Holst's *United States,* II, 479-486; J. Q. Adams's *Memoirs,* XI, 113-115; Wilson's *Rise and Fall of the Slave Power,* I, Chap. 31; Benton's *Thirty Years' View,* II, Chap. 98.

The work of this statesman is treated in Byron R. Long's *Joshua R. Giddings, A Champion of Political Freedom* and in George W. Julian's *Life of Joshua R. Giddings.* See also J. B. Moore's *International Arbitrations,* I, 417.

right to legislate on this question and that the question of slavery should be decided by those persons who would settle in the said territory.

About the year 1850, when the antislavery agitation was at its height and the various laws of interest to the many contending elements emerged in the form of the Omnibus Bill, several constitutional questions of importance were

The crisis of 1850. raised. There came up the question of the admission of California, the paying of certain Texas claims, the organization of territory acquired from Mexico, the abolition of the slave trade in the District of Columbia, and the provision for a more effective fugitive slave law. The friends of slavery objected to having the State of California admitted without passing through the territorial probation period, and did not agree with Henry Clay, who contended that slavery in that State illegally existed. They believed that slavery existed everywhere unless it had been positively prohibited by law. Many northerners objected to paying claims incurred by the acquisition of slave territory and were not disposed to hurry up with the organization of slave States to be formed therefrom.[3] As to the prohibition of slavery in the District of Columbia, the southerners were still of the opinion that the Constitution had not given Congress any power to legislate regarding slavery. On the other hand, the friends of freedom were of the opinion that the proposed fugitive slave law, intended to impress into the service of slave-catching men who had no inclination to perform such a task, interfered with a man's rights as a citizen, and that it was unconstitutional because it did not guarantee the suspects any right of trial by jury and did not permit a fugitive to testify in his own behalf. In the midst of so many conflicting efforts to bring about a compromise between two militant sections, far-sighted men like William

[3] This is well expressed by Giddings's speech in the Appendix.

H. Seward [4] and Henry Ward Beecher saw no hope for peace in the Omnibus Bill, which emerged from the chaos of sectional claims.

Then followed the popularization of *Uncle Tom's Cabin*. This was a sentimental novel written by Harriet Beecher Stowe. As the wife of a professor in Lane Seminary in Cincinnati, a way-station to freedom just across the slave border, she had ample opportunity to learn the horrors of slavery. It was published in 1852, as a protest against the fugitive slave law, but did not do its work until a few years thereafter. Finding in this book the lofty feeling of a sensitive soul outraged by an iniquitous institution, the whole country was deeply moved. It even became so popular abroad that it had to be translated into many languages. It was a book

HENRY WARD BEECHER, a champion of freedom

which human beings could not easily read without having an impulse to do something for the destruction of slavery. The South, therefore, resented this picture of slavery, outlawed the book in that section, and attacked elsewhere all thinkers influenced by such sentiments. The book, however, became a factor in politics and proved to be one of the disastrous blows to slavery.

This book doubtless helped to complicate matters

[4] See Appendix for Seward's *Higher Law*.

when it was proposed to organize Kansas and Nebraska without regard to slavery. Stephen A. Douglas, the champion of this movement, seemed to stultify himself in trying to harmonize his theory of squatter sovereignty with that **The Kansas-** of the freedom of the people in determining **Nebraska** for themselves how the new commonwealth **question.** should come into the Union. How Douglas could make it possible for a man to take his slaves wherever he would and still hold them as goods and chattels, while at the same time the law would guarantee to the people in a new commonwealth, when framing the Constitution, the right to decide for themselves whether or not the State should be free, was never satisfactorily explained to the increasing number of antislavery men.

The most formidable of all these antislavery men, however, was not among the first to appear. He was a backwoodsman born in Kentucky and developed to manhood in Indiana and Illinois. As a rail-splitter he could understand the hardships entailed upon those compelled to engage in drudgery. When a young man he went on a **Lincoln on** flatboat on a trading trip to New Orleans. On **slavery.** the market square there he saw human beings auctioned off like cattle. Being deeply impressed with the evil thereof, he said to himself that if he ever had a chance to strike slavery he would strike it and would strike it hard. Some years later, when Elijah Lovejoy was killed at Alton, Illinois, by the proslavery leaders because of his diatribes hurled at the bold defenders of that institution, the legislature of the State passed a resolution which seemingly condoned that murder. Thereupon this representative joined with Daniel Stone in a protest to the effect that "they believed that the institution of slavery is founded on both injustice and bad policy." This man was Abraham Lincoln.[5]

[5] See Lincoln's speech in the Appendix.

Against all temporizing and compromising efforts to placate the many proslavery advocates, Lincoln persistently warned his fellow-countrymen. In his celebrated debates with Stephen A. Douglas in 1858, Lincoln said that by the continuation of the policies of the proslavery party the country had decided upon a fatal course of winking at a terrible evil. "Under the operation of that policy," said he, "that agitation has not only not ceased, but has constantly augmented. In my opinion it will not cease until a crisis shall have been reached and passed. 'A house divided against itself cannot stand.' I believe this government cannot endure permanently half slave and half free. I do not expect the Union to be dissolved—I do not expect the house to fall—but I do expect it will cease to be divided. It will become all one thing, or all the other. Either the opponents of slavery will arrest the further spread of it, and place it where the public mind shall rest in the belief that it is in the course of ultimate extinction; or its advocates will push it forward till it shall become alike lawful in all the States, old as well as new, North as well as South." [6]

The culmination of the proslavery discussion was the Dred Scott decision. This was the case of a Negro who had been taken from the slave States into free territory a second time. He then instituted proceedings to obtain his freedom. The case passed **The Dred Scott decision.** through the local and higher courts and finally came before the Supreme Court of the United States. It decided that at the time, when the Constitution of the United States was adopted, Negroes were not regarded as citizens of this country and they could not, therefore, sue as such in the United States courts. That tribunal, then, had no jurisdiction in such a case, and it was dismissed. This was to say that the Negro, so far as the United States Government

[6] Abraham Lincoln, *Speeches and Debates* (New York, 1907), p. 36.

was concerned, had no rights that the white man should respect, and that although certain sections of the country were generally free by regulations to that effect, any part of the country might become slave, should persons owning Negroes choose to settle therein. Slavery was therefore national, while freedom was sectional.

Against this interpretation of the Constitution to justify such encroachment upon the rights of the individual, the friends of freedom persistently protested. William Henry **Increasing** Seward, then figuring also as a spokesman **opposition.** of those who dared to engage in the battle for the right of citizens under the constitution, accepted the challenge in his ''Impending Crisis'' and ''Irrepressible Conflict.'' [7] Salmon P. Chase and Charles Sumner, though not at first militant abolitionists, had reached the conclusion that slavery would have to yield ground to free soil, free speech and free men. The slavery debate then ceased to be a constitutional question and became largely political. The organization of the Republican party in 1854, and its all but successful campaign in 1856 with John C. Fremont on the platform of prohibiting the extension of slavery, **Slavery in** made this question the dominant thought of **politics.** most forward-looking men. Here we see the agitation for the rights of man connecting opportunely with modern economic movements to reduce slave labor to the point of a death struggle with free labor. Although aware of the fact that the civilized world had proscribed slavery, the South was willing to remain in a primitive state to retain it. The North was determined not to yield any more ground to an institution in which it had no interest and against which it had many reasons to be opposed.

Working in another way, but not through sentiment, was Hinton Rowan Helper in his book entitled *The Impending Crisis of the South.* The importance of this book may be

[7] See Appendix for Seward's thought on the crisis.

understood by the difficulty experienced in the House of
Representatives in the election of the speaker in 1859. A
member from Missouri introduced a reso- **The impending
crisis.**
lution to bar from the speakership any one
who had endorsed this book. It was not until the first of
February that this body could finally elect Pennington, a
conservative Republican of New Jersey. The doctrine set
forth in this work was a severe indictment of slavery by a
non-slaveholder of the South. It was at the same time an
appeal to get rid of the leadership of slaveholders. Its
language seemed bitter, but it presented logically the economic situation of the South as it really was. It alarmed
the slaveholding States. It could be easily seen that in a
country where there were only 225,000 persons who actually owned slaves or only one out of every five who had an
interest in slaves, if the non-slaveholding element combined
against the institution, it would be doomed.

The Impending Crisis was the voice from the crushed
industrialism of the South. For a number of years it had
been plainly evident that industrialism could not develop
far in the South when that section with its unskilled slave
labor had to compete with the free labor of **Industrialism
in the South.**
the North. Some whites, not all of them of
the poor class, deplored the comparative decline of the
South on a purely agricultural basis. Even those who
seemed to defend slavery could not fail to see the weakness
of that section, should it have to depend on others from
without to supply all except its agricultural needs. Certain men in the South had, therefore, advocated for some
years the repeal of Southern laws prohibiting Negro education. They wanted their Negroes taught at least to the
extent of being able to "read and cipher." Agricultural
societies in the South, observing also how that section was
running behind the North in both commerce and industry,
took the same position. From such bodies there went to

the legislatures memorials praying for some modification of these restrictive measures to improve the efficiency of Negro labor by mental development and thus give the South a new chance in industry. Such a measure was introduced in North Carolina in 1855, and about the same time one all but passed both houses of the legislature of Georgia.

There were also actual experiments in industry in the South. Some of the efforts were made to show that industrialism was compatible with slavery, and others to show how poor whites properly encouraged could be used to develop industries in the South. The latter, however, sometimes assumed the phase of enterprises conducted by Northern white men in the South to show the advantages of free labor. Eli Thayer made such an experiment at Ceredo, Virginia (now West Virginia), where he established a factory for matches and other such articles.

The efforts, however, had come too late. The North and South had already become divided. The only thing, then, remaining to be done was to effect a separation. The bloodshed in Kansas was the beginning of the Civil War. Out of this stormy district John Brown came with a definite program for the liberation of the slaves and the establishment of a free republic in the South. In 1858, he made an excursion into slaveholding Missouri, which one historian refers to as "a dress rehearsal for the final tragedy." His original headquarters, where the scheme for servile insurrection was worked out, were at Chatham, Canada. He hoped to establish himself in the mountains of the South at some strategic point to which slaves might be attracted in sufficiently large numbers to defend themselves and maintain an independent government. He stopped first at Kennedy Farm, about five miles from Harpers Ferry. Proceeding from this point with only $2,000, about 200 rifles, and some pikes, he began his mission by taking possession of the arsenal at Harpers Ferry in October, 1859.

Intensely excited by this unexpected blow at slavery, the Virginia government and the United States authorities immediately dispatched troops to capture the invaders and to bring them to justice. John Brown and his followers made a desperate defense; but, being overwhelmed, those who were not killed and did not succeed in escaping were captured and imprisoned. On December 2, 1859, John Brown was hanged. He faced his doom like a martyr. He said that he was sustained by the peace of God which passeth all understanding and the testimony of a good conscience that he had not lived altogether in vain. Believing that his death would do vastly more to advance the cause of freedom than all he had done in life, he was willing to die to seal his testimony for God and humanity with his blood.

Although the slaves had not the opportunity to join Brown, as he desired, five Negroes figured conspicuously in this raid. Among the ten killed were Lewis Sheridan Leary, a free Negro native of Fayetteville, North Carolina, and Dangerfield Newby, formerly a slave of Fauquier County, Virginia, both at that time citizens of Oberlin, Ohio. Two of the seven hanged were John Anthony Copeland, a free man of color, born in Raleigh, North Carolina, but later transplanted to Oberlin for education, and Shields Green, a fugitive from Charleston, South Carolina, known as the protégé of Frederick Douglass. One of the five who escaped was Osborn Perry Anderson, a printer born at Fallowfield, Pennsylvania. He served with distinction in the Civil War and later wrote an account of the venture entitled *A Voice from Harpers Ferry*.

This event, like that of the strife in Kansas, was an act of Civil War. It was not a disconnected deed of an insane man, as some persons of clouded vision contend. Although John Brown overestimated the effect of his exploits, he did drive home the fact that a number of people in the North had thought so seriously of slavery as to endanger their lives in the effort to exterminate the institution. It made the country realize that something would have to be done to bring the matter to a conclusion, and the conflict of the two sections was the crowning event of this long drawn out contest. John Brown, therefore, takes his place among the greatest martyrs of the world. His lofty purpose was vindicated by the ultimate triumph of his cause within six years after his martyrdom.

1860

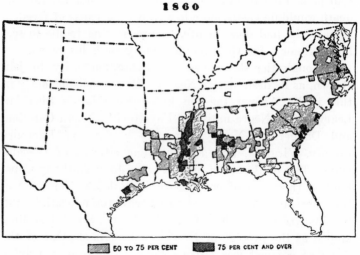

50 TO 75 PER CENT   75 PER CENT AND OVER

THE DISTRIBUTION OF THE NEGRO POPULATION IN 1860
By permission of the United States Bureau of the Census

Then came the division of the truncated Democratic party, the accession of Northern liberals to the ranks of the Republicans, and the triumph of the Republican party in 1860. The Southern States, believing that their last chance to maintain slavery in the Union had passed, thereupon seceded to establish a confederate government in keeping with their institutions. South Carolina took such action December 20, 1860, and before Lincoln had been inaugurated the following March all of the cotton States had followed her example.

The last stand of the South.

Was secession constitutional? James Buchanan, the weak executive then finishing his term as President, said that these commonwealths had no right to leave the Union, but he did not believe that he had any constitutional power to interfere with their going. This was the most critical period through which the Union had passed. Persons who had for some years observed the development of disintegrating forces doubted that the Union would weather the storm.

BENJAMIN F. WADE, the defier of the Secessionists

When the Federal Constitution was framed and adopted few persons were conscious of the fact that the foundation for a durable union of the States had been laid. The very language of the Constitution itself indicates that a consolidation of the States ratifying that agreement was not clear in the minds of the framers. In the course of time, however, the country developed into a Union. The majority of the States took the position that it could not be broken. Some States were in doubt as to whether a State could secede at the time of the agitation of the Alien

The nature of the Union.

and Sedition Laws which culminated in the high ground taken by Virginia and Kentucky in their threatening resolutions. More strength for the Union was evidenced when New England, because of its dissatisfaction with the conduct of the War of 1812, felt disposed to make an effort at secession. The Union sentiment was much more pronounced at the time of the nullification efforts of South Carolina in 1833. It indicated, as Benjamin F. Wade of Ohio boldly asserted, that there was little chance for a State to leave the Union of its own accord.[8]

In spite of this nationalistic attitude, however, the South had become so much attached to slavery and the North so far removed from it that this institution tended to force a conflict. To carry its point the South had threatened the country with secession for three

Threats of secession.

decades. Before the two participants in this contest lay the promising West. Each was making an effort to invade that domain to establish there States which would support their respective claims. As a free society expands much more rapidly than a slave community, the North easily outstripped the South. In seeking an advantage in the interest of free labor by preventing the expansion of slavery, the North forced the South to the radical position of undertaking secession. These threats were very much pronounced during the ardent slavery debates of 1849 and 1850, and left certain sores which the all-comprehending compromise of 1850 failed to heal. And when the agitation had seemingly been all but settled by these arrangements, it broke out anew in the effort to provide a government for Kansas and Nebraska and in the bloody conflict there between the representatives of the North and South. This was the Civil War itself, although it required several years for the excited American people to realize it.

[8] See Appendix for Wade's speech.

CHAPTER XXII

THE NEGRO IN THE CIVIL WAR

WHEN the war broke out, Lincoln, hoping to curry favor at home, openly declared that it was not his purpose to interfere with the institutions of the South. He meant, of course, that he had no desire to attack slavery in those commonwealths in which it existed. The South, on the other hand, was anxious to win favor abroad. Knowing how it would harm its cause in foreign countries to have it said that it had undertaken a war to promote slavery, the Confederacy declared its position one of self-defense to maintain its right to govern itself and to preserve its own peculiar institutions. Negroes, therefore, were not to be freed; and, to be sure, were not to take a part in the war. It was considered a struggle between white men. This does not mean, however, that Abraham Lincoln had lost sight of the fact that he had been elected by a party opposed to the extension of slavery, nor that he ceased to put forth efforts, whenever possible, to check the institution as he had formerly declared. After the war had been well begun and it was evident that such efforts as the peace convention could not succeed, Lincoln took up with the Border States the question of setting the example of freeing the Negroes by a process of gradual emancipation.[1]

Evading slavery.

[1] J. K. Hosmer, *The Appeal to Arms* and his *Outcome of the Civil War;* J. W. Burgess, *Civil War and the Constitution;* James Ford Rhodes, *History of the United States,* Vol. III; J. B. McMaster, *History of the United States,* Vol. VIII, p. 473; James Schouler, *History of the United States,* VI, 1861-1865, *passim;* William Wells

ABRAHAM LINCOLN

Before the war had proceeded very far, however, the Negroes came up for serious consideration because of the many problems which developed out of the peculiar situation in which they were. In the first place, **The Negro** there were in the North free Negroes who, **involved.** knowing that the success of the South meant the perpetuation of slavery, were anxious to do their share in defeating the purposes of the Confederate States. There were in the North, moreover, white men who were of the opinion that free Negroes should share a part of the burden entailed by waging the Civil War. Furthermore, as soon as the invading Union armies crossed the Mason and Dixon line into the South, disturbing the plantation system and driving the masters away from their homes, the Negroes were left behind to constitute a problem for the army. There arose the question as to what was the status of such Negroes. Nominally they were slaves; actually they were free: but there was no law to settle the question. A few slaves who had been taken over by the Union armies from persons in rebellion against the United States, were confiscated by virtue of the legislation providing for this disposition of such property of the Confederates. Yet there were Negroes who did not wait for the invading armies. When their masters had gone to the front to defend the South, they left their homes and made their way to the Union camps.[2]

The first effort to deal with such slaves was made by General Butler at Fortress Monroe in 1861. **Butler's** Such slaves as escaped into his camp in flight **contrabands.** from their masters, he accepted as contraband of war on the grounds that they had been employed in assisting the

Brown, *The Rising Son*, 341-381; George W. Williams, *History of Negro Troops in the War of the Rebellion, passim;* William Mac-Donald, *Select Statutes of United States History*, 34-39; and A. B. Hart, *American History Told by Contemporaries*, IV, 181-458.

[2] The best authority on the Civil War is James Ford Rhodes. See his *History of the United States from the Compromise of 1850 to the Final Restoration of Home Rule in the South;* Volumes I-IV.

Confederate armies and could be confiscated in the same sense that one would take over other supplies of the Confederates. Much discussion was aroused by the action of General Butler, and there was doubt as to whether or not it would be supported by the President. This plan, however, was followed by General Wood, Butler's successor,

NEGROES IN THE SERVICE OF THE CONFEDERATES

and by General Banks when he was operating in New Orleans. General Halleck, while fighting in the West, at first excluded slaves from the camps, as did also General Dix in Virginia. Some generals, like General McCook and General Johnson, permitted slave hunters to come into their lines and reclaim their fugitive slaves. Later, however, General Halleck evidently receded from his early position. General Grant refused to give permits to those seeking to recapture the Negroes who had escaped from their former masters. He used the blacks at such labor as the building of roads and fortifications, very much as they were first used by General Butler. This anticipated a policy which was later followed by the United States Army.[3]

In the course of time, however, the national government saw the necessity of treating the Negro ques- **The Negro** tion more seriously. It was evident that if **question** the South continued to use the Negro slaves **serious.** in building fortifications and roads and bridges and, in

U. S. GRANT

fact, to do practically all of the labor required in the army, it was incumbent upon the Union armies operating in the South to do likewise. Lincoln, therefore, soon accepted the policy of using the slaves in this capacity. He receded from his former position of thinking that, should the slaves be given any encouragement to leave their homes they might start a servile insurrection, and in promoting such he would weaken himself in his hold on the North.

At first these Negroes did not find their life a pleasant one. They were suddenly thrown among strange men from the North, who had never had much dealing with such Negroes and whose first impression of them **The Negro in** was not favorable. Arriving among these **the camps.** soldiers, naked, hungry, diseased, and utterly lacking the

[3] G. W. Williams, *History of the Negro Troops in the War of the Rebellion, passim;* William Wells Brown, *The Rising Son;* and John Eaton, *Grant, Lincoln, and the Freedmen.*

initiative to provide for themselves what the average freeman was expected to do, moreover, these wanderers presented a piteous spectacle which baffled the skill of the army. The refugees were finally organized under directions sent out from headquarters of the army, and placed in charge of a superintendent having under him sufficient assistants to relieve most of the cases of distress and to make some use of the able-bodied Negroes.

Most of these refugees were sent to Washington, Alexandria, Fortress Monroe, Hampton, Craney Island, Yorktown, Suffolk, Portsmouth, Port Royal, South Carolina, and certain camps of the West near Memphis. At one time, in the camp at Arlington, just across from Washington, there were as many as 30,000 Negroes. This number increased to almost 100,000 in the various camps near Washington, in the proportion that the war advanced and the territory of the Confederates was overrun by the invading Union armies.[4] It was easy to find employment for those in camps near cities. Some of them were put to work on deserted plantations. Others were incorporated into the army as teamsters, mechanics, and common laborers. Sojourner Truth, who served the Union army as a messenger and a spy, rendered valuable service in these camps by teaching the refugees cleanliness and habits of industry.

It was arranged also to send a number of these Negroes from the congested districts in the loyal States as fast as opportunities for their employment presented themselves. Those found near cities and manufacturing points, where **Fugitives sent North.** there was a demand for labor, were employed, in some cases, to do work in which white men sent to the war had been engaged. A good many passed

[4] For more extensive treatment, see John Eaton, *Grant, Lincoln and the Freedmen*; E. L. Pierce's *The Freedmen of Port Royal, South Carolina*; G. W. Williams's *The History of Negro Troops*, 90-98; E. H. Botume's *First Days Amongst the Contrabands*, and *The Atlantic Monthly*, XII, 308.

through Cairo, Illinois, into the West, and some others went through York, Columbia, Harrisburg, and Philadelphia to points in the North. This, however, did not continue to a very great extent, for the reason that there was some apprehension that the North might be overcrowded by such freedmen. Several schemes were set forth to deport this population. When this number was still further increased by the thousands of Negroes emancipated in the District of Columbia in 1862, Abraham Lincoln himself thought to get rid of these freedmen by colonizing them in foreign parts.

To carry out this plan as he desired, he sent a special message to Congress to show the necessity for Congressional action in the way of an appropriation to finance such an enterprise. Thinking that certain nations could be induced to accept Negro emigrants from this country, the Secretary of State opened correspondence with various countries having colonies settled partly by Negroes. He thus brought the matter before Great Britain, Denmark, France, Sweden and all of the South American countries. In the beginning it became evident that only two countries, Liberia and Haiti, each of which were settled by Negroes, were willing to admit these refugees. But the Negroes themselves, because of their prejudice against Liberia and the unsuccessful effort at colonization in Haiti, did not care to emigrate to those countries. Favorable replies, however, finally came from the Island of Vache, a part of Haiti. The government immediately planned to send a colony to that settlement by virtue of an appropriation made by Congress. Bernard Koch approached the government and induced the authorities to make with him a contract for the transportation of Negroes to this island.

At the same time Koch connected himself with certain business men in New York. In return for commercial advantages to be gained there, they agreed also to finance the enterprise. When this double dealing was discovered the United States Government severed connection with Koch.

The double dealing of Koch. The capitalists, however, still determined to conduct this enterprise, engaged the services of Koch as governor. Accordingly a number of Negroes were sent to this island in the year 1862; but, owing to the unfavorable conditions and their lack of initiative, unusual suffering ensued. Because of the many complaints received therefrom, it was necessary for the Government to send a special investigator to report on the situation. Finally, on account of his unfavorable report, the Government dispatched a transport to bring the emigrants back to the United States.

James Watson Webb, United States Minister to Brazil, proposed that the freedmen be colonized in that country. To emphasize the feasibility of this project he submitted to Lincoln and Seward various arguments. Brazilian Negroes were decreasing, labor was scarce in that country, the free Negroes would make progress there since Brazil allowed an open door to all honors and had social equality. A treaty with Brazil was suggested; but, thinking that the slavery question was too acute for such a far-reaching plan, the administration declined to undertake it.[5]

Lincoln, however, remained fundamentally antislavery in spite of the failure of the colonization schemes, although he religiously adhered to his gradual emancipation plans. He would not permit the abolition sentiment of the country to force upon him the policy of instant emancipation. As there were in the field generals availing themselves of every opportunity to weaken the slave power much vigilance had to be exercised to avoid extreme measures which might embarrass the Federal Government. Taking the advanced position that the slaves should be free, Fremont issued a decree abolishing slavery in Missouri. It was necessary for

[5] *Journal of Negro History*, XI, 35-49.

Lincoln to say to him on September 2, 1861: "I think there is great danger that the closing paragraph, in relation to the confiscation of property and the liberating of slaves of traitorous owners, will alarm our southern Union friends and turn them against us; perhaps ruin our rather fair prospect for Kentucky. Allow me, therefore, to ask that you will, as of your own motion, modify that paragraph so as to conform to the first and fourth sections of the act of Congress, entitled *An Act to Confiscate Property used for Insurrectionary Purposes.*"

The following May, Lincoln had to deal similarly with Major-General Hunter, then stationed at Port Royal, South Carolina. This commander had issued a declaration to the effect that the commonwealths within his jurisdiction, having deliberately declared themselves no longer under the protection of the United States of America and having taken up arms against the United States, it became a military necessity to declare martial law; and as slavery and martial law were incompatible in a free country, the persons of these States held to service were declared free. Lincoln then issued a proclamation declaring that neither General Hunter nor any other commander or person had been authorized by the government of the United States to take such action and that the supposed proclamation in question, whether genuine or false, was altogether void so far as respects such a declaration. He considered it sufficient at that time to rely upon his proposed plan for the gradual abolition of slavery on the compensation basis recently accepted by Congress.

Writing Hunter again on the eleventh of the same month, Lincoln said: "The particular clause, however, in relation to the confiscation of property and the liberation of slaves appeared to me to be objectionable in its nonconformity to the act of Congress passed the 6th of last August upon the same subjects; and hence I wrote you, expressing my wish that that clause should be modified accordingly. Your answer, just received, expresses the preference on your part that I should make an open order for the modification, which I very cheerfully do. It is, therefore, ordered that the said clause of such proclamation be so modified, held, and construed as to conform to, and not to transcend, the provisions on the same subject contained in the act of Congress, entitled *An Act to Confiscate Property used for Insurrectionary Purposes.''*

It was growing more and more apparent, however, that the Negro would have to be treated as a citizen of the United States. In the army he had demonstrated his ca-
A convincing pacity as a man. He had shown that he could
record. become industrious, that he was thrifty, and that he would serve unselfishly. Where he had an opportunity to toil upward he succeeded. It was, therefore, recommended by a number of men, and among them General Grant himself, that certain Negroes be so equipped and trained that they might be employed not only as teamsters and mechanics and the like, but as soldiers. This change of policy was necessary not merely for sentimental reasons but because the North, in its effort to subjugate the haughty South, had found those warriors too well trained and too spirited to be easily conquered. In most of the important engagements the South had won. Farragut had captured New Orleans, Thomas and Grant had won a few victories in the West, and the *Monitor* had held its own with the *Merrimac* in defending the nation's cause, but the Union army had been twice ingloriously defeated at Manassas, and McClellan had lost in his Peninsular campaign and had thrown away his advantages gained at Antietam. As the army was unsuccessful under Burnside at Fredericksburg, and under Hooker at Chancellorsville, the North, growing tired of the war, was becoming fertile ground for seeds of a second secession sown by copperheads secretly

planning to establish another republic in the Northwest. It was deemed advisable, therefore, to bring the Negro into the army that he might help to save the Union. By this time, too, the Federal Government had reached the position

That on the first day of January in the year of our Lord, one thousand eight hundred and sixty-three, all persons held as slaves. within any state, or designated part of a state, the people whereof shall then. be in rebellion against the United States, shall be then, thenceforward, and forever free. and the executive government of the United States, will, and maintain the freedom of cognize. such persons, and will do no act or acts to repress such persons, or any of them in any efforts they may. make for their actual freedom.

FACSIMILE OF THE ORIGINAL DRAFT OF THE EMANCIPATION
PROCLAMATION

that slavery, the root of most of the evils of the country and

The Emancipation Proclamation. the actual cause of the war, would have to be exterminated. Congress passed sweeping confiscation acts by virtue of which the armies could take over slaves; and, in 1862, Lincoln came forward with the Emancipation Proclamation, declaring that after the first of January in 1863 all slaves in those parts of the country where the people might remain in rebellion against the United States, should be declared free.

Northern men like General DePeyster, General Thomas W. Sherman, General Hunter, Governor Yates of Illinois, Henry Wilson, and Charles Sumner, had been emphatic in urging the United States Government to arm the Negroes to weaken the South. And well might the United States Army take this action, for the seceders had not only made use of the Negroes as laborers, but in Tennessee and Louisiana had actually organized free Negroes for military service in the Confederate Army. Yet, although the confis-

The arming of Negroes. cation acts and other legislation justified the employment of Negroes, Lincoln hesitated to carry out these provisions. In 1862, however, General David Hunter, commanding in South Carolina, issued an order for recruiting a Negro regiment, which in a few months was in the field. This caused much dissatisfaction among the Unionists, who did not feel that Negroes should be called on to fight the battles of a free republic. An effort was made to embarrass General Hunter, but he emerged from the investigation without being reversed, although he did not have the support of Lincoln. General J. W. Phelps, under General B. F. Butler in Louisiana, undertook to carry out Hunter's policy, but his superior was then willing to use the Negroes as laborers only.

Certain leaders in the North, however, were becoming a little more aggressive in their demand for the employment of Negroes as soldiers. On August 4, 1862, Governor Sprague of Rhode Island urged Negro citizens to enlist, and that same month Butler himself appealed to the free people of color of Louisiana to come to the defense of the Union. The next month a regiment of Negroes marched forth to war as the "First Regiment of Louisiana Native Guards,'' soon changed to the ''First Regiment Infantry Corps d'Afrique.'' There was later organized the ''First Regiment Louisiana Heavy Artillery.'' Other Negro regiments soon followed, and before the end of 1862 four Negro regiments had been brought into the military service of the United States. Then came the

ROBERT GOULD SHAW LEADING THE FIFTY-FOURTH MASSACHUSETTS REGIMENT

''Kansas Colored Volunteers'' early in 1863. When the Emancipation Proclamation had been signed Lincoln officially authorized the raising of Negro troops. Then followed the famous Fifty-fourth and Fifty-fifth Massachusetts and so many other troops that there was established in Washington a special bureau for handling affairs respecting these units. Before the end of the war they aggregated 178,975.

In keeping with the custom which was all but followed during the First World War, the Negro troops were commanded almost altogether by white officers. There was some doubt that the Negro would make a good soldier; and, of **The use of** course, the Negro officer was then almost im- **Negro troops.** possible. Massachusetts, however, commissioned ten Negro officers, Kansas three, and the military authorities a considerable number in Louisiana. Negroes held altogether about seventy-five commissions in the army during the Civil War. Among these officers were Lieutenant Colonel William N. Reed of the First North Carolina, a man well educated in Germany. He made a gallant charge with his regiment at the battle of Olustee, Florida, where he was mortally wounded. In the Kansas corps there were Captain H. Ford Douglass, First Lieutenant W. D. Matthews and Second Lieutenant Patrick A. Minor. In the U. S. C. T. One Hundred and Fourth Regiment, there were Major Martin R. Delany and Captain O. S. B. Wall of Company K. Dr. Alexander T. Augusta, who was surgeon of the U. S. C. T. Seventh Regiment, was finally breveted with Lieutenant-Colonel. Dr. John V. DeGrasse was assistant surgeon of the U. S. C. T. Thirty-fifth Regiment. Charles B. Purvis, Alpheus Tucker, John Rapier, William Ellis, Anderson R. Abbott and William Powell were hospital surgeons at Washington, D. C.

One might inquire, too, as to exactly what was the status of the Negro troops. In the first place, they were not treated as the equals of white men. There was objection to giving them the same compensation offered the whites. **The status of** In the matter of bounties there was a dis- **the Negro** crimination against Negro soldiers who were **soldiers.** slaves on April 19, 1861. This caused dissatisfaction among the Negro troops, whose families thereby seriously suffered. Sergeant William Walker was shot by order of court martial because he had his company stack arms before the captain's tent for the reason that the Government had failed to comply with its contract. The Fifty-fourth and Fifty-fifth of Massachusetts refused to receive their pay until it had been made equal to that of the whites. Negro troops, moreover, were often used by white troops for fatigue duty. Because of this notorious discrimination many of these soldiers became restive, sullen and even insubordinate.

COL. THOMAS W. HIG-GINSON, a commander of Negro troops

Yet, these Negroes distinguished themselves as soldiers. Men under whom these troops fought in battle were loud in praise of their gallantry and martyrdom. Negroes served in almost all parts of the South. They engaged in the perilous South **Valuable service.** Edisto Expedition to burn a bridge above Walton Bluff to aid General Sherman, and participated in the action at Honey Hill. Speaking of their behavior in the expedition to Dobey River in Georgia, General Rufus Saxton said that they fought with most determined bravery. Surgeon Seth Rogers, operating in South Carolina, said that braver men never lived. Colonel T. W. Higginson himself believed that "it would have been madness to attempt with the bravest white troops what he successfully accomplished with the black." Even in the failure to carry Fort Wagner, a point necessary for the capture of Charleston, the Negro troops bore the severest tests of valor. They sacrificed themselves along with their gallant leader, Colonel Robert Gould Shaw, who in this charge fell mortally wounded.

In the Mississippi Valley they fought still more bravely. Negro troops made six such desperate charges on a fort at Port Hudson that a reporter said that the deeds of heroism

Bravery in the West. performed by these black men were such as the proudest white men might emulate. General Banks said in referring to their behavior: "It gives me great pleasure to report that they answered every expectation. Their conduct was heroic; no troops could be more determined or more daring." Other troops from Louisiana showed themselves equally brave at Milliken's Bend. Reporting this battle, Captain Matthew M. Miller said: "So they fought and died, defending the cause that we revere. They met death coolly, bravely; nor rashly did they expose themselves, but all were steady and obedient to orders." And so went others to death in the massacre at Fort Pillow in Tennessee. There the Confederates, in keeping with their bold declaration not to give quarter to the slaves striking for their own freedom, slaughtered them as men kill beasts.

In the Department of the Potomac the Negro maintained there his reputation as a soldier. Under General Wild, at Fort Powhatan in 1864, the Negro soldiers bravely held

Bravery along the Potomac. their ground against the heavy onslaught of Fitzhugh Lee's brilliant soldiers, who were badly worsted in the conflict. When General Grant was endeavoring to reduce Petersburg, a brigade of Hinck's Negro division brilliantly dashed forward and cleared a line of rifle-pits and carried a redoubt ahead. They did valiant work of the same order at South Mountain and died bravely in carrying the fortified positions of the Confederates at New Market Heights and nearer to Petersburg. In the dash along the James and in the pursuit of Lee's weakened forces, the Negroes under arms maintained their bearing as brave men and came out of the Civil War as heroes.

In the course of the Civil War many constitutional questions arose. Chief among these was the suspension of the writ of habeas corpus in the cases of certain copperheads or "pacifists" in the North, who arrayed themselves against the United States Government and at one time even threatened the country with an additional secession. The Constitution provided for the sus-

Constitutional questions.

pension of the writ in times of great danger, but it is not clear whether the framers of the Constitution contemplated that this power should be exercised by the President of the United States. Furthermore, those who asserted that the writ could be suspended under certain conditions did not concede the right of the President to suspend it in sections where the courts were open and where the armies were not in operation. The most important case of this kind was that of Mil-

BISHOP DANIEL A. PAYNE, an Educator and Churchman active during the Civil War

ligan in 1864. By operation of the courts the plaintiff undertook to secure his liberty through a writ of habeas corpus and the President of the United States interfered.

There arose also other questions. The Government, it was charged, was unduly taxing the people to support an administration waging war to coerce certain States, interfering with the freedom of the press, enforcing conscription acts, compelling men to fight

Taxation.

against their will, and finally promoting by action of Congress gradual emancipation in certain border States and the abolition of slavery in the District of Columbia. Whether Congress could constitutionally legislate respecting slavery was still a question, but the Civil War gradually brought the country to a realization that Congress, representing the people of the United States, had adequate power in the premises. Because of vesting the President with dictatorial power to wage the war effectively, however, there came from certain sources a bitter antagonism which led to the organization of a party of opposition advocating the "Union as it was and the Constitution as it is."

The most important constitutional matter coming up during the Civil War was that of the Emancipation Proclamation itself. Lincoln had for some time wondered whether or not he had such authority. He long hesitated **The emancipation problem.** to issue this mandate declaring free all the Negroes in the districts then in rebellion against the United States. Fremont, Hunter and Butler, in charge of Union armies, had undertaken to do this, but had to be restrained. One of the members of Lincoln's cabinet was of the opinion that he had no such power and that such a step would doubtless do more harm than good. In the end, however, just after a number of encouraging Union victories, the Emancipation Proclamation was issued and had its desired effect; but to become legal it had to be fortified by the Thirteenth Amendment. It declared that neither slavery nor involuntary servitude, except as a punishment for crime, should exist within the United States. This was passed in Congress and ratified by the States by December 18, 1865. Few persons have since questioned the Thirteenth Amendment, although peonage still exists in parts of the United States. However, the Fourteenth and Fifteenth which followed thereupon have since given rise to all sorts of constitutional questions involving the rights of the Negroes and of others.

The reasons for these different attitudes on constitutional matters cannot be readily understood now by the layman. We are so far removed from that time that we cannot easily appreciate the underlying reasons for the positions which statesmen of that day took. Negroes of to-day, for example, severely criticize Abraham Lincoln for his inaction and hesitancy in matters re- **Lincoln and** specting the emancipation and recognition of **the Negro.** the race; and they, therefore, laugh at the idea of recording him in history as the "Great Emancipator." Lincoln often expressed his contempt for abolitionists like Sumner and Stevens. They worried him by urging the instant liberation of the "d——d niggers." He repeatedly said that he would save the Union with slavery or that he would save it without slavery. His chief purpose was to save the Union. Few persons of that day understood that the Union with slavery was impossible. Lincoln could not easily come to the position of immediate emancipation. He had thought only of gradual and compensated emancipation to be completed by the year 1900.

With respect to Negroes after they became free, moreover, he was not very liberal. He did not care to have Negro soldiers in the Union Army, and when finally all but forced by circumstances to admit them, he did not desire to grant them the same pay and the same treatment accorded white soldiers. He believed, moreover, that Negroes, if liberated, should be colonized abroad, inasmuch as they could not hope to remain in this country and become socially and politically equal to white men. His attitude was made clear in 1862, when after the liberation of the Negroes in the District of Columbia, he summoned certain of their group to urge them to emigrate. "And, why," said he, "should the people of your race be colonized and where? Why should they leave this country? You and we are different races. We have between us a broader difference than exists between almost any other two races. Whether it is right or wrong I need not discuss, but this physical difference is a great disadvantage to us both, as I think. Your race suffer very greatly, many of them, by living among us, while ours suffer from your presence. In a word we suffer on each side. If this is admitted, it affords a reason why we should be separated.''

Lincoln, however, should not be unsympathetically condemned as the Negro's enemy who sought to exterminate slavery merely because it was an economic handicap to the white man. It must be remembered that Lincoln was not elected on an abolition platform. His party had merely repudiated the Dred Scott decision and opposed the extension of slavery. Lincoln, himself, had borne eloquent testimony against mob rule, lynching and slavery throughout his career.

Lincoln sympathetically pathetically considered.

In Congress he had worked for gradual and compensated emancipation, and he had kept this plan before the slave States as the best solution of their problem. To say that he would save the Union with or without slavery does not necessarily show a lack of interest in emancipation. No one will hardly think that emancipation would have had much of a chance if the Union had been lost. It succeeded with the Union saved. In his hesitancy as to emancipation and the arming of the Negroes there may be evidence of statesmanship rather than lack of interest in freedom and democracy. As he often well said, the main thing was to win the war. Everything depended upon that. Had Lincoln immediately declared the Negroes free and turned them armed upon their masters he would have lost the war. Many of the people in the border slave States, who were kindly disposed to the Union, were nevertheless proslavery.

A considerable number of the people in the free States,

moreover, especially the "Copperheads" in the Northwest, objected to the "coercion" of the South. They would have risen in protest against anything resembling a servile insurrection. The war was not an effort to free slaves. Lincoln, as President of the United States, could not carry out his own personal plans. In a situation like this an executive must fail if he undertakes a reform so far ahead of the time that his very coworkers cannot be depended upon to carry out his policies. The abolitionists were a small minority. Men had to be gradually brought around to thinking that immediate emancipation would be the proper solution of the problem. There was much fear that such a radical step would lead to inter-racial war. For this reason Lincoln and others connected deportation with emancipation. As the experiment had not been made, the large majority of Americans of Lincoln's day believed that the two races could not dwell together on the basis of social and political equality. A militant minority of the descendants of those Americans do not believe it now. The abolitionists themselves were not united on this point. Lincoln, moreover, gradually grew unto the full stature of democracy. Observing finally that the Negroes would remain permanently in this country, he urged upon the States in process of reconstruction to make some provision for the education of the freedmen, and suggested that the right of franchise be extended to those who were intelligent and owned property. Whatever Lincoln did was what he thought best for all concerned. He was not prejudiced against any race in the sense that men are to-day. Frederick Douglass said that Lincoln was the first white man he ever met who did not say or do something to make him feel that he belonged to a different race.

CHAPTER XXIII

RECONSTRUCTION

RECONSTRUCTION began in the schoolhouses not in the State houses, as uninformed persons often say. Misguided men of that day did not know it. Having the idea that voting and holding office are privileges for oppressing the **Actual recon-** weak rather than opportunities for serving **struction.** humanity, they have emphasized unduly the part played by messages of governors, the proceedings of conventions, and the measures of legislatures. The missionary teacher was at work in the South long before it was known how the war would end. As the Union armies gradually invaded that area the soldiers opened schools for Negroes. Regular teachers came from relief societies and the Freedmen's Bureau. These enlightened a fair percentage of the Negroes by 1870. The illiteracy of the Negroes was reduced to 79.9 by that time When about the same time these freedmen had a chance to participate in the rehabilitation of State governments in the South, they gave that section the first free public school system, the first democratic education it ever had. This was the real reconstruction and the only thing which will bring the South out of its present medieval state. Some of these days there will arise in the South a white man fair-minded enough to propose the building of a monument to these Negroes who were so far ahead of their exploiters.

The first substantial support for education in the South came from philanthropists. Following up the good work done by the Union soldiers in teaching Negroes coming

382

within their reach during the Civil War, these philanthropists sent the best blood of the North as missionary teachers. They gave their lives as a sacrifice for the enlightenment of the Negro.

Reconstructing agencies.

The unselfish teachers engaged by the Bureau of Refugees, Freedmen and Abandoned Lands, established March 3, 1865, were early in the field. They had paved the way for the expansion of the work. For example, as early as 1861, Lewis Tappan, the treasurer of the American Missionary Association, learned by communication with General Butler, in charge at Fortress Monroe, that education was the immediate need of the freedmen. He, therefore, sent C. L. Lockwood to establish at Hampton the first dayschool for the freedmen. The first teacher of this

GEN. O. O. HOWARD, head of the Freedmen's Bureau and founder of Howard University

school was Mrs. Mary S. Peak, an educated free woman of color. Other such schools followed at Norfolk, Newport News, and at Hilton Head and Beaufort, South Carolina. In the West, the Rev. John Eaton was giving some attention to the education of the freedmen in the camps. There were 83 of these missionary teachers in 1863 and 250 in 1864. Many of them were preachers.[1]

These Christian workers, however, cared not so much about proselyting as they did about education. This was

[1] *Journal of Negro History*, VIII, 1-40; IX, 322-345; XI, 379-415.

the greatest need of the freedmen.   The Baptists and Methodists, who had considerable communicants among the Negroes prior to the Civil War, took the lead in this move-

The first schools.   ment.   They opened at strategic points schools which they believed would become centers of culture for the whole race.   The Baptists established Shaw University at Raleigh in 1865; Roger Williams at Nashville, and Morehouse at Atlanta, in 1867; Leland at New Orleans in 1869 and Benedict at Columbia in 1871.   The Free-will Baptists founded Storer College at Harpers Ferry in 1867.   The Methodists, who were no less active, established Walden at Nashville in 1865, Rust at Holly Springs in 1866, Morgan at Baltimore in 1867, Haven Academy at Waynesboro in 1868, Claflin at Orangeburg in 1869, and Clark at Atlanta in 1870.   The Presbyterians, who could not compete with the Baptists and Methodists in proselyting Negroes, restricted their efforts to a few small schools and to the establishment of Biddle at Charlotte in 1867. They promoted also the work begun at Lincoln University in Pennsylvania, established as Ashmun Institute in 1854. The Episcopal Church established some small institutions: St. Augustine at Raleigh in 1867, and the Bishop Payne Divinity School in Petersburg, in 1878.

Another factor was equally effective in this uplift of the freedmen.   This was the American Missionary Association. These earnest workers established Avery Institute at Charleston, Ballard Normal School at Macon, and Washburn at Beaufort, North Carolina, in 1865.   They founded,

The American Missionary Association.   too, Trinity at Athens, Alabama; Gregory at Wilmington, North Carolina; and Fisk at Nashville in 1866.   Then came Talladega in Alabama, Emerson at Mobile, Storrs at Atlanta, and Beach at Savannah in 1867.   Next appeared Hampton Institute in Virginia, Knox at Athens, and Burrell at Selma, now at Florence, and Ely Normal in Louisville in 1868.

Straight University opened at New Orleans, Tougaloo in Mississippi, Le Moyne in Memphis, and Lincoln at Marion, Alabama, in 1869. Dorchester Academy began at McIntosh, and the Albany Normal in Georgia in 1870. The Congregationalists, moreover, figured with the Freedmen's Bureau in the establishment of Howard University. This institution was chartered by the United States Government in 1867 with provisions for the education of all persons regardless of race.

GEN. SAMUEL C. ARMSTRONG
A Friend in War and Peace

Some other less effective forces were at work during this **Missionary educators.** period accomplishing here and there results seemingly unimportant but in the end productive of much good. In 1862 Miss Towne and Miss Murray, members of the Society of Friends, established the Penn School on St. Helena Island, South Carolina. Cornelia Hancock, a Philadelphia woman of the same sect, founded the Laing School at Mount Pleasant, near Charleston, South Carolina. Martha Schofield, another Friend of Pennsylvania, opened at Aiken in 1868 the Schofield Industrial School. In 1864 Alida Clark, supported by Friends in Indiana, engaged in relief work among Negro orphans in Helena, Arkansas, and in 1866 established near that city what is now known as Southland College. The Reformed Presbyterians maintained a school at Natchez between 1864 and 1866, and in 1874 established Knox Academy at Selma, Alabama. The United Presbyterians opened a sort of clandestine school in Nashville in 1863, and in 1875 established Knoxville College as a center for a group of schools for Negroes in Eastern Tennessee, Virginia, North Carolina, and Northern Alabama. Franklinton Christian College, maintained by the American Christian Convention, was opened in 1878 and

TEACHING THE FREEDMEN

chartered in 1890. Stillman Institute was established by the southern Presbyterians at Tuscaloosa in 1876. Paine College was founded at Augusta for the Colored Methodists in 1884. Lane came later.

The Freedmen's Bureau and the relief agencies were chiefly effective in educational work between 1865 and **Agencies in** 1870. During the first year of the war, the **this field.** Bureau itself reported the establishment of 4,239 schools with 9,307 teachers and 247,333 students in the various States. These schools were free and tended to emphasize the necessity for democratic education at public expense. When these schools closed as a result of the withdrawal of Federal support in 1870, they had probably brought under instruction ten or fifteen per cent of the Negro children. In 1870 twenty-one per cent of the Negroes were literate largely as a result of these efforts. The work of the Freedmen's Bureau was turned over then to various agencies, mainly to the American Missionary Association. This body had been organized some years earlier, prior to the Civil War as an interdenominational effort, but in 1881 it came under the control of the Congregational Church.

The other agencies participating in this effort were the Pennsylvania Freedmen's Relief Association, the Tract Society, Pennsylvania Friends Freedmen's Relief Association, the Old School Presbyterian Mission, the Reformed Presbyterian Mission, the New England Freedmen's Aid Committee, the New England Freedmen's Aid Society, the New England Freedmen's Mission, the Washington Christian Union, the Universalists of Maine, the New York Freedmen's Relief Association, the Hartford Relief Society, and the National Freedmen's Relief Association of the District of Columbia. Along with these forces should be mentioned the liberal elements of the South, represented by Haygood, Curry, Ruffner, Northern, and Vance, who urged upon the people the importance of enlightening the freedmen. High upon the roll of honor Negroes inscribe as immortal apostles to the lowly Myrtilla Miner in the District of Columbia,[2] Corey at Virginia Union, Packard and Giles at Spelman, Cravath at Fisk, Ware at Atlanta, Armstrong at Hampton, Graves at Morehouse, and Tupper at Shaw. They left the comforts of a modern home and went into a benighted land to face social ostracism, persecution, and sometimes death, in spending their lives in the uplift of the Negro. These men and women

[2] *Journal of Negro History*, V, 448-457.

gave the world a new meaning of what their Great Teacher had in mind when he said: "Greater love hath no man than this, that a man lay down his life for his friends."

The Negro church was equally effective in working out reconstruction in the South. In fact, what has been said above with respect to the extensive work undertaken by the schools is also a sketch of the operations of the church. Christian work-

Reconstruction through the church. ers learned in the be- ginning of this effort that the extensive proselyting and thorough Christianization of the Negroes would be impossible until the schools could do their work of enlightening the freedmen. The whole educational movement then may be properly styled as a work of missionary teachers inspired and largely supported by the church.

RICHARD DeBaptiste

Most of the first teachers sent to the Negroes were persons who taught during the week and preached on Sunday. Schoolhouses were churches, and churches were schoolhouses. However, this was not a revival of anything like the church combined with the state. Denominations forgot their sectarian differences and unselfishly coöperated in the general uplift of the Negro.

The further development of the Negro churches as such after the war, however, was also a factor in reconstruction in the South. The church went forward under distinguished ministers like Bishop Daniel A. Payne and James Poindexter in Ohio, Rufus L. Perry in New York, and Richard DeBaptiste in Illinois. In the South where the majority of the freedmen were found, the Negro church had its real opportunity. Thousands of them had been communicants segregated in the pews of white churches or ministered unto at different hours or in separate buildings. With the spirit of freedom, these Negroes went out to establish a religious system of their own. Under the leadership of Bishop W. H. Miles and Bishop R. H. Vanderhorst, the Colored Methodist Episcopal Church began its eventful career in 1870. Later this work was decidedly stimulated by Bishop L. H. Holsey. After the removal of the restrictions which handicapped independent religious efforts there prior to emancipation, the work of the

W. H. MILES

African Methodist Episcopal Church was extended rapidly through the South by Bishops A. W. Wayman, R. H. Cain, H. M. Turner, and W. B. Derrick. The African Methodist Episcopal Zion Church invaded the same field with unusual success, especially in the State of North Carolina, where it was efficiently aided by Bishops J. W. Hood and J. J. Clinton. The Negro membership of the Methodist Episcopal Church, maintaining its connection with the North, went also into this field of a waiting harvest and accomplished much in the enlightenment of the freedmen. The Baptists at the same time were blazing the way through such men as Henry Williams, James Holmes, Walter H. Brooks, and Richard Wells in Virginia; through J. J. Worlds, George W. Lee, and E. M. Brawley in North Carolina; J. P. Brockenton and J. J. Durham in South Carolina; W. J. White in Georgia; and W. R. Pettiford in Alabama.[3]

The political reconstruction, however, attracted the attention of the whole country. As soon as the

Lincoln's reconstruction.

Union armies began to occupy a considerable portion of the territory of the so-called seceded States, there was some thought about the rehabilitation of these commonwealths.[4] As to the exact position of these commonwealths which had undertaken to withdraw from the Union, there was a wide difference of opinion. Lincoln himself was of the impression that a State could not get out of the Union. "Once in the Union, forever in the Union," was his theory. Lincoln therefore issued,

J. W. HOOD

[3] These facts are given in detail in Woodson's *History of the Negro Church*. See also *The Journal of Negro History*, IX, 346-364; and XI, 425-458.

[4] There are no scientific studies of the nation-wide reconstruction in which the Negroes took a part. W. L. Fleming, James F. Rhodes, W. A. Dunning and J. W. Burgess have written works in this field, but they are biased and inadequate. Almost a score of other so-called scientific studies of Reconstruction in the various States have

on December 8, 1863, a proclamation setting forth a plan
for the reconstruction of these commonwealths. He proclaimed full pardon to the people in the Confederate States
with the restoration of all rights of property except as to
slaves if they should take and subscribe to an oath of
allegiance to the United States Government and thenceforward keep and maintain this oath inviolate. He made exception of those who had served in the civil or diplomatic
service of the Confederate Government or in judicial stations, of those who had served in the army or navy with
rank above colonel, or who had abandoned Congress to
aid the rebellion, resigned commissions in the army, or
cruelly treated Negroes or white persons in charge of them.

Lincoln further proclaimed that whenever in any of these
States there should be loyal persons to the number of not
less than one-tenth of the votes cast in such States at the
Presidential election of the year 1860, each having taken
this oath and not having violated it and being **The ten per
cent basis.**
a qualified voter by the election law of the
State existing prior to the secession, the commonwealth
should establish a State government. This government
should be democratic, should be recognized as the true government of the State, and should receive the benefits of the
constitutional provision which declares that the United
States shall guarantee to every State in this Union a
republican form of government.

Lincoln also proclaimed that any helpful provision which
these commonwealths thus restored might adopt in relation
to the freed people within their limits would not be objected

been made, but these merely try to make a case for the white man's
side of the question as to whether the reduction of the Negro to
serfdom was just. John R. Lynch in his *Facts of Reconstruction,*
and W. E. B. DuBois in his *Reconstruction, and Its Benefits* (in the
American Historical Review, XV, No. 4) have undertaken to point
out these defects. Some other views of John R. Lynch are given
in the *Journal of Negro History,* II, 345-368; III, 139-157; V,
420-436.

to by the President. He wanted the States to recognize and declare their permanent freedom, and provide for their education by way of some temporary arrangement **Interest in** which might be consistent with their con-**the freedmen.** dition as a laboring, landless and homeless class. The President was of the opinion that the name of the State, the boundary, subdivisions, constitution, and the

JAMES POINDEXTER

former code of laws should be maintained, subject only to the modification made necessary by the conditions elsewhere stated in the proclamation. He did not object to other measures, not contravening the conditions of the proclamation, if deemed expedient by those framing the new State government.

Upon this basis Lincoln undertook the reconstruction of the States of Louisiana, Arkansas, and Tennessee prior to the close of the Civil War as soon as loyal men to the number of one-tenth of the voters exercising suffrage in the presidential election of 1860 were **States** found in those commonwealths. Believing **reorganized.** that Lincoln's position in this case was sound, Andrew Johnson, his successor, undertook to carry out this policy. When the cessation of arms finally came, several of the rebellious commonwealths, thinking that the States as such could never be destroyed, proceeded to organize similar governments. The rebellious States complied with the conditions of repudiating the Confederate debts, declared allegiance to the Union, and ratified the Thirteenth Amendment. Thinking, therefore, that they would be immediately admitted to the Union with the rights and privileges formerly enjoyed by the Southern States, they elected representatives and senators to sit in Congress. This, however, was not acceptable to the statesmen then in control of affairs, and the right of such persons to serve as representatives of these commonwealths was questioned.

They found in Congress men led by Charles Sumner and Thaddeus Stevens. These men were of the opinion that inasmuch as the Southern States had rebelled and had failed to maintain their cause, they were then subject to the same treatment as any other people in a conquered territory. This, to be sure, con- Various theories. flicted with certain other views, as it admitted that secession had been temporarily successful, and conflicted with the administrative plans of Lincoln and Johnson. They held that secession was merely an unsuccessful effort and that the States were still in the Union. Shellabarger contended that secession was a nullity. Although disloyalists could not assume control of the territory in which secession existed, it nevertheless worked a loss of the status of a member of the Union. The citizens remaining therein were, therefore, exclusively subjected to the jurisdiction of the United States Government. This was endorsed by Sumner, Fessenden and Wilson, and became, in fact, the theory of the reconstructionists in Congress. This meant antagonism to the administration and led to the long differences of opinion between that body and Johnson, which finally culminated in the impeachment of the President.

There came also to the national capital various reports which further convinced the gentlemen in charge of affairs in Congress that the South was unwilling to grant the

Negro the right to enjoy the fruits of the victory of the
Civil War. The freedmen were being oppressed almost to
The unwill- the extent of being enslaved. Disorder fol-
ing South. lowed. Native whites undertook to "manage" or "control" the freedmen as they were handled when
slaves. If the freedmen objected, they were beaten or
killed. Referring to South Carolina an authority said:
"The pecuniary value which the individual Negro formerly
represented having disappeared, the maiming and killing
of them seemed to be looked upon by many as one of those
venial offenses which must be forgiven to the outraged
feelings of a wronged and robbed people." "E. H.
Johnson, a Virginia clergyman, killed a Negro soldier in
1865." According to the *Richmond Enquirer* on November 3, 1866, "J. C. Johnston, a law student of Lexington
charged with killing a freedman, was acquitted." For a
trivial reason one Queensbury, a planter in Louisa County,
killed a Negro in his employ. Because of slight misunderstandings, R. N. Eastham of Rappahannock, and
Washington Alsworth of Lunenburg killed Negroes in their
service. On November 24, 1866, the *Enquirer* reported that
Dr. James Watson, "one of the most respectable gentlemen
of Rockbridge county," killed a Negro for driving into his
vehicle. These criminals were not punished.[5]

A bloody race-riot broke out in Memphis in the spring of
1866. In the following July a more serious conflict took
place in New Orleans when freedmen on the way to a political meeting clashed with native whites. Going into the hall
where they were to assemble, they found themselves surrounded by their pursuers aided by the police. Forty
Negroes were killed and about a hundred were wounded.
Twelve of the whites were killed and a few were wounded.

The first official reports on conditions in the South were
brought in by General Grant and Carl Schurz. The former

[5] *Journal of Negro History*, XI, 325.

contended that the Southerners were in the main willing to accept the changes effected by the Civil War, and the latter that the rebellious commonwealths were not loyal and intended to reënslave the Negroes. Some of these States were enacting black codes providing for apprentice-ship, penalizing the vagrancy of Negroes, and interfering with the civil rights of the freedmen. Many of the blacks, having wandered about or flocked to the towns where they too often were reduced to poverty and subject to tempta-tions and vicious influences, tended to retrograde rather than advance. The vagrancy laws, therefore, generally provided for fines, corporal punishment, indenturing for a certain period of service, and in a few cases required that every Negro should be attached to some employer.

Some of these measures will bear detailed treatment here. Virginia, for example, empowered officers to bring the vagrant before a justice of peace. If condemned as such, he was to be hired out for a period not **Vagrancy** exceeding three months. If during this time **Acts.** the vagrant absconded without cause, he would be penalized by adding another month, or the employer could shackle the vagrant with ball and chain to prevent such an escape. Such a fugitive might be placed in the public service of the county, or he might be imprisoned and fed on bread and water. Five classes of persons were defined as vagrants. These included "all persons who shall unlawfully return into any county or corporation whence they have been legally removed''; "all persons who, not having where-with to maintain themselves and their families, live idly and without employment, and refuse to work for the usual and common wages given to other laborers in the like work in the place where they then are''; "all persons who shall refuse to perform the work which shall be allotted to them by the overseers of the poor as aforesaid''; "all persons going from door to door, or placing themselves in the

streets, highways or other roads, to beg alms, and all other
persons wandering abroad and begging, unless disabled or
incapable of labor''; and ''all persons who shall come from
any place without this commonwealth to any place within
it, and shall be found loitering and residing therein, and
shall follow no labor, trade, occupation or business, and
have no visible means of subsistence, and can give no reasonable account of themselves or their business in such
places.''

In South Carolina orphan children of color were subjected to compulsory apprenticeship like that provided for
a servant under contract. Practically all Negroes were
compelled to enter the service of some planter. They had
to sign an indenture of service and be bound thereby.
Servants should rise at dawn in the morning, feed, water
and care for the animals on the farm, do the usual and
needful work about the premises, prepare their meals for
the day, if required by the master, and begin the farm
work or some other task by sunrise. All losses of
implements and supplies not caused by the act of the master
would be deducted from the wages of the servants and also
the cost of food and other necessaries in cases of sickness
necessitating absence from work. No person of color should
pursue or practice the art, trade or business of an artisan
or shopkeeper, or any other trade without a license from
the Judge of the District Court. Vagrancy was defined
very much as in the case of Virginia. Such offenders
might be sentenced to imprisonment and hard labor. One
or both should be fixed by the verdict not exceeding twelve
months. The defendant, if thus sentenced, might be hired
for such wages as could be obtained for his service to
any owner or lessee of a farm, or might be hired for
labor on the streets, roads or public buildings. The person
receiving such a vagrant should have all the rights and
remedies for enforcing good conduct and diligence at

labor. No person of color should immigrate into the State unless within twenty days he could give bond for his good behavior.

Aggravating the situation still more, Mississippi provided in its black code, "that if any apprentice shall leave the employment of his or her master or mistress, said master or mistress may pursue and recapture said apprentice, and bring him or her before any justice of peace of the county, whose duty it shall be to remand said apprentice to the service of his or her master or mistress; and in the event of a refusal on the part of said apprentice so to return, then said justice shall commit said apprentice to the jail of said county."

For the improvement of the social conditions of the Negroes, these codes provided also for the marriage of the freedmen according to law and vested the children of the former unions during slavery with the right of inheritance of the property of their parents. The Negroes were also granted the right to own property and that of suing and being sued in the courts. They could give testimony in cases in which only Negroes were concerned. They could not serve on a jury or in the militia; and, of course, could neither vote nor hold office. Their right of locomotion was restricted in that they were forbidden to assemble under certain circumstances. Furthermore, there had set in a general intimidation of Negroes.

Assured that the situation was deplorable, Congress passed the Civil Rights Bill in 1865 to secure to Negroes the full enjoyment of social and civil privileges. The body then proceeded to draft the Fourteenth Amendment as a condition of readmission of a seceded State to the Union. The aim was to prevent any State from making or enforcing a law which would encroach upon the privileges or immunities of citizens of the United States, deprive them of life, liberty or property without due process of law, or withhold from any one within its jurisdiction the equal protection of the law. It guaranteed to all persons the enjoyment of the privileges and immunities of citizens without regard to race, color, or previous condition of servitude. Congress also deemed it necessary at this juncture to bring the South under military rule. Then came the establishment of military districts into which the unreconstructed States were organized for the rule of the army. In 1870 came the Fifteenth Amendment declaring that the right to vote shall not be denied on account of race, color or previous condition of servitude. In this way the South, by taking a radical position in its unwise application of its power to deal with persons over whom it would have been given more control, brought upon itself a military rule from which it would not have suffered if it had been disposed to treat the freedmen humanely.

The official reports led also to the extension of the work of what is known as the Freedmen's Bureau, the commission established for the protection and the assistance of the freedmen. Several times some such idea had been expressed in both houses of Congress. On March 3, 1865, therefore, Congress established in the War Department "a bureau of refugees, freedmen and abandoned lands." This action was taken after hearing numerous suggestions as to how the Government should control and manage the freedmen coming within the lines of the Union Army. The **The Freed-** actual work of this bureau, however, fol- **men's Bureau.** lowed after the Civil War. In their struggle with President Andrew Johnson, the reconstructionists in Congress sought to increase these powers of the Federal Government, although this had been done in a measure passed in 1865. A bill to this effect, however, was proposed in 1866. The measure was debated long and carefully by both houses. Some doubted the necessity for such a grant of additional military power in the time of peace. The

Reconstruction

SOME FACTORS IN THE RECONSTRUCTION
WILLIAM P. FESSENDEN   SAMUEL SHELLABARGER
CARL SCHURZ
FREDERICK T. FRELINGHUYSEN   THADDEUS STEVENS

measure to give the department additional powers was vetoed by President Johnson. In presenting his reasons he so antagonized the leaders in Congress as to widen the irreparable breach between the executive and legislative departments. This bill, with certain objectionable features removed, was later passed over the President's veto, but it had to be amended.

The act provided for the appointment of a commissioner with a number of assistants under the administration of the President to care for the freedmen in the districts in rebellion or controlled by the Union Army. Primarily the Freedmen's Bureau was intended to aid refugees and freedmen by supplying them with provisions and by taking up abandoned lands in the South. These were to be distributed in parcels of not more than forty acres each. On account of misrepresentations many Negroes expected from this quarter forty acres of land and a mule for each of the landless freedmen. This prospective charity tended to produce vagrancy and shiftlessness among people indulged as dependent children. The Freedmen's Bureau was vested with the power to build schoolhouses and asylums for the Negroes, and it was proposed to give it unusual power in its jurisdiction over all civil and criminal cases where equality in civil rights and in the application of justice was denied on account of race, color, or previous condition of servitude. With this unusual power vested in machinery coming from without the State and intended to benefit persons recently enslaved, the Freedmen's Bureau became a source of much irritation to the whites of the South. Grant thought that the officers of the Freedmen's Bureau were a useless set of men and recommended that the work be placed in charge of army officers. For a number of years the Freedmen's Bureau was directed by General O. O. Howard, who founded Howard University with sums appropriated to the use of the Freedmen's Bureau.

When Congress finally decided to ignore Johnson's reconstruction schemes, a committee was appointed to work out a more acceptable plan. After some deliberation these gentlemen returned with a majority and a minority report. The majority report, representing the views of the Unionists, was to the effect that the attempted secession of eleven States had resulted in the loss of their status and in their becoming **Congressional reconstruction.** disorganized communities, but that although the State governments in the same had been destroyed, the commonwealths had not escaped the obligations of the Constitution and the authority of the United States Government. The minority report, representing the secessionist theory, was that a State could never be anything less than a State, regardless of what its deeds may be, and each was, therefore, entitled to the same powers, rights and privileges under the Constitution as those given any other State. It is needless to say that under these circumstances the minority report had little weight.

Congress thereupon proceeded in accordance with the views of the majority to work out a plan for the control of the disorganized States. In spite of the President's opposition and his vetoes, it was decided to divide the seceded States into five military districts, to each of which the President would assign an army officer **Military districts.** of not lower rank than a brigadier general, with a sufficient force to enable him to carry out the laws of the Union. The commanders were to govern these districts by martial law as far as in their judgments the reign of order and the preservation of public peace might demand. No sentence of death, however, could be carried out without the approval of the President. To escape from this military government, a rebellious State had to accept universal manhood suffrage of all male citizens of twenty-one years of age without regard to color, race or previous condition of servitude. At a special election the State might provide for the framing of a State constitution through delegates to be chosen among persons who were not disqualified by participation in the rebellion. There would have to be a ratification of this constitution by a

majority of the voters as designated by the same law of suffrage for the delegates of the convention. These States, moreover, would have to ratify the Fourteenth Amendment. This new measure of freedom provided that no State should abridge the privileges or immunities of citizens of the United States, nor should any State deprive any person of life, liberty, or property, without due process of law, nor deny to any

JOHN M. LANGSTON

person within its jurisdiction the equal protection of the laws. The South had refused to ratify this amendment.

Some of the States immediately availed themselves of this opportunity to be relieved of the military régime, for there was among them a natural antagonism

Different courses followed. to such a rule. Hoping to find a better solution of the problem by adopting the policy of watchful waiting, however, other States, Virginia, Georgia and Texas, refused to take advantage of this opportunity. The citizens of these States found out that the military government was more acceptable than the governments so quickly organized in some of the other Southern States. They decided then for the time being to obey the dictum of the army. In the course of time there was an enlargement of the white minority by the extension of the terms of granting pardon to those who had participated in the rebellion. As there was already a larger percentage of white persons than Negroes in these three States, when the time did come for them to organize State governments, there soon developed a majority opposed to liberal reconstruction. The other States in the South, from 1868 to about 1872, became subjected to what is commonly known as "Negro carpet-bag rule."

To call this Negro rule, however, is very much of a mistake. As a matter of fact, most of the local offices in these commonwealths were held by the white men, and those Negroes who did attain some of the **Not a Negro regime.** higher offices were usually about as competent as the average whites thereto elected. Only twenty-three Negroes served in Congress from 1868 to 1895. The Negroes had political equality in the Southern States only a few years, and with some exceptions their tenure in Congress was very short.

JOHN R. LYNCH, a member of Congress

Hiram R. Revels of Mississippi completed an unexpired term in the Senate, and B. K. Bruce served there six years. John M. Langston, the Negro member from Virginia, served in the House one term. From North Carolina went to the United States House of Representatives John A. Hyman for one term and James E. O'Hara, H. P. Cheatham and George H. White for two terms each. Jefferson F. Long represented a district of Georgia a part of a term. Josiah T. Walls of Florida served in the House two terms. Alabama elected to Congress Jere Haralson, Benjamin S. Turner and James T. Rapier, who served one term each. Louisiana sent Charles

SOME NEGRO CONGRESSMEN

ROBERT B. ELLIOTT
ROBERT C. DeLARGE

JOSIAH T. WALLS
RICHARD H. CAIN

E. Nash for one term, and Mississippi John R. Lynch for two. South Carolina had the largest number of Negro representatives in the House. Joseph H. Rainey of that Commonwealth sat in Congress five terms; Richard H. Cain, two; Robert C. DeLarge, one; Alonzo J. Ransier, one; Robert B. Elliott, two; Robert Smalls, five; Thomas E. Miller, one; and Geo. W. Murray, two. J. W. Menard, of Louisiana, was not recognized. At one time all the Representatives of South Carolina were Negroes.

The charge that all Negro officers were illiterate, ignorant of the science of government, cannot be sustained. In the first place, the education of the Negro by Union soldiers in the South began in spots as early as 1861. Many of the Negro leaders who had been educated in the North or abroad returned to the South after the war. Negro illiteracy

H. R. REVELS, U. S. Senator from Mississippi

had been reduced to 79.9 by 1870, just about the time the freedmen were actually participating in the reconstruction. The masses of Negroes did not take a part in the government in the beginning of the reconstruction.

It is true that many of them were not prepared to vote, and decidedly disqualified for the positions which they held. In some of the legislatures, as in Louisiana and South Carolina, more than half of the Negro **Negroes** members could scarcely read or write. They, **capable.** therefore, had to vote according to emotions or the dictates of the demagogues. This, of course, has been true of legislatures composed entirely of whites. In the local and State administrative offices, however, where there were frequent chances for corruption, very few ignorant Negroes ever served.

Some of the Negro officeholders had undergone consider-

Literacy of voters and officers. able training and had experienced sufficient mental development to be able to discharge their duties

with honor. Hiram R. Revels spent two years in a Quaker seminary and probably was later instructed at Knox College. B. K. Bruce had considerable practical education. Jere Haralson learned enough to teach. R. H. Cain studied at Wilberforce. James T. Rapier was well educated in a Catholic school in Canada. Benjamin Turner clandestinely received a fair education in Alabama. James E. O'Hara obtained a secondary education. According to Frederick

B. K. BRUCE, U. S. Senator from Mississippi

Douglass, Robert Brown Elliott, educated at Eton College, England, had no peer in his race except Samuel R. Ward. John M. Langston, after finishing both the college and theological courses at Oberlin, practiced law in Ohio. John R. Lynch, as evidenced by his addresses and writings, was well educated by his dint of energy, although he had only a common school training. Most Negroes who sat in Congress during the eighties and nineties, moreover, had more formal education than Warren G. Harding, once President of the United States.[6]

Other Negro officeholders, furthermore, were liberally trained. Richard T. Greener, a reconstruction officeholder in South Carolina, was the first Negro graduate of Harvard College. F. L. Cardozo, another functionary in the same State, was educated at the University of Glasgow, Scotland. E. D. Bassett, who distinguished himself as an educator and as Minister to Haiti, studied the classics, mathematics and general literature at Yale after being graduated at the Birmingham Academy and the Connecticut State Normal School. P. B. S. Pinchback admirably united common sense with his fundamental e d u c a t i o n obtained largely at Gilmore's High School in Cincinnati, Ohio, prior to the War for Southern Independence.

JOSEPH H. RAINEY, a member of Congress

Most of the local, State and Federal offices, however, were held not by Negroes but by southern white men, and by others who came from the North and profited by the prostration of the South. They were in many respects selfish men, but not always utterly lacking in principle. The northern whites, of course, had little sympathy for the South. They depended for their constituency upon the Negroes, who could not be expected to placate the ex-slaveholders. Being adventurers and interested in their own affairs, the carpet-baggers became unusually corrupt in certain States. They administered af-

White men in control.

[6] *Journal of Negro History*, VII, 127-171.

fairs selfishly. Most Negro officers who served in the South came out of office with an honorable record. Such was the case with J. T. White, commissioner of public works and internal improvements in Arkansas; M. W. Gibbs, city judge in Little Rock; J. C. Corbin, superintendent of schools of the same commonwealth; Jonathan C. Gibbs, a Dartmouth graduate elected also as superintendent of public instruction in Florida, and F. L. Cardozo, State treasurer of South Carolina.

Reconstruction history, however, was distorted by J. W.

Burgess, a slaveholder of Giles County, Tennessee, who was educated in the North and finally attained distinction as a teacher and writer at Columbia University; and by W. A. Dunning, the son of an industrialist of Plainfield, New Jersey, who became the disciple of Burgess. The two trained or influenced in the same biased way the sons and sympathizers of former slaveholders who prostituted modern historiography to perpetuate the same distortion. These pseudo-historians refused to use the evidence of those who

JAMES T. RAPIER, a member of Congress

opposed slavery, discredited the testimony of those who favored Congressional Reconstruction, and ignored the observations of travellers from the North and from Europe. These makers of history to order were more partial than required by the law of slavery, for they rejected the evidence from Negro sources and thus denied the Negro not only the opportunity to testify against the white man but even to testify in favor of himself.

CHAPTER XXIV

POLITICAL RECONSTRUCTION UNDONE

WHETHER the free Negro was capable, whether he was honest, however, had little to do with the southern white man's attitude toward the Negro officeholders. To produce evidence that the Negroes lacked these essentials, the whites well knew, would help them to justify themselves to the world for using such harsh measures to over- **Prejudice a** throw the new régime. But the Negro was **factor.** unacceptable merely because he was black, because he had not enjoyed the distinction of wringing his bread from the sweat of another's brow. Government, as the Southern man saw it, should be based on an aristocratic exploitation of the man far down. As the slaveholders had for centuries enjoyed this exclusive privilege, they could not but bear it grievously that it had been suddenly taken away.

Wherever they could, the native whites instituted government by investigation to expose all shortcomings of Negro officials. The general charge was that **Corruption** they were corrupt. The very persons who **explained.** complained of the corruption in the Negro carpet-bag governments and who effected the reorganization of the State governments in the South when the Negroes were overthrown, however, became just as corrupt as the governing class under the preceding régime. In almost every restored State government in the South, and especially in

Mississippi, the white officers in control of the funds defaulted. These persons who had been so long out of office came back so eager to get the most out of it that they filled their own pockets from the coffers of the public. No exposure followed.

In contradistinction to this rule of stealing from the public treasury, there stood out Dubuclet, the Negro who served as Treasurer of the State of Louisiana. When the government of that State was taken from the reconstructionists by the restored aristocrats, he had still two years to serve. He was investigated with a view to finding out some act of misuse of the public funds that he might be impeached and thrown

Excellent record of Dubuclet.

Bishop L. H. Holsey, a factor in Reconstruction through the Church

out of office. The committee, of which E. D. White, later Chief Justice of the United States Supreme Court, was chairman, reported after much deliberation that his funds had been honestly handled and that there were no grounds on which proceedings against him could be instituted. In these investigations the political purpose was clear. For example, the Negro treasurer of South Carolina was declared a criminal for diverting funds appropriated for a definite purpose, although no theft was shown. The white treasurer of "Conservative" Virginia during the reconstruction repeatedly thus diverted the money appropriated to education, but no white person thought of him as a criminal.

The gravest charge against the Negroes seemed to grow out of the unwritten law that the "superior" white race should not be ruled by its "inferiors." That there should be unusual friction in communities where persons, who a few years prior to their elevation to citizenship had served as goods and chattels, should excite little sur-

Haughtiness.

prise. The South could not appreciate a Negro in uniform or in office. But true students of history know that the Negroes were not especially anxious to put themselves forward. While there were a good many among them seeking to be placed where they could not serve, the majority of the blacks were anxious to secure the coöperation of the best whites. But the former slave-holders refused to coöperate. They believed that the Negroes should have no part in the government at all. They hoped that they could in some way effect the complete elimination of the Negro from politics, as they have done in recent years. The result, therefore, was that the Negroes were compelled in the beginning to support for office white men who had never been tried and who in some cases had given evidence of dishonest purposes.

The argument against this, however, is that the Negroes should not have been enfranchised and that the government should have been organized among the loyal whites. To this it may be replied that there were

Enfranchise-ment question.

few loyal whites, and many of those who pretended that they were and undertook to organize governments, proved to be just as oppressive as they ever had been. In fact, they undertook to reëstablish slavery. Had there been a close coöperation among the best whites in the South and a gradual incorporation of the intelligent freedmen into the electorate, many of the mistakes made would have been obviated; and the recent steps backward towards peonage, segregation and lynching might not have been made.

Another trouble, too, was the fear of a social upheaval. It seemed to be more probable at that time than ever before in the history of this country. The prejudice of a

large number of persons of that day was based on caste rather than on color. A few white men who had long
Fear of a so-cial upheaval. looked with wishful eyes upon Negro women prior to the war and could associate with them only clandestinely married such women after emancipation. A few white women, having long since known of the relations of white men and Negro women, dared to

W. R. Pettiford

A Reconstructionist in the Church

break over the social barrier to marry Negro men. For this change of attitude there were various reasons. Just after emancipation the Negroes were looked upon as the "coming people." Thousands of persons were working for their uplift through the church and school. They could vote and hold office. More industrious, too, than the poor whites, the freedmen often became the more progressive element in the community. Prosperous Negro men, therefore, sometimes seemed more attractive to white women than males of their own race. Consequently a number of intermarriages followed in the various Southern States. Against this admixture, however, the press of the conservative whites persistently inveighed, but it continued in some places clandestinely a generation after emancipation.

The whites seriously objected to the granting of civic privileges to Negroes also on the ground that this would ultimately lead to miscegenation. Interpreting the liberal reconstruction constitutions and the Federal Civil Rights Law as granting mixed schools and an open door to inns, hotels and public places of amusement, moreover, Negroes endeavored to avail them- selves of these opportunities. The whites as a majority bit- terly opposed any such democratization of our institutions. Almost before the public schools could be established Southerners who had never been enthusiastic about educa- tion at public expense began to oppose the system because a few interpreted the Federal Civil Rights Law to mean the coeducation of the races. They believed that it was better to have no education at all than to have the two races at- tending the same school. The public schools were finally made separate, and custom and public opinion generally kept the races apart in social matters until specific laws of the restored reactionaries to this effect could be placed on the statute books.[1]

The attack on the policies of the carpet-bag governments, moreover, had the desired effect among the poor and igno- rant whites. Reared under the degrading influences of slavery, they could not tolerate the blacks as citizens. The Negroes thereafter were harassed and harried by disturbing elements of anarchy, out of which soon emerged an oath-bound order called the Ku Klux Klan, established to terrorize the Negroes with lawlessness and violence. The Ku Klux Klan started in Tennessee in 1865. It did its work of intimidation here and there largely by clandestine methods. In the early seventies the order proceeded to its task in bolder fashion and drew into action other lawless combinations which helped to spread terror and dismay among the Negroes. Negroes and their friends could not make a case against

Social privileges.

Ku Klux Klan.

---

[1] For a discussion of this social upheaval see *The Journal of Negro History*, IX, 249-251; and XI, 294-309.

these agents of disorder, because only native whites of proslavery sentiment could join. Proceeding at night, too,

A hooded order. in hooded white attire shaped and decorated in scarecrow fashion, they easily terrified ignorant Negroes.

Congress, therefore, deemed it necessary to pass a series of repressive measures, known as "force bills," to protect the Negroes in the enjoyment of the civil and political rights. The President was authorized to suppress insurrection in the Southern States where and when local authorities were powerless and to suspend the writ of habeas corpus. The jurisdiction of the Federal courts was so extended as to take cognizance of cases in which Negroes complained of being deprived of their rights. This legislation also contemplated the use of Federal troops to secure fair election in these States. While these measures offered temporary relief they caused such deep resentment in the South, especially among those whites who were endeavoring to suppress mob violence, that the South tended to become a smoldering volcano awaiting an opportunity for eruption.

Some of the clashes became almost as serious as the battles of the Civil War. The United States Government appointed a committee in 1870 to investigate these opera-

Inter-racial clashes. tions. The committee went throughout the reconstructed territory, sitting in various cities to take evidence. The report which the committee made consists of many volumes. The facts set forth therein show that the situation was alarming. At the same time the report shows how difficult it was to obtain evidence there because of the organized opposition of the native whites and the determination to dispatch unceremoniously any one who disclosed their operations. Men were killed at their post of duty, innocent persons were shot down in cold blood, and groups of Negroes were massacred.

The most cruel of these massacres was that which took place at Hamburg, South Carolina, in 1876. This was a sequel of the solid native white party organization which was then taking shape in the State. This was the election year of 1876, when by such methods the native whites won the day in South Carolina. The leaders of the movement had passed the word to get rid of the new **The Hamburg** régime even if it had to be done by foul **Massacre.** means. To do this they had to dispose of the Negro militia. This state guard which, under the reconstruction laws, admitted Negroes, worked the exclusion of the whites in South Carolina. Because of caste the native whites would not join. The very uniform on Negroes enraged them as a red flag does a bull. This made the fight on the militia a bloody one in South Carolina.

At Hamburg the outbreak developed in this way. Thomas Butler and Henry Getzen interfered with the drill of the local Negro militia on a back street in Hamburg on July 4, 1876. On the following day the plot was further developed by preferring against these Negroes in the local court of a Negro justice of the peace the charge of blocking the streets. By postponement for various excuses the matter was prolonged until the following Saturday. Under the direction of General M. C. Butler, of Confederate fame, the agents of disorder had then had time to organize their forces and assemble them. Hundreds of armed white men began to reach the town. The trial was ordered by Butler. After some hesitation the Negro justice of the peace appeared upon the scene. Butler then called on the Negro militiamen to apologize for the offense of blocking the streets and to surrender their arms. This they refused to do. Butler then went to Augusta, Georgia, and cannon and other munitions soon followed. The Negroes, seeing that they were outnumbered and surrounded, asked Butler whether he would protect the people if the guardsmen gave up their arms. Butler, however, gave no definite assurance. The Negroes then inquired as to whether it would be acceptable to Butler if they shipped the arms to the Governor of the State. To this he replied: "D—— the Governor." The Negroes then repaired to the armory to protect themselves, but the native whites had already begun firing. When the Negroes heard of the cannon brought from Augusta they tried to escape from the town. Two of the guardsmen had then been killed. The native whites captured twenty-seven others. Five of these were shot down in cold blood after they had surrendered. James Cook, the Negro chief of police of the town, was murdered in like manner. Commenting on this in an exaggerating fashion characteristic of pagan civilization, the *Sumter True Southron* said: "As usual in all these outbreaks the whites behaved with calmness and moderation. But we solemnly warn the colored people that these things occur too often. The white people of this State do not intend to be ridden over by ignorant and foolish Negroes who lead these riots. We may not be able to carry the State at the ballot box, but when it comes to a trial of the cartridge box we do not entertain any doubt of the result. The whites seek no contest with the colored people, but the latter must behave themselves and submit to the laws which they have made, and to office-holders whom they or their friends have placed in power."

The dénouement came from President Rutherford B. Hayes in the withdrawal of the troops to the support of whom he probably owed his doubtful election. Reconstructionists defeated by fraud and intimidation in South Carolina asked for troops to sustain them in office. Hayes said: "In my opinion there does not now exist in that State such domestic violence as is contemplated by the Constitution as the ground upon which the military power of the National Government

The withdrawal of troops.

The New Freedom, the first mixed jury in the District of Columbia

may be invoked for the defense of the State, but these are settled by such orderly and peaceable methods as may be provided by the Constitution and laws of the State. I feel assured that no resort to violence is contemplated in any quarter, but that, on the contrary, the disputes in question are to be settled solely by such peaceful remedies as the Constitution and the laws of the State provide.''

The withdrawal of the national troops from the South gave much relief to the whites in that section. It pleased a majority of the Northern citizens, who, despite the efforts of the Southerners to break up the Union, could not support the policy of forever afflicting them with martial law. The Negroes and their sympathizers, however, have always considered this the most unstatesman-like act any President has committed since the war. They contend that by a corrupt bargain for the South Carolina electoral vote Hayes immediately restored to power the unreconstructed element. Because of the color and former condition of the freedmen, these reactionaries have segregated, disfranchised and lynched Negroes to the extent that the United States can now be criticized for not complying with that clause of the Constitution guaranteeing every State a republican form of government. These troops should have undoubtedly been withdrawn by gradual process, in the proportion that the districts thus relieved exhibited evidence of the ability to protect all citizens in the enjoyment of their rights and privileges.

The closing chapter of political reconstruction is its undoing. The reactionaries reclaimed the State governments from the liberal functionaries. Not only were they determined to assume exclusive control of things, but to prevent the Negroes from further participation in politics the restored caste later enacted measures which eliminated most Negroes from the electorate. This has been done on the grounds that they

The undoing of the reconstruction.

could not read and write, did not own property of a fixed value, or were not descendants of persons who had voted prior to 1866. The method last mentioned has been referred to as the "grandfather clause" because it permitted all white persons to vote if their grandfathers had formerly exercised that privilege. Mississippi set the example in 1890 by passing a law disfranchising the Negroes, South Carolina followed in her footsteps in 1895, and Louisiana added the "grandfather clause" in 1898. Other restrictive suffrage measures reaching the same end were enacted by North Carolina in 1900, by Virginia and Alabama in 1901, by Georgia in 1907, and by Oklahoma in 1910. All of these laws hedged around the Fifteenth Amendment which provides that the right to vote shall not be denied or abridged by the United States or by any State on account of race, color, or previous condition of servitude.

The reactionaries further curtailed the privileges of Negroes, moreover, by segregation laws dealing first with railway accommodations and then with schools and places of amusement. This was made possible by a number of reactionary decisions of the United States Supreme Court by which the Civil Rights Act of 1875 has been finally nullified. The first of these decisions was that of 1869 in the case of *Hall* v. *De Cuir*. In this case this tribunal set aside as unconstitutional a law of Louisiana enacted in 1869 to prevent discrimination against Negroes on railroads. The Supreme Court was of the opinion that this particular law interfered with the regulation of interstate commerce; but it has not yet felt this way about laws enacted since that time to provide for the separation of the races. Its decision in the case of *Plessy* v. *Ferguson* upheld such State measures as valid. The Fourteenth Amendment provides that no State shall make or enforce any law which shall abridge the privileges or immunities of citizens of the United States; nor shall any State deprive any person

THREE SURVIVORS OF THE RECONSTRUCTION

M. W. GIBBS   P. B. S. PINCHBACK   JAMES LEWIS

M. W. Gibbs was municipal judge in Arkansas. P. B. S. Pinchback was elected lieutenant governor of Louisiana, served a short period as acting governor, was elected United States senator, but was not seated. James Lewis was for some years the collector of New Orleans' port.

ᴏₗ life, liberty, or property, without due process of law, nor
deny to any person within its jurisdiction the equal protection of the laws. According to these decisions, the act serves
merely as a restriction on the States rather than on individuals, and it does not deprive the States of the police
power exercised in forcing the Negro into the ghetto.

The chief reason given for thus abandoning the Negroes
to their fate was that the State governments which they
had assisted in establishing had become too corrupt for
honest people to support. If rumors and misrepresentations be taken as facts, such a conclusion might easily be
reached. However, investigation has shown **Corruption**
that the Negro carpet-bag governments were **general.**
just as clean as the governments of other States at that
time and as clean as that of the United States itself. If
those of the South were too corrupt to be sustained we had
ample reason for abandoning government altogether. Never
before had the country heard of such malfeasance as that
implied in the transactions of the "Tweed Ring," the
"Credit Moblier," the "Whisky Ring," and the "Star
Route Frauds." The country had gone mad with economic development. Railroads were being built here and
there, sometimes in unprofitable fields, only to bring ruin
to their promoters. Enterprises without capital were being
financed at the expense of the people. Connected in one
way or another with these corrupt machines were some of
the most distinguished ex-Confederates. Men prominent
in life permitted themselves to be drawn into these "get-
rich-quick" schemes with the understanding that they would
use their influence to build and operate them out of the
public treasury. The reconstructed States suffered from
the same sort of corruption; but the actual corruption in
the South was grossly exaggerated for political purposes.

The wave of fraud in the South, furthermore, had passed
before reconstruction was undone. For example, in South

The Negro In Our History

Carolina, the most maligned of the reconstructed States, Governor Chamberlain had actually cleaned up every department of the State. He gave the commonwealth the

Fraud at end. most respectable administration it has ever had. According to the native whites themselves, Chamberlain broke the backbone of the "Ring" and "restored decent government." He corrected the abuse of the pardoning power, appointed competent and honest men to office, rejected fraudulent claims, refunded the State debt, reduced taxes, and diminished the expenses of the State enough to save $1,719,488 in two years. *The Greenville Enterprise and Mountaineer,* therefore, said in 1875: "If Governor Chamberlain continues in the course he has so far pursued, and we have faith that he will do so, he will place his name high on the roll of great men, who have adorned the history of South Carolina. The honest citizens of the State will have reason to rejoice that he came from New England to take part in our public affairs."

Whatever may be said about the corruption in the reconstructed States, moreover, should not leave any stigma attached to the Negroes. They were participants in the rehabilitation of these commonwealths, but not the actual powers in control. At no time did the Negroes have con-

Negroes exonerated. trol of the whole government of one of these States. With the exception of South Carolina and Mississippi, moreover, the Negroes never even controlled a legislative, judicial, or executive department of these States. White men who came into the South after the Civil War and the native whites of the section coöperating with them kept the control of things during the reconstruction. This situation was aptly presented by a writer in the *Nation* in reference to South Carolina when he said that "in the distribution of its spoils, the poor African gets the gilt and plush, the porcelain spittoons, the barbaric upholstery, while the astuter Caucasian clings to the solider and more durable advantages.''

In a broader sense, however, we cannot speak of reconstruction as having been undone. The far-reaching reforms set going by this upheaval can never be overcome. The reconstructionists accomplished definite results which will continue to bear fruit as long as political and social institutions exist in this country. In overthrowing the proslavery aristocratic régime these reformers democratized the governments of the new South by establishing free manhood suffrage and apportioning representation on the basis of population rather than on interests. To enlighten the poor whites as well as the Negroes the reconstructionists provided for the first public school system the South ever had. Finally, the reconstructionists instituted a social reform in abolishing such relics of barbarism as the whip-

Reconstruction a success.

W. J. Simmons

A Reconstructionist in Education

ping post, the branding iron, and the stocks. ''By forty odd years,'' says Louis F. Post in reference to South Carolina, ''those Negroes forestalled Lloyd George with his proposal for old age pensions; by nearly four they preceded Henry George in apprehending the deadly import of land monopoly.'' In fact, so acceptable were the new constitutions providing for these reforms that they were not

"Reform Reconstruction Members of the First South Carolina Legislature after Emancipation and Enfranchisement of All Citizens"

altered for one or two generations after the overthrow of
the reconstructionists, and then largely to eliminate the
Negro from politics. The fundamental principles of social
justice proclaimed in the reconstruction constitutions still
remain. It is true enough that the Negro was thrown out
of office, driven to the ghetto and denied education, but the
very forces which the enfranchised freedmen set going are
now gradually having such effect on the whites that they
are beginning to understand how they handicap themselves
by trying to keep the Negro down.

CHAPTER XXV

FINDING A WAY OF ESCAPE

THE abridgment of the Negroes' rights came as a calamity. For a generation following the restoration of the reactionaries to power, the Negroes were in a state of confusion; and they could not extricate them-

The untoward condition.

selves from their difficulties.[1] There then ensued a most cruel persecution of the blacks by the degraded and impecunious poor whites. Although assured that under the circumstances the Negroes could not soon regain their political rights, certain criminal communities found special delight in killing and lynching Negroes on account of offenses for which a white man would hardly be accused, if the complainant happened to be black. By the art of psychological appeal to the race prejudice of the masses the leading newspapers easily succeeded in convincing the public that the general cause of these lynchings was criminal assault; but statistics show that ordinary misdemeanors of Negroes were the excuses for three out of every four of these lynchings.

The extent to which the country has been disgraced by

[1] George W. Williams, *History of the Negro Race*, II, 375-380; C. G. Woodson, *A Century of Negro Migration*, chs. VII and VIII; *The Atlantic Monthly*, XLIV, page 222 *et seq.;* *The Vicksburg Commercial*, May 6, 1919; *The Nation*, XXVIII, 242, 386; *The American Journal of Social Science*, XI, 1-35; *Public Opinion*, XVIII, 370 *et seq.;* *The American Law Review*, XL, 29, 52, 205, 227, 381, 547, 590, 695, 758, 865, 905; *Reports of Committees of the Senate of the United States for the First and Second Sessions of the Forty-sixth Congress, 1879-1880,* pp. iii-xiii.

the institution of lynching may be more easily estimated by
a few statistics. According to General Sheridan, 3,500
persons were killed in the South during the
Lynching. first decade after emancipation; 1,884 were
killed and wounded in 1868, and probably 1,200 between
1868 and 1875. Most of these massacres occurred in the
disturbed area of Louisiana. Following that period the
number of Negroes annually lynched in the whole country
aggregated between fifty and a hundred, and the whole
number for the reconstruction and readjustment periods
not less than 2,500. As the Negroes were no longer valu-
ables attached to owners, as horses or cattle, there was little
to restrain the degraded class from murdering them in communities where few white men had any conception of the
blacks as persons entitled to life, liberty, and the pursuit
of happiness.

The economic situation in the South in the meantime became critical. The poor whites, who were unwilling to
labor themselves, so disturbed the Negroes that their em-
The economic ployment was precarious. The ex-slavehold-
situation. ers, moreover, imposed upon the Negroes willing to work. The Negroes were the only dependable laboring class in the South, and too many were trying to live on
the fruits of Negro labor. Whether aware or not of.
being duped, the Negroes had to seek employment by the
whites, as they had no capital to operate farms and factories independently. Some of those who, during the hap-
piest days of reconstruction, succeeded in acquiring property, saw it seized thereafter on the plea of delinquent taxes
and transferred to the master class to satisfy fraudulent
claims.

The land in the South, moreover, remained mainly in
large tracts held by planters. Except in the case of poverty, they never desired to dispose of it; and even if they

had been thus inclined, the Negroes, under the existing régime, could not quickly earn sufficient money to purchase holdings. There was then no chance for the Negroes to develop at once into a desirable **Land tenure.** class of farmers. They then became mainly a wage-earning element dependent on the will of their employers. As few of the Negroes could read and write, they were cheated in signing contracts and had to suffer the consequent privations aggravated by cruelty, if they unduly complained.

Except in the sugar district, the wage system of the South early failed to give satisfaction. The planters then made the experiment of working on shares, but had to abandon this because the employer was not **Wage system** always able to advance the Negro tenant sup- **tried.** plies pending the growth of the crop, and some insisted that the Negro was too indifferent and lazy to make the partnership desirable. It was then decided to resort to the renting system, which became the accepted tenure in the cotton district. While this system apparently threw the tenant on his own responsibility, it frequently made him the victim of his own ignorance and the rapacity of his landlord. As the Negroes could do no **Rent system.** better, they had to pay such high rent that they hardly derived from their labor adequate returns to support their families.

The worst feature of the rent plan was its iniquitous concomitant, the credit system. Having no capital to begin with, a Negro tenant became dependent on his landlord for advance of supplies of tools, food and clothing **The credit** during the year, secured by a lien on the **system.** crop. As these new tenants had had only a few years of freedom to learn business methods, they became a prey to dishonest men. Through their stores and banks they extorted from the Negroes practically all of their earnings before the end of the year. A few honest planters desired to protect the Negroes by supplying them at reasonable prices; but, subject to usury themselves, their efforts availed little. It was necessary then for the Negro tenant to begin the year with three mortgages, covering all he owned, his labor for the coming year, and all he expected to acquire during that twelvemonth. According to an observer of the time, he paid "one-third of his product for the use of the land; he paid an exorbitant fee for recording the contract, by which he paid his pound of flesh; he was charged two or three times as much as he ought to pay for ginning his cotton; and, finally, he turned over his crop to be eaten up in commissions, if any was still left to him."

Various means of escape from these conditions were therefore considered. Believing that a reconstructed Republican Party would again interfere in southern affairs to relieve the freedmen, some Negroes looked forward to a change in politics. Others had the idea that religion would be the solution of the problem. They insisted that the calamities of the race resulted as an affliction with which they had been visited because of their wandering away from God. He would right their wrongs as soon as they heeded His pleading voice.

Remedies proposed.

The unrest, however, first found a safety valve in the exodus of the Negroes. During the seventies a considerable number of them moved from North Carolina to Indiana. Because of the pivotal political situation in that State their hasty migration gave rise to the accusation that they were being brought thither for the purpose of carrying doubtful States for the Republican Party. A Congressional investigation proved that these charges were absurd. The larger number of the Negroes who were induced to migrate during this period went not to Indiana but to Kansas, because of its known attitude towards the black man as evidenced by its willingness to bleed in behalf of freedom.

This movement was organized. It was promoted by two men who were not widely known as race leaders but attained distinction as the organizers of one of **The exodus** the most disturbing migrations ever effected **to the West.** among Negroes. They were Henry Adams of Louisiana and Benjamin, or "Pap," Singleton of Tennessee. Seeing that the Negroes had almost lost the fruits of their emancipation and that there was little hope that their situation would be greatly improved, they had organized a committee which they later increased by the hundreds. They circulated information as to the intolerable oppression of the blacks and the opportunities in the West for relief. In this way, according to these promoters, they interested 100,000 or 200,000 Negroes, although not more than one-fourth or one-fifth of this number actually went West.

This unusual movement of the Negroes threatened the South with economic ruin. The thinking class saw that the section was soon to lose the economic foundation of its prosperity, and that if something were not speedily done the land would doubtless become a waste place in the wilderness. Meetings, therefore, were called among the whites and the blacks to induce the latter to remain where they were. The most important meeting of this kind was that held at Vicksburg, Mississippi, on May 6, **Alarm among** 1879. There were assembled the representa- **the planters.** tives of the best of both races seeking to reach some conclusion as how to deal with the situation. Frank expressions as to the causes of the grievances were made on both sides, and most persons concerned were willing to make such sacrifices of personal feeling and opinion as to remedy the evils of which the Negroes complained.

Unwilling to rely upon moral suasion, however, the whites resorted to force to stop the exodus. They denied the Negroes transportation and imprisoned them on false

charges. But Negroes to the number of many thousands
The resort continued their way West despite this opposi-
to force. tion—despite even the discouragement of their
greatest leader, Frederick Douglass. He advised them to
the contrary, believing that it would be better for the
blacks to remain in the South where they would have suffi-

R. T. Greener

cient numbers to wield political
power. The promoters of the
movement were fortunate in
having the support of Richard
T. Greener and John M. Langston. Having sufficient foresight to see that the United
States Government would not
soon interfere in behalf of the
Negroes in the South, these men
advised them to flee from political oppression to a free country.
They considered it a hopeful
sign that the blacks had passed through that stage of
development of appealing to philanthropy into that of
appealing to themselves.

This rapid migration was soon checked, but the Negroes
gradually found their way into the West, into the Southwest
and into the industrial centers of the Appalachian Moun-
The migration tains. The masses of the Negroes, however,
checked. became settled in the South in a condition not
much better than their former state; for the planters forgot
their promises of better treatment just as soon as the exodus
ceased. The economic adjustment after the Civil War,
culminating in the resumption of specie payments in 1879,
however, brightened somewhat the dark age through
which the South was passing. Yet during the eighties
and nineties, the masses of Negroes could do little more
than eke out an existence. Following this period some

of them prospered sufficiently to appreciate the difference between free and slave labor. The income of the average Negro even then, however, was very small. The most fortunate Negro tenants or farmers did not generally come to the end of the year with more than they needed to keep them while producing their crop during the next. The rural wage earner did well to receive for his toil, from sunrise to sunset, twenty-five to forty cents a day, including board restricted to half a gallon of meal and half a pound of fat bacon. Mechanics believed that they were highly favored when they earned from seventy-five cents to a dollar and a half a day.

In the midst of such circumstances the Negroes could not establish homes and educate their children. It was of much assistance to the Negroes in the

J. C. Price

South, however, that the North raised considerable money and sent some of its best citizens to found institutions for the enlightenment of the freedmen. This philanthropic scheme presupposed that educa- **Education tried.** tion in the classical field was the urgent need of Negroes, in that it was essential to a proper understanding of the problems of government, and that when this was supplied the masses thus enlightened would have an advantage by which they could triumph over all opposition. Heeding this call to avail themselves of such opportunities, Negroes not only crowded such institutions as Howard,

Fisk, Lincoln, Morehouse, and Atlanta, but began to establish higher institutions of their own. Out of the schools came not many scholars, but enthusiastic teachers devoted to the enlightenment of their people, a large number of race-

KELLY MILLER

leading preachers proclaiming religion as the solution of the problem, many orators, like J. C. Price and William Pickens, and educating controversialists, like W. M. Trotter, Kelly Miller and W. E. B. DuBois. Under different conditions these men, no doubt, would have been historians, scientists, or mathematicians, but their race was passing through the ordeal of kith and kin democracy. Their talent had to be impressed into the service of exposing the folly of the reactionaries promoting the return to medieval civilization in proscribing the citizenship of the Negroes.

The majority of the Negroes in the South finally became **Resignation** settled to conditions as they were, endeavor-**to fate.** ing to make the most of an undesirable situation; but Negroes who had experienced mental development and had had their hearts fired with the desire to enjoy the rights so eloquently set forth by their uncompromising leaders, contrived to escape from their political and civic humiliation. To these Negroes of talent it seemed that the South would never be a decent place to live in;

for even the North was then turning a deaf ear to the pleadings of their spokesmen sent thither to portray to the children of the Negroes' former friends exactly how the fruits of their victory for human rights had been so quickly permitted to perish from the earth. After the reconstruction period the North was too busy in developing its industries and had established too close relations with the South to think of severing these ties. The prevailing opinion was that the South should be permitted to deal with the Negroes as it felt disposed.

As the South, in this position of renewed supremacy, became increasingly intolerant of the talented freedmen, many of them left. To this the whites offered no objection whatever. The exodus of the intelligent Negroes was much desired by the southerners. *Cruelty of the restored South.* Every one migrating diminished the chances of the Negro for mental development, a thing which most southerners believed spoils the Negro. It has been the policy of most Anglo-Saxon nations to keep in ignorance the exploited races, that in their undeveloped state the one group may be arrayed against the other to prevent them from reaching the point of self-assertion. In keeping with that same policy southerners would not only discourage but would have little dealing with the talented Negroes; and in making desire father to the thought, insisted that there were no intelligent Negroes. Well might some sections reasonably reach this conclusion as to the mental development of the Negroes, if it is to be judged by the amount of money spent for their education. In its backward state the South could not afford large appropriations for education; but in most of the districts the Negro public schools were almost a mockery. With the exception of the State industrial schools almost no provision at all was made for the higher education of the Negro after the undoing of reconstruction. Elementary schools were generally neglected

and secondary schools hardly existed at public expense.
The per capita expenditure for educating the Negro child
was about one-fourth of that for the white.

In the effort to get away from the South there was a
renewal of the colonization scheme under the leadership of
Colonization Bishop H. M. Turner. With the encourage-
again. ment of Senator Morgan, of Alabama, it
seemed that the plan might prove feasible. After the reactionaries had well completed the task of depriving the

BISHOP H. M. TURNER, a fearless
spokesman for his people

Negroes of their rights,
Morgan believed that
they should then go to a
foreign land to develop
independently a nation of
their own. Some thought
again of Africa as the
place of refuge, but the
memory of the antebel-
lum struggle of the free
Negroes to defeat that
enterprise made that con-
tinent too frightening to
attract many. In the
early nineties a few Ne-
groes emigrated to Ma-
pimí, Mexico, from which, after some hardships, they returned to their homes in Georgia and Alabama. Resorting
to Africa, then, 197 Negroes sailed from Savannah, Georgia,
for Liberia in 1895. The expedition to Liberia was not as
unsuccessful as that to Mexico, but in carrying out their
plan the deportationists soon discovered that it is impossible to expatriate a whole race. Liberia at that time, moreover, was not doing well. Under President Edward James
Roye, the country made the all but fatal mistake of borrowing £100,000 from the British. The transaction was

handled in such a manner that Liberia lost rather than gained by this supposed aid. Gloom and depression consequently hovered over Liberia for years to come.

Many of the talented Negroes who had been conspicuous in politics, thereafter decided to yield to the white man's control, and devoted themselves to the accumulation of wealth. But, as hell is never full and the eyes of man are never satisfied, the mere domina- **Terrorism.** tion did not meet all of the requirements of the degraded class of whites. Slavery had made them brutal. They had been accustomed to drive, to mutilate, to kill Negroes, and such traits could not be easily removed. The reign of terror, ostensibly initiated to overthrow the carpet-bag governments by means of the Ku Klux Klan, continued; and it became a special delight for the poor whites to humiliate and persecute the Negroes who had acquired education and accumulated some wealth. The effort was to make the Negro realize that he lives in a white man's country in which law for the Negro is the will of the white man with whom he meets. The Negroes had to undergo punishment for presuming to assume the reins of government during the reconstruction. They had to be convinced that this country will never permit another such revolution. Further legislation to restrict suffrage inalterably to the whites, to deprive Negroes of the right to serve in the State militia, to segregate them in public conveyances, and to exclude them from places of entertainment, soon followed as a necessity for maintaining white supremacy, so precarious has its tenure at times seemed.

At the same time the laboring Negroes not only saw themselves overwhelmed by a rent and credit system which would not pass away, but lost further ground in the new form of slavery called peonage. This once had **Peonage.** legal sanction in Alabama, Florida, Georgia, Mississippi, North Carolina, and South Carolina. It was a sort of involuntary servitude by which the laborer is considered bound to serve his master until a debt he has contracted is paid. The origin of this was in a custom in Mexico, and the opportunity lay in the poverty of the Negroes who had to borrow from the whites. In working to pay these debts they must still borrow to live. As the white man was the bookkeeper and his statement of account was law in the courts, it was the former master's prerogative to say how much the peon owed, to determine exactly when he should leave his service, or whether he should ever leave it.

Peons during these years were recruited from the chain gang. In collusion with courts arranging with the police **Peonage and** to arrest a required number of Negroes to **the courts.** secure the desired amount in fees and fines, innocent Negroes were commonly apprehended. When fined in court they had to agree to enter the service of some white man who would pay their fines for the opportunity to reduce them to involuntary servitude. A brief account from one of these peonage districts is sufficient to illustrate this point. Passing along the street where a Negro was employed by a white man, a sympathetic observer noticed that his employer frequently kicked and cuffed the Negro when he was not working satisfactorily. ''Why do you stand this? Why do you not have this man arrested for assault?'' inquired the observer. ''That is just the trouble now,'' responded the Negro. ''I complained to the court when another white man beat me, and the judge imposed upon me a fine which I could not pay, so I have to work it out in the service of this man who paid it to have the opportunity to force me to work for him.'' Inasmuch as some Negroes died of starvation and exposure in unhealthy quarters while others were actually killed, the fate of the chain gang peon might have been the lesser of two evils. The Supreme Court of the United States undertook to put an end to peonage in 1911 by declaring the Alabama law unconstitutional. But in the many districts, where there is no healthy public opinion to the contrary or where the employer is a law unto himself, peonage has continued in spite of the feeble effort of the Federal Government to eradicate the evil.

These increasing encroachments convinced many thinking Negroes that they should no longer endure such humiliation. They could not adequately educate their children at public expense, although taxed to support the public schools; they enjoyed little security **Negroes going North.** in the possession of property, and dared not defend their families from insult. Their first thought, then, was to go North. For more than a century the North, despite its lack of hospitality for the Negroes, had remained in their minds as a place of refuge. From time immemorial Negroes had gone to that section, and sometimes in considerable numbers. During the nineties and the first decade of the present century these numbers decidedly increased and brought nearer home to the North the so-called race problem.

There went first the dethroned politicians who, when failing to secure employment in Washington, endeavored to solve the problem by migration. A few Negroes well established in business, moreover, closed up their affairs and moved out. The educated **Politicians leaving the South.** Negroes—especially the Negro college graduates who were imbued with the principles of justice set forth by Pickens, Trotter and DuBois—had too much appreciation for freedom to remain longer where they were politically and socially proscribed. A few professional men, who under the undesirable conditions were reduced to-want, also made their escape. Intelligent laborers who knew that they were not receiving the proper returns from their labor tired also of the ordeal and went in due time to try life in other parts. In fact, this slow but steady migration was a gradual drawing off from the South of the most advanced classes, those best qualified to lead the race more rapidly toward achievement. In its backward state, however, the South could not appreciate this loss, so willing has it been to pay the high cost of race prejudice.

The undesirable feature of this migration was that it was mainly to the cities. The hostility of the trades unions to the Negroes was already a handicap rendering

The rush to cities. their presence in large northern cities a problem. The increase of numbers resulting from this new influx aggravated the situation. It was further aggravated in the course of time when, because of the increasing popularity of the North, many Negroes "just happened" to go. Some went on excursions to Columbus, Indianapolis, Chicago, Cleveland, and the like, and never returned South. In the North, moreover, educated Negroes had to follow drudgery. Not many could practice professions or work at skilled labor as they could in the South. Hoping that at some time the fates would bring it to pass that they would secure an economic foundation in the North, they were, then, willing to pay this price for social and political rights. The attainment of the economic objective, notwithstanding some encouraging events, however, has been a battle against well-established precedents in the effort to maintain the supremacy of the laboring whites. They feel that they should not be compelled to compete with Negroes. In labor, as in other things, they contend, the sphere of great remuneration must be restricted to the white man, and drudgery to the Negro.

Some systematic efforts were made to break down the barriers of these trades unions. White men, like Eugene V. Debs, high in the councils of these bodies, attacked this medieval attitude of the white laborers, but to no avail.

As Negroes in the North and West, therefore, were pitted against the trades unions, they engendered much feeling between the races by allying themselves with the capitalists to serve as strikebreakers. **Trades unions.** In this case, however, the trades unions themselves were to be blamed. The only time the Negroes could work under such circumstances was when the whites were striking, and it is not surprising that some of them easily yielded then to the temptation. In those unions in which the Negroes were recognized, they stood with their white co-workers in every instance of making a reasonable demand of their employers. Some of these unions, however, accepted Negroes merely as a subterfuge to prevent them from engaging in strikebreaking. When the Negroes appealed for work, identifying themselves as members of the union in control, they were turned away with the subterfuge that no vacancies existed, while at the same time white men were gladly received.

As a rule, therefore, the Negroes migrating to the North had to do menial service. It was pathetic for the traveler to see Negroes, once well established in business in the South, reduced to service as porters to earn **In menial** a living in the North. The Negroes were so **service.** scattered in the North that they did not supply the opportunity for mutual help. Since the whites were not willing to concede economic opportunity, the northern Negroes were isolated, so to speak, in the midst of a medieval civilization founded on the caste of color. While the migrating Negroes of intelligence hid their lights under a bushel in the North, the illiterate Negroes in the South, in need of their assistance in education and enterprise, too often fell into the hands of the harpies and **Results in** sharks. Many of these white impostors had **the South.** the assistance of unscrupulous Negroes in plundering these unfortunates.

There came forward then a Negro with a new idea. He said to his race: ''Cast down your buckets where you are.'' In other words, the Negroes must work out their salvation in the South. He was a native of Virginia. He had **Booker T. Washington's idea.** been trained at Hampton and under adverse circumstances had founded a school in Alabama, which afforded him the opportunity to study the Negroes in all their aspects. Seeing that the

need of the Negro was a foundation in things economic, he came forward with the bold advocacy of industrial education of the Negroes ''in those arts and crafts in which they are now employed and in which they must exhibit greater efficiency if they are to compete with the white men.'' The world had heard this before from Pestalozzi, Owen, Douglass and Armstrong, but never before had an educator so expounded this doctrine as to move the millions. This man was Booker T. Washington.

BOOKER T. WASHINGTON

The celebrated pronunciamento of Washington was well set forth in his address at the Atlanta Exposition in 1895. **The Atlanta address.** His educational theory and practice have not since ceased to be a universal topic. He insisted that since the Negroes had to toil they should be taught to toil skillfully. He did not openly attack higher education for Negroes, but insisted that in getting an education they should be sure to get some of that which they can use. In other words, the only education worth while is that which reacts on one's life in his peculiar situation. A youth, then, should not be educated away from his environment, but trained to lay a foundation for the future in his present situation, out of which he may emerge into something above and beyond his beginnings.

Washington's plan was received by the white people in the South as a safe means by which they could promote Negro education along lines different from those followed in the education of the white man. They desired to make education mean one thing for the whites and another for the Negroes. The North was at first divided on the question. The sympathetic class felt that such a **Washington's** policy would reduce the Negroes as a whole to **plan accepted.** a class of laborers and thus bar them from the higher walks of life through which the race must come to recognition and prominence. The wealthy class of whites in the North took the position that there was much wisdom in Washington's policy. With the encouragement which they have given his industrial program, with the millions with which they have endowed Tuskegee and Hampton, and with the support given the many other schools established on that basis, they brought most northern people around to their way of thinking in less than a generation.

With exception of a small minority, however, the Negroes regarded this policy as a surrender to the oppressors who desired to reduce the whole race to menial service, and they proceeded militantly to attack Washington. They branded him with the opprobrium of a traitor **Opposition to** to his people. In the course of time, however, **Washington.** the South, following the advice and example of Washington, reconstructed its educational system for Negroes and began to supply these schools with faculties recommended

by men interested in industrial education and too often by
Washington himself. The South thus gradually elevated
to leadership many Negroes who, in standing for industrial
education, largely increased the support of Washington
among his people. When, moreover, his influence as an
educator extended into all ramifications of life, even into
politics, to the extent that he dictated the rise and fall of

W. E. B. DuBois

all Negroes occupying po-
sitions subject to the will
of the whites, that con-
stituency was so generally
increased that before he
died there were f e w
Negroes who dared criti-
cize him in public or let
it be known that they
were not in sympathy
with his work.

Against this policy,
however, there always
stood forth some Negroes
who would not yield
ground. The most out-
spoken among these were
W. M. Trotter and W. E.
B. DuBois. These men
have had the idea that
the first efforts to secure
recognition for the Negro must come through agitation for
higher education and political equality. What they demand for the Negro is the same opportunity,
the same treatment, generally given the white
man. To accept anything less means treachery. Feeling
that Washington's position was a compromise on these
things, they persistently denounced him from the rostrum

**Trotter and
DuBois.**

and through the press in spite of the great personal sacrifices which they thereby suffered. DuBois lost the support of white friends who could not understand why all Negroes do not think alike, and Trotter suffered imprisonment because he undertook by unlawful means to break up one of Washington's meetings in Boston.

This agitation exhibited evidences of unusual vitality. It gave rise to several widely circulated organs which stand for equal rights and equal opportunities — in short, for a square deal for all men regardless of race, color or previous condition of servitude. One of these, *The Crisis*, became a self-supporting popular magazine with a circulation of several thousands. It is the organ of the National Association for the Advancement of Colored People, a movement launched by the remnant of the abolitionists in connection with the militant Negroes. Among its makers stood William English Walling, a popular author; Charles Edward Russell, a most liberal journalist; Mary W. Ovington, the indefatigable worker; W. E. B. DuBois, the radical thinker; Oswald Garrison Villard, the grandson of William Lloyd Garrison; Moorfield Storey, one of the most prominent members of the American Bar Association; Joel E. Spingarn, a famous scholar; Jane Addams, the social reformer; and A. H. Grimké, a fearless advocate of equality for all. While at times the Association and its promoters may have gone rather far in blaming Washing-

OSWALD GARRISON VILLARD

ton for his silence, it has nevertheless kept before the Negroes the ideal which they must attain if they are to count as a significant factor in this country.

Washington's long silence as to the rights of the Negro, however, did not necessarily mean that he was in favor of the oppression of the race. He was aware of the fact that **An unjust criticism.** the mere agitation for political rights at that time could not be of much benefit to the race, and that their economic improvement, a thing fundamental in real progress, could be promoted easily without incurring

the disapproval of the discordant elements in the South. He may be justly criticized for permitting himself to be drawn into certain entanglements in which he of necessity had to make some blunders. As an educator, however, he stands out as the greatest of all Americans, the only man in the Western Hemisphere who has succeeded in effecting a revolution in education. A few centuries hence, when this country becomes sufficiently civilized to stand the truth about the Negro, history will record that Booker T. Washington, in trying to elevate his oppressed people, so admirably connected education with the practical things of life that he effected such a reform in the education of the world as to place himself in the class with Pestalozzi, Froebel and Herbart. Seeing that the white

MOORFIELD STOREY, for years President of the National Association for the Advancement of Colored People

people have realized that industrial education is not only a good thing for the Negro but a blessing to the white man, the Negroes as a whole have little to say now against Washington's educational policy. The whites accordingly have proceeded to spend millions of dollars for buildings and equipment to secure these advantages to their youth. Washington's advocacy of industrial education, moreover, in spite of all that has been said, was not a death blow to higher education for the Negro. That movement has lived in spite of opposition. Washington himself frequently stated that industrial education, as he emphasized it, was for the masses of the people who had to toil. Knowing that the race had to have men to lead it onward, he did not object to higher education. To-day Hampton and Tuskegee, the exponents of this idea, are offering college courses and may soon be reorganized as universities.

CHAPTER XXVI

ACHIEVEMENTS IN FREEDOM

DURING these stormy years most Negroes had all sorts of advice. They were told how they might emerge from the muddle of controversy about the best solution of their problems; but they did not spend all their time in academic discussion. Building upon the foundation that they made before the Civil War, the Negroes soon developed into one of the most constructive elements in our economic system.[1] The census of 1910 shows that, although the Negroes constituted about thirty per cent of the population of the South, more than half of the agricultural laborers of that section were Negroes. In the main, moreover, the Negroes were useful citizens, showing little tendency to become peddlers, agents, and impostors who make their living robbing the people. On the corners of the streets in some cities there might be found a few Negroes who were not disposed to work for a living, but these constituted a small fraction of one per cent of the Negro population of the United States.

The census reports will help us further to determine what the Negroes in this country had been doing. In 1910, 5,192,535, or 71 per cent, of the 7,317,922 Negroes between

An era of progress.

---

[1] The statistics bearing on the progress of the Negro are found in the *United States Census Reports*. Other valuable facts may be obtained from Monroe N. Work's *Negro Year Book* and the files of *The Crisis*. There is also Mr. Henry E. Baker's informing article on *The Negro in the Field of Invention* (in the *Journal of Negro History*, II, 21-36). Dr. Thomas J. Jones's *Negro Education* in two volumes throws light on what has been going on in that field during the last half century. The book, however, is biased.

the ages of ten years and over were engaged in agriculture, forestry and animal husbandry. In the number employed in agriculture were included 893,370 farmers, planters and overseers; 218,972 were owners, 672,964 tenants, and 1,434 managers. Owners free of debt possessed 8,835,857 acres, owners having mortgaged farms had 4,011,491, and part owners, 2,844,188. There were 12,876,308 acres operated by cash tenants, 13,691,494 by share tenants, and 349,779 by managers. This area of 42,279,510 acres will appear more significant when one realizes that it is as large as New England, or Belgium and Holland combined.

Occupations of Negroes.

The field in which most Negroes had been employed was agriculture, and next to that domestic and personal service. While in most of the unskilled occupations the Negroes constituted a larger percentage than their percentage of the entire population, the increasing number of skilled laborers had reduced the percentage of unskilled laborers from a very high mark to about seventy per cent. So much improvement in the unskilled Negro laborer had been made during the previous generation that his increasing efficiency had rendered difficult the distinction between the skilled and unskilled laborer. The standard of the unskilled laborer, moreover, had been raised, peonage had been gradually giving way to a system of wages, and the intelligence of the workmen had been increased. Negro laborers had become so dependable that, despite the large influx of immigrants, they had been able to withstand the competition.

Unskilled labor.

Other statistics as to the number of Negroes employed at skilled labor will further emphasize this point. According to the census of 1910 there were among the males, 12,401 brick and stone masons, 9,727 blacksmiths, 8,035 glaziers, painters and varnishers, 6,175 plasterers, 5,188 locomotive firemen, 4,802 stationary

Skilled labor.

A Negro Country Seat, the home of Scott Bond

engineers, 3,296 machinists and millwrights, 2,304 coopers, 2,285 plumbers, and gas and steam fitters, 2,156 molders, and 4,652 tailors. At the same time there were among the females, 38,148 dressmakers and seamstresses, 8,267 operators in cigar and tobacco factories, and 6,163 employed in general manufacturing.

Building upon these achievements in labor, the Negroes had towered higher and higher in the professions. In 1910 one Negro out of every 146 was engaged in some professional pursuit, whereas one white person in **Negroes in** every 51 was thus engaged. The proportion **professions.** of clergymen among Negroes exceeded that among the whites, but in the other cases the whites showed the excess of the ratio of population to professional workers. While it appears that professions among Negroes were still undermanned, a decided increase in this direction had been noted during the preceding generation. It meant a great deal to be able after forty-five years of freedom to produce 29,485 teachers; 5,606 musicians and teachers of music; 3,077 physicians and surgeons; 478 dentists; 798 lawyers; 123 chemists, 329 artists, sculptors and teachers of art; 247 authors, editors and reporters; 59 architects; and 237 civil engineers. That in half a century they had achieved enough in the professions to bring them within the range of comparison with the whites is striking evidence of the ability of the Negro to meet the test of competition.

This growing usefulness of the Negro in the new fields had made a corresponding reduction in the numbers of those disposed to waste their time. The criminal class of the Negroes in America, therefore, had decidedly improved, despite the reports to the **Less crime.** contrary. These false alarms were based largely on unwarranted charges growing out of the convict lease system and the imposition of unjust fines for ordinary misdemeanors and such petty offenses as vagrancy. The attitude of the Negroes themselves toward maintaining the peace was well reflected in their efforts to better conditions by establishing law and order leagues working in coöperation with the local governments. To further this cause the Negroes once had the coöperation of Southern white men who, believing in justice for all, had tried to

THE RESIDENCE OF MADAME C. J. WALKER

improve rather than exterminate the Negro. These citizens were endeavoring to understand the causes of crimes of the whites against Negroes, as well as crimes of the latter. Both races, too, were much aided by the abolition of the liquor traffic.

The actual forces which have effected in general the improvement in the Negro race, however, have been strictly Negro organizations themselves. Chief among these were the Negro churches, social welfare agencies, and schools.

Achievements In Freedom

PROMINENT CHURCHMEN OF THEIR TIME

BISHOP G. C. CLEMENT   BISHOP R. A. CARTER

BISHOP R. E. JONES   BISHOP B. F. LEE

In 1906 the Negroes of white denominations had 6,210 churches with 514,571 communicants, 5,330 Sunday schools, 293,292 scholars, and property worth $12,107,-655. The independent Negro denominations had 33,220 churches with 3,789,898 communicants, 30,999 Sunday schools, 1,452,095 scholars, and property valued at $45,191,422. These churches were in the main Baptist and Methodist. The latter comprised four distinct groups, known as the African Methodist Episcopal Church, the African Methodist Episcopal Zion Church, the Colored Methodist Episcopal Church, and the Negro membership of the Methodist Episcopal Church. But the Baptists, until the schism of 1916, had only one national organization. This exercised loose supervision over the whole denomination. Although smaller in numbers, however, these various Methodist churches succeeded in accomplishing much by their well-constructed organizations through their forty-three well-informed bishops and enterprising general officers. The work of other denominations, like the Episcopalians, the Presbyterians, Congregationalists and the Catholics, became very effective also in Negro uplift wherever they secured a following.

Churches as factors.

Coöperating with these churches labored the 3,555 physicians, surgeons and dentists, preachers of health, supplementing the work of the ministers of the gospel. They were able to direct the attention of entire communities to the necessity of observing the laws of health and of making the community a decent place to live in. These well-trained Negroes thereby decidedly supplemented the serious work of the Anti-Tuberculosis League and the American Hygiene Association, and extended the operations of the annual school conferences held at Atlanta University, Hampton, and Tuskegee. So much good was so readily accomplished by the staff of workers lecturing to the soldiers in the camps on social hygiene that national

Physicians.

bodies promoting health later paid more attention to the problems of Negroes. As a result of this persistent struggle against ignorance, poverty and negligence, the mortality rate among Negroes decreased and much improvement was noted in their physique.

To do for the race some of the things which the church had not accomplished, social welfare work was undertaken among Negroes decades ago. The first colored Young Men's Christian Association was organized in Washington, D. C., in 1853 by Anthony Bowen, a man of color; the second in Charleston, South Carolina, in 1866; and the third in New York City in 1867. **Work of the Y. M. C. A.** The first colored Student Association was organized at Howard University in 1869. E. V. C. Eato, of the New York City Branch, attended the Montreal Convention in 1867 as the first Negro delegate thus to serve. In 1876 George D. Brown, ex-Confederate soldier, was appointed to supervise the Negro branches of the Young Men's Christian Association throughout the country. In 1888, however, the lamented William A. Hunton, a man of color, who had served as general secretary of the Negro Young Men's Christian Association of Norfolk, Virginia, was appointed to succeed Brown. Thereafter the work was placed altogether under the supervision of Negro secretaries.

The work was widely extended with some difficulty. It was given much needed impetus by the accession to the ranks of enterprising secretaries laboring in many cities and in most Negro schools of the South. Interesting here and there the many persons who were against the movement because of its discrimination as **The growth.** to race, these gentlemen gradually worked their way into the very hearts of indifferent communities. Now in almost all of the large cities where Negroes are found in considerable numbers, business and professional men of both races, thanks to the noble example set by the large donations of Julius Rosenwald, have united to establish for Negroes branches of the Young Men's Christian Association. In these hospices they enjoy a comradeship and homelike life which the transient of color could not theretofore find in those cities. Thereafter an effort was made to provide for young women in these centers the same facilities. The success of the useful branches of the Young Women's Christian Association readily established in New York, Washington, Louisville and St. Louis, was sufficient encouragement to the authorities in charge to provide elsewhere similar facilities for women of color.

As a result of the work of these agencies the home life of the Negroes decidedly improved. Every Negro, of course, did not heed the advice of his friends, and the fact that **Improvements in homes.** some lagged far behind while others went forward made it no longer possible to speak of all Negroes as belonging to two classes. Before the Civil War Negroes were referred to as slaves and worthless free persons of color. Negro homes after the emancipation showed the same difference in standards as found among the whites. The majority of Negroes advanced beyond the point of being satisfied with a one-roomed hut conspicuous by its lack of ordinary comforts. They bought land and built houses of several rooms. Prosperous Negroes decorated their homes and supplied them with adequate furniture. Negro children attending school read the latest books, newspapers and magazines. Where the evidence of such progress was not manifest it was possible in most cases to show that, because of economic conditions, the Negroes concerned had been too much handicapped by poverty to improve their situation as they would like. Later improvements in their economic situation, however, made these conditions exceptions to the rule.

For the remaking of Negroes most credit must be given to the schools at work among them. The enterprising teacher made the school, the school figured mainly in the making of the home, and the home produced a new civi- **The efforts** lization. Yet, despite the efforts of kindly **of schools.** disposed educators like Ruffner, Curry, and Dillard, the facilities for education offered Negroes in the public schools of the South continued to be meager, hardly extending beyond that of teaching them to read and write. But there

were offered in private schools maintained in the South by Northern philanthropy opportunities for so much enlightenment that teachers going out from these institutions came to their people like missionaries inspired to preach a new gospel to the lowly. Lincoln and Wilberforce with much zeal set a high standard for the education of the Negroes prior to the Civil War. Howard University, under its

JULIUS ROSENWALD

distinguished founder, General O. O. Howard, undertook to equip for leadership a number of youths of color to toil for the enlightenment of their people in higher pursuits. This was the first Negro university. A large number of other philanthropists having the same ideals as the founders of these institutions, established schools like Fisk, Atlanta, Tougaloo, Talladega, **Industrial** Morehouse, Livingstone, Knoxville, Lane, and **schools.** Straight. Then came Hampton, Tuskegee and the like, to direct attention primarily to the education of the masses in things fundamental so as to enable the youth to begin with life where he is and to make of it what his opportunities will permit.

Meeting thus in a way almost every need for Negro education, offering facilities for training of all sorts, the Negro schools were decidedly successful. They owe much to the impetus given them by such philanthropists as William H. Baldwin, Jr., Robert C. Ogden, H. H. Rogers, John D. Rockefeller, Andrew Carnegie, and Julius Rosenwald through their liberal contributions

Aid from philanthropists.

to the establishment and the development of various institutions. Negro education may at times have been ill-directed, in that persons, without giving due consideration to their capacity and opportunities, have wasted time undertaking to master things to which they were not adapted and which they would never have to do; but the readjustment finally worked out in such

ANDREW CARNEGIE. The donor of $600,000 to Tuskegee. The first philanthropist to set the example of giving large sums of money for the elevation and development of the Negro race.

a way that Negroes, like the whites, now have opportunities to equip themselves for whatever they feel disposed to do. In action they have exhibited the same mental endowment found among the ranks of all other races.

The good work of these institutions became effective in putting the race on its feet, so to speak, in enabling the Negro to do for himself what the thousands of sympathetic and benevolent whites of the missionary spirit had to do

Achievements In Freedom

JOHN D. ROCKEFELLER AND HIS SON. Through appropriations of the General Education Board and the Laura Spelman Rockefeller Memorial large sums have come from these philanthropists to agencies engaged in the uplift and the education of the Negro.

Copyright by Underwood & Underwood.

for the helpless freedmen immediately after the Civil War. Out of these schools soon came thousands of Negroes of **Trained leadership.** scholarly tendencies. In devoting their time and means to the study of educational problems and school administration, they equipped themselves for leadership in education in the South. For some time it was a matter of much regret that white persons in charge

R. R. Moton, the Principal of Tuskegee

of schools in the South, maintained by philanthropy, failed to recognize this ability of the Negro and long adhered to the policy of restricting them to subordinate positions. Negroes bore it very grievously that they had to contend with many white persons who feel that whenever a Negro is given a position of responsibility he needs careful watching or supervision by some wise white man that it may be done in keeping with an established policy of Negro control.

Many Negroes not only learned lessons in religion, education and health, but showed unusual progress in the business world. They **Progress in business.** accumulated so much property in the rural districts that they constituted a desirable class of small farmers. In the cities in which took place during the migration the concentration of large numbers of Negroes, enterprising men of color acquired businesses formerly monopolized by whites. Near a Negro church one would find an undertaker of color. In almost any Negro urban community one observed a successful real estate dealer, a reliable contractor, an insurance office, and sometimes a bank. It became so popular for Negroes to deal with their own people that white men owning businesses in Negro sections learned to employ considerable Negro help.

The Negro in business, however, was not a new thing. The point to be noted here is the unusual stride of the race in this field after emancipation. It was more **Unusual** than encouraging, moreover, to observe how **achievements.** easily certain Negroes learned the lesson of pooling their efforts in larger enterprises. To promote the economic progress of the race, Negroes were soon wise enough to organize several efficient agencies. The first of these to attain importance was the National Business League founded by Dr. Booker T. Washington. There arose also the National Negro Bankers' Association, the National Association of Funeral Directors, and the National Negro Retail Merchants' Association. Negro fraternal organizations, although established for social purposes, assumed a business aspect in later years in providing for the purchase of property and the insurance of the lives of their members. In some parts of the South the Negroes used no other insurance. The managers of this work constituted in reality an industrial insurance company. Negroes had a score of banks and a number of insurance companies, four of which were regular old line life insurance companies. In 1910, 3,208 Negroes were employed in banking and brokerage, 2,604 in insurance, and 1,095 in real estate.

Among these captains of industry thus pressing forward should be mentioned John R. Hawkins, financial secretary of the A. M. E. Church and president of the Prudential Bank of Washington; Samuel W. Rutherford, **Captains of** secretary of the National Benefit Association **industry.** of the same city; Isaiah T. Montgomery, the capitalist of Mound Bayou, Mississippi; John Merrick, founder of the North Carolina Mutual and Provident Association; C. C. Spaulding, later the promoter of these same interests; Mrs.

FACTORS IN THE ECONOMIC PROGRESS OF THE NEGRO

MRS. A. E. MALONE
HEMAN E. PERRY

JOHN MERRICK
SAMUEL W. RUTHERFORD

A. E. Malone, the noted manufacturer of the Poro products in Chicago; Madame C. J. Walker, the manufacturer of toilet articles, out of which she accumulated more than a million dollars' worth of property; Jesse H. Mitchell, banker and real estate dealer of Washington, D. C.; and Major R. R. Wright, Sr., banker and promoter of business in Philadelphia. The Negroes in the United States have owned property worth more than a billion dollars.

In the midst of the busy bustle and the economic development of the United States since the Civil War Negroes not only demonstrated their ability to accumulate a portion of the world's goods, but by their inventive genius contributed much toward the economic **Inventive** progress of the country. As to exactly how **genius.** many Negroes have appeared in the field of invention we are still in doubt. The United States Patent Office has not kept in all cases a record as to the race of the applicants. While in many instances the racial connection has been easily determined, an investigation has shown that many inventors of color have not disclosed facts to this effect because the value of the invention might thereby be depreciated. By correspondence with patent attorneys and the inventors themselves it has been established as a fact that there are in the United States Patent Office a record of 1,500 inventions made by Negroes. This number, no doubt, is only a fraction of those which have been actually assigned to persons of color.

Some of these inventions have been remarkable. Probably the most significant one of them is that of a machine for lasting shoes invented by Jan E. Matzeliger, a Negro born in Dutch Guiana in 1852. Early in his youth Matzeliger came to this country and **Matzeliger.** served as an apprentice at the cobbler's trade in Philadelphia and in Lynn, Massachusetts. Undergoing unusual hardships which undermined his health, Matzeliger applied his brain to working out a labor-saving device by which his trade might be relieved from drudgery. He invented, therefore, a lasting machine which adjusted the shoe, arranged the leather over the sole, and drove in the nails. Matzeliger died in 1889, in his thirty-seventh year, before he could realize the value of his invention. The patent was bought by Sydney W. Winslow. Upon the advantages derived from this machine he established the well-known United Shoe Machinery Company, which absorbed over forty smaller corporations. This company was soon operating with a capital stock of more than $20,000,000, employing 5,000 operators in factories covering more than twenty acres of ground. Within the twenty years from the time of its incorporation its product increased from $220,000 to $242,631,000 and the shoes exported increased from 1,000,000 to 11,000,000. As a result the cost of shoes decreased 50 per cent, the wages of the operators decidedly increased, the working hours diminished, and laboring conditions improved.

Some other inventions of Negroes of less consequence were of much value and deserve mention. J. H. Dickinson and S. L. Dickinson, both of New Jersey, were granted **Valuable inventions.** a dozen patents for mechanical appliances used in player piano machinery. W. B. Purvis of Philadelphia accumulated much wealth by his inventions of machinery for making paper bags, most of which were later sold to the Union Paper Bag Company of New York. A. B. Albert, a native of Louisiana, invented a cotton-picking machine a few years later. Charles V. Richey of Washington, D. C., invented and patented several devices for registering calls and detecting the unauthorized use of the telephone. Shelby J. Davidson invented a mechanical tabulator or adding machine; Robert A. Pelham, a pasting machine; and Andrew F. Hilyer,

Achievements In Freedom

J. E. MATZELIGER
LASTING MACHINE

No. 274,207.

PATENTED MAR. 20, 1883

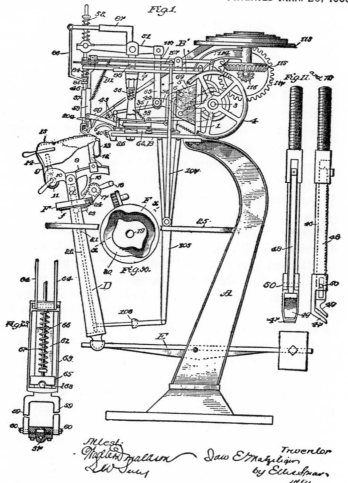

AN ILLUSTRATION SHOWING THE MODELS MADE BY MATZELIGER TO ILLUSTRATE
HIS INVENTIONS IN SHOE MACHINES.

two hot-air register attachments. Benjamin F. Jackson of Massachusetts invented a heat apparatus, a gas burner, an electrotypers' furnace, a steam boiler, a trolley wheel controller, a tank signal, and a hydrocarbon burner system. Frank J. Ferrell of New York obtained about a dozen patents for improvements in valves for steam engines. George W. Murray, a former member of Congress from South Carolina, patented eight inventions of agricultural implements. Henry Kreamer of New York made seven different inventions in steam traps. William Douglass of Arkansas secured six patents for inventions of harvesting machinery. James Doyle of Pittsburgh devised the automatic serving system so as to dispense with the use of waiters in cafés.

Fred J. Lowden, known to fame as one of the Fisk Jubilee Singers, patented in 1893 a fastener for the meeting rails **Useful** of sashes, and a key fastener the following **appliances.** year. J. L. Pickering of Haiti, James Smith of California, W. G. Madison of Iowa, and H. E. Hooter of Missouri, were granted patents for inventions in airships. No less significant, moreover, was the patent, in 1897, of Andrew J. Beard, of Alabama, for an automatic car-coupling device, sold to a New York car company for more than $50,000. William H. Johnson of Texas invented a successful device for overcoming dead center in motion, one for a compound engine, and another for a water boiler. While keeping a hotel in Boston, Joseph Lee patented three inventions for kneading dough. Brinay Smart of Tennessee invented a number of reverse valve gears. J. W. Benton of Kentucky invented a derrick for hoisting heavy weights. John T. Parker invented screws for tobacco presses with which he established a thriving business as the Ripley Foundry and Machine Company of Ripley, Ohio.

The most useful inventor with a career extending into the twentieth century, however, was Granville T. Woods.

He doubtless surpassed most men in his field in the number and the variety of his devices. He began **Granville T.** in Cincinnati, Ohio, in 1889, where he ob- **Woods.** tained his first patent on a steam boiler furnace. Then came an amusement machine apparatus in 1889, an incubator in 1900, and electrical air brakes in 1902, 1903, and 1905. He then directed his attention to telegraphy, producing several patents for transmitting messages between moving trains, and also a number of transmitters. He thereafter invented fifteen appliances having to do with electrical railways and a number of others for electrical control and distribution To further his interests he organized the Woods Electrical Company, which took over by assignment all of his

GRANVILLE T. WOODS

early patents. As in the course of time, however, he found a better market for his devices with the more prosperous corporations in the United States, the records of the patent office show the assignment of a large number of his inventions to the General Electric Company of New York, the Westinghouse Air Brake Company of Pennsylvania, the American Bell Telephone Company of Boston, and the American Engineering Company of New York. During this period of his larger usefulness he had the coöperation of his brother, Lyates Woods, who himself invented a number of such appliances of considerable commercial value.

Another inventor of consequence was Elijah J. McCoy. He was unique in that he was the first man **Elijah J.** to direct attention to the need for facilitating **McCoy.** the lubrication of machinery. His first invention was patented in 1872 as a lubricating cup. From that day his fame as an inventor of this useful appliance went throughout this country and abroad. In responding to the need for still further improvements in this work, he patented about fifty different inventions having to do with the lubricating of machinery. His lubricating cup became of general use on the leading railroads in the United States and abroad and on the vessels on the high seas. In his work, however, Mr. McCoy was not restricted to lubricating machinery. He patented a variety of devices for other purposes, and he was long active in the production of other mechanical appliances in demand in the industrial world.

The achievements of the Negroes in this field become much worthier of mention when one takes into consideration the hard problems of the inventor of color. In this

Difficulties of the inventor. country it has not been a very easy matter for white men with ample protection of the law to secure to themselves by patents the full enjoyment of the fruits of their own labor. The achievements of Eli Whitney and Robert Fulton are cases in evidence. Henry A. Bowman, a Negro inventor of Worcester, Massachusetts, therefore, found himself facing the same difficulty. After he had established a thriving business on the basis of his invention of a new method of making flags, he discovered that a New York firm was outstripping him by using his invention. As he was unable to hire competent attorneys to protect his interests, he was soon compelled to abandon his business. The experience of E. A. Robinson of Chicago is another case in evidence. He invented a number of devices, such as the casting composite for car wheels, a trolley wheel, a railway switch and a rail. His patents, however, were infringed upon by two large corporations, the American Car and Foundry Company and the Chicago City Railway Company. To restrain these corporations from appropriating his property to their use, he instituted proceedings in the local courts and finally in the Supreme Court of the United States; but he was unable to have his patent protected.

Exhibiting this same sort of genius ever manifesting itself despite difficulties, Negroes have shown in other fields evidences of unusual attainment. In music the world saw the lowly life and higher aspirations of the Negro in J. W. and F. W. Work, Will Marion Cook, Nathaniel Dett, and Harry Burleigh, who followed in the footsteps of Samuel Coleridge Taylor. In sculpture the race was well represented by Meta Vaux Warrick Fuller, who won fame by her first work in clay in the Philadelphia School of Industrial Art. She studied in Paris, where she attracted the attention of the great sculptor, Rodin. In 1893 she exhibited the highly prized model of art, *The Wretched,* her masterpiece. She added thereafter some other works, *The Dancing Girl, The Wrestlers,* and *Carrying the Dead Body.* In the same field appeared also Mrs. May Howard Jackson, whose works have elicited honorable mention in many circles. E. M. Bannister, William A. Harper, and William E. Scott attracted considerable attention by their paintings.

The most distinguished Negro in the field of art, however, was Henry O. Tanner. With the white artist, Sargent, Tanner represented the best America has produced in painting. He had little encouragement in this field, but early attracted attention by *The Bagpipe Lesson,* portraying a workman sitting on a wheelbarrow observing the efforts of a youth on a musical instrument. Lacking in this country the atmosphere conducive to the development of the best in man, Tanner went to the city of Paris in 1891. There, under the instruction of Jean Paul Laurens and Benjamin Constant, he mastered the principles of art. In contact there with men in his own sphere, he developed into one of the greatest artists of his time.

His first painting of value was exhibited in 1894. The following year he completed *The Young Sabot Maker;* but it was not until 1896 that, with the encouragement given him by the great artist Gérôme, Tanner won recognition as a painter. In 1897, however, his *Raising of Lazarus* attracted so much attention far and wide that thereafter

H. O. TANNER'S *Christ and Nicodemus*

there was little doubt in the circles of art as to the greatness of this man. This picture was awarded the gold medal by the French government and placed in the Louvre. In 1898 he presented to the public *The Annunciation* at the Academy of Fine Arts in Philadelphia, where it elicited favorable comment. His *Judas,* presented to the public in 1899, was bought by the Carnegie Institute of Pittsburgh. That same year *Nicodemus,* awarded the Walter Lippincott prize of $300, was purchased by the Pennsylvania Academy of Fine Arts. For his *Daniel in the Lions' Den* he was awarded second class medals at the Universal Exposition in Paris in 1900, at the Pan-American Exposition in 1901, and at the St. Louis Exposition in 1904. In 1906 his *The Disciples at Emmaus* was awarded the second gold medal and purchased by the French government. That same year his *The Disciples at the Tomb* was declared the best painting at the annual exhibition of art in Chicago and was awarded the N. W. Harris prize of $300. In 1908 appeared *The Wise and Foolish Virgins,* which was characterized as a masterpiece of a sincere artist.

As a painter, Henry O. Tanner directed his attention largely to religious and lowly life, as evidenced by the names of his paintings. He no doubt owed this attitude to the fact that he was the son of a bishop of the African Methodist Episcopal Church, and early in life was encouraged to apply himself to theology. As an artist his productions have a reverent atmosphere, and his pictures are clean-cut and luminous. In his paintings there are subtle power, purity of line, and thorough charm, with sentiment prevailing over technique. While the shades are luminous, the coloring is neither heavy nor muddy. "He always brings out of all his work," says one, "an admirable dramatic sentiment given full value and fully expressed."

In the field of literature the Negroes are sometimes considered as beginners, but much progress in this field is evident. Kelly Miller, W. E. B. DuBois and William Pickens did remarkably well in controversial literature. George W. Williams, John W. Cromwell **In literature.** and Booker T. Washington made contributions to history. Following in the wake of Jupiter Hammon, Phyllis Wheatley and Frances E. W. Harper, writers of interesting verse, Paul Laurence Dunbar came before the public in the early nineties as a man endowed with the unusual gift of interpreting the lowly life of the Negro. As an elevator boy in a hotel, writing a few lines in dialect, he himself did not realize his poetic genius. Succeeding, however, in having a few of these published in daily papers and magazines, he attracted attention. It was not long before several of his literary contemporaries became interested in his works and proclaimed him to the world as a poet worthy of the

The rise of Dunbar. consideration given Whittier, Lowell and Longfellow. Dunbar had fortunately reached that unusual stage in the development of a belated people

PAUL LAURENCE DUNBAR

of having his education react upon his environment. He saw the Negro as he is, saw something beneath the surface of his mere brogue, in fact, saw a philosophy for which the world wanted an interpretation. This interpretation came in his first book, *Oak and Ivy,* and was still better exhibited in his second w o r k, *Majors and Minors,* appearing in 1895. Very soon then appeared such comments on him as that coming from William Dean Howells, saying that Dunbar was the first black man to feel the life of the Negro esthetically and to express it lyrically.

Dunbar made an attempt at novel writing, in the production of his *The Uncalled.* This was a character study upon which fortunately his reputation as a literary man does not rest, for it does not come up to the standard of his verse. Unstinted praise awaited him upon his publication of *Lyrics*

*of Lowly Life, Folks from Dixie, Lyrics of the Hearth-
side, Poems of Cabin and Field, The Strength of Gideon,
The Love of Landry, The Fanatics, The Sport of the Gods,
Lyrics of Love and Laughter* and *Candle Lighting Time.*
Some of the popular poems in his collection which are
worthy of special mention are ''When Malindy Sings,''
''When the Co'n Pone's Hot,'' ''The Party'' and ''The
Poet and His Song.''

Dunbar's literary success was due much to his originality.
There had appeared from time to time scores of whites and
blacks who had undertaken to write verse in Negro dialect; but Dunbar was the first to put into it such thought
and make of it such a portraiture of the feeling and the
aspirations of the Negroes as to give his work the stamp of
originality.   While he was always humorous, his poetry
showed deep pathos and sympathy.   With no problems
to solve and no peculiar type to represent, he went into the
Negro life, saw it as it was, and emerged portraying
it with living characters exhibiting the elasticity, spirit,
tone, and naturalness in the life about him.

In life Dunbar was respected and known throughout this
country and abroad.   In 1897 he visited England, where
because of his fame as a poet he was received with marked
honor.   Upon returning to this country his literary engagements became such that he could devote himself entirely to work in his field.   His health early began to decline, however, and he died at the age of thirty-four at his
home in Dayton, Ohio.   Thanks to the interest of sympathetic persons of both races, this home is now maintained
as a monument to remain as a museum in honor of the
poet, Paul Laurence Dunbar.

Since the days of Dunbar a number of other Negro
writers of prominence have considerably interested the
public.   Among these should be mentioned Angelina W.

Grimké, a woman of poetic insight; Benjamin Brawley, an author of many interests; Jessie R. Fauset, a writer of

Other writers. varying purpose; Georgia Douglas Johnson, whose interesting poems have made a very favorable impression; Leslie Pinkney Hill, distinguished by his *Wings of Oppression;* Joseph Seaman Cotter, known to the public through his poems contributed to various magazines and his collection entitled the *Band of Gideon;* and James Weldon Johnson, whose gripping verse first appeared in the volume, *Fifty Years and Other Poems.* He wrote also two books of spirituals, *Black Manhattan, God's Trombones, Along This Way* and *The Autobiography of an Ex-Colored Man.* These poets were at their best in writing verse which has no bearing on the life of the Negro. In this field they exhibited evidences of the thought, feeling and imagination found in the best literature. In taking up Negro life, however, they did not reach the standard of Dunbar. Their difficulty was that because of suffering from social proscription in the white man's world they faced their task with a problem to solve; and, unlike Paul Laurence Dunbar, who went into life and merely portrayed what he saw, they prejudiced their readers against them by a premature introduction to an unpleasant atmosphere. The younger writers like Jean Toomer, Nella Larsen, Eric Walrond, Rudolph Fisher, Arna Bontemps, and Claude McKay had a different approach, and in their natural way produced some of the best literature in the United States.

A few other writers deserve more extensive comment. Countée Cullen has to his credit poems collected as *Color, Copper Sun, The Ballad of the Brown Girl, The Black Christ and Other Poems, One Way to Heaven, The Medea and Some Other Poems,* and *Caroling Dusk.* Langston Hughes first brought out *The Weary Blues.* Next came *Fine Clothes to the Jew.* He then wrote a novel entitled

Not Without Laughter, followed by a collection of stories, *The Ways of White Folks. The Dream Keeper* and *A New Song* were the next in order. Later Langston Hughes took to the drama and wrote a number of plays, the most important being that on the Scottsboro Boys and "I Want to Be Free." His *Mulatto* had a long run on the New York stage. His timely autobiography, *The Big Sea,* is a readable work. Zora Neale Hurston, an anthropologist and writer of charming stories, has to her credit novels entitled *Jonah's Gourd Vine* and *Their Eyes Were Watching God.* She produced also such collections of tales as *Mules and Men, Tell My Horse,* and an autobiography entitled *Dust Tracks on a Road.* Recently Richard Wright with his *Native Son* all but created a national sensation in giving the radical's picture of the plight of the present-day Negro. The book came to Americans as a challenge. Honorable mention belongs here to Walter White, whose novels, *Fire in the Flint* and *Flight,* have attracted much attention. *Rope and Faggot* was widely read some years ago.

One of the most remarkable writers of Negro blood since Dunbar is William Stanley Braithwaite. As a writer he is not a Negro. Although realizing the fact that the race has obstacles to surmount, that it is in a great struggle, and that the battle is being hard **Braithwaite.** fought, Mr. Braithwaite, by his literary production and criticism, has won much consideration for the Negroes, not by singing of their woes, but by demonstrating that the Negro intellect is capable of the same achievements as that of the whites. Because of his poems, his annual publication, the *Anthology of Magazine Verse,* and his numerous literary criticisms appearing from time to time in the leading publications of this country, Mr. Braithwaite, although a man of African blood, is accepted as one of the literary critics of our day.

CHAPTER XXVII

IN THE COURT OF THE GENTILES

In spite of these achievements, however, most white men were still reluctant to concede the right of the Negro to enjoy the full measure of citizenship. His rise to a position Citizenship of usefulness in the North often brought him begrudged. into competition with white men who selfishly endeavored to proscribe him in the economic sphere, and most Southern spokesmen boldly proclaimed that any effort on the part of the Negro to improve his social and civil status would not be countenanced in that section. The Negro was to be tolerated there only in recognized inferiority. It was in vain, then, that Negroes pointed to their economic progress, intellectual development, contribution to art, and preservation of the Christian religion.

Stating the matter much more frankly, some white men openly asserted that the Negro thrives too rapidly. They observed that he is more anxious than the poor white citizen to educate his children. To prevent the enlightenment of the Negro, then, public education must be discouraged, although it might be beneficial to the poor whites. They noted with some regret, too, that Negroes acquire land more readily than the poor whites and do not willingly alienate it. To prevent the Negroes from outstripping their unprofitable neighbors, therefore, the former must be further handicapped.

This desire for concerted action against the Negro, however, had resulted somewhat from an increasing feeling that the Negro, being socially inferior to the white man, was a menace to his civilization. From the point of view of most of these whites, it mattered not what the Negro had accomplished, he is nevertheless inherently inferior to the most despicable white man on earth, and any attempt to change his status must be visited with condign punishment inflicted by "law." While the race, they believed, would some day become extinct, the whites could not await that solution of the problem. There must not, therefore, be any contact with the Negro except that of master with servant.

The Negro called a menace

This feeling had been intensified by the work of pseudoscientists who endeavored to prove that Negroes are carriers of social diseases. As a matter of fact, however, history shows that these evils originated among whites and were never known among Negroes until thus contaminated by Caucasians. These diseases once worked ravages among Negroes because time had not then established in them the immunity found in the whites who have so long been accustomed thereto. Education, moreover, the very thing which has proved to be the significant factor in removing man from the grasp of social diseases, these same whites denied the Negroes. Further support to this bias came from unscientific reports circulated by prejudiced authors like Edgar G. Murphy, Thomas Dixon, Thomas Nelson Page, A. H. Stone, Jerome Dowd, Ulrich B. Phillips and Avery O. Craven. They undertook to prove the inefficiency of Negro labor and other such fallacies by uprooting the contention of science that one race cannot be inherently inferior to another.[1]

The influence of biased writers.

[1] For this point of view see E. G. Murphy's *Problems of the Present South;* Thomas Dixon's *Clansman;* Thomas Nelson Page's *In Olv Virginia, Red Rock,* and *The Negro; The Southerner's Problem;* A. H. Stone's *Studies in the Race Problem;* U. B. Phillips's *Plantation and Frontier, Documentary History of American Industrial Society, American Negro Slavery,* his lectures and reviews of books, and E. B. Reuter's *The Mulatto in the United States.*

NEGROES OF CREATIVE GENIUS

MRS. G. D. JOHNSON   ROLAND HAYES
GBERT AUSTIN WILLIAMS   CHARLES S. GILPIN

To preclude, then, the possibility of changing the Negro's situation by overcoming the obstacles already thrown across his path, others had to be added under the guise of the "mutually beneficial system of segregation." The Negroes had already been despoiled of their pro rata share of public school funds, ingeniously disfranchised, and denied the democratic use of public utilities; but now it must be made utterly impossible for them to profit by any good which may accrue to the benefit of the white community. Negroes, therefore, were deprived of the right to frequent public places of amusement, to move into city blocks where white people were in the majority, to purchase farm land in sections restricted to white ownership, or to serve with whites in civil service.

Segregation.

The more desirable districts must be reserved to whites, some argued, because lazy Negroes attached such a stigma to labor that white men would not work among them at certain occupations. The Negroes, they further contended, had a low standard of living; their wants were easily supplied. Yet the facts prove that proportionately Negroes have excelled white men in the establishment of homes and in the purchase of land. The census of 1920 showed that 218,612 Negroes had bought land. This land increased from about 6,000,000 acres in 1880 to 13,948,512 in 1920. In addition to this large number of owners of farms there were 705,070 Negro tenants cultivating an acreage of 27,077,582,[2] worth together with buildings $1,676,315,864.

The argument
for social
distinctions.

Statements as to the laziness of Negroes, however, are fraught with downright prevarication. It requires only a trip of forty-eight hours through the South to prove that

---

[2] These figures were a little higher in 1910. As a result of the migration the Negro farm owners decreased from 218,978 to 218,612 in 1920. These figures are for Negro farmers, not for colored farmers among whom are included Japanese, Chinese, Indians and the like.

the Negroes constitute the working class in that section. As the race makes progress, however, a large number **Biased** of Negroes become economically independent **statements.** of the white people not only to the extent of employing themselves, but to that of requiring the assistance of other Negroes. Under different circumstances these would enter the service of whites. Inasmuch as so many whites have never learned to work and instead have made their living exploiting Negroes, they now bear it grievously that the Negroes available for this purpose are comparatively diminishing.

Persons who have advocated residential segregation have tried to disguise their real feeling by advancing other arguments. Business men have said that the presence of **The Negro** Negroes in a white community depreciates the **and property** property. If they have in mind the "color- **values.** phobia" which seizes white residents when a Negro becomes their neighbor and the race prejudice which impels them to dispose of their property quickly below cost; or if they take into consideration the abandoned condition in which the local government generally leaves a Negro residential section, this contention is right. But it is not the Negro causing the depreciation. This fault lies at the door of the whites. The value of property, moreover, is determined by its income, and history has shown that as soon as Negroes move into a section formerly occupied by whites, the landlord receives from such property a larger income than before. The rent is often increased from 15% to 30%.

While custom, city ordinance, and acts of legislatures accomplished the purpose of segregation in various parts, **Temples of** in the State of Oklahoma this movement as- **injustice.** sumed the form of open robbery in collusion with courts of the commonwealth. Negroes, who had freely interbred with Indians there, came into the possession of

valuable oil lands by special federal legislation guaranteeing the inheritance of persons having even an infusion of
Indian blood. To deprive their Negro offspring of their
property the courts appointed white men as guardians of
such Negroes under age. To extend this guardianship the
courts often declared such wards irresponsible or of unsound mind. These guardians received a percentage of the
income from the valuable oil properties, but this was not
sufficient. Often in collusion with the purchaser they disposed of the properties altogether on the condition that the
guardian should share in the fortunes made from oil found
on the lands sold.

In this movement for the social degradation of the Negro,
moreover, the majority of the church finally joined.
Having in the preachment of men like Lyman Abbott, justification for segregation in the "court of **Doughfaced**
the gentiles," the "Christians" of the me- **"Christians."**
dieval type could more boldly proclaim the injustice of
forcing their members to break bread with devotees whom
the god of race hate has not made their social equals.
Churches in which Negroes had worshiped with whites
from time immemorial contrived to organize their Negro
membership as separate bodies. These were usually provided for by a make-shift inadequate system of religious
institutions. Bishops, moreover, soon tired of the ministrations entailed by their communicants of color. There
arose, then, a clamor not only for complete separation of
the races in the edifices, but for a separate church administration throughout the whole system.

This, however, would cause as many problems as it
would solve. White men were reluctant to serve Negroes
in their special groups. Yet it was considered **Hypocrisy**
"impracticable" to exalt Negroes to positions **supreme.**
of trust in the mixed churches. Furthermore, while many
churchmen disliked contact with Negroes, they believed

that it would be a mistake thus to abandon the control of Negro religious thought as the Southern churches did after the Civil War. This mingled feeling once blocked the movement for the unification of the Methodist churches. Some of the Northern Methodists stood out for at least as much recognition under the proposed system as this connection had hitherto given the Negro, but the Methodist Episcopal Church, South, would accept communicants of color only on the basis of adherents to be tolerated as undeveloped children. They finally compromised and united.

Social agencies undertaking the work which the church never performs faced the same problem. The Young Men's Christian Association and the Young Women's Christian **The compro-** Association had for years maintained sepa-
mise of social rate branches of their work for Negroes
agencies. in the South. For a long time after the Civil War race prejudice was not sufficiently rampant to exclude the few Negroes in the North from the occasional use of these conveniences. But race hate would not down, and in those centers, too, Negroes were socially proscribed when their numbers increased as a result of the migration. This problem was worked out by the compromise of constructing in urban centers separate buildings for the accommodation of men and women of African blood. These establishments have been very useful as hospices for transients; but their branches have had difficulty in finding a definite function among Negroes whose situation, made unlike that of the whites by law and custom, requires social uplift effort different from that applied to persons otherwise circumstanced. The Negroes in charge of the branches of these agencies, however, are not responsible for this situation, since they have never been left to their initiative in working among Negroes.[3]

Some believed with Senator J. B. Foraker that this segre-

[3]*Journal of Negro History*, IX, 127-138.

gation rage was stimulated by Theodore Roosevelt's dishonorable dismissal of the Negro soldiers charged with raiding Brownsville, Texas, in 1906. Eloquent defenders of Roosevelt, however, assert that he did so much for the social and civic recognition of the race in dining with Booker T. Washington and in forcing upon the Senate and the Southerners the appointment of Dr. William D. Crum as collector of the port of Charleston, that such a motive could not have thus actuated him. But there is little doubt that this accentuation of caste was decidedly aided by the policy of William H. Taft. In his inaugural address he announced that he would not appoint Negroes to office where they were not wanted by the whites. Interpreted broadly, this finally would mean that, with the increasing prejudice against the race, no Negroes at all could secure appointments to civil positions of usefulness. Taft thereby abetted segregation.

Policies of Roosevelt and Taft.

Wishing to secure universal approval of this reactionary program, legislators from the unprogressive districts of the country endeavored to enact special laws for further segregation of the races in all ramifications of life. The courses of study in State schools were further changed, and threats were made to cut off the appropriations of Negro institutions of learning altogether. These legislators advocated also the prohibition of persons of African blood from immigrating into and becoming citizens of this country, and the exclusion of Negroes from employment in certain capacities desirable for white men. Florida and Kentucky enacted laws making it a crime for a white person to teach a Negro.

Efforts for further segregation.

Where there were no special laws or ordinances providing for segregation, the end was reached another way. Negroes purchasing homes in desirable white residential districts were often warned not to move into them. If they did they were often terrorized

Riots rampant.

Co-workers in Various Causes

George E. Haynes   E. K. Jones
C. W. Chesnutt   W. S. Braithwaite

by having their homes stoned or bombed from day to day as in the cases of Kansas City, Baltimore, Philadelphia, and Chicago. In fact, this effort to prevent the expansion of the Negro residential districts was a cause of the race riots in Newbern, Tulsa, East St. Louis, Chester, Knoxville, Washington and Chicago during the migration of 1916-18 and its aftermath. In these cases the mob acted in the absence of the "law." Many assert, moreover, that in some of these instances the Negro section was burned primarily to force them into less desirable quarters in order that the property of Negroes might be used for the extension of the business districts. Some Negroes were thus deprived of their property thereafter by s p e c i a l ordinances requiring rebuilding on such expen-

Dr. L. K. Williams, a prominent factor in socializing the Church

sive plans as to force the homeless to sell out and establish themselves in the suburbs of the cities.

The worst of all in this perplexing situation was that men who formerly had been counted upon to speak for the Negroes advised them to accept the situation philosophically. Few white men encouraged Negroes to criticize adversely anything which members of the **Non-resist-** haughty race might inflict upon persons of **ance advised.** color. Negroes were told that it is unwise to infuriate a lion when you have your head in his mouth. Charles F.

Dole, voicing the sentiments of the majority of whites, said: "Don't antagonize, don't be bitter; say the conciliatory thing; make friends and do not repel them; insist on and emphasize the cheerful and good, and dwell as little as possible on wrong and evil."

This advice could not be followed, as Dr. DuBois well said, when Negroes were denied education; driven out of the Church of Christ; excluded from hotels, theaters and public places; labeled like dogs in traveling; refused decent employment; forced to the lowest wage scale; compelled to pay the highest rent for the poorest homes; prohibited from buying property in decent neighborhoods; ridiculed in the press, on the platform, and on the stage; disfranchised; taxed without representation; d e n i e d the right to choose their friends or to be chosen by them; deprived by custom and law of protection for their women; robbed of justice in the courts; and lynched with impunity.

CLAUDE McKAY

Negroes had recourse to "law," but without much avail. Many in cities in the North appealed to State civil rights acts which protected the individual against discrimination in the use of such places as theaters, hotels, railroads, steamboats and the like; but the biased courts usually evaded the issue by some sort of fallacious reasoning, or merely allowed nominal damages. The Civil Rights Act which forbade such discrimination had long since been declared unconstitutional so far as it undertook to forbid citizens of States to do these things. The rest of the act was nullified by a decision of the United States Supreme Court in 1913. A Negro woman sued a steamship company under this statute because she was denied equal accommodations with white passengers solely on the ground of color. She was not traveling within a State, but on the high seas from a port in one State to a port in another. This decision was reached by misapplying the rule of construction that when an act has been passed, the parts of which must stand or fall together, because the legislature would evidently not pass it at all unless it could pass it as a whole; then, if one part was beyond the power of the legislature and must fall, the rest must fall with it. The court held that "if Congress had known that it could not forbid the citizens of the various States from discriminating against each other on the ground of color, it would not have attempted thus to restrict the citizens of Territories, or other people subject in this respect to the control of Congress." No candid thinker, well read in Civil War history, will agree with the court, that, even if Congress had known that it could not enact such a measure which would bind the citizens of States, it would not have made it extend so far as it could by applying it to the citizens of districts subject to the direct legislation of Congress. In this case, then, the Supreme Court of the United States was merely giving its sanction to caste.

An unconstitutional decision.

In several other decisions more favorable to democracy there was offered a little hope that this high tribunal might some day ally itself altogether with justice and truth. One of these decisions was that covering three cases testing the validity of State laws imposing the literacy qualifica-

The "grandfather clause" unconstitutional.

tion for voters but exempting from its operation those persons whose grandfathers could vote prior to 1866, which was before the Negroes had been granted this privilege. In 1915 the Supreme Court decided that while the literacy test was legal and not subject to revision, it was so closely connected with the "grandfather clause" that both were unconstitutional. The standard of voting set by these measures, this tribunal held, was in substance but a revitalization of conditions which, when they prevailed in the past, had been destroyed by the self-operative force of the Thirteenth Amendment.

The decision in 1917 as to the validity of ordinances of various cities endeavoring to segregate Negroes in residential districts, was also favorable. It had been argued **Residential** that such measures preserve the purity of the **segregation** races, maintain the public peace, and prevent **outlawed.** the depreciation of property. The court conceded the seriousness of the situation, and admitted the right of a State to make race distinction on the basis of equal accommodations, but it could not go so far as to sanction the deprivation of Negroes of such rights altogether. It held, then, that a law to prevent the selling of property to a person of color is not a legitimate exercise of the police power of the State, and is in direct violation of the fundamental law enacted in the Fourteenth Amendment of the Constitution preventing State interference with property rights except by due process of law.

Another of these decisions was that in the case in which Negroes legally protested against the law of Oklahoma **A favorable** which deprived them of the rights guaranteed **opinion.** inter-State passengers using common carriers. Giving the opinion of the court in 1914, Justice Charles E. Hughes upheld the validity of separate coach laws applying to passengers within a State, but contended that so much of the Oklahoma act as permitted carriers to provide sleeping cars, dining cars, and chair cars exclusively for whites and provide no similar accommodations for Negroes, denies the latter the equal protection of the laws guaranteed by the Fourteenth Amendment of the Federal Constitution.

During these years, moreover, the Negroes did not remain inactive. They felt powerless but they would not despair.

BISHOP JOHN HURST, distinguished by valuable services for freedom within and without the Church

It was just **Propaganda** this plight **organizations.** of the Negro that brought into existence the National Association for the Advancement of Colored People. It sprang from whites and blacks who believed that some good can be accomplished by publicity, by agitation, and by memorializing the State Legislatures and Congress for a redress of these grievances.[4] These evils were well set forth also in 1911 in a memorial by the National Independent Political Rights League at its meeting in Boston. This body drafted a petition for the enforcement of the Constitution. It prayed Congress to stop disfranchisement and peonage, to pass a Federal "Anti-Jim Crow" law for inter-State passengers, to give Federal aid to education, to enact a national anti-lynching bill, and to reinstate the soldiers discharged for connection with the Brownsville riot in 1906.

[4] *Journal of Negro History*, IX, 107-116.

Forced by the logic of Negro agitators attacking these evils, some white men justified this medievalism on the ground that the leaders of the Negroes themselves have advocated the separation of the races in things civic and social. If they had in mind those Negroes, who to curry favor in using white persons to reach an end have pretended that they accept their point of view, there may be a bit of truth in such a statement. Too often, moreover, when a Negro complained of the hardships of travel, or of the denial of the ease and comforts provided for the public, the personnel responsible for these injustices referred to Booker T. Washington as the outstanding Negro whose career and teachings support segregation. As a matter of fact, however, neither Washington nor any other self-respecting Negro has ever countenanced segregation.

Misrepresentation of the Negro's attitude.

Booker T. Washington, on the contrary, was one of the worst enemies of segregation. Believing in the helpful contact of the races, he associated with the best white people, dined with President Roosevelt, and feasted among the crowned heads of Europe. In an article of his in the *New Republic* in 1915, he forcibly characterized segregation as unjust because it invites unjust measures. He believed that it would not be productive of any good, "because practically every thoughtful Negro resents its injustice and doubts its sincerity." "Any race adjustment based on injustice," said he, "finally defeats itself. The Civil War is the best illustration of what results where it is attempted to make wrong right or seem to be right. It is inconsistent," said he further; "The Negro is segregated from his white neighbor, but white business men are not prevented from doing business in Negro neighborhoods. There has been no case of segregation of Negroes in the United States that has not widened the breach between the two races. Wherever a

Booker T. Washingon opposed to segregation.

form of segregation exists, it will be found that it has been administered in such a way as to embitter the Negro and harm more or less the moral fiber of the white man. That the Negro does not express this constant sense of wrong is no proof that he does not feel it.''

Segregation thus at its worst left the Negroes in a morbid state of mind with a feeling of despair mingled with revenge. Because their former friends were weakening under the stigma of loving the race, the Negroes thought seriously of turning to their enemies. They were all but convinced that the attitude of the Southern white man toward the Negro is **Negroes in a quandry.** due in a measure to the attachment of the Negro to the ideals of the Northerner, whom the Southerner still hates. With a change in the political affiliations of the Negro, moreover, many politicians proclaimed, there would dawn a new day for the race in the South. This accounts for the large Negro vote given Woodrow Wilson

W. M. TROTTER, a fearless opponent of segregation

for the presidency in 1912, especially since he promised such Negroes that, if elected, he would see that they received justice abundantly.

Never were constituents more disappointed. The very functionaries whom they had elected manifested more enmity than ever. With the sanction of Wilson, Negroes were eliminated from all of the higher positions in the Government and segregated in the civil service. Some **Disappointed** check to segregation was effected by the **by Wilson.** numerous memorials coming from indignation meetings of the Negroes throughout the country. These protests were fostered in the main by the National Association for the Advancement of Colored People through its various branches, and by the National Equal Rights League, of which Monroe Trotter was the moving spirit. Trotter secured an interview with Wilson to protest against the injustice of segregation in the government service; but the President, whose attitude toward the Negro was actually that of the reactionaries, suddenly took umbrage at the serious tone in which Trotter fearlessly criticized the policy and abruptly terminated the conference.

In the meantime, moreover, the voice of former white friends of the Negro could not be heard except as expressed in occasional editorials and resolutions suggested by Negroes who persistently kept the offense before the **Apathy of** country. On the other hand, the whole coun- **the public.** try generally heard with conviction the misrepresentation of the race and found some delight in seeing the *Birth of a Nation,* the dramatization of Thomas Dixon's *Clansman.* This film exaggerated the part played by the Negro during Reconstruction and idealized the aristocracy which instituted a régime of blood to reëstablish its rule. After all, the reactionaries had brought it to pass that a large number of citizens had begun to think that this is a white man's country and, if the Negro remains here, he must be content with an inferior status.

Segregation, moreover, was extended abroad wherever the United States Government controlled or wherever its white citizens had influence. It has been decided by the United States Supreme Court that the Constitution does not necessarily follow the flag, but it cannot be denied that the caste of color does. The intervention of the United States in the war of Cuba with Spain, the **Segregation** consequent acquisition of territory from the **carried** latter, the construction of the Panama Canal, **abroad.** the conquest of helpless Haiti, and the purchase of the Virgin Islands by the United States, all opened promising fields for the extension of our Caucasian autocracy into the West Indies, where persons of color had formerly been treated as members of the human family. Citizens of the United States established the rule of the white man in Cuba; they carried segregation into the Canal Zone; they subjected the Haitians to the will of descendants of slave drivers; and they deprived the natives of the Virgin Islands of the opportunities for development enjoyed under the control of Denmark. Because of the protests of Negroes against the dishonorable conquest and occupation of Haiti by the United States, President Harding thought that he would placate some of them in 1922 by appointing a commission headed by W. T. B. Williams to report on the situation in that island. For a similar purpose President Coolidge sent to the Virgin Islands in 1924 a commission headed by George H. Woodson. The other members of the commission were W. H. C. Brown, C. E. Mitchell and J. S. Coage. So far as could be observed, however, there was no change in the condition of these natives as a result of these investigations.

Hitherto Liberia has been spared from these iniquities, but the encroachment of ill-designing foreigners has invited the segregating Americans. Under James S. Payne, President in 1876, the country did not rapidly recover. In the administration of Anthony W. Gardiner, however, the hope for the republic seemed to be practically lost. England and France were slicing away the territory of Liberia. Because certain natives maltreated some shipwrecked Germans, their country's warships bombarded Nana Kru and forced the payment of damages. The colony had become involved in troubles with England and Germany. Its numerous debts could not be paid. The French and English, therefore, were endeavoring to take over the country. This sort of situation continued through the administrations of Hilary R. W. Johnson, Joseph James Cheeseman, William D. Coleman and Arthur Barclay from 1884 to 1896. To secure further relief the Government authorized in 1906 another British loan of £100,000 through the Liberian Development Company. The understanding was that a stipulated sum of this money would be used to meet the pressing obligations while the other was for the development of the country. It soon appeared, however, that this scheme, backed by Sir Harry H. Johnston, was another effort to defraud the Liberian Government and encroach upon its territory. It was fortunately prevented by the Government of the United States. Upon hearing of the untoward condition of Liberia, the Taft administration sent to that country in 1909 a commission of inquiry of the following persons: Roland P. Faulkner, George Sale, and Emmett J. Scott. This commission made definite recommendations to eradicate the evils affecting Liberia. The United States, they said, should aid Liberia in settling its boundary disputes, in refunding its debt, in reforming its finances and in organizing a defense force. Some opportunity for aggression appeared in the recommendation that the United States should establish and maintain a research station in Liberia and should reopen the question of establishing there a coaling station. The commission, however, did not provide any means, although it forestalled the theft projected by the Liberian Development Company. Colonel Charles Young was sent twice to Liberia to reorganize its military force in keeping with one of the recommendations, but, seeking rest from hardships, he died in Lagos in 1921.

The Republic of Liberia then turned to the United States Government for a loan of $5,000,000. Charles D. B. King, inaugurated President in 1920, spent some time thereafter in this country in the interest of this loan. Such a grant was finally proposed in Congress, but the measure provided for the expenditure of this money almost altogether by Americans. This left little possibility for the republic to profit thereby. It was fortunate, then, that the country did not finally receive such expensive aid. Liberia was later ''assisted'' by a grant from Firestone, the exploiter of rubber, who received concessions which have netted him a strangle-hold of the republic. The League of Nations promised much and authorized investigations but offered the country no practical help. The United States Government continued to be indifferent as to the fate of that republic.

The ''civilized Liberians,'' it is said, have done very little to develop the resources of the interior. Dependent mainly on trade which has rapidly declined because of the competition of European imperialists, Liberia with little or no wealth to tax, has had to resort to expensive loans from land-grabbing neighbors. Cultivation in Liberia is primitive and workers are underpaid. Firestone says that he would pay the natives higher wages, but the ruling class in Liberia objects. Unfortunately those in control took their cue for the treatment of the natives from the slaveholders of the United States by whom their forbears were liberated and sent to Africa. For this reason the country has been kept at a standstill, and its most important achievement is its survival. Backwardness has been true of many other countries during their first century; but with the recent establishment of a military base there during the Second World War and other improvements now being made toward modernization, Liberia may enter upon a new era.

CHAPTER XXVIII

THE TENDER MERCIES OF THE WICKED

As the second decade of the century found President Taft officially advocating the elimination of the Negro from politics in the South and his successor upholding racial segregation in the government service, the majority of the

Taft and Wilson. Northern people easily acquiesced in the policy of abandoning the Negro to whatever lot his enemies might grant him. By this time the immigration of unsympathetic Europeans had gone to such an extent and the third generation was so far removed from the social upheaval of the Civil War that the Negro and his problems tended to pass from the public mind in the North. Elihu Root did warn the South in one of his speeches in the Senate not to go so far in the oppression of the Negro as to invite again the interference of the North; but most statesmen, while deprecating the awful plight in which the Negro was, expressed the belief that the North would never again champion such a cause.

The country, however, registered no striking protest against the appointment of various Negroes whom President Taft placed in positions of trust outside of the South.

Few Negroes in office. His most important appointment was that of William H. Lewis, an Amherst and Harvard man, who had distinguished himself as a member of the Massachusetts Legislature and as an Assistant United States District Attorney in Boston. Lewis was made an Assistant Attorney General of the United States under George Wickersham, who fearlessly defended him when the Southern members of the American Bar Association endeavored

494

to keep him out of that body on account of his color.   In making this particular appointment, however, Taft did not show any more courage than Woodrow Wilson.   Upon the recommendation of his Attorney General James C. Mc-Reynolds, he renominated Judge Robert H. Terrell for the municipal bench in the District of Columbia and kept his

OFFICEHOLDERS BECAUSE OF MERIT

WILLIAM H. LEWIS   ROBERT H. TERRELL

name before the Senate until he was confirmed despite the efforts of the reactionaries to the contrary.

Such loyaty to a Negro, however, was exceptional.   The chief interest manifested in the race during these years was the effort of philanthropists to support the "optimistic, constructive, educational program" of Tuskegee and Hampton, where they said the training of the Negroes was "rightly directed."   The South accepted this educational

The optimistic program popular.

policy, hoping to make of the Negro a sort of super-servant. But, as Ray Stannard Baker said, the very system itself turned out instead independent, upstanding, intelligent men and women who acquired property and thus came into sharper competition with whites. A man's mental power may develop just as easily in studying chemistry to improve the soil as in learning languages to appreciate the classics. During that generation, therefore, Negroes in spite of themselves developed in the direction of agitative organization under leaders who controlled or influenced the press.

This development more than anything else accounts for the return of the Negro to politics in certain States. The old line politicians, who figured conspicuously in Republican conventions, corralled the Negroes and delivered more than a million votes merely for such positions as Recorder of Deeds in the District of Columbia and Register of the Treasury, lost their influence. Negroes began to clamor not for office, but for issues. They desired to know what candidates had done, or would pledge themselves to do for equality and justice regardless of race or color. Most Negroes finally realized that the party of Lincoln and Grant went down with them into their graves. In the Border States and in the North, therefore, it became difficult to determine beforehand how the Negro would vote. Recognizing this wise use of power by Negro voters, citizens elected some meritorious men of color to the State Legislatures in Massachusetts, New York, Missouri, New Jersey, Pennsylvania, West Virginia, Ohio, Indiana, and Illinois. Liberal voters chose also deserving Negroes to represent them in the municipal councils in New York City, Baltimore, and Chicago. The unusual migration of Negro voters to the North in later years, moreover, brought home to the public

The Negro in politics again.

the possibility of electing Negroes to Congress in certain urban centers of the North.

On the other hand, many Negroes of foresight saw little hope in the unsatisfactory results obtained in politics. They looked to constructive agencies by which political affiliations are determined and controlled.

The Negro, they believed, will gain little in **The constructive program.** this sphere unless his claims for social and civic recognition are supported by economic achievement. Therefore, whereas the talented Negroes just after the Civil War took up politics, teaching, or preaching, and the next generation of their group directed its efforts toward mechanical pursuits and practical professions, the educated Negroes of the third generation went into business. This change took place so rapidly that the schools, churches, and social agencies of the race were left largely in the hands of Negroes who had not the initiative to succeed in commercial pursuits. Once it had been considered exceptional to find a Negro succeeding in business, but after this change of objective one observed in every large urban community of Negroes a considerable number rising to commanding positions in the economic development of the race. The Negro had learned that his chief hope is to develop from within and he was carrying out this program.

Some of the most encouraging signs for a brighter day for the Negro, however, came from without; and, strange to say, from the South, from the enlightened, thinking men and women of the South. These workers were not politicians themselves and had little or no concern **The awakening of the South.** with the movement to restore the political power of the Negro. These were educated persons of vision, students of history and government sufficiently informed to realize that the repression of the Negro was merely developing an evil which in the future would react most unfavorably on the white man himself. They knew, according to history, that in all cases of oppression, the oppressor loses his moral sense and pristine vigor in the long run while developing against himself entwining social, economic, and political forces which eventually work his own destruction. Let us come together, then, they said, and do something to constrain both races to work out their destiny in harmony and brotherly love. In short, having particularly the interests of the white man at heart, these leaders of the new thought in the South had begun to appreciate the force of Booker T. Washington's wisdom when he said: "I will let no man drag me down so low as to make me hate him."

This very movement was an open confession that customary methods of violence had failed. The South, the reformers observed, was handicapping itself by impoverishing the Negro and preventing his mental and moral **Unrest among** development. The Negroes decreased their **Negroes.** illiteracy of persons over 10 years of age from 79.9 per cent in 1870 to 22.9 per cent in 1920, but most of this progress was above the Lower South. Negroes were, therefore, in a state of unrest; and as long as this continued there could be no security in any effort for economic amelioration dependent upon him as a stable factor. The farming sections were rapidly losing Negro labor as a result of their flocking to the cities of the South in quest of a larger return for their labor and better educational facilities, offered in the main by Northern philanthropy. The Negroes found it impossible to accumulate much on the worn-out soil; and, being generally unable to buy land, they held it tempora-**Beginnings** rily only on terms of a stringent land lease **of the** which deprived them of practically all of their **migration.** earnings. This was especially true when most of such Negro farmers, in addition to these inconveniences, had to bear that of paying usurious rates of interest and had to endure brutal treatment if they succeeded in maintaining themselves independently of the whites. These Negroes, moreover, were not remaining in the Southern cities. For a number of years the talented tenth of the Negroes in the South had lost large numbers to the North,

JOHN R. HAWKINS, a business man, an educator, and a factor in the Church

and the laboring element gradually found its way to the same centers.

Those who had refused to treat the Negro as a man were then having trouble **The failure of intimidation.** in using him merely as an instrument. Gradually it had become evident that you cannot settle a question by satisfying only one of the parties concerned, that nothing is settled until it is settled right. For the first time in the history of the South the thinking class began to believe that the country had been actually befuddled by politicians like Ben Tilman, Hoke Smith, Cole Blease, and James K. Vardaman. For generations they had ridden into office on the worn-out issue of "Down with the Negro."

Among a few of the educated aristocracy of the South the effort for reform became largely publicity. **Southern** After much academic discussion the proposals **Sociological** for racial coöperation took form under the **Congress.** Southern Sociological Congress founded by Mrs. Anne Russell Cole and inaugurated at Nashville in 1912 by Governor

Ben W. Hooper of Tennessee. All of the persons presenting themselves did not have the same ideas as to how racial harmony could best be promoted. They differed as to what should or should not be done for the Negro. It was noteworthy, too, that the Congress appointed a Committee on Race Problems, among the members of which were such workers among the Negroes as Miss Belle H. Bennett, Bishop W. P. Thirkield, Miss Grace Bigelow House, Dr. J. D. Hammond, Dr. H. B. Frissell and Dr. George W. Hubbard. At this first meeting of the Congress, too, there was formed what is known as the University Commission on Race Questions consisting of representative educators of ten Southern State Universities. Negroes were permitted to join the Sociological Congress, and at the second annual meeting five of them were invited as speakers. But the body did not grant the Negroes any significant share in the administration of the society, and in choosing its Negro speakers the management carefully selected those leaders who have always been known to be conservative. This policy caused the impatient element of Negroes to question the movement and to doubt its sincerity.

This Southern coöperative movement, however, was not organized to solve the race problem. Its program was "to study and improve social, civic and economic conditions in the South, to make the South better by promoting brotherhood and to enlist the entire South in a crusade of social **Efforts to improve conditions.** health and righteousness." To do all of these things the leaders of the movement realized that the coöperation of all races was necessary and for the first time in the history of the South a group of high-minded white men said to the Negroes: "Come and let us reason together." "The Negro," said they, "is the weakest link in our civilization and our welfare is indissolubly bound up with his."

The Southern leaders of thought, moreover, felt that while they could not accomplish everything at once, they might do much good in directing attention to a few urgent needs. As far as these gentlemen went in the direction of helping the Negro was to attack mob violence and request the extension of educational opportunities for the race. Appealing to college trained men to influence public opinion in favor of these things, they did some good in convincing the better element of the South that the lynching of Negroes brutalizes the white man and that the mentally undeveloped laborer is an economic handicap to the nation.

The appeal to the college man.

Endeavoring not to alienate the rabid white man, however, the leaders of the movement lost the confidence of many Negroes when they proclaimed their belief in the integrity of races and emphasized for the Negro only that sort of education which is "rightly directed." It did not help matters to hear one of the workers say: "Agencies controlled by ideals in accord with the spirit of the South should be provided for training Negro ministers, teachers, and supervisors of schools." And it did not seem encouraging to have so many insist that before much could be done for the education of the Negro, more facilities would have to be provided for the mental development of the poor whites. Yet, there resulted a somewhat increasing respect for the Negro, a wider interest in industrial education, and a bold attack on the strongholds of lynching, all of which began to become effective by 1915.

Difficulties in facing the issue.

This Southern coöperative movement, like its successor. the interracial effort, did not succeed in obtaining definite results. This may be accounted for by the lack of confidence in the movement, the stupendous task undertaken, and the failure to secure adequate funds to finance the work. Educated

Definite results wanting.

Negroes severely criticised the University Commission because it was undertaking to solve the race problem without officially coöperating with the race by taking on their staff representatives of Negro schools. In connection with the Phelps-Stokes Fund, however, the Commission made a step forward in the actual study of the Negro. It established at the universities of Virginia and Georgia fellowships of $1,250 each, supporting white graduate students

WORKING ON THE ROAD

desiring to exploit this field. Scholars, however, did not look favorably upon the all but undergraduate type of dissertations produced by these students. The *New York Evening Post*, moreover, expressed the thought of many in saying: "While some of the educated colored people will feel like endowing scholarships elsewhere for the scientific study of the white man and of his failure to adjust himself to American civilization by lynching from Coatesville to the Gulf and his persistent nullification of the Constitution with regard to suffrage, the experts will agree that these gifts are usefully bestowed."

Such an effort as that of these few advanced Southern thinkers, however, could not immediately succeed. Unfortunately, too many of the so-called friends of the Negro had then surrendered to the reactionaries. Few white men then contributed anything to the support of propaganda in behalf of the rights of the Negroes. A Negro known to be anxious to break down social barriers or to have the rights of his race respected made as little headway in raising funds in one section of the country as in another. In most cases of financial aid to institutions it had to be known beforehand that the management was safely conservative or that some white man would supervise the expenditure of the funds contributed. The Negro, according to this idea, must be carefully guarded and directed from without. One should not leave a Negro to his own initiative, for nobody knew what he would do. The Negro might run amuck and advocate social equality, or demand for his race the privileges of democracy when he should restrict himself to public health, economic improvement, and industrial education.

The Negro battling by himself.

The use made of the Phelps-Stokes Fund strikingly illustrated how "friends of the Negroes" often served them. This factor in the life of the Negro resulted from the bequest of $900,000 by Miss Caroline Phelps-Stokes in 1909. The income from this fund was to be used for the improvement of tenement houses in the city of New York, for the relief of poor families there, "for the education of the Negro both in Africa, and in the United States, North American Indians, and needy and deserving white students." Almost immediately after conforming to the provisions for the execution of this will, the trustees offered the United States Bureau of Education the

Misdirected philanthropy.

coöperation of this foundation in studying the private
and higher schools for Negroes.   The offer was accepted by
Commissioner Claxton.   Upon the recommendation of Dr.
Hollis B. Frissell, and despite the proposal of Dr. Booker T.
Washington, Thomas Jesse Jones was chosen to make this
study.   He had the assistance of Ocea Taylor, Thomas
Jackson Woofter, and Walter B. Hill, all of whom had not

THE NEW HOME IN THE MAKING

been adequately trained in methods of scientific investigation.

Their report made in 1917, then, pertained largely to
such matters as attendance, number of teachers, income,
value of property, organization, and methods of administration.   A standard which Americans and Europeans have
spent centuries reaching was agreed upon as the test for
Negro schools in operation for less than fifty years.   Those
which did not measure up accordingly were pronounced

unworthy of support. Partiality was shown to those schools for Negroes directed or controlled by white persons.

It was proper for these investigators to expose and thereby close up many institutions which were mismanaged or used as a means for imposing upon the public; but this report worked a gross injustice to those schools founded and supported by enterprising Negroes themselves. Thomas Jesse Jones did not find much virtue in this type of school. Some of such institutions are still unable to employ adequate teachers, or purchase necessary equipment; but they are living monuments to the initiative of these pioneers. Many useful Negroes of to-day would not have received any education at all, had .it not been for these very institutions. Their students did not always thoroughly learn mathematics or science; but seeing men of their own race in action, they received that better boon, the inspiration to achieve in spite of difficulties. As Jones's idea of uplifting the Negroes does not get beyond that of the benevolent tutelage of children to be developed as useful instruments for the whites, there would be no need for such initiative in Negroes. Jones would have Negro schools and social uplift agencies brought under direct control of the whites or placed in charge of Negroes whom white men can use.

Negro initiative discouraged.

By persons who knew little about the Negro this report made by Thomas Jesse Jones was evaluated as one of the most important achievements in the history of Negro uplift. A little examination of the situation, however, shows that this report redounded not to the good of the Negro but to the aggrandizement of the man who made it. The work favorably impressed many philanthropists, who, having little time to study the Negro institutions in which they were interested, welcomed this biased investigator as their guide in contributing to Negro education. Booker T. Washington had often spoken

An unusual liability.

for the race, but now they had some one better qualified, a white man to serve as the almoner of the despised group. After working out the salvation of the Negro on this wise in America, moreover, he appointed himself as redeemer of the heathen in Africa through the control of its missions. This last step was a direful calamity in the life of the Negro, for Jones was too narrow-minded to understand that all of the wants of the race cannot be supplied by agencies of one sort, and the program for its uplift cannot be carried out by one man.

A careful investigation of the methods of Jones, moreover, revealed startling facts. He proscribed the many Negroes who criticised his policies, and he conducted a general campaign among philanthropists to prevent their giving to institutions in which such Negroes were working. Furthermore, he might be personally interested in an agency, but if he happened to have a misunderstanding with its Negro administrative officer, he would insidiously lie in wait for every opportunity to destroy the work to wreak vengeance upon the person in charge. And worst of all, he never fought in the open, or permitted his victim to know that he was doomed to slaughter. He proceeded always by indirection, writing letters of misrepresentation and holding conferences by which he influenced persons against those whom he sought to destroy. His efforts, then, gradually degenerated into those of a bureau of espionage directed by a destructively vindictive man. He was detested by the majority of thinking Negroes. Among them his name was mentioned only to be condemned.

A bureau of espionage.

CHAPTER XXIX

WHILE the Negroes were suffering from persecution in the South and economic proscription in the North, the world plunged almost unexpectedly into a universal struggle which materially affected the interests of the blacks.[1] The heir-presumptive to the **A factor in the war.** Austro-Hungarian throne was shot at Serajevo June 28, 1914. Blaming the Serbs for this crime, the Austrian government sent Serbia an ultimatum demanding that the offenders be brought to trial by a tribunal in which Austria should be represented. Serbia refused to yield to these demands and was supported by Russia in this position; but, feeling that if such an act passed without punishment, it would soon be impossible for the crowned heads of Europe to maintain their empires, Germany upheld Austria. England, France, and Italy recommended that the matter be adjusted by arbitration; but Germany, contending that mobilization of the Russian army was in reality a declaration of war against her, declared war on Russia the first of August and on France two days later. England sympathized with France, to which she was attached by various ties, and accordingly entered the war against Germany. When Germany showed such disregard of her treaty obli-

---

[1] The history of the World War has not yet been written. There have appeared several subscription volumes for the purpose of making money rather than to publish the whole truth, and they have been extensively sold. As to the rôle of the Negro in this drama there is but scant reliable information. Emmett J. Scott has written a popular account of the achievements of the Negroes in this struggle, but it is hoped that this may soon be followed by a scientific treatise.

gations as to invade Belgium, a neutral country, she lost
the sympathy of the advanced European and American
countries, most of which finally joined the allies to curb the
power of the Hohenzollerns.

The United States deeply sympathized with the struggle
against autocracy, but did not deem the interference with
our commerce and even the sinking of our neutral ships
sufficient cause for intervention. This coun-
Prosperity. try, then, entered at once upon an unprece-
dented period of commercial prosperity in becoming the
source of supply for almost everything needed by the numerous nations involved in the war. Industries, formerly
in a struggling state, received an unusual impetus; new
enterprises sprang up in a day; and persons once living
merely above want multiplied their wealth by fortunate investments. The aggressions of Germany upon our commerce, resulting in the death of our citizens upon ships
destroyed on the high seas, became so numerous, however,
that thousands of Americans, led by Theodore Roosevelt,
insisted upon a declaration of war against Germany. But
our trade with the Allies was so lucrative that it was difficult to convert a majority of the people of the country to
the belief that it would be better for us to disturb the era
of commercial prosperity to go to war for the mere principle that Germany wronged us in trying to break up our
lawful commerce with the belligerents in Europe.

This continued prosperity brought on a new day for the
laboring man and consequently a period of economic advancement for the Negro. The million of immigrants an-
A new day nually reaching our shores were cut off from
for labor. this country by the war. Labor in the United
States, then, soon proved to be inadequate to supply the
demand. Wages in the industrial centers of the North and
West were increased to attract white men; but a sufficient
number of them could not be found in this country, so

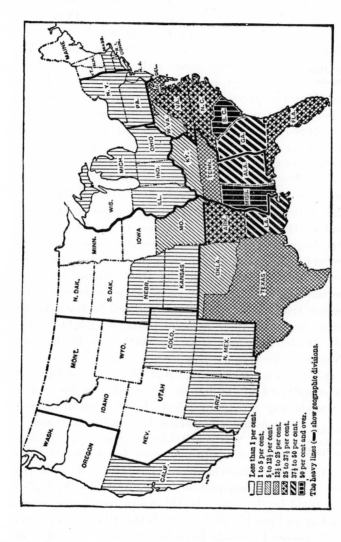

THE PERCENTAGE OF NEGROES IN THE POPULATION OF THE UNITED STATES IN 1920

great was the demand in the industrial centers, the plants, and cantonments, making preparations for war. Departing then from the time-honored custom in the North, the needy employers began to bid for Negro labor of the South. All **Negro labor** Negroes who came seeking unskilled labor **in demand.** were hired, and occasionally skilled workmen of color found employment. But the Negroes of the South were not merely invited; they were sent for. Those who first ventured North to find employment wrote back for their friends; and when this method failed to supply the demand, labor agents were sent for that purpose wherever they could find men. The Mississippi Valley, for several reasons, proved to be the most favorable section. Throughout this section conditions had at times become unsettled on account of the periodical inundations of the Mississippi; and the Negroes in those lowlands, usually the greatest sufferers, welcomed the opportunity to go to a safer and more congenial part. Throughout the Gulf States, however, where the boll weevil had for years made depredations on the cotton crop, Negroes were also inclined to move out to a section in which their economic progress might be assured. In short, the call from the North came at the time the Negroes were ready and willing to go.

It may seem a little strange that Negroes who had for years complained of intolerable persecution in the South never made any strenuous efforts to leave until offered **Economic** economic advantages in the North. Such a **advantages** course was inevitable, however; for, intoler- **in the North.** able as conditions were in the South, the Negro had to live somewhere and he could not do so in the North. There the monopoly of labor maintained by trades unions stood in the way. In this more recent movement, instead of making his way to the North where among unfriendly people he would have to eke out an existence as a menial, he was invited to come to these industrial centers

where friends and employment awaited him. History,
moreover, does not show that large numbers of persons
have migrated because of persecution. If not assured of
an equally good economic foundation elsewhere, the majority of those persecuted have decided in the final analysis to
bear the ills they have rather than fly to those they know
not of.

The oppression of the Negroes in the South, however,
was also a cause of the exodus, though not the dominant
one. When men from afar came to tell the Negroes of a
way of escape to a peaceful and law-abiding **Oppression,**
place, they were received as spies returning **a cause.**
from the inspection of a promised land. While the many
migrated with the hope of amassing fabulous sums, they all
sighed with relief at the thought that they could at last
go to a country where they could educate their children,
protect their families from insult, and enjoy the fruits of
their labor. They had pleasant recollections of the days
when Negroes wielded political power, and the dream of
again coming into their own was a strong motive impelling
many to leave the South. Negro leaders primarily interested in securing to the race the full enjoyment of its rights
rejoiced that they were going North, while the conservative,
sycophantic, toady classes advised them to remain in the
service of their employers in the South.

In the North the Negroes readily entered upon the full
enjoyment of many privileges denied them in the South.
Here and there, however, they were brought into close competition with the radical white laboring ele- **Troubles in**
ment. At Chester, Youngstown, and East St. **the North.**
Louis they precipitated riots in trying to get rid of Negro
labor. At East St. Louis in July, 1917, Negroes long
harassed by this element finally became the object of onslaughts by the whites. They were overcome by the mob,

which was supported by the silence of the militia sent to maintain order. They permitted individuals to take their guns to drive the Negroes into their congested quarters, where 125 were massacred and burned. The administration of justice in this Northern State seemed no better than that in the South; for, although the whites were the aggressors in

A RESULT OF THE MIGRATION. A NEGRO TEACHER WITH PUPILS OF BOTH RACES

the riot, the court inflicted more punishment on the Negroes than on the whites. One Negro was sentenced to life imprisonment but later acquitted. Ten other Negroes were to serve fourteen years, whereas four white men were imprisoned for from fourteen to fifteen years, five for five years, eleven for less than one year; eighteen were fined, and seventeen acquitted.

These outbreaks, of course, justified the predictions of Southern employers that the Negroes would not be welcomed in the North and encouraged certain seriously thinking Negroes in proclaiming that the prosperity of the Negro in the industrial centers was merely temporary. It was said that the trades unions, **Differing reflections.** when strengthened by the immigrants from Europe after the war, would eventually force the Negroes out of employment after they had severed the ties which bound them to the South. Other Negroes had little fear from the immigrants. Believing that the depopulation of Europe during this war would render a large immigration from that quarter an impossibility, others urged the Negroes to continue their coming North in spite of all conflicts and difficulties. They rejoiced that they were then migrating in such numbers as to be mutually helpful and to wield economic and political power.

Knowing that the South was losing the only sort of labor it can use in its exploiting system, employers of that section considered the exodus a calamity. They, therefore, took steps to impede and, if possible, to stop the **The exodus** movement. Moral suasion was first used. **a calamity.** Negroes were told of the horrors of the North and especially of the hard winters. When letters to Negroes from friends who were easily braving these hardships reached the South, another sort of argument was necessary. Labor agents were first handicapped by requiring a high license. By special ordinances, they were then prohibited from inducing Negroes to leave, and finally they were driven out of the South. As the mail proved to be almost as good an avenue for reaching the prospective migrant, those seeking to prevent the exodus found their efforts still futile. Negroes going North were then driven from the railway stations, taken from trains, and imprisoned on false charges to delay or prevent their departure from southern cities. But the Negroes continued to go North. The movement was not checked until after the intervention of the United States in the war. The administration spent so much money in the South while hurrying the preparation for war that wages so rapidly increased and work became so general that it was unnecessary for the Negroes to go North to improve their economic condition.

The intervention of the United States in the First World War marked another epoch in the history of the Negro in this country. In the first place, few people in America **The interven-** were anxious to go to the front, although a **tion of the** majority of our citizens felt that the Hohen- **United States.** zollern autocracy should be destroyed. Men had to be converted to the war. German spies had long been abroad in this country, and millions, because of their German descent, felt bitter toward the United States for going to the aid of the Allies. There was then much appre· hension as to the attitude of the Negroes. Throughout this country they had been treated as pariahs, unprepared for the full measure of that democracy for which Woodrow Wilson desired to fight in Europe that the world might be a decent place to live in. As a matter of fact, German spies **German spies.** did approach Negroes; and a few of them expressed themselves as being in sympathy with Germany. A still larger number boldly advocated making this country a decent place for the Negroes before taking Negroes to Europe to secure to the oppressed there privileges which the blacks could not enjoy at home.

In thinking that the Negro would prove disloyal to the United States, however, the white man showed that he did not understand the race. The Negroes of this country **The Negroes** love their native soil and will readily die, if **loyal.** necessary, to defend it. However, they do not love the reactionaries, who during the last seventy years of their control of the Federal Government have failed to live up to their oath to carry out the Constitution of the United States, which guarantees to the Negroes the enjoyment of every right, immunity, and privilege, found in the most liberal democracy on earth. The Negroes have continued to be loyal to their country, with the hope that the degraded elements in control may become sufficiently civilized to abandon medieval methods for government based on liberty, equality, and fraternity. As the principle is worth fighting for, and as the struggle for it must not be hopeless in view of the interest occasionally shown in the man far down, the Negroes would not permit their dispositions to sour; they forgot their wrongs and offered themselves to fight the battles of humanity.

The reactionary class, however, although ready to brand the Negroes with suspicion and to prosecute them for disloyalty, urged the government not to recruit Negroes. The Negroes, according to the whites of this attitude, constituted an inferior **Reactionaries against Negroes.** class which should not participate in the struggle of white men. Many Southerners who, in their faulty judgment, "have solved forever" the race problem by depriving Negroes of social, political and civic rights, moreover, considered it alarming to train them in the arts of war; for men who have waded through blood to victory are not easily intimidated into subjection to the insult and outrage legalized in the backward districts. The efforts of the reactionaries were futile, however, and the Negroes were drawn into the army in much larger numbers than they should have been. Although constituting one-tenth of the population, the Negro element furnished thirteen per cent of the soldiers called to the colors. At the same time the European nations had not sufficient prejudice to hesitate as did Americans in deciding the question of employing Negro troops. There were 280,000 Senegalese who had helped to repel the Germans on the Ourcq and the Marne, 30,000 Congolese, and about 20,000 from the British West Indies, who also did their part in saving France from autocracy.

When the American Negro was finally decided upon as

desirable for the army, the same reactionaries in control of the Federal Government endeavored to restrict them in the

Restriction in the service required.
service. Negroes had to register under methods of discrimination, that they might not be confused with the whites. No pro-vision in the beginning was made for training Negro offi-cers, and southern congressmen urged that all Negroes be confined to stevedore regiments to labor under white com-missioned and non-commissioned officers. Fearing that this would be done, Negro leaders protested. They charged the War Department with conscripting Negroes for labor. The Secretary of War, of course, assured them that noth-ing of the sort was planned when it was actually being done.

To the Service of Supply regiments most Negro draftees were sent. Not less than three-fourths of the 200,000 of the Negroes sent to France were reduced to laborers. It re-sulted that one-tenth of the population of the nation was compelled by a country fighting for democracy abroad, to

In the Service of Supply.
supply three-fourths of the labor of the ex-peditionary force. They were commanded, moreover, largely by illiterate, prejudiced white men, and finally all but enslaved in the Service of Supply divisions abroad by unsympathetic officers, the majority of whom were reactionaries on the order of slave drivers. These Negroes were subjected to unnecessary rigor; they were assigned unusually hard tasks; they were given inadequate recreation, while white soldiers in the same camp were ex-empted from these hardships. Abusive language, kicks, cuffs and injurious blows were the order of the day in dealing with the Negroes impressed into this branch of service. As there were in these camps no Negroes in touch with the outside world except the Young Men's Christian Association secretaries, and the slave-driving officers suc-ceeded in displacing some of these, there was no one to

whom these Negroes could take a complaint. The Bureau of Negro Economics directed by George E. Haynes in the Department of Labor was very busy with various plans during the war; but these efforts did not continue long enough to effect much of a change in the status of the Negro laborers in civil life, and the Bureau was not required to deal with those in the army.

The Negroes drafted accepted their lot as good soldiers. Loyal to the cause of humanity, they faced humiliation, hardships and insult without murmur. But the universal opinion is that the Negro stevedore, in spite of all he had to endure, was the best laborer in the war and that without this efficient service the Allies could not have been supplied with food and munitions rapidly enough to save them from exhaustion. Negroes were stationed at the English and French ports and at depots like that at Givres. Millions of American wealth handled by 25,000 men there passed through enormous masses of warehouses with 140 miles of interior railroad lines for the handling of freight. They unloaded the transports, prepared the vehicles to convey the supplies to the interior, and built depots for storing them. When the way to the expeditionary force lay through woods and over hills, the labor battalions built roads from the port of entry to the front. Moreover, they buried the dead, salvaged war material, and detonated explosives scattered over France by the enemy.

Loyal in spite of discrimination.

The Negroes were diplomatically told that they would be drafted to fight in the ranks as other men. The War Department, however, was not at first sure that the army could make use of the Negro as an officer. This situation offered little hope to the thousands of well-educated Negroes, who in the army would be serving under inferior whites. Therefore, the students and a few members of the faculty of Howard University instituted a nation-wide campaign for a training camp in which Negroes of certain educational qualifications should have the opportunity to qualify as officers in the national service. As this movement soon had the support of all Negro schools of consequence and was promoted, too, by many white and black citizens, the War Department was forced to take the matter under advisement. After some hesitation the administration decided to

The demand for Negro officers.

COL. CHARLES YOUNG
The aggrieved Negro graduate
of West Point

establish at Fort Des Moines a camp for the training of colored officers. There was, however, much apprehension as to how the experiment would work out and still more as to whether the United States Government would actually commission a large number of Negro officers. Six hundred and seventy-five of the twelve hundred accepted at the camp, however, were commissioned in October, 1917, and the country saw going hither and thither the largest number of Negroes who had ever worn the stripes and bars.

The Negro officer, however, had already been proscribed. The administration had granted the Negro this recognition to secure the support of the Negroes for the war, but the Negro officer was not desired in the army, and the personnel in control did not intend to keep him there. Colonel Young was soon retired because of high blood pressure from which he did

Proscription of the Negro officer.

not dreadfully suffer until in a time of rapid promotion it seemed likely that he would advance high enough to command too many white men and disturb race superiority in the United States. Then followed in the cantonments the campaign to discredit and force the Negro officer out of the army. Through the Secretary of War, Emmett J. Scott, his assistant, was able to counteract some of these efforts made within the limits of the United States.

This attack, however, finally centered on the Negro officer in action in France, as it was a little difficult to do here some things which could be effected abroad before the War Department could intervene. In the **Fighting the** 92nd Division, in which most of the Negroes **Negro officer** trained at Fort Des Moines served, the Negro **in France.** officer suffered unusually. The division was placed in command of an incompetent man, General Ballou. Surrounded by officials prejudiced against the Negro, he became unduly influenced thereby and shaped his policy accordingly. He showed very little judgment in trying to force his division to accept race discrimination, and still less in criticizing Negro officers in the presence of their subordinates. He said that they were failures before they had been tested. Wherever Negro officers were stationed, morover, a systematic effort was made to get rid of them by bringing them as early as possible before efficiency boards to find excuses for their retirement or assignment to labor battalions. In regiments where there were all Negroes the same end was reached. This happened in the case of the New York Fifteenth, from which Colonel Hayward, the white commander, secured the transfer of all Negro officers after retiring a few for inefficiency. The staff could then contend that, as additional officers thereafter were necessary and other Negro officers could not be supplied, the regiment would have to take on white officers altogether,

Many superior officers openly asked that white officers be sent to their regiments regardless of the question of efficiency.

To carry out this purpose grave complaints were filed against the Negro officers. They were often charged with cowardice, although the Negro soldier was by the same man praised for his bravery. Such was the experience of four officers of the 368th Regiment. Having received the orders first to advance and then to withdraw, they obeyed both and withdrew to their former positions. As a matter of fact, these troops had not been prepared for this attack. They were without maps, without hand grenades, and without adequate ammunition, and wholly without artillery support. The "high command," as evidenced by orders, had no intention of sending these troops "over the top" in the first phase of this offensive, but had reserved for them the duty of combat liaison unit between the Seventy-seventh Division on the right and the French Chasseurs à Pieds on the left. Contrary to orders, however, these troops thus ill equipped were sent "over the top at zero hour." Major Merrill, a white officer supposed to be leading them, was nowhere to be found during the engagement. Two companies of the Second Battalion became disorganized on account of confusion in orders and Major Max A. Elser, the battalion commander, was not near enough to the front to be communicated with. He had gone well to the rear as soon as the fire became intense. Major Elser later made charges of inefficiency against four of the officers of this battalion, and regardless of his dishonorable conduct under fire he was later promoted to the rank of Lieutenant Colonel. An investigation by Newton D. Baker, the Secretary of War, showed that the Negro officers were not to be blamed and he exonerated them. He took occasion to laud these and other Negro officers and soldiers for their valor and patriotism.

In keeping with the policy of eliminating Negro officers

The New York Fifteenth in the World War

from the army, Colonel Allan J. Greer addressed a letter
to Senator K. D. McKellar, in violation of a law which, in
a country believing in justice, would subject him to court
martial. Pointing out the so-called weakness in the Negro
officer, he said: "Now that a reorganization of the army

A step be- is in prospect . . . I think I ought to bring
yond bounds. a matter to your attention that is of vital
importance, not only from a military point of view but
from that which all Southerners have. I refer to the question of Negro officers and Negro troops.

"The record of the division," said he, "is one which
will probably never be given full publicity, but the bare
facts are about as follows: We came to France in June,
we were given seven weeks in the training area instead of
the four weeks in training area as usually allotted, then
went to a quiet sector of the front. From there we went
to Argonne, and in the offensive starting there on September 26, had one regiment in the line, attached to the 38th
French Corps. They failed there in all their missions, laid
down and sneaked to the rear, until they were withdrawn.
Thirty of the officers of this regiment alone were reported
either for cowardice or failure to prevent their men from
retreating, and this against very little opposition. The
French and our white field officers did all that could possibly have been done; but the troops were impossible."

While these white officers of superior rank were persistently trying to weed out the Negro officers on the
Praised by grounds of their inefficiency, the French, with
the French. whom some of the Negro officers and troops
were fortunately brigaded, had nothing but words of praise
for their gallant leadership. Among the French officers of
consequence who thus complimented them was the unbiased
leader, General Goybet. In fact, the French officers, easily
observing that the trouble with the Negro officer and his
American superior was merely a question of color, often

interfered to save many a Negro officer from humiliation and from dishonorable discharge from the army. That there was no truth in the reports as to the general inefficiency of the Negro officer is evidenced by the fact that the 370th, the 8th Illinois, which was officered throughout by Negroes, rendered such gallant service that it received more citations and croix de guerre than any other American regiment in France. And many wondered how it could be possible for a Negro to be such a good soldier and have no possibility for leadership.

It is true that some Negro officers were inefficient; and so were many whites, thousands of whom could not stand the ordeal. It is true also that it does not make for the morale of the army to criticize, abuse and **The criticism** humiliate an officer in the presence of his men. **unjust.** If by army regulations the white officers could not be forced to respect the Negro officers, how could the Negro soldiers be expected to do so? Yet it is not true that the Negro soldiers in France did not respect and follow their Negro officers. Unusually proud of the honor conferred upon men of their race, they rather treated them with every mark of respect. The Negro officers were not lowered in the estimation of the Negro soldiers by the whiff and scorn of the white officers higher in the ranks, for the same dart of prejudice hurled at the Negro officer was also directed against Negro soldiers. They, all in common, were to be socially proscribed in France by Americans while fighting to make the world safe for democracy.

A few cases in evidence will be interesting. Certain colored troops were ordered to sail on the battle ship *Virginia,* but after going aboard, the officer in charge had these troops removed on the ground that no **Insult.** colored troops had ever traveled on board a United States battleship. Where under ordinary circumstances it would have been sometimes necessary for officers of both races to eat together, special arrangements were made so as to have the whites report to certain quarters while the blacks went elsewhere.   In most of these cases the blacks had inferior accommodations.   Planning for a reception of General Pershing at one of the forwarding camps, General Logan ordered that all troops except Negroes should be under arms.   Negro troops not at work were to be in their quarters or in their tents.

Every effort was made to separate the Negro soldiers from the French people.   General Ervin, desiring to reduce the Negro soldier to the status of undesirables, issued **Prejudice in** among other regulations in his order *Number* **the army.** *40,* a proclamation that Negroes should not associate with French women.   The order, of course, was not obeyed, but an effort was made to enforce it even in the case of Negro officers.   Some Negro officers who were in school at Vannes accepted the invitation to attend certain entertainments given for charity as Franco-American dances requiring an admission fee.   Upon hearing of this, General Horn prohibited their attendance by ordering that no officer of the 167th Brigade should be permitted to attend a dance where a fee was charged, although the white officers at this same school, but belonging to other brigades, could attend.

To extend systematically the operation of race prejudice throughout France the Americans had issued, August 7, 1918, through a French mission from General Pershing's **A bold** headquarters, certain *Secret Information con-* **slander.** *cerning Black American Troops.*   The Americans proclaimed that it was important for French officers in command of black Americans to have an idea as to the status of the race in the United States.   The Negroes were branded as a menace of degeneracy which could be escaped only by an impassable gulf established between the two races.   This was an urgent need then because of the tendency of the blacks to commit the loathsome crime of assault, as they said the Negroes had already been doing in France. The French were, therefore, cautioned not to treat the Negroes with familiarity and indulgence, which are matters of grievous concern to Americans and an affront to their national policy. The Americans, it continued, were afraid that the blacks might thereby be inspired with undesirable aspirations. It was carefully explained that although the black man is a citizen of the United States, he is regarded by the whites as an inferior with, whom relations of business and service only are possible; and that the black is noted for his want of intelligence, lack of discretion, and lack of civic and professional conscience. The French Army then was advised to prevent intimacy between French officers and black officers, not to eat with

MAJOR JOEL E. SPINGARN, an enemy of prejudice in the army

them nor shake hands nor seek to talk or meet with them outside of the requirements of military service. They were asked also not to commend too highly the black American troops in the presence of white Americans. Although it was all right to recognize the good qualities and service of black Americans, it should be done in moderate terms strictly in keeping with the truth. The French were urged also to restrain the native cantonment population from spoiling the Negroes, as white Americans became greatly incensed at any deep expression of intimacy between white women and black men.

From accessible evidence it is clear that if some of the American soldiers had struggled as hard to defeat the Germans as they did to implant race prejudice in France, the army would have been much nearer the Rhine when the armistice was signed. They failed, however, to bring the French around to their way of seeing liberty; and the Negroes, in appreciation for the democracy of France as they saw it and felt it, willingly sacrificed their lives to save this beautifully humane people. Whether in Champagne, in the Argonne Forest or at Metz, it was the history of the Negro repeating itself—unflinching stand before a brutal enemy, eagerness to engage in the conflict, and noble, daring endurance in the heat of the battle. Many a white soldier, many a white officer, testified that these Negro soldiers were braver than any white men that ever lived. They fought the enemy from behind and in the front and still came out victors. But they were not merely victors. A score of them, like Roberts and Johnson of the New York Fifteenth, returned as heroes decorated by France for their bravery in action and their glorious triumph over Germans by whom they were greatly outnumbered.

The Negro as a fighter.

Thinking that the record of the Negro in France might be taken as a reason for enlarging his measure of democracy for which he had fought, the Negro-hating element in the army, navy, and civilian life organized to prevent this even before the close of the war. They tried so to intimidate the Negroes on their return home that they might remain content to continue in a position of recognized inferiority. The temper of editorials appearing in reactionary newspapers indicated a

The welcome home.

hostile reception for Negro soldiers returning from the war, and soon certain editors openly declared that demands for equality would be firmly met with opposition typical of the Ku Klux Klan.

Taking it for granted that a race war might thus result, Woodrow Wilson endeavored to forestall the matter in the usual fashion of whites dealing with Negroes. He had Dr.

FIRST SEPARATE BATTALION OF THE DISTRICT OF COLUMBIA
receiving the Croix de Guerre in France

Robert Russa Moton go to France to speak to the Negro soldiers in the camps before their departure for the United States. Practically everywhere he went Thomas Jesse Jones, the self-appointed inspector of Negroes, was somewhere nearby evidently to check up on the message Dr. Moton delivered in order to determine whether or not the program of white supremacy was thereby advanced. Dr. Moton bluntly told the Negro soldiers that on their return home they must not expect in the United States the democracy they had enjoyed in France, that they must remain content with the same status they had before experiencing democracy abroad.

This message infuriated the Negro soldiers. They felt that it would be insult enough for someone of another race to speak to them in this manner, but to have one of their own number thus convey to them the dictates of the oppressor was more than they could easily bear. Some of these soldiers talked of doing Dr. Moton bodily injury, but the discipline of the Army prevented any such development. This insult was remembered, however, and when noised abroad among the Negroes of the United States, made Dr. Moton very unpopular. His mission to France was very unfortunate, for it made bad matters worse. It tended to make the Negro soldiers more determined than ever to resist any effort toward social repression, and in spite of all that had been said and done, race riots followed.

The Negro soldiers returning to the South were objects of contempt. To the reactionary the uniform on a Negro was like a red rag thrown in the face of a bull. Negro soldiers clamoring for equality and justice were beaten, shot down, and lynched, to terrorize the whole black population. They were not guilty of the violation of any law, but the barbarians considered it advisable to lynch a few Negroes even when it was known that they were innocent; for it generally resulted in intimidating others who might otherwise insist that they be treated as men.

This post-war down-with-the-Negro propaganda finally reached Washington, the capital of the nation, itself. Because of exaggerated reports that Negroes had assaulted white women and the rumor that the wife of a marine had been thus attacked there appeared in the **Race war in Washington.** streets of Washington on July 19, 1919, a number of soldiers, sailors, and marines, who proceeded to the southwest section of Washington where they beat several innocent Negroes. On Sunday, the following day, these whites on leave from the United States Army and Navy, supported by civilians, had effected a better organization to carry out their purposes. Negroes were pulled from vehicles and street cars and beaten into unconsciousness. One was thus taken possession of by the mob and beaten unmercifully right in front of the White House. Other Negroes were shot and left to die on the streets.

The events of the following day, however, showed that this mob had misjudged the Washington Negroes. They took the offensive when the white mob attempted to invade Negro quarters, although Thomas Armistead, charging in defense of the Negroes, fell mortally wounded. Whereas the whites wounded about 300 Negroes the Sunday night when they were not expecting the attack, the casualty list of Monday night showed two Negroes and four whites killed and a much larger number of whites than Negroes wounded.

A riot almost of the same order broke out in Chicago a few weeks later. In that city the large migration of Negroes to its industrial plants and the invasion of desirable residential districts by these newcomers incensed the whites to the point of precipitating a race war. The trouble started there by an interracial clash at a bathing beach, but there had already been much bombing of recently purchased Negro homes on the best streets. The Negroes, however, showed by the number of whites killed the same tendency of the Washington Negro to retaliate when attacked by cowards. The Negro helped to save democracy abroad, but he must fight to enjoy it at home.

CHAPTER XXX

THE NEGRO AND SOCIAL JUSTICE

DURING the last quarter of a century the Negro has had some ground for hope in the forces which bid fair to bring about a social readjustment involving the leveling of society **Impending** if not the elevation of the underman to rule **crisis.** over his hitherto so-called superiors.[1] All elements of our population during this period have been subject to change by these evolutionary movements at work among the masses. The laboring man is no longer a servile employee of serf-like tendencies, but a radical member of a dissatisfied group, demanding a proper division of the returns from his labor. He is made more potential in this position by a recent propaganda to the effect that, so far as the laboring man is concerned, political affiliation means little, since all parties have been under the influence of aristocratic leaders. Taking advantage of the ignorance of their constituents, they have been able to rule this country for the benefit of those that *have* rather than in the interest of those that *have not*. In conformity then with the cycles of government borne out by history, this country has passed through the stage of aristocracy to that of the white man's democracy and bids fair to be revolutionized in the near future by the rule of the mob represented by so-called organized labor. In other words, the country has

[1] This study may be further extended by reading W. E. B. DuBois's *The Soul of Black Folk*, his *The Negro*, William Pickens's *The New Negro*, Kelly Miller's *Race Adjustment*, *Out of the House of Bondage* and *Appeal to Reason*, Alain Locke's *The New Negro*. The *Atlanta University Studies* and the *Occasional Papers of the American Negro Academy* are helpful. The files of *The Crisis*, *The Messenger*, *The Crusader*, *The Boston Guardian*, *The Chicago Defender* and *The New York Age* should be consulted.

developed from aristocracy to frontier democracy, from frontier democracy to progressivism and from progressivism almost to socialism.

This has been all but true even in the South where this social upheaval has expressed itself politically in the rise of the poor white man. During the days of slavery the South and, to some extent, the whole country, continued under the domination of aristocratic slaveholders. The poor whites, driven to the uplands and the mountains where slavery was unprofitable, never accumulated sufficient wealth to attain political recognition enjoyed by those living near the coast. There followed, therefore, a long train of serious clashes, urgent debates, charges, and counter-charges coming from discordant elements among the mountain whites requiring an equalization of political power. When, however, after 1850 and especially after the Civil War there resulted an extension of the franchise, making it universal free manhood suffrage, the poor whites did not long delay in realizing the power given them through the ballot. Under the leadership then of men like James K. Vardaman, Benjamin Tillman, and Cole Blease, these uplanders finally came into their own. Lacking that sympathy for the Negroes found among the ex-slaveholders, these poor whites, in getting control of the southern governments, however, effected sufficient changes to deprive the blacks of their civil and political rights and even of some economic opportunities. Giving so much attention to the perpetuation of caste, the molders of public opinion in the South never permitted the radically democratic movements to invade that section. There it was discovered that it would be impossible to live up to the principles set forth without giving the Negroes a larger share of social and political privileges. In the North, where a smaller number of Negroes have been found, there has not been any serious handicap to such movements. So far **The situation in the North.** as the Single Taxers, the Socialists, and the *Bolsheviki* are concerned, the Negro may share at their table the same blessings vouchsafed to others. Yet the rank and file of the people have hesitated to recognize the Negro. Leaders in the North are still trying to decide how large a share of social **Conservatism of the Negro.** justice, how much of the world-wide democracy, the Negro should enjoy.

James Weldon Johnson, Former Secretary of the National Association for the Advancement of Colored People, now Professor of Creative Literature at Fisk University

The Negro, however, has been loath to drift into anarchy. His claim f o r social justice is rightly based on his work as a conservative and constructive force in the country. Although the present-day encroachment on the part of the degraded class of whites has forced many Negroes to take up arms in self-defense, as in Houston, Washington, Chicago, Elaine in Arkansas, Knoxville in Tennessee, and Tulsa in Oklahoma, the blacks have not and do not desire to become disorderly. Increasing persecution, however, is gradually forcing Negroes on the defensive into the ranks of the Socialists and Radicals. Negro preachers, editors, and teachers, who have for years pleaded at the bar of public opinion for the recognition of the Negro as a man, now find themselves unconsciously allied with the most radical forces in the United States. This, of course, if not arrested by a more sympathetic consideration of the Negro's rights, may increase the ranks of the malcontents to the extent of effecting a general upheaval in this country.

It is well to note that there no longer exists a frontier with all of its opportunities for free arable land. In the midst of so many changes there the frontiersmen passed so rapidly through the various stages of the civilization of the backwoods, the farm, the town and the city that in a generation they became thoroughly Americanized. Since 1890 we have been confronted with the aftermath of the frontier—the increase of restlessness, pessimism and revolutionary sentiment, aggravated by the presence of un-Americanized foreigners who, no longer able to go West, must remain in our large cities to wage war against the capitalists whom they now consider the source of all their evils.

Labor and capital now face each other in the cities in a restricted area, and each has to combine to protect its interests. The combination against capital was **The conflict** impossible when land was abundant and in- **in cities.** dividualism was strong. To protect the weak we are now reduced to a new sort of radicalism. This differs from that of the European Socialists in that while the latter are trying to build a democracy out of the remains of monarchical life, our malcontents are resorting to various political experiments to hold on to the ideals of the frontier which have been shattered by the concentration of the population in cities. There has followed, therefore, such assimilation of the black and white people to urban conditions as to mark an epoch in the making of our civilization. It means a revolution not only in industry but in politics, society, and life itself. The rural society has been destroyed by commercialism, which has transformed the majority of the American people into commercial beings. As more than half of the people of the United States now live in urban communities of over 5,000 inhabitants, the problems of this country to-morrow will be the problems of the city. As the

MARY WHITE OVINGTON, chairman of the Board of Directors of the National Association for the Advancement of Colored People

cities are now in control of the most radical elements in the United States, it is only a matter of time before the national policy will be dominated by radical thought. Men disposed to hold on to the best in republican government have utterly failed to think of the danger of driving by persecution into the ranks of this unrestrained element the Negroes, who constitute the most conservative and the most constructive stock in America.

With the migration of a large number of Negroes to Northern cities, however, there have been tendencies indicating that wherever Negroes are numerous enough to impress themselves upon the community, disturbing race prejudice develops. We hear, therefore, of the agitation for separate schools in Philadelphia, Pittsburgh, Columbus, Indianapolis, and Chicago.

Race conflict.

There is also a desire among certain whites, not necessarily to segregate the Negroes by special ordinances to that effect, but to restrict them by owners' personal covenants to certain parts of the cities where they may not come into such close contact with the so-called superior whites. Race prejudice in these parts, then, has become much more volcanic at times than it is in certain sections of the South, as was evidenced in 1917 by the riots at Chester in Pennsylvania, Youngstown in Ohio, East St. Louis, and Chicago. Although it does not appear that any part of the North has developed into what may be properly styled a criminal community, as in the case of the regions devoted to lynching, it has shown possibilities in that direction.

The greatest difficulty of all which the Negroes have had in the North has been the problem of earning a living. When the North had few Negroes on its hands it was an unusually pleasant experience for **The economic** a Negro to go to that section and spend **problem.** his money without restriction. He enjoyed all of the social privileges usually denied the Negroes in the South. But until recently it had always been extremely difficult for the same persons of color permitted to worship in a white church or to attend a white school, to earn a living among these same sympathetic persons. It is only since 1916, when Negroes went North in such large numbers as to enable employers to hire enough of them to take over the entire operation of plants, that they have easily succeeded in finding employment.

This difficulty has seemed a problem impossible of solution. The reason is that back of the protests against the employment of Negroes in higher pursuits have been the trades unions. They wield such power that in the economic world their will has been **Trades unions.** law. Many years ago the American Federation of Labor declared that its purpose was for the organization of all working people without regard to class, race, religion, or politics; that many organizations affiliated with the American Federation of Labor had within their membership Negro workmen with all other workers of trades; and that the American Federation of Labor had made and was making every effort within its power for the organization of these workmen. This, however, was largely diplomacy; but a change of attitude was evident as early as 1910 when the national council of the American Federation of Labor unanimously passed a resolution inviting persons of all races to join. The body gave instructions for making a special effort to organize Negroes, in 1913. It required the dearth of labor during the First World War, however, to give the Negroes such a basis for economic freedom in the North as to secure actual consideration from the trades unions. Seeing that Negroes had to be employed and that they would be worth so much more to the trades unions than the latter would be to the Negroes, the American Federation of Labor feebly expressed a desire for the organization of Negro workers as units of the various trades unions.

Dr. F. J. Grimké, a preacher of the New Democracy

In carrying out this program, however, the American Federation of Labor was taking high ground. In fact, it found itself far in advance of the sentiment favorable to the Negro in the rank and file of the local trades unions **The position** themselves. There was a tendency to ad**of the unions.** mit the Negroes nominally to the union when it was found that their competition was such as to necessitate their admission. By certain excuses and evasion thereafter, moreover, the employers would take white men in preference to the Negroes, although the latter might be members of the union. During the migration, however, the American Federation of Labor had to take another stand. At the annual meeting of the American Federation in 1916, therefore, it was reported that the Negroes who were then being brought North were to fill the places of union men demanding better conditions; and it was, therefore, felt necessary to take steps to organize these Negroes who were coming in rather large numbers to be checked by strikes and riots.

The following year, the American Federation of Labor, after giving more attention than ever to the situation of labor conditions among the blacks, found itself **Attention** somewhat handicapped. This was due to the **given** fact that not only was there an antipathy of **Negroes.** the Negro toward labor unions, but they were not informed as to their operations and their benefits. It was, therefore, urged that a Negro organizer be appointed to extend the work of these trades unions among them. Many of the delegates assembled thought it advisable to suggest that at the peace table closing up the World War the American people should endeavor to influence the nations participating in this conference to agree upon a plan of turning over the continent of Africa or certain parts thereof to the African race and those descendants of the same residing in this country.

At the meeting of the American Federation of Labor in Atlantic City in 1919, there was reached the decision to admit Negroes indiscriminately into the various trades unions, to grant them the same privileges as **The American** the whites. Proclaiming thus so boldly the **Federation of** abolition of race distinction in the labor **Labor in 1919.** organizations, the American Federation of Labor had at least laid the foundation for the economic advancement of the blacks. This declaration, however, had to be accepted merely as a basis upon which the Negro might take his stand for the economic struggle before him. Broad as the decision might seem, this, like any other law or constitution, must be carried out by persons who, if not sympathetically disposed, might give this decision such an interpretation as to make it mean nothing. Liberal as the American Federation of Labor might then be, moreover, the Negroes had before them a struggle. To enjoy economic freedom they must still bring about such changes in the laws and constitutions of the labor locals as to permit the carrying out of the purpose of the national body. As the matter stood, then, the victory had been won in the national council, but the battle was yet to be waged in the locals.

A number of Negroes, not content with the efforts for their economic advancement made from without, endeavored to remedy their own evils through agencies either established by Negroes or by white persons closely co-operating with them. One of the factors in **Efforts among Negroes.** effecting the proper distribution of labor during the First World War and in securing for them justice in many communities where they would have otherwise been imposed upon, was the National League on Urban Conditions among Negroes. This is an organization with fifty odd branches dealing with the Negro laboring, dependent, and delinquent classes in the various large cities. The Negroes organized also in New York a Negro labor union intended mainly to find employment for Negroes rather than to secure an increase in their wages. In the Southwest, there was organized the Inter-State Association of Negro Trainmen of America, launched to perfect the union of all unorganized railway employees of color. During the First World War there were several such organizations following in the wake of this. Still later an effort was made to effect the organization of a national body which would be for the Negroes just what the American Federation of Labor has been for the whites.[2]

Negroes sought justice, moreover, not by trying to force themselves socially on the whites, but by certain improvements in the situations in which they were at that time. One of their attacks was directed against the poor railroad accommodations in the separate cars and stations assigned Negroes in the South. They complained also of the inadequate school facilities. They contended that it is poor logic to insist that the Negroes must be denied certain privileges because of their undeveloped state and at the same time be refused those opportunities for improvement necessary to make themselves worthy of those privileges which they are denied. Negroes insisted that certain recreational facilities be given the race in the interest of their contentment and health. These are essential to the maintenance of that physical strength necessary to efficient labor. Negroes wisely contended also that if the white man is the superior of the two, the black must be brought into sufficiently close contact with the white to learn by his example. Segregation will tend to keep one part of a community backward while the other is hopelessly struggling to go forward.

A just complaint.

A. H. GRIMKÉ, "A Defender of his People"

[2] *Journal of Negro History,* IX, 117-127.

In spite of this effort, however, the South spoke out more boldly than ever for a more radical segregation of the race. The motive here was to prevent miscegenation.

Radical reaction. Southern leaders believe that if you permit Negroes to be elevated to positions of importance, it will be only a matter of a few generations before they will be sufficiently attractive to white persons to promote the intermarriage of the races. Inalterably attached to their own ideal and believing in their superiority as the chosen people of God in line of succession with the Jews, the whites have insisted upon all sorts of social and political proscription, in fact, every measure necessary to discourage the recrudescence of the miscegenation of the races. There has been, therefore, among those Southerners who have endeavored to fall in line with the radical democratic and social movement, a tendency to accept the program so far as it does not include the Negroes. As a natural consequence, then, such leaders have brought around to their way of thinking a large number of Southern men who have gradually gained control of the Northern press. They are idealizing the institutions of the South and pitying that section because of being handicapped by the presence of the Negro. They are demanding for the freedman exemption from unusual cruelties and persecution only, while ignoring the clamor for recognition as a real citizen of the United States.

To justify this position there have come forward a number of writers disguised as scientific investigators to prove by psychology and anthropology that the Negro is a sort of **Biased investigators.** inferior being. They disregard the contention of the world's best scientists that no race is essentially inferior to any other race and that differences in civilization have resulted from varying opportunities and environments. Loath to give up this theory of superiority, however, they have devised various schemes to make a case for the natural superiority of the white man. Among these methods have been the collection of data intended to show that the Negro is naturally a criminal. Some have made psychological measurements of various types of humanity with a view to proving that the Negro is mentally weaker than other peoples. Others are busy writing history of the countries outside of Africa to prove that the Negroes in Africa are inferior to races without.

A passing remark as to these methods may be worth while. In almost all of the investigations as to the crime of the Negroes the evidence is *ex parte*. No man should be condemned as a criminal merely on the **Unscientific** testimony of his enemies. In the matter of **conclusions.** criminal statistics of the Negro the evidence is always questionable, for the white man is the sole judge. He makes the arrest, determines the guilt of the Negro, and applies the penalty. Just as during the days of slavery prejudiced masters spoke of the crimes of their slaves and branded free Negroes as pariahs of society, so now we hear the same concerning the Negroes. In other words, all of this evidence is from those persons who, making desire the father of thought, have issued statements without evidence to support them. Such so-called statistics of the whites adversely critical of the Negroes, against whom they are intensely prejudiced and to whom they have denied the rights and privileges of men, are worthless in seeking the truth.

In making some of the psychological measurements the experiments have been very interesting. One man found in a white school a Negro who showed more mental capacity than any other member of the institu- **Measurements** tion. To explain this away in keeping with **used.** his theory that the Negro is inferior, he contended that the Negro far off in the North among the white people by himself was better selected than the whites. In another case, in which the purpose of the experiment was to prove that the Negro was inferior both to the Indian and white man, it was discovered that the Negro stood between the Indian and the white man. Adhering to the contention that the Negro was still inferior even to the Indian, the biased writer attributed the Negro's superior mental capacity to his closer contact with the white man. Such a little is known of the Negro race as a whole, however, that these conclusions must pass as facetious. Because the whites of modern times succeeded in finding in Africa slaves for exploitation at the time when the country was torn to pieces by wars of migrating hordes, they have concluded that these weak captives in war, whom they enslaved and debased, must be taken as a sample of what the Negro is capable of. Yet if the Negroes of this country are to serve as an indication of the capabilities of the race, it is both unscientific and unjust to expect the Negroes to pass through two hundred and fifty years of slavery and in four generations achieve as much as the whites have during as many centuries. **If Negroes could do such a thing**, instead of thereby showing that they are equal to the whites, they would demonstrate their superiority.

To disabuse the public mind of this slander proceeding from ill-designing investigators, C. G. Woodson organized the Association for the Study of Negro Life and History **The study of** in Chicago in 1915, hoping to save and pub-**the Negro.** lish the records of the Negro, that the race may not become a negligible factor in the thought of the world. The work of this Association is to collect sociological and historical data, to publish books on Negro life and history, to promote studies in this field through schools and clubs with a view to bringing about harmony between the races by interpreting the one to the other. The supporters of the movement have been well known philanthropists like Moorfield Storey, Julius Rosenwald and

John D. Rockefeller, Jr.; writers like Roland G. Usher, John M. Mecklin, Justice W. R. Riddell, E. A. Hooton, J. Franklin Jameson, and Charles H. Wesley; and publicists like Frederick L. Hoffman, Talcott Williams, and Oswald Garrison Villard. For thirty-two years the Association has published *The Journal of Negro History,* a quarterly scientific magazine, and for ten years a magazine for students, known as *The Negro History Bulletin.* The Association has published also scientific works bearing on various phases of Negro life and history.

CARTER GODWIN WOODSON

A new note in the progress of the Negro has been sounded in the appeals of the churches and the civic organizations in behalf of a square deal for the Negro. As the murder of Negroes has led to the murder of white men, many citizens [3] have begun to cry out for a halt all along the line. Citizens of both races have been appointed by mayors, governors and the like to effect an agreement by which both races may live together for the greatest good of the greatest number. An effort also has been made to bridle the radical press. By playing up in bright headlines the crimes of Negroes and suppressing the similar crimes of whites, this agency has inflamed the public mind against the Negroes as a natural criminal class. Nevertheless, a new day is dawning.

[3] See Lincoln's speech on lynching in the Appendix.

CHAPTER XXXI

COURAGEOUS EFFORTS

SELF-HELP among Negroes, however, has become significant. In the first place, it has made impracticable the program of those bodies accustomed to meet for the mere academic discussion of the race problem. Their efforts were fortunately superseded to some extent by **Ku Klux Klan** agencies designed to translate beautiful **again in the** theories into action. Mere talk did not suffice **saddle.** when the Ku Klux Klan was terrorizing the country by exciting the poor white Protestants against the Catholics, the Negroes, and the Jews. The public had winked at the sporadic outburst of mob violence in backward communities, but unusual horror struck the public mind on seeing the agents of anarchy effecting a national organization. Once more in the history of this country some white men dared to say that the continued infringement upon the rights of the Negro will eventually mean the loss of the privileges of citizenship by white men. The churches which formerly winked at the lynching of Negroes by criminals whom they too often welcomed among them to pray and preach, began to work out plans for interracial cooperation.

These efforts have recently taken the form of local, State and national bureaus primarily organized to find a basis **Interracial** on which the sane leaders of the two races **cooperation** may meet as citizens of a common country **versus racial** and dispassionately solve their problems. **antagonism.** These workers at last have seen from experience that the perpetuation of race hate only complicates the problem of readjustment and that if any improvement

544

Courageous Efforts

REPRESENTATIVE WOMEN

MARY CHURCH TERRELL
MARY M. BETHUNE

MARY B. TALBERT
NANNIE H. BURROUGHS

of the situation is possible, it must come from allaying antagonisms and promoting toleration. The Negroes have been told not to expect everything they want, and white men have been entreated to cultivate a more tolerant spirit and more generous sympathy, to emphasize the best rather than the worst features of interracial relations, and to secure greater publicity for those views which are based on reason rather than on prejudice. These agencies set to work in the South to reshape public opinion, and in a short while the number of the local interracial committees exceeded a thousand.

This timely work was finally given a national aspect through Secretaries W. W. Alexander and Dr. George E. Haynes of the Interracial Commission of the Federal Council of the Churches of Christ of America. A large share of the success, however, was due to the stimulus given the cause by men and women of both races. The whites were well represented in this work by persons of the type of Mrs. Luke Johnson, Mrs. L. H. Hammond, Miss Belle H. Bennett, Dr. Plato T. Durham, Dr. M. Ashby Jones, and Dr. C. B. Wilmer. The case of the Negro was very ably stated in such councils by spokesmen like E. K. Jones, James Bond, C. S. Johnson, J. R. E. Lee, and by these useful women: Mrs. Booker T. Washington, Mrs. Charlotte Hawkins Brown, Mrs. Mary McLeod Bethune, Mrs. Mary Church Terrell, Mrs. Mary B. Talbert, Miss Jane E. Hunter, and Miss Nannie H. Burroughs.

Fearless workers.

To say that these achievements in racial adjustment were due altogether to the personnel of these agencies, however, would be putting effect for cause. Such a claim would do injustice to the Negro pulpit and press, and especially to the National Association for the Advancement of Colored People. By publicity and agitation directed by Dr. DuBois, this society did much to stimulate the South

National Association for the Advancement of Colored People.

to action by making it feel ashamed of itself. Much credit is due especially to James Weldon Johnson, the statesman-like secretary of this organization, for the indefatigable manner in which he earnestly labored to unite the Negroes in this movement and the success with which he often urged State Legislatures to pass laws proscribing mob violence. How he influenced Congress to the extent of forcing it to do as much as take notice of the Anti-Lynching Bill was an achievement in itself, great as is the credit due its sponsor, Mr. L. C. Dyer. Such a bill is still pending.

It meant a great deal for reform for the country to learn and to be repeatedly reminded that from 1885 to 1918 there were 3,224 persons lynched in the United States, that 702 of these were white persons and 2,522 Negroes, or 21.8 per cent whites and 78.2 per cent Negroes. It was alarming to intelligent per- **Lynching exposed.** sons in the sections concerned to observe from scientific treatments that these lynchings were restricted in the main to the Lower South with the occurrence of a dimin-ishing number in the Upper South, and that the number in the South as a whole reached 2,834. The public, too, was not permitted to forget the Atlanta massacre of 1906 repeated in bloody fashion in East St. Louis, Elaine, Wash-ington, and Chicago, during the upheaval of the First World War.

A large share of the praise for developments favorable to Negroes belongs to the press. Without the aid of the Negro newspaper this program of publishing to the world the grievances of the race could not have been carried out. Yet when one thinks of the ridicule **The Negro press.** formerly evoked on the mention of a Negro newspaper, one has to wonder how this agency has been so effective in the development of the race. The Negro press as such has contrived to exist from time imme-morial. For many years Negroes appreciated the influence of such weeklies as the *Cleveland Gazette*, *Philadelphia Tribune*, *Richmond Planet*, *New York Age*, *The Freeman*, *The Guardian*, *The Dallas Express*, and *The Atlanta Independent*. Most of these papers, however, moved along in an uninteresting way without showing signs of any more growth than some which came and went prior to the emancipation of the race. The First World War, however, taught the Negro newspaper how to conduct a "drive," how to popularize an idea. Upon applying these methods, many of these weeklies like the *St. Louis Argus*, the *Pittsburgh Courier*, the *Norfolk Journal and Guide*, the *Baltimore Afro-American*, *Opportunity*, and the *Crisis*, soon found themselves with an increasing list of subscribers, additional advertisements, and correlated business which assured them a promising future.

The Negro newspaper had its opportunity in restricting itself largely to matters in which Negroes are interested,

Influence of the Negro newspaper. but which find no place in the white press. The Negro gets publicity among whites only for the crimes committed by the race. Seeing this opportunity, the Negro press displayed race wrongs, race protest, race progress, and race aspiration. During the period from 1916 to 1920, the Negro press had much to say about the migration. In fact, the Negro newspaper was one of the causes of the migration; and, in turn, the development of the Negro newspaper into a more effective force in Negro life resulted from the migration.

In no case was this more strikingly exemplified than in the rise of the *Chicago Defender*. This publication was started in 1905 by Robert S. Abbott, an all but penniless Hampton graduate. He began on the small scale of issuing the publication as copies of handbills, which he himself distributed. Abbott at once learned the value of glaring headlines featuring the sensational to attract the average man, while at the same time he filled his paper with strong editorials in defense of his race. The paper developed unexpectedly. During the migration of 1916-1918, the *Chicago Defender* became a sort of "Bible" to the Negro seeking to escape from his lot in the South. Exploiting this demand for enlightenment, Mr. Abbott attracted an efficient editorial staff, built an up-to-date printing plant, expanded the circulation beyond 200,000 and made this one of the most influential weeklies in the world.

ROBERT S. ABBOTT

The increasing power of the Negro press, moreover, has tended to solidify large num-**Achievements of the Negro editor.** bers of Negroes in the effort to extricate themselves from their present difficulties. It has not yet meant unification, but the race does not have to reach this end to carry out far-reaching schemes. The Negroes of to-day are far from thinking all alike. Public opinion among them is rapidly developing. They have not the attitude which they had just after the Civil War. The Negro leader denounced as a radical a generation ago is now branded a sycophantic conservative. A few impatient Negroes followed the fortunes of the National Equal Rights League. The majority of thinking Negroes have long believed in the sanity and feasibility of the program of the National Association for the Advancement of Colored People. This wide movement, however, now seems lukewarm to the more socialistic element.

The discontented natives from the West Indies, augmented by some ambitious Negroes of this country, attached themselves to the fortunes of the Back-to-Africa movement headed by Marcus Garvey. To most men Garvey's idea of transplanting Negroes to Africa seemed insanely Utopian. In spite of his fraudulent methods, unsound economics and **The Back-** unwise politics, however, Garvey made himself **to-Africa** one of the noted characters of his time. He at- **movement.** tracted a larger personal following than any other Negro in the Western Hemisphere. His incarceration for misuse of the mails merely made him a hero. He found further support among Negroes, an unexpected thing which some tried to account for in the ignorance of his followers. Garvey's power, however, was due to his frank facing of the issue. Most Negro reform agencies do not do this. Believing that two separate and distinct races can live together in harmony, they are undertaking the impossible in trying to break down the social and civil barriers without promoting miscegenation. Garvey knew enough history to understand that as long as one race is white and the other black there will always be a race problem. The races must either amalgamate or separate. Garvey advocated the latter as the line of least resistance. While the deportation to Africa soon proved impracticable, many contended that the emigration of a few Negro captains of industry to that land of undeveloped resources would mean much more to the Negro than the distant protest of those who from afar decry the white man's exploitation of the natives.

The Garvey movement made a more successful appeal to the multitudes than the Pan-African idea advanced by Dr. DuBois. The latter hoped to ''establish some common meeting ground and unity of thought among **The Pan-** the Negro people'' of the whole world **African idea.** through biennial meetings of the Pan-African Congress.

This body began operation in 1917 and found limited support among talented Negroes in the United States, the West Indies, and Europe. No definite program was promulgated except that of keeping alive an idea, holding to the ideal of establishing a continuity of action toward unity and coöperation in the solution of the universal Negro problem. To use the words of the *Crisis:* "The problems of the American Negro must be thought of and settled only with continual reference to the problems of the West Indian Negroes, the problems of the French Negroes and the English Negroes, and above all, the problems of the African Negroes. This is the thought back of the Pan-African movement in all of its various manifestations."

As few white men expect any solution of the Negro problem and only a small number of any race can understand such an idealistic movement, the Pan-African Congress was generally referred to as visionary. The case But the movement went on. At the meeting of Africans held in London in 1922 thirteen countries stated. and six of the commonwealths of the United States had representatives. From the resolutions of this meeting one may grasp an idea of the objectives of these reformers. They asked for peoples of African descent a voice in their own government, access to the land and its sources, trial by juries of their peers under established forms of law, free elementary education for all, broad training in modern industrial technique, and higher training for selected talent. They demanded, moreover, the development of Africa for the benefit of Africans rather than for the profit of Europeans, the abolition of the slave trade and of the liquor traffic, the organization of commerce and industry so as to make the main objects of capital and labor the welfare of the many rather than the enriching of the few. World disarmament and the abolition of war, they urged; but failing this, as long as white folk bear arms against black folk, these memorialists demand the right of blacks to bear arms in their own defense.

Kelly Miller saw little virtue in the hazy schemes for world-wide reform in behalf of the Negro. This race had too long looked to others; it must now look to itself. The

Uniting all agencies of the race. Negro in this country could not be indifferent to the fate of the race as a world unity, but he must first show his competency to deal with his own domestic problems before he can assume leadership and direction of the millions of his blood now dispersed over the face of the globe. Miller projected, therefore, an all-comprehending race conference known as the Negro Sanhedrin. This body differed from other such agencies in that, instead of burdening the race with another organization, it was to serve as a harmonizing medium to reduce these fractional agencies to a common denominator. Miller was endeavoring to make the Sanhedrin a clearing house through which might be pooled all interests which they hold in common. It was to be not so much an organization as an influence, a union of organizations which could speak with the consent and authority of them all.

On the other hand, some of Kelly Miller's best friends branded his scheme as more visionary than that of the Pan-African idea or the Back-to-Africa movement. They pointed out the impracticability of thus uniting all of the agencies working among Negroes. Self-interest, they said, would prevent the union of any large number of organizations, and if thus brought together, they could not proceed far without differing so widely as to make impossible the construction or execution of any definite program. Soon various race leaders began to array themselves against the movement. It actually failed.

All of these reformers, of course, could not have been right. Somebody must have been wrong. It is essential to the makeup of these reformers, moreover, that they think themselves right and everybody else wrong. Although one may not agree with their ideas and methods, however, he must give them credit for continuing a hard fight. This becomes more evident when one takes into consideration the number of Negroes who acquiesce in the program of racial distinc-

TWO NEW FACTORS IN BUSINESS

C. C. SPAULDING   ANTHONY OVERTON

tions. Many innocent Negroes advocate separate playgrounds, separate schools, and the like to provide for themselves and their children employment which **The profits of** would not be available in the case of keeping **segregation.** these institutions open to all races. They are at the same time fighting segregation elsewhere, because they are inconvenienced or do not profit thereby. They show very little judgment in failing to understand that if they once yield the principle of equality and justice, there can be no hope for democracy and all their rights which they may

now have are held only by precarious tenure. Other
Negroes who thoroughly understand the inevitable result
from such a surrender give up the fight for democracy
in return for the profits of segregation. The extension
work of church organizations, social welfare agencies,
and institutions of learning controlled by white advocates
of caste have all been brought under the direction of
Negroes who have sealed their lips as to actual democracy.
Such Negroes are approached beforehand and thoroughly

A Julius Rosenwald School Taking the Place of a Ram-
shackle Structure

tested as to their stand on race matters. If they conform to
the requirements of genuflecting toadyism they are placed
in these commanding positions to use their influence in
keeping the Negroes content with their lot. Most Negroes,
however, cannot be thus bought and paid for.

Certain very hopeful signs of vitality in the Negro, moreover, have caused reactionary whites to redouble their
efforts to keep the Negro down. Further legislation is
Unending   unnecessary since the Negro has been socially
opposition.   and politically proscribed in the South. The
new step toward repression, then, has been characterized

by personal methods. Negroes known to have radical views have been dismissed from positions. Negro business men regarded as thus inclined have been refused the coöperation of whites. Negroes seeking loans to buy property in desirable districts or to conduct a business interfering with the trade of the whites have not been given any consideration in the larger business world. This has forced upon the race a crisis, to meet the exigencies of which Negro financial institutions without adequate means have risen. In other words, the struggle has become more intense on both sides— a discouraging aspect to some, but a hopeful sign to those who feel that in fighting it out the situation must become worse before it becomes better.

In this struggle, too, the so-called protection of the law has sometimes been lacking. In the decision of the Corrigan *vs.* Buckley in 1926 the Supreme Court partly undid what protection that tribunal had theretofore guaranteed the Negro. The Court held that no federal **Due process** question is involved and refused to reverse **of law.** state courts which have upheld as valid contracts the covenants of white citizens who draw up agreements not to sell property to Negroes within a specified time and enforce these agreements by law. In other words, although the government cannot legislate to this effect individuals may combine to reach the same end. Upon thinking people this decision makes the impression of a vicious tendency in the interpretation of law, which may ultimately destroy the foundation upon which rests the liberty of all citizens.

On the other hand, in the case of the appeal of the victims of peonage in the "riot" in Elaine, Arkansas, who in 1923 were condemned to be hanged because they struck back at their oppressors, the Supreme Court of the United States decided that their trial and conviction **Residential** by a mob court was a denial of due process of **segregation.** law as set forth in the Fourteenth Amendment. This part

NEW FIGURES IN POLITICS

JUDGE JAMES A. COBB	CONGRESSMAN OSCAR DE PRIEST
JUDGE ALBERT B. GEORGE	JUDGE EDWARD W. HENRY

of the Constitution provides that no state shall make or enforce any law which shall abridge the privileges or immunities of citizens of the United States; nor shall any state deprive any person of life, liberty, or property without due process of law; nor deny to any person within its jurisdiction the equal protection of the laws. The Supreme Court was of the opinion that, although these Negro victims had been given such "justice" as is meted out to their race in certain parts, they had not been given what the majority of the people of the United States considered due process of law.[1]

The Supreme Court, likewise, dealt a blow to the movement to keep the Negro out of politics. As a result of the efforts of the Ku Klux Klan and the terrorism inaugurated later by the poor whites the Negroes and the **One party** party with which they affiliated were actually **politics.** eliminated from politics in the South. With only one party in the field, then, the primary election adopted at that time in the South was actually final. Whoever received the nomination in the Democratic primary was assured of election because he would have no opposition in the final contest. But this was not sufficient to silence the Negro in politics forever. Certain states, therefore, passed laws providing that Negroes should not participate in the Democratic primaries. In the decision in the case of Herndon *vs.*

---

[1] "Due process of law" has been identified as having the same significance as the English term "the law of the land," but unfortunately the real meaning of it is a much mooted question. It was somewhat cleared up by Mr. Justice Bradley in 1883 when he said: "In all cases that kind of procedure is due process of law which is suitable and proper to the nature of the case, and sanctioned by the established customs and usages of the courts." "Perhaps no definition," says Judge Cooley, "is more often quoted than that given by Mr. Webster in the Dartmouth College case: 'By the law of the land is most clearly intended the general law—a law which hears before it condemns; which proceeds upon inquiry, and renders judgment only after trial. The meaning is that every citizen shall hold his life, liberty and property, and immunities under the protection of the general rules which govern society.' "

Nixon in 1927, however, the Supreme Court held that inasmuch as the Democratic primaries in such states were equal to regular elections such laws were in violation of the Fifteenth Amendment because they virtually deprived the Negroes of the right to vote.

This decision upset the plans of politicians. During those years there was an understanding between the larger **"Friends"** parties in the country where the Republicans **and enemies.** had a little chance for success that the Democrats would refuse the Negroes' votes while the Republicans, although accepting their support, would neither appoint nor elect them to office and would do nothing to redress the wrongs from which they suffered. Choosing the lesser of two evils, the Negroes would never divide their strength, but would stand with the party which formerly championed their liberation, for, although doing nothing for the Negroes, the party of such memories would be doing nothing against them. In some cases, however, Republicans in the South went so far as to exclude Negroes from the councils of the party. John J. Parker, whom Herbert C. Hoover worked hard to have confirmed for Associate Justice of the United States Supreme Court, was defeated for that office partly by the opposition of Negroes who showed that as a Republican Candidate for Governor of North Carolina in 1920 he took this position and contended that Negroes are not qualified to discharge the functions of citizenship.

In keeping with this policy of granting Negroes no consideration at all, the Federal Government has been gradually eliminating them from its service. Even positions like **Elimination** those of the Register of the Treasury and the **from the** Minister to Haiti, which were once allotted **civil service.** Negroes in segregated fashion, were filled thereafter by "deserving" whites, and thousands of Negro clerks once in the civil service were reduced to a few hundred during the Taft, Harding, Coolidge, and Hoover administrations. To keep satisfied the Negroes in the border and northern states where their votes were desired some few Negro politicians were made special assistants in departments where they were segregated and often had no special function except to keep Negro voters in line.

The Negro in politics, however, is still a factor. The migration of the Negroes to the industrial centers, although

A. W. SCOTT

A. W. MITCHELL

aggravating race prejudice, has increased the political power of the Negroes in those parts. Here and there they are still being elected to local and state offices, and some have been appointed to positions in which they have made a good record. **In politics in spite of handicaps.** Among these should be mentioned the appointment of James A. Cobb and Armond W. Scott as municipal judges in the District of Columbia, the success of E. W. Henry as magistrate in Philadelphia, the elevation of Albert B. George to the bench in Chicago, the election of C. **E. Toney** and J. S. Watson as judges by the Democrats of New York City, the appointment of Myles A. Paige and Jane Bolin to the

Courageous Efforts

SCHOLARS OF NATIONAL STANDING

ERNEST E. JUST   GEORGE W. CARVER
CHARLES H. TURNER   JULIAN H. LEWIS

bench, and Hubert Delany as tax commissioner in the same city. Still more significant was the election of Oscar De Priest to Congress from Illinois and his reëlection when many of his party were swept out of office. Since that time Arthur W. Mitchell has been four times elected as a Democrat from the same district.

All Negroes, however, did not permit this crisis to diminish their interest in science, letters, and art. In music appeared men and women of prominence like Florence Cole-Talbert, Marian Anderson, Roland Hayes, Etta Moten, Anne Wiggins Brown, and Dorothy Maynor, performing their parts **Achievements of the talented tenth.** more beautifully than those of old. Charles S. Gilpin and Egbert Austin Williams became stars on the stage. Years later Paul Robeson, Ethel Waters and Richard B. Harrison played well their parts also in the histrionic sphere. Scholars among Negroes, moreover, have steadily developed; and there followed an extensive recognition of their achievements. The late Dr. Charles H. Turner of St. Louis made an all but universal reputation for himself in his studies of animal behavior. Dr. E. E. Just, a product of Dartmouth and Chicago, and an instructor at Howard University, won professional standing as an authority in marine biology. Dr. Julian H. Lewis, a specialist in pathology, attained the rank of an assistant professor in pathology in a research institute connected with Chicago. A. A. Taylor and Charles H. Wesley in history, L. D. Turner in English, Allison Davis in anthropology, Rayford W. Logan in diplomatic history, and Charles S. Johnson and E. Franklin Frazier in sociology have achieved prominence. Dr. George Washington Carver, head of the Agricultural Experiment Station at Tuskegee, made himself a world character by his achievements in the chemistry of agriculture. He developed more than a hundred products from the sweet potato, over a hundred and fifty uses for the peanut, upwards of sixty articles from the pecan, and extracted useful dyes from the clay of Southern soils.

CHAPTER XXXII

EDUCATIONAL DEVELOPMENT

BECAUSE of the failure of the Negroes' neighbors to understand that the education of all elements is a necessity schools for the freedmen during the first three generations after emancipation had to be supported in part by persons and boards from without. Although undertaking a hard task, however, some of these agencies have obtained significant results. The Slater and Jeanes Funds, once under the direction of Dr. James H. Dillard, did a systematic work which has been outstanding. The first of these was created by a bequest of $1,000,000 as a trust fund in March, **Educational** 1882, by John F. Slater of Norwich, Connec-**foundations.** ticut, for the purpose "of uplifting the lately emancipated population of the Southern States and their posterity." The income from this fund was once used for the support of public and private schools, which had proper standards of efficiency and maintained normal and industrial departments. In the course of time, however, one of its chief concerns became the education of Negro rural **County Train-** teachers in a system of County Training **ing Schools.** Schools. These were supported in part by this fund on the condition that the local school district contribute its pro rata share and accept these institutions as a part of the public school system. There are now more than three hundred of these schools with more than fifteen hundred teachers. The Peabody Fund aided the effort with an appropriation of $2,000,000. The General Education Board once gave sums for the building and equipment of school houses.   The work in the County Training Schools was abandoned in 1937 by the Slater Fund except to aid a little thereafter in building.

The other agency known as the Rural School Fund, Anna T. Jeanes Foundation, was established in 1907 to carry out the terms of a bequest of $1,000,000 by the lady whose name it bears.   Her aim was to help "the small rural schools."   The trustees, therefore, decided to apply the income of this fund to country schools by employing teachers trained in the handicrafts, each to serve several schools in a supervising capacity.   They work under the direction of the county superintendents and endeavor to help and encourage the rural teachers.   They introduce into the small country schools simple home industries, give talks and lessons on sanitation and cleanliness, promote the improvement of the school houses and the grounds, and organize clubs for the betterment of the community.

Helping the rural schools.

The system has so expanded that there are now employed more than 450 Supervising Teachers paid partly by the counties and partly by this fund.   Among these teachers have appeared workers like Miss Virginia E. Randolph in Virginia, who deserves honorable mention as the first Jeanes teacher to carry the work over her whole county.   The success of the work throughout the South was due to the efficient State Agents connected with the State Departments of Education and to the indefatigable efforts of Mr. B. C. Caldwell and Dr. W. T. B. Williams, who were Dr. Dillard's assistants.   On July 1, 1937 the John F. Slater Fund and the Anna T. Jeanes Foundation were consolidated as the Southern Education Foundation under a new board with Arthur D. Wright as president. Dr. Dillard died in 1940, years after having retired.

The Julius Rosenwald Fund, working in coöperation with these agencies, contributed toward the erection of

"COMPLETE CONSOLIDATION"

AN OLD BUILDING YIELDS GROUND TO THE NEW

These are striking examples of what the Julius Rosenwald Fund has done to build modern schools for Negroes in the South and to make it possible for them to reach these social centers. Some of the States make no provision for the transportation of Negro pupils in working toward the consolidation of schools.

5,357 public school buildings in 15 Southern States (4,977 school houses, 217 teachers' homes, and 163 shops or vocational units), costing $28,408,520. Of this amount, according to the official report of July 1, 1932, the **The Rosen-** Negroes themselves gave $4,725,871 (16.64 **wald Fund.** per cent) in cash, labor and materials; their white neighbors $1,211,975 (4.27 per cent); the public school boards $18,105,805 (63.73 per cent); and the Julius Rosenwald Fund $4,364,869 (15.36 per cent). The teacher capacity of these so-called Rosenwald schools was 14,747 and the pupil capacity 663,615—accommodation for more than 40 per cent of the rural Negro teachers employed and pupils enrolled that school year in these 15 states. While the public school authorities gave only 63.73 per cent on all the buildings constructed, it is interesting to note that approximately three-fourths of the cost of these buildings came from public funds. The buildings range in size from one-teacher to twenty-teacher, the average being approximately a three-teacher type and the average size of the school site slightly over three acres. In 1933 the Fund discontinued its aid to the construction of school buildings after having stimulated local agencies and educational authorities to the extent of their assuming this responsibility. The depression of 1929 tended to make difficult the effort to keep these buildings in repair.

In addition to the program of schoolhouse construction, the Fund gave until 1933 aid toward the purchase and operation of school busses for transporting Negro pupils to consolidated and high schools, where the **Consolida-** public authorities had not supplied this need **tion of** for both races. The Fund has contributed one- **schools.** third the cost of 5,058 elementary libraries and 1,884 high school libraries for Negro schools, costing $281,883.00. In recent years this board has given several millions to public health, higher education and research.

POTTAWATOMIE COUNTY TRAINING SCHOOL, BROOKSVILLE, OKLAHOMA

THE SCHOOL IN THE COMMUNITY SUITE

Proceeding independently of these agencies, Mr. Pierre S. Dupont all but revolutionized Negro education in Delaware by a grant of several million dollars which was used to improve Negro rural schools. By the first of March in 1931, $2,157,547.22 had been spent in building 201 rooms in 89 schools. These buildings had capacity for 7,520 pupils and required 175 teachers. In addition there had been spent also $167,781.59 on the State College for Negro Students. The result was more than a mere stimulus to Negro education. Inasmuch as it appeared that these improved facilities for Negroes excelled those for whites in certain communities, more was done for the latter. The system has further expanded. *Schools in Delaware.*

This increase in the efficiency of Negro rural schools made possible the development of the Negro college separate and distinct from secondary work. This became the tendency at Shaw, Wiley, Claflin, Morehouse, Spelman, Straight, Tougaloo, Talladega, Fisk, and Atlanta. It facilitated also the expansion of the work of industrial schools. Tuskegee, under Dr. R. R. Moton, for example, considerably raised the standard of its secondary academic work and began to do accredited college work in teacher training, agriculture, and business practice. During the administration of Dr. James E. Gregg, Hampton not only enriched its secondary course, but established a college department offering degrees in education and agriculture. Through these improved schools, too, it was possible to do so much more than formerly to improve the farming methods, the health, and the home building of the Negro peasantry. *The development of the Negro college.*

Increasing interest in Negro education during recent years, moreover, has assured the growth of a larger number of Negroes unto the stature of the talented class. The number of those attending high school and college has multiplied in recent *Increasing interest in education.*

years, and those who have taken their positions in the higher spheres have shown more academic preparation. In this respect Negroes, as a rule, have excelled poor whites who have had more opportunity than their despised neighbors of color but have shown less inclination to sacrifice to obtain an education.

Systematic assistance for the higher strivings of the Negro has come also from the General Education Board which has helped in the development of rural schools. According to an official statement made in 1940, this foundation had appropriated $40,864,207 for the education of **General** Negroes in the United States during the preced-**Education** ing thirty-eight years. Payments amounting to **Board.** $36,292,761 on account of these appropriations had been paid at the close of December 31, 1940. Of the total sum appropriated $28,762,705 went to colleges and secondary schools, $4,525,473 to Negro medical education, and the major portion of the remainder to public education, chiefly for rural work. These institutions included the group of independent and denominational institutes and colleges established by various Northern associations and churches and tax-supported colleges like Howard University. Since 1922 the Board has strengthened the faculties of these institutions by granting hundreds of their promising teachers fellowships for further study—a wise step toward standardization.

When the trying period of the First World War and the succeeding period of depression placed a difficult burden on Negro schools, the General Education Board's assistance was largely devoted to annual grants for teachers' salaries and other current expenses. As the schools have become better established, this form of assistance has been gradually reduced to insure the continuance of improved standards at a few colleges, but with the increasing interest of the States in the development of the State colleges and nor-

Educational Development

EDUCATORS OTHERWISE INTERESTED

MORDECAI W. JOHNSON
JOHN HOPE

H. L. McCROREY
JAMES E. SHEPARD

mal schools, the Board has been giving assistance in other forms, particularly in plant improvements.

Appropriations for medical education have been made to such institutions as Meharry Medical College, Nashville, Tennessee; Howard University, Washington, D. C.; and the Medical College of Virginia—St. Philip Hospital, Rich-

Medical education. mond, Virginia—for buildings and permanent improvements. A small part of the Board's appropriations was made for current purposes and a portion was given for improved facilities for training Negro physicians, dentists, and nurses. When the total sum appropriated had been paid the amount thus given was considerable.

The General Education Board, in dealing with the problem of Negro education in the South, has consistently tried to aid the various educational agencies of the States in their

State agencies. endeavors. In 1910 the Peabody Education Fund and the Southern Education Board enabled Virginia to employ a state agent for Negro rural schools. The following year the General Education Board took over the support of this work and extended the offer to the other Southern States. Kentucky, Alabama, and Arkansas responded at once and were closely followed by North Carolina and Tennessee. By 1914 Georgia was added, and by 1919 each of the Southern States had appointed a State agent for Negro rural schools as a member of the staff of the State department of education.

The work has grown steadily. In North Carolina, for example, there is a Division of Negro Education in the State Department of Public Instruction employing a score

Efforts in North Carolina. of people of both races. This Division is larger than the whole Department of Education was thirty-five years ago. The State spends about $25,000 a year for the support of this office. These functionaries are well trained men and have gone about the task of improving the Negro rural schools in a businesslike manner.

Educational Development

EDUCATORS IN CHARGE OF LAND GRANT COLLEGES

From the beginning their service and counsel have been sought by school officers of the State and they have had a large share in all of the recent improvements.

The education of the Negro, however, has continued in the hands of the whites, the Negroes themselves being largely the objects of such efforts. This results from the fact that in the main it is a concern of the government and Negroes are not permitted to figure conspicuously in this sphere. The philanthropists are not to be blamed for this, for they are merely dealing with the situation as they find it. The public functionaries believe that it inures to their special program to direct the mental development of the Negro along lines which will not be prejudicial to their interests; and some of them, disregarding the economic principle that the consumer pays the tax, boldly assert that since they are financing the education of the Negro, they have the right to direct it as they will. The education of the Negro, therefore, has been largely a process of telling the Negro what some one else wants him to say or do and watching him do it in automaton fashion.

An object of education.

In view of the large number of Negroes engaged in education, persons have expressed their surprise that they have not influenced the course of things differently, but such is impossible when the Negroes thus employed are products of the system which they serve and they are not permitted to develop the power to think for themselves. And even if one happens to learn to think he is too often unwilling to sacrifice an easy livelihood by going so far as to insist on any radical change. The education acquired by Negroes, therefore, has little bearing on their uplift because what they are taught is intended for persons who are otherwise circumstanced.

In the Negro private schools where one would expect a different program among their educators, it appears that, under similar influences, most of them have developed the same way. These private institutions must follow the course of public education because the certification of teachers and professional men is a matter in the hands of the government and to compete for students and public support all schools must supply the same need. In the teaching of languages, mathematics and natural science little harm results and much good is accomplished; but in matters of social science, as pointed out by James Harvey Robinson, we are not doing any better now than the people of ancient times. Most of the literature used in both kinds of schools is practically the same and consequently produces the same result. Negro students are taught to admire the Hebrews, the Greeks, the Latins and the Teutons and to despise themselves and all other races which are now subject to exploitation. Whatever is is right. Nothing tending to question the present order of things is allowed to enter books adopted for classroom instruction, and teachers found discussing such matters are not tolerated.

Private schools like others.

Dr. James H. Dillard

The inevitable result, then, is that the Negro himself has had difficulty in escaping from the conviction that he is an inferior and should be content with an underprivileged status. Not a few "highly educated" Negroes produced by the system have been

Crushing the spirit.

known to advocate or acquiesce in segregation and other disabilities forced upon their race. This sort of education was stimulated by the recent degradation of psychology through the popular tests and measurements used on the soldiers during the First World War to test intelligence. The protagonists of racial inequality took up these devices to discredit the mental capacity of oppressed races.

The result of present-day education, then, has been not only to inflame the whites against the Negroes but to cause the Negroes to despise their own. Struggling under the supposedly heavy load of their inferiority, some have lost their ambition to fight against their odds. They cannot be inspired from within because their teachers themselves are not informed as to the background in the achievement of Africans, and few boards of education or colleges permit the use of books presenting such achievements of the Negroes in art, literature and philosophy. When Negroes complete their college work they can be useful only in serving the race as teachers in the way they themselves have been served.

Here and there, then, Negroes with vision are insisting upon a reconstruction of the curricula in Negro schools. They have none of the once popular idea that a Negro does **Educational** not need to study the higher branches **reform** which are offered in white schools or that **required.** the Negro is incapable of conceiving such advanced ideas. The thought is that the Negroes in their segregated position, denied the economic opportunities of other races in this country, must be educated from within rather than undergo the process of tacking on something from without. Instead of being told what to say or do and forced to do it, Negroes must be led to work out their own problems and thus carve out their own future.

For this reason Negroes are turning upon the remaining

Educational Development

HOWARD UNIVERSITY MEDICAL SCHOOL

FISK UNIVERSITY LIBRARY

white teachers from the North now left in their schools, because the latter, whether they will or not, are compelled **Negroes in Negro schools.** by custom to remain not of them, although among them. These teachers cannot thus help the Negroes from afar as they could if they were free to become thoroughly identified with them. This feeling among Negroes has resulted in troublous disturbances which required changes of administration at Howard, Hampton and Fisk. At Howard the trustees did the new thing of electing to the presidency Mordecai W. Johnson, a Negro who has made a good record, and Atlanta University, reconstructed under John Hope, has developed satisfactorily under R. E. Clement. Lincoln recently made H. M. Bond its first Negro president. Fisk has likewise chosen Charles S. Johnson. Other large Negro institutions, however, continue under the control of whites.

Recently friends of social progress have been giving considerable millions for the development of Negro colleges. Because of their poverty they have been kept too long down on the level of high schools. Now they **The development of the Negro college.** are to be developed into accredited institutions. Most of these private grants have come from the General Education Board and the Julius Rosenwald Fund, but these benefactions have come as a result of larger sums appropriated by the United States Government for Howard University and by the fourteen Southern State Governments for their Negro State schools. According to the plans now published abroad, Negro education will be further developed at four centers: at Howard in Washington, D. C.; at Fisk University in cooperation with the Meharry Medical School in Nashville; at the reconstructed Atlanta University cooperating with Spelman, Morris Brown, Clark, and Morehouse; and at Dillard University, to be developed from the merger of Straight College and New Orleans University with the Flint Hospital.

These Negro schools unfortunately have not been urged to study themselves, their own people, and their African background. The new effort is largely an importation of ideas; and it is complained, moreover, that Negroes the Negro church, the only institution which not studying the Negroes in this country have developed themselves. and controlled, has been practically omitted from the program. The majority of the whites in the country do

ATLANTA UNIVERSITY

not find any need for the religion of Jesus in their lives and have turned their churches into social centers from which the Negroes, as a rule, are excluded. Most Negroes, however, are fundamentalists because of the furnace of affliction through which they have gone. Negroes have a psychology, a religion, and a philosophy of life which are peculiarly their own. To teach the Negro youth to serve successfully as leaders among them they must learn to approach the race with an accurate knowledge of this background. Unless this program of education is radically reconstructed in the near future, then, it is said, these better equipped institutions can do nothing more than to contribute further to the alienation of the enlightened class from the lowly Negroes who need elevation.

One of the foundations thought seriously along this line. The Laura Spelman Rockefeller Memorial became interested in the interracial problems of America and in the social and economic problems of the American **The Laura Spelman Rockefeller Memorial.** Negro some years ago. It gave support to certain researches and investigations in these fields and a limited support to certain social welfare organizations. It made contributions to the general budgets of such organizations as the Commission on Interracial Coöperation, the National Urban League and the Association for the Study of Negro Life and History. It encouraged research work in Negro folk studies, and in Negro social and economic studies at such institutions as the University of North Carolina and at Vanderbilt University at Nashville, particularly where these studies were parts of systematic efforts dealing with wider social groups. The Memorial also made appropriations to the Department of Records and Research of Tuskegee Institute and to the Department of Social Science of Fisk University. In 1929 the Memorial was merged with the Rockefeller Foundation, and some of these interests were taken over by that board which has done much to stimulate further these researches. Recently the Carnegie Corporation under Dr. F. P. Keppel, appropriated a quarter of a million dollars to make a national survey of the Negro. The work was undertaken by a Swedish sociologist, Gunnar Myrdal, assisted by a staff of white and colored scholars. The large portion of the matter collected was finally analyzed and published in 1943 as *The American Dilemma*. It has been widely read and variously evaluated.

CHAPTER XXXIII

HEALTH AND SPIRIT

WITH such ill adapted education as the Negroes have had it is little wonder that their health has been neglected. Here and there persons have become preachers of the gospel of sanitation, but the neglected and uninformed populace has not always responded. Throughout this gloom, however, may be seen some light. The truth is now gradually dawning upon the multitude, and some help has come from without. The recent progress in health has been restricted mainly to the urban centers. The rise of the Negro physicians has been the large contribution to this result. They have advanced the cause of health by their close contact with Negro patients who more freely disclose to them the origin and history of their complaints than they would to the physicians of another race. Negro physicians in later years, too, have demonstrated the capacity to interpret and apply the principles of advanced medicine with special reference to laboratory work and institutional service.

The handicaps of health.

The increasing interest of the Negro physicians in preventive medicine with some support of Negro insurance companies has been another favorable development in spite of the fact that Negro physicians have not been given a large place in either official or voluntary agencies dealing with the health problems. In some cases they are not permitted to man the hospitals established for their race, neither Negro physicians nor internes being allowed. Dr. Roscoe C.

Special Service of Negro Physicians.

PIONEERS IN MEDICINE AND SURGERY

DR. GEORGE C. HALL   DR. DANIEL H. WILLIAMS
DR. A. M. CURTIS   DR. S. L. CARSON

Brown of the United States Public Health Service, Franklin O. Nichols, and Ralph B. Stewart of the American Social Hygiene Association, and Dr. A. B. Jackson of the Howard University Public Health Department stimulated health education among Negroes. The National Negro Health Week, instituted by Booker T. Washington at Tuskegee, but now enlarged into a program for a year around movement with headquarters at the Nation's Capital, has been helpful to the same end.

In the rural districts where the Negro population is numerous in this country, however, such interest in health is not generally found. The main reason for giving such little attention to the health of the Negroes in the **Rural health problems.** rural districts is *ignorance,* among both the Negroes themselves within such areas and among persons outside of such places. It was formerly thought that the health of man was well taken care of by nature itself when he lived in the country. It was said that he breathed pure air, ate fresh food, drank limpid water, and evaded the attacks of germs which make inroads on the health of people in urban communities. Most people of our day, however, have learned to question these assertions: but unfortunately the neglected Negroes in the rural communities have remained embalmed in their ignorance of the laws of health. They have not had sufficient education and contact to learn how to live.

In such ignorance it does not help the case when, in better circumstances, these people build ceiled or lathed and plastered homes to take the places of the log huts in the rural districts; for, with such habits, they are more **Unfortunate habits.** fortunate in cabins where the air can find its way into the rooms through apertures in the walls. Statistics show also that these people from the country easily fall as victims to pulmonary troubles when they migrate to urban centers and live thus in modern homes. Physicians constantly report the difficulty of keeping these patients' windows open. These inadequately clad people cannot get rid of the idea that cold air is injurious to health while warm air is most conducive thereto.

With respect to the Negroes in the remote districts, it may be said that the public is not working systematically to **Lethargy** improve these conditions. Health at public **with respect** expense is almost as slow a development as **to health.** education at public expense. For centuries many persons opposed the tax on property of citizens to educate the youth; and, so far as the Negro is concerned,

DELIVERING TO A NEGRO HOSPITAL A PATIENT WHO HAS JUST BEEN OPERATED ON AND BROUGHT THROUGH THE STREETS IN AN AMBULANCE FROM A WHITE HOSPITAL WHERE THE OPERATION WAS PERFORMED

certain parts of the United States still maintain this position. The majority of the people in the area of the dense Negro population are still indifferent about the health of any of its citizens. They are yet unable to understand that a country with a healthy people is naturally more prosperous than one of a diseased population. With respect to the Negroes there is still more lethargy. Vitiating race prejudice precludes the possibility of their getting as much consideration as the members of the other race; and for some reason there seems to be an unexpressed belief that the Negroes can survive with less provision for their health than other members of the human family.

Carrying out a health program among Negroes has been hindered, too, by the lack of hospital facilities. In the remote districts there are practically no hospitals for these unfortunate people. There are, mainly in urban **Lack of** centers, about two hundred Negro hospitals **hospitals.** and a few white institutions which provide a number of beds for persons of color. Sixteen of the one hundred and twenty visited in 1928 were of A grade, forty-three of grade B, thirty of grade C, twenty-seven of grade D or unworthy of support, four not entitled to the name. These proportions have shown change toward better conditions in recent years. Of these Negro hospitals only 13 had been approved for internship by the Committee on Hospitals and Medical Education of the American Medical Association in 1939, and of the approximately one hundred and fifty Negro medical students completing their courses each year only about seventy or seventy-five could secure internships. Since there are only about two hundred socalled Negro hospitals with a total bed space of about seven thousand, or an average of one bed for each two thousand Negroes, the situation has not much chance for improvement. Every white patient has fourteen times as good a chance for hospitalization as the Negro. In the case of tuberculosis the Negro has only one chance out of twenty-five.

Another handicap is that the general public is not interested in the extension of hospital service, and the rustic people themselves are too backward to appreciate the use of hospitals. Among the rural Negroes and poor whites hospitals are unpopular. Many of them have never seen such institutions and, therefore, retain the notion that they are still poorly equipped asylums kept like the alms-houses of old. Some few rural Negro patients who have sympathetic and intelligent employers learn better and seek distant hospitals for treatment. Inasmuch as up-to-date hospitals for Negroes, even in cities, are rarities, as indicated above, however, this trip may involve transportation to a place a hundred or two hundred miles away, and the patient may die en route. And in numerous cases white hospitals have let Negro patients die of neglect while knocking at their doors for emergency ministration. Such cases have been reported from Delaware, West Virginia, Alabama, and Georgia.

A rural attitude.

Still another handicap to the protection of health is that Negro physicians are inadequate to the demand among their people. There is one such physician for about every thirty-two hundred Negroes whereas the whites have a physician for about every five hundred. The profession is undermanned to the extent that few Negro physicians extend their practice far into the outlying rural districts, and a still smaller number live beyond the limits of cities and towns. The Negroes in the rural districts are not able to pay for modern medical treatment; and even if they were, the prejudice against Negro physicians is often such that it is uncomfortable for them to dwell there. The Negroes in the remote districts, then, are dependent upon such ministrations as the casual visits or calls for resident white physicians or visiting Negro practitioners will permit. Inasmuch as most of those rural blacks are found in that section of the country where race prejudice is most acute, the disinclination or the refusal of white physicians to attend promptly patients in dire distress sometimes results in serious loss of life.

Lack of physicians.

The Negroes so unfortunately situated, therefore, must die. Figures show that the death rate in the registration

area was 18.2 per cent in 1925; 17.6 per cent in 1924; and
17.7 per cent in 1923. This was 48 per cent higher **Death**
than the white rate in 1924 and 62.5 per cent **rate.**
higher than in 1925, while the Negro death rate was higher
in the cities than in rural districts, being 23.5 per cent and
15.2 per cent, respectively, in 1925. The rural death rate

DR. CONSTANTINE C. BARNETT   DR. C. V. ROMAN

of Negroes in the South, however, was 14.8 per cent whereas in the North it was 23.4 per cent. In 1925 it was shown
that while the death rate a thousand population for rural
whites was 10.84 per cent, that of the Negroes was 16.13
per cent. In recent years this rate has declined.

The death rate of the Negro, then, although high, is remarkably low when we consider these handicaps. It is
little wonder that it is not more than two to one. The
wiseacres, studying this death rate, have begun to say
that the Negro is on the way to extermination when as a

matter of fact experience has shown that adequate attention
given to the health of these people will cause the pendulum
to swing the other way.

To meet these needs for prolonging the life of the Negro
one finds here and there various suggestions for a new
health program.   The extension of hospital service, of
course, is desirable, and there is a chance for a

**New
health
program.**   more general use of those already available in
cities inasmuch as the improved roads make the
transportation easier.   There is some effort to increase the
number of county nurses, but only here and there has this
idea been actually translated into an action.   Philanthropists have thought of establishing health centers from
which nurses and physicians may operate as their base
very much as the rural teachers do in the schools.   A few
institutions like Freedmen's Hospital, maintained by the
Federal Government in the District of Columbia, and
Provident Hospital in Chicago, now being reconstructed
for the medical education of Negroes, are carrying out
such a program in training persons for service in remote
parts.

The Julius Rosenwald Fund and the General Education
Board, long interested in the Negro, have made appropriations to sustain these efforts.   It is hoped that the Negroes
themselves will become alive to the situation and that a
much larger number of friends will give their support in
working toward an efficient health program to which this
philanthropy points.   Here, as in other cases, the Negroes
who have given their centuries of service to enrich others
are unable to provide for themselves the ordinary facilities
of health.   Those whom they have faithfully served are
being entreated to come to their rescue and in so doing
free the whole nation from the fetters of ill health and
disease.

With education in ancient rather than in practical

Health and Spirit

A Pioneer Effort, the Red Cross Sanitarium in Louisville, An Effort of Negroes Themselves to Provide for their Health in View of the Fact that the Public is not Sufficiently Interested.

West Virginia State Hospital. Dr. Constantine C. Barnett in Charge. A Demonstration of what a State Has Done in Providing Equal Health Facilities for the Races.

theology the Negro in the spiritual realm as in health finds himself making effort without a program. The lack of

Ancient knowledge of man's actual relation to his
religion. Maker, and the dependence upon ancient religious practices have sometimes prevented the development of a health program. Things have changed little in this sphere. Divine healing is still popular, and Negroes in the backward districts neglect their health to prepare for the coming of the "Great Physician." From the point of view of the Negro peasant things of the spirit constitute the most important concern of man. In the rural communities the pastor is still the outstanding man in the group in that he plays the important rôle of its spiritual adviser.

This situation has changed somewhat with respect to the whites and the Negroes in urban centers; but the rural Negroes, who because of custom and social and economic handicaps cannot develop any other professional class, must look to their clergy. Some white neighbors of the rural Negroes are glad to have it so. Under almost any sort of pretext a Negro lawyer, physician, or dentist may be driven out of a rural community, if a few whites decide that he should go; but the Negro preacher is seldom disturbed, if he "sticks to the Bible." He is regarded as a factor in making the church a moral police force to compel obedience to what is known as imperfect obligations. He is also an asset in that he keeps Negroes thinking about the glorious time which they will have beyond this troublesome sphere and that enables them to forget their oppression here. White people, therefore, give more readily to religious work among the Negroes than to any other of their needs, although what they do give is inadequate.

The Negro rural church, therefore, is in no sense decadent, as it sometimes seems in the case of the rural white churches. Statistics show encouraging progress, in numbers at least, from year to year. The rural Negroes maintain about three times as many churches as the urban Negroes do, and the same proportion holds with respect to the Sunday schools. The number of churches in the city would be comparatively smaller, if there were not so many urban store-front churches which are really country churches moved to town. **Increase of Negro churches.**

The stability and progress of the Negro church is due to the fact that it is generally orthodox. The large majority of the Caucasians have abandoned real Christianity and treat it as reminiscence, but among them are still found a few of the orthodox who hope to see this religion preserved through the blindly faithful Negroes. And well might they think so, for the Negro churches exhibit practically none of the tendencies toward modernism. They are composed almost altogether of fundamentalists. Negro communicants are largely of the simple Protestant faith, chiefly Methodists and Baptists, who with the exception of the difference of opinion on immersion are very much alike throughout the country. In their own way Negroes contend for the principles originally promulgated by the Protestant Church fathers. Negro communicants are served by their own ministers, "inspired men" who are not always educated but have great influence among their people. **Negro fundamentalists.**

The appeal of the Negro church, then, very much like that of the whites, is based upon fear. God is not so much the loving Father who has provided many good things for His obedient children. He is rather Jehovah, Lord of Hosts, working the destruction of those who do not heed His commands. This attitude is natural since this institution is without an educational program. The chief aim of the church, in backward communities, is to fire the communicants' emotion from time to time and to keep people sufficiently scared of evil by referring fre- **Fear as a motive.**

A CHURCH BY THE WAYSIDE

AN UNUSUAL CHURCH FOR THE RURAL COMMUNITY

The disproportionate amount spent by Negroes in building expensive churches shows how Christianity has gripped the mind of the Negro while it is losing ground among others from whom the Negroes learned what they know about this religion. It seems to suit the Negro's Oriental mind.

quently to the horrors of the damned and the blessings of the "beautiful island of by and by." There may be a Sunday school, but this does not always follow the church, and the children attending it are presented catechism formulas rather than an exposition of the Bible with respect to right living. The Sunday school, moreover, not the nursery of the church, is conducted rather as a separate institution directed by workers who do not figure conspicuously in the work of the church itself, and only a smaller number attend the Sunday school. As a rule the church has no week day religious school to train the youth. Few of them take religious periodicals, and the teaching in their Sunday schools is antiquated. Furthermore, you may learn all you can in the auxiliaries of the Church, but you must still be "converted" before you are permitted to join the church.

From the point of view of the uplift agencies of the whites, the Negro churches have no system of religious education. Problem project **Lack of religious education.** teaching, story telling, dramatization, instruction through manual activities and arts, or supervised discussion are not general in Negro churches; yet these churches are backward by choice. Negroes are not anxious to have their church take over too many things which the community requires. The church must not engage in things which are not at once spiritually uplifting. All these influences are not needed to save humanity. What man needs most is the grace of God in his heart. To see that he is thus supplied, they say, is the particular business of the church.

This criticism of the Negro church does not apply altogether to congregations composed of certain intelligent groups of urban Negroes who do not represent the masses. In almost every large city there **A few model churches.** are a few churches which are conducted on the order of the most progressive congregations of the whites in the United States. Most of these city churches, too, have a program of religious education as it has been worked out during recent years. Such churches often have the atmosphere of community centers, generally referred to as institutional churches. Among these one finds the Abyssinian Baptist Church of New York City; the First Baptist Church of Lexington, Kentucky; the Plymouth Congregational Church in Springfield, Massachusetts; the Church of the Good Shepherd, of Chicago; the Episcopal Church, of Miami; and the Bethel Baptist Church, of Jacksonville, Florida. The majority of the Negroes in the cities, however, proceed religiously in the way of their fathers of old. A considerable number of these persons who have come under the influence of the primitive ideas of sanctification, holiness and divine healing concentrate their efforts in the store front churches of the cities which show more primitiveness than is usually found in the most backward parts of the rural districts.

Yet the Negro church is the greatest asset of the race. It has been the clearing house for all other useful activities. As the Negro church is the only institution which the race **Achievements** in America controls, its leaders have had to **of the church.** use it to promote other interests. The Negro would be practically helpless today without the church. The teacher often has to reach the parents of her pupils through the local church, the physician coming into the small community must be introduced by its pastor, and the business man must get his support largely from the communicants of the shrine at which he bows.

The Negro church, handicapped as it has been, has accomplished some things apparently impossible. In spite of the increasing influence of the public schools with largely augmented resources the church schools have continued and in poverty have produced the outstanding men of the race. With their limited resources these church schools report a larger number of influential ministers than those richly endowed. A poverty-stricken institution like the Virginia Theological Seminary and College has produced more efficient ministers than Howard University with its thousands.

With a more intelligent ministry the Negro church is beginning to become more systematic in its efforts. The institution is now giving attention to proper records, the wise use of funds, the diminution of rank denominational bias, over-churching, and the wreckage resulting from rather ambitious churchmen. Some have gone so far as to say that if the Negro church. which understands the people, could secure the funds now being used for secular education in schools which do not understand the people, great results would follow in the near future. It is clear, however, that although the Negro church is far behind the procession of advanced religionists. the institution is proceeding in the way of developing the Negro from within while the schools have been attacking the problem from without. If the Negro churches were united rather than divided and hostile as they are, they could accomplish much more than what they do.

Appearance of system.

Recently the Negro Church has been given unexpected prominence by divine healers and new prophets who profess to have the power to deal with the awful plight of the Negroes by supernatural methods. The hungry, the sick, and the heavy laden have been asked to cast their troubles upon these divines and be free for evermore. Behind these cult leaders have developed powerful followings who acclaim these prophets as gods. At first the thing looked ridiculous, and the intelligent Negroes laughed at these people, but they have so rapidly multiplied among the poverty-stricken and the helpless during the depression and after that they must be taken into account.

CHAPTER XXXIV

TOWARD ECONOMIC EFFICIENCY

IN the economic sphere the Negroes have been largely workers rather than manufacturers and merchants. Of the larger aspects of business most Negroes still know too little, although certain individuals have made an impression in this sphere. Negroes, as a rule, have had little chance

Lack of experience in business. for the experience necessary to such success, and those who have undergone business training have not been taught in the light of what their situation requires of them. Yet in various ways there has been sufficient development to require an analysis of the situation. We do not yet know what businesses apparently controlled by Negroes are actually owned by whites and what white promoters are using Negroes to get the trade which under other circumstances might go to merchants of color. We have not yet found out the actual percentage of Negroes who deal with Negro local business men or the extent to which the Negroes constitute the market of the merchants of their own race. No one has yet come forward with a constructive program to supply the Negro business men's need for capital, with a remedy for the lack of coöperative enterprise among them, or with a plan to stimulate their short-lived establishments.

Up to 1917 the status of such Negro business as then existed was not very favorable. In the Southland where large

Discouraging aspects. numbers of the race might have made enterprise more general it seemed that conditions were becoming worse. Efforts of the Negroes to undertake

594

the larger tasks of life were belittled by members of their own race and discouraged by the whites. The businesses which endured, however, received great stimulus during the inflation of the First World War. All classes learned to co-operate and especially to do the "impossible" in "drives." Negroes, therefore, began to appreciate the value of their savings when pooled. If they could do as much as they did to raise funds to carry on the war they could do something for their own good. Race riots like those in Washington and Chicago, moreover, taught Negroes how to come together for mutual help. These Negroes thus racially conscious became economically conscious, and they began to enter business in a larger measure. Centers of business sprang up here and there in cities throughout the South.

Prior to this awakening no Negro business man could be found in the average community except the barber, the keeper of the poolroom, or probably the undertaker; but thereafter could be seen Negroes competing **Increase** in all lines of commercial endeavor. Local **in business.** enterprises rapidly developed. The Negroes increased the small number of banks to eighty-two, and brought the number of prosperous insurance companies up to thirty-two, not including fraternal and smaller industrial insurance companies. One of the first things said in one's observation on a visit to the Negroes of a town or city usually turned on the point as to whether they were developing any business. In several cases the number of establishments increased more than one hundred per cent between 1910 and 1920. Some of these, too, were businesses in spheres which Negroes had not formerly penetrated, such as houses of dealers in furniture, piano merchants, florists, sellers of advertising novelties, automobile agencies, bond agents, investment bankers, and manufacturers of vehicles.

A real picture of the situation during the inflation period, however, is impossible today if one considers the numerous

A Log Camp

Home Economics Demonstration in the Country

The schools have done much to stimulate local industry among Negroes during recent years, but the recent radical changes effected by machines make necessary a reconstruction of their work along this line.

enterprises which, launched during the First World War, had to be abandoned as soon as things began to return to their normal state. Unsettled conditions following 1920, moreover, caused other failures. An investigator discovered that from one-half to two-thirds of the small business establishments of Negroes like butcher shops, groceries, cafes, and the like, listed in 1920, could not be found in 1927.

The Negro in business, moreover, still had his problems to solve. Many of these adventurers in various spheres were untrained. They had to learn in the costly school of experience. Again, these businesses were conducted in most cases on the individual plan **Lack of business** rather than coöperative as large corporations **training.** which are backed by the capital of many people. The lack of coöperation, however, was not always the fault of the Negro promoter but that of the Negroes who suffer from the inferiority complex as a result of their teaching and traditions. Most Negroes of means not only refused to take stock in such enterprises but patronized white establishments with the thought they would get more for their money than from novices of their own race starting in an all but forbidden field. The Negro business man, therefore, lacking capital, credit and buying power, had a dark future.

Because of the background of the circle in which the Negro business man operated, too, he faced also the difficulty of inefficient employees and unintelligent management. Having to borrow money at handicap, **Difficulties** and buy goods at higher prices, while depend- **of business.** ing upon an inefficient force, he could not compete with white merchants who did not have these problems to solve. At the same time the Negro business man had to depend upon a clientele accustomed to deal with lodges and churches on the basis of friendship which cannot be employed in strict business. Catering, also, to people of small income, he often found the demand for credit much greater than his small capital was able to stand. If the business succeeded, moreover, and the enterprise developed into a gigantic corporation, it sometimes outgrew the capacity of the enterprising but inexperienced merchant who began it. A step in the wrong direction at this point usually meant disaster.

Inasmuch as the Negro in business has not developed sufficiently to employ large numbers the most significant fact in the history of the Negro since the emancipation of the **Making** race has been its success in making a living in **a living.** spite of terrorism, peonage, and the proscription of trades unions. In this effort Negroes have shown the ability to triumph over difficulties and to break through apparently impassable barriers. During the first two generations of freedom the Negroes seemed to remain permanently employed in agriculture and domestic and personal service. As early as 1900 there was evidence of a little change in the relative occupational status of the Negro. This slight variation was a tendency away from farm labor and domestic employment toward industry.

During the decade from 1900 to 1910, the number of Negroes engaged in agriculture and domestic and personal service collectively decreased 5.2 per cent, dropping from **On the farm** 86.7 in 1900 to 81.2 in 1910. The decline, **and at home.** however, was not common to both fields, for the number engaged in agriculture showed a numerical increase of 738,300, which raised the total percentages of all Negroes engaged in agricultural pursuits to 55.7 per cent. The unusual increase may be partially explained by the disproportionate number of Negro women and children returned in error as agricultural laborers in 1910.

In domestic and personal service, during this same decade, there was a decline in the relative percentage of Negroes employed. This resulted from dissatisfaction with Negro servants, the invasion by whites of this field hitherto monopolized by Negro natives, the preference for immigrants as menials, and the breaking of Negroes **Domestic** into occupations hitherto closed. By 1900 con- **service.** sequently came a decline of 6.9 per cent in the total number of Negroes engaged in domestic and personal service. The percentage had diminished from 33.0 in 1900 to 26.1. There was a numerical increase in both agricultural pursuits and domestic and personal service during this decade, but it actually represented a decline in the total percentage of Negroes engaged in these occupations in 1910 as contrasted with 1900. The percentage in 1900 was 86.7 and in 1910 it was 81.6.

Along with the decrease in the percentage of Negroes engaged in domestic and personal service, however, came a remarkable increase in the Negro in manufacturing and mechanical pursuits and trade and transporta- **Decline in** tion. For this change there were several causes. **domestic** In the first place, Negroes were used as strike **service.** breakers in the coal and iron mines and in the iron and steel mills; the public began to realize that Negroes, given an opportunity to adapt themselves under patient and unprejudiced supervision, would render the same service as other workers; a number of Negroes were reluctantly admitted to labor unions during the increasing industrialization of the South; and because of their greater tractability Negro laborers were sometimes preferred to others. The number of Negroes engaged in manufacturing and mechanical pursuits in 1910 showed an increase over a hundred per cent rising from 275,116 in 1900 to 552,815 in 1910. Though some were skilled laborers, the vast majority were unskilled workers.

The number of Negroes engaged in trade and transportation increased also during these ten years by 63,272, or 43.4 per cent. While this indicated progress it was evident

MEAT PACKING

WORKING WITH METALS

that more advance was a necessity. The hindrance had
been the unpreparedness of the Negroes for work in business enterprises, the small number of Negro   In trade
business men able to hire assistants, and the   and trans-
general reluctance of white business men to   portation.
employ Negroes in this capacity. The number of Negroes
engaged in manufacturing and mechanical industries increased from 6.9 per cent in 1900 to 10.6 per cent in 1910,
a rise of 3.7 per cent. In trade and transportation there
was a comparatively smaller percentage increase from 5.2
per cent in 1900 to 6.4 per cent in 1910, an advance of 1.2
per cent. The movement of the Negroes from menial service
is clearly seen, for by that year 18.2 per cent of all Negroes
were gainfully employed in industry and professional
service.

By 1920 the industrialization of Negro labor along with
a further decrease in agricultural pursuits and domestic
service had become significant. By 1920, in agricultural
pursuits and domestic and personal service in   Going into
which seven-eighths or 87.3 per cent of all   industry.
Negroes gainfully occupied were employed in 1890, the
proportion of Negroes engaged in these two occupations had
declined to 67.06 per cent. This was a percentage decline
of 20.24 below that of 1890 and a decrease of 14.44 per cent
since 1910.

The industrial advance of Negro labor which began in
1910 reached much higher ground by 1920 when 1,506,255
Negroes or 31.2 per cent of all those gainfully employed,
were engaged in manufacturing and mechanical industries
and trade and transportation. Within twenty years 19.1
per cent of all the Negroes gainfully employed had gone
into industrial occupations. Fourteen and two-tenths per
cent of all Negro laborers had thus changed their status
since 1910. These percentages doubtless ran higher during
the First World War, when probably a million Negroes were

employed in industry. The data herein supplied was collected in 1920 after a general depression in industry. Many Negroes engaged as marginal workers were the first to be laid off.

Several tendencies of Negroes in occupations since 1890 are significant. In the first place, the Negroes constitute a greater percentage of all persons gainfully occupied than

Significant tendencies. of the total population. In the second place, since 1890 the Negroes have a higher proportion of persons gainfully employed within their group than any other large element of the population. In the third place,

A CANDY FACTORY

a relatively larger number of Negro women have been gainfully employed than of any other group in the population. Most significant of all has been the transition from employment in agricultural pursuits and domestic and personal service to manufacturing and mechanical pursuits and trade and transportation.

The actual gains of the Negroes in industry, trade, and transportation, however, cannot be accurately estimated because of the differing wage scales maintained for the two races. In case of unskilled work in the North little difference is made between the wages of the Negroes **Gains** and whites who are not affiliated with unions; **estimated.** but in the South, as a rule, the compensation of the unskilled blacks falls considerably below that of whites of the same status. When employed for skilled work in the North Negroes receive the same wages granted the whites according to the union scale, but Negroes are generally kept out of such work by the various provisions and subterfuges. When engaged for piece work in the North the Negro laborers are not paid on a different scale, but here again the distinction is made by limiting the number of Negroes to be thus engaged. Southern plants, however, not only keep down the number of Negroes assigned to piece work, but have also a different scale for such Negro employees.

It is highly important, however, for the Negroes to hold the position which they have won in industry. In leaving the agricultural sections many of them have burned their bridges behind them. Years ago when white employers, deserted by Negroes on farms, **Burning the** learned to do their own work they thereby **bridges be-hind them.** precluded the possibility of the return of the Negroes from the industrial centers in case of unemployment. The recent depression, aggravated by natural forces, reëmphasized this fact. A few Negroes at these points, therefore, are developing businesses to give employment to members of their own group. A still larger number of Negroes have learned to run ice wagons, fruit carts, and peanut stands, which were once monopolized by foreigners. Furthermore, while there is a general tendency of white employers to lay off Negroes first in case of an industrial slump, the Negroes have counteracted some of this by inaugurating the policy of refusing to spend their money where they cannot work.

The position of the Negroes in the higher pursuits of

labor, however, cannot be made secure until they are fully recognized by the trades unions. This means a difficult

Barrier of trades unions. task of overcoming race prejudice. Trades unions have made no serious attempt to unionize black laborers. Wherever this has been done, the chief motive has been not to improve the general status of Negro workers but primarily to lessen the menace which the Negroes by virtue of their formidable numbers con-

SHOEING THE ANIMAL.

stituted in various occupations in the case of taking the places of strikers.

It is little wonder, then, that the majority of Negro workers in trades unions have been, and still are mainly

Race distinctions. common laborers or miners. In 1900, although the number of Negro union workers reported, 32,569, was almost ten times that of 1890, the increases followed along the lines of common labor. Those unions which cover largely unskilled work or menial service naturally have the largest numbers of Negro workers. In most of such cases there is some line of separation of the races, as in that of the Freight Handlers which is controlled by Negroes and the Pullman Porters recently organized by A. Philip Randolph. Some unions admit Negroes freely but only to mixed unions. Both skilled and semi-skilled Negroes are found in the coal fields of West Virginia and Western Pennsylvania. The Garment Workers Union with no Negro membership before the World War now has 6,000 Negro constituents. That this industry is chiefly controlled by Russian Jews who are more or less friendly toward the Negro workers may account for this increase.

As a rule, the unions representing the highest pursuits of labor exclude the Negroes either by subterfuge, ritual, or constitutional provisions. Such are the Railway Car Men, Boiler Makers, Dining Car Conductors, **Exclusion** Sleeping Car Conductors, Railway Conductors, **from** Machinists, Engineers, Firemen, Switchmen, **unions.** Telegraphers, Train Dispatchers, Trainmen, Yardmasters, Railroad Workers, Wire Weavers, Clerks, Freight-Handlers, Express and Station Employees, Masters, Mates and Pilots, the Railway Mail Association, and the Neptune Association. Other unions in this class are the Electrical Workers, the Sheet Metal Workers, the Plasterers' Union, and the Plumbers and Steam Fitters. These unions, while not excluding Negroes expressly, achieve the same purpose through circumvention. As a result there are virtually no Negro plumbers or electricians in labor unions, although there were more than 4,000 of these workers in 1930. Of the 7,000 Negro plasterers, only 782 are organized.

The building trades unions admit Negroes, but do not seek their membership. The only exception to this has been in the South, where the numerous Negro mechanics in this field could handicap artisans by underworking them. Yet, although there were more than 34,000 Negro carpenters in this country, only 592 were members of the Carpenters and **The build-** Joiners Union in 1930. Out of approximately **ing trades.** 9,000 Negro painters, only about 279 were union men. In the South, the Negroes have unions of their own; in the North they are so few that their only chance for unionization is with the white locals. The total number and proportion of Negro union workers, however, still remains insignificant when brought into comparison with the whites. In 1930 the Negro membership was estimated as varying between 45,000 and 65,000 with a possible average of 55,000. It has been impossible to overcome the prejudice of narrow-minded white laborers who either cannot, or refuse to see that the elevation of the working classes demands the protection of all laborers alike, regardless of their color, race, or creed. A recent increase has been due to the work of the Congress of Industrial Organizations which, seeing that the unionization of Negroes is essential to labor success in general, has refused to draw the color line.

Dark as the uninviting prospects seemed the thinking classes of both races believed that hope for improving the status of Negro labor lay in the success in bringing closer together the workers of both races. Negro workers must be made union-conscious, and they must ally themselves with the labor organizations. While discrimination must be expected for years to come, Negro workers at least nominally connected with unions have more influence when thus attached than when operating at low wages and to break strikes. At the same time white workers must be convinced of the unwisdom of racial discrimination, which ultimately proves prejudicial to the economic welfare of the nation and defeats the very purpose of the trades unions.

These efforts to improve the economic status of the Negro, however, received a tremendous setback when the depression came upon the United States in 1929 and hovered over the land until another war prosperity struck the nation. Nobody knew the real cause of the depression and nobody could remedy it. During the Hoover administration nothing was done to dispel the gloom except to advance loans to the employers in the hope that, in an improved situation, they would provide work for the laboring classes. Unemployment, however, became more widespread than ever; and Negro workers, always the "last hired and the first fired," suffered more than any other class. Finally in 1933, when the banks over the centire country were closing in a panic, a change came with the administration of Franklin Delano Roosevelt. He endeavored to bring back prosperity by spending the funds of the United States Government to make work for people and to relieve those who for the time being could not be employed. In this way thousands of families of both races were relieved. Inasmuch as this "made work" was so directed as to employ whites in preference to Negroes, a disproportionate number of Negroes had to live on relief doled out by the Federal Government. For example, in Chicago, where Negroes constituted one-tenth of the population, they received forty per cent of the relief. The situation was about the same in New York City.

In the rural areas of the South, however, where the Negroes received their allotments through administrators whose tradition is never to give a Negro the equal of what the white man receives, the reverse was the rule. There were brought to light a number of cases of actual robbery of the Negroes of what was allotted them by the Government. Ill-designing whites actually secured loans in the names of Negroes and used the money for their own private purpose. Through such channels Negroes could hardly profit at all by the subsidies provided for farmers and business men, and where such advances were made they came often through hands in which they were so shaved that the Negro received little or nothing of what was originally provided. When the acreage was reduced to prevent over-production of agricultural products the subsidies given went to the landlords while the tenants and sharecroppers, having no land to till, were turned out to shift for themselves. Negroes knowing that they were thus being treated were afraid to complain, for the perpetrators in most cases were the local officers of the law and complaint might mean lynching on the spot. For the southern Negroes, then, as so many of them said, the "New Deal" was a "Dirty Deal."

These acts of maladministration were due, however, neither to President Roosevelt nor to most of his advisers. The central administration actually tried to be fair to the Negro. These inequalities and injustices in administering relief were the deeds of the reactionary element of his party —adherents still unable to follow the President in the effort to uplift all men. In the bureaucratic machinery set up by the Federal Government to administer relief more than a hundred Negroes were given policy-making positions. As many as 140,000 Negro boys and girls participated in the benefits of the National Youth Administration, in which Mrs. Mary McLeod Bethune was an important administrator with a definite program of enabling them to continue their courses in college. The Out-of-School Work Program provided employment at which experience for better jobs in industry was acquired; 9,000 Negro youths in college, and 55,000 in grade and high schools were employed on student work; 30,000 youths and veterans of the First World War were rehabilitated through the Civilian Conservation Corps which for instruction and supervision employed 150 Negro college graduates and 25 physicians, chaplains, and reserve officers. By 1940 as many as 12,000 enrollees completed the course and 10,000 learned to read and write. A yearly average of 500,000 heads of Negro families found employment through the Work Projects Administration, and many thousands of Negro workers at building trades shared in the $1,500,000,000 paid in wages by the Public Works Administration for developing 34,500 projects. By 1940 the United States Housing Authority spent $250,485,-384 for 54,201 new homes for Negroes.

Through other agencies some additional help came to the Negroes. The Social Security Board gave assistance to the aged, to the blind and to dependent children. The Farm Security Administration of the Department of Agriculture gave a helping hand where its efforts were not blocked by race-distinction administrators. Likewise the Agricultural Extension Service thus served. At the same time the United States Public Health Service made extra efforts to preserve the health of Negroes. In the Government offices in Washington where a larger personnel was required to take care of the new interests of the Federal Administration thousands of Negroes found employment as clerks. Some citizens objecting to such a large outlay for the unfortunate, insisted that the Roosevelt Administration was building up thereby a political machine to perpetuate itself in office with the support of the laboring classes and the Negroes. As a matter of fact, he received the large majority of the votes of these classes in 1936, 1940, and 1944, but it is doubtful that his motives were so political.

CHAPTER XXXV

NEGRO ART IN ITS NATURAL SETTING [1]

ON this side of the Atlantic where Americans are slowly emerging from the surfeit of material things we can see the beginning of an appreciation of art. Some few Americans have been making a small æsthetic contribution, but the atmosphere has been too cold to supply the required stimulus to persistent endeavor. People themselves may be artistic without knowing it. They sometimes go abroad in quest of art when they have it at home.

Art in its broad sense is the expression of beauty in form, color, sound, speech, and movement. It embraces, then, not only drawing, painting, sculpture and architecture, but poetry, music, dancing and dramatics. We refer to it sometimes as fine art, which is the creation of objects of imagination and taste for their own sake and without relation to the utility of the object produced. Art sometimes begins in such personal adornment as painting and tattooing the body. It expresses itself too in beautifully shaped designs as decorations on jewelry, clothing, utensils, furniture, the adornment of buildings and objects of worship. Finally, when more keenly appreciated, pictures, statues and the like once used only for the ornamentation of objects are produced for their own sake by themselves, separate and distinct from other things. Decorative art, then, becomes fine art. When these objects are produced also in conventional form according to our ideals of grace,

[1] For a more detailed treatment of Negro Art see the following: Guillaume and Munro's *Primitive Negro Sculpture*, Alain Locke's *New Negro*, pp. 19-25, and James A. Porter, *Modern Negro Art*.

ENTRANCE TO A PALACE

From the collection of works of art discovered at Benin by the Punitive Expedition in 1897, and now in General Pitt River's Museum at Farnham, Dorset. A few pieces of this art may be found in museums in Philadelphia, New York and Boston.

harmony, beauty, and the laws of perspective, we call it modern art. Modern art, then, does not rely so much upon imagination as it depends upon the imitation of nature.

The art of the African, however, is not imitative of nature. The African artist depends more upon his imagination. He is, therefore, more original. Without any training in the art of speech the African becomes a most dramtic orator; he easily expresses the rhythm of life in soul-stirring verse; and he pours out from his throat the richest of music. A study of the past of Africa, too, reveals all but wonderful paintings on its cliffs, and archæologists have found there sculptures in metal and stone which evoke the admiration of the world. Among these are pointed out the ornamented pottery, the terra cotta decorations, the exquisite ivory carving, and the stone and metal productions like the megaliths of Gambia, the figures of Sherbro, and the antique works of art of Benin.

ART AS THE AFRICAN
UNDERSTANDS IT

When the public began to hear of these things, some frankly said that the popular theory as to the inferiority of the African must be revised at least to the extent of conceding that he has excelled in the fine arts. Later those same observers have found so many other evidences of the significant contributions of the Negro that they have further revised their opinions. They now say that there is nothing in anthropology or psychology to support the theory of inferiority of people according to race. One race may have accomplished more than another, but this difference in progress is largely the result of a difference in opportunity offered by environment. It is generally agreed now, moreover, that the Negro has more of a spiritual makeup than other races. He has not permitted his mind wholly to dominate his body. He feels things deeply and he can express them emotionally. If a man is capable of deep impression he can give vivid expression. The explanation of Negro art, then, is found in his temperament or in his natural gifts.

A little study of the past of the Negroes will explain exactly why they have had little chance to make their art known. When they were carried away captive by **Negro Art Suppressed.** the Europeans who did not understand their art they were dissuaded from following their native artistic bent. Negroes were encouraged to imitate their captors, and most of them are still doing it. Negroes suppressed the promptings of their own native religious instinct and ceased to give free exercise to their imagination. They were religiously taught by Europeans and Americans to forget their fondness for music, dancing,

AN AFRICAN IDEA

pageantry, and ceremony in general. Their education consisted solely of imitating the Caucasian. Negroes, then, lost their self-confidence and initiative.

Art, however, tends to reproduce itself. Nothing is ever destroyed altogether. All that the Negro accomplished in Africa was not lost. His art tended to revive in the slave on the American plantation. It appeared in the tales, proverbs and riddles of the plantation Negroes. The tribal chants of the African paved the way for the spirituals, the religious expression of the slave. The harmony of this music was in keeping with the aim of the lowly to satisfy the desire for another world better than this one of discordant note. John W. Work di- **Negro Art Returns.** rected the attention of the public to the spiritual and æsthetic value of this music. It has gradually grown upon the public until the people think of it as a work of art. Churches, schools and theaters now make a general

LESLIE PINCKNEY HILL

use of Negro music. Several have been ambitious enough to work certain fragments of it into an opera.

From the study of primitive African sculpture, moreover, art has recently received new life. Contemporary art, it is said, suddenly lost its creative powers. It was about to decline again as art did in **Negro Art a Stimulus.** Italy in the Sixteenth and Seventeenth Centuries. Fortunately at this juncture some artist received from Negro primitive sculpture a new impetus for creative work in plastic art, in music, and in poetry. In the painting and sculpture of Picasso, Matisse, Modigliani, Lipchitz, and Soutine this influence is seen. The Negro spirit appears in the music of Satie, Auric, Honneger, Milhand, Poulenc and Talliaferro. This influence may be traced also to the works of Stravinsky and Diaghlieff. The same spirit is found in the prose and poetry of Guillaume Apollinaire, Jean Cocteau, Max Jacob, Blaise Cendrars, and Reverdy. The Negro motive in this sculpture has somewhat changed modern dress through its influence on decorative art. This is not a discovery of something entirely foreign but a recovery of an element in the past of European art. Some say that Greek art received its first stimulus from Africa.

Observing Negro sculpture, however, the layman would wonder why it is referred to as art. These figures do not show beauty as we understand it to-day. Human beings do not resemble them, and we are taught to **How to Understand African Art.** look for imitation. They do not seem to express any high ideals. Their significance lies in *sculptural design*, a thing which the untrained observer is apt to miss. If one can learn to appreciate design he can understand African art. Thomas Munro, therefore, says: "As in other arts, it is achieved by taking certain basic themes or motifs, then repeating, varying, contrasting and interrelating them to form a unified, harmonious whole. In music, the composer takes as these certain melodic phrases and chord-progressions; the painter takes certain distinctive lines, color, spaces and areas of light and dark. What has the sculptor to use that is analogous to these themes? Sometimes he too uses color, but not often; mainly he depends on lines (grooves, ridges and contours of objects as seen in silhouette), on surfaces of different curvature, angularity, texture and degree of smoothness, and on masses of different shape, such as cylinders, spheres, and irregular approximations to these and other shapes. From these he can select a few particular forms, vary, and combine them in countless different ways.

"The repetition of similar lines, planes and masses tends to give an effect of rhythmic sequence, as of beats in music, which is satisfying to the instinctive craving for rhythm which all human beings, and even animals, possess innately.

Negro Art In Its Natural Setting

IVORY UTENSILS FROM BENIN

"The real African," says Leo Frobenius, "need by no means resort to the rags and tatters of bygone European splendor. He has precious ornaments of his own, of ivory and feathers, fine plaited willowware, weapons of superior workmanship. Nothing more beautiful, for instance, can be imagined than an iron club carefully wound round with strips of metal, the handle covered with snake skin." And Dr. Franz Boas has recently called attention to the "dainty basketry" of the Congo and the Nile Lakes, the "grass mats of the most beautiful patterns" made by some of the Negro tribes, and "the beautiful iron weapons of Central Africa, which excel, in symmetry of form, and many of which bear elaborate designs inlaid in copper, and are of admirable workmanship."

A characteristic rhythm pervading the various parts of an object also tends to give it the appearance of harmonious unity, which satisfies another innate desire, that of order and equilibrium. Yet if the similarity of parts is too complete, the design tends to become monotonous, so an imaginative artist will introduce unexpected and surprising variations and contrasts, taking care at the same time not to let these destroy the underlying sense of harmony.

"Ordinary European and American sculpture, which imitates the Greek and Renaissance, shows comparatively little systematic use of rhythmic design. An occasional swirl is repeated in drapery; an angle of the elbow may be repeated in that of the knee; but these few conventional rhythms are used over and over again to the point of tiresome banality. Outside these few rhythms, many

The Use of Rhythmic Design.

R. Nathaniel Dett

of the parts of an ordinary statue are plastically unrelated, thus destroying unity; many curves, features, limbs, have little definite resemblance to others. This must always be the case when art is dominated by the aim of exact representation, for if the artist must conform to the actual proportions of anatomy and clothing, including a host of details as they exist in nature, he can never bring them into a simple, harmonious and original design. Selection of certain aspects and elimination of others is the essence of all art, and the sculptor who merely copies nature, though he may astonish us with his technical skill, is no more creative than the maker of a plaster cast. In the interest of creative design, the sculptors of all great past traditions, such as the Egyptian, early Greek, Hindu and Chinese, have not hesitated to depart from natural anatomical proportions.

In other words, the "distortion" which perplexes many observers in Negro sculpture is not peculiar to the art of the Negro. In no other form of sculpture, however, is the body altered so freely and extensively, with the resulting achievement of a wealth of strik- **Distortion an Art.** ing and different rhythms. Since these rhythms are composed of fully shaped masses as well as lines and surfaces, the typical Negro statue has an effect of vigorous three-dimensional solidity, and presents a variety of designs when seen from different points of view. Since in the best pieces every part is plastically related to every other with firm subordination of decorative detail to underlying structure, there results a high degree of harmonious unity and cohesive strength. These, in general, are the qualities for which Negro sculpture is to-day so highly prized. Such results, it should be needless to say, are never the outcome of mere savage crudity or lack of skill in accurate representation. The Negro's mastery of the medium is amply demonstrated by a complex unity of organization and a delicate precision of detail, which require quite as much purposeful technique as most accurate representation."

We are just beginning also to appreciate the Negro poet. The Negro is born a poet. He is not so much concerned with scientific precision as with things in the concrete, "the immediate and colorful." He likes the at- **Poetry of Art.** mosphere of fancy. We were amused by Paul Laurence Dunbar. Few persons saw the depths of the philosophy which he presented in his lyrics

MASKS

A mask, as we understand it, is a cover for the face used for disguise or protection by dancers, fencers, and athletes. We know also that the Greek and Roman actors used the mask partly as a symbol of the character represented and partly to concentrate the sound of the voice. In the grotesque form, the mask has been widely used at carnivals. It seems that the African made all of these uses of the mask and in addition to this employed it in serious matters like worship. This probably accounts for the numerous works of this sort of art discovered in various parts of Africa. The unusual art displayed in making them may be explained by this extensive use.

of lowly life. The spirit of a great people was imbedded there, but we did not know it. The story has been told again by James W. Johnson, Angelina Grimké, Langston Hughes, Countee Cullen, Joseph S. Cotter, Georgia D. Johnson, Claude McKay, Sterling A. Brown, and Bessie Woodson Yancey. As A. C.

LANGSTON HUGHES

Barnes says of this poetry of art: "The images are vivid and full of color; they express the personal sorrows, hopes and aspirations of the poet, transfigured by imagination and given universal human significance. They have the emotional harmony, the rhythmic surge, the poignancy and rapture which are the authentic note of poetic inspiration. In the work of the Negro novelists at its best, the same vivid realism is combined with imaginative vision. The modern literary movement among the Negroes is rapidly advancing; and, in conjunction with the new interest in Negro sculpture and music, is undoubtedly the chief agent in making the Negro aware of his actual spiritual stature." Through its investigations, reports, and publications the Association for the Study of Negro Life and History is doing much to bring this to pass. "When this consciousness is fully spread through his own race and the race of his oppressors, the Negro will be assured of the high place he deserves in American civilization."

The interest in Negro art has developed to the extent that persons question Negroes for devoting their time to the in-

terpretation of the art of others when they might be so much
more successful in interpreting the art of their own race.

A criticism of Negro art.   The Negro artist, then, should find among his
own people the material for his artistic ex-
pression. When a Negro sings a folk song, it is said, one
gets "an impression of unique mastery and significance
which, with all his gifts one does not receive from his singing of a Scotch ballad or a German song. For the same

Kru women and children. Monrovia Liberia.

NATIVE AFRICANS

reason no Scot or German can give the Negro spiritual quality a competent colored artist can give it. In this thought,
however, there is no invidious comparison, no question of
superiority of one culture over another. It is simply a matter of the sources of creative work which are in the artist's
intimate experience, not merely his individual but his racial
experience. Shakespeare is a universal poet in idea, but he
is also an Englishman. 'Macbeth' and 'Hamlet' as works
of art would have been something very different if written
by a German or Latin."

JANE HUNTER   LUCY LANEY
A. F. HERNDON   F. D. PATTERSON

Other critics, however, contend that while this attitude toward art is a truism it is subject to misunderstanding. Some have a rather narrow definition of Americanism in art. "They are preoccupied with certain striking aspects of American life, its material accomplishment **A narrow** especially, and think an American composer or **definition.** writer must get his inspiration exclusively from them. He must celebrate the skyscraper, the stockyards, and the automobile. He must find in contemporary activities, in business, or politics, or social relations themes and forms peculiarly American. Fortunately the strong creative mind will not submit to any such restrictions. Its inspiration obeys the profound laws of its own being and will choose themes and forms wherever the wings of imagination have carried it. Nevertheless it is at home only in its culture, and whatever it produces is formed and deeply colored by racial character and racial memories."

"A distinctive American art," says one, "will not be confined to expressions of present-day American life, however significant they may seem to us. It will draw upon the past, which has its roots in the race **A broader** life of many different peoples. The American **view.** was not born in a vacuum, and the springs of American inspiration are many, though in time they will flow together and produce something independently racial and peculiar, as is the literature and music and art of England, of France, of Germany, of Scandinavia, of Ireland or Scotland, of Russia or China. To this broad current the American Negro will make his own special contribution of rhythm, of form and color, of thought and feeling." These contributions were being made and were being recognized as the rumblings of the Second World War were heard, and history marched on.

CHAPTER XXXVI

THE SECOND WORLD WAR

During the last generation the civilized world has had to direct attention to the discordant elements in Europe which would not abide by the treaty of peace closing the war of 1914-18. Italy contended that she did not receive her share of the spoils. Germany groaned under the burden of reparations imposed because of the guilt of the Hohenzollerns, who had to flee to Holland to escape execution. The nations with which the United States was allied defaulted in **Treaties** their debt payments to us when we had actu- **violated.** ally financed them during the war. Soon Germany, revolutionized as a republic, refused to meet the demands upon her and proclaimed to the world that she would no longer "pay tribute." Evidently one nation after another reached the conclusion that it was not compulsory to carry out the Treaty of Versailles.

The worst, however, was yet to come. The large powers, as of old, began to swallow the small nations. Japan conquered Manchuko in 1932, and Italy subdued Ethiopia in 1937 while the moribund League of Nations could do no more than to threaten to invoke sanctions against the aggressors. In the meantime Hitler's party got control of the German Government and undertook to unite all German-speaking peoples in the effort to conquer the world and keep the Teuton above all other people. In carrying out this program he conquered the Rhineland, annexed the Saar, subdued Austria, seized the Sudetenland, and snatched back Danzig and the Polish Corridor. This con-

COLONEL SPENCER C. DICKERSON GREETS MRS. MARY McLEOD BETHUNE

quest was sufficient for a joint declaration of war on Germany, but the other nations were not prepared whereas Germany had secretly spent years in building up an armed force which would overrun all Europe. The trembling border nations therefore resorted to "appeasement." However, when the Nazis wantonly extended their conquests beyond the area of the German-speaking people, the other large powers of Europe, in order to maintain the balance of power, had no other remedy but to declare war on Germany. Knowing that her opponents were not prepared, Germany proceeded by blitzkrieg methods through Belgium and Holland and conquered France. The Nazis would have taken England had not the English Channel proved to be such a barrier, but even then it seemed that with their formidable air force they might destroy the British. Matters became aggravated because the Soviet Government at first co-operated with Germany; but the latter soon turned upon the former, and the allies had to go to the rescue of the Soviets, who finally checked the Nazis in the decisive battle of Stalingrad and thereafter gave efficient aid to the allies.

Looking at the conflict in one way, many Americans justified our remaining neutral. Let them fight it out among themselves was the position which so many assumed. The **Working** President of the United States, however, in- **toward war.** sisted that the United States would be the next victim of the Nazis, and that it was all but unmanly for us to hide behind the British Navy. He insisted that we should do our part in saving democracies like France and England and thus assure the continuation of our own way of life, inasmuch as the Nazis were trying to bring the whole world to the recognition of Fascism. On this point the President was severely excoriated in 1940 for trying to get the country into war to perpetuate himself in office, and mothers were stirred up to appeal to him not to plow their boys under foreign soil. The Congress of the United States hesitated but did go far enough to adopt a lend-lease system to give aid to all unoffending nations attacked by the Nazis. It supported also the policy of defending our commerce against the submarine attacks of the Nazis who destroyed as contraband of war our vessels and whatever we shipped to the prostrate nations. The relations between the United States and Germany became more and more strained as the days went by. Finally Japan, aggrieved because we were friendly toward China which she was conquering and would not grant Japanese rights they desired, declared war on the United States on December 7, 1941. At that very moment she was raiding our naval base at Pearl Harbor and attacking us on Guam, on Wake and in the Philippines. Germany and Italy, her allies, made similar declarations the following day. The United States Government responded likewise with declarations of war against all three of these countries. Isolation, then, was no longer possible and the "appeasers" had to change their tune, although we had done much to bring the war to America.

The Negroes of the United States had no particular interest in waging the Second World War to make democracy safe for everybody but themselves. With three of the leading world powers declaring war against us in **Negroes concerned.** a state of unpreparedness like that of other nations that had been battered down, the United States had to require the Negroes of the country to bear every burden they could shoulder. A tremendous army and navy had to be built up and equipped with munitions of war. Those who could not go to the front were called to the war industries which immediately multiplied to accelerate the preparation to meet the enemy off our shores, threatening to invade the mainland. Negroes, not desiring to be placed in the same position where they were in 1917, raised the question of equality and justice in the ranks. A delegation led by Walter F. White, executive secretary of the National

Association for the Advancement of Colored People, called on President Roosevelt to inquire what Negroes might expect from the administration. The President promised that Negroes would be admitted to all branches of the armed forces, but he neither stated the proportion in which they would be incorporated into these branches nor promised to abolish segregation. What was hailed first as a victory soon turned out to be only half of the battle won. The Presi-

PREPARING FOR THE ENEMY

dent, when facing the menace of a march of thousands of Negroes on Washington, led by A. Philip Randolph, head of the Brotherhood of Sleeping Car Porters, however, issued an order that in war industries there should be no discrimination in employment on account of race, religion, or national origin. To carry out this order the President appointed a Fair Employment Practices Committee, the membership of which underwent so many changes and experienced so many rebuffs from the unreconstructed race-hating element, large industries, and certain trades unions that it was difficult to carry out this order. Negro-baiting members of Congress went off in a tirade and voted solidly to kill the Committee, and this encouraged the railroads and factories in their part of the country to defy the order.

In the army, of course, the same sort of impediments were thrown across the path of Negro soldiers. They could not serve here, and they could not go there. The discrimination was brought before Secretary of War Henry L. Stimson who, because of his strong intellectual prejudice against the Negro, would not **Demand for equality and justice.** budge from his position. The protests against the conscription of Negroes merely for labor battalions, when it is known that they make good soldiers, evoked finally from him the comment that Negroes were not being used in some branches of the service because they are unable to learn the use of war machines. Negroes arose in holy horror at such a misrepresentation and boldly contended that Stimson's prejudice and ignorance disqualified him to be the Secretary of War. About this time, too, Judge William H. Hastie, civilian aide to this functionary, resigned in protest against such discrimination, especially that encountered by Negroes seeking to enter the Air Corps. Dr. Robert L. Weaver, of the United States Office of Production Management, resigned his position also and went to a task in private life because he found out that race prejudice blocked almost everything constructive which he desired to do for all people without regard to race or color.

In the Navy the Negroes had less chance than in the Army. The policy which had recently restricted Negroes in the Navy to the mess was hard to overcome, for in the gateway stood the late Secretary of War Frank L. Knox who, believing all the propaganda against the Negroes in the First World War, said that Negroes could not be depended upon to hold their ground in hotly contested battles and therefore should not be accepted in commanding positions. The Negroes desired to serve the country but not like dumb driven cattle. Yet they had little hope for finding the opportunity with these two doors closed in their faces. The President apparently was not living up to his promise to admit Negroes to all branches of the service. Knox threatened to resign, if the President forced him to change his policy. The attack on Pearl Harbor, however, forced Knox to reverse himself. Forrestal, who succeeded him, adopted the liberal policy of equal opportunity for all. Likewise the War Department had to yield.

Another difficulty was encountered when the Negroes conscripted as privates were sent to the camps in the South for training. Many of these Negroes had no acquaintance with the segregation codes of the South and ignored their regulations in transportation and recreation. The land of the caste of color arose in protest against settling such Negroes there. Senator Bankhead, of Alabama, requested that in order to avoid clashes with Negro soldiers no northern Negroes be sent to the South. The War Department refused to grant any such request. All men were being sent south because the milder climate there assured a longer time for training than the harsher climate of the North, and the preparation for war had to be expedited.

The South, however, continued its protest in the considerable number of Negro soldiers shot down sometimes in cold blood by railway conductors, policemen and indignant defenders of caste; and the War Department did little or nothing to bring the offenders to justice. On the contrary, the Secretary of War simply said that the Federal Government could not abrogate the laws of the States, and the soldiers must obey them; but even so, defenders of real democracy contended, the United States could have prosecuted those who went to the extent of killing a soldier for not changing his seat on a street car, for getting on trains from which Negroes were barred altogether, or for seeking food and recreation in places from which Negroes were excluded. Negroes, like all other soldiers, had to go from

GOING TO WAR

place to place according to orders. These handicaps upon the egress and regress of Negro soldiers actually retarded our preparation for the war and, in a crisis, might have proved unusually serious.

The War Department and the Navy Department, more-over, refused to break up segregation in the camps where the Federal Government had full jurisdiction. The policy seemed to leave the Negro soldiers at the mercy of communities in which they were located. In the North, the East and the West appeared in less virulent form the same prejudice against the Negro found in the South, but there was no law to enforce it as was the case in the land of cotton. Yet the migration of Negroes during the Second World War aggravated the situation at industrial centers. Matters probably would have grown much worse than they finally became had the migration of Negroes been more concentrated at a few centers as was the case in 1916-18. In the Second World War the Negroes went in practically all directions. Cities like Philadelphia, Pittsburgh, Cleveland, and Chicago received an increase in the Negro population but in no such proportions as did the cities on the Pacific like Los Angeles, Pasadena, San Francisco, Portland, and Seattle. For example, San Francisco, which had only a few thousand Negroes in 1930, now has about 25,000. With this much wider distribution of Negro migrants less trouble developed in the East than in the First World War. Riots of fearful proportions, however, broke out in New York, Los Angeles, and Detroit to match those in Mobile and Beaufort.

Several practices continued to keep the Negro mind inflamed against traducers of the race. There remained the segregation of the blood plasma contributed for the armed forces. The American Red Cross adhered to its policy of keeping the blood of the two races separate and distinct, and the advocates of caste raving in and out of Congress exhibited their ignorance of science in madly demanding that no white person be given an injection of Negro blood. It is doubtful, however, that any considerable number of the officials in the armed forces observed this demand of madness. The Army Nurse Corps closed its doors to Negroes but finally accepted Negro nurses on a non-segregated basis. The Red Cross sent a considerable number of workers overseas to labor among Negro soldiers only. Negro women were accepted in the Women's Auxiliary Army Corps, and they later broke down the barriers of the corresponding order in the Navy. In 1942 the Marine Corps began to accept Negroes. Finally, moreover, Secretary of War Stimson issued an order against racial discrimination.

Naturally the question arises as to what was done with the other Negroes in the armed forces, aggregating in proportion to the Negro population more than those drawn from any other element of the population. **In labor** Most Negroes in the armed forces were put **battalions.** to work. Instead of being supplied with guns they were given hand trucks, picks and shovels to serve in what the authorities euphemistically styled as the Engineer Corps. In the First World War these units were called labor battalions, now they were designated as the "Engineers."

Yet, in spite of these restrictions a number of Negroes distinguished themselves in the Pacific, in Africa, in Europe, and especially in the defeat of the Nazis in the "Bulge." The most conspicuous of the heroes were Dorie Miller, shooting down six planes at Pearl Harbor December 7, 1941; Colin P. Kelly, Jr., sinking the Japanese heavy cruiser *Ashigary* three days later; Robert H. Brooks at Fort Stotsenburg in the Philippines; Woodall I. Marsh in Italy; Mack B. Anderson and Ralph Snell in Northern India; George Watson in the Southern Pacific; Charles Jackson French on the *Gregory;* Elvin Bell on the *Lexington* in the Battle of the Coral Sea; Christopher Columbus Sheppard on the *Borie;* Charles W. David on a Coast Guard Cutter in icy seas; William Pinckney on the *Enterprise;* and Leonard Leroy Harmon on the *San Francisco* in the Solomon Islands. The Negro has never been a traitor to this country. He loves his native soil and will sacrifice as much as any other American to defend it. This does not mean, of course, that the Negro loves those who ad-

ON THE WAY TO THE FRONT

minister the Government for the good of one race and eternally delight in trying to humiliate, segregate, lynch and massacre the members of the Negro race.

If doubt determines the attitude of the Federal Government, as so many men of foresight fear, it is a fatal mistake which will work disastrously in the end. In the beginning of the Second World War, England lost her possessions in Asia by her failure to make use of the native people while Japan succeeded in uniting them by exposing the racial autocracy of the British Empire. If a nation is to defend its frontiers in the world of tomorrow and continue its course in peace, it must learn to unite all elements and eliminate all discordant groups desiring to perpetuate the caste of color. The winning of the Second World War will mean very little unless the victorious nations win at the same time a victory over racial domination and exploitation. To crush temporarily the forces which have brought on a world conflict because of the malefactions in both the so-called democracies and dictatorships will amount to nothing more than the postponement of a more destructive clash to come in a few years.

For this reason there was, and still is, an urgent desire among certain whites for a mixed army. Some white soldiers themselves asked that units be mixed in order that blacks and whites, while learning to fight side **Mixed army** by side, might learn to live together without **proposed.** friction; but the white-supremacy policy of the Federal Government proved to be so satisfactory to the oppressors that no such consideration could be given the oppressed. Some few officers in the armed forces had the courage to remove a little of the segregation. Negro and white officers in the Second World War were trained together, whereas in that of 1914-18 the Negroes were sent to a special camp at Fort Des Moines, Iowa. In the Navy certain mixed groups mess and sleep together amicably, although certain ones to the contrary endeavor to separate the races as they were formerly. There were mixed crews in the Merchant Marine, and some ships had Negro captains. Armed forces with the races mixed throughout, however, seem to be a far distant prospect, and there is little assurance that the Negro officer will be saved in the merger.

The advocates of the abolition of segregation cannot derive much consolation from the treatment received by Negro units which have distinguished themselves in various wars. Before the outbreak of the Second World War the Ninth and Tenth Cavalry and the Twenty-fourth and Twenty-fifth Infantry had been demilitarized for special

BLAZING THE WAY

service to white troops, too often of a menial nature. From the beginning of World War II the Negro units drawn from the National Guard of certain States suffered the same fate when incorporated into the armed forces of the nation. New York's 369th, known also as the 15th New York, answered the call with Colonel Chauncey Cooper in command. In Hawaii this unit was broken up and mixed with a white unit, leaving Colonel Cooper in charge with white officers and enlisted men under him. Soon, however, according to the reports from the front, the Negro regiment was completely broken up, and Colonel Cooper returned to the United States for a medical discharge. Other Negro officers awaited the same fate. The 8th Illinois had already been thus broken up. The 372nd, also commanded by Negro officers, was slated for the same treatment; and possibly the 366th, the only remaining regiment with Negro officers, which, the last time it was reported intact, was doing guard duty in Italy.

Writers have commented to the effect that President Roosevelt was reluctant to grant the Negro more for fear that he might completely alienate his followers in the race-hating areas and thus fail of reelection for a fourth term in 1944. Certain voters of the **Politics and war.** Lower South had long murmured because of the administration's desire to repeal the Poll Tax, the admission of a Negro to the President's Press Conference, and the operations of the Fair Employment Practices Committee. So many citizens first interpreted as a new charter of freedom his executive order setting up this commission. These same discordant followers of the President bore it grievously that Negroes had been given even as much recognition on the segregated basis as they had received. When the United States Supreme Court declared unconstitutional a law of Texas excluding Negroes from the White Primary, the recalcitrants bolted the Democratic party. They insisted that in a long train of acts favorable to the Negro and hostile to the white supremacy the Roosevelt Administration had dynamited every tradition of the South. That section therefore must rise in its might and defend the encroachment upon its institutions.

The complaint must have had some effect, for to placate these complainants the Administration permitted the bosses of the National Democratic Convention in 1944 to ditch Henry A. Wallace, of Iowa, then a candidate for the nomination to succeed himself as Vice President of the United States. In his place was set up Senator Truman, of Missouri, an all but unknown factor in the nation, whereas Wallace had declared himself a liberal opposed to the poll tax, segregation, mob rule and any other device which defeats democracy. The ditching of Wallace, on the other hand, alienated many a Negro voter who had supported the President in all his appeals for reelection because, although not going so far as the Negroes desired, he had shown them more consideration than any other incumbent in the White House since Abraham Lincoln. The majority of Negro voters, however, supported Roosevelt in his reelection in 1944. Roosevelt died in 1945, and Truman succeeded him.

The demands of the Negro have had some weight in national and local situations because the Negro is a greater factor in politics today than he was a generation ago. Negroes have learned to divide their vote. They have therefore been elected and appointed to useful and commanding positions in cities like New York, Philadelphia, Cleveland, Cincinnati, and Chicago. Arthur W. Mitchell, the successor of Oscar DePriest, a Republican from the first district of Illinois, served as a Democrat in Congress four terms; and he was succeeded by William L. Dawson, another Democrat. A. Clayton Powell, Jr., of the Harlem area in New York City, with the endorsement of the two parties, came to Congress in 1944 as the first Negro in that state to attain such distinction. With two Negroes in Congress in contradistinction to the situation between 1901 and 1928 when no Negroes at all sat in that asembly, the Negro has a chance for a better hearing in political circles. Today Negroes are in the strategic position of holding the balance of power in pivotal states, and in the exercise of it many of the Negro New Deal adherents abandoned the bunglesome leadership of Truman in 1946 and gave the control of Congress to the Republicans.

After 1946, the relations between the United States and the Soviet Union began to deteriorate. Little progress was made toward the settlement of the Berlin question and there arose the Berlin Blockade and the so-called "Cold War," which limited the road traffic be- **The Cold War.** tween Berlin and Western occupation zones. An Airlift was conducted which demonstrated the plan of the Western powers not to yield to Russian demands for the occupation of Berlin. The Truman Doctrine developed into the Marshall Plan for aid to foreign peoples. An Atlantic Pact for Western Europe was drawn up and the prevention of world conquest by communism through the Soviet Union was planned. All of this meant that the military establishment had to be continued, the maintenance of troops abroad would be undertaken and the policy of aid to Europe and Asiatic peoples would have to be developed.

The invasion of the Republic of Korea by North Korean troops under the direction of Russia drew from the United Nations Security Council the demand for the cessation of hostilities and the withdrawal of troops to the 38th Parallel in Korea. When the members of the United Nations were called upon to carry out this demand, President Harry Truman calling the intervention "a police action," on June 27, 1950, ordered General Douglas MacArthur to Korea. On request of the United Nations he was named Commander of the Armed Forces in Korea. The first phase of this occupation culminated in the checking of the North Korean drive to occupy South Korea. **Korea.** The second phase was the attack of the Chinese army and its crossing of the Yalu River and entrance into South Korea. United Nations troops attacked and pushed the Chinese back across the 38th Parallel. Negro soldiers were engaged in these military endeavors. The 25th Infantry Division which had been stationed in Japan was made up of one Negro regiment and two white regiments.

Congressional Record

of July 1950

PROCEEDINGS AND DEBATES OF THE 81st CONGRESS, SECOND SESSION

First United States Victory in Korea Won by Negro GI's

But, Mr. Chairman, at this time I want to speak of another matter which I think is of importance to the House.

For day after day, a gallant band of American kids had been falling back under the hammer blows of Korean Reds who were superior in numbers, guns, and armor—superior in almost every element of ground fighting except raw courage.

Their families and neighbors back home were becoming restless and worried, fearing another disaster like Bataan.

When would this one-sided battle turn for the better?

People were switching their radio dials right past high-class entertainment, trying to catch the latest war bulletins. Newspapers were being bought, not daily, but by editions, searching for the first ray of hope, no matter how slim it might be, that would pierce the gloom of strategic withdrawals.

It came on July 20, when the Army's oldest Negro infantry regiment, spearheading the Twenty-fifth Division which had just come into the line, counterattacked and drove the Reds out of Yechon

It was the Twenty-fourth Infantry Regiment that did the trick and braced morale where it was needed most, back in the United States of America where hoarding and profiteering reflected uncertainty over the immediate situation.

And you have heard something about that as the first order of business today, Mr. Chairman.

Mr. GROSS. Mr. Chairman, will the gentleman yield?

Mr. LANE. I yield.

Mr. GROSS. The gentleman recognizes that we are still withdrawing, does he not?

Mr. LANE. I certainly do.

Mr. Chairman, all of us should offer a prayer of thanks to the regulars of this Negro regiment for shaming us out of

899957—50

our fears. They demonstrated, the hard way, their faith in a common cause that has no room for the ignorance and selfishness of racism and bigotry.

Communist propaganda took it on the chin at Yechon when the Korean Reds were blasted by American Negro troops who believed not only in the United States as it is, but in the better Nation that it will become when intolerance is also defeated.

They fought and won for all of us.

Segregation is on the way out in this world, and we are in this fight, among other things, to hasten its departure.

Our Army is becoming truly democratic, and in this respect is far ahead of our social and economic organization.

If the present crisis should spread, young draftees would become better soldiers if they had some veterans of the Twenty-fourth at their side to steady them in their baptism under fire.

Let us pay tribute, then, to the men of the Twenty-fourth, who have added battle honors to those they first started winning against the Comanche Indians over 70 years ago.

This old-line outfit, stems from the two Negro companies that were organized in 1866, at Jefferson Barracks, Mo.

It is the oldest and perhaps the last Negro infantry regiment in view of the fact that from now on all our soldiers will be Americans, without any stigma of segregation .

But give credit where credit is due, and the Twenty-fourth has earned it by being the first to push the enemy back. It may be temporary and only local, but it is a morale builder that should stir every one of us to give his best.

Take heart. We are in this thing together, as equals, and we will win as equals, with such men as those of the fighting Twenty-fourth to show us the way.

U. S. GOVERNMENT PRINTING OFFICE: 1950

The fighting in Korea had significant beginnings for Negro officers. Second Lieutenant William M. Benefield, Jr., of Kansas City, Missouri, was a member of the 77th Combat Engineer Company, 25th Infantry Division and was killed in combat while attempting to clear a mine field near Sangju, Korea, in July 1950. He was awarded posthumously the Distinguished Service Cross. A second Negro, a Platoon Leader, Chester J. Lennon was also awarded the Distinguished Service Cross for gallantry. He was a Captain and had served as Professor of Military Science at Hampton Institute in Virginia. There were Air Force officers who were Negroes and were cited for bravery during the Korean Conflict. Several received the Distinguished Flying Cross: Lieutenant Colonel Daniel James of Pensacola, Florida; Captain Ernest Craigwell, Jr. of Brooklyn, New York; Major George Gray of Welch, West Virginia and Captain Dayton Ragland, a Military Instructor at Howard University. Another officer, as a member of an integrated unit in Korea was Captain Luther N. McManus of Washington, D. C., who was awarded the Distinguished Service Cross for gallantry in action. His citation reads, "Inspiring the troops with his personal fearlessness, Lieutenant McManus called them to fix their bayonets and then led them in a determined charge against the hostile position."

Awards in heroic combat in Korea.

This development has continued as Negro officers and enlisted men have served the nation in defense in many areas. The highest ranking officer in the United States Armed Forces as the fifties advanced was Major General Benjamin O. Davis, Jr., who was serving as Deputy Chief of Staff for Operations, the United States Air Force, Europe, and was scheduled to return to the high command at the Pentagon. He was confirmed as a Major General by the Senate in 1959 and became the highest ranking Negro-American ever to serve in the

Officers of high rank.

The Negro In Our History

MAJOR-GENERAL BENJAMIN O. DAVIS, JR.

Armed Forces. Brigadier General B. O. Davis, father of Major General Benjamin O. Davis, Jr., had served in the Army and was retired after fifty years of Army service. He continued to serve the country as a member of the American Battle Monuments Commission. These men as officers and as soldiers made an enviable record for service in World War II and in Korea. During the period 1940 to

COLONEL CAMPBELL C. JOHNSON, Office of Selective Service Records

COLONEL VANCE MARCHBANKS, JR., Medical Monitor for Project Mercury, highest ranking Negro professional officer in the U. S. Air Force Project.

1960 there were twenty-five Negro officers who attained the rank of full Colonel on active duty either in the organized Reserve or as members of the National Guard.

A partial list of Negro full Colonels on active duty during World War II includes the following: Colonel West A. Hamilton and Colonel Howard D. Queen, 366th Infantry Regiment; Colonel Campbell C. Johnson, Selective Service

System; Colonel Edward O. Gourdin and Colonel Howard C. Gilbert, 372d Infantry Regiment; Colonel Chauncey M. Hooper, 369th Coast Guard Artillery; Colonel Midian O. Bousefield, Commanding Officer, Station Hospital, Fort Huachuca, Arizona; Colonel Benjamin O. Davis, 332d Fighter Group and Colonel Anderson F. Pitts, 184th Field Artillery Regiment. Colonel Gourdin was later promoted to Brigadier General of the Massachusetts National Guard. Colonel Vance Marchbanks, Jr., was medical monitor for Project Mercury, one of the space projects, and was the highest ranking Negro professional on the U. S. Air Force programs.

For the first time in history the Negro was allowed to fight as an integrated soldier. As the years passed, President Truman's Executive Order in 1948 had established a legal basis for an armed policy of "equality of treatment and opportunity for all without regard to race, color or national origin." The U. S. Navy announced its policy June 7, 1949, stating, "It is the policy of the Navy Department that there shall be equality of treatment and opportunity for all persons in the Navy and Marine Corps without regard to race, color, religion or national origin."

Following these announcements against discrimination in the military service, several states between 1948 and 1955 barred segregation in the National Guard. These included the states of California, Connecticut, Illinois, Maryland, Massachusetts, Michigan, Minnesota, New Jersey, New York, Pennsylvania, Washington and Wisconsin. Early in 1950 the Army dropped quotas for Negro enlistment and the Selective Service eliminated questions on race for draft registrants. Segregation was reported to be entirely eliminated in the Air Force, the Army, the Marines and the Navy.

There was the testimony of a large number of white officers that the service of Negroes was not only acceptable but commendable and that some performed better than their white associates. The record of the Korean Conflict showed practically no difference in the rate of disease and the non-battle injuries between white and colored troops and the gap in venereal disease was closed markedly. The Negro was able as result of integration to achieve a status comparable to the white soldier. Near the end of World War II only eighteen per cent of the Negro enlisted men held the rank of Sergeant or better, whereas there were thirty-one per cent of the whites who held this rank. However, as the result of the endeavors which took place after 1950, twenty-eight per cent of the Negro enlisted men were in the top grades compared with twenty-six per cent of the white men. They were being admitted to the Army schools and were attending them with some success. In 1951 the Army and the Air Force announced that integration had taken place in nearly all of their units. The Navy stated that segregation had been eliminated.

Military integration

DR. JAMES C. EVANS, Civilian Assistant, Office of the Assistant Secretary of Defense

Dr. J. C. Evans, Civilian Assistant, who had been quietly and effectively at work in the program of upgrading the Negro soldier and officer, reported that "the accelerated impetus of racial integration in the Armed Forces during the post-war years has given Negro personnel the opportunity to demonstrate their skill and ability without limitations imposed by race," and he added that "many Negroes

SARGEANT ELIJAH MCLAUGHLIN of Rockingham, N. C., leads his squad to begin an advance in Korean hills.

Fighting with the 2nd Infantry Division in Korea, MAJOR L. CLEVELAND of Fort Valley, Georgia, points out enemy to his machine gun crew.

in uniform are now holding responsible and important positions on a fully integrated basis."

This development of integration was due also to the initiative of civilian organizations, and notably the National Association for the Advancement of Colored People, as well as the pronouncements of statesmen and the rise of a liberal military leadership. This was facilitated through the increase and development of the qualifications of young Negroes

Civilian organizations at work.

WACS IN ENGLAND

who entered the services both with aptitudes, skills and with education and technical preparation. The Reserve Officers Training Corps has contributed to the development of the military preparation of many of these successful officers. The Reserve Officers Training Corps (ROTC) assisted in the training of students as officers who graduated from colleges with ranks of 2nd Lieutenants. There were Army ROTC units at two colleges with predominantly Negro enrollments in 1940 and 14 such colleges in 1951, of 322 institutions offering these programs.

However, social change in many of its aspects had brought it about that the Negro during the fifties was evaluated and promoted on the basis of his ability, skill and usefulness and not retarded in terms of his color. For the first time in American history Negroes in the Army had an equal opportunity to show what they could do except in some cases where they were prevented by circumstances related to race and color, from manifesting their abilities equally with others.

Troops Returning from Korea, August, 1953.

CHAPTER XXXVII

THE YEARS OF CHANGE—
CITIZENSHIP AND ECONOMIC ADVANCEMENT

The years 1945 and 1946 and the period of the fifties were years of significant events in world history. In 1945 the offensive of the allied troops had proved to be a successful one. In May, Mussolini and Hitler died and Germany surrendered. Two months later the first atomic bomb was exploded in New Mexico, and in August of this year the bombs were used on Hiroshima and Nagasaki and Japan surrendered. The war had come to an end, and preparations for peace among men and the establishment of better human relations were the next considerations at home and abroad.

During the war there had been marked improvement in the establishment and protection of Civil Rights for all peoples, particularly those engaged in war services. Later, on December 5, 1946, President Truman by **Civil Rights** Executive Order 9808 established the Presi- **in the forties.** dent's Committee on Civil Rights. This committee was to inquire into and determine whether the civil rights of the people were being safeguarded, and a report was to be made to the President.

This report was made in 1947, under the title, *To Secure These Rights.* It dealt with the American heritage as the promise of freedom and equality. By refer- **To secure** ence to the record, it was indicated how **these rights.** short we were of the goal in the legal and practical establishment of these fundamental rights. The committee de-

649

To Secure These Rights

THE REPORT

OF THE PRESIDENT'S COMMITTEE

ON CIVIL RIGHTS

". . . *to secure these rights governments*

are instituted among men . . ."

—THE DECLARATION OF INDEPENDENCE

UNITED STATES GOVERNMENT PRINTING OFFICE

Washington : 1947

To Secure These Rights

clared that they were sensitive to the general existence of prejudices which were continuing and stated that it would take time to remove them. And then it was added, "How much time will depend in a large measure of how quickly and aggressively we inaugurate the program of action under the leadership of the federal government." The committee regarded the avenues of governmental action and education as indispensable to the attainment of the accepted goals.

Gains were made rapidly in civil rights, education, housing, public accommodations and voting. The separate but equal doctrine dating from *Plessy v. Ferguson* in 1896 had led to attempts to establish equal courses and departments at Negro institutions. In 1946 the rise of the Ada Lois Sipuel Case in Oklahoma, *Sipuel v. Board of Regents,* inaugurated a new era in regard to individual constitutional rights to public education. The **Oklahoma** United States Supreme Court in 1948 ordered the State of Oklahoma to provide her with a legal education as it did for other applicants, and the case was remanded to the Oklahoma Supreme Court. In 1949 she was admitted to the University, although there had been established at Langston University, the Langston Law School.

In Kentucky, Lyman Johnson, a high school teacher in Louisville, was denied admission to graduate study at the University of Kentucky under the state's Day Law. Johnson appealed to the Federal District Court and the court ruled that facilities at Kentucky State College at Frankfort were not equal to those furnished white students at the University of Kentucky, and that colored students must be admitted there on the same **Kentucky** basis as white, although the court upheld the separate but equal doctrine. The legislature then passed an amendment to the Day Law which went into effect in 1950 providing that Negroes who were above the high school level may attend any public or private school provided school authorities so elect, and that an equal course was not available at Kentucky State College. This decision resulted in the closing of the Louisville Municipal College as the Negro branch of the University of Louisville. One member of the faculty, Dr. Charles Parrish, was retained as a member of the faculty of the University of Louisville, and became the first Negro member of a formerly white public college in the state of Kentucky.

In 1950 the United States Supreme Court, in the case of *McLaurin vs. Oklahoma* and the case of *Sweatt vs. Painter,* ordered that rules compelling Negroes to sit apart from classmates at a state university or to attend a school with inferior educational opportunities were unconstitutional. These decisions in effect terminated the practice of legal segregation in state graduate and professional schools.

Other cases in 1950 included the University of Delaware case known as *Parker vs. University of Delaware,* in which **Oklahoma,** it was ruled that the Negro applicant was **Delaware and** entitled to admittance to the State Univer-**Virginia.** sity of Delaware at Newark. Another case arose in 1950, *Swanson vs. the University of Virginia.* While the court ruled that he was entitled to secure a post-graduate course in law at Virginia State College, the institution primarily for Negroes, it was also ruled that he could not be restrained from admission to the University of Virginia.

The culmination of these legal efforts was reached on May 17, 1954, when the U. S. Supreme Court's unanimous decision was announced, ruling that segregation in public education was unconstitutional under the Fourteenth Amendment to the U. S. Constitution. Said the Court, "In approaching this problem, we cannot turn the clock back to 1868 when the amendment was adopted, or even to 1896 when *Plessy v. Ferguson* was written. We must consider public education in the light of its full development and its present place in American life throughout the nation." The responsibility of the states was then set forth and they were to proceed "with all deliberate speed" to equalize education for all Americans.

Desegregation moved slowly over the country. In the autumn of 1954, beginnings were undertaken in Wilmington, Baltimore, Washington, D. C., and scattered counties in Missouri, Arkansas and West Virginia. By 1958, the process of desegregation was in process in ten of the seventeen states which had legal segregation in 1954. New desegregation moves appeared slowly in the remaining seven states, but it was again on the move in 1958-1959.

In higher education in 1958, two Negroes were admitted to the University of Florida. The admission of two Negro applicants in 1961 to the University of Georgia, Charlayne Hunter and Hamilton Holmes, marked a historic occasion. This action was the result of court order of U. S. District Judge William A. Bootte of Macon, Georgia. This left only three states, Alabama, South Carolina and Mississippi, with no bi-racial classes in any tax supported school.

The developments of sentiment through public statements went along with the court actions in the opening of educational opportunities to Negroes. In 1949, the Catholic Commission of the South urged all Catholic institutions of higher education to admit Negroes without discrimination. In the same year the university presidents, deans and officials of over 100 universities met at the annual conference of the American Council **Pronouncements** on Education and adopted resolutions urging the elimination of college admission quotas based on race, religion or national origin. The President's Commission on Higher Education condemned segregation and discrimination in colleges and professional schools. The platforms of both major political parties embodied statements committing

PERCENT OF NEGRO PUPILS ENROLLED IN PUBLIC SCHOOLS OF THE DISTRICT OF COLUMBIA AND SELECTED SOUTHERN STATES HIT BY DESEGREGATION DECISION - 1955

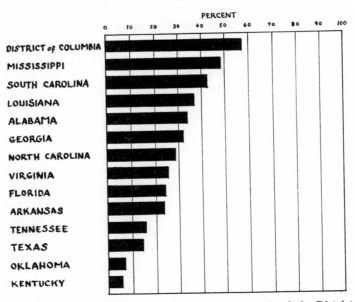

Per Cent of Negro Pupils Enrolled in Public Schools of the District of Columbia and Selected Southern States Hit by Desegregation Decision, 1955.

them to the attainment of civil rights for all citizens. The U. S. Civil Rights Commission issued a report in 1961 of 356 pages entitled *Equal Protection of the Laws in Public Higher Education,* which proposed that the federal government cease disbursing funds to publicly controlled colleges and universities practicing racial exclusion, whether of Negroes or of whites. The commission divided its votes on the withholding of funds from private institutions and

The Years of Change

IN THE

Supreme Court of the United States

October Term, 1953

No. 1

OLIVER BROWN, ET AL., *Appellants,*

VS.

BOARD OF EDUCATION OF TOPEKA, ET AL., *Appellees.*

No. 2

HARRY BRIGGS, JR., ET AL., *Appellants.*

VS.

R. W. ELLIOTT, ET AL., *Appellees.*

No. 4

DOROTHY E. DAVIS, ET AL., *Appellants,*

VS.

COUNTY SCHOOL BOARD OF PRINCE EDWARDS COUNTY, *Appellees.*

No. 10

FRANCIS B. GEBHART, ET AL., *Petitioners,*

VS.

ETHEL LOUISE BELTON, ET AL., *Respondents.*

APPEALS FROM THE UNITED STATES DISTRICT COURT FOR THE DISTRICT OF KANSAS, THE EASTERN DISTRICT OF SOUTH CAROLINA AND THE EASTERN DISTRICT OF VIRGINIA, AND ON PETITION FOR A WRIT OF CERTIORARI TO THE SUPREME COURT OF DELAWARE, RESPECTIVELY

BRIEF FOR APPELLANTS IN NOS. 1, 2 AND 4 AND FOR RESPONDENTS IN NO. 10 ON REARGUMENT

CHARLES L. BLACK, JR.,
ELWOOD H. CHISOLM,
WILLIAM T. COLEMAN, JR.,
CHARLES T. DUNCAN,
GEORGE E. C. HAYES,
LOREN MILLER,
WILLIAM R. MING, JR.,
CONSTANCE BAKER MOTLEY,
JAMES M. NABRIT, JR.,
DAVID E. PINSKY,
FRANK D. REEVES,
JOHN SCOTT,
JACK B. WEINSTEIN,
    of Counsel.

HAROLD BOULWARE,
ROBERT L. CARTER,
JACK GREENBERG,
OLIVER W. HILL,
THURGOOD MARSHALL,
LOUIS L. REDDING,
SPOTTSWOOD W. ROBINSON, III,
CHARLES S. SCOTT,
Attorneys for Appellants in Nos. 1, 2, 4 and for Respondents in No. 10.

The Supreme Court of the United States October Term, 1953, Brief for Appellants

the authorization to the U. S. Attorney General to initiate suits.

During the same period, action was taken which led to the removal of discriminatory pressures in public accommodations. A Federal District Court in 1949 sustained the right of the Civil Aeronautics Administrator to prohibit **Public accommodations.** discrimination and segregation at the Washington National Airport, although by the state of Virginia there was provided compulsory segregation. A year later the United States Supreme Court in *Henderson vs. the United States* outlawed segregation in dining cars on interstate travel, and in 1951 the United States Court of Appeals at Richmond, Virginia, held that segregation on interstate railroads violated the United States Constitution. In this way within a short period of years and especially at mid-century there was beginning to develop a change in the pattern of segregated education, housing and public accommodations.

The same development began in the right to vote. In 1948 the Federal District Court enjoined the Democratic Party of the State of South Carolina from barring Negro voters from primaries and from participation in party politics. In 1949 the United States Supreme Court in *Schnell vs. Davis* upheld the Federal District **Voting** Court decision that stringent education requirements set up by Alabama for voting were unconstitutional. Under the impact of these factors and the trends which were taking place in the development of representative democracy, the number of Negro voters steadily increased.

In 1957 Congress passed a Civil Rights Act, the first in 85 years. This Act established a Commission on Civil Rights to be appointed by the President as an independent agency which had the power to study, investigate, appraise and make recommendations concerning civil rights. This commission was to determine whether citizens were being denied their right to vote and to collect information concerning this denial. In 1959, the Attorney-General of the United States was empowered to seek court injunctions against interference with the voting rights of any individual. A Civil Rights Division was established in the Department of Justice headed by an Assistant Attorney-General.

In 1960 Congress passed a supplemental Civil Rights Act. This Act provided that any attempt to obstruct a court order was a punishable offense. The most important provision was to insure the right of qualified citizens to vote by providing for the appointment of Federal Voting Referees. As a result of this judicial ac- **Civil Rights** tion, the growth of favorable sentiment and **and voting.** initiative by Negro citizens and organized groups, there was a considerable increase in the number of qualified Negro voters in the South. From 1940 to 1947 there was an increase of Negro voters from 4,000 to 47,000 in Arkansas; from 20,000 to 125,000 in Georgia; from 20,000 to 80,000 in Tennessee and from 30,000 to 100,000 in Texas. By 1950 the number of Negroes of voting age was approximately seven million five hundred thousand, but only about 25 per cent of the Negro citizens in the Southern States of voting age were registered to vote. The U. S. Department of Justice filed suit in 1961 to cause to cease the discriminations against Negroes seeking to vote in Clarke and Forrest Counties, Mississippi. Attorney General Robert Kennedy has said of the responsibility of the Department in this connection, "It is our responsibility under the law to guarantee this right and we will meet that responsibility in these counties and elsewhere."

These voters were most influential in the election in 1946, when two Negro Congressmen, thirty State Legislators, including State Senators in Ohio, Michigan and Indiana were elected. There were forty members of state

THURGOOD MARSHALL

legislatures who were Negroes in 1956. Negroes were members of City Councils and school boards and were represented in federal, state and local offices. By   **Immediate**
1958 there were four Negroes in the United   **results.**
States House of Representatives: William R. Dawson,

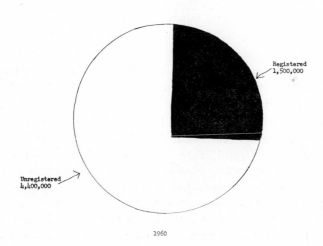

THE NEGRO AND THE BALLOT

THE SOUTH

(Eleven states of the Confederacy)
Negroes of voting age: 5,900,000 (est.)

Registered
1,500,000

Unregistered
4,400,000

1960

elected from Chicago, Illinois, first in 1943, who later
served as Chairman of the powerful Operations Committee
of the House of Representatives; Adam Clayton Powell,
first Negro Congressman from New York City, elected in
1945, who later served as Chairman of the House Commit-

tee on Education and Labor; Charles C. Diggs, first Negro
Congressman elected from Detroit, Michigan who served in
the 84th-86th United States Congresses; and Robert Nix
of Philadelphia, elected in 1957 to the U. S. House of
Representatives from Pennsylvania.

Advancement in civil rights were due largely to the
initiative of the National Association for the Advancement
of Colored People and its leadership. Celebrating its for-
tieth year in 1949, this Association launched a national organization which met in New York City and formulated
a "Declaration of Negro voters." This statement was intended to serve as a guide in the vote for candidates in the
Emphasis   elections. One of the emphases was placed
on voting.   upon the value of the Negro vote and the
demonstration of its power in the vote for President Truman in the pivotal states. The margin by which the President carried each state was exceeded by the Negro vote,
which was given to him mainly "as the forthright spokesman for civil rights."

At the 50th anniversary in 1959 the chronicle of achievements of the Association included, the outlawing in the
courts of the Grandfather Clauses; municiple residential
segregation; the all-white jury system; the all-white party
primaries; Negro exclusion from tax-supported colleges
and universities; segregation in interstate and intrastate
transportation; and the Negro exclusion from publicly
owned recreation facilities. Agitation and protest led to
the reduction of lynching and mob violence, the convening
of conferences and conventions in hotels excluding Negroes
and the Jim-Crow policy in labor unions. Motivation and
action were contributed to the adoption of state and city
Fair Employment Practice Acts.

The growth of membership to 385,000 in 45 states and
the District of Columbia in the NAACP was due directly to

WILLIAM L. DAWSON
Chicago

A. CLAYTON POWELL, JR.
New York

CHARLES C. DIGGS
Detroit

ROBERT NIX
Philadelphia

NEGRO CONGRESSMEN IN 1961

these accomplishments. Its annual membership growth was accompanied by Life Memberships under the leadership of **NAACP growth and service.** a committee of three co-chairmen: Kivie Kaplan, Jackie Robinson and George Cannon. The NAACP Legal Defense and Educational Fund was established headed by Thurgood Marshall as Director-Counsel, who had conducted the procedures for legal gains; Attorney Robert Carter with Dr. John W. Davis, formerly President of West Virginia State College as Special Director, Teacher Information and Security. The NAACP and the Legal Fund have won 42 major victories on civil rights and its outstanding victory was the 1954 U. S. Supreme Court decision on desegregation.

The Congress of Racial Equality, known as CORE, conducted its first Sit-In in Chicago in 1942 and an aggressive and yet non-violent activity was undertaken against segregation. The Freedom Riders and Sit-Ins re-**CORE** ceived support from this organization, led by James Farmer, National Director of the organization with 50 chapters and 25,000 members. He sounded a warning to those who would divide the objectives of his organization from those of the NAACP, when he declared in 1961, "Let no one mistake debate on tactics for division on goals. Let us by cooperation in action serve notice on the enemies of racial equality that they waste their time when they seek to divide us."

The same philosophy was spoken by Martin Luther King, Jr., President of the Southern Christian Leadership Con-**Southern conferences.** ference. The leadership of this movement has centered around the personality of this spokesman of nonviolence, who in Alabama conducted the successful Montgomery bus boycott in 1956, issued calls from Atlanta for continued Freedom Rides and conducted a campaign to register a million Negro voters in the South. Another conference, the Southern Conference Educational

Dr. John W. Davis
Former President, West Virginia State College; Special Director, Teacher Information and Security, NAACP Legal and Defense Fund.

JUDGE WILLIAM H. HASTIE
Judge of the United States Circuit Court of Appeals for the Third
Circuit.

Fund with its publication, *The Southern Patriot,* has dedicated itself to the ending of segregation and discrimination based on race, creed, color or national origin. The Southern Education Reporting Service published a monthly, *Southern School News,* which presented impartial and factual coverage of school segregation and desegregation.

The Federal Judiciary has had Negro representatives serving as judges. The first of this group was William H. Hastie, Amherst College and Harvard University Law graduate, Assistant Solicitor U. S. Department of the Interior, Judge of the U. S. District Court of the Virgin Islands, Dean of the Howard University Law School, Civilian Aide to the Secretary of War, member of the Caribbean Commission, Governor of the Virgin Islands and Judge of the United States Court of Appeals for the Third Circuit. Judge Harold A. Stephens *Judges* who had served as Judge of General Sessions Court, New York City was appointed as Judge of the New York Supreme Court. Scovel Richardson after serving as Chairman of the United States Parole Board was named to the United States Maritime Court. Irvin C. Mollison was appointed Judge of the United States Customs Court in 1945. President John F. Kennedy appointed Judge James B. Parsons of Cook County (Illinois) Court as Judge of the United States District Court for the Northern District of Illinois. This is a life-time appointment and is the first time a Negro has been appointed to the Federal District Court in the Continental United States. In addition, more than fifty Negroes have served as judges in the courts of cities mainly in the North. Judge Juanita K. Stout was the first Negro woman appointed as judge in Pennsylvania, thereby making history.

Federal officeholders have included J. *Governmental* Ernest Wilkins and George Weaver, both *service.* serving as Assistant Secretaries of Labor; E. Frederick

JUDGE JUANITA K. STOUT

First Negro woman appointed as a Judge in Pennsylvania, being congratulated by Judge Raymond Pace Alexander of the Common Pleas Court and his wife, Attorney Sadie Mossell Alexander.

Morrow, Administrative Officer for Special Projects, the White House Staff, and Andrew T. Hatcher, White House Press Aide; Campbell C. Johnson, Assistant to the Director of Selective Service; James C. Evans, Civilian Aide to the Secretary of Defense; Robert C. Weaver, Harvard trained, Head, Housing and Home Finance Agency, the highest U. S. position ever held by a Negro. The total number of Negroes in governmental service, federal, state and local had increased from 214,000 in 1940 to 855,000 in 1960.

The Negro population according to census reports had been increasing continuously during the past twenty years. In 1940 their number had increased to 12,865,000. By 1950, the total Negro population was above 15,000,000 and in 1960 it was 18,871,831 or about 10.5 per cent of the total population. The Negro population had increased 25.4

The Years of Change

CLIFFORD WHARTON
Ambassador to Norway; former
Head of Mission to Rumania.

CECIL POOLE
First Negro appointed by Presi-
dent Kennedy as United States
District Attorney.

ANDREW T. HATCHER
Associate White House Press Aid, with President Kennedy and Press
Chief Pierre Salinger

DR. ROBERT C. WEAVER
Administrator, Housing and Home Finance Agency

per cent from 1950 to 1960, whereas the white population had increased 17.5 per cent. This was a more rapid increase for Negroes than in any previous decade in the twentieth century. **Growth of Negro population.**

By 1950 as a result of continuous shifts, sixty-eight per cent of the Negro population lived in the South and thirty-two per cent in the North. In the same period there were over two million and a half Negroes who were born in the South and were living in other sections of the nation. Six states had a Negro population of over one million. New York had 1.4 million; Texas had 1.2 million; Georgia and North Carolina had about 1.1 million and Louisiana and Illinois had about one million each.

The 1950 census revealed that twenty per cent of the Negro farm population were in medium or high income farm areas as against sixty per cent of the white farm population in the same areas. The Negro **Farm population.** population to the extent of forty per cent lived in the low income sections. It has been found that the Negro farm families had only half as much money as white farm families in the South from their farming ventures, and they had only one-third as much as the white farm families in the entire United States.

The U. S. Census Bureau revealed a continuous shift of the Negro population to northern states and cities. For instance, in 1950, New York State was behind Georgia, North Carolina, Mississippi, Alabama and Texas in Negro population totals. In 1960 New York had jumped ahead of all states in this respect. At the same time, three-fourths of the Negro population were living in urban centers. The statistics of the twenty-five cities show higher percentages of increases of Negro population in these cities **Migration to cities.** than in other areas. There were 7,781,984 in 1960 in New York City, an increase of 14.0 per cent over 1950; 3,550,404 in Chicago, an increase of 22.9 per cent;

2,823,183 in Los Angeles-Long Beach, California, an increase of 12.2 per cent; 939,024 in Baltimore, an increase of 34.8 per cent; 763,956 in Washington, D. C., an increase of 53.9 per cent; 487,455 in Atlanta, Georgia, an increase of 38.3 per cent, and in New Orleans there were 627,525, an increase of 37.2 per cent. In nine cities the Negroes formed more than one-fourth of the total population. With the movement of the white population to the suburbs of cities and the settlement of Negroes in the vacated areas, changes were taking place in home and community life for the better in Negro life.

Occupational differences between Negroes and whites were still numerous, but since 1940 there has been an increase of occupational opportunities of Negroes. By 1960, one-fourth of the white males and less than seven per cent of the non-whites were in professional or managerial occupations. Over fifty per cent of non-whites were in manual occupations but less than ten per cent were working as skilled craftsmen or foremen, whereas twenty per cent among the whites were working in the latter capacities. In **Occupational differences.** the service occupations, about fifteen per cent of the non-whites were found, and the same number in farm work, compared with six per cent of whites in service occupations and nine per cent in agricultural occupations. While these percentages represent gains for both groups, the gains for Negroes were less than those for whites.

Negro women were engaged more largely in domestic service both in 1940 and 1960 than were white women. **Negro women.** However, the number of Negro women workers decreased from fifty-eight to thirty-seven per cent over this twenty year period. Negro women earn a little more than one-half as much as white women, but Negro men earn about sixty per cent as much as white men. However, employment opportunities were continuing to expand.

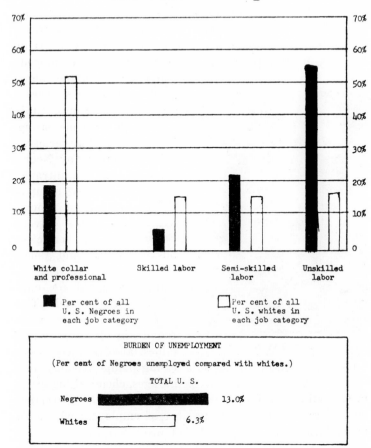

JOBS HELD BY NEGROES AND WHITES, 1960

There was an increase in clerical workers for Negroes but a far larger number were found among white. Negroes have been confined to jobs in the manufac- Occupational turing industry, mainly as laborers, truck changes. drivers or janitors. There were relatively few in positions as managers or officers. A break through the barrier of exclusion of managerial opportunities had begun to take place in the fifties. However, while 22 per cent of white college men became proprietors, managers and officials in business, only 5 per cent of Negroes were so employed.

CAROL TAYLOR
Air-line Hostess, Mohawk Air-Lines, First Negro Hostess

Change was taking place as Negroes prepared themselves for these opportunities which were increasing in number and in variety.

Three-fourths of Negro workers were concentrated in nine groups of occupations. The largest groups **Occupational** were drivers **concentration** of trucks, busses, taxis and such transportation vehicles, which accounted for one-third of their total. The other large groups were found in lumber mills, mines, laundries, food processing plants, parking lots, garages, chemical factories, metal refineries, foundries and power plants. Nevertheless, there was a growing number of employees who were being hired, trained, placed and promoted without reference to their color. This type of integration has been expanding. White persons have continuously averaged higher income from wages and salaries than Negroes, but **Wages and** the gap has been decreased. The median in- **salaries** come during the decade 1950-1960 of the Negro family was $3,233, a little more than one-half of the white median of $5,835. This relationship in the Southern states was much less for the Negro family, where all families had less income. Negroes were constantly getting jobs at higher pay in industry. In 1940 one in every ten Negroes were workers in industry but in 1960 this had increased to one in every six men.

With large numbers of Negroes who were living in cities, and particularly in cities with 50,000 or more in the population, and the increase in their income the **The Negro** Negro market was a thriving urban market and **market.** had become of increasing importance. This market was estimated in 1960 to be twenty billion dollars annually. Having more money to spend Negroes had become buyers of brand name products which constituted a good market for sellers, particularly of such things as clothing, home appliances, record players, T-V sets, home furnishings, toiletries and better quality merchandise. A marketing expert has reported that Negroes in the United States own four and one-half million automobiles or one for every five

AT WORK IN THE MACHINE SHOP

NEGRO OWNERSHIP OF APPLIANCES*
(from Research Company of America)

Appliance:	New York City	Northern N.J.	South Atlantic	East-South Central	West-South Central	Boston	Pacific Coast	East-North Central	West-North Central
Refrigerator	10.7	2.8	8.4	5.9	2.0	37.2	47.5	59.7	56.3
Home Freezer	1.1	0	3.1	2.6	2.6	0	1.9	3.9	0.7
Vacuum Cleaner	17.3	29.3	16.2	10.4	8.8	31.5	38.1	41.4	36.2
Sewing Machine	15.4	23.5	11.1	14.5	12.4	33.3	18.1	22.3	27.6
Washer	5.8	23.5	17.2	16.0	23.1	16.2	35.0	42.6	44.2
Iron	52.7	45.7	48.0	41.5	44.1	57.6	30.0	37.0	42.8
Toaster	42.6	51.5	30.5	18.5	23.2	56.6	40.6	44.0	48.7
Clock	30.2	40.0	23.9	21.1	31.4	36.4	38.1	49.2	48.1
Electric Shaver	7.6	16.7	8.7	9.9	5.6	11.1	10.0	14.0	13.8
Radio	87.1	93.7	84.6	68.4	86.2	92.0	89.4	88.7	86.5
Radio-Phonograph	30.6	38.5	26.6	34.5	31.2	36.4	35.6	39.7	44.2
Records	31.3	40.0	25.8	23.8	33.1	39.4	38.1	40.6	39.1

*By per cent of Negro population

THE NEGRO MARKET IN ONE PURCHASING AREA

Negroes in the United States. Advertisers were now using Negro models for their products and hiring Negroes for sales and promotion work.

An important factor in the economic advancement of Negroes had been the changing attitude of **The unions and race.** the unions, both national and local. When a merger was agreed upon and the constitution of the American Federation of Labor and the Congress of Industrial Organizations was adopted in December, 1955, there was a change expressed in the attitude of organized labor, for one of its objectives was listed as "to encourage all workers without regard to race, creed, color, national origin or ancestry to share equally in the full benefits of union organizations."

This merger was followed by the election of two Negro

labor leaders, A. Phillip Randolph of the Brotherhood of Sleeping Car Porters, and Willard W. Townsend, President of the Independent Brotherhood of Red Caps, as Vice-Presidents of the united AFL-CIO. There was then established a Civil Rights Committee and a Civil Rights Department. These committees functioned to assist the Executive Council in bringing about the implementation of the principle of non-discrimination which was adopted in the constitution. Two regional **Labor committee leadership.** committees had been appointed to help carry out this purpose. The Southern Advisory Committee on Civil Rights was made up of the presidents of the AFL-CIO bodies in the Southern states. A Mid-Western Advisory Committee on Civil Rights was organized in 1960, and was composed of the representatives of the union bodies in Ohio, Indiana, Illinois, Michigan, Wisconsin and Minnesota, with each of these states also having a Civil Rights Committee.

Action by unions against discrimination was undertaken, and changes were being made in the restrictive constitutions. In 1960 the Brotherhood of Railway Trainmen voted four to one for the removal of the clause "white only" from its constitution. Other International Unions during the sixties have been considering the removal of these clauses, and the change seems to be in- **Removal of barriers.** evitable. Many local unions still discriminate in various ways against Negro workers. They were either refused membership, or they were segregated in local unions of their own, or they were barred from the skilled trades or from apprenticeship training. The cause for such barring was not always directly on the basis of color. It happened ofttimes that Negroes were not trained for these jobs, since they had not had the training and also were barred from apprenticeships, and accordingly there was an excuse which unions and employees had for not spreading employment to include them.

One of the actions of Negro workers against these conditions was the formation in 1959 of the Negro-American Labor Council which held a second session in Washington, D. C., in 1960. This council was formed under the leadership of A. Phillip Randolph. Its aim was to secure equal **Negro-American** treatment for Negroes in labor organiza**labor council.** tions, in policy making, in apprenticeship, and in all aspects of labor relationships. Having had a successful development in the Brotherhood of Sleeping Car Porters which was also organized by A. Phillip Randolph, it is quite probable that the Negro-American Labor Council may prove to be an effective organization operating within the labor movement.

Other influences have helped to raise the status and wage level of Negro workers and especially those in cities. Fair Employment Practices Acts banning exclusion and wage **Fair employment** discrimination because of race or color **practice.** were adopted by 1960 in sixteen states having about one-half of the total population of the United States and about one-fourth of the Negro population. Fair employment practice had contributed to the improved status of Negro workers.

In this connection, the Federal Government had undertaken a series of acts to develop equality for work under government contracts. Executive Order 8802, June 25, 1941, announced a policy of participation in the defense program by all persons regardless of race, creed, color or national origin. The agencies of the Federal Government were ordered to include in each defense contract a pro**Additional influences** vision obliging the contractor not to **—executive orders.** discriminate against any worker. A Fair Employment Practice Committee was established to investigate and report grievances. A second Executive Order, 9346, May 27, 1943, gave reaffirmation to the policy of non-discrimination in government contracts and was intended to cover apprenticeship. It also established a seven

A. Phillip Randolph
International President of the
Brotherhood of Sleeping Car
Porters; President, National
Negro Labor Council

Dr. Earl B. Dickerson
President, Supreme Liberty
Life Insurance Company

Dr. Asa T. Spaulding
President, North Carolina
Life Insurance Company

John H. Johnson
Editor and Publisher
Johnson Publishing Company

member committee in the Office of Emergency Management to enforce this policy. Another step was taken when a Committee on Government Contract Compliance was established by Executive Order, 10308, December 5, 1951, which established a committee with advisory and educational powers.

An Executive Order, 10479, August 13, 1953, created the President's Committee on Government Contracts which was made up of sixteen high ranking government, business and labor leaders who were appointed on a non-partisan basis. The Vice President of the United States became the Chairman and the Secretary of Labor the Vice Chairman. **President's committee on government contracts.** This committee was charged with strengthening the enforcement of non-discrimination policies in federal contracts. On September 3, 1954, another Executive Order, 10557, added a standard non-discrimination provision in contracts and ordered that it should be included in all future contracts. Between August, 1953 and May 16, 1960, the committee received 970 complaints involving several thousand jobs and entire industries. There were 718 of these complaints which were disposed of and 252 were under investigation. Educational endeavors have also been made by the Committee on Government Contracts. These have included conferences on equal job opportunity, youth training incentives, minority community resources and one with religious leaders.

Discrimination against Negroes in housing has been a national problem. The problems incident to the Negro population in housing were due in part to their low incomes and to enforced residential segregation. These two factors have produced sub-standard housing, an insufficient supply of residential units and a market of segregated housing. In 1940 it was reported that of every ten dwelling units occupied by whites, four and a half were in need of major repairs or deficient in plumbing. It was reported for Negroes that eight and a half out of every ten dwelling units were in need of the same repairs. A larger proportion of Negroes were living in sub-standard housing. In most of the large industrial areas, north, south, east and west, the housing available to Negroes had never caught up with the demands resulting from the mass migrations which took place from South to North during and after World War I. One of the agencies used to limit **Restrictive** housing for Negroes was the restrictive cov- **covenants.** enant. This was an agreement by home owners not to sell their properties to certain racial or religious groups and to restrict the ownership of their community to a particular population group. For many years these agreements were not enforceable by the courts. In 1948 the United States Supreme Court ruled that neither state nor federal courts would enforce racial or religious covenants. Again in 1953 the court ruled that it would not award damages for the breach of restrictive covenants.

One of the fundamental areas of discrimination was in housing and in the aid which was being given to its development by the federal government. In 1949 the Federal Housing Administration and the Veterans Administration declined to make federal loans for new housing with discriminatory deeds or clauses, and the United States Supreme Court ruled in *Shelby vs. Kraemer* and in *Hurd vs. Hodges* that the court could not enforce racial restrictive covenants. These events opened the way for the development of federal housing without legal discriminatory clauses.

Fifteen states and a number of cities prohibited discrimination in housing developments which received government assistance. Four states have instructed housing commissions to prevent discrimination in the sale, rental or occupancy of private as well as public housing. The government agencies have given assistance to this program. Housing and Home Finance Agency has declined federal mortgage assistance to builders who violate New York's law against discrimination in public housing. The Veterans Administration has joined with New York and New Jersey in barring discrimination in Veterans Administration housing developments in these states.

Federal and state action in housing.

Negro housing in spite of the persistence of discrimination and segregation has improved. This is due to the rise in the income of the Negro population which has given them more funds to pay rents as well as to buy property, and also to federal assistance. Negro home ownership has increased. In 1940 only twenty-four per cent of the non-white families lived in homes they owned, as compared with forty-six per cent of white families. By 1956 the percentage had risen to thirty-six per cent for Negro ownership and sixty-three per cent for white ownership. The situation however for both groups has been improving. As whites have moved out of the central portion of cities into the suburbs, Negroes have moved in and occupied these vacancies, and many whites have remained in their homes and declined to move, electing to live side by side with Negro home owners.

Home ownership.

Housing commissions have been appointed to improve housing in a large number of cities. Along with this, real estate agents, mortgage financing companies and citizens groups have been urged to support campaigns for housing improvement, and to develop a free housing market. There is progress being made toward the development of decent homes for all Americans and the elimination of slums. It is reported that twenty-seven million Americans or nearly one-sixth of the

Housing commissions and homes for all.

United States population are limited in their opportunities to live in neighborhoods of their choice because of their race, color, or ethnic origins. Negroes are not alone in this respect for other groups suffer from these restrictions. These include eighteen million seven hundred thousand non-whites, five million Jews, two million five hundred thousand persons of Mexican ancestry and eight hundred thousand Puerto Ricans.

Negroes have made considerable progress in American business, although they are only a minor part of the total financial structure of the United States. When they are judged by the depths from which they have come, their economic advance is remarkable. There were approximately sixty-five Negro owned life insurance com- *Negroes in* panies in 1958. These companies have over *insurance.* two hundred fifty million dollars in force. Some names stand out prominently in this field: William J. Kennedy and Asa Spaulding of the North Carolina Mutual Insurance Company; Earl Dickerson and Truman K. Gibson, Sr., of the Supreme Life Insurance Company; A. F. Herndon and Norris Herndon of the Atlanta Life Insurance Company; Charles H. Mahoney and Louis C. Blount of the Great Lakes Life Insurance Company, and the Houstons of the Golden State Life Insurance Company.

The North Carolina Mutual Life Insurance Company in its sixty-second year had assets of $67,699,000 and its policyholders numbered 752,278. These policyholders lived in nine states and the District of Columbia. Other life insurance companies with major assets included the Atlanta Life Insurance Company of Georgia with assets of some $46,000,000. The Supreme Liberty Life Insurance Company which was founded in 1921 as the Liberty Life Insurance Company, merged with the Supreme Life and Casualty Company of Columbus, Ohio and the Northeastern Life Insurance Company of Newark, New Jersey and took the name Supreme Life Insurance Company. In 1958 it merged with the Dunbar Life Insurance Company of Cleveland, Ohio, to form a company then with combined assets of $22,000,000 and insurance in force of $143,000,000. The recent important step taken by this company was in its expansion in 1960 when the Beneficial Life and Friendship Mutual Life of Detroit and the Federal Life Insurance Company of Washington, D. C., were purchased and linked with the Supreme Liberty Life. The company now has nearly $160,000,000 worth of insurance in force. The Great Lakes Mutual Life Insurance Company of Detroit and the Golden State Life Insurance Company of Los Angeles, California, are among companies which are aiding the Negro poulation in many beneficial ways, and providing capital for housing and Negro enterprise.

There were eleven Negro banks in 1943 with resources of over $15,000,000 and deposits amounting to $14,000,000. There were thirteen banks controlled by Negroes in 1958. **Banks** Their assets had increased to more than $40,000,000 in 1960. There were approximately thirty-three Negro savings and loan associations holding mortgages valued at $75,000,000. Individually some have assets of over $10,000,000 and more. Their financial assistance has helped to loosen the loans of white institutions to Negroes for homes and business projects.

There were 155 Negro owned newspapers, which constituted an important part of Negro business. Nearly all of these were weekly newspapers but there were two daily papers in Chicago and Atlanta, Georgia, the *Chicago Daily World* and the *Atlanta World*. Negro newspapers have been published in 32 states, and in nearly all large cities there was at least one Negro weekly newspaper. There have been continuous improvements in the journalistic activities and in the movement toward professionalism in these newspapers. The expansion of printing plants and the quality of reporting have advanced tremendously, and the Negro press now represents one of the big businesses in Negro life. These papers included: The *Pittsburgh Courier* under the leadership of Mrs. Robert Vann, successor to Robert L. Vann; the *Chicago Defender* under the leadership of John H. Senstack, successor to its **Newspapers** founder Robert H. Abbott; the *Atlanta Daily World* under C. C. Scott; the *New York Amsterdam News* under C. B. Powell; the *Norfolk Journal and Guide* under P. B. Young; the *Cleveland Call and Post* under William O. Walker; the *Philadelphia Tribune* under E. Washington Rhodes and the *Afro-American* under Carl J. Murphy. Some city daily newspapers have also employed Negro reporters. A few of these were Ted Poston with the *New York Post;* Carl Rowan with the *Minneapolis Tribune;* Roi Ottley with the *Chicago Tribune* and Luther P. Jackson, Jr. of the *Washington,* D. C. *Post.*

Publishing companies among Negroes were few. However there were magazines which were the result of corporate ventures. The magazine with the longest continuous existence among Negroes was *The Crisis,* which began its fiftieth year of publication in 1960. It was the official organ of the National Association for the Advancement of Colored People. *Opportunity,* the journal of **Negro** the National Urban League ceased publica- **magazines.** tion in 1949. *The Journal of Negro History* launched in January 1916 by Carter G. Woodson for the Association for the Study of Negro Life and History, Washington, D. C., has had continuous publication since its inception. *The Journal of Negro Education,* edited by Charles H. Thompson and the Bureau of Educational Research, Howard University, Washington, D. C. began its thirtieth year of quarterly publication in 1962. *Phylon,* a literary journal edited and published at Atlanta University for two decades continued its effective service and scholarly presentations.

One of the spectacular magazine publications was *Ebony*, launched by John H. Johnson of Chicago in 1947 and published by the Johnson Publishing Company. Its circulation mounted rapidly, reaching a circulation of a half million in a few years, as it depicted Negro life in graphic ways, developing race pride and self-respect in its colored readers throughout the world, and amazement on the part of its white readers who knew so little of these aspects of Negro life presented in *Ebony*. In rapid succession there were offsprings of this magazine under the Johnson Publishing Company: *Tan*, a magazine of personal confessions and romance; *Jet*, a weekly news chronicle; *Hue*, a smaller *Ebony* and the *Negro Digest*.

The Associated Publishers, an affiliate of the Association for the Study of Negro Life and History was the lone **Negro publishers.** Negro-officered publishing company among Negroes during the fifties. Its objective has been the publication primarily of textbooks concerning history, although other books on Negro subjects have also been published by this agency. It was organized by Carter G. Woodson and has continued to pursue its original purpose with successful results, from the period when it was organized in 1921 "to make possible the publication and circulation of valuable books on the Negro not acceptable to most publishers."

CHAPTER XXXVIII

The years of change since World War II witnessed not only the emergence of Negro-Americans as a political and economic power in the United States, but also the continuous advancement in the areas of education and in individual and group attainment. In spite of conditions of poverty, segregation, discrimination, inadequate housing and disadvantaged environments, there were Negroes who were being educated in schools, colleges and universities and there were individuals who ranked among the attainers. When there were frustration and obstacles based on race and color, incentives and motivations were contributed by some devoted parents, churches and organizations.

Two facts stand out in the education of Negroes. One is the gradual improvement in educational facilities offered to Negroes since the first decade of the twentieth century, but these gave far less opportunties to Negroes to be educated than was given to whites. The second is the continued inferiority of this education as contrasted with the education of white youth even in 1950. At this period, one of every five Negroes in the South who reached adulthood had obtained **The status of the education of Negroes.** only five years of schooling. Three times as many male Negroes as whites had completed less than five years in school. The proportion of white boys who had graduated from high school was almost three times as high as the number of Negro boys. Although advances had taken place in

685

education in the North, the proportion of whites who went to high school far exceeded the proportion of Negroes. At all levels of education, Negro youth were far behind white youth. This was due not to ability or race, but to environment, motivation, low family income and discriminatory employment practices, adverse conditions under which many Negro families lived, and inadequate preparation for jobs which would assist in continuance in school.

The education of Negroes had continued to improve rapidly in the period since World War II. While statistics showed that their education was below the level reached by whites, there were rapid steps being taken to close the gaps. The deficiencies in education had often been due to weaknesses in the environment as well as in the schools which had been attended. However, the statistics of literacy, school attendance and expenditures per pupil in the South have shown progress toward a closer relationship to the expenditures for whites. In three states, North Carolina, **Comparative** Florida and Alabama, the result was to raise **data.** the average instruction expenditure per pupil in Negro schools to more than ninety per cent of the rate in white schools. In Mississippi the large percentage increase brought the average expenditure in Negro schools per pupil up to only forty-four per cent of the rate for whites. In no southern state was the expenditure for either Negro or white children reported in 1953-1954 as high as the national average.

The educational opportunities for the Negro population were advanced greatly by mid-century. Through community **Increase of** ty leadership, better qualified teachers, the **opportunities** actions of an enlightened citizenry and the **for education.** increasing intelligence of hundreds of thousands of parents of both racial groups, there had developed the motivation and inspiration which had increased the educational capacities and desires of communities. Southern leadership had grown more liberal and the number of those who believed that the education of Negroes should be restricted to special spheres was decreasing; and on the contrary, the number of those who believed that the education of Negroes should be equal to that of the whites had been increasing rapidly. The result was that more money was secured, better buildings and equipment and better teachers were being obtained, and with the lengthening of

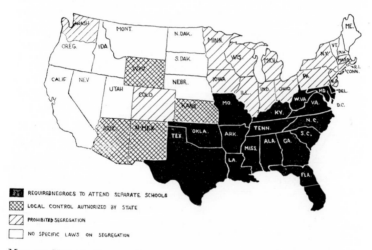

REQUIRED NEGROES TO ATTEND SEPARATE SCHOOLS
LOCAL CONTROL AUTHORIZED BY STATE
PROHIBITED SEGREGATION
NO SPECIFIC LAWS ON SEGREGATION

MAP OF UNITED STATES SHOWING SEGREGATED AND NON-SEGREGATED SCHOOLS, 1954

school terms, an increasing consideration was given to the advancement of the public schools.

The United States Supreme Court's decision of 1954 declaring that in the field of public education "the doctrine of separate but equal" could not be maintained, had affected directly the education of all youth by states and cities. This decision declared that separate educational facilities on racial bases were unequal. It was stated that separate educational facilities were unequal and were not related to any proper governmental objective. Again in 1955, the Supreme Court held that "a prompt and reasonable start, must be made in the process of desegregation" and was to proceed, according to the court order, "with all deliberate speed," in a "systematic and effective" way and within a "reasonable time."

There had been the development of sentiment and action for and against segregation. Thirty-three of the fifty states have had integrated public schools, although four states before the decision,

Public school desegregation —North.

Kansas, Arizona, New Mexico, and Wyoming, had permitted segregation, as well as some northern states. West Virginia and Washington, D. C., had legally desegregated their formerly segregated schools except for the influence of residential segregation. Six states had begun integration in a large portion of their schools, five had made small beginnings and in five others no public school desegregation had occurred. In northern states, there had been some segregated schools maintained due largely to all-Negro or all-white residential areas. Efforts had been made and were being made to cease the operation of these schools by either

WHITE CHILDREN

1957 - 1958

2,299,445

NEGRO CHILDREN

1957 - 1958
402,403

1956 - 1957

2,000,000

1956 - 1957
350,000

1955 - 1956

1,823,908

1955 - 1956
319,184

DESEGRATION BY NUMBERS, 1955-1958, estimated by *Ebony*, January, 1959; see also *Southern School News*, October, 1959

integrating them or having the families send their children to other areas.

In 1959-60, about seven per cent of the Negro public school children in seventeen southern and border states were in school districts that had been deseg- **Public school** regated. Anti-desegregation laws have been **desegregation** adopted by several legislatures providing for **—South.** the closing of public schools if necessary and for the assignment of pupils to specific schools by school boards.

Grade by grade desegregation is being tried in some states and cities. While there has been opposition to this decision, there has been the continuance of public school education. Some Negro teachers have lost their positions because of sympathetic action with desegregation groups, but as a whole the Negro teacher continues to maintain his place in education. In 1960, the Southern Education Reporting Service, a fact finding agency of white and Negro southerners, reported that ninety-four per cent of the South's Negro students still attended segregated classes in spite of the Supreme Court Decision of 1954. Of three million and thirty-nine thousand Negroes, there were

MRS. DAISY BATES of Little Rock Fame

five hundred and twenty-four thousand four hundred and twenty-five who were in integrated school districts. The dramatic highlights of this period were the Little Rock incidents in which Mrs. Daisy Bates was a leader and the New Orleans effort to desegregate the schools there, with the court case being initiated by Attorney A. P. Tureaud.

In the area of higher education, the progress had been continuing. The number of such institutions and the total enrollment of Negroes had increased. By 1950 there were 28.4 times as many students in colleges for Negroes as there were in 1900. For every one person who received a bachelor's degree in 1900, there were 84 who received this degree in 1950. There were 23,000 Negroes in colleges and universities in 1940. In 1950 there were 113,735 Negroes enrolled in colleges and pro-

Higher education.

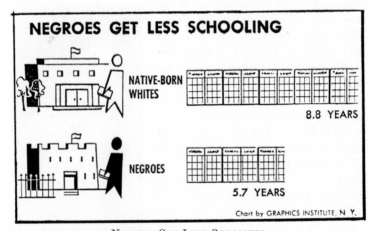

NEGROES GET LESS SCHOOLING

NATIVE-BORN WHITES

8.8 YEARS

NEGROES

5.7 YEARS

Chart by GRAPHICS INSTITUTE, N. Y.

Negroes Get Less Schooling

fessional schools, and in 1958, this number had increased to 212,000 enrollees. This was an increase of 86.4 per cent. It was during this period that the United States Supreme Court Decision of 1954 was also having effect in higher education. However, integration in some colleges had preceded this decision. Several private institutions had taken this action first and were followed by public ones. Other institutions continued to be all-white and all-Negro mainly because applications had not been received from Negroes or whites, or because of hesitations on the part of those who would apply. In other states, the number of Negroes who had been admitted to institutions for higher education for whites remained small. Complete segregation continued in South Carolina, Alabama and Mississippi.

Many basic factors operated to keep Negroes from going to college. The relatively lower **Other basic factors.** family income, the lack of motivation, inadequate guidance and poor counseling, the limited primary and secondary school preparatory programs for Negroes which resulted in inadequate preparation for college. Many of these weaknesses were being remedied in community after community although controversy had continued. The National Defense program of education was also contributory to good results. Salaries of teachers had improved and were reaching planes of equality with teachers of similar training and experience. These changes were due primarily to articulate spokesmen among Negroes who in association with liberal white citizens compelled a reevaluation of inequalities.

Applications of larger numbers of Negroes to professional schools were due to the opening of these institutions on the non-segregated basis. These professional schools included those for medicine, medical technology, dentistry, dental hygiene, engineering, law, pharmacy, theology and veterinary medicine. There were two medical and dental colleges primarily for Negroes, the Meharry **Professional education.** Medical College, Nashville, Tennessee and Howard University Medical School, Washington, D. C. These institutions, together with those which were gradually admitting Negroes in some token way to their professional schools, were developing the possibilities for an increasing number of professionally trained Negroes to serve their communities. There were in 1947-48, only ninety-three Negroes in twenty predominantly white medical schools. In 1955-56, there were 216 Negro students in 48 of these medical schools. It was expected that as segregation declined, that there would be an expansion of the professions open to Negroes and additional openings in professional education.

This was greatly to be desired because while Negroes made up about ten per cent of the total population, Negro physicians constituted only 2.2 per cent of all physicians.

DR. JAMES M. NABRIT, JR.
President of Howard University

The ratio of Negro physicians to white physicians was one physician to 770 people in the total population of the United States but only one Negro physician **The need for** **professionals.** to 4,567 of the Negro population. Negroes had been admitted to the associations of medical specialists. Twenty-nine Negro surgeons have been inducted into the

American College of Surgeons since 1945. They were members of the American College of Physicians, the International College of Surgeons, the American College of Chest Physicians, the American Academy of Pediatrics, the American Academy of Dermatology and Syphilology and the College of Radiology. Negro student nurses were accepted in over 300 nursing schools.

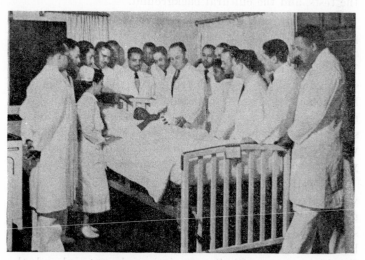

DR. CHARLES R. DREW (center)
who developed new procedures in surgical shock, fluid balance and the blood bank; Spingarn Medalist, with his students at the Howard University Medical School.

A considerable discussion had developed in American educational circles over the intelligence capacity of Negroes. Some psychologists who had worked in the testing programs with them had drawn assumptions and conclusions which had been too **Intelligence tests.** readily accepted by the unthinking public. These results had led to the additional conclusions that since the test results showed that Negroes were "inferior," they should not have the same "rights as others." We now know that the psychological tests were not perfect instruments of measurement. Then too, the measurement of intelligence depends on other factors than this factor by itself—the experiences as well as the education of the individual, his motivation and purpose of making a satisfactory score on the test, his acquaintance with testing and the subjects of the tests, and the cultural background.

The latter is of great importance so far as the Negro population is concerned. For while their status in American life had been advanced, they are still handicapped. The schools attended by them were not the equals of the schools for whites, although the gap was closing. The family income was less, as has been stated. The Negro community was not maintained by the municipalities on the same level as other communities. The environment as a whole was less conducive to full participation by adults or youth in the various activities of American life.

It is well to remember that there were individual Negroes who scored higher than individual whites. Groups of Negroes have also scored higher. Tests of World War I have shown that Negroes from several Northern states scored higher on psychological tests than whites from several Southern states. Similar variations have produced the accepted conclusion that skin color was not an index of future success for a group or of group superiority.

There are other factors to be considered. In World War II, white men who were examined for military induction showed that they had completed about twelve years of school, whereas Negro men had completed about eight years of school. Nearly three-fourths of these whites scored on the qualification tests for the Armed Forces in Group III, or above, as compared with one-fourth of the Negroes who scored in the three highest groups. The difference in scores was attributed to the difference in schooling.

Concluding on these experiments and others, the National Manpower Commission declared, "Most social scientists now believe that there are no inborn differences in intellectual potential between Negroes and the rest of the population, or that such differences, if they exist, are very small. Yet, a study made a few years ago of college freshmen, showed that the average freshman in a Negro college scored only a little higher on aptitude tests than the lowest-ranking freshman in the average college. This finding testifies both to the sensitivity of the test to prior educational experience and to the great differences between the educational opportunities of Negroes and whites."

By 1950, Negro writers were moving into the American mainstream of literature. While using Negro themes, they were also moving out of the use of the stereotype that had confined them to a special type of writing and they were using universal themes although they also described Negro life. There were demands of the literary market **Literary** which wanted the concepts of the myths which **concepts.** had grown up concerning Negro life and character. Gradually, however, the old concept was fading and the writer was relieved of the necessity to depict the Negro tradition or to praise it. This new concept would appear to have been due to the progress of integration.

Richard Wright had been impelled to describe Southern pressures and the Northern ghetto with their influences upon the Negro, and, with his *Native Son* in 1940 and *Black Boy* in 1945, there were successful sales of these volumes. They were both Book-of-the-Month selections. Langston Hughes, poet, author and play- **Negro writers—** wright, published books, short stories, **men.** plays, poems, opera librettos and songs. One of his plays, *Mulatto,* had a year's run on Broadway, and *The Barrier* has had repeated performances as an opera. His books have been translated into several languages. He was awarded the Springarn Medal for 1960 for "the highest achievement of an American Negro."

Frank Yerby's first endeavor toward success was a short story written in *Harper's Magazine* in 1944. In the same year, his first novel which was a best seller, *Foxes of Harrow,* soon sold into millions of copies, and within a decade he had published twelve best sellers with an average sale of around a million copies for each publication. He

RICHARD WRIGHT
Novelist and Writer of International Standing.

LANGSTON HUGHES
Poet, Author and Playwright

did not use race themes, and he was not known as a Negro writer. Many readers were unaware of his racial identification. Willard Motley wrote his *Knock On Any Door,* a powerful moving novel of the experiences of an Italian boy in an American city. This was followed by his *Let No Man Write My Epitaph.* Ralph Ellison, with his first book *Invisible Man,* won acclaim as an author of the first rank. The National Book Award for 1953 was awarded to him at the same time when Hemingway was under consideration for the same award. James Baldwin began his career with the writing of short stories and in 1961 brought out his *Nobody Knows My Name.* This volume declaring that "Negroes wanted to be treated like men" went through its third printing within a few months. It was described as "a passionate, probing controversial book." Dr. W. E. B. DuBois, although beyond ninety years of age, completed a triology of books on *Mansart,* a typical Negro teacher in the South, backgrounded by some of the DuBois experiences.

Among the female writers was Ann Petry. Her first writings were short stories, one of which appeared in *The Crisis.* She received a literary fellowship from the Houghton Mifflin Company which enabled her to complete her first novel, *The Street,* describing the **Negro writers—** struggle of a Negro mother with her son **women.** in the slum areas of New York. Gwendolyn Brooks wrote poetry from her youth in Chicago, first for her high school paper, then for *The Chicago Defender.* Her book of poetry *A Street in Bronzeville,* made her a Pulitzer Prize Winner. She was also a winner of the Poetry Workshop Award.

The Negro writer had arrived by Mid-Century and was portraying Negro life but writing about it like an American author. This list of Negro writers continued to grow as their subject scope widened so that there has been an increase in literary output and in acceptance.

Music has been a vital part of the life of the Negro-American and outstanding contributions have been made by Negroes to American music. These con- **Musical** tributions have extended all the way from **Composition** the music of the plantation and the levy, to the mello voices of concert singers and the composition of symphonies. The deep sense of rhythm, grace and poetic musical expression have been parts of these attainments. Both

W. E. B. DuBois
Scholar, Author and Provocative Thinker

GWENDOLYN BROOKS
Winner of the Pulitzer Prize in Poetry, first Negro to be awarded
this prize.

in the realm of popular music and in the more serious areas of music, abiding contributions have been made.

In the period of the fifties the names of Marian Anderson, Paul Robeson, Roland Hayes, Dorothy Maynor and Todd Duncan as concert singers were preeminent. Many others have attained prominence: Adele Addison, Mattiwilda Dobbs, Gloria Davy, Robert McFerrin, Leontyne Price, William Warfield, Camella Williams, Charlotte Holloman and Lawrence Winters. Marian Anderson, born in Philadelphia and moving forward from the church choir to the concert stage in Europe, the United States and ultimately around the world, singing in the languages of the people with a repertoire of many hundred of songs, was the first Negro to sing in the Metropolitan Opera. She has become one of the ambassadors of America to the world. She was followed by Robert McFerrin, Baritone in 1955, Mattiwilda Dobbs, Soprano in 1956, Gloria Davy in 1957 and Leontyne Price in 1961. Dorothy Maynor **Singers** making her debut in the forties was one of the nations leading sopranos. She was guest soloist for a number of international music festivals, and sang throughout America and Europe. Todd Duncan a native of Kentucky, educated at Butler University and Columbia University, appeared in the production of *Cavalleria Rusticana* in New York and was engaged by George Gershwin later for the leading role in *Porgy and Bess*. He has pursued widely successful concert tours in Europe, Latin America, Australia and the United States.

The list of modern Negro composers manifests its best with William Grant Still whose name ranks high in original American music. His symphonic trilogy **Composers** *Africa*, the *Afro-American Symphony* and the *Symphony in G Minor* was written at the request of Leopold Stokowski. His opera *Blue Steel* was followed by the use of Negro themes in other works. *Trouble Island,* a

MARION ANDERSON
Internationally Known Contralto

TODD DUNCAN
Artist and Musician

ROBERT McFERRIN
Metropolitan Opera Baritone

LEONTYNE PRICE
Metropolitan Opera Star

Southern Interlude, *A Bayou Legend* and *Lenox Avenue,*
are evidences of his symphonic contributions. Howard
Swanson was the only American composer represented at
the Edinburgh Festival of 1951. His short symphony was
performed there. William Dawson was another of the current composers whose work in the development of choral
music based on Negro themes was evidence of a distinguished contribution to the musical culture of America.

Dean Dixon was the first Negro conductor to win both
national and international acclaim. After playing in high
school orchestras he organized a little symphony orchestra
at the Harlem YMCA composed of white and colored
players and then was invited to conduct the Chamber Orchestra of the League of Music Lovers at Town Hall. In
the meantime, he continued to pursue his studies at Columbia University. David Sarnoff, head of the Radio Corporation of America, invited Dixon to fill in as a
Conductors   summer conductor of the NBC Symphony. He
served other symphonic groups in Europe as conductor and
was selected as permanent conductor of the Gothenburg
Symphony Orchestra and Director for Radio Koln in West
Germany. Clarence Cameron White was the outstanding
violinist and orchestra conductor, as well as a composer
basing his compositions upon Negro and Haitian themes.

In Jazz and popular musical forms, the Negro was represented by unusual individuals. Heading this list was
W. C. Handy who had been playing in dance orchestras
and yet seeking constantly to secure a musical education
for himself. His first outstanding composition was entitled
Memphis Blues. He sold this song to a
Jazz composers.   New York publisher for $50.00, and it
was soon sweeping the country. He then turned to produce his famous *St. Louis Blues.* He was more careful with
this song in a financial way, and it sold more copies
perhaps than any other single piece of music produced by
a Negro composer.

WILLIAM GRANT STILL
A Distinguished Composer

DEAN DIXON
A Distinguished Conductor

WILLIAM C. HANDY
Originator of the "Blues;" Composer and Music Publisher

DUKE ELLINGTON
Composer and Band Director

PAUL ROBESON
Actor and Singer

One of the outstanding exponents of jazz in song was Bessie Smith. Her renditions were of the highest order and were heartily received. While she had very little training, her natural voice enabled her to receive the acclaim of critics of jazz. She made over 150 records, although she died in 1937, her records have continued to be used and references are frequently made to her presentations. Lena Horne has been an **Jazz exponents.** attractive singer and a unique personality in American entertainment. She was engaged for singing roles in the film *Panama Hattie* in 1942 and *Cabin in the Sky*. She also appeared in the productions of *Stormy Weather*, and *Jamaica*, starring with Bojangles Robinson, the dancer.

Duke Ellington, another of the composers of popular music, has been an outstanding personality in the production of the best in this field. He has produced a number of classics in the field of jazz and has been given a number of awards for these contributions. A critic has said of him that his melodies move against each other in the harmonies of rich counterpoint and that the off beat rhythm weaves threads that move in and out of his works. He has been called "the most original music mind in America." While this may border upon extravagance, nevertheless, it indicated that here was an original mind contributing to American music which was being accepted by the millions. He was given the Springarn Medal in 1960, and was the first from the world of Jazz so cited.

There have been some exponents of music who have become roving goodwill ambassadors. Among these was Count Basie, master of sophisticated rhythm. Another was Dizzy Gillespie who was **Jazz ambassadors.** sent on tours by the U. S. Department of State. Louis Armstrong, known as Satchmo, carried his music and his trumpet not only throughout America and Latin America and Europe but also into Africa. Lionel Hampton and others have followed the same tours. The audiences of these individuals have been far larger than those attending their concerts because their records and sound productions have sold into the millions.

Negro names have continued to dominate the jazz area of music, with folk and gospel singers also receiving acclaim. Among these were Mahalia Jackson, Clara Ward, Josh White. In the popular music field there were names **Folk and** which continued to make headlines: Harry **gospel singers.** Belafonte, Cab Calloway, Nat King Cole, Sammy Davis, Jr., Billie Eckstine, Ella Fitzgerald, Errol Garner, Lionel Hampton, Louis Jordan, Carmen McRay, Hazel Scott, Sarah Vaughn, Dinah Washington and Mary Lou Williams.

Plays with Negro characters and concerning Negro life have had acceptance by the theatrical world. These plays have been by white playwrights in which Negroes appeared as part characters and plays by Negroes or whites with **The theatre.** all-Negro plays. Among these were *Anna Lucasta,* in which Hilda Sims, a 1943 graduate of Hampton Institute, took the leading role; *Cabin in the Sky,* in which Ethel Waters played the lead; *Carmen Jones,* written by Oscar Hammerstein, II, produced by Billy Rose in 1944, and with the leads played by Muriel Smith and Muriel Rahn; *Porgy and Bess* with Todd Duncan and William Warfield in the roles, with lyrics by DuBose and Dorothy Heyward and the music by George Gershwin; *Show Boat* by Jerome Kern and Oscar Hammerstein, II, with Kenneth Spencer and Paul Robeson in the lead roles, of which "Ol' Man River" was a long time hit song; and others such as *Strange Fruit, Native Son, Run Little Chillun, St. Louis Woman* and *Jamaica.* Paul Robeson's "Othello" made history for him as a Shakespearian actor.

The American Negro Theatre was organized in 1940 under the inspiration of Frederick O'Neal for the purpose of aiding Negro actors to secure dramatic jobs in the theatre rather than continue in the non-dramatic roles offered to Negroes. This group hoped to launch and build its own theatre. The Negro Actor's Guild of America was organized to assist Negro actors and to promote their welfare.

The dramatic success of *A Raisin in the Sun* written by Lorraine Hansberry and performed by an all Negro cast headed by Sidney Poitier and Claudia McNeil was a high mark in the presentation of drama. It had a long run as a play and subsequently was put into a motion picture.

There has been a long time resentment by the Negro people against the image which Hollywood and its producers have been making of them. The Negro Press, the National Association for the Advancement of Colored People and organizations of artists have made protests against the pattern as it has been presented. The export of these films to foreign countries also attracted criticism and protest. A resolution submitted by Dr. Nnamdi Azikiwie a member of the Nigerian Legislative Assembly in 1949, urged the prohibition of "films which are derogatory and humiliating to the Negro race." It was against the *Uncle Tom* theme and the *Birth of the Nation* pattern that these protests were being made. The *Rastus* and *Sambo* films were descendants of this idea. **First motion pictures.**

A second type of film followed this group and endeavored to show the dilemma of the mulatto. The film *Pinky* was one of the earliest of this concept, although it was an improvement over the old type. Films have appeared during the last two decades **The second group of motion pictures.** which have been based upon good relations between white and colored people but have frequently introduced the continuation of the *Uncle Tom* tradition in modern dress. In the fifties pictures began tc appear with racial themes presenting Negro actors playing leading roles. The Negro market was one reason for these presentations and a widening of the liberal market of whites was another basis for it. There was the absence of the clowning, the buffooning and the brute concepts. The films *Home of the Brave, Cry the Beloved Country, Lost Boundaries, Intruder in the Dusk, The Defiant Ones* were presentations of racial themes which it would have been difficult to have made in earlier periods.

Television had not grown up entirely in this respect and yet it was on its way. There were television and theatrical **Television** appearances of Harry Belafonte, who had his **and radio.** own television company, Nat King Cole, Dorothy Dandridge, Lena Horne, Pearl Bailey, Ethel Waters, and Eartha Kitt. Several groups have appeared on radio and television: The Deep River Boys, The Eva Jessye Choir, the Ink Spots, The Mills Brothers, The Golden Gate Quartette and many well-known bands, orchestras and singers. There had been a greater change in the appearance of Negroes on radio than in television. The latter moved more slowly but progress of major proportions was made in the appearances of Leontyne Price in *Tosca* with NBC and of other able Negro artists.

A change had taken place also in Negro dancing. Instead of the tap dance of which Bill Robinson was the incomparable exponent, the buck and wing patterns and the Broadway appearance of Florence Mills and Josephine Baker, a change had taken place in the forties in the serious Negro dance pattern. During the period, Katherine Dunham developed creative dancing which was readily accepted by the American people. With a Rosenwald Fellowship she went to Haiti, Jamaica, Martinique and Trinidad, studying their dances, rhythm and costuming. She stated her point of view in the following, "For my part, I am satisfied to have been at the base of the awakening of the American Negro to the fact that he had roots somewhere else, and to have presented dark-skinned people in a manner delightful and acceptable to people who have never considered them often even as persons." She and her dance company had been on the concert stage and in Hollywood and had served with the Moscow Art Theatre, and had appeared in concerts in some fifty countries. Several years thereafter, other concert dancers made appearances. Janet Collins appeared in 1949 with the Metropolitan Opera Company in "Aida." Pearl Primus of Trinidad, a graduate of Hunter College, danced in New York following her career in college and moved into dancing as a career through the Works Progress Administration. In 1959, President Tubman invited her to Liberia to head the African Performing Arts Center in Monrovia. Carmen de LaVallade, described as "one of the most beautiful dancers in America, both physically and technically," appeared with the New York City Opera and in motion pictures. James Truitte, Sherly Talley, Alvin Alley, Talley Beatty and Louis Johnson were among other talented dancers.

The cold war, shortages of material and men in critical areas, gave opportunities for Negroes to be used in the laboratories of corporations, research divisions, the chemical industries and research staffs of corporations and businesses. Without notice the colleges and universities had turned out individuals who were moving into these vacancies and filling these needs. George Washington Carver who had worked at Tuskegee Institute and established a reputation for creative work in chemurgy had died in 1943. There was no dramatic personality such as his to fill this particular gap but there were serious Negro scientists who were coming forward by the hundreds located in various parts of the nation silently at work developing the dominion of man over nature and its products.

Negroes in scientific pursuits.

CHARLES R. DREW
Surgeon known also for his success with the Blood Bank.

Charles R. Drew of the Howard University Medical School accomplished a significant job in his cooperative work with the organization of the blood bank and the blood collection service for the British and American governments. Dr. Elmer S. Imes, Professor of Physics at Fisk University, engaged in research in molecular physics and was regarded as one of the first to establish that the quantum theory could be expanded to include the rotational status of the molecule. Dr. Percy Julian who had served as a Professor of Chemistry, and as a chemist in the laboratories of Glidden and Company of Chicago, opened the Julian Laboratories under his own direction and rapidly won acclaim for himself with his synthesis of products from soybeans and other natural products. His research in cortisone, sex hormones and soy products marked him out as a distinguished chemist. Lloyd Hall, industrial chemist was a specialist in food products and was chemical director of the Griffith Laboratories in Chicago. Dr. Hildrus A. Poindexter, a graduate of Lincoln University (Pa.), Harvard University (M.D.), and Columbia University (Ph.D.), became Professor of Bacteriology and Preventive Medicine in the Howard University School of Medicine. His contributions to medical journals were significant ones in his field. He has served the U. S. Public Health Service and the Federal Government in health assignments in foreign countries.

Teachers of science.

There were professors in colleges and universities who had been training Negro youth and who had gone into the scientific laboratory areas. Dr. Robert P. Barnes and Dr. Lloyd Ferguson of the Department of Chemistry at Howard University were among the leaders in this endeavor who had also been contributing to chemical research journals. Dr. Herman Branson of the Department of Physics at Howard University was another productive scholar with similar objectives. Dr. N. O. Calloway of Tuskegee Insti-

PERCY L. JULIAN
Chemist noted for useful products from the Soybean.

GEORGE WASHINGTON CARVER
Agricultural Chemist, experimenting with peanuts and potatoes.

tute, Fisk University and the University of Chicago had
been interested in contributions of chemistry to endo-
crinology. George Washington Carver, Chemurgist of
Tuskegee Institute, donated his Humanitarian Award of
$1,000 from the Variety Clubs of America and finally his
estate for the establishment of the George Washington
Carver Foundation, for the continuance of the research in

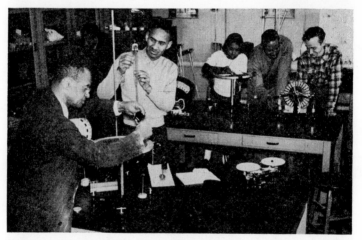

TECHNICIANS AND PHYSICISTS working in the laboratory on intricate
modern problems.

agricultural products and foods in which he had major interests. Dr. Theodore K. Lawless, a graduate of Talladega
College and the Medical School of Northwestern University, a physician in Chicago and a lecturer at Northwestern
had had remarkable success in the treatment of skin diseases. These men had their counterparts in other colleges
and universities where there was dynamic activity in the
expansion of knowledge and in investigating and exploring
natural products with the purpose of discovering better
ones and in improving the processes for securing remedial

ways for better living. The Space Age, and the Government support for education and research had influenced large numbers to select scientific fields for study.

With the technical advance of America it was inevitable that Negroes would move into the areas of engineering and architectural advance. Archie Alexander, who was later Governor of the Virgin Islands, was the **Engineering and** builder of a sewage treatment plant for **architecture.** the city of Des Moines, Iowa and the engineer and builder of the tidal basin bridge from Washington, D. C., across the Potomac to the Virginia side. He was a builder of airports, sewage plants, and power plants. Paul Williams is the best known name among Negroes in architecture, having been architect in California for the homes of such Hollywood stars as Grace Moore, Coreen Griffith and Zasu Pitts, and for such show places as Beverly Wilshire Hotel, Twentieth Century Fox, Sunset Plaza Apartments, Saks Fifth Avenue and for the palatial home of the Columbia Broadcasting executive, William Paley.

Graduates of the engineering and architectural departments of Howard University, an accredited engineering school, were serving in laboratories of aircraft, electronic, automotive and chemical industries. As America was advancing in technology, colored youth were steadily moving in the same direction.

One of the significant areas of change was the collapse of racial barriers in sports. There had been a long reign of Negro boxing champions but the great change in sports came when professional baseball abolished its color line. Joe Louis had a reign of twelve years as world's heavyweight champion. Henry Armstrong held **Sports** three world championships, the featherweight, the lightweight and welterweight championships at the same time. Sugar Ray Robinson also won the welterweight champion-

MUSIC CORPORATION OF AMERICA—BEVERLY HILLS—
PAUL WILLIAM, Architect.

ship in 1946, the middleweight championship in 1951 and regained the middleweight crown in 1959. Floyd Patterson became heavyweight champion in 1956 and defended his title in 1957, 1958 and 1959, the latter defense was against Ingemar Johansson of Sweden. Other Negro champions were represented by Archie Moore, Jersey Joe Wolcott, Ezzard Charles.

The performance of Negroes in boxing was spectacular, but this was soon topped by their appearance in professional baseball. The pioneer in this field was Jackie Robinson who was signed by Branch Rickey, manager of the Brooklyn Dodgers and became the first Negro to break into major league baseball with the Montreal Baseball Team of Canada in 1946. The next year he was signed for the Brooklyn Dodgers. Robinson was born in Cairo, Georgia and later moved with his parents to Pasadena, California, where he attended the public schools, the Pasadena Junior College and the University of California at Los Angeles. He earned twenty-four athletic letters in his career and then served as First Lieutenant in World War II. He was voted "Rookie of the Year" in 1947, and in 1949 as the "Most Valuable Player" in the National League. Robinson's brilliant playing and his undaunted courage together with his exemplary conduct gave acceptance to him as a player and helped open the way for others to follow. He retired from baseball in 1956 and became Vice-President in charge of Personnel of the Chock-Full-O-Nuts Corporation in New York City and was active in civil rights programs and in the work of the National Association for the Advancement of Colored People.

Roy Campanella, who was a catcher and Robinson's teammate on the Dodgers, was voted in 1951 the "Most Valuabe Player Award" in the National League. The same award went to Willie Mays in 1954, Don Newcombe in 1956, Hank Aaron in 1957 and Ernie Banks in 1958. Other

JOE LOUIS
speaks as a soldier—aiding the War Effort.

leading players were Minnie Minoso of Chicago, Wes Covington of Milwaukee. Sam Jones, one of the outstanding pitchers, broke the twenty-five year old strike-out record of Dizzy Dean of 200 batters by striking out 201 batters and also pitched a major league no-hit game in 1955. He was the first Negro pitcher to perform this feat, although Don Newcombe pitched nine hitless innings, then allowed one hit in the tenth inning in 1954. In the years from 1958 to 1961, Negroes were playing on a number of teams in the major leagues and in almost every position. It was not unusual to find these teams having one or more Negro players. In 1959 there were over fifty Negro players in major league baseball.

Negro college football players were quite common and they became gridiron stars in many instances. Basketball after 1950 became another sport in which Negroes were prominent. This **Football and baseball.** was followed by professional football in which the racial barriers were also considerably reduced.

Mal Whitfield of Ohio State University in 1948 and 1952 established the Olympic 800 meter record, and Harrison Dillard was the Olympic champion during the same period. Rafer Johnson in 1958 of the University of California established a new world record in the Decathlon at Moscow. Milton Campbell won the Decathlon in the Olympic game at Melbourne, Aus- **Track and tennis.** tralia in 1956. Ralph Boston was a Broad Jump sensation. Rafer Johnson and Wilma Rudolph carried the stars and stripes to victory in the Olympic games and won gold medals as Americans. Althea Gibson was the women's single champion in 1957 and in 1958 and teamed with associates to become Mixed Doubles Champion in 1957. She ranked at the top of the world's women athletes and was the winner in two annual tournaments of the National Championship Singles for Women at Forest Hills, New

JACKIE ROBINSON

ALTHEA GIBSON and DARLENE HARD
whom Miss Gibson defeated for Championship honors

York and in state and regional contests. She traveled extensively and won international contests on several occasions. Her rise and development as a tennis champion was due primarily to her participation in the American Tennis Association Tournaments held at colleges predominantly for Negroes. These contests led to her first championship experience. She and other young Negroes had their first experiences in tennis tournaments through opportunities provided by this association of tennis players and enthusiasts.

Negro life has had, as is true of American life in general, a large number of organizations. Alexis DeTocqueville in his *Democracy in America,* pointed out that people in aristocratic countries do not have the same reason to unite in order to create action by government as in a democratic nation where people have to learn voluntarily to help one another. This trend has been very active in Negro history in particular and in American history generally. These organizations have also formed a type of school for the people's self-government.

The church has been one of these main factors in Negro life. Its members have been largely fundamentalists in their religious beliefs. The largest numbers have been in the Baptist and Methodist Churches. Outstanding leaders have given direction to religious organizations so that there has been the development of a capable community leadership. Of 100 Negroes in Who's Who in America in 1936-1937, there were thirty-three who were leaders in the Negro Church. Names like those of Dr. **The church.** Joseph H. Jackson of Chicago, Illinois; Dr. Benjamin Mayes of Morehouse College; Dr. James H. Robinson of New York City; Dr. Howard Thurman of Boston University; Dr. Gardner Taylor of Brooklyn, New York; Dr. Adam Clayton Powell of New York City; Bishop J. W. E. Bowen of Atlanta, Georgia; Bishop William J.

WILMA RUDOLPH
International Track Athlete, welcomed to New York after Olympic
Championships

DR. HOWARD THURMAN
Dean of March Chapel
Boston University

DR. BENJAMIN E. MAYS
President of Morehouse College

DR. ARCHIBALD J. CAREY
Alternate Delegate to the United
Nations; Chairman of the Presi-
dent's Committee on Government
Contracts; Chicago Attorney and
A.M.E. Clergyman

BISHOP W. J. WALL
A.M.E. Zion Church

Wall of the A. M. E. Zion Church; Dr. Martin Luther King, Jr., of Atlanta, Georgia; Dr. William J. Faulkner of Chicago; Dr. Arthur D. Gray of Talladega College; Dr. Archie J. Cary, Jr. of Chicago; and hundreds of others including Bishops of Churches with Episcopal government, are representatives of a leadership which has been contributing to the advancement of the Negro population both in religious and social endeavors.

The development of student life in colleges and univer-

MARY CHURCH TERRELL
Educator and Lecturer

MARY MCLEOD BETHUNE
Educator and Public Servant

sities in the United States gave rise to the organization of fraternities and sororities. These organizations dated in the main from the early decades of the twentieth century and directed their interests toward men and women in the colleges. They adopted programs which were for the benefit and advancement of their communities and the people whom they would serve, and not exclusively for themselves. There were fraternal societies of men and women which were organized not only for benefits to their membership

EUGENE KINCKLE JONES
Executive Secretary and General
Secretary, National Urban
League

LESTER B. GRANGER
Executive Secretary, National
Urban League; President; In-
ternational Conference of Social
Work; President, National Con-
ference of Social Work.

MRS. W. H. BALDWIN, JR.
National Urban League Founder

in the case of emergencies but also for the maintenance of scholarship assistance and gifts to needy causes. These organizations gave the people of color great opportunity to become acquainted with organized efforts and also to exercise their abilities as leaders in the development of the fraternal spirit. These organizations included the Prince Hall Grand Lodge of Masons, the United Order of Odd Fellows, The Supreme Grand Lodge of Pythians, the Improved Benevolent Protective Order of Elks of the World, and similar national organizations. The National Association of Colored Women's Clubs has had a history dating from 1896 when Mary Church Terrell began to serve as its first president. The National Council of Negro Women of which Dr. Mary McCleod Bethune was founder-president was also an organization of great influence.

Fraternal organizations and clubs.

The National Urban League, originally known as the National League on Urban Conditions among Negroes, was spreading its influence and services through the work and direction of Dr. E. Kinckle Jones and Dr. Lester B. Granger, its respective Executive Secretaries. They were devoted and loyal in their interracial activities as was one of its founders, Mrs. W. H. Baldwin, Jr., who on retiring as Chairman of the Board of Directors said, "Let us work not as colored people nor as white people for the narrow good of any group alone, but, as American citizens for the common good of our common city, our common country."

The progress which has been made since World War II in the advancement of the Negro people in the United States has been paralleled by developments in human relations. There have been and there are still numbers of obstacles which have prevented and continue to prevent complete solutions of the problems involved in the differences among mankind of race and color. Nevertheless, gains have been made which would indicate that there will be the triumph of the ideas and practices of equality of opportunity for all people.

In this connection, the concept of race has been experiencing new interpretations since World War II. New interpretations and investigations in the fields of anthropology, history, psychology and genetics have thrown new

Differences in people come from the things they learn

They come from the way they live — the chance they have for decent homes, schools, medical care, jobs

DIFFERENCES IN PEOPLE

light on the problem of race. We are now aware that race is partly a physical concept as well as a social one created by society, and that the differences between so-called races based upon the color of skin, the form of the head, the differences in stature and physiognomy, and the texture of hair do not indicate or decide with dogmatism the differences on the bases of capacity between peoples. These physical traits were not to be confused with cultural traits and we have found that the conclusions reached by scientists who worked with

Concept of race.

these problems were quite different from the conclusions drawn in popular ways.

Rapid changes have come in the physical sciences with reference to the atomic bomb, the hydrogen bomb, the use of radar, space discoveries and new discoveries which have affected the relations of peoples and nations. In the field of human relations we have been moving all too slowly. While we would not think of building a world through the physical sciences based upon ignorance, we are endeaving to build such a world in **Human relations.** human relations based upon the lack of knowledge of one another and of the sympathetic understanding of what the groups of the population want. This lack of knowledge concerns also the darker peoples in the United States and the world. We know that knowledge is not enough and there must be motivation and interest toward learning about them. We are aware that an acquaintance and a proper understanding of race must exist or else there will continue to be relationships between people based upon false assumptions of differences between color and intelligence, race and culture.

There are no pure races. There is no exclusive or pure white race or black race or brown race or yellow race, for all of these are crossed races and mixed races, and these mixtures show differences on physical bases. There is no proof that there is a superior race, either on the basis of the measurement of intelligence by the so- **Is there a** called objective tests or by the measure- **superior race?** ments of achievement. There have been principal population stocks of mankind through history but these have become so mingled one with the other through population migrations across the centuries, that it is entirely unscientific to set people apart under a single racial designation.

The United States is one of the great borrowers of civilization as well as a great developer of civilization. All of our early inventions were borrowed from other peoples. The elementary ones, as we well know, the wheel, the lever, and the alphabet were borrowed from the peoples whom we know as backward peoples in Asia, Africa and the Near East. The American colonists who came to the United States borrowed from the Indians and even certain principles of our democratic government were borrowed from Europe and given our interpretations. Then too, not only England and Germany but also Africa had historical experiences with representative government. The peoples who have come to the United States known as immigrants, white and black, have made their contributions to our American life.

The descendants of the darker peoples of Africa have not been so primitive and simple a people as had been gen-
Contributors to civilization. erally supposed, for they have contributed historically to a cultural life in their own communities. It has been said truthfully by Franz Boaz, a professor of Anthropology at Columbia University, "The achievements of the Negro in Africa demonstrates that the race is capable of social and political accomplishment; that it will produce its great men here as it has done in Africa; and that it will contribute its part to the welfare of the community."

Racial prejudice which denies this truth can be overcome through education, experiences and contacts with the people who are disliked before we know them. They are disliked on the basis of what we have heard from other prejudiced persons or what we assume because of their physical differences of color, features hair, nose, lips, language, religion or custom, and we believe that they must be inferior and kept in inferior places because they are different. Separation breeds further prejudice. When it is realized that one race or one color or religion or custom is not superior to another and that attainment has been made by individuals of all races, colors, religions and custom, equal opportunity can then be given without hesitation in the interest of national well being. The glory of America can be in its differences, its *e pluribus unum*—its many in one, rather than its single likeness. It should be known and recognized that peoples of different racial and physical appearances, different religions and different cultures have contributed to American civilization, that they as population groups can live side by side in peace and in understanding, and that there are superior individuals in each group who have qualities for leadership and cooperation. These people should be utilized and given opportunity for the greater advancement of all American life.

IMMIGRANTS ALL

CHAPTER XXXIX

THE DARKER PEOPLES ABROAD IN TRANSITION

The study of the Negro in the United States ofttime failed to take into consideration the broader aspects of the peoples of color in the world. With the end of isolation in international affairs, so far as separate nations were concerned, there was need for information concerning other darker peoples. Race and color were not such great walls of separation between nations of people as they were within the United States. Discriminations had not been practiced against them as they had against Americans of color. However, with the extension of the influence and contacts of the United States over the world, there was a fear among peoples that the color line might also be extended. This belief gave an international aspect to the problem of color in the United States. The relationships were so close that the Negro in our history had become the Negro in world history.

International aspects of color.

This was due mainly, as perceptive Americans know, to the known fact that the colored peoples of Asia, Africa and the islands of the seas totaled two-thirds of the people of the world. These people could think rarely about the United States without considering its 19,000,000 darker people. They could see that mainly on account of their color, these black and brown people like themselves, were denied their fair share of the nation's substance and opportunity. This fact gave a hollowness to our protestations and excuses about these conditions, in spite of the progress which these darker people were making in our history.

732

In this connection, the use of the word "Negro" for the designation of persons of color abroad was subjected to limitation and non-use. The tendency was to confine its uses to persons of color in the United States. Others of the same color abroad were designated by the national names of the countries of their birth and allegiance. They were Nigerians, Ghanians, Liberians, and Haitians. Although they were of the same color, their national relationships induced Americans to use the names of their nations. Embarrassments to which foreign persons had suffered in the United States for having been mistaken for Negro-Americans had demonstrated how shallow this difference was and these instances have had international repercussions. On the other hand, colored peoples in the lands outside of the United States had been concerned also with the superior attitudes of European peoples who had colonized their lands and taken possession of their governments and resources. These situations had been equally the concerns of the colored people in the United States. Thousands in the United States had identified themselves with the struggles of black peoples abroad for recognition, independence and mutual respect. The limitations and frustrations at home had given a basis for these sympathies abroad.

The designation of Negro.

Opposition to the use of the word "Negro" had developed over the years. Richard B. Moore of New York City, author of *The Name "Negro," Its Origin and Evil Use.* (1960), believed that "the proper name for peoples has thus become, in this period of crucial change and rapid reformation on a world scale, a vital factor in determining basic attitudes involving *how,* and even *whether,* peoples will continue to live together on this shrinking planet." The *Afro-American* declined to use the word "Negro" in its newspaper and used in its stead "colored." Still others were more concerned with the basic historical facts which

gave racial character to darker peoples, particularly in the
United States, whatever the name, and were of the view
that these facts were primary considerations. They preferred to make the name "Negro" more worthy by reveal-
ing the facts that would give it a different connotation and
meaning rather than to accept the interpretation of others
and run away from its use.

The special considerations given to African diplomats
by Americans were sources of irritation, mirth and laughter as the ridiculous aspects of fair treatment of black and
brown representatives from outside the United States were
Attitudes of compared with the experiences of darker
Africans. Americans at home. These Africans being
mistaken for Americans had discriminations practiced on
them in housing, restaurants and travel. A palliation of
these situations came through official apologies and the
appointment of persons to assist and guide them away
from embarrassments, and also to make adequate provision
for them. Then, Negroes in the United States saw the
difference which a turban, a type of dress and a foreign
relationship would make, and they wondered about their
treatment as American citizens.

A program which gave Negro-American leaders an opportunity to interest their group in foreign aspects of color
was in the meetings of the Pan-African Congresses. The
first of these Congresses met in Paris in 1921, under the
leadership of W. E. B. DuBois and Rayford W. Logan.
The second meeting was in London in 1923, the third in
1924, the fourth in 1927 in New York. There
Congresses was a gap of years and again there was the
fifth Pan-African Congress at Manchester, England in
1945. In initiating these Congresses, Dr. DuBois had said
that the Negro-American problem had to "be thought of
and settled only with continual reference to the problems
of French Negroes, and English Negroes, and above all, of

the African Negroes." A plan was undertaken by the League of Colored Peoples established in London in 1931 for an all African Congress in 1944. This Congress was to plan cooperation with an expected peace conference after World War II. This conference was called in the interest of "the peoples of African descent all over the world."

These conferences manifested the interest which the darker peoples had in one another. These people in the United States wanted to know more of the colored peoples in the states abroad. Information concerning the colored people in the United States had also become of interest to colored peoples abroad. The U. S. Office of Information had as one of its purposes the furnishing of information concerning the United States to na- **A knowledge of** tions and peoples of other countries. **darker peoples** This office sent out information abroad **abroad and at home.** with reference to the Negro and his progress in the United States. The United Nations and the international relations of the United States had contributed to this interest. These relationships were of great importance to Americans of color to learn more of the colored peoples outside of the United States, for their past and their future affected our history.

The most important event near the close of World War II was the assembly of the United Nations Conference on International Organization at San Fran- **United Nations** cisco, California, April 25 to June 26, **conference.** 1945. The charter of the United Nations was drawn up and signed by forty-one nations, and by 1961 the membership had reached 100 nations. Among the nations admitted as charter members were the governments of the darker peoples of India, Egypt, Ethiopia, Haiti and Liberia. Accredited representatives who were Negroes included Dr. Ralph Bunche, the Acting Chief then of the Division of Dependent Territories of the U. S. Department of State;

Dr. W. E. B. DuBois and Dr. Walter White of the NAACP; Dr. Mordecai W. Johnson, President of Howard University; Dr. Mary McLeod Bethune of the National Council of Negro Women and Negro newspaper representatives. Negroes followed these deliberations with deep interest be-

WALTER WHITE

cause they knew that protests against discriminations in South Africa would have their repercussions on discriminations in the United States.

The charter pledged the nations who signed it to maintain international peace and security and to cooperate in

RALPH BUNCHE
Deputy Secretary General, United Nations

the establishment of conditions favorable to these goals. The nations pledged themselves in the charter to prevent

United Nations'— war, to reaffirm faith in fundamental
the charter. human rights and in the dignity and
worth of human persons, to establish justice and respect for obligations by treaty, to promote social progress, to practice tolerance and to employ international machinery for the promotion of economic and social advancement of all people. This was the first international organizational assembly of governments to which the colored peoples of the world were brought in as full members. Peoples of color saw in this organization and its charter, the foundation for the continuance of their own efforts for freedom from discrimination.

After the first assembly of the United Nations opened in London, January, 10, 1946, and the United Nations Securi-

League of Nations ty Council met in its first meeting at
and United Nations Hunter College, New York City,
commissions. March 25, the League of Nations in
Geneva, Switzerland, voted itself out of existence and turned over its physical assets to the United Nations on April 18. The United Nations with its Security Council, Trusteeship Council, Economic and Social Council, the International Court of Justice and the Commission on Human Rights, were among its important agencies. Dr. Ralph Bunche, Professor of Political Science, Howard University, and a member of the Division of Dependent Territories of the U. S. Department of State, served as Director of the Trusteeship Council and later as Deputy Secretary-General. He was awarded the Nobel Peace Prize in 1950 in recognition of his work as mediator for the United Nations in the Palestine quarrel.

Negroes have served as Alternate Delegates to the General Assembly of the United Nations. They were Edith Sampson, Chicago Attorney; Archibald J. Carey, Jr., Chicago Clergyman and Attorney; Channing H. Tobias,

New York YMCA Executive; Robert L. Brokenburr, Indianapolis Attorney; Marian Anderson, Concert Artist; Charles Anderson, Louisville Attorney; Zelma George, Lecturer and Musician. **Negro delegates.** Charles H. Mahoney, Detroit Attorney and Insurance Executive, was the first Negro-American to serve as a full delegate to the General Assembly. These representatives

CHANNING H. TOBIAS
International YMCA Secretary; Chairman NAACP Board of Directors; Alternate Delegate to United Nations.

CHARLES H. MAHONEY
Former President, Great Lakes Mutual Life Insurance Company; First Negro Delegate to the United Nations.

worked with the skill and statesmanship which characterized other American delegates.

A conference for the establishment of the educational, scientific and cultural organization of the United Nations was initated by the government of the United Kingdom and the government of France in London, November 1-16, 1945. Forty-five nations were represented at the meeting and seven international organizations with observers. It was approved that the seat of

United Nations educational, scientific and cultural organization—UNESCO.

Unesco would be Paris. The constitution was adopted in its preamble stated the following: "That since wars begin in the minds of men, it is in the minds of men that the defenses of peace must be constructed; that ignorance of each other's ways and lives has been a common cause throughout the history of mankind of that suspicion and mistrust between the peoples of the world through which their differences have all too often broken into war; that the great and terrible war which is now ended was a war made possible by the denial of the democratic principles of the dignity, equality and mutual respect of men, and by the propagation, in their place, through ignorance and prejudice, of the doctrine of the inequality of men and races."

Unesco was to become one of the important international organizations working in the area of the minds of men in order to produce more effective human relations between nations and peoples. Dr. Charles S. Johnson, President of Fisk University, was a member of the United States delegation to this first Unesco meeting in Paris. **Negro-American representatives to UNESCO.** He served also as a member of the Executive Committee of the U. S. Commission for Unesco and as an American corresponding member of the Unesco Project for Scientific and Cultural History of Mankind. Dr. E. Franklin Frazier, Professor of Sociology at Howard University, Washington, D. C., was the Chairman of the Committee of Applied Sciences of Unesco which reported modern studies of race.

Negroes were encouraged by these evidences of equality of representation for darker nations and the references to human rights which were announced in the Charter of the **Discrimination—a United Nations issue.** United Nations, and the work of the United Nations Educational, Scientific and Cultural Organization. When the racial discriminations in South Africa were considered in the United

Nations, the Negro Press continued to express the view that discriminations in the United States, although a domestic problem, might also be a subject for consideration as an international one at some later period. Negro scholars, such as Dr. W. E. B. DuBois in his *Color and Democracy* (New York, 1945), and Dr. Rayford W. Logan in his *The Negro and the Post War World* (Washington, 1945) were writing and speaking about colonialism, and the problems of Africa and the darker peoples.

The growth of the Asian-African bloc in the United Nations represented increased strength against colonialism. Japan and India as nations which are colored—from whatever angle they are viewed—have demonstrated that cultural attainments can be made with Western techniques and their applications to their materials. The people of color in Africa realize that these achievements prove that they have nothing to do with color superiority and they are confident that they can do it too.

The admission of African states to the United Nations has increased the influence of the Asian-African states in the United Nations. Hearty welcomes have been given by all representatives of the Nations in the United Nations to the newly independent African states. One of these expressions came from Zulfekor Ali Bhutto, leader of the Pakistan delega- **Asian-African bloc.** tion. On September 20, 1960, he spoke of the "tremendous youth and vigor these new states would bring to the United Nations." He said further, "The tremendous upsurge of freedom which we have witnessed in the African continent during the last year or two now reaches culmination in the admission of all these states to the United Nations. Colonialism bows out of Africa. This moment is a point of time when all nations, big and small, rededicate themselves to one purpose—of a world free from fear, in which we live as good neighbors, in peace, in unity, and above all, in dignity."

RAYFORD W. LOGAN
Author: *The Negro and the Post War World; Diplomatic Relations between the United States and Haiti.*

A more direct approach was made by Dr. Nnamdi Azikiwe, Governor-General of Nigeria in his inaugural address, entitled "Respect for Human Dignity," "We regard all races of the human family as equal. **Dr. Azikiwe's** Under no circumstances shall we accept **inaugural address.** the idea that the black race is inferior to any other race. No matter where this spurious doctrine may prevail, it may be in Lodmar or Sharpville or Decatur, we shall never admit that we are an inferior race, because if we accept the Christian or Muslin doctrine that God is perfect, and that man was made in the image of God, then it would be sacriligious, if not heretical, to believe that we are an inferior race. We cannot concede that it is in our national interest to fraternize with such nations which practice race prejudice and we must not acquiesce in such an outrageous insult on the black race. In fact, we must regard it as a mark of disrespect and an unfriendly act if any country with whom we have friendly relations indulges in race prejudice in any shape or form, no matter how it may be legally cloaked."

There were Negroes who represented the United States Government in foreign lands and participated in our diplomatic relations. The ranking Negro diplomat continued to be as in previous years, the United States Ambassador to the Republic of Liberia on the West Coast of Africa. Richard Jones, Chicago busi- **Negro diplomatic** nessman, had served in this position and **representatives.** also as an alternate delegate to the United Nations. However, he was succeeded by a white appointee. There was unfavorable reaction among Negroes to this appointment. The hope was often expressed in the Negro Press that this may have meant that Negroes would be appointed to non-Negro countries in the diplomatic service. Clifford R. Wharton, graduate of Boston University, entered the U. S. Foreign Service in 1925. He was assigned to foreign service as representative of the United States, to Liberia, the

NNAMDI AZIKIWE
Governor-General, Nigeria

Canary Islands, Madagascar, Portugal, and the Azores. In 1957 he was appointed Ambassador to Romania. This was the first time that a Negro had served in such a capacity to a non-Negro country. Attorney John R. Wilkins was appointed Legal Counsel of the International Cooperation Agency in Southeast Asia. Attorney Robert K. Shoecraft, a graduate of Central State College and Ohio State University was appointed Attorney of the Trust Territory of the Pacific Islands including Guam. Three Negroes were in the 1,140 Foreign Service Reserve and 38 in the Foreign Staff Corps of 3,527.

While these were appointments of the diplomatic and

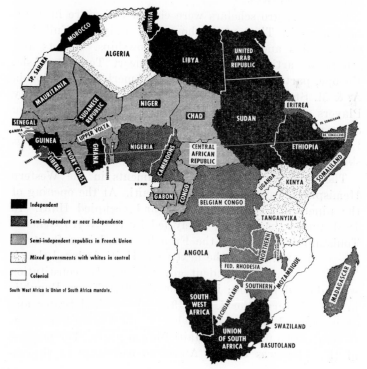

AFRICA IN 1960

advisory ranks in which Negroes had served, the office of Governor of the Virgin Islands was another appointment in which Negroes had served. Archie Alexander of Des Moines, Iowa, and W. C. Gordon of California, have served recently as Virgin Island Governors. There have been other appointments also to the staffs of American officials abroad. Frank Snowden, Dean of the College of Liberal Arts, Howard University, served as Cultural Attache to the United States Embassy at Rome, Italy. Rupert Lloyd was First Secretary of the United States Embassy in Paris, France. Negroes were with the agents of the United States Information Agency, the Point IV Program and other international services.

Selected Negro scholars were chosen to lecture in countries abroad. They were chosen to study on Fulbright Scholarships and other foreign fellowships. Artists and groups of artists were sent on Concert Tours to Asia, Europe, parts of Africa, and South America. The Florida A. & M. State University Players, the Howard University Players and the Howard University Choir toured foreign areas giving concerts and recitals. Negroes also went to Liberia, Ethiopia, India and other countries to serve as skilled instructors to the peoples.

The oldest of the Negro governments in the Western Hemisphere was the Republic of Haiti. At the opening of the nineteenth century, France had occupied Haiti. In 1803, under the Haitian Army led by the Negro General, Touissant L'Ouverture, the French were driven from the island, and in the next year, Haiti declared that it **Haiti** was an independent government. Its constitution was adopted in 1805; it became the first Negro Republic in the Western World. In 1915, the United States and Haiti entered into a treaty, whereby the United States was to control the finances of Haiti for ten years. The purpose of this plan was to give American assistance in the improvement of the finances of Haiti. This was known as the American Occupation of Haiti. A second treaty was signed extending the time of occupation to another ten years. The Haitians protested against this occupation. The American troops were kept in Haiti until 1934, having been there for nineteen years.

After the American withdrawal, Haiti continued its way as an independent government with changes taking place

FRANCOIS DuVALIER
President of Haiti

TOM MBOYA
Brilliant Young Nationalist
Leader in Kenya

in its presidency from time to time, due to elections and at times changes by revolution. Haiti with its mountains, rivers, market places, primary peasant life, its French customs, music and dances, drew its historical traditions and influences from Africa and France. It was the only French-speaking country in the Western Hemisphere. This Black Republic had relationships to our history which made its peaceful continuance of importance to our government and people.

AFRICAN DELEGATES to the African Student Conference at Howard University, on the steps of the National Capitol, Washington, D. C., June, 1953.

Since World War II, the independent and republican
movements in Africa have been rapid and have increased
in rapidity. The old colonial map of Africa   **African**
has completely changed as black nationalism   **independence.**
has spread over the entire continent either as independent
governments or as governments within the British Empire
or the French community. Portugal has felt this pressure
in 1961.

The movement has traveled rapidly within ten years.
Only Liberia and Ethiopia were independent in 1950.
Libya joined these ranks in 1951, Egypt and United Arab
Republic in 1953, although its constitution dated from
1922; Tunisia and Sudan in 1956; Guinea in 1958, Morocco
in the same year, and Nigeria in 1960. These changes became more rapid with 1960. Who in the West would have
predicted one year before that, 14 African nations, including the Congo would be added to the list of free states in
Africa in 1960, which included the Cameroons, Togoland,
Mali Federation, Malagasy, Somalia, Somaliland, Nigeria,
Dahomey, Ivory Coast, Niger, Upper Volta, Central African Republic and the territories of the French Community? The year 1960 closed with 24 independent states
in Africa including the Malagasy Republic on the Island
of Madagascar off the Southeast Coast. In 1961 Sierra
Leone and Uganda, among others became independent.
The tide of independence swept on, additional governmental changes were impending, and the end of the trials and
errors of freedom in Africa had not come. It is estimated
that 83 million Africans in 1961 had governments of their
own making.

In 1953, the first stirrings of overt unrest began in the
Continent of Africa, although there were long-time evidences of dissatisfaction with colonialism as conducted by
European nations. Kenya in East Africa was the
scene of the activity of the Mau Mau Society, a   **Kenya**
secret organization opposing white dominance and de-

manding better land for the use of black Kenyans. Following a raid on Lari, near Nairobi on March 26, over five hundred arrests were made. Jomo Kenyatta, a courageous African leader and President of the Kenya African Union was sentenced to imprisonment although he had denounced the Mau Mau activities. These activities were declared illegal. Kenyatta was released in 1959, only to be sent to a lonely isolated post, but he was again released in 1961. However, the uncertainties were continued, as black Kenyans pressed for changes under the active leadership of Tom Mboya, James Gichuru and Dr. Kiano.

A second change in Africa in 1953 was the proclamation of Egypt as a Republic on June 19, through military action under General Mohammed Naguib, who was named Premier. The former was removed from the Presidency on
Egypt October 26, 1954, after the reports of an attempted assassination of Gamal Abdul Nasser, who had led in the ousting of King Farouk. In 1956 Nasser nationalized the Suez Canal and seized control of the Canal Company. Israel and Egypt agreed to a cease fire proposal of the United Nations in 1957. One year later, the United Arab Republic was formed of Egypt and Syria, with Yemen in a federated agreement, and with Nasser as President. Closely associated with these movements are the stirrings for independence in Tunis, Algeria and North Africa. These movements will have effects upon the continued rise of African nations in the sixties.

The Republic of Liberia for nearly a century was the only African independent government on the West Coast of Africa. It had its beginnings in the efforts of the American Colonization Society which was organized in 1817 to settle free Negroes in West Africa. These efforts were
Liberia never very successful but there were Negroes from the United States who settled in this West African area. In spite of many discouragements and misunderstandings between the Africans and the new settlers,

the Colony was declared on July 26, 1847, as the Free and Independent Republic of Liberia. Its progress was slow, because of its hot, dry climate, its lack of a commercial harbor and its few contacts with the larger nations.

When its resources became known, a loan was made in 1912 to Liberia for its development by the J. P. Morgan Company of New York. In 1926, learning of the possibility of profit from rubber, the Firestone Rubber Company of Ohio established plantations in Liberia for the planting and development of rubber and made a loan to the Liberian government. This company has, in Liberia, the largest rubber plantations in the world. The first loan with the Morgan Company was paid off with funds from the Firestone loan. The harbor was dredged and built so that deep-water ships could use the ports of Monrovia. The water supplies, the sewerage system, and roads were constructed. Iron was discovered and began to be mined by the Republic Steel Company of Cleveland, Ohio. The production of Liberia's natural resources expanded rapidly.

The Technical Assistance Program of the United States, known also as Point IV, sent technicians, scientists and teachers to Liberia, and among them was Dr. John W. Davis, former President of West Virginia State College. The Country began a period of prosperity under the leadership of President William V. S. Tubman, who was inaugurated for the third time as President in 1955. Liberia ranked fourth among the nations of the world in ships under its registration in 1955. It was fourth after Great Britain, the United States and Norway. While these ships were registered by Liberia, they were more often owned by other nations, but they were carrying Liberian products to many parts of the world.

One of the oldest of African states was Ghana. Its early history revealed a civilization of significant merit. It was from this area that millions of slaves were brought to the United States. After wars with the Ghanians, and

PRESIDENT WILLIAM V. S. TUBMAN OF LIBERIA

especially with the war-like Ashanties, Ashanti was annexed by the British Government. A protectorate was declared over the Northern territories in 1897 and Ashanti
was annexed by the British Crown in 1901. During the
First World War and following the Second World
War, Ghanians began to show more active interest   **Ghana**
in the independence of their governments than at any
other period in their history. The Gold Coast, as Ghana

PRIME MINISTER KWAME NKRUMAH of Ghana and PRIME MINISTER
JAWAHARAL NEHRU of India, representative leaders of black and
brown peoples.

was then known, was the first African Government to
achieve its independence. This little country of 4,911,000
people was one of the richest of Great Britain's colonies.
More of the Gold Coast people were educated and prosperous than in most African colonies. Its properity was due
largely to the growth of cocoa. The Gold Coast produced
more than one-half of the world's supply. There are also

gold mines, large forests of mahogany and valuable trees and plants.

Gold Coast voters went to the polls in 1956 to give their decision upon independence and home rule. By the vote of the people, an independent government with an All-African assembly was requested of Great Britain. This was the first colonial nation on the West Coast of Africa since the establishment of the Republic of Liberia. Dr. Kwame Nkrumah, a graduate of Lincoln University in Pennsylvania and the University of Pennsylvania after being released from prison under British authority, led his political party in victory and became the first African government representative in Ghana. The announcement of its independence on March 5, 1957, marked the end of the British Colony of the Gold Coast and the birth of Ghana as a free country within the British Commonwealth of Nations.

This new nation took its place beside the smaller nations in the British Commonwealth, Canada, New Zealand and India. Ghana was different because it was an all-Negro government and the first Negro West African state to appear in the twentieth century. Nevertheless, Prime Minister Nkrumah said, "the independence of Ghana is meaningless unless it is linked with the total liberation of the whole of Africa." A new republican constitution was approved by the people's vote and became effective on July 1, 1960.

The advance toward self-government in West Africa showed itself also in Nigeria. It was the largest all-Negro country in the world, with a large literate population. It was three times the size of Britain. It had a popu-

Nigeria lation of 32,000,000 with only 16,000 white persons. Its three main sections were striving for educational and economic development as the beginning of self-government. These sections of the nation were also divided in

Peoples Abroad In Transition

PRESIDENT KWAME NKRUMAH of Ghana in
African Costume

PRESIDENT KWAME NKRUMAH of Ghana, Addressing
the U. N. General Assembly, March 7, 1961.

their planning and were divided further by such forces as family, clans, tribes and leaderships.

In Eastern Nigeria, the smallest of Nigeria's three regions, Dr. Nnamdi Azikiwe a graduate of Lincoln University and First African Governor-General, worked to bring industry into his area, to stimulate markets and to build schools, hospitals and roads. He made visits to the United States and tried to interest American businessmen in erecting plants and engaging in business in Nigeria. Harbor improvements, railroad and road building and bridge construction were the bases of prosperity for this section of Nigeria.

Dr. Nnamdi Azikiwe— Eastern region.

In Western Nigeria, there was an area of 45,376 square miles and a population of 6,352,472. Premier Obafemi Awolowo had been interested in improving the economic life of his people and through his travels and invitations to business influenced the more rapid development of this territory. He visited the United States and Canada in 1956 for this purpose. This section had many educated leaders, and was the most developed and richest in Nigeria. In this region, the Yoruba art with its bronzes, terra-cottas and wood carvings have been prized in the museums of the world.

Awolowo— Western Nigeria.

The Northern section looked toward the same goals of education and economic advance. This Northern region under Premier Alhaju Ahmadu embraced more than three-fourths of the total area of Nigeria and had more than one-half of the total population. Farming and cattle raising were the leading pursuits of the people. The Mohammedan religion predominated in this section. It was the last of the three regions to become self-governing.

Northern region.

The first step toward unity in independence was taken in 1956 with the Nigerian Constitutional Conference held in London, England. Each of the three regions was repre-

PREMIER ABAFEMI AWOLOWO
West Nigeria

PREMIER ALHAJI AHMADIE
North Nigeria

NNAMDI AZIKIWE
Governor General of Nigeria

ABUBAKAR BALEWA
Prime Minister of Nigeria

sented by delegates. Steps were taken at this meeting for the independence of Nigeria, within the British Commonwealth of nations. These three sections formed the Federation of Nigeria, with the Capitol at Lagos, and each with its own government.

The Prime Minister, Sir Abubakar Tafawa Balewa is British educated and one of the capable Nigerians of his day. He has said boldly, "As long as other nations are interested in ruling other people in Africa, there will be trouble." Nigeria was an undeveloped country but economic advances were being made by Nigerians. Agricultural products were increasing. Their export of tobacco was 25,000 pounds in the first nine months of 1956, compared with 2,000 pounds for the same period in 1955. Orders were placed for the installation of 30,000 more telephones in Nigeria by 1960. There were then forty daily air flights to and from its capitol city. Nigeria was destined to play a leading role in Africa's economic and political future.

The Belgium Congo had been a Belgian Colony since 1885 and became an independent state in 1960. Belgium had not encouraged education in the Congo so as to prepare its people for self-government. This situation was different from the results in Nigeria and Ghana. It was **Congo** not difficult for strife and division to develop or to be motivated in the Congo. Patrice Lumumba had led in the termination of Belgium rule. He was elected Prime Minister of the Republic of the Congo. His death, attributed to the divisive elements, and through which he became somewhat of a hero, led to a struggle between pro-Lumumba and anti-Lumumba forces. In the Katanga Province, the Kasai Province and the rivalries of Congo President Moise Tshombe of Katanga, President Joseph Kasavubu of the Congolese Central Government, Antione Gizenga at Stanleyville, Lieutenant General Joseph D. Mobutu, Commander of the Congolese forces of the Cen-

PRESIDENT KASAVUBU OF THE CONGO

tral Government, Albert Kalonji, President of South Kasai, and others, the future seemed to be clouded. However, the call for a Parliament for united action in the Congo, through representation of all elements under urgings of the United Nations, was promising.

Located in East Africa, Ethiopia is an agricultural country of 16,000,000 darker people. Its history goes back to Biblical days when the royal family began with Menelik, **Ethiopia** the son of King Solomon and the Queen of Sheba. Menelik II became Emperor in 1889 and the tribes of Ethiopia were brought under his rule as emperor. For five years, Italy waged war in an effort to conquer Ethiopia. On March 1, 1896, the Battle of Adowa was fought, and a great victory was gained by the Ethiopians over the Italians.

Haile Selassie I became emperor in 1930, with a Council of Ministers, a Senate, and a Chamber of Deputies. He began to bring modern economic methods to Ethiopia and to train an army. Italy continued to plan to regain its control over Ethiopia. Finally in 1936, Italian troops invaded Ethiopia, in spite of the opposition of the League of Nations and Addis Ababa, the Ethiopian capital was **Haile** captured. Ethiopia then was made a part of **Selassie.** Italy's East African territory. World War II brought freedom to Ethiopia. It was the first of the nations to be retaken by the armies of the Allied Nations. The Italian Army surrendered to the British and Ethiopian Army on November 27, 1941, and the recognition of its independence came in 1942. Five years after his expulsion, Haile Selassie again entered his capital, Addis Ababa. The British troops left Ethiopia in 1948.

Illiteracy was very high in this country, and it was reported that over 70 per cent of the people could not read or write in 1956. However, emphasis was being placed on education and in 1953-54, there were 431 state primary

EMPEROR HAILE SELASSIE OF ETHIOPIA

schools with 69,000 pupils and 11 secondary schools with
2,155. Foreign missions also maintained schools. New
New methods were introduced in agriculture and in-
methods. dustry, and Ethiopia, while moving more slowly than Ghana and Nigeria, seemed to be moving forward
to take its place among the African nations of the world.
Whether or not the attempt of 1961 to overthrow the
regime of Haile Selassie will lead to the introduction of
reforms more rapidly, will be for future decision.

The African peoples in all parts of the African Continent were in movement at mid-century toward self-government and self-determination—a word used widely since
World War I. The drums were beating their discontent in
all Africa. One by one, the former colonies were demanding
independence and participation in government. They were
budding states with English, French, Belgian, Portuguese
legacies. They were determined to bring political order out
of the chaotic conditions temporarily created and assisted
by imperialism in its decadence.

Parts of East Africa, North Africa, Central Africa and
South Africa were feeling the effects of this movement
African among peoples for freedom. They were striv-
movements. ing to achieve unity among themselves and
economic and political democracy for their people, although
Africa is plagued by rivalries and traditions. These divisions are not too different historically from those in
Europe and the United States which have also broken into
war and hindered progress. Numerous tribes with their
leaders regarded themselves as the equals of others. Unfortunately this is the way of mankind, white or black.
Tribalism was then challenged by the movement of freedom which was spreading with tremendous speed in every
direction.

It was well-known to them that if they could achieve in
the ways of united government and make wise use of their

PRIME MINISTER SEKOU TOURE
Guinea

MADAME SEKOU TOURE
Guinea

PROMINENT
AFRICAN
LEADERS

DR. HASTINGS BANDA
Nyasaland

PRIME MINISTER PHILBERT
TSIRANANO, Madagascar

QUEEN SALOTE
Tonga

natural and human resources, African freedom would be advanced. There has been an awakening of all Africa,

African awakening. through the activities of educated Africans, the introduction of new industry, the movement of the people from the hut in the African bush and village to the city and town. Similar changes in govern-

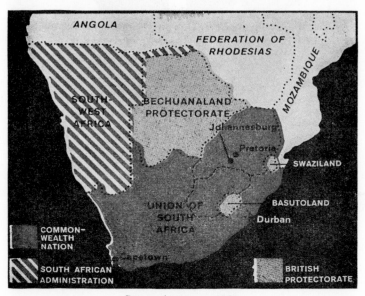

SOUTH AFRICA IN 1960
South Africa has administrative control of South West Africa, once German controlled. Swaziland, Basutoland and Bechuanaland are British Protectorates.

ment and life were seen in 1960 in Guinea, the Sudan, the Cameroun Republic, Somalia, Togoland, British Cameroons, Gambia, Mali, Ivory Coast, the Federation of Rhodesia, and in Nyasaland, Tanganyika, Uganda, Sierra Leone, the French Community and the Portuguese area.

South Africa, with its 3,000,000 whites, 10,000,000 blacks

and 1,500,000 persons of mixed or Asiatic ancestry, has adopted a policy of white rule and superior privileges for whites. South Africa's defense of *apartheid* and its determination to maintain it have pointed the way **South** backward for Africa and have damaged race **Africa.** relations in all Africa. This attitude was continued despite the opposition of the Asian-African bloc in the United Nations. The African National Congress, the Pan-Africanist Congress and other organized opposition groups developed more overt opposition and non-violent activities to the principles and practices of the government party in control of the South African Parliament. There were explosion and smoldering revolution all over Africa. Where the next abrupt change will take place no one knows.

In meeting these changes in Africa, the American Government moved slowly, but our African relationships and interests must be accelerated. Too little and too late should not be our policy. Our military was aware of the strategic importance of African areas. Our Department of State created an African Division in its work. Our plans must be speeded up because of East-West competition as well as the needs of Africans themselves. In spite of our treatment in history of the Negro-Americans, Africans still look to the United States for assistance, leadership and cooperation.

Black and brown peoples were in various parts of the Latin American states to the South of the **Latin** United States. It is estimated that there were **America.** 25,000,000 such people in these areas at the middle of the century. The Negro background could be seen plainly in Haiti, Cuba, the Dominican Republic, Panama and Brazil. Such countries as Venezuela, Columbia, Ecuador and parts of Central America have Negroes in the populations varying from one-tenth to one-third. Even Argentina has a number of Negroes in its population. Color has been and can continue to be a factor of contention in these geographical areas, for Africa has left its imprints on the populations of the areas south of the United States.

These people have had individuals who have distinguished themselves, not as Negroes but as men in these countries, and as leaders and soldiers in their campaigns for independence in the Western world. Their talents in music, literature, art, the dance and rhythm manifested qualities which have received recognition. Negroes have had considerable influence on the folklore and customs of Latin Americans, and to overlook this fact is to ignore a great factor in their history and cultural tradition.

The term "West Indies" is applied to the islands which form a curve extending from Florida south to the Northern Coast of South America and eastward. They begin nearest Florida with Cuba and the Bahama Islands and end with Trinidad off the coast of South America. Jamaica, Haiti, San Domingo and Puerto Rico are called the Greater Antilles. The Lesser Antilles include the smaller islands which seem to be mere dots in the Caribbean Sea. Following the voyages of Columbus and his successors, these **The West** islands passed under the control of Spain in **Indies.** the sixteenth century. The continuous flow of tropical products to Europe, such as sugar, coffee, tobacco, rice, cotton and pimento—led other nations to seek to claim and occupy some of these islands. As a result, Western European nations finally built up colonial empires. It was against these empires and their colonialism that these peoples have protested and self-government had developed. They were still striving for better status and for the cooperation of the United States.

The word "Negro" needs some consideration as it is related to the West Indies. From the earliest periods, there were persons known as "Free Persons of Color" and "Free Blacks." Either of these would have been classed as

CENTRAL AMERICA AND THE WEST INDIES

"Negroes" in the United States. However, since the fixed color line had developed in parts of the British Empire,

The word "Negro" in the West Indies. the thoughtful people in the Negro population were realizing that they must work together in order to reach the goal of equality. As a result, they were more willing to accept the term "Negro," although they looked upon themselves as Jamaicans, Barbadians, or West Indians.

The islands of the British West Indies became the British West Indies Federation on April 22, 1957, when the legislature of the Federation was welcomed by Her Royal Highness Princess Margaret of Great Britain. A University College of the West Indies had been established in Jamaica.

The British Colonies entering the Federation were: Trinidad-Tobago, Barbadoes, the Windward Islands of Grenada, Saint Vincent, Saint Lucia and Dominica and the

West Indian leadership. Leeward Islands of Antiqua, Saint Kitts, Monserrat and Jamaica, although Jamaica had subsequently withdrawn. Leaders in this project were: Eric Williams, First Minister and Premier of Trinidad-Tobago; Norman W. Manley, Chief Minister of Jamaica; Sir Grantley H. Adams, Premier of Barbadoes and Sir W. Alexander Bustamente of Jamaica. These islands were dependent upon the production of agricultural products, with sugar as the chief product.

These darker peoples in various parts of the world have come to realize that they have a common origin and related heritage—Africa; and that they have come out of slavery and reconstruction and are making their way to freedom. They have seen the value of history and they are making history. These endeavors contribute to their need and ours for knowledge of Africa's history.

Just as marked changes had taken place in Africa within the past two decades, a change had also occurred in Africa's historical tradition. New viewpoints on African peoples and their civilizations were being accepted by peoples of the Western world, just as they were compelled to revise their views of the "heathen" peoples of Japan, China and India. There had been the old tradition of Africa as uncivilized, savage, cannibalistic, a child-like continent, there had been reaction against it, and there had been a renewal of this reaction. The reactions to Africa and African history have been

Africa's historical tradition.

BRANTLEY H. ADAMS
Barbadoes

NORMAN W. MANLEY
Founder of the International
Peoples Party of Jamaica

the results of a resurgence of historical truth, and the breath-taking transformations in Africa which have presented challenges to all the world.

The historical truth about Africa and its peoples was announced in its organization aspects with the establishment of the Association for the Study of Negro Life and History under the leadership of Dr. Carter G. Woodson on September 9, 1915. The Association was incorporated under the

laws of the District of Columbia on October 3, 1915. In
January, 1916, the Founder, Dr. Woodson, brought out the
The ASNLH. first issue of the *Journal of Negro History,*
which since then has been published regular-
ly every quarter in the year without missing a single issue.
Ten years later, in 1926, the Association began the celebra-
tion of *Negro History Week* and in 1937 the *Negro History
Bulletin* was issued. Throughout all this period, the cause
of African historical truth was proclaimed at annual sessions and at the annual Negro History Week periods, and
this work continues.

In spite of these scholarly endeavors and the widespread
popularization of African history and culture, there was
the continuance of the acceptance of the "old African tradition." Just as the Government of the United States had
regarded Africa as a dependent continent into which European nations could have the right of expanding their
colonial empires, Negro-Americans followed this view also
and looked down their noses at Africans. Africans lost
little love on their brothers of color in the United States,
who had been slaves and were regarded as inferiors by
white Americans, and they as Africans would prefer not
to be regarded and classed with these inferior persons.
These situations and points of view are changing rapidly.
Dr. Woodson in commenting upon this situation said in
1945, "With a more sympathetic approach, a few Negroes
have recently become more intelligently interested in the
fate of the man of African blood in the crucible of international affairs."

Here in the United States all immigrant peoples have
striven to become primarily Americans. There was nothing
Immigrants except color—and this too was absent at times
all. —which seemed to show the relationships of
Negro-Americans to Africa. They have been taught and
have learned the language and the social techniques of this

country in which they have lived from early periods. There were few traces of African culture in Negro life in America and the Negro-Americans seemed not to be essentially different in this respect from the Irish-Americans, the German-Americans, the Scotch-Americans, or any other types so far as the indigenous culture of the lands of their ancestors were concerned. They have become parts of the American population and have been seeking to become American citizens in the largest measure rather than only part American.

Quite unlike the homelands of the peoples who have come from England, Ireland, France, Germany, Spain, Holland and other lands, the homeland of Africa had not had its history and civilizations listed, **Homelands of** taught, or referred to in educational circles. **Americans.** The contributions of other countries from which the peoples have come have been included in the modern study of history but the study of Africa was left more completely to the technical studies of Anthropology and Ethnology rather than to History. As a result scholars have concluded that Africa had been a land without a civilization or a history. Nevertheless, just as there was a European background, there was also an African background. Neither of these should be neglected in the interest of historical truth.

The dramatic emergence on the world scene of African peoples seeking self-government was accompanied by a change in the tradition that Africa was without a history. This tradition, created mainly by Europeans **The dark** and Americans, had made Africa into "the **continent.** dark continent." This designation with its connotations, was continued through centuries not only on account of the dark hues of its peoples but also because little was known of Africa except that it was the land of the unknown, of mystery and legend. It was in its first discovery the land of "Sheba," "Ophir," "Prester John" and "King Solomon's

Mines" and was a rich and fabulous area which could become also a land of potential slaves. It was regarded as a land of savagery and barbarism. These opinions became a tradition, fixed and unchanging. The exact disregard and the omission of the African people from history's accounts contributed to the building of this tradition and to the dilemma created by differences in culture and color. Such people, it was believed, could not have had a history until their continent had been penetrated by Europeans.

Contrary to such dogmatic statements and their acceptance by peoples all over the world, Africans have kept their history alive for themselves by continuing its oral transmission. They were never the savages they were said to be and never was there an Africa of the old geography books. The councils of the elders kept the true record active in the legends and stories of tribal histories. These accounts with their facts, myths, legends, and imagery were often terminated when an African state was conquered by another, and its historical traditions would pass away with it. This past, was described by Leo Frobenius, Anthropologist and Historian in his *Voice of Africa* as follows: "The ruins of the mighty past lie slumbering within the bosom of the Earth but glorified in a memory of the men who live beneath the sun," and he referred to "the Godlike strength of memory in those who lived before the advent of the written word."

African history transmitted.

Today, with the rise of independent darker peoples and their governments, the false is giving way to the true. The truth about black and brown folk is being made known for the first time. This change in their historical tradition has begun as scholars, scientists, and specialists have worked successfully in the search for the historical truth. They began to dig beneath the soil unearthing material objects, studying the available documents and reports of excavations, checking these with oral

The truth revealed.

traditions, and holding meetings for the presentation of prepared historical papers on aspects of pre-history and history. Scholars in the universities expanded this work and inspired others to additional researches. Governments have undertaken steps to safeguard their monuments and materials for history. Use was being made by researchers of archaeological materials, oral traditions, linguistic evidence, ethnological data and material culture. As the darker peoples achieved self-government and independence. and were admitted to the Unitd Nations, their histories became factors of importance to them and to all students of history. This truth was now a part of *our history* and could be neglected no longer by students of historical truth.

BIBLIOGRAPHY

I. *Bibliographies and Collections of Source Materials*

APTHEKER, HERBERT, *A Documentary History of the Negro People in the United States.* New York, 1951. 2 Vols.

Association for the Study of Negro Life and History—*Woodson Collection*—Source Materials.

Atlanta University—*Henry Slaughter Collection.*

BARNES, GILBERT H., and DUMOND, DWIGHT L., *Letters of Theodore Dwight Weld, Angelina Grimke Weld and Sarah Grimke, 1822-44.* New York, 1934. 2 Vols.

Boston Public Library. *Manuscript Collections.*

BROWN, STERLING A., DAVIS, ARTHUR P. and LEE, ULYSSES, *The Negro Caravan: Writings by American Negroes.* New York, 1941.

Calendar of the Writings of Frederick Douglass in the Douglass Memorial Home. Washington, D. C., 1940.

CATTERALL, HELEN T., *Judicial Cases Concerning American Slavery and the Negro.* Washington, D. C., 1926-1937. 5 Vols.

COOK, P. A. W., *A Guide to the Literature on Negro Education.* Teachers College Record, Vol. XXXIV, 1933; 671-677.

Cornell University Library Bulletin, May Collection. Antislavery Periodicals.

DONNAN, ELIZABETH, Documents *Illustrative of the History of the Slave Trade to America.* Washington, 1930-1935.

DREER, HERMAN, *American Literature by Negro Authors.* New York, Macmillan, 1950.

DUBOIS, W. E. B., *A Select Bibliography of the Negro American for General Readers.* Atlanta, 1905.

DUBOIS, W. E. B., and JOHNSON, GUY B., *Encyclopedia of the Negro: Preparatory Volume with Lists and Reports.* New York, 1945.

DUNLAP, M. E., "Special Collections of Negro Literature in the United States," *The Journal of Negro Education,* Vol. IV, 1935, 482-489.

FONER, PHILIP S., *The Life and Writings of Frederick Douglass.* 4 Vols. New York, 1950.

FOWLER, JULIAN S., *A Classified Catalogue of the Collection of Anti-Slavery Propaganda in the Oberlin College Library.* Oberlin, 1932.

Fisk University Library, *Negro Collection.*

Frederick Douglass Papers, Frederick Douglass Home, Washington, D. C.

GREEN, ELIZABETH L., *The Negro in Contemporary Literature: An Outline for Individual and Group study.* Chapel Hill, 1928.

GRIFFITHS, JULIA, *Autographs for Freedom.* Auburn, 1854.

Hampton Institute, *A Classified Catalogue of the Negro Collection.* Hampton, 1940.

HARPER, FRANCIS P., *Catalogue of Unusual Collection of Books and Pamphlets relating to the Rebellion and Slavery.* New York, 1894.

Harvard Guide to American History. Cambridge, 1954.

Harvard University—*Collections.*

Historical Society of Pennsylvania. Philadelphia.

International African Institute, *Select Annotated Bibliography of Tropical Africa.* New York, 1956.

Journal of African History, The, 1960 — Cambridge University Press, England.

Journal of Negro Education, The, 1932—Howard University, Washington, D. C.

Journal of Negro History, The, 1916—Association for the Study of Negro Life and History, Washington, D. C.

LEWINSON, PAUL, *A Guide to Documents in the National Archives: For Negro Studies.* Washington, D. C., 1947.

Library of Congress. Division of Bibliography.
—*List of Books relating to the West Coast of Africa,* 1908.
—*List of recent references on the Negro,* 1935.
—*A List of References on Negro Migration,* 1923.
—*List of References on Negro Segregation in the United States,* 1927.
—*List of References on the Negro and the European War,* 1919.
—*Select List of References on the Negro Question,* 1926.
—*Select List of References on the Negro Question. Compiled*

under the direction of Appleton Prentiss Clark Griffin. Washington, D. C., 1906.
—*Booker T. Washington: A Register of his Papers.*
—*Manuscript Collections.*
—*Negro Newspapers on Microfilm,* 1953.

Massachusetts Historical Society. Boston.

MAY, SAMUEL JOSEPH, *Catalogue of Antislavery Publications in America.* New York, 1864.

National Archives and Records Service. Washington, D. C.

Negro Year Book, The, edited by J. P. Guzman, V. C. Foster and W. H. Hughes. Tuskegee, 1947.

New York Historical Society. New York.

New York Public Library, 135 Street Branch. *Schomburg Collection of Negro Literature and History.*

——————, *The Negro: A Select Bibliography.* New York, 1935.

New York Public Library Bulletin.
—*List of Works relating to the American Colonization Society.* July, 1902.

PORTER, DOROTHY B., *A Catalogue of the African Collection in the Moorland Collection.* Howard University, Washington, D. C., 1958.

——————, *A Selected List of Books by and about the Negro.* Washington, D. C., 1936.

——————, *"Early Manuscript Letters Written by Negroes." Journal of Negro History,* XXIV, 1939.

PORTER, DOROTHY B., HUNTON, MARGARET R. and WILLIAMS, ETHEL, *A Catalogue of Books in the Moorland Collection.* Howard University, Washington, D. C., 1939.

QUARLES, BENJAMIN, "Letters from Negro Leaders to Gerritt Smith." *The Journal of Negro History*, Vol. XXVII (1942); 432-453.

ROSS, FRANK ALEXANDER and KENNEDY, LOUISE VENABLE, *A Bibliography of Negro Migration*. New York, 1934.

SCHOMBURG, ARTHUR ALFONSO, *A Bibliography Checklist of American Negro Poetry*. New York, 1916.

University of Michigan, Clements Library, Manuscript Collection.

WESLEY, CHARLES H., *Negro Labor in the United States, 1850-1925. A Study in American Economic History*. New York, 1927, List of References.

WILLIAMSON, HARRY A., *The Negro in Masonic Literature*. Brooklyn, 1922.

WIESCHHOFF, HEINRICH A., *Anthropological Bibliography of Negro Africa*. New Haven, American Oriental Society, 1948.

WOODSON, CARTER G., *Free Negro Owners of Slaves in the United States in 1830*, Washington, D. C., The Association for the Study of Negro Life and History, 1925.

————, *Negro Orators and their Orations*. Washington, D. C., 1925.

————, *The African Background Outlined or Handbook for the Study of the Negro*. Washington, D. C., 1936.

————, *The Mind of the Negro as Reflected in Letters Written during the Crisis*. Washington, D. C., 1926.

————, *The Works of Francis J. Grimke*. Washington, D. C., The Associated Publishers, 1942.

Yale University Library: Special Collections.

II. *General Works*

ALEXANDER, WILLIAM T., *History of the Colored Race in America*. Kansas City, 1887.

ALLPORT, GORDON, *The Nature of Prejudice*. Cambridge, 1954.

ASHLEY—MONTAGUE, *Man's Most Dangerous Myth. The Fallacy of Race*. New York, 1942.

BENEDICT, RUTH, *Race: Science and Politics*. New York, 1940.

BENEDICT, RUTH and ELLIS, MILDRED, *Race and Cultural Relations: America's Answer to the Myth of the Master Race*. Washington, D. C., 1942.

BENEDICT, RUTH and WELTFISH, GENE, *The Races of Mankind*. New York, 1943.

BONTEMPS, ARNA, *The Story of the Negro*. New York, 1955.

BRAWLEY, BENJAMIN, *A Short History of the American Negro*. New York, 1939.

BROWN, INA CORRINNE, *The Story of the American Negro*. New York, 1936.

CHAMBERS, LUCILLE A., *America's Tenth Man*. New York, 1956.

CROMWELL, JOHN W., *The Negro In American History*. Washington, D. C., 1914.

DAVIE, M. R., *Negroes in American Society*. New York, 1949.

DuBOIS, W. E. B., *Black Folk, Then and Now: An Essay in the History and Sociology of the Negro*. New York, 1939.

————, *The Gift of Black Folk*. Boston, 1924.

————, *The Ordeal of Mans-*

art.—A Triogy, The Black Flame. New York, 1957.

————, The Negro. New York, 1915.

————, The Souls of Black Folk. New York, 1953.

EDWARDS, G. FRANKLIN, The Negro Professional Class. Glencoe, Illinois, 1959.

ELKINS, STANLEY M., Slavery, A Problem in American Institutional and Intellectual Life. Chicago, 1959.

EMBREE, EDWIN R., Brown Americans: The Story of a Tenth of the Nation. New York, 1944.

EPPSE, MERL R., The Negro, Too, In American History. Chicago, 1943.

FRANKLIN, JOHN HOPE, From Slavery to Freedom: A History of American Negroes. New York, 1947, 1956.

————, The Militant South, 1800-1860. Cambridge, 1956.

————, "The New Negro History." The Journal of Negro History, Vol. XLIII (1957); 89-97.

FRAZIER, E. FRANKLIN, The Negro in the United States. New York, 1957.

GARFINKEL, HERBERT, When Negroes March. Glencoe, Illinois, 1959.

HUGHES, LANGSTON, Famous American Negroes. New York, 1954.

HUGHS, LANGSTON, and MELTZER, MILTON, A Pictorial History of the Negro in America. New York. 1956.

JOHNSON, CHARLES S., The Negro in American Civilization. New York, 1930.

JOHNSON, EDWARD, A School History of the Negro Race in America. Raleigh, 1891.

LEWIS, R. B., Light and Truth, Collected from The Bible and Ancient and Modern History, Containing the Universal History of the colored and the Indian Race. Boston, 1851.

LOCKE, ALAIN, The Negro in America. Chicago, 1933.

LOGAN, RAYFORD W., The Negro in American Life and Thought: The Nadir, 1877-1901. New York, 1954.

————, The Negro in the United States: A Brief History. New York, 1957.

MACLACHLAN, JOHN M., This Changing South. Gainesville, Florida, 1956.

MANDEL, BERNARD, Labor: Free and Slave; Workingmen and the Anti-Slavery Movement in the United States. New York, 1955.

MURDOCK, GEORGE PETER, Africa, Its Peoples and Their Cultural History. New York, 1959.

MYRDAL, GUNNAR, An American Dilemma: The Negro Problem and Modern Democracy. 2 Vols New York, 1944.

National Planning Association. Selected Studies of Negro Employment in the South. Washington, D. C., 1955.

NEARING, SCOTT, Black America. New York, 1929.

PENNINGTON, JAMES W. C., A Textbook of the Origin and History of the Colored People. Hartford, Connecticut, 1841.

REDDING, J. SAUNDERS, They Came in Chains: Americans from Africa. New York, 1950.

RICHARDSON, BEN, Great American Negroes. New York, 1956.

SCHRIEKE, B., *Alien Americans: A Study of Race Relations.* New York, 1936.

TILLINGHAST, JOSEPH A., *The Negro in Africa and America.* New York, 1902.

VAN DEUSEN, JOHN, *Black Man in White America* Washington, D. C., 1944.

WASHINGTON, BOOKER T., *The Story of the Negro: The Rise of the Race from Slavery.* 2 Vols. New York, 1909.

WEATHERFORD, W. D., *The Negro from Africa to America.* New York, 1924.

WILLIAMS, GEORGE WASHINGTON, *History of the Negro Race in America.* 2 Vols. New York, 1882.

WOODSON, CARTER G., and WESLEY, CHARLES H., *The Story of the Negro Retold.* Washington, D. C., 1959.

III. *Selected References*

ADAMS, ALICE, *The Neglected Period of Anti-Slavery in America, 1808-1831.* Boston, 1908.

ADAMS, JAMES T., "Disfranchisement of Negroes in New England." *American Historical Review,* XXX, 1925.

AFRICANUS, JOANNES LEO, *The History and Description of Africa.* London, 1896.

ALLAND, ALEXANDER, and WISE, JAMES W., *The Springfield Plan.* New York, 1945.

ALLEN, CUTHBERT E., "The Slavery Question in Catholic Newspapers." *U. S. Catholic Historical Society Record.* Vol. XXVI; 99-169.

ALLEN, JAMES E., "The Negro and the 1940 Presidential Election." (Unpublished Master's Thesis.) Howard University, 1943.

ALLEN, JAMES S., *The Negro Question in the United States.* New York, 1936.

ALLEN, WILLIAM G., *A Refugee from American Despotism. The American Prejudice Against Color.* London, 1853.

ALPENFELS, ETHEL, *Sense and Nonsense about Race.* New York, 1946.

American Assembly, The, Columbia University. *United States and Africa.* New York, 1958.

American Colonization Society (1818-60), *The African Repository.* Washington, D. C., 1825-92.

ANDREWS, CHARLES C., *The History of the New York African Free Schools.* New York, 1830.

ANDERSON, MARIAN, *My Lord, What A Morning.* New York, 1956.

Annals of the American Academy of Political and Social Science. "Racial Desegregation and Integration," March, 1956.

Appeal of Forty Thousand Citizens, Threatened with Disfranchisement, to the People of Pennsylvania. Philadelphia, 1838.

APTHEKER, HERBERT, "Maroons within the Present Limits of the United States," *Journal of Negro History,* XXIV, April, 1939.

————, "Militant Abolition," *The Journal of Negro History,* Vol. XXVI, pp. 438-484.

————, "Negro Casualties in the Civil War," *Journal of Negro History,* XXXII, January, 1947.

————, *Negro Slave Revolts in the United States.* 1526-1860. New York, 1939.

————, "The Negro in the Abolitionist Movement," *Science and Society.* Winter, 1941.

————, *The Negro in the Civil War*. New York, 1938.

ARMSTRONG, LOUIS, *Satchmo. My Life in New Orleans*. New York, 1954.

ARNETT, ALEX M., *The Populist Movement in Georgia*. New York, 1922.

ASHMORE, HARRY S., *The Negro and the Schools*. Chapel Hill, 1954.

ATWOOD, J. H., ET AL., *Thus Be Their Destiny*. Washington, 1941.

AZIKIWE, BEN N., "In Defense of Africa," *The Journal of Negro History*, Vol. XVII, pp. 30-50.

BACOTE, CLARENCE A., "Some Aspects of Negro Life in Georgia, 1880-1908," *The Journal of Negro History*, Vol. XLIII, 1958; 186-213.

BAKER, HENRY E., "Benjamin Banneker, The Negro Mathematician and Astronomer," *The Journal of Negro History*, Vol. III, April, 1918; 99-118.

————, "The Negro in the Field of Invention," *The Journal of Negro History*, Vol. II, 1917; 21-36.

BAKER, PAUL, *Negro-White Adjustment*. New York, 1934.

BAKER, RAY S., *Following the Color Line*. New York, 1908.

————, "The Negro Goes North," *World's Work*, XXXIV, July, 1917.

BALL, CHARLES, *Slavery in the United States*. New York, 1837.

BALLACH, J. C., *A History of Slavery in Virginia*. Baltimore, 1902.

————, *White Servitude in the Colony of Virginia*. Baltimore, 1895.

BANCROFT, FREDERIC, *Slave Trading in the Old South*. Baltimore, 1931.

BARDOLPH, RICHARD, *The Negro Vanguard*. New York, 1959.

————, "The Negro in Who's Who in America, 1936-1955,"

The Journal of Negro History, Vol. XLII, 1957; 261-282.

————, "Social Origins of Distinguished Negroes, 1770-1865," *The Journal of Negro History*, Vol. XL, 1950; 211-249.

BARNES, GILBERT, *The Antislavery Impulse, 1830-1844*. New York, 1933.

BARNES, GILBERT H., and DUMOND, DWIGHT L., *Letters of Theodore Dwight Weld, Angelina Grimke Weld and Sarah Grimke, 1822-44*. 2 Vols. New York, 1934.

BARNETT, IDA WELLS, "Our Country's Lynching Records." *Survey*, Vol. XXIV, January, 1913.

BARTLETT, IRVING H., *From Slave to Citizen: The Story of the Negro in Rhode Island*. Providence, 1954.

BARTON, REBECCA C., *Witnesses for Freedom: Negro Americans in Autobiography*. New York, 1948.

BASSETT, JOHN S., *Anti-Slavery Leaders in North Carolina*. Baltimore, 1931.

BASSETT, JOHN SPENCER, *Slavery and Servitude in the Colonay of North Carolina*. Baltimore, 1896.

————, *The Southern Plantation Overseer as Revealed in His Letters*. Northhampton, 1925.

BAUER, RAYMOND and BAUER, ALICE, "Day to Day Resistance to Slavery," *Journal of Negro History*, Vol. XXVII, October, 1942; 388-419.

BAXTER, WILLIAM E., *America and the Americans*. London, 1855.

BAYTON, JAMES A., "The Psychology of Racial Morale," *Journal of Negro Education*, Vol. XI, April, 1942.

BEALE, HOWARD K., *The Critical Year, A Study of Andrew Johnson and Reconstruction*. New York, 1930.

————, "On Rewriting Reconstruction History," *American*

Historical Review, Vol. XLV, July, 1940.

BEER, GEORGE L., *African Questions at the Paris Peace Conference.* New York, 1923.

BELL, ANDREW, *Men and Things in America.* London, 1838.

BELL, HOWARD H., "National Negro Conventions of the Middle 1840's: Moral Suasian vs. Political Action," *Journal of Negro History,* Vol. XLII, 1957; 247-260.

——————, "The Negro Convention Movement, 1830-61: New Perspectives," *Negro History Bulletin,* Vol. XIV (1959); 103-105, 114.

——————, "A Survey of the Negro Convention Movement, 1839-61," (unpublished Ph.D. Dissertation; Northwestern University, 1953).

BELL, J. W., "The Teaching of Negro History," *The Journal of Negro History,* Vol. VIII, 1923; 123-127.

BELTRAN, AGUIRRE G., "Races in Seventeenth Century Mexico," *Phylon* VI, Third Quarter, 1945.

BENTLEY, GEORGE R., *A History of the Freedmen's Bureau.* Philadelphia, 1955.

BILLINGTON, RAY ALLEN, "James Forten: Forgotten Abolitionist," *Negro History Bulletin,* Vol. XIII, November, 1949.

——————, (edited by), *The Journal of Charlotte Forten.* New York, 1953.

BIRD, MARK B., *The Black Man: Or Haytian Independence.* New York, 1869.

BIRNEY, JAMES G., *The American Churches, the Bulwarks of American Slavery.* Newburyport, Mass., 1842.

BISHOP, MORRIS, *The Odyssey of Cabeza de Vaca.* New York, 1933.

BLAKE, WILLIAM O., *The History of Slavery and the Slave Trade.* Columbus, 1860.

BLAKISTON, HARRY S., "Lincoln's Emancipation Plan," *Journal of Negro History,* Vol. VII, July, 1922; 257-277.

BOAS, FRANZ, *Africans are Old African Civilizations.* Atlanta, 1906.

——————, *General Anthropology.* Boston, 1938.

——————, *The Mind of Primitive Man.* New York, 1938.

BOND, FREDERICK W., *The Negro and the Drama.* Washington, 1940.

BOND, HORACE MANN, *Negro Education in Alabama: A Study in Cotton and Steel.* Washington, D. C., 1939.

——————, *The Education of the Negro in the American Social Order.* New York, 1934.

BONE, ROBERT, *The Negro Novel in America.* New Haven, 1958.

BONTEMPS, ARNA, *Black Thunder,* New York, 1936.

BOTUME, ELIZABETH HYDE, *First Days Amongst the Contrabands.* Boston, 1893.

BRACKETT, JEFFREY R., *The Negro in Maryland: A Study of the Institution of Slavery.* Baltimore, 1889.

BRADLEY, PHILLIPS (ed.), *Tocqueville, Democracy in America.* New York, 1951, 2 Vols.

BRAMELD, T H E O D O R E, *Minority Problems in the Public Schools.* New York, 1946.

BRAWLEY, BENJAMIN, *Africa and the War.* New York, 1918.

——————, *Early Negro American Writers.* Chapel Hill, 1935.

——————, *Negro Builders and Heroes.* Chapel Hill, 1937.

——————, *The Negro Genius: A New Appraisal of the Achievements of The American Negro in Literature and the Fine Arts.* New York.

——————, *The Negro in Litera-ture and Art*. New York, 1918.

——————, *Women of Achieve-ment*. Chicago, Woman's Ameri-can Baptist Home Mission So-ciety, 1919.

BRAZEAL, B. R., *The Brotherhood of Sleeping Car Porters*. New York, 1946.

BREASTED, JAMES H., *History of Egypt*. New York, 1905.

BREWER, W. M., "Henry Highland Garnet," *The Journal of Negro History*, Vol. XIII, 1928; 36-52.

——————, "John B. Russwurm," *Journal of Negro History*, Vol. XIII, 1928; 413-422.

BRODERICK, FRANCIS L., *W. E. B. DuBois, Negro Leader in a Time of Crisis*. Stanford, 1959.

BROEK, JACOBUS TEN, *The Anti-slavery Origins of the Fourteenth Amendment*. Berkeley, 1951.

BROWN, EARLY, and LEIGHTON, GEORGE R., *The Negro and the War*. New York, 1942.

BROWN, GEORGE W., "Haiti and the United States," *Journal of Ne-gro History*, Vol. VIII, April, 1923; 134-152.

——————, *The Economic History of Liberia*. Washington, D. C., 1941.

——————, "The Origins of Aboli-tion in Santo Domingo," *Journal of Negro History*, Vol. VII, Oc-tober, 1922; 365-376.

BROWN, HALLIE Q., *Homespun He-roines and Other Women of Dis-tinction*. Xenia, 1926.

BROWN, STERLING, *The Negro in American Fiction*. Washington, D. C., 1937.

——————, *Negro Poetry and Drama*. Washington, D. C., 1937.

BROWN. W. O., "Racial Inequality: Fact or Myth," *The Journal of Negro History*, Vol. XVI, 1931; 43-66.

BROWN. WILLIAM WELLS, *Sketches of Places and Peoples Abroad*. New York, Jewett, Proctor and Worthington, 1855.

——————, *The American Fugi-tive in Europe*. Boston, 1855.

——————, *The Black Man: His Antecedents, His Genius and His Achievements*. New York, 1863.

——————, *The Negro in the American Rebellion: His Hero-ism and Fidelity*. Boston, 1867.

——————, *The Rising Sun or the Antecedents and Advance-ment of the Colored Race*. Bos-ton, 1874.

BROWNING, JAMES B., "Negro Companions of the Spanish Ex-plorers in the New World," *How-ard University Studies in His-tory*, No. 11, November, 1930.

——————, "The Beginnings of Insurance Enterprise Among Negroes," *The Journal of Negro History*, Vol. XXII, 1937; 417-432.

——————, "The Free Negro in Ante-Bellum North Carolina." *The North Carolina Historical Review*, Vol. 15; 23-33.

BRUCE, KATHLEEN, *Virginia Iron Manuufacture in the Slave Era*. New York, 1930.

BRUCE, P. A., *Economic History of Virginia in the Seventeenth Cen-tury*. New York, 1895, 1907.

BUCKLER, HELEN, *Doctor Dan: Pioneer in American Surgery*. Boston, 1954.

BUCKMASTER, HENRIETTA, *Let My People Go*. New York, 1941.

BUNCHE, RALPH J., *A World View of Race*. Washington, D. C., 1936.

——————, "The Negro in the Political Life of the United States," *The Journal of Negro Education*, Vol. X, July, 1941.

——————, "The Programs of Or-ganizations Devoted to the Im-provement of the Status of the American Negro," *The Journal* of *Negro Education*, Vol. VIII, July, 1939.

BUTCHER, MARGARET JUST, *The Negro in American Culture: Based on Materials left by Alain Locke.* New York. 1956.

BUTCHER, PHILIP, *George W. Cable: The Northhampton Years.* New York. 1959.

BUTSCH, JOSEPH, "Catholics and the Negro," *The Journal of Negro History*, Vol. II, 1917; 393-410.

CADBURY, HENRY J., "Negro Membership in the Society of Friends," *The Journal of Negro History*, Vol. XXI, April, 1936; 151-213.

CADE, JOHN B., "Out of the Mouths of Ex-Slaves," *The Journal of Negro History*, Vol. XXI, 1935.

CALIVER, AMBROSE, *A Personnel Study of Negro College Students.* New York, 1931.

CANNON, POPPY, *A Gentle Knight, My Husband Walter White.* New York, 1952.

CARPENTER, JESSE, *The South as a Conscious Minority*, 1789-1861. New York, 1930.

CARPENTER, MARIE E., *The Treatment of the Negro in American History School Textbooks.* Menasha, Wisconsin, 1941.

CARROLL, JOSEPH C., *Slave Insurrections in the United States, 1800-1865.* Boston, 1938.

CAYTON, HORACE and MITCHELL, GEORGE S., *Black Workers and the New Unions.* Chapel Hill, 1939.

CHAMBERLAIN, ALEXANDER FRANCIS, "The Contribution of the Negro to Human Civilization," *The Journal of Race Development*, Vol. II, April, 1911.

————, *A History of Art in Ancient Egypt.* London, 1883.

CHAMBERS, WILLIAM, *American Slavery and Colour.* London, 1857.

CHANNING, EDWARD, *History of the United States*, Vol. I, II, III, IV, V, VI, New York, 1902-1925.

CHAPMAN, BARBARA (tr.), *Beaumont, Marie; Or, Slavery in the United States.* Stanford, 1958.

CHAPMAN, CHARLES E., *Colonial Hispanic America: A History.* New York, 1933.

————, "Palmares, The Negro Numantia," *Journal of Negro History*, Vol. III, January, 1918; 29-32.

CHESTNUTT, HELEN, *Charles Waddell Chestnutt.* Chapel Hill, 1952.

CHEW, ABRAHAM, *A Biography of Colonel Charles Young.* Washington, 1923.

Chicago Commission on Race Relations, *The Negro in Chicago, A Study of Race Relations and a Race Riot.* Chicago, 1922.

CLARKE, JAMES FREEMAN, "Condition of the Free Colored People of the United States," *The Christian Examiner* Vol. LXVI, Fifth Series, Iv (1859).

CLARKSON, THOMAS, *History of the Abolition of the Slave Trade.*

CLEMENT, RUFUS E., "Legal Provisions for Graduate and Professional Instruction for Negroes in States Operating Separate School Systems," *Journal of Negro Education*, VII, April, 1939.

CLEVEN, N. ANDREW, "Some Plans for Colonizing Liberated Negro Slaves in Hispanic America," *Journal of Negro History*, Vol. XI, January, 1926; 35-49.

COAN, JOSEPHUS R., *Daniel Alexander Payne, Christian Educator.* Philadelphia, 1935.

COFFIN, LEVI, *Reminiscences.* New York, 1876.

COLEMAN, J. WINSTON, *Slavery Times in Kentucky.* Chapel Hill, 1940.

"Color, Unfinished Business of

Democracy," *Survey Graphic*, XXXI, November, 1942.

CONRAD, EARL, *Harriet Tubman*. Washington, D. C., 1943.

COOK, MERCER, "The Literary Contribution of the French West Indian," *Journal of Negro History*, Vol. XXV, October, 1940.

COOLEY, HENRY S., *A Study of Slavery in New Jersey*. Baltimore, 1896.

COPPIN, BISHOP L. J., *Unwritten History*. Philadelphia, 1919.

CORNISH, DUDLEY T., *The Sable Arm: The Negro in the Union Army, 1861-1865*. New York, 1956.

CORWIN, E. H. L., and STURGES, GERTRUDE E., *Opportunities for the Medical Education of Negroes*. New York, 1936.

COULTER, E. MERTON, *The South During Reconstruction, 1865-1877* (A History of the South, Vol. VIII), Baton Rouge, 1947.

COULTER, ELLIS M., *A Short History of Georgia*. Chapel Hill, 1933.

COUPLAND, REGINALD, *The British Anti-Slavery Movement*. London, 1933.

COX, O. C., *Class and Race*. New York, 1948.

CRAVEN, AVERY O., "Poor Whites and Negroes in the Ante-Bellum South," *The Journal of Negro History*, Vol. XV, 1930; 14-25.

CRAWFORD, GEORGE W., *Prince Hall and His Followers*. New York, 1913.

Crisis, The

CROGMAN, W. H., and KLETZING, H. F., *Progress of a Race*. Atlanta, Georgia, **1897.**

CROGMAN, W. H., and GIBSON, J. W., *The Colored American from Slavery to Honorable Citizenship.*. Atlanta, Georgia, 1902.

CROMWELL, JOHN W., *The Early Negro Convention Movement*. Washington, 1904.

CRONON, EDMUND D., *Black Moses, The Story of Marcus Garvey and the Universal Negro Improvement Association*. Madison, 1955.

CURRENT, GLOSTER, "Why Nixon Lost the Negro Vote,' *The Crisis*, January, 1961, Vol. 68; 5-14.

CURRY, J. L. M., *Difficulties, Complications and Limitations Connected with the Education of the Negro*. Baltimore, 1895.

CURTI, MERLE, *The Social Ideas of American Educators*. New York, **1935.**

DABNEY, WILLIAM P., *Cincinnati's Colored Citizens, Historical, Sociological, Biographical*. Cincinnati, 1926.

DALY, JOHN JAY, *A Song in His Heart* (James A. Bland). Philadelphia, 1951.

DANIEL, SADIE, *Women Builders*. Washington, D. C., 1931.

DANIELS, JOHN, *In Freedom's Birthplace, A Study of the Boston Negroes*. Boston and New York, 1914.

DAVENPORT, F. M., *Primitive Traits In Religious Revivals*. New York. 1905.

DAVIDSON, BASIL *Lost Cities of Africa*. Boston, 1959.

————, *Old Africa Rediscovered*. London, 1959.

DAVIE, MAURICE R., *Negroes in American Society*. New York, 1950.

DAVIS, ALLISON, and DOLLARD, JOHN, *Children of Bondage*. Washington, 1940.

DAVIS, H. P., *Black Democracy*. New York, 1936.

DAVIS, HARRY E., "John Malvin. A Western Reserve Pioneer." *The Journal of Negro History*, XXIII. October, 1938; 426-434.

DAVIS, JOHN W., "George Liele and Andrew Bryan," *The Journal of Negro History*, Vol. I, 1916; 202-205; Vol. III, 1918, pp. 119-127.

DAVIS, T. R., "Negro Servitude in the United States," *The Journal of Negro History*, Vol. VIII, pp. 247-283.

DAVIS, WILLIAM J., "The Role of the Adviser on Negro Affairs and the Racial Specialist in National Administration, 1933-1940," (unpublished Master's Thesis). Howard University, 1940.

DeCOSTA, B. F., *Three Score and Ten—The Story of St. Phillip's Church*. New York, 1889.

DELAFOSSE, MAURICE, *The Negroes of Africa: History and Culture*. Washington, D. C., 1931.

DELANY, MARTIN R., *The Condition, Elevation, Emigration and Destiny of the Colored People of the U. S. Politically Considered*. Philadelphia, 1852.

DENNY, JOHN F., *An Enquiry into the Political Grade of the Free Coloured Population, Under the Constitution of the United States and the Constitution of Pennsylvania*. Chambersburg, Pa., 1834.

DETT, R. N., *Religious Folk-Songs of the Negro as Sung at Hampton Institute*. Hampton, Va., 1927.

DETWEILER, FREDERICK G., *The Negro Press in the United States*. Chicago, 1922.

DEUTSCH, MORTON, *Interracial Housing*. Minneapolis, 1951.

DIGGS, IRENE, "Color in Spanish America," *The Journal of Negro History*, Vol. XXXVIII, 1953; 403-427.

DIGGS, MARGARET A., *Catholic Negro Education in the United States*. Washington, D. C., 1935.

DIXON, ROLAND, *The Racial History of Man*. New York, 1923.

DOLLARD, J., *Caste and Class in a Southern Town*. New Haven, 1937.

DONALD, HENDERSON, "The Negro Migration, 1916-1918," *Journal of Negro History*, Vol. VI, 1921; 383-498.

DORO, GEORGE F., *Slave Ships and Slavery*. Salem, 1927.

DOUGLASS, FREDERICK, *The Life and Times of Frederick Douglass*, Hartford, Connecticut, 1884.

—————, *My Bondage and My Freedom*. New York and Auburn, 1855.

DOUGLASS, FREDERICK, WATKINS, WILLIAM J., and WHITFIELD, JAMES M., *Arguments, Pro and Con, on the Call for A National Emigration Convention, to be held in Cleveland, Ohio, August, 1854*. Detroit, 1854.

DOUGLASS, WILLIAM, *Annals of the First African Church in the U. S. A.* Philadelphia, King and Baird, 1862.

DOWD, JEROME, *The Negro in American Life*. New York, 1926.

—————, *The Negro Races*. New York, 1907-1914.

DOYLE, BERTRAM W., "Racial Traits of the Negro as Negroes Assign them to themselves," (unpublished Master's Thesis) University of Chicago, 1924.

—————, *The Etiquette of Racial Relations in the South*. Chicago, 1937.

DRAKE, ST. CLAIR, and CLAYTON, HORACE R., *Black Metropolis: A Study of Negro Life in a Northern City*. New York, 1945.

DREER, HERMAN, *The History of Omega Psi Phi*, Washington, D. C., 1940.

DREW, BENJAMIN, *Northside View of Slavery*. Boston, 1856.

DREWRY, W. S., *Slave Insurrections in Virginia, 1830-1865*. Washington, 1900.

DuBOIS, RACHEL DAVIS, *Build Together Americans*. New York, 1945.

DuBOIS, W. E. B., *Black Recon-*

struction. New York, Harcourt Brace, 1939.

—————, *Color and Democracy: Colonies and Peace*. New York, Harcourt Brace, 1945.

—————, *John Brown*. Philadelphia, G. W. Jacobs and Co., 1909.

—————, *Dusk of Dawn*, New York, 1940.

—————, "Reconstruction and Its Benefits," *American Historical Review*, XV, July, 1910.

—————, *Some Efforts of American Negroes for their Own Social Betterment*. Atlanta, 1898.

—————, *Souls of Black Folk*. Chicago, A. C. McClurg and Co., 1911.

—————, *The College-Bred Negro*. Atlanta, 1900.

—————, *The Gift of Black Folk*. Boston, The Stratford Co., 1924.

—————, *The Negro*. New York, Henry Holt and Co., 1915.

—————, *The Philadelphia Negro: A Social Study Together with a Special report on Domestic Service by Isabel Eaton*. Philadelphia, 1899.

—————, *The Suppression of the African Slave Trade to the United States*. Boston, 1896; New York, 1954.

—————, *The World and Africa*. New York, 1947.

DuBois, W. E. B., and Washington, Booker T., *The Negro in the South*. Philadelphia, G. W. Jacobs and Co.

Dumond, Dwight L., *Antislavery Origins of the Civil War in the United States*. Ann Arbor, 1939.

—————, *Anti-slavery. The Crusade for Freedom in America*. Ann Arbor, 1961.

—————, "The Fourteenth Amendment. Triology in Historical Perspective," *The Journal of Negro History*, Vol. XLIII, 1958; 171-185.

—————, *Letters oj James Gillespie Birney, 1831-57*. New York, 1938, 2 Vols.

—————, *The Secession Movement*. New York, 1931.

Dunbar, Paul Laurence, *Lyrics of Lowly Life*. New York, Dodd, Mead and Co., 1896.

Dyer, Brainerd, "The Treatment of Colored Union Troops by the Confederates, 1861-1865," *Journal of Negro History*, XX, July, 1935.

Dykes, Eva B., *The Negro in Romantic Thought*. Washington, D. C., 1942.

Easton, Hosea, *A Treatise on the Intellectual Character, and Civil and Political Condition of the Colored People of the United States; and the Prejudice Exercised Towards Them*. Boston, 1837.

Eaton, Clement, "A Dangerous Pamphlet in the Old South," *Journal of Southern History*, Vol. II, 1936.

—————, *Freedom of Thought in the Old South*. Durham, 1940.

Eaton, John, *Grant, Lincoln and the Freedmen*. New York, 1907.

Eckenrode, H. J., "Negroes in Richmond in 1864," *The Virginia Magazine of History and Biography*, Vol. XLVI, July, 1938.

Edmonds, Helen G., *The Negro and Fusion Politics in North Carolina, 1894-1901*. Chapel Hill, 1950.

Edmonds, Randolph, *The Land of Cotton and Other Plays*. Washington, D. C., 1942.

Epstein, Abraham, *The Negro Migrant in Pittsburgh*. Pittsburgh. 1918.

Edwards, Paul K., *The Southern Negro as a Consumer*. New York, 1932.

ELLIS, A. B., "White Slaves and Bond Servants in the American Colonies," *Popular Science Monthly*, Vol. XL.

ELLIS, GEORGE W., *Negro Culture in West Africa*. New York, 1914.

EMBREE, EDWIN R., *Thirteen Against the Odds*. New York, Viking Press, 1946.

Encyclopedia of Social Sciences, Vol. 7, "Race"; 25-36.

EPPSE, MERL R., and FOSTER, A. P., *The Negro, Too, In American History*, Nashville, Tennessee, 1949.

ERNST, ROBERT, "The Economic Status of New York City Negroes, 1850-63," *Negro History Bulletin*, Vol. XII, March, 1949.

EVERETT, DONALD E., "Emigres and Militiamen; Free Persons of Color in New Orleans, 1803-1815," *The Journal of Negro History*, Vol. XXXVII, 1953; 377-402.

FAGE, J. D., *An Introduction to the History of West Africa*. London, 1959.

FAIRCHILD, H. P., *Race and Nationality in American Society*. New York, 1947.

FARRISON, W. EDWARD, "Booker T. Washington: A Study in Educational Leadership," *The South Atlantic Quarterly*, Vol. XLI, July, 1942.

FAUSET, ARTHUR HUFF, *Sojourner Truth, God's Faithful Pilgrim*. Chapel Hill, 1938.

FERRIS, WILLIAM H., *The African Abroad, Or, His Evolution in Western Civilization*. New Haven, 1913. 2 Vols.

FILLER, LOUIS, *The Crusade Against Slavery, 1830-60*. New York, 1960.

FISHER, MILES M., *Negro Slave Songs in the United States*. Ithaca, 1953.

—————, *The Master's Slave: Elijah John Fisher*. Philadelphia, 1922.

FITCHETT, E. HORACE, "The Origin and Growth of the Free Negro Population of Charleston, South Carolina," *The Journal of Negro History*, Vol. XXVI, 1941; 413-420.

FITE, EMERSON D., *Social and Industrial Conditions in the North during the Civil War*. New York, 1910.

FLACK, HORACE E., *The Adoption of the Fourteenth Amendment*. Baltimore, 1908.

FLANDERS, RALPH B., *Plantation Slavery in Georgia*. Chapel Hill, 1933.

—————, "The Free Negro in Ante-Bellum Georgia," *The North Carolina Historical Review*, Vol. 9; 250-272.

FLEISCHER, NAT, *Black Dynamite: The Story of the Negro in the Prize Ring from 1782 to 1938*. New York, 1939.

FLEMING, BEATRICE J., and PRYDE, MARION J., *Distinguished Negroes Abroad*. Washington, D. C., 1946.

FLEMING, WALTER L., *Civil War and Reconstruction in Alabama*. New York, 1905.

—————, *The Freedmen's Savings Bank*. Chapel Hill, 1927.

FLETCHER, TOM, *100 Years of the Negro in Show Business*. New York, 1954.

FOSTER, CHARLES I., "The Colonization of Free Negroes in Liberia, 1816-35," *The Journal of Negro History*, Vol. XXXVIII, 1953; 41-66.

FOX, DIXON RYAN, "The Negro Vote in Old New York," *The Po-*

litical Science Quarterly, Vol. XXXII.

FOX, EARLY L., *The American Colonization Society, 1817-1840*. Baltimore, 1919.

FOX, JOHN, *Opinion . . . Against the Exercise of Negro Suffrage in Pennsylvania*. Harrisburg, Pa. 1838.

FRANKLIN, CHARLES L., *The Negro Labor Unionist of New York*. New York, 1944.

FRANKLIN, JOHN HOPE, (ed.), *The Civil War Diary of James T. Ayers*. Springfield, Illinois, 1947.

————, (ed.), *The Free Negro in North Carolina, 1790-1860*. Chapel Hill, 1946.

FRAZIER, E. FRANKLIN, *The Free Negro Family, A Study of Family Origins before the Civil War*. Nashville, **1932**.

————, *The Negro Family in the United States*. Chicago, 1934.

————, "The Negro Slave Family," *The Journal of Negro History*, Vol. XV; 198-259.

————, *The Negro in the United States*. New York, 1949.

————, *Negro Youth at the Crossways*. Washington, 1940.

————, *Freedom's Journal*. 1827-1828. New York.

FREYRE, GILBERTO, "Social Life in Brazil in the Middle of Nineteenth Century," *Hispanic American Historical Review*, Vol. V, 1922.

————, *The Masters and the Slaves: A Study in the Development of Brazilian Civilization*. New York, 1946.

FROBENIUS, LEO, "Early African Culture as an Indication of Present Negro Potentialities," *The Annals of the American Negro Academy*. Vol. 140, November, 1928.

————, "The Origin of African Civilizations," *Annual Report of the Smithsonian Institution*, 1898.

FULLER, THOMAS O., *History of the Negro Baptists of Tennessee*. Memphis, 1935.

GAINES, FRANCIS PENDLETON, *The Southern Plantation: A Study in the Development and the Accuracy of a Tradition*. New York, 1925.

GALLAGHER, BUELL G., *American Caste and the Negro College*. New York, 1938.

GARA, LARRY, *The Liberty Line*. Lexington, 1961.

GARRISON, LLOYD, *Thoughts on African Colonization: Or, An Impartial Exhibition of the Doctrines, Principles and Purposes of the American Colonization Society*, etc. Boston, 1832.

GARRISON, WILLIAM LLOYD, *The Liberator* (1831-65).

GARRISON, W. P. and F. J., *William Lloyd Garrison*. Boston and New York, 1894. 4 Vols.

GIBSON, WILLIAM M., *The Social Element in Negro Education, 1865-1935*. Worcester, Massachusetts, 1935.

GINZBERG, ELI, *The Negro Potential*. New York, 1956.

GLASS, EDWARD L. N., *The History of the Tenth Cavalry, 1866-1901*. Tucson, 1921.

GLEASON, ELIZA ATKINS, *The Southern Negro and the Public Library*. Chicago, 1941.

GLOSTER, HUGH, *Negro Voices in American Fiction*. Chapel Hill, 1948.

GOODELL, WILLIAM, *Slavery and Anti-Slavery*. New York, 1852.

GOSNELL, HAROLD F., *Negro Politicians, The Rise of Negro Politics in Chicago*. Chicago, 1935.

————, "The Negro Vote in Northern Cities," *National Municipal Review*, XXX, May, 1941.

GOVAN, THOMAS P., "Was Plantation Slavery Profitable," *Journal of Southern History*, Vol. VIII, 1942.

GRAHAM, SHIRLEY, *There was Once A Slave: The Heroic Story of Frederick Douglass.* New York, 1947.

GRAVES, JOHN TEMPLE, "The Southern Negro and the War Crisis," *Virginia Quarterly Review*, Vol. XVIII, Autumn, 1942.

GREAVES, IDA C., *The Negro in Canada.* Orillia, 1930.

GREEN, ELIZABETH L., *The Negro in Contemporary American Literature.* Chapel Hill, 1928.

GREENE, H. W., *Negro Holders of the Doctorate.* Boston, 1948.

GREENE, LORENZO J., WOODSON, C. G., and CALLIS, M. C., *The Employment of Negroes in the District of Columbia.* Washington, D. C., 1930.

GREENE, LORENZO J. and WOODSON, C. G., *The Negro in Colonial New England, 1620-1776.* New York, 1943.

GREENE LORENZO J .and WOODSON, C. G., *The Negro Wage Earner.* Washington, D. C., 1930.

GREENE, LORENZO J., "Mutiny on the Slave Ships," *Phylon*, Vol. V, Fourth Quarter, 1944.

————, "Slaveholding New England and Its Awakening," *The Journal of Negro History*, Vol. XIII; 492-533.

GRIMES, JOSEPH, *A Study of the Negro Historian, 1844 - 1920.* (Unpublished Master's Thesis.) University of Iowa, 1935.

GRIMKE, ARCHIBALD H., *The Life of Charles Summer: The Scholar in Politics.* New York. 1892.

————, *Papers of the American Negro Academy.* Washington, D. C., 1915.

————, *William Lloyd Garrison, The Abolitionist.* New York, 1891.

GROSS, BELLA, "Freedom's Journal and the Rights of All," *The*

Journal of Negro History, Vol. 17; 241-286.

————, "Life and Times of Theodore S. Wright," *The Negro History Bulletin*, Vol. III, No. 9.

————, "The First National Negro Convention," *The Journal of Negro History*, Vol. XXXI, October, 1946.

GUERIN, DANIEL, *The West Indies and their Future.* London, 1961.

GUILLAUME, PAUL and MUNRO, THOMAS, *Primitive Negro Sculpture.* New York, 1926.

GUTHRIE, JAMES M., *Camp-Fires of the Afro-American or The Colored Man as a Patriot.* Cincinnati, 1899.

GUZMAN, JESSIE P., *The Negro Year Book.* New York, 1952.

HAGOOD, L. M., *The Colored Man in the Methodist Church.* Cincinnati, Ohio, 1880.

HAILEY, LORD, *An African Survey.* London, 1938.

HAINSWORTH, R. W., "The Negro and the Texas Primaries," *Journal of Negro History*, Vol. XVIII, 1933; 426-450.

HAMBLY, W. D., *Ethnology of Africa.* Chicago, 1930.

————, "Racial Conflict in Africa," *Journal of Negro History*, Vol. XII, 1927; 577-589.

————, *Source Book for African Anthropology.* Chicago, 1937.

HAMILTON, JOSEPH G. DEROULHAC, *Reconstruction in North Carolina.* New York, 1914.

HANDY, W. C., *Father of the Blues: An Autobiography by W. C. Handy.* Edited by Arna Bontemps. New York, 1944.

HANKINS, FRANK H., *The Racial Basis of Civilization: A Critique of the Nordic Doctrine.* New York, 1926.

HANSBERRY, LEO, "Sources for the Study of Ethiopian History,"

Howard University Studies in History. November, 1930.

——————, "The Material Culture of Ancient Nigeria," *The Journal of Negro History,* Vol. V, 1921; 261-295.

HARDY, CHARLES O., *The Negro Question in the French Revolution.* Menasha, Wis., 1919.

HARE, MAUDE CUNEY, *Negro Musicians and Their Music.* Washington, D. C.

HARLOW, RALPH V., *Garrett Smith, Philanthropist and Reformer.* New York, 1939.

HARRIS, ABRAM L., "The Negro Problem as Viewed by Negro Leaders," *Current History,* Vol. XVIII, June, 1923.

——————, *The Negro as Capitalist.*

HARRIS, N. D., *The History of Negro Servitude in Illinois.* Chicago, 1904.

HARRIS ROBERT J., *The Quest for Equality: The Constitution, Congress and the Supreme Court.* Baton Rouge, 1950.

HART, ALBERT BUSHWELL, *Slavery and Abolition.* New York, 1906.

HARTGROVE, W. B., "The Negro Soldier in the American Revolution," *The Journal of Negro History,* Vol. I, 1916; 110-131.

HATCHER, WILLIAM E., *John Jasper, The Unmatched Negro Philosopher and Preacher.* New York, 1908.

HAY, THOMAS R., "The Question of Arming the Slaves," *Mississippi Valley Historical Review,* VI, June, 1919.

HAYES, LAURENCE J. W., *The Negro Federal Government Worker.* Washington, 1941.

HAYNES, GEORGE E., *The Negro at Work in New York City.* New York, 1912.

——————, *The Trend of the Races.* New York, 1922.

HELPER, HINTON R., *The Impending Crisis of the South: How to Meet It.* New York, 1957.

HENDERSON, EDWIN B., *The Negro in Sports.* Washington, D. C., 1939, 1949.

HENRY, HOWELL M., *The Police Control of the Slave in South Carolina.* Emory, Virginia, 1914.

HENSON, JOSIAH, *The Life of Josiah Henson.* Boston, 1849.

HENSON, MATTHEW A., *A Negro Explorer at the North Pole.* New York, 1912.

HERSKOVITS, MELVILLE J., *Dahomey: An Ancient West African Kingdom.* New York, 1938.

——————, *The American Negro: A Study in Racial Crossing.* New York, 1928.

——————, "The Ancestry of the American Negro," *The American Scholar,* 1938-1939.

——————, *The Anthropometry of the American Negro.* New York, 1930.

——————, *The Myth of the Negro Past.* New York, 1941.

——————, "The Significance of West Africa for Negro Research," *The Journal of Negro History,* Vol. XXI, 1936. 15-30.

HESSELTINE, WILLIAM B., "Some New Aspects of the Proslavely Argument," *The Journal of Negro History,* Vol. XXI, 1936; 1-14.

——————, *The South in American History.* New York, 1943.

HEYWOOD, CHESTER D., *Negro Combat Troops in the World War: The Story of the 371st Infantry.* Worcester, 1928.

HICKOK, C. T., *The Negro in Ohio.* Cleveland, 1896.

HICKS, JOHN D., *The Populist Revolt.* Minneapolis, 1931.

HIGGINSON, THOMAS W., *Army Life in a Black Regiment.* Boston, 1870.

HILL, HERBERT, "Negro Wage-Earner and Apprenticeship

Training," *The Crisis.* June-July, 1961, Vol. 68; 325-341.

HILL, HOWARD C., *Roosevelt and the Caribbean.* Chicago, 1927.

HILL, T. ARNOLD, *The Negro and Economic Reconstruction.* Washington, 1937.

HIRSCH, LEO H., JR., "The Negro and New York, 1783-1865," *The Journal of Negro History,* Vol. XVI, 1931; 382-473.

HOFFMAN, FREDERICK L., *Race Traits and Tendencies of the American Negro.* New York, 1896.

HOFSTADTER, RICHARD, "U. B. Phillips and the Plantation Legend," *The Journal of Negro History,* Vol. XXIX, 1944; 109-124.

HOLMES, DWIGHT O. W., *The Evolution of the Negro College.* New York, 1934.

HOPKINS, VINCENT C., *Dred Scott's Case.* New York, 1951.

HORNE, LENA, *In Person Lena Horne* (as told to Helen Arstein and Carlton Moss). New York, 1950.

HOWE, SAMUEL G., *The Refugees from Slavery in Canada West.* Boston, 1864.

HUGGINS, WILLIS N. and JACKSON, JOHN G., *An Introduction to African Civilizations.* New York, 1937.

HUGHES, CARL M., *The Negro Novelist:* A Discussion of the Writings of American Negro Novelists, 1940-1950. New York, 1953.

HUGHES, LANGSTON, *The Big Sea: An Autobiography.* New York, 1940.

HUGHES, LANGSTON and BONTEMPS, ARNA, *The Poetry of the Negro, 1746-1949.*

HUNTON, ADDIE, *William A. Hunton.* New York, 1938.

HUNTON, ADDIE W., and JOHNSON, KATHERINE M., *Two Colored Women with the American Ex-peditionary Forces.* New York, 1920.

HURD, J. C., *Law of Freedom and Bondage in the U. S.* New York, 1858-1862.

INGLE, EDWARD, *Southern Sidelights.* New York, 1896.

ISAACS, EDITH J. R., *The Negro in the American Theatre.* New York, 1947.

JACK, ROBERT L., *History of the National Association for the Advancement of Colored People.* Boston, 1943.

JACKSON, GEORGE PULLEN, *White Spirituals of the Southern Uplands.* Chapel Hill, 1933.

JACKSON, LUTHER P., *A History of the Virginia State Teachers Association.* Norfolk, 1937.

——————, "Elizabethan Seamen and the African Slave Trade," *The Journal of Negro History,* Vol. IX, 1924; 1-17.

——————, *Free Negro Labor and Property Holding in Virginia.* New York, 1942.

——————, *Negro Office-Holders in Virginia.* Norfolk, 1945.

——————, "Religious Development of the Negro in Virginia from 1760 to 1860," *Journal of Negro History,* Vol. XVI, 1931; 168-239.

——————, "The Educational Efforts of the Freedmen's Bureau and Freedmen's Aid Societies in South Carolina, 1862-1872," *The Journal of Negro History,* Vol. VIII, 1923; 1-40.

——————, "Virginia Negro Soldiers and Seamen in the American Revolution," *The Journal of Negro History,* Vol. XXVII, 1942; 247-287.

JACQUES-GARVEY, AMY, *Philosophy and Opinions of Marcus Garvey.* New York, 1923.

JAHN, JANHEINZ, *Muntu: An Out-*

line of the New African Culture. New York, 1961.

JAMES, C. L. R., The Black Jacobins: Toussaint Louverture and the San Domingo Revolution. New York, 1939.

JAY, JOHN, Caste and Slavery in the American Church. New York and London, 1843.

JAY, WILLIAM, Inquiry into the Character and Tendency of the American Colonization, and American Anti-Slavery Societies. New York, 1835.

————, On the Condition of the Free People of Colour in the United States. New York, 1839.

JENKINS, WILLIAM S., Pro-Slavery Thought in the Old South. Gloucester, 1960.

JERNEGAN, MARCUS W., Laboring and Dependent Classes in Colonial America, 1607-1783. Chicago, 1931.

JOHNSON, CHARLES S., Education and the Cultural Process. (n. p., 1943.)

————, Growing Up in the Black Belt. Washington, 1941.

————, The Economic Status of Negroes. Nashville, 1933.

————, The Negro College Graduate. Chapel Hill, 1938.

————, The Negro in American Civilization. New York, 1930.

JOHNSON, EDWARD A., Adam vs. Ape-man and Ethiopia. New York, 1931.

————, History of Negro Soldiers in the Spanish-American War. Raleigh, 1899.

JOHNSON, FRANKLIN, The Development of State Legislation concerning the Free Negro. New York, 1919.

JOHNSON, GUION G., Ante-Bellum North Carolina. Chapel Hill, 1937.

JOHNSON, GUY B., Folk Culture on St. Helena Island, South Carolina. Chapel Hill, 1930.

————, "Some Factors in the Development of Negro Social Institutions in the United States," American Journal of Sociology, Vol. XXX, November, 1934.

JOHNSON, JAMES WELDON, Along This Way; The Autobiography of James Weldon Johnson. New York, 1933.

————, Black Manhattan. New York, 1930.

————, Native African Races and Culture. Charlottesville, 1927.

————, The Book of American Negro Poetry. New York, 1922.

————, The Book of American Negro Spirituals. New York, 1925.

————, The Second Book of Negro Spirituals. New York, 1926.

JOHNSON, JOHN C. DEGRAFT, African Glory. The Story of Vanished Negro Civilizations. New York, 1954.

JOHNSON, JOSEPH T., The Potential Negro Market. New York, 1952.

JOHNSON, WILLIAM, Natchez: The Ante-Bellum Diary of a Free Negro. Baton Rouge, 1951.

JOHNSTON, SIR HARRY H., The Negro in the New World. London, 1910.

————, The Colonization of Africa by Alien Races. Cambridge, 1913.

JOHNSTON, JAMES H., "A New Interpretation of the Domestic Slave System," The Journal of Negro History, Vol. XVIII, 1933; 39-55.

————, Miscegenation in the Ante-Bellum South. Chicago, 1939.

————, "The Mohammedan Slave Trade," The Journal of Negro History, Vol. XIII, 1928; 418-491.

JOHNSTON, RUBY F., *The Development of Negro Religion*. New York, 1954.

JOHNSTON, WILLIAM, *Slavery in Rhode Island, 1755-1776.* Providence, 1894.

JONES, RUFUS M., *The Quaker in the American Colonies*. London, 1911.

Journal of Negro Education, A Quarterly Review of Problems Incident to the Education of Negroes, 1932—and Yearbook Issues.

Journal of Negro History, Quarterly, 1916—

KENDRICK, BENJAMIN B., *The Journal of the Joint Committee of Fifteen on Reconstruction*. New York, 1914.

KENNEDY, LOUISE V., *The Negro Peasant Turns Cityward*. New York, 1930.

KERLIN, ROBERT T., *The Voice of the Negro 1919*. New York, 1920.

KESSELMAN, LOUIS, *The Social Politics of FEPC*. Chapel Hill, 1948.

KING, JAMES F., "Negro History in Continental Spanish America," *The Journal of Negro History*, Vol. XXIX, 1944; 7-23.

KINZER, ROBERT H. and SAGARIN, *The Negro in American Business. The Conflict Between Separtism and Integration*. New York, 1950.

KLINE, BURTON, "America Discovered Many Times Before Columbus," *The World's Work*, Vol. 10.

KLINEBERG, OTTO, *Race Differences*. New York, 1935.

KLINEBERG, FRANK J., *An Appraisal of the Negro in Colonial South Carolina*. Washington, 1941.

———, *T h e Anti-Slavery Movement in England*. New Haven, 1926.

KOGER, A. BRISCOE, *History of the*

Negro Baptists of Maryland, 1836-1936. Baltimore, 1935.

KORNGOLD, RALPH, *Citizen Toussaint*. Boston, 1944.

KREHBIEL, H. E., *Afro-American Folksongs*. New York, 1914.

KUPER, LEO, *Passive Resistance in South Africa*. New Haven, 1960.

LAPRADE, WILLIAM T., "The Domestic Slave Trade in the District of Columbia," *The Journal of Negro History*, Vol. XI, January, 1926.

LAWSON, ELIZABETH, *Study Outline History of the American Negro People, 1619-1918*. New York, Workers Book Shop, 1939.

LEAVELL, ULLIN W., *Philanthropy in Negro Education*. Nashville, 1930.

LEGER, JACQUES N., *Haiti, Her History and Detractors*. New York, 1907.

LEVY, LEONARD W., and PHILLIPS, HARLAN B., "The Roberts Case: Source of the 'Separate but Equal' Doctrine," *American Historical Review*, Vol. LVI, 1951.

LEWINSON, PAUL, *Race, Class, and Party; A History of Negro Suffrage and White Politics*. New York, 1932.

LEWIS, ROBERT B., *Light and Truth*. 1st edition, 1836, Boston, Massachusetts; 2d edition, Portland, Maine, 1844.

LEYBURN, JAMES G., *The Haitian People*. New Haven, 1941.

LINCOLN, C. ERIC., *The Black Muslims in America*. Boston, 1961.

LIPSCOMB, A. A., *North and South, Impressions of Northern Society Upon a Southerner*. Mobile, Alabama, 1853.

LITTLE, ARTHUR W., *From Harlem to the Rhine, The Story of New York's Colored Volunteers*. New York, 1936.

LITWACK, LEON F., *North of*

Slavery: The Negro in the Free States, 1790-1860. Chicago, 1961.

LIVERMORE, GEORGE, *An Historical Research Respecting the Opinions of the Founders of the Republic on Negroes as Slaves, as Citizens, and as Soldiers.* Boston, 1862.

LOCKE, ALAIN, *A Decade of Negro Self-Expression.* Charlottesville, Virginia, 1928.

————, *Negro Art: Past and Present.* Washington, D. C., 1935.

————, (ed.) *The New Negro: An Interpretation.* New York, 1925.

————, *The Negro and His Music.* Washington, D. C., 1935.

LOCKE, ALAIN and GREGORY, MONTGOMERY, *Plays of Negro Life: A Source Book of Native American Drama.* New York, 1927.

LOCKE, MARY S., *Anti-Slavery in America from the Introduction of African Slavery to the Prohibition of the Slave Trade.* Boston, 1901.

LOGAN, RAYFORD W., *African Mandates in World Politics.* Washington, D. C., 1948.

————, *Diplomatic Relations between the United States and Haiti, 1776-1891.* Chapel Hill, 1941.

————, "Educational Segregation in the North," *Journal of Negro Education,* Vol. II, January, 1933.

————, "Estevanico, Negro Discoverer of the Southwest," *Phylon,* Vol I, Fourth Quarter, 1940.

————, *The Attitude of the Southern White Press Toward Negro Suffrage.* Washington, D. C., 1940.

————, *The Negro and the Post-War World.* Washington, D. C., 1945.

————, *The Negro in American Life and Thought, 1877-1901.* New York, 1954.

————, *The Operation of the Mandate System in Africa.* Washington, D. C., 1942.

————, (ed.) *What the Negro Wants.* Chapel Hill, University of North Carolina Press, 1944.

LOGGINS, VERNON, *The Negro Author.* New York, 1931.

LOGUEN, THE REV. J. W., *The Rev. J. W. Loguen as a Slave and a Freeman.* New York, 1859.

LONN, ELLA, *Desertion During the Civil War.* New York, 1928.

LOVE, E. K., *History of the First African Baptist Church.* Savannah, Georgia.

LUGARD, FLORA LOUISA, *A Tropical Dependency.* London, 1905.

LUNDY, BENJAMIN, *Genius of Universal Emancipation,* (1821-38)..

————, *The Diary of Benjamin Lundy,* edited by Fred Landon. Toronto, 1922.

LYNCH, JOHN R., *Some Historical Errors of James Ford Rhodes.* Boston, 1922.

————, *The Facts of Reconstruction.* New York, 1915.

LYNK, MILES V., *The Black Troopers, or the Daring Heroism of the Negro Soldiers in the Spanish American War.* Jackson, 1899.

MABRY, WILLIAM A., *Studies in the Disfranchisement of the Negro in the South.* Durham, 1933.

MACKAY, CHARLES, *Life and Liberty in America: Or, Sketches of a Tour in the United States and Canada in 1857-58.* London, 1859. 2 Vols.

MACY, J. C., *The Anti-Slavery Crusade.* New Haven, 1921.

MALVIN, JOHN, *Autobiography.* Cleveland, 1879.

MANGUM, CHARLES S., *The Legal Status of the Negro.* Chapel Hill, 1940.

MARCUS, LLOYD, *The Treatment of Minorities in Secondary School Textbooks.* New York, 1961.

MARSHALL, HERBERT, *Ira Aldridge, the Negro Tragedian.* New York, 1958.

MARSH, Z. A. and KINGSWORTH, G. W., *An Introduction to the History of East Africa.* London, 1959.

MARTIN, ASA EARL, *The Anti-Slavery Movement in Kentucky Prior to 1850.* Louisville, 1918.

MARTIN, FLETCHER, *Our Great Americans: The Negro Contribution to American Progress.* Chicago, 1954.

MARTIN, JOHN T., LT. COL., *The Negro Officer in the Armed Forces of the United States of America.* Office of the Assistant Secretary of Defense. Washington, D. C., 1960.

MARTIN, ROBERT E., *Negro Disfranchisement in Virginia.* Washington, 1938.

MATTHEWS, BASIL, **Booker T.** *Washington, Educator and Racial Interpreter.* Cambridge, 1948.

MAY, SAMUEL J., *Recollections of Our Anti-Slavery Conflict.* Boston, 1869.

——————, *The Right of Colored People to Education Vindicated.* Brooklyn, Conn., 1833.

MAYS, BENJAMIN E., *The Negro's God as Reflected in His Literature.* Boston, 1938.

MAYS, BENJAMIN E., and NICHOLSON, JOSEPH W., *The Negro's Church.* New York, 1933.

MAZYCK, W. H. *George Washington and the Negro.* Washington, D. C., 1932.

McCLOY, SHELBY T., *The Negro in France.* Lexington, Ky., 1961.

McCRADY, EDWARD, *The History of South Carolina under Proprietary Government, 1670-1719.* New York, 1897.

McKAY, CLAUDE, *Harlem: Negro Metropolis.* New York, 1940.

MECKLIN, JOHN M., *The Klu Klux Klan: A Study of the American Mind.* New York, 1924.

MEHLINGER, LOUIS R., "The Attitude of the Free Negro toward African Colonization," *The Journal of Negro History,* Vol. I, 1916; 276-301.

Memorial of Thirty Thousand Disfranchised Citizens of Philadelphia to the Honorable Senate and House of Representatives. Philadelphia, 1855.

MILLER, HERBERT A., *Races, Nations and Classes.* Philadelphia, 1924.

MILLER, KELLY, *Kelly Miller's History of the World War for Human Rights.* Washington, D. C., n. d.

——————, *Race Adjustment,* New York, 1909.

——————, *The Everlasting Stain.* Washington, D. C.

MILLER, KELLY and GAY, J. R., *Progress and Achievements of the Colored People.* Washington, D. C., 1917.

MILLER, MARGERY, *Joe Louis: American.* New York, 1945.

MOON, HENRY LEE, *Balance of Power: The Negro Vote.* New York, 1948.

MOORE, GEORGE H., *Historical Notes on the Employment of Negroes in the American Army of the Revolution.* New York, 1862.

——————, *Notes on Slavery in Massachusetts.* New York, 1866.

MORGAN, EDWIN W., *Slavery in New York.* Washington, 1891.

MOTON, ROBERT R., *Finding a Way Out.* Garden City, 1921.

MURRAY, FLORENCE, *The Negro Handbook.* New York, 1946.

MURRAY, PAUL, *State Laws on Race and Color.* Cincinnati, 1951.

MYRDAL, GUNNAR, *An American Dilemma: Negro Problem and Modern Democracy.* New York 1944. 2 vols.

NATIONAL URBAN LEAGUE, *Economic and Social Status of the Negro in the United States, 1961.* New York, 1961.

NAVILLE, EDOUARD HENRI, "The Origin of Egyptian Civilization," *Annual Report of the Smithsonian Institution,* 1907.

NEEDLES, EDWARD, *An Historical Memoir of the Pennsylvania Society for Promoting the Abolition of Slavery, the Relief of Free Negroes Unlawfully Held in Bondage, and for Improving the Condtion of the African Race.* Philadelphia, 1848.

NELL, W. C., *Colored Patriots of the American Revolution.* Boston, 1855.

————, *Colored Americans in the Wars of 1776 and 1812.* Philadelphia, 1902.

————, *Property Qualification or No Property Qualification.* New York, 1860.

————, *Services of Colored Americans in the War of 1776 and 1812.* Boston, 1855.

NELSON, BERNARD, *The Negro and the Fourteenth Amendment Since 1912.* Washington, 1946.

NELSON, DENNIS D., *The Integration of the Negro into the United States Navy.* New York, 1951.

The New Negro Thirty Years Afterward, edited by the Division of the Social Sciences of Howard University. Washington, 1955.

NEWCOMB, HARVEY, "The Negro Pew": *Being an Inquiry concerning the Propriety of Distinctions in the House of God on Account of Color.* Boston, 1837.

NICHOLS, LEE, *Breakthrough on the Color Front.* New York, 1954.

NOBLE, JEANNE L., *The Negro Woman's College Education.* New York, 1956.

NOBLE, PETER, *The Negro in Films.* London, 1946.

NORTHRUP, HERBERT R., *Organized Labor and the Negro.* New York, 1944.

NYE, RUSSEL B., *Fettered Freedom: Civil Liberties and the Slavery Controversy.* East Lansing, 1949.

Occasional Papers of the American Negro Academy. Washington, D. C.

Official Opinions of the Attorneys General of the United States Washington, D. C., 1791-1948 40 Vols.

OLBRICH, EMIL, *The Development of Sentiment on Negro Suffrage to 1860.* Madison, Wis., 1912.

OLMSTED, FREDERICK L., *A Journey in the Seaboard Slave States.* New York, 1863.

————, *The Cotton Kingdom: A Traveler's Observations in Cotton and Slavery in the American Southern States.* New York, 1862.

OTTLEY, ROI, *Black Odyssey: The Story of the Negro in America.* New York, 1948.

————, *New World A-Coming.* New York, 1943.

————, *The Lonely Warrier, The Life and Times of Robert S. Abbott.* Chicago, 1955.

OVINGTON, MARY W., *How the National Association for the Advancement of Colored People Began.* New York, 1914.

OVINGTON, MARY W., *Portraits in Color.* New York, 1927.

PAGAN, BOLIVAR, *Puerto Rico: The Next State.* Washington, 1942.

PARKER, GEORGE W., "The African Origin of Grecian Civilization," *The Journal of Negro History,* Vol. II, 1917; 334-344.

PATTERSON, CALEB P., *The Negro in Tennessee.* Austin, 1927.

PAYNE, DANIEL A., *Recollections of Seventy Years.* Nashville, Tennessee, 1888.

PEIRCE, PAUL S., *The Freedmen's*

Bureau, A Chapter in the History of Reconstruction. Iowa City, 1904.

PENN, I. GARLAND, *The Afro-American Press and its Editors.* Springfield, 1891.

PENNINGTON, JAMES W. G., *The Fugitive Blacksmith.* 3d Ed., London, 1850.

PERRY, RUFUS, *The Cushites or the Children of Ham as seen by the Ancient Historians.* Springfield, Massachusetts, 1893.

PHILLIPS, P. L., "The Negro, Benjamin Banneker: Astronomer and Mathematician," *Records of the Columbia Historical Society,* Vol. XX, Washington, 1917.

PHILLIPS, ULRICH BONNELL, *American Negro Slavery, A Survey of the Supply, Employment and Control of Negro Labor as Determined by the Plantation Regime.* New York, 1918.

PIERCE, JOSEPH A., *Negro Business and Business Education.* New York, 1947.

PIERSON, DONALD, *Negroes in Brazil: A Study of Race Contract at Bahia.* Chicago, 1942.

PIERSON, DONALD, "The Negro in Bahia Brazil," *American Sociological Review.* 4:524-533, 1939.

PITMAN, FRANK W., "Slavery on the British West India Plantations in the Eighteenth Century," *The Journal of Negro History,* Vol. XI, 1926; 584-682.

PORTER, DOROTHY B., "David M. Ruggles, An Apostle of Human Rights," *The Journal of Negro History,* Vol. XXVIII, 1943; 23-50.

———, "Early American Negro W r i t i n g s: A Bibliographical Study," *The Papers of the Bibliographical Society of America,* Vol. XXXIX, 1945.

———, "Organized Educational Activities of Negro Literary Societies, 1828-1846," *The Journal of Negro Education,* Vol. 5, pp. 555-576.

PORTER, JAMES A., *Modern Negro Art.* New York, 1943.

PORTER, KENNETH W., "Relations between Negroes and Indians within the Present Limits of the United States," *The Journal of Negro History,* Vol. 17, 1932: 287-367.

PORTER, KIRK H., *A History of Suffrage in the United States.* Chicago, 1918.

POWDERMAKER, HORTENSE, *Probing our Prejudices.* New York, 1944.

PRESTON, E. O., "The Genesis of the Underground Railroad," *The Journal of Negro History,* Vol. XVIII, 1933; 144-170.

———, "The Underground Railroad in Northwest Ohio," *The Journal of Negro History,* Vol. XVII, 1932; 409-435.

President's Commission on Civil Rights, To Secure These Rights. Washington, D. C., 1947. (See Reports.)

President's Commission on Higher Education, *Higher Education for American Democracy.* Washington, D. C., 1947.

PUCKETT, NEWBELL N., *Folk Beliefs of the Southern Negro.* Chapel Hill, 1926.

QUARLES, BENJAMIN, *Frederick Douglass.* Washington, D. C., Associated Publishers, 1948.

———, "Letters from Negro Leaders to Gerrit Smith," *The Journal of Negro History,* Vol. XXVII, 1942; 432-453.

———, "Ministers without Portfolio," *Journal of Negro History,* Vol. XXXIX, 1954; 27-42.

———, (ed.), *Narrative Life of Frederick Douglass,* An American Slave, Written by Himself. Cambridge, 1960.

———, "The Breach Between

Douglass and Garrison," *The Journal of Negro History*, Vol. XXIII, pp. 144-154.

————, *The Negro in the Civil War*. Boston, 1953.

QUILLEN, FRANK U., *The Color Line in Ohio*. Ann Arbor, 1913.

RAGATZ, LOWELL J., *The Fall of the Planter Class in the British Caribbean, 1763-1833*. New York, The Century Co., 1928.

RAMMELKAMP, JULIAN S., "The Providence Negro Community, 1920-42," *Rhode Island History*, VII, 1948.

RAMOS, ARTHUR, *The Negro in Brazil*. Washington, 1939.

RANSOM, LEON A., "Legal Status of Negro Education Under Separate School Systems," *Journal of Negro Education*, VIII, July, 1939.

RAPER, ARTHUR, *The Tragedy of Lynching*. Chapel Hill, 1933.

RAUCHAMES, LOUIS, *Race, Jobs and Politics*. New York, 1953.

RECORD, WILSON, *The Negro and the Communist Party*. Chapel Hill, 1951.

REDDICK, L. D., *Crusader without Violence: a Biography of Martin Luther King*. New York, 1959.

————, "The Negro in the Navy, in World War II," *The Journal of Negro History*, Vol. XXXII, 1947; 201-219.

————, "The Negro Policy of the American Army Since World War II," *The Journal of Negro History*, Vol. XXXVIII, 1953; 196-215.

REDDING, J. SAUNDERS, *No Day of Triumph*.

————, *On Being Negro in America*. Indianapolis, 1951.

————, *The Lonesome Road*. New York, 1958.

REID, IRA DE A., *The Negro Immigrant*. New York, 1939.

REINSCH, PAUL S., "The Negro Race and European Civilization," *American Journal of Sociology*. Vol. 11:145-167, 1905.

REUTER, R. B., *The American Race Problem, A Study of the Negro*. New York, 1927, 2d ed., 1938.

RICHARDSON, BEN, (Revised by William A. Fahey) *Great American Heroes*. New York, 1956.

RICHARDSON, WILLIS, *Plays and Pageants from the Life of the Negro*. Washington, D. C., 1930.

RICHARDSON, WILLIS and MILLER, MAY, *Negro History in Thirteen Plays*. Washington, D. C., 1935.

RIDER, SIDNEY S., *An Historical Inquiry Concerning the Attempt to Raise a Regiment of Slaves by Rhode Island During the War of the Revolution*. Providence, 1880.

RIPPY, J. FRED, "The Negro and the Spanish Pioneers in the New World," *The Journal of Negro History*, Vol. VI, 1921; 183-189.

RODABAUGH, JAMES H., "The Negro in Ohio," *The Journal of Negro History*, XXXI, 1946; 9-29.

ROEDER, BILL, *Jackie Robinson*. New York, 1950.

ROGERS, BEN F., "William E. B. DuBois, Marcus Garvey and Pan-Africa," *The Journal of Negro History*, Vol. XL, 1950; 154-165.

ROGERS, J. A., *Africa's Gift to America*. New York, 1959.

————, *Sex and Race*, Vols. I, II, III. New York, 1904-1944.

————, *World's Great Men of Color*. 2 vols. New York, 1947.

ROGERS, W. MCDOWELL, "Free Negro Legislation in Georgia," *Georgia Historical Quarterly*, XVI, March, 1932.

ROSE, A. M., *The Negro's Morale*. Minneapolis, 1950.

ROWAN, CARL, *South of Freedom*. New York, 1952.

RUCHAMES, LOUIS, "Jim Crow Railroads in Massachusetts," *American Quarterly*, VIII, 1956.

————, "Race, Marriage and Abolotionism in Massachusetts," *The Journal of Negro History*, Vol. XL, 1955; 250-273.

RUSSELL, J. H., *The Free Negro in Virginia, 1619-1865*. Baltimore, 1913.

RUSSELL, JOHN H., "Colored Freemen as Slave Owners in Virginia," *The Journal of Negro History*, Vol. I, 1916; 233-242.

SAVAGE, WILLIAM S., *The Controversy over the Distribution of Abolition Literature*. Washington, D. C., 1939.

SCARBOROUGH, RUTH, *The Opposition to Slavery in Georgia Prior to 1860*. Nashville, 1933.

SCHOENFELD, SEYMOUR J., *The Negro in the Armed Forces*. Washington, 1945.

SCHOOR, GENE, *Roy Campenella, Man of Courage*. New York, 1959.

————, *Sugar Ray Robinson*. New York, 1951.

SCOTT, EMMETT J., *Negro Migration during the War*. New York, 1920.

SCOTT, EMMETT J. and STOWE, LYMAN BEECHER, *Booker T. Washington*. New York, Doubleday, Page and Co., 1918.

SELLERS, JAMES B., *Slavery in Alabama*. University, Ala., 1950.

SHANNON, FRED, "The Federal Government and the Negro Soldier, 1861-65," *The Journal of Negro History*, XI, October, 1926.

————, *The Organization and Administration of the Union Army*. Glendale, 1928. 2 Vols.

SHEELER, J. REUBEN, "The Struggle of the Negro in Ohio for Freedom," *Journal of Negro History*, XXXI, 1946.

SHEPPERD, GLADYS B., *Mary Church Terrell: Respectable Person*. Washington, 1959.

SHUGG, ROGER WALLACE, "Negro Voting in the Ante-Bellum South," *The Journal of Negro History*, Vol. XXI, 1936; 357-364.

————, *Origins of Class Struggle in Louisiana*. University, La., 1939.

SIEBERT, WILBUR HENRY, *The Mysteries of Ohio's Underground Railroads*. Columbus, 1951.

————, *Underground Railroad from Slavery to Freedom*. New York, 1898.

SIMKINS, FRANCIS B., *A History of the South*. New York, 1953.

SIMKINS, FRANCIS B. and WOODY, R. H., *South Carolina During Reconstruction*. Chapel Hill, 1932.

SIMMONS, W. J., *Men of Mark*. Cleveland, Ohio, 1887.

SMITH, LILLIAN, *Killers of the Dream*, New York, 1943.

SMITH, SAMUEL D., *The Negro in Congress, 1870-1901*. Chapel Hill, 1940.

SMITH, THOMAS P., *An Address Before the Colored Citizens of Boston in Opposition to the Abolition of Colored Schools*. Boston, 1850.

SOUTHERN REGIONAL COUNCIL, *Questions and Answers: The Schools and the Courts*. Atlanta, 1953.

SPEARS, JOHN, *The American Slave Trade*. New York, 1900.

Special Reports of the Commission of Education on the Condition and Improvement of Public in the District of Columbia, Submitted to the Senate, June, 1868 and to the House with additions, June 13, 1870. Washington, D. C., 1871.

SPENCER, SAMUEL R., JR., *Booker T. Washington and the Negro's Place in American Life*. Boston, 1955.

SPERO, S. D., and HARRIS, A. L., *The Black Worker*. New York, 1931.

STAFFORD, A. O., "The Tarikk Es-Soudan," *The Journal of Negro History*, Vol. II, April, 1917.

STAMPP, KENNETH M., *The Peculiar Institution, Slavery in the Ante-Bellum South*. New York, 1956.

STEINER, BERNARD C., *History of Slavery in Connecticut*. Baltimore, 1893.

STEPHENSON, GILBERT T., *Race Distinctions in American Law*. New York, 1910.

STEPHENSON, N. W., "The Question of Arming the Slaves," *American Historical Review*, XVIII, January, 1913.

STEWARD, AUSTIN, *Twenty-Two Years a Slave and Forty Years a Freeman*. Rochester, 1857.

STEWARD, THEOPHILUS G., *How the Black St. Domingo Legion Saved the Patriot Army in the Siege of Savannah 1779*. Washington, D. C., The Negro Academy, Occasional Papers No. 5.

———, *The Colored Regulars in the U. S. Army, with a Sketch of the History of the Colored American*. Philadelphia, A. M. E. Book Concern, 1921.

———, *The Haitian Revolution, 1791 to 1804*. New York, 1914.

STILL, WILLIAM, *The Underground Railroad*. Philadelphia, Porter and Coats, 1872.

STONEY, SAMUEL G., and SHELBY, GERTRUDE MATHEWS, *Black Genesis*. New York, 1930.

STOWE, LYMAN B., *Booker T. Washington, Builder of a Civilization*. Garden City, 1916.

SUMNER, CHARLES, *Argument of Charles Sumner, Esq., Against the Constitutionality of Separate Colored Schools, in the Case of Sarah C. Roberts vs. the City of Boston*. Boston, 1849.

SUTHERLAND, ROBERT L., *Color,* *Class and Personality*. Washington, 1942.

SWEENEY, JAMES J., *African Negro Art*. New York, 1925.

SWINT, HENRY L., *The Northern Teacher in the South, 1862-1870*. Nashville, 1941.

SYDOR, CHARLES S., *Slavery in Mississippi*. New York, 1933.

———, "The Free Negro in Mississippi before the Civil War," *American Historical Review*, XXXII, July, 1927.

TANNENBAUM, FRANK, *Slave and Citizen*. New York, 1947.

TAPPAN, LEWIS, *The Life of Arthur Tappan*. New York, 1870.

TATE, MERZE, "The War Aims of World War I and World War II and their Relation to the Darker Peoples of the World," *The Journal of Negro Education*, XII, Summer, 1943.

TAYLOR, ALRUTHEUS A., *The Negro in South Carolina During the Reconstruction*. Washington, D. C., 1924.

———, *The Negro in Tennessee, 1865-1880*. Washington, D. C., 1941.

———, *The Negro in the Reconstruction of Virginia*. Washington, D. C., 1926.

TAYLOR, JULIUS H.; DILLARD, CLYDE R.; PROCTOR, NATHANIEL K. and BRANSON, HERMAN R., *The Negro in Science*. Baltimore, 1955.

TAYLOR, R. H., *The Free Negro in North Carolina*. Chapel Hill, 1920.

The Pennsylvania Society for Promoting the Abolition of Slavery and the Society of Friends, *The Present State and Condition of the Free People of Color of The City of Philadelphia*. Philadelphia, 1838.

———, *Statistics of the Colored People of Philadelphia*. Philadelphia, 1856.

THORNBROUGH, EMMA LOU, *The Negro in Indiana.* Indianapolis, 1957.

THORPE, EARL E., *Negro Historians in the United States.* Baton Rouge, 1958.

TINDALL, GEORGE, *South Carolina Negroes, 1877-1900.* Columbia. 1952.

TORRENCE, RIDGELY, *The Story of John Hope.* New York, 1948.

TREMAIN, MARY M., *Slavery in the District of Columbia.* University of Nebraska Papers, 1892.

TRENT, WILLIAM J., *Development of Negro Life Insurance Enterprises.* Philadelphia, 1932.

TREXLER, HARRISON A., *Slavery in Missouri, 1804-1865.* Baltimore, 1914.

TURNER, E. R., *The Negro in Pennsylvania, 1639-1861.* **Washington, 1911.**

TURNER, LORENZO J., *Anti-Slavery Sentiment in American Literature Prior to 1865.* Washington, D. C., 1929.

UNESCO (ed.), *Race and Science.* New York, 1961.

U. S. DEPARTMENT OF COMMERCE, BUREAU OF CENSUS, *Negro Population in the United States, 1790-1915.* Washington, D. C., 1918.

—————, *Negroes in the United States, 1920-32.* Washington, D. C., 1935.

U. S. OFFICE OF EDUCATION, *Biennial Survey of Education Statistics of State School Systems.*

VAN DEUSEN, JOHN G., *The Black Man in White America.* Washington, D. C., 1944.

VANDERCOOK, JOHN W., *Black Majesty, the Life of Christophe, King of Haiti.* New York, 1928.

VILLARD, OSWALD GARRISON, *John Brown, 1800-1859; A Biography Fifty Years After.* New York, 1910.

WALKER, DAVID, *Appeal in Four Articles.* Boston, 1830.

WARD, SAMUEL RINGOLD, *Autobiography of a Fugitive Negro.* London, 1855.

WARNER, ROBERT A., *New Haven Negroes, A Social History.* New Haven, 1940.

WASHINGTON, BOOKER T., *Frederick Douglass.* Philadelphia, 1906.

—————, *The Story of My Life and Work.* Atlanta, 1901.

—————, *The Story of the Negro.* New York, 1909. 2 Vols.

—————, *Up From Slavery.* New York, 1901.

WASHINGTON, E. DAVID, (edited) *Selected Speeches of Booker T. Washington.* Garden City, 1932.

WAXMAN, PERCY, *The Black Napoleon: A Study of Toussaint Louverture.* New York, 1931.

WEAVER, ROBERT C., *Negro Labor, A National Problem.* New York, 1946.

—————, *The Negro Ghetto.* New York, 1948.

WESLEY, CHARLES H., *A History of the Improved Benevolent Protective Order of Elks of the World, 1898-1954.* Washington, D. C., 1956.

————— "International Aspects of the Negro's Status in the United States." *Negro History Bulletin,* Vol. XI, (1948); 113-118.

—————, "Lincoln's Plan for Colonizing the Emancipated Negro," *Journal of Negro History,* Vol. IV, (1919); 7-21.

—————, *Negro Labor in the United States, 1850-1925.* New York, Vanguard Press, 1927.

—————, "Negro Suffrage in the Period of Constitution Making, 1787-1865," *Journal of Negro History,* Vol. XXXII (1947); 143-168.

—————, *Richard Allen, Apos-*

tle of Freedom. Washington, D. C., 1935.

————, *The Collapse of the Confederacy.* Washington, D. C., 1937.

————, "The Concept of Negro Inferiority in American Thought," *The Journal of Negro History* (1940); 540-560.

————, "The Employment of Negroes as Soldiers in the Confederate Army," *Journal of Negro History,* Vol. IV (1919); 239-253.

————, *The History of Alpha Phi Alpha.* Washington, D. C., 1927, 1961.

————, (ed.) *The Negro in the Americas.* Washington, D. C., 1940.

————, "The Negro in the Organization of Abolition," *Phylon,* II, 1941; 223-235.

————, "The Participation of Negroes in Anti-Slavery Political Parties," *The Journal of Negro History,* Vol. XXIX, (1944); 32-74.

————, "The Reconstruction of History," *The Journal of Negro History,* (1935); 411-427.

————, "The Treatment of the Negro in the Teaching of United States History," *Social Education,* Vol. VII, (1943).

WHARTON, VERNON L., *The Negro in Mississippi, 1865-1890.* Chapel Hill, 1947.

WHITE, WALTER, *A Man Called White.* New York, 1948.

————, *How Far the Promised Land.* New York, 1955.

WHITING, HELEN A., *Negro Art, Music and Rhyme for Young Folks, Book II.* Washington, D. C., 1938.

————, *Negro Folk Tales for Pupils in the Primary Grades.* Washington, D. C., 1938.

Who's Who in Colored America, 1927, 1928-1929, 1933-1937, 1950.

WIENER, LEO, *Africa and the Discovery of America.* Philadelphia, 1920, 1922. 3 Vols.

WILEY, BELL IRVIN, *Southern Negroes, 1861-1865.* New York, 1938.

WILKES, LAURA E., *Missing Pages in American History.* Washington, D. C., Press of R. L. Pendleton, 1919.

WILLIAMS, ERIC, *Capitalism and Slavery.* Chapel Hill, 1944.

————, *The Negro in the Caribbean.* Washington, D. C., 1942.

WILLIAMS, GEORGE W., *History of the Negro Race in America from 1619 to 1880.* New York, 1883 2 Vols.

————, *History of the Negro Troops in the War of the Rebellion, 1861-1865.* New York, 1888.

WILLIAMS, MARY W., *The People and Politics of Latin America.* Boston, 1938.

WILSON, C. D., "Negroes Who Owned Slaves," *Popular Science Monthly,* Vol. LXXXI, November, 1912.

WILSON, HENRY, *The Rise and Fall of the Slave Power in America.* New York, (1872) 2 Vols.

WILSON, JOSEPH T., *The Black Phalanx.* Hartford, 1888.

WISH, HARVEY, "American Slave Insurrections before 1861," *The Journal of Negro History,* Vol. XXII (1937); 299-320.

————, "Slave Disloyalty under the Confederacy," *The Journal of Negro History,* Vol. XXIII (1938); 435-450.

WOODSON, CARTER G., *A Century of Negro Migration.* Washington, D. C., 1918.

————, "Fifty Years of Negro Citizenship as qualified by the United States Supreme Court," *The Journal of Negro History,* Vol. VI, 1921; 1-53.

—————, *Free Negro Heads of Families in the United States in 1830*. Washington, 1925.

—————, *Free Negro Owners of Slaves in the United States in 1830*.

—————, *Negro Orators and their Orations*. Washington, D. C., 1926.

—————, *The African Background Outlined or Handbook for the Study of the Negro*. Washington, D. C., 1936.

—————, *The Education of the Negro Prior to 1861*. Washington, D. C., 1915.

—————, *The History of the Negro Church*. Washington, D. C., 1921, 1944.

—————, *The Mind of the Negro as Reflected in Letters Written During the Crisis, 1800-1860*. Washington, D. C., 1926.

WOODWARD, C. VANN, *Origins of the New South, 1877-1913*. Baton Rouge, 1951.

—————, *The Strange Career of Jim Crow*. New York, 1955.

—————, *Tom Watson, Agrarian Rebel*. New York, 1938.

WOOFTER, THOMAS J., *Negro Problems in Cities*. Garden City, 1928.

WORK, MONROE, "The Passing Tradition and the African Civilization," *The Journal of Negro History*. Vol. I, (1916); 34-41.

WRIGHT, JAMES M., *The Free Negro in Maryland*. New York, 1921.

WRIGHT, R. R., *The Encyclopedia of the A. M. E. Church*, Philadelphia, 1948.

—————, "The Negro Companions of the Spanish Explorers," *The American Anthropologist*, Vol. IV, (1902).

WRIGHT, MARIAN T., *Education of Negroes in New Jersey*. New York, 1941.